CONTENTS

LIST OF MAPS

ABOUT THE AUTHORS

Michael Luongo has written on Argentina for the *New York Times, National Geographic Traveler, Bloomberg News, Out Traveler,* and many other publications. He is also the author of *Frommer's Buenos Aires*. His debut novel, *The Voyeur,* was published by Alyson Books in 2007, and he has written several other travel books. He has visited more than 80 countries and all seven continents, but few places have stolen his heart like Argentina. Highlights include riding Juan Perón's coffin through the streets of Buenos Aires during his 2006 reburial, and wearing a dab of perfume from the last bottle of fragrance Evita used before her death to a dinner party. Visit him at www.michaelluongo.com and www.misterbuenosaires.com.

Charlie O'Malley is an Irishman who lives and works in Mendoza, Argentina. He has worked on several *Frommer's* guidebooks for countries all over South America and Central America. He edits his own magazine in Argentina called *Wine Republic*.

Christie Pashby has written for Frommer's for a decade. She covers western Canada and the southern regions of Chile and Argentina. By the time she was 25, Christie had lived in Berlin, the Cote d'Azur, Chile, and Costa Rica, and studied in three Canadian provinces, earning degrees from McGill University and University of King's College. But the mountains were calling; along with her Argentine husband, she splits her time between homes in Canmore, Alberta, and Bariloche, Argentina, two of the world's finest alpine playgrounds. She is a freelance translator, journalist, and also runs a small guiding business in Patagonia. Her website is www.patagonialiving.com.

ACKNOWLEDGMENTS

Michael Luongo

A big thanks to my editors Lorraine Festa and Maureen Clarke and to Kathleen Warnock for introducing me long ago to the Frommer's bunch, and to Pauline and Arthur Frommer for their advice and guidance over the years, as well as so many others at the Hoboken office. Thanks to Ines Segarra of the Argentina Tourism Office in New York, and the rest of Consulate General of Argentina in New York, and Eduardo Piva of the Argentina Tourism Office in Miami, Carlos Enrique Mayer in Buenos Aires, and to their staff, for answering all of my questions over the years. Thanks to Gabriel Miremont of the Museo Evita for all of his knowledge over the years, to Sandra Borello and her staff at Borello Travel for all their advice, and to Luis Formaiano and Lawrence Wheeler who are like my two big brothers in Buenos Aires, without whom I could never get anything done, and to so many others who have helped over the years.

Charlie O'Malley

Many thanks to Frank Pirhalla and Brian Gregory for adding an extra dimension to my trip to Salta and letting me use their fine-tuned criticisms. I'd like to thank Martha Chocobar, Luciana Salaun, and Sandra Yreta for their hospitality and for making the road less lonely. A special thanks to Rosa Maria Aguilera for her insights on Cordoba and a special, special thanks to her sister Ana who happens to be my wife, assistant, and mother to my baby son and future assistant, Finbar.

Christie Pashby

Covering such an expansive territory is no easy task. Fortunately, there are new wines to taste, dear friends to sip *mates* with, and superb fly-fishing to keep the author motivated! I'd like to thank my conversational pilots Max and Gabriela for making the thousands of kilometers fly by, as well as Pascale in El Calafate, Gabriel and Sil in Puerto Madryn, and my *compañeros* Mike and Charlie. My task was made much easier by Isobel and Julie at Destino Argentina, and *gracias* to my brother-in-law Cristian who kept our truck running under immense pressure. I couldn't have made this round happen without the enduring support of my sisters in Toronto, Kathy and Karen.

HOW TO CONTACT US

In researching this book, we discovered many wonderful places—hotels, restaurants, shops, and more. We're sure you'll find others. Please tell us about them, so we can share the information with your fellow travelers in upcoming editions. If you were disappointed with a recommendation, we'd love to know that, too. Please write to:

Frommer's Argentina, 3rd Edition
Wiley Publishing, Inc. • 111 River St. • Hoboken, NJ 07030-5774
frommersfeedback@wiley.com

ADVISORY & DISCLAIMER

Travel information can change quickly and unexpectedly, and we strongly advise you to confirm important details locally before traveling, including information on visas, health and safety, traffic and transport, accommodation, shopping and eating out. We also encourage you to stay alert while traveling and to remain aware of your surroundings. Avoid civil disturbances, and keep a close eye on cameras, purses, wallets and other valuables.

While we have endeavored to ensure that the information contained within this guide is accurate and up-to-date at the time of publication, we make no representations or warranties with respect to the accuracy or completeness of the contents of this work and specifically disclaim all warranties, including without limitation warranties of fitness for a particular purpose. We accept no responsibility or liability for any inaccuracy or errors or omissions, or for any inconvenience, loss, damage, costs or expenses of any nature whatsoever incurred or suffered by anyone as a result of any advice or information contained in this guide.

The inclusion of a company, organization, or website in this guide as a service provider and/ or potential source of further information does not mean that we endorse them or the information they provide. Be aware that information provided through some websites may be unreliable and can change without notice. Neither the publisher or author shall be liable for any damages arising herefrom.

FROMMER'S STAR RATINGS, ICONS & ABBREVIATIONS

Every hotel, restaurant, and attraction listing in this guide has been ranked for quality, value, service, amenities, and special features using a **star-rating system.** In country, state, and regional guides, we also rate towns and regions to help you narrow down your choices and budget your time accordingly. Hotels and restaurants are rated on a scale of zero (recommended) to three stars (exceptional). Attractions, shopping, nightlife, towns, and regions are rated according to the following scale: zero stars (recommended), one star (highly recommended), two stars (very highly recommended), and three stars (must-see).

In addition to the star-rating system, we also use **seven feature icons** that point you to the great deals, in-the-know advice, and unique experiences that separate travelers from tourists. Throughout the book, look for:

special finds—those places only insiders know about

fun facts—details that make travelers more informed and their trips more fun

kids—best bets for kids and advice for the whole family

special moments—those experiences that memories are made of

overrated—places or experiences not worth your time or money

insider tips—great ways to save time and money

great values—where to get the best deals

The following abbreviations are used for credit cards:

AE	American Express	**DISC**	Discover	**V**	Visa
DC	Diners Club	**MC**	MasterCard		

TRAVEL RESOURCES AT FROMMERS.COM

Frommer's travel resources don't end with this guide. Frommer's website, **www.frommers. com**, has travel information on more than 4,000 destinations. We update features regularly, giving you access to the most current trip-planning information and the best airfare, lodging, and car-rental bargains. You can also listen to podcasts, connect with other Frommers. com members through our active-reader forums, share your travel photos, read blogs from guidebook editors and fellow travelers, and much more.

THE BEST OF ARGENTINA

The distance from Argentina's northern tip to Tierra del Fuego spans 3,650km (2,263 miles). The scope of experiences you can find here is no less grand, ranging from the cosmopolitan bustle of Buenos Aires to the tropical jungles and pounding falls of Iguazú or the thunderous splash of icebergs in Los Glaciares National Park. Whether you've come to meander the quiet towns of the Lake District or dance the night away in a smoky, low-lit Argentine tango bar, your trip to the Southern Hemisphere won't disappoint. In this chapter, we've selected the best that Argentina has to offer—museums, outdoor adventures, hotels, and even side trips to Chile.

THE best TRAVEL EXPERIENCES

- **Experiencing Tango in Buenos Aires:** *Milongas,* or tango salons, take place every night of the week throughout the Argentine capital; the most famous are in the San Telmo neighborhood. Most visitors will be content just to watch as dancers of all generations (most of them amateurs) go through the beautiful paces of traditional Argentine tango. Both the dance and the complex social ritual that frames it are mesmerizing. Brave onlookers can choose to dance as well; most *milongas* offer lessons before the floor opens up to dancers. Walking into **El Niño Bien** is like taking a step back in time as you watch patrons dance in an enormous Belle Epoque–era hall. **Salon Canning** is equally beautiful, and the large space allows onlookers to sit in the background as voyeurs to this intimate, beautiful spectacle. **El Querandí** offers a historically based tango show, tracing the dance's roots from brothel slums, when only men danced it, to its current leggy sexiness. See chapter 5.
- **Paying Respects at a First-Class Necropolis** (Buenos Aires): In the chichi neighborhood of Recoleta is the beautiful **Recoleta Cemetery,** where enormous, expensive mausoleums compete for grandeur. Among the scant few nonaristocrats buried here is Eva Perón, or "Evita." Children won't be bored either, delighting in playing with the more than 80 cats living among the tombs. See p. 125.
- **Enjoying the Capital's Best Nightlife Street** (Buenos Aires): Whether you want to dine at a *parrilla* (grill), try some nouvelle cuisine, barhop, or go dancing, **Calle Báez** in Las Cañitas is the place to go. Though it's often overshadowed by the more tourist-trod Palermo Soho, which is always making the news, ask locals about this busy street full of great

restaurants—including **Novecento** and **El Estanciero**—and some of the most intensely packed nightlife on any 3 blocks of Buenos Aires. See chapter 5.

o **Facing the Abyss at Iguazú Falls:** Two hundred seventy-five plummeting waterfalls fed by the Iguazú River make this one of the world's most spectacular and dramatic sights. In addition to the falls, Iguazú encompasses a marvelous subtropical jungle with extensive flora and fauna. See chapter 7.

o **Wrestling with Anaconda in Esteros del Ibera:** A 12,950-sq.-km (5,000-sq.-mile) stretch of waterways and vegetation is the perfect habitat for yellow-backed anaconda, caiman, marsh deer, and the largest rodent in the world. Look up (if you dare) and you'll spot over 300 colorful species of birds such as storks and kingfishers who hang out in this marvelous slice of Eden in the northeast province of Corrientes. See chapter 7.

o **Driving the Quebrada de Humahuaca:** A taste of real South America is offered by this rainbow-colored mountain range that extends all the way to Bolivia. The windy road reveals dusty adobe villages, such as **Pumamarca** and **Tilcara,** set amidst striking red-rock formations. Quechuan women herd goats amid Inca ruins in the distance while brand-new luxury lodges let you experience the real Andean South America without having to slum it. See chapter 8.

o **Taking a Train to the Clouds:** The **Tren a las Nubes** is one of the world's great railroad experiences. The journey through Argentina's Northwest is a daylong excursion that takes you 434km (269 miles) through tunnels, turns, and bridges, culminating in the breathtaking La Polvorilla viaduct. Cross magnificent landscapes while making your way from the multicolored Lerma valley through the deep canyons and rugged peaks of the Quebrada del Toro, and on to the desolate desert plateau of La Puña. See chapter 8.

o **Having a Tribal Gathering in Tafí del Valle:** Argentina's best-kept secret is a lush green valley and lake set above a scorching red desert in the tiny province of Tucumán. Wander a field of mysterious standing stones or marvel in the lost, fortress city of Quilmes where the locals kept the conquistadors at bay for 300 years. See chapter 8.

o **Touring the Jesuit Ruins of Córdoba:** Magnificent colonial architecture set in the rolling green hills of the Córdoba sierras reveals a lost utopia of arts and learning. It's one of the few examples of harmonious cooperation between indigenous people and European colonizers. See chapter 9.

o **Sampling Torrontes Wine in Cafayate:** This sun-kissed village has blossomed with new hotels and restaurants. Charming wineries and vineyards are within strolling distance in this valley of pink sand and cactus-dotted canyons famous for producing an aromatic white wine called Torrontes. See chapter 8.

o **Traveling the Wine Roads of Mendoza:** Less commercialized than their European and American counterparts, Mendoza's wineries spread out along roads known locally as Caminos del Vino. The spectacular high Andes form a dramatic backdrop. About 80 wineries formally offer tours and tastings, with those in the southerly Valle de Uco the most fascinating. See chapter 10.

o **Cruising to Chile with Cruce Andino:** Why fly or drive when you can sail through the Andes? With three boats and three bus trips, you can go from Bariloche, Argentina, to Puerto Montt, Chile, in a day on the Cruce de Lagos tour. Turning it into an overnight trip, with a stay on the Chilean side, gives you time to take in the beauty of the temperate rainforest and the magic of these mountains. See chapter 11.

- **Whale-Watching at Península Valdés:** From April to December, the massive Southern Right Whale heads to the protected bays off the Península Valdés to relax, reproduce, and recharge. The boats that head out hourly from Puerto Pirámides get remarkably close to these friendly giants. You can spot sea elephants, penguins, ostrichlike *choiques,* and sometimes even orca whales on the peninsula. See chapter 12.

- **Seeing a Million Penguins Guarding Their Nests:** Every autumn, over a million penguins return to mate on a hillside overlooking the Atlantic, in a remote area of Patagonia. At **Punta Tombo National Reserve,** you can walk among these friendly creatures and, if you're lucky, get to see them guarding the babies in their nests. See chapter 12.

- **Watching Ice Calve off the Perito Moreno Glacier:** It's worth the journey to remote El Calafate to simply sit still and gaze at the majestic tongue of ice that stretches into Lago Argentino. When you see a giant chunk of ice (the size of a bus!) crackle off the glacier into the lake, you'll feel chilled by the power of nature. See chapter 12.

THE most CHARMING SMALL TOWNS

- **Colonia del Sacramento** (Uruguay): Just a short ferry trip from Buenos Aires, this is Uruguay's best example of colonial life. The Barrio Histórico (Old Neighborhood) contains brilliant examples of colonial wealth and many of Uruguay's oldest structures. Dating from the 17th century, this beautifully preserved Portuguese settlement makes a perfect day trip. A few resorts and *estancias* (Argentine ranch farms, dating mostly to the mid- to late 19th c.) in the area offer the chance to spend the night. See chapter 6.

- **Salta:** Nestled in the Lerma valley of Argentina's Northwest, Salta has an eternal spring-like climate and the nation's best-preserved colonial architecture. It's surrounded by the fertile valley of the provincial capital, the polychrome canyons of Cafayate, and the desolate plateau of La Puña. See chapter 8.

- **Cafayate:** Set amid a pink, sandy landscape of cactus-dotted vineyards, the sleepy town of Cafayate has donkeys grazing on the central plaza and heaps of unlocked bicycles outside schools and churches. The sun-drenched area offers palatial-style wineries and luxurious wine lodges. See chapter 8.

- **Purmamarca:** A little white adobe church surrounded by cactus sits in front of a rainbow-colored mountain in the northern Jujuy province. It is a picture that could be used in every Argentine travel brochure—and is. See chapter 8.

- **Villa Carlos Paz:** A quick getaway from Córdoba, Villa Carlos Paz surrounds the picturesque Embalse San Roque. Although it's actually a reservoir, vacationers treat San Roque like a lake, and they swim, sail, and windsurf in its gentle waters. Year-round, visitors come to Carlos Paz to play outdoors by day and party by night. See chapter 9.

- **La Falda:** An excellent base from which to explore the Punilla, La Falda lies between the Valle Hermoso (Beautiful Valley) and the Sierras Chicas. Argentines come here for rest and relaxation, not wild entertainment. Crisp, clean air, wonderful hikes, and quiet hotels are the draw. See chapter 9.

o **Chacras de Coria:** Once considered a summer getaway for wealthy Mendoza families, Chacras de Coria is just 20 minutes from downtown Mendoza, but it's offset by its shady, gentle, rural lifestyle. The town has great bistros, excellent small inns, a lovely town square with an antiques market on Sundays, and a great ice-cream shop. See chapter 10.

o **Villa La Angostura:** With cottages owned by a "who's who" of Porteños, Villa la Angostura is becoming something of a jet-set stop in Patagonia. It has plenty of coastline along the north shores of Nahuel Huapi Lake for sailing, fishing, swimming, and sunning. The sweet main street is tidy and quaint, with good shops and some excellent restaurants. The eastern suburb of Bahia Manzano has a collection of cozy wooden lodges that hug the shore. In the winter, the local ski hill Cerro Bayo may be Patagonia's best-kept winter secret. See chapter 11.

o **San Martín de los Andes:** City planners in San Martín had the sense to do what overdeveloped Bariloche never thought of: limiting building height to two stories and to mandate continuity in the town's alpine architecture. The result? Bariloche is crass, whereas San Martín is class, and the town is a year-round playground to boot. Relax, swim, bike, ski, raft, hunt, or fish—this small town has it all. See chapter 11.

o **El Chaltén:** If you've ever wanted to relive the Wild West, you just might get your chance here in El Chaltén. On the verge of modernity, the area is influenced above all by the ever-present wind and by the beautiful granite spires of Cerro Torre and Mt. FitzRoy, which tower above town. It's a ramshackle place, with little town planning, lots of half-built homes, and a remarkable selection of good restaurants. The vibe is for adventurers and nature lovers who are willing to sacrifice some comforts for awe-inspiring nature and friendly locals. See chapter 12.

THE best OUTDOOR ADVENTURES

o **Strolling the Parks of Buenos Aires:** The Palermo park system in Buenos Aires is one of the world's most beautiful. Within the system are numerous parks, such as the Rose Garden and the Japanese Garden, as well as museums such as the **Museo de Arte Latinoamericano de Buenos Aires** (MALBA) and the **Museo Nacional de Bellas Artes.** See chapter 5.

o **Bird-Watching in Esteros del Ibera:** The flat marshlands of Corrientes province are a nature lover's paradise and can be explored by boat or horseback. See chapter 7.

o **Getting Wet Beneath Iguazú Falls:** Take an exhilarating boat ride beneath Iguazú's plummeting waterfalls. A number of tour companies operate rafts that speed toward the falls, soaking their awe-struck passengers along the way. This is the best way to experience the sound and fury of Iguazú's magnificent *cataratas*. See chapter 7.

o **Traveling Beyond the Falls into the Iguazú Jungle:** This is a place where birds such as the great dusky swift and brilliant morpho butterflies spread color through the thick forest canopy. You can easily arrange an outing into the forest once you arrive in Iguazú. See chapter 7.

- **Mountain Biking in the Valley of Dinosaurs:** Power pedal through Argentina's version of the Grand Canyon, **Talampaya National Park,** which boasts some of the largest dinosaur fossils in the world, mysterious stone etchings, and weird and wonderful rock formations. See chapter 8.

- **Paragliding in La Cumbre:** Jumping off a 300m (984-ft.) cliff and flying with condors is what attracts world-champion paragliders to this laid-back valley in the Córdoba sierra. See chapter 9.

- **Raging Down the Mendoza River:** Mendoza offers the best white-water rafting in Argentina. During the summer months, when the snow melts in the Andes and fills the Mendoza River, rafters take on Class IV and V rapids here. Rafting is possible year-round, but the river is colder and calmer in winter months. See chapter 10.

- **Skiing Las Leñas:** One of South America's top ski destinations, Las Leñas boasts more slopes than any single resort in the Americas, with 40 miles of runs, excellent snow, and typically small crowds. Las Leñas also hosts an active nightlife in winter. See chapter 10.

- **Skiing Cerro Catedral:** With a huge investment in new lifts, new development at the base, and consecutive years of heavy snowfall, Bariloche's Catedral is the best ski resort in Argentina. The après-ski scene includes chocolate shops, live music, and happening slopeside lounges. And the views take in the Andes and the beautiful Nahuel Huapi Lake. See chapter 11.

- **Rafting the Río Manso:** There are two sections to this gorgeous emerald river south of Bariloche. The Inferior makes for a great family outing, with bird-watching and fun paddling. The Frontera section takes you through an adrenaline-heavy set of 10 rapids toward the border with Chile. Either way, it's a trip through a beautiful undiscovered mountain valley. See chapter 11.

- **Fly-Fishing in Patagonia:** Few places in the world are as appealing to expert fly-fishers, and as rewarding to beginners and novices, as Argentina's Patagonia. Remote rivers from Junín de los Andes all the way down to Tierra del Fuego draw fanatics who long for solitude, gorgeous scenery and, of course, very big trout. Great guides become lifelong friends. See chapter 11.

- **Lahuen Co Hot Springs:** If your idea of the outdoors includes gentle pampering and peace and quiet, this remote thermal spa deep in Lanín National Park will wow you. Small, natural pools (indoor and out) are heated by natural thermal waters in a volcanic area in the middle of a temperate rainforest outside San Martín de los Andes. See chapter 11.

- **Horseback Riding the Patagonian Steppe:** Discover your inner gaucho on a horseback ride across a beautiful horizon on the wild steppe or into the deep Andes. Horses are cherished here, lovingly cared for by dedicated, actual gauchos. See chapter 11.

- **Hiking to Laguna Torre:** One of the world's finest day hikes takes you from the door of your inn in El Chaltén to the base of the needle-shaped granite spire of Cerro Torre, a legendary challenge for mountaineers and rock climbers. The hike's pinnacle is on the shores of the blustery Laguna Torre, where the wind feels like it just may blow you over. Back in the shelter of the FitzRoy River valley, you'll head back to town refreshed and exhilarated. See chapter 12.

- **Hiking Big Ice in Perito Moreno Glacier:** Tour operators have been offering guided walks on the Perito Moreno Glacier for years, and guests from around the world strap on some crampons and head out for an hour or so. Those with a good level of fitness can now head much deeper into the glacier with a full-day hike. Peer into deep ice canyons, navigate your way along a frozen ridge, and try to grasp the sheer grandeur of this UNESCO World Heritage Site. See chapter 12.

THE best HOTELS

o **Palacio Duhua–Park Hyatt Buenos Aires** (Buenos Aires; ✆ **11/5171-1234**; www.buenosaires.park.hyatt.com): In Recoleta, this hotel combines the Belle Epoque mansion of the once powerful Duhau family with an adjacent tower. Guests have a choice of suites within the mansion or the modern tower, which are connected by a spectacular multilevel garden that's worth checking out even if you're not staying here. See p. 86.

o **Alvear Palace Hotel** (Buenos Aires; ✆ **11/4808-2100**; www.alvearpalace.com): This hotel, dating to the Belle Epoque era, is the city's most exclusive and one of the top hotels in the world. The Alvear leaves you wanting for nothing; its luxurious bedrooms and suites even have private butler service. The hotel's guest list reflects the top names in Argentina and visitors from abroad. See p. 85.

o **Four Seasons Hotel** (Buenos Aires; ✆ **11/4321-1200**; www.fourseasons.com/buenosaires): In 2002, the Four Seasons took over what was already one of Buenos Aires's most luxurious properties. This landmark hotel has two parts—the 12-story Park Tower, housing the majority of the guest rooms, and the turn-of-the-20th-century French rococo La Mansión, with seven elegant suites and a handful of private event rooms. See p. 85.

o **Killa Cafayate** (Cafayate; ✆ **3868/422254**; www.killacafayate.com.ar): This lovely Mediterranean-inspired property offer spacious rooms that overlook the village rooftops. Outdoors, follow the long, delightful walkway of terra-cotta tiles and ceramic urns to a splendid pool and courtyard. The Killa's friendly owner Martha never leaves the front desk. See p. 226.

o **Iguazú Grand Hotel Resort & Casino** (Puerto Iguazú; ✆ **3757/498-050**; www.iguazugrand.com): The best luxury hotel near the falls cannot be faulted. The giant rooms feature beautiful decor, and the helpful staff keeps everybody happy. See p. 196.

o **Posada Puerto Bemberg** (Puerta Libertad; ✆ **3757/496500**; www.puertobemberg.com): It hardly gets more exclusive than this with a private boardwalk overlooking a jungle river surrounded by a lush jungle that is your own private reserve, shared with howler monkeys and toucans. Ample rooms and ampler gardens complete the formula at this gorgeous lodge 30km (19 miles) south of Puerto Iguazú. See p. 200.

o **Hotel Kkala** (Salta; ✆ **0387/439-6590**; www.hotelkkala.com.ar): If you like your hotels to appear like something from a Le Corbusier catalogue, Kkala will not disappoint. Meticulously designed rooms surround a handsome deck in a modernist suburban house in a quiet neighborhood overlooking this historic city. See p. 218.

o **Estancia Los Potreros** (La Cumbre; ✆ **011/6091-2692**; www.ride-americas.com): This genuine Argentine ranch located in the rolling green hills of northern Córdoba, offers gracious hosts, authentic rooms, and superb horses to make for a memorable stay. See p. 257.

- **Finca Adalgisa** (Chacras de Coria; ✆ **261/496-0713;** www.fincaadalgisa.com. ar): Hotels around the world, let alone in Mendoza, all try to reproduce what this small wine lodge has: authenticity, charm, and superb service. From the simple pool surrounded by 100-year-old Malbec vines and the relaxed outdoor lounge serving only fresh local tapas, to espresso at breakfast and a full-service concierge, your stay here will get the absolute most out of the real Mendoza. See p. 283.

- **Park Hyatt Mendoza** (Mendoza; ✆ **261/441-1234;** www.mendoza.park.hyatt. com): The best-located hotel in Mendoza looks out on the bustling Plaza Independencia. Sipping a glass of Malbec on the front courtyard patio, you're likely to feel like royalty. Rooms are modern, luxurious, and large. The hotel hosts regular events here that celebrate the amazing food and wine of the area. See p. 270.

- **Llao Llao Hotel & Resort** (San Carlos de Bariloche; ✆ **02944/448530;** www. llaollao.com): With its stunning alpine style, top-notch service, a golf course, a lovely pool, and a plethora of activities, the Llao Llao has it all. It's considered one of the top resorts in the world, with a price to match. Inside, the style is that of an upscale yet cozy hunting lodge. The unbeatable location, perched on a hill surrounded by mountain lakes, offers sublime views from every window. Come here for an unforgettable splurge. See p. 318.

- **Río Hermoso Lodge** (Paraje Río Hermoso; ✆ **02972/410485;** www.riohermoso. com): A sunny fishing lodge nestled in a lush, green landscape, this small lodge has done everything right. From the cozy rooms to colorful cushions, it's wonderfully relaxing and quiet here. And you're only 20 minutes from the adventures waiting in San Martín de los Andes. See p. 340.

- **Correntoso Lake and River Hotel** (Villa la Angostura; ✆ **02944/15-619728** [mobile]; www.correntoso.com): A historic landmark that's been carefully restored, this hotel keeps getting better. A unique spa, lovely pool, great lakeside restaurant, and natural decor make this a wonderful base camp in the Lake District. Oh, and one of the finest fly-fishing holes in the entire world is right out front. See p. 330.

- **Eolo Patagonia's Spirit** (El Calafate; ✆ **02902/492042;** www.eolo.com.ar): A friendly and relaxed home amid the powerful emptiness of the Patagonian Steppe, Eolo is influenced by traditional *estancias* (Argentine ranch farms), but it has modern amenities such as a spa, a wine bar, and a library. It's a place to come live, breathe, and be wowed by the vastness of Patagonia. See p. 374.

- **Los Notros** (Perito Moreno Glacier, near Calafate; ✆ **02902/499510;** www. losnotros.com): Location is everything at the Los Notros hotel, which boasts a breathtaking view spanning one of Argentina's great wonders, Perito Moreno Glacier. The hotel blends contemporary folk art with a range of colorful hues. Impeccable rooms come with a dramatic view of the electric-blue tongue of the glacier, making this lodge one of the most upscale, unique lodging options in Argentina. The hotel arranges excursions around the area and occasional informative talks. Plenty of easy chairs and lounges are strewn around the property, so guests can sit and contemplate the glorious natural environment. See p. 380.

- **Los Cauquenes Resort & Spa** (Ushuaia; ✆ **2901/441300;** www.loscauquenes. com): Situated right on the Beagle Channel at the end of the world, this inn has just about everything you could want—a great wine bar, scenic terraces, a spa, and a gentle feel. Unforgettable. See p. 403.

THE best DINING EXPERIENCES

- **El Obrero** (Buenos Aires; ✆ 11/4362-9912; www.bodegonelobrero.com.ar): Widely considered one of the best *parrillas* (grills) in Buenos Aires, El Obrero remains authentic due to its out-of-the-way location in La Boca and its emphasis on Boca Junior soccer fans. The beef is thick and juicy, and the Italian dishes spectacular. Started by two Spanish brothers decades ago, the restaurant remains in family hands. See p. 109.

- **Café Tortoni** (Buenos Aires; ✆ 11/4342-4328; www.cafetortoni.com.ar): This legendary cafe might not have the best service in town, but its historical importance and old-world beauty more than make up for it. Café Tortoni was and remains Argentina's meeting place of choice among intellectuals who co-exist with the throngs of tourists. See p. 151.

- **La Bourgogne** (Buenos Aires; ✆ 11/4805-3857): Jean Paul Bondoux is the top French chef in South America, brandishing his talents in the kitchen of this restaurant tucked inside the Alvear Palace Hotel (a second La Bourgogne is in Mendoza). A member of Relais & Châteaux, La Bourgogne serves exquisite cuisine inspired by Bondoux's Burgundy heritage. See p. 105 and 286.

- **José Balcarce** (Salta; ✆ 387/421-1628): The best restaurant in Salta serves incredibly imaginative Andean cuisine in an elegant setting. Guests can sample llama carpaccio or roasted llama medallions with prickly pear sauce, accompanied by Andean potatoes grown in the verdant hills on the outskirts of the city. They're all delicious. See p. 220.

- **1884** (Mendoza; ✆ 261/424-2698; www.1884restaurante.com.ar): Celebrity chef Francis Mallmann's restaurant in Mendoza has been number one in town for several years now, and it remains the ultimate Argentine dining experience in the country's food and wine capital. Located inside a century-old *bodega,* or wine cellar, the restaurant serves rugged and tasty local specialties such as *chivito* (kid) and *lechón* (piglet). See p. 272.

- **Lunch at a Bodega:** Mendoza is home to dozens of places where visitors can learn more about wine—from how the grapes are grown to how the barrels are chosen. And the lessons usually come with a relaxed outdoor lunch served on a *bodega* patio, with the towering Andes in the distance. The experience is indulgent, informative, and so very relaxing. Try the lunch at **Ruca Malen** in the Luján area or at **Andeluna** or **O. Fournier** in the Valle de Uco. See chapter 10.

- **Lakeside Gourmet Dining in Bariloche:** The capital of Northern Patagonia has some truly excellent restaurants. The best, such as **Butterfly** and **Cassis,** are right above the giant mountain lakes, offering views that match the outstanding dining. Be sure to arrive well before sunset! See chapter 11.

- **Patagonian Asado:** The gaucho gets things going early. The coals take time to warm up, and they place the lamb on a cross in front of the heat and leave it there to roast for hours. Served with a simple salad and a few bottles of Malbec, it's home cooking like you've never eaten. *Estancias* from the Lake District to Los Glaciares National Park humbly offer this tradition daily to visitors. In El Calafate, sample local lamb at the **Estancia 25 de Mayo.** See chapter 12.

ARGENTINA IN DEPTH

by Charlie O'Malley

Argentina is a nation that once was among the wealthiest in the world. It long reigned as the preeminent power on the South American continent. Every building in Buenos Aires, every legend emerging from the Pampas, every abandoned church in the missions, overgrown with vines, tells of this vast country's glorious past. Even the faces on the streets of Argentina's cities are a reflection of a history full of accidents, desires, and the sheer force of a nation's will to shape itself and its perception within the outside world.

ARGENTINA TODAY

Compared to the surging profiles of its neighbors Chile and Brazil, Argentina seems to be locked in as the underachiever in the southern cone of South America. Under the administration of President Cristina Fernández de Kirchner, the country remains unattractive to foreign investors as state interventionist policies, opaque business dealings, sinister union agitation, and endemic corruption take a toll on its international image. Add to this rampant inflation, a worsening education system, and an increasing wealth gap and its no wonder most Argentines shrug their shoulders with depressed resignation when discussing their country's politics.

Nevertheless, Argentina is well placed in what is an emerging and increasingly self-confident continent. Just look at the thousands of Brazilian tourists that now flock the streets of Buenos Aires and tour the wine roads of Mendoza. They have come for something that only Argentina does well: Old World sophistication with a vibrant, South American flavor. Despite a global crisis, Argentina is still booming, not just from tourism but exports of commodities that vary from soya to wine, meat to wheat. Its vast mineral wealth remains largely untapped and its huge open spaces are becoming a rarity in this crowded world.

The sudden death of Nestor Kirchner in October 2010 shocked the country. Suffering in the polls at the time, his posthumous legacy is somewhat brighter and he is now recognized for bringing stability to the country after the trauma of the 2001 economic crisis. He is also credited with finally bestowing some closure to the terror of the Dirty War by prosecuting and jailing many of its perpetrators. His wife and current president Cristina experienced a brief recovery in popularity after her husband's death but at press time had yet to declare if she will run for office again in November 2011. One significant act of hers was to legalize gay marriage in 2010, making Argentina the only country in South America to allow it. As well as leading to an upsurge in gay tourism (wedding planners in Buenos Aires are apparently working overtime), it has further enhanced the image of Argentina as culturally open, sophisticated, and most of all, very friendly.

Yet despite the looming clouds, nobody is expecting the chaos of 2002, when police shot protestors on the street. Argentina is certainly a more stable country, and the fact that you hold this book in your hand means you are one example of the millions who have come to Argentina as a guest, eager to experience its rich, diverse culture and excellent quality of life. The country is now celebrating its 200-year-old existence, and a new era in the nation's history has begun.

LOOKING BACK AT ARGENTINA'S SETTLEMENT & COLONIZATION

Well before the arrival of Europeans, several distinct indigenous groups populated the area now called Argentina. The Incas had made inroads into the highlands of the Northwest. Most other groups were nomadic hunters and fishers, such as those in the Chaco, the Tehuelche of Patagonia, and the Querandí and Puelche (Guennakin) of the Pampas. Others (the Diaguitas, of the Northwest) developed stationary agriculture. The Mapuche Indians, a warrior tribe based at the very bottom of Patagonia in both Argentina and Chile, were the only Indian tribe never conquered by the Spanish.

The Argentina we know today took shape only after repeat attempts at colonization by the Spanish. Much of Spain's effort was initially aimed at staving off Portuguese expansion in what today is Brazil. The first European known to have laid eyes on the area that would become Buenos Aires was Juan Díaz de Solís, who sailed up what is now the Río de la Plata and named it the Mar Dulce, or Sweet Sea. Ferdinand Magellan retraced the route in 1520, thinking he had stumbled upon a passageway that would take him to the Pacific Ocean. Sebastian Cabot returned on a treasure-hunting expedition in 1526. An exchange with local Indians yielded trinkets of gold and silver, and so Cabot renamed the Mar Dulce the Río de la Plata, or River of Silver, in expectation of riches he hoped to find. Then he returned to Spain to convince the crown that more wealth was to be had in the region.

In 1535, Spain—victorious after having conquered Peru, yet aware of Portugal's presence in Brazil—sent an expedition, headed by Pedro de Mendoza, to settle the region. Mendoza was initially successful in founding Santa María del Buen Aire, or Buenos Aires (1536), but the lack of food proved fatal. Mendoza, mortally ill and discouraged by Indian attacks, sailed for Spain with a hundred of his men in 1537. He died on the way, and his body was cast out to sea.

The Spanish had greater success in other parts of the country. In 1573, Jerónimo Luís de Cabrera founded Córdoba in central Argentina. The city was a Jesuit stronghold, and the religious order established the Universidad Nacional de Córdoba in 1613, one of the oldest universities in South America. Córdoba remained an important city through much of colonial Argentina. To this day, it's Argentina's most important education center, where one out of five residents is a student.

Mendoza, in the shadows of the Andes, was settled in 1561 by Pedro del Castillo. He had pushed into the region from an expedition based out of Santiago, in modern Chile. In 1535, the Spaniards began exploring the Northwest, as they expanded down through the recently conquered Inca Empire, and founded the city of Salta in 1582.

In 1580, Juan de Garay resettled Buenos Aires. His expedition sailed from Asunción, in Paraguay, down the Paraná River. At the time, Asunción was a significant city within the Spanish Empire, and Jesuit missions on the border of what is today Argentina, Brazil, and Paraguay thrived, providing economic output and the ability to control the frontiers. Garay had with him about 45 men and, uniquely, one woman, Ana Díaz. Díaz's role has been obscured by time, and it is unknown whether she was a prostitute from Asunción who accompanied the troops or whether she should be exalted as a female conquistador. In any case, a woman's touch on the expedition proved to be the charm. Upon the second attempt to colonize, the city continued to grow into a permanent, though small, colonial establishment. Ana Díaz's colonial landholdings were on what is today Calle Florida.

While today Buenos Aires is the cultural and political capital of Argentina, it was a backwater region for a long time during the colonial period. More important were Córdoba, Salta, the Jesuit missions, and other parts of the country closer to Lima and Asunción, the centers of power in the Spanish Empire. Buenos Aires was logistically important in defending the lower half of the Spanish Empire from the Portuguese. Constant skirmishes continued between the two empires, with neighboring Uruguay as a disputed territory. Tiny Colonia, across the Río de la Plata from Buenos Aires, passed back and forth, and its buildings reflect the styles of the two ruling powers. With access to the Río de la Plata and the open Atlantic, however, it was inevitable that Buenos Aires—at first a lonely outpost on the edge of the vast Pampas—would grow to be one of the continent's most important cities.

Independence & Warfare

All revolutions are political as well as economic, and Argentina's was no exception. By the late 1700s, Buenos Aires was the preeminent port within the region, and cattle hides became a major component of the economy. The trade, however, was heavily taxed and strictly regulated by the Spanish crown, so smuggling and circumventing became the norm, along with illicit trade with the British. Downtown Buenos Aires is still riddled with underground tunnels. Many of them opened directly to what had been the port area along the Río de la Plata, and cargo passed untaxed through them during this time period. To this day, it is not clear whether the Jesuits may have built them, even farther back, as secret passageways. In any case, the merchants' desire to end taxation began to foment, feeding a greater drive for overall political independence.

Indirect trade was not enough for the British. Sensing that the Spanish Empire was weakening, they attacked Buenos Aires in 1806 and 1807. The battles were known as the Reconquista and the Defensa. These battles are memorialized in the names of the streets of Buenos Aires that feed into the Plaza de Mayo, which were the routes the Argentine armies used to oust the British. Able to defend themselves without the aid of Spain, many Argentine-born Europeans began to debate the idea of self-government in Buenos Aires.

The Revolution of Buenos Aires was declared on May 25, 1810, marking the beginnings of the independence movement. On July 9, 1816 (Nueve de Julio), Buenos Aires officially declared its independence from Spain, under the name United Provinces of the Río de la Plata. Several years of hard fighting followed before the Argentines defeated the Spanish in northern Argentina, and the Europeans remained a threat until Perú was liberated by General José de San Martín, considered the national hero of Argentina, and later by Simón Bolívar, from 1820 to 1824. With Lord

George Canning as their main representative, Britain officially recognized Argentina's independence. Argentina's relationship with this European world power, however, would remain tenuous.

Spain's defeat, however, did not mean that Argentina had peace. Boundaries and the power structure were still unclear. Strongmen with private armies, called *caudillos*, controlled remote regions, as was the case in other areas of South America after independence. Even with a national constitution, the territory that now constitutes modern Argentina was frequently disunited until 1860. The national debate included the question of whether Buenos Aires would be the new capital.

The internal and external struggles were brutal, changing both the physical and ethnic structure of the country. In 1864, the War of the Triple Alliance (also known as the Paraguayan War) broke out between Paraguay and an alliance of Argentina, Brazil, and Uruguay. Paraguayan president Francisco Solano López saw himself as an emperor and hoped to give the country an Atlantic port. The war, which devastated Paraguay, lasted 6 years and was among the bloodiest fighting ever on South American soil.

Of the three countries fighting Paraguay, Argentina recovered from the war quickest, and it served as an impetus for unification. From this point on, Argentina was the most powerful and wealthiest country on the continent—and remained so for nearly 80 years.

Modern Argentine historians dispute this subplot, but the Argentine army fought its battles by placing black soldiers at the front lines, where they faced immediate slaughter, ahead of white soldiers. For this reason, Argentina, unlike much of South America, is home to few descendants of slaves brought from Africa.

Argentina's ethnic makeup was further altered in the late 1870s by General Julio Argentino Roca's Campaign of the Desert. Essentially, he drew a line out from Buenos Aires and slaughtered virtually every Indian within it. He claimed to do so in the name of national defense and the economy, in light of the fact that some Indian populations stole cattle and attacked the various *estancias* and forts within the Pampas and Upper Patagonia. The destruction of the native population further consolidated Buenos Aires's control of the hinterlands and led to a wave of new ranches and *estancias*, as well as the unimpeded development of the railroads. Now only within the north and the very south of Argentina (areas untouched by Roca) do Indians exist in any substantial numbers.

It was these two specific genocidal policies—toward descendants of African and indigenous South American folk—that laid the ground for the largely white and European culture that Argentina was to become. Needless to say, however, Argentines have a sensitive relationship with this period and often gloss over it in historical accounts. Many historians account for the lack of an African population by arguing that blacks died out naturally or simply intermarried with the millions of white immigrants until pure Africans no longer existed.

The fact that Africans existed in Argentina is most evident, however, in the nation's most important cultural contribution to the world—the tango. Like all musical and dance forms native to the Americas, it owes its roots to slave culture. Photographs of gauchos from the late 1800s also show that many were clearly of African descent. The overwhelmingly white society of greater Buenos Aires that tourists see today was not simply the proud result of millions of Italians and Spaniards descending from boats after a long Atlantic voyage, but was instead the result of a deliberate government policy of genocide.

Buenos Aires, the Capital

Genuine unification of Argentina did not occur until 1880, 300 years after the permanent founding of Buenos Aires. On this anniversary, the city was officially made the capital. The return of San Martín's body that year, to a permanent tomb within the Catedral Metroplitano on Plaza de Mayo, solidified and symbolized the city's absolute authority.

From then on, Buenos Aires experienced a period of explosive growth and wealth, laying the foundations for the glory days that Argentines remember about their country. Trade with Europe expanded, with cattle and grain from the newly conquered hinterlands serving as the main exports. Millions of immigrants came from Italy, Spain, and other countries, filling the city's slums, primarily in the southern sections of La Boca and San Telmo. To this day, there are almost as many Italian last names as Spanish in Argentina. Even the language spoken in Argentina seems almost like Italian-accented Spanish, with its rhythm and pitch. *Lunfardo,* the street dialect associated with tango, owes many of its words to immigrant Italian.

The exponential growth of this time means that Buenos Aires—unlike Salta, Córdoba, and other old Argentine cities—retains few colonial buildings besides its churches. In fact, by the late 1800s, the capital made a conscious effort to completely rebuild much of its cityscape, following a pattern loosely based on Haussman's plans for rebuilding Paris under Second Empire France. Much of this was to be done in time for the 1910 Independence Centennial celebrations.

Developers laid new boulevards over the original Spanish colonial grid. The most important was Avenida de Mayo, which opened in 1893 and would serve as the government procession route, linking the Casa Rosada or Presidential Palace on its eastern end with the new Congreso on its western terminus. Lined with Beaux Arts and Art Nouveaux buildings, according to the styles of the time, it became the cultural and nightlife center of the city. Diagonal Norte and Diagonal Sud were also laid out (though not completed for many years later). The widest boulevard in the world, 9 de Julio, was planned in 1888 as well, but its construction didn't begin until 1937. Technically, it remains incomplete.

The majority of Buenos Aires's most iconic structures were built at this time—the Teatro Colón, the Water Palace, the Subway System, Congreso, Retiro Station, and the innumerable palaces and mansions that still line the streets in the northern sector. For nearly 30 years, the city was an ongoing construction site, as it forcefully rebuilt itself with a European image. While Argentina had the wealth and resources to pay for the massive rebuilding, however, it lacked the know-how and had to import its talent, labor, and even materials from Europe. The capital's planners, architects, and engineers came from the Old World, bringing with them the beautiful structural materials that now grace the city. A sticking point for many years was the fact that the British built and controlled the railroads.

Today, as a visitor mindful of Argentina's past several decades of political and economic chaos, it is difficult to make sense of the ostentatiously built infrastructure that remains from this earlier time. In essence, between 1880 and 1910, Argentina assumed the height of its wealth and power. Built at great expense of labor, money, and determination, Buenos Aires was the imperial capital of a country hungry to assert its importance on the world stage. Indeed, at the turn of the last century Argentina was one of the 10 wealthiest countries in the world.

Cultural Growth in the 1920s & 1930s

The economic expansion, wealth, and sense of power Argentina had during this time laid the groundwork for strong cultural growth by the 1920s and 1930s. During this period, traditions that had always existed among the lower classes within Buenos Aires bubbled to the surface and came into international recognition. Tango has its roots in slave culture, and immigrants (mostly Italian) adopted the dance as they moved to Argentina. While the dance had always been associated with the slums of the lower classes, one man changed all of that. In 1917, Carlos Gardel, who began his career singing as a child in Buenos Aires's Abasto Market, recorded what is considered the first important tango song—"Mi Noche Triste," which launched him to stardom. Throughout the 1920s, Gardel toured in France. Seeing that Parisians accepted tango, the upper classes within Argentina began to embrace it as well. By the middle of the 1920s, tango became the country's most important musical form; its history and eventual acceptance internationally is akin to the rise of jazz in the United States. Gardel recorded numerous songs and toured Europe, South America, and the United States, making musical movies along the way. He died young, at the age of 44, on June 24, 1935, in a plane crash in Colombia, which solidified his status as one of Argentina's most important cultural icons.

The same period saw a flowering of literature and live theater. Jorge Luis Borges published short stories that often spoke of the struggles of the gangsters and lower classes in Buenos Aires and other parts of Argentina. Along with other colleagues, Borges launched the short-lived literary magazine *Proa* in 1924. By the 1930s, amid political chaos, eminent civil war, and repression in Spain, Buenos Aires became the preeminent center of Spanish-language culture. Among the most important Spanish artists who came during this period was the playwright Federico García Lorca, who lived in Buenos Aires briefly during 1933 and 1934, staying at the Castelar Hotel on Avenida de Mayo.

The 1930s were also a golden age for Argentine radio and cinema. Many stars came of age at this time, including Tita Morello and Libertad Lamarque. The Argentine film industry's only South American rival was in Rio de Janeiro. Even there, however, stars such as Carmen Miranda, long before Hollywood discovered her, emulated the style of Buenos Aires movie stars who set the trends on the continent. By the 1930s, Avenida Corrientes was also widened, many theaters moved to this new location, and many new ones opened.

Viewed from the edges, the city of Buenos Aires glittered as the cultural capital of Argentina, pulling many a young man and woman in from the provinces to seek fame. In 1934, one teenage girl from the city of Junín in the Province of Buenos Aires would come to do just that, changing Argentine history forever with her determination beyond the obvious glamour of the stage and screen. Though accounts differ as to exactly how Maria Eva Duarte came to Buenos Aires—whether she was escorted by members of her family or by her purported lover, Augustin Magaldi, one of the country's top tango singers—she was in Buenos Aires for her very first time at the tender age of 15. With little but her looks, charm, and persistence, Ms. Duarte moved through a succession of jobs and men in theater, radio, and film. Many claimed she lacked talent, but with her connections, she became a force to be reckoned with. Various bosses hired her knowing only who her current powerful boyfriends were. Eventually, with success as an actress, she would meet her most powerful boyfriend of all.

The Perón Years

Few eras of Argentina's history play into its modern-day politics like the Perón era. In 1943, the military overthrew Argentina's constitutional government in a coup. Perón was put in charge of the National Labor Office, making him popular among the working class. Unique among members of the military, he had a flare for public relations, courting members of the media as well as young stars. Even during this period, he was revealing what would eventually be part of his persona: He is often the only member of the military smiling in photographs.

Perón's popularity was anchored by an earthquake that occurred on January 15, 1944, in San Juan, a city near Mendoza in the shadows of the Andes. Ten thousand people died and nearly half the city was left homeless. The tragic event became the ultimate public relations opportunity for Perón, as he rallied support for the region. Perón arranged a fundraiser for the victims of the earthquake with a star-studded concert in Luna Park, a stadium in Buenos Aires. Legend has it that at this event, he met 24-year-old actress Eva Duarte, changing Argentina's history forever. (In fact, photographic evidence makes clear that the two had met before, in Buenos Aires.)

Fearing his rise to power, the military government arrested Perón and imprisoned him on Juan García Island in the Tigre Delta. A near revolt occurred in Buenos Aires, and the government quickly released him. On October 17, 1945 (the most important date in the Peronist calendar), Perón spoke to a crowd gathered from a balcony at the Casa Rosada and announced that elections would be forthcoming. Feeling the need to legitimize their relationship with elections pending, Eva and Perón married secretly in Los Toldos, the town of her birth, using the civil registry. They later married in a Catholic ceremony in La Plata, the provincial capital of Buenos Aires Province. Ordinarily, the Catholic Church would not have sanctioned the marriage, given Duarte's reputation as a "tainted" woman, but the priest was a relative of Perón's.

Perón became president in 1946 in an election marked by fraud and brutality on both sides. Though Juan was technically the power, he could not have retained his popularity without Eva (nicknamed Evita by the people) at his side. Knowing that their power was based in worker's unions, the couple launched numerous economic and work initiatives, many along the lines of communist-style 5-year plans, and employment and wages spiked under the new regime.

The modern middle class of Argentina, now weakened by more recent economic policies, owes its existence to this period. Eva used her position to create the Eva Perón Foundation, which was as much a public relations tool as a charity service for the first lady. Under the official economic plans and the foundation, contributions were forced from workers and the wealthy alike; land, buildings, and factories were seized from the oligarchs; and the railroads, formerly in the hands of the British, were nationalized in lieu of payment for unpaid war debts owed by Great Britain to Argentina. Throughout the country, the couple built hospitals, schools, and playgrounds for lower-class citizens and their children. One children's park, the Ciudad de los Niños in La Plata, served as the model for Walt Disney when he designed Disneyland, in California. The popularity of the power couple soared among the poor, but the two were despised by the upper classes and the military alike.

After Evita's long insistence, women received the right to vote in 1947, and the presidential elections of 1951 were the first in which women participated. Wanting to legitimize her power within the government, Evita sought to be vice president on the 1951 election ballots, but Perón forced her to decline. Stricken with cervical cancer, Evita was dying, and forfeiting this final fight worsened her health. She voted in the elections from her hospital bed. She was so weak for the inaugural parade through Buenos Aires that they doped her up with painkillers and strapped her body to a wood frame, hidden by an oversize fur coat, so she could wave to crowds.

On July 26, 1952, Evita finally died. A 2-week mourning period ensued, and millions poured into Buenos Aires to pay their final respects. More than a dozen people died and hundreds were injured in the commotion as mourners lined up for days to view Evita's body in its glass coffin. Knowing that without Evita his days might soon be over, Perón commissioned a monument to her, which was never completed, and had her body embalmed to be preserved forever.

A period of economic instability ensued, exacerbated by Perón's own policies. He had, in essence, robbed the country of its wealth by spending on social causes (and siphoning much for his own use). In 1955, the military deposed Perón and stole Evita's body, sending it on a journey that lasted nearly 17 years before it resurfaced. Images of the Peróns were banned in Argentina; even uttering their names was an offense.

Perón bounced through several countries—Paraguay, Panama, Venezuela, the Dominican Republic—before finally settling in Spain, ruled by his longtime ally Francisco Franco. During his time in Panama, he met his future third wife and vice president, Isabel Martínez, a nightclub dancer.

While Perón was exiled in Spain, Evita's body was returned to him, and his power base in Argentina strengthened, allowing his return to the presidency in 1973. Still, his arrival was wrought with chaos. Gun battles broke out at Ezeiza Airport when his plane landed, leaving several of his followers and rivals dead. When he died in 1974, Isabel replaced him. Neither as strong as her husband nor his previous wife, Isabel could not hold onto the country for very long. She took on the nickname Isabelita, to bring back the memory of her predecessor, and, as an occultist, she supposedly held séances over the coffin of Evita in order to absorb her power. Despite her efforts, terrorism and economic instability persisted during her short reign, and on March 24, 1976, she was deposed in a military coup.

The Dirty War & Its Aftermath

The regime of Jorge Rafael Videla, established in the junta, carried out a campaign to weed out anybody suspected of having Communist or Peronist sympathies. (Ironically, it was in this period that Evita was finally laid to rest in her current tomb in Recoleta Cemetery.) Congress was closed, censorship imposed, and unions banned. Over the next 7 years, during this "Process of National Reorganization"—a period now known as the Guerra Sucia (Dirty War) or El Proceso—between 10,000 and 30,000 intellectuals, artists, activists, and others were tortured or executed by the Argentine government. The mothers of these *desaparecidos* (the disappeared ones) began holding Thursday afternoon vigils in front of the presidential palace in Buenos Aires's Plaza de Mayo as a way to call international attention to the plight of the missing. Although the junta was overturned in 1983, the weekly protests continue to this day in Buenos Aires and in other large cities in the country.

With the Argentine population growing increasingly vocal about human rights abuses and the increasingly worsening economy, the military dictatorship sought a patriotic distraction.

Argentines have long laid claim to the Falkland Islands, known locally as the Islas Malvinas. The basis for the claim is that the territory, which was used for a penal colony beginning in 1828, was part of the Spanish Empire that Argentina conquered when it won independence. Argentina's early military rivals for power over the islands included both Britain and the United States. Argentina proved to be too young a nation with too little power to control such a remote region: The British seized the islands in 1833 by simply sending warships and a gentlemanly note to the Argentine commander in charge, José María Pinedo.

The taking of the Falklands had always been a sticking point among Argentines. In the early 1980s, Argentine President Leopoldo Galtieri assumed that invading the Falklands would be easy and bring much-needed support to his government. Galtieri believed the invasion would go almost unnoticed by the United Kingdom (unbelievable in retrospect) because the U.K. didn't really want the islands and would not tolerate a loss of life to protect its far-flung turf. At the United Nations, Argentina had made several attempts to bring up their claim to the Falklands before the invasion, without any response from Great Britain.

The Argentines tested the waters by first invading the South Georgia Islands on March 19, 1982. On April 2, Galtieri launched the full-fledged invasion of the Falklands. The invasion was ill-fated, ill-planned, and tragic; nearly 900 people died in the short war. Most of Argentina's military forces remained on the Chilean border out of concern that British ally Augusto Pinochet of Chile would use the war as a reason to invade his eastern neighbor. Losses were heaviest on the Argentine side, including the sinking of the battleship *General Belgrano* with nearly 300 sailors aboard. Officially, neither side declared war on the other during the entire dispute. While no other powers contributed to the military effort, much of Latin America sided with Argentina, while Europe and the United States sided with Great Britain.

The war was a diplomatic nightmare for the United States, whose Monroe Doctrine—penned nearly 180 years before—technically required it to declare war on Great Britain. However, the war meant the end of the military regime and the solidification of power for Great Britain's Prime Minister Margaret Thatcher. Virtually forgotten in the greater world, it's almost a joke among English-speaking nations that Argentina would challenge one of the world's greatest naval powers. But the war is a serious issue for Argentines, who still lay claim to the Falklands.

Galtieri's defeat brought about his greatest fear: the collapse of his government. An election in 1983 restored constitutional rule and brought Raúl Alfonsín, of the Radical Civic Union, to power. In 1989, political power shifted from the Radical Party to the Peronist Party (established by Juan Perón), the first democratic transition in 60 years. Carlos Saúl Ménem, a former governor from the province of La Rioja, won the presidency by a surprising margin.

The Pizza & Champagne Years

A strong leader, Ménem pursued an ambitious but controversial agenda with the privatization of state-run institutions as its centerpiece. With the peso pegged to the dollar, Argentina enjoyed unprecedented price stability, allowing Ménem to deregulate and liberalize the economy. For many Argentines, it meant a kind of prosperity they had not seen in years. The policies had a dark side, however. The new money controls devastated local manufacturing, and the country's entire export market virtually dried out. World financial crises in the late 1990s, including those in Mexico, East Asia, Russia, and Brazil, increased the cost of external borrowing and further reduced the competitive edge of Argentine exports and industries. The chasm between rich and poor widened, squeezing out much of the middle class and eroding the social support systems put in place over the decades. This destroyed investor confidence, and the national deficit began to soar. Ménem was seen as a corrupt purveyor of cheap glamour. His favorite food-and-wine combination was pizza and champagne and some journalists adopted this moniker to describe the crass materialism of the era when Argentina no longer looked to Europe, but to Miami, for inspiration. His wife, Cecilia, the former Miss Chile and Miss Universe, was hated by many and regarded as a trophy wife. Rumor has it that members of his government had a hand in the bombings of the Israeli Embassy and the AIMI Jewish Community Center bombings. Some of the accusations bear a racial tinge, given that he was Argentina's first president of Arabic descent.

After 10 years as president—and a constitutional amendment that allowed him to seek a second term—Ménem left office. By that time, an alternative to the traditional Peronist and Radical parties, the center-left FREPASO political alliance, had emerged on the scene. The Radicals and FREPASO formed an alliance for the October 1999 election, and the alliance's candidate, running on an anti-corruption campaign, defeated his Peronist competitor.

Economic Crisis

Less charismatic than his predecessor, President Fernando de la Rúa was forced to reckon with the recession the economy had suffered since 1998. In an effort to eliminate Argentina's ballooning deficit, de la Rúa followed a strict regimen of government spending cuts and tax increases recommended by the International Monetary Fund. However, the tax increase crippled economic growth, and political infighting prevented de la Rúa from implementing other needed reforms designed to stimulate the economy. With a heavy drop in production and a steep rise in unemployment, an economic crisis was looming.

The economic meltdown arrived with a run on the peso in December 2001, when investors moved en masse to withdraw their money from Argentine banks. Government efforts to restrict the run by limiting depositor withdrawals fueled anger through society, and Argentines took to the streets in sometimes violent demonstrations. De la Rúa resigned on December 20, as Argentina faced the worst economic crisis of its history. A series of interim governments did little to improve the situation, as Buenos Aires began to default on its international debts. Peronist President Eduardo Duhalde unlocked the Argentine peso from the dollar on January 1, 2002, and the currency's value quickly tumbled. Within a few months, several presidents came and went in the ensuing crisis, and several citizens died in street protests throughout the country. The country's default to the IMF was the largest in history.

Argentina's economic crisis severely eroded the population's trust in the government. Increased poverty, unemployment surpassing 20%, and inflation hitting 30% resulted in massive emigration to Italy, Spain, and other destinations in Europe and North America. Anyone who had the passport to do so fled to Miami, Milan, and Madrid in particular. *Piqueteros* and *cartoneros,* the protestors and the homeless, became a visible presence throughout Buenos Aires and other large cities, as the unemployed in rural areas picked garbage for a living. Many of the protestors, it is claimed, have been paid off or fomented by various factions in government seeking to further destabilize the country and bring visible chaos to the streets.

The K Era

Ironically, those who could not flee the country in the midst of the economic chaos stayed behind and built a stronger nation. While under Ménem, Argentina idolized Europe and the United States, now citizens had to look to their own historical and cultural models, the things that were authentically Argentine. The tango—long expected to die out as a dance for the older generation—found new enthusiasts among the young. It had always been seen as a dance that alleviated pain, and there was more than enough of that to go around.

The country further stabilized by 2003, with the elections of Nestor Kirchner, the governor of the Province of Santa Cruz in Patagonia, a province made wealthy by oil exploration. Kirchner had proven his economic savvy by sending the province's investments overseas just before the collapse of the peso. A left-wing Peronist, he saw many of his friends disappear under the military regime. He reopened investigations into this dark period in Argentina's history and also went after the most corrupt of Ménem's regime. A consolidator of power, he and his senator wife, Cristina Fernandez de Kirchner, became the country's most important political couple. Under Kirchner, economic stability returned, with exports of soy, oil, and meat pumping the economy, a cheap peso and an overall global boom meant there was a hungry market for the raw material Argentina produces, especially with China and other Asian economies. Tourism became the third-most-important economic sector under his administration, with many well-off foreigners deciding to stay and invest in property and business.

Yet Kirchner could hardly be called a reformist and Argentine politics remained mired in a myriad of bitter rivalries, exacerbated by a weak bureaucratic civil service and compromised judiciary. Corruption scandals, such as public works bribes and a Venezuelan cash-in-suitcase election donation, failed to dent the president's popularity, buoyed by a consumer boom and relative prosperity. Sure to win a second term, Kirchner surprised everybody when he put his wife forward instead and she won the presidency in October 2007 with 45% of the vote, making her the country's first elected female leader.

Cristina Kirchner's term as president was anything but boring. Early on she picked a fight (egged on by her husband) with the powerful farmers' unions that led to road blockades and fuel shortages and much antigovernment sentiment. Runaway inflation saw prices rise 30%, though government statistics insisted it remained at 7%, discrediting the administration further. The farmers' crisis came to a head when congress split evenly in two, and the deciding vote of the vice president, Julio Cobos (a supposed ally of the Kirchners), dramatically sided with the farmers. The deep global recession in 2008 had many observers questioning Argentina's ability to service its huge foreign debt, but a raid on the central bank's reserves staved off another crisis. Cristina's popularity rating was extremely low, and it was expected that her husband (the real power behind the throne) would attempt to retake the reins at the next election in 2011. However, Argentine politics are never so predictable and what appeared to be a brilliant plan to share power for 2 decades was upset by the sudden death of Nestor Kirchner in October 2010. Cristina was on her own.

THE LAY OF THE LAND

Argentina is 5,000km (3,107 miles) in length and 1,800km (1,118 miles) wide in parts, making it the world's eighth-largest country with a landmass of almost 3 million sq. km (1.2 million sq. miles). Such vastness means great contrasts regarding geographical features.

THE PAMPAS This flat terrain is an agricultural powerhouse and where a third of the population resides. It consists of the central eastern provinces of Buenos Aires and La Pampa and the southern parts of Santa Fe and Córdoba. The climate is

Argentina

BOLIVIA

San Pedro
de Atacama

San Salvador
de Jujuy

Antofagasta

ATACAMA DESERT

Salta

GRAN CHACO

PARAGUAY

Pilcomayo

Paraná

BRAZIL

Asunción

Iguazú Falls

San Miguel
de Tucumán

Salado

Resistencia

Corrientes

Posadas

Santiago
del Estero

Paraná

Uruguay

La Serena

ANDES

Mar
Chiquito

San
Juan

La Falda

Córdoba

Villa
Carlos
Paz

Santa Fe
Paraná

Lagôa
dos Patos

Lagôa
Mirim

OCEAN

Valparaíso

Mendoza

Rosario

URUGUAY

Santiago

San Rafael

Buenos
Aires

Montevideo

ARGENTINA

Las Leñas

La Plata

Río de la Plata

Concepción

Colorado

Salado

Cabo San Antonio

CHILE

Bahía
Blanca

Mar del Plata

Negro

Bahía
Blanca

Puerto
Montt

San Carlos
de Bariloche

Puerto
Madryn

Golfo San Matías

Península
Valdés

Argentino

Isla de
Chiloé

Esquel

Chubut

Trelew

Mar

ATLANTIC

CORDILLERA DE LOS

PACIFIC

Archipiélago
de los Chonos

Chico

Golfo de
San Jorge

OCEAN

ARGENTINA

Deseado

Cabo Tres Puntas

FALKLAND ISLANDS
(ISLAS MALVINAS)
(U.K.)

Bahía Grande

West
Falkland

East
Falkland

Puerto Natales

Río Gallegos

Archipiélago
Reina Adelaida

PATAGONIA

Estrecho de Magallanes
(Strait of Magellan)

Punta
Arenas

Tierra del Fuego

Ushuaia

Cabo San Diego

Cabo de Hornos
(Cape Horn)

0   300 mi

0   300 km

humid, with lots of rainfall (900mm/35 in. a year) and sweltering summers that force much of the population to decamp to the Atlantic coast on its eastern fringe.

PATAGONIA   Desolate and romantic, Patagonia is like a country within a country, consisting of four provinces and huge contrasts. The northern alpine Lake District is far away from the arid steppes that host lots of sheep and few humans and the spectacular glaciers farther south. The Andes form a wall of ice, blocking rain from Chilean Patagonia on the other side. Comodoro Rivadavia is an oil town, while Río Gallegos is sustained by agriculture.

TIERRA DEL FUEGO   The Andes mountains are pulled eastward, forming one large island and a multitude of smaller ones holding famous bays and inlets such as the Beagle Channel and the Magellan Straits. Because of this tectonic shift, Ushuaia is the only Argentine town on the other side of the Andes and is surrounded by icy peaks. The northern half of the island is a desolate plain of brown furze that supports sheep and llama.

MESOPOTAMIA & EL CHACO   The northeastern part of Argentina is hot and humid, with the border province of Misiones resembling a jungle frontier. Here you'll find the famous Iguazú Falls and the triple border shared with Brazil and Paraguay and formed by the Rio Uruguay and Rio Parana. The vast wetlands of Esteros del Ibera lie farther south in Corrientes province. Farther north and east, the land becomes a dry, inhospitable shrub, known as El Chaco, which extends all the way to Bolivia.

THE ANDES   The Andes form the backbone of Argentina, stretching the whole way from Bolivia to Tierra del Fuego and rising as high as 6,960m (22,835 ft.) at Mt. Aconcagua in Mendoza province, the highest peak outside the Himalayas. The huge differences in altitude mean the landscape varies dramatically, with the red desert plateaus of Salta province contrasting with the temperate lakes of Tafi del Valle and the humid cane fields of Tucuman. Farther south, the provinces of San Juan and Mendoza consist of vast desert scrub with little rain. Yet together they are one of the most prolific wine regions in the world, thanks to melted snow channeled toward the vineyards through a vast network of canals.

ARGENTINE WAYS & MANNERS

Argentines have a dramatic disposition. Witness the spontaneous street protests where neighbors spill out on the street to bang pots and pans, usually prompted by an electricity cut or burglary. A football game can be communal chaos. The deafening chanting amid rocket flares and mammoth banners covering huge crowds watched by heavily armed riot police is at once terrifying and electrifying. Or sit back in any cafe and watch the exaggerated gesticulations of the patrons who have been there since 8am complaining about the politicians, the heat, and the crime, but then gush over the photos of the adorable newborn nephew. Everything is animated, including the exaggerated greetings and farewells when everybody rises to cheek kiss and hug, including the men. Argentines are a gregarious bunch, and they would rather sit around until 4am with friends and drink *mate* tea than sit in silence in front of a TV. It is therefore not surprising that the most popular TV programs are chat shows.

The country's psyche is somewhat schizophrenic. Deep pride is counterbalanced by strong self-doubt. Famous on the rest of the continent for being arrogant and self-confident, Argentina's brashness was somewhat sullied after the economic crisis in 2001. An identity crisis ensued where a period of navel gazing saw the nation's intellectuals wondering whether they were First World or Third World. Argentines will freely criticize the politicians they keep electing or the system they keep supporting but soon switch to the defensive if a foreigner offers a negative opinion. Such contradictions are evident in their attitude to the British. Argentines act aggrieved regarding the Las Malvinas defeat, triumphant regarding football victories, and fawning regarding British culture, with ubiquitous pop on every radio station and the middle class dropping English phrases at every opportunity.

> **Impressions**
>
> *An Argentine is an Italian who speaks Spanish, acts like a French man, but secretly wishes he were English.*
> —Argentine proverb

Of course it is dangerous to generalize a whole race of people, especially when their characteristics differ greatly depending on class and location. The usual capital-and-provincial rivalry exists here just as anywhere else. Perhaps in Argentina it is a little more pronounced as Buenos Aires is overpopulated and the vast countryside underpopulated. Those from the provinces regard Porteños as loud, brash, and untrustworthy. The capital dwellers feel less strongly about their country cousins; but whatever opinion they have, it is usually twinged with disdain and condescension. What they all have in common is love of family, food, and football; pride in their country's natural beauty; disregard for watches and all known timepieces; and utter contempt for taxes. The famous footballer Maradona illustrates Argentina perfectly. Despite his many faults, he is like his country, loved by everybody.

ARGENTINA IN POPULAR CULTURE

Recommended Books

Fiction lovers have a rich seam to mine regarding Argentine writing. Jorge Luis Borges is the country's grandfather of literature, with his elegant short stories combining symbolism, fantasy, and reality to create metaphysical narratives that have been translated all over the world. *Labyrinths* and *A Universal History of Iniquity* are just two of his collections from a prolific career. Julio Cortázar is another giant of letters who, like Borges, was very much influenced by European ideas and lived abroad for many years in Paris. His novel *Hopscotch* has an unconventional narrative that requires reading twice to give two different versions. His story *The Droolings of the Devil* was adapted into the famous art-house movie *Blow Up* by Michelangelo Antonioni. Another Borges-influenced writer is Ernesto Sábato, whose *On Heroes and Tombs* is one of the most thorough artistic expressions of Buenos Aires ever written. *The Tunnel,* by the same author, is a compelling read about an obsessed painter. Less lauded abroad but more indicative of Argentine rural life is the work of Horacio Quiroga. A tragic figure (he committed suicide in 1937), Quiroga's stories are mostly set in the jungle frontier of Misiones; they combine the supernatural and bizarre to create stories that are enjoyed by young and old alike and can be seen as a predecessor to magical realism. *The Decapitated Chicken* and *The Exiles* are both short story collections that are available in English. A seminal book in Argentine literature is the 19th-century gaucho poem *Martin Fierro,* by José Hernández, a compulsory read for all Argentine students.

Popular modern writers include Manuel Puig, whose *Kiss of the Spider Woman* was adapted into a movie of the same name. It deals with sex and repression, using popular movies and cultural references to keep the narrative flowing. Puig's background as a screenwriter can also be seen in other books such as *Betrayed by Rita Hayworth* and *Heartbreak Tango.* Osvaldo Soriano's *Shadows* and *A Funny Dirty Little War* are popular critiques of Argentine society, while Federico Andahazi's *The Anatomist* is an entertaining and somewhat bawdy work of historical fiction.

For an outsider's take on Argentine culture, read *In Patagonia* by Bruce Chatwin, one of the most famous travelogues ever written. *Chasing Che* by Patrick Symmes is an eloquent description of the writer's attempt to retrace the road trip of the famous revolutionary. Miranda France's *Bad Times in Buenos Aires* is an excellent impression of an expat's frustrating attempt to live in Argentina. For something lighter and more frivolous, read *Kiss and Tango,* by Marina Palmer, the warts-and-all confessions of a tango-dancing *gringa.*

Recommended Films

Despite limited funding and very little exposure, the Argentine movie industry has a prodigious output, with movies veering from slick mainstream features to grim independent offerings and an occasional award-winning gem in between. Themes such as the breakdown of society, the dirty war, the Malvinas war, and the sex wars provide rich pickings for young creative directors with little money but lots of talent.

Maria Luisa Bemberg is probably the most famous late-20th-century Argentine filmmakers and specialized in period dramas. Her *Camila* (1984) and *Miss Mary* (1986) both deal with the feminine experience in Argentina, with Julie Christie starring in the latter. *The Official Story* (1985), by Luis Puenzo, and *The Night of the Pencils* (1986), by Hector Olivera, are two powerful dramas about the military dictatorship and how the repression even reached the nation's children. *Man Facing Southeast* (1986) and The *Dark Side of the Heart* (1992) are two compelling movies by Eliseo Subiela, the former having a sci-fi theme and the latter an intriguing love story. The Italian neorealist style of filmmaking is a strong influence in Argentine cinema, and nowhere is it more evident than in the movies of Pablo Trapero. *Crane World* (1999) and *El Bonarense* (2002) are two gritty working-class features, with the former a stark portrait of police corruption. Another master of everyday themes and deadpan comedy is Carlos Sorin. *Historias Minimas* (2003) and *Bombon the Dog* (2004) deal with love, life, and dogs. For something more mainstream but just as hilarious, *Tiempo de Valientes* (2008), by Damian Szifron, concerns two favorite Argentine subject matters—crime and psychoanalysis. *Blessed by Fire* (2004), by Tristan Bauer, is possibly one of the best movies made about the Falklands War, while grifter movie *Nine Queens* (2001), by Fabian Bielinsky, is so good that it was remade in Hollywood.

Unfortunately Hollywood's take on Argentina is not so illustrious and fraught with clichés. One of the first mainstream movies is a lighthearted musical called *Down Argentine Way* (1940), by Irving Cummings. Robert Duvall's *Assassination Tango*

(2002) and Christopher Hampton's *Imagining Argentina* (2003) are uninspiring and best forgotten, and the less said about Alan Parker's *Evita* (1996) the better. The best foreign movies about Argentina are those that make the setting speak for itself—in most cases, the rich, atmospheric backdrop of Buenos Aires. Two great examples of this are *Happy Together* (1997), by Wong Kar Wai, and *Tango* (1998), by Carlos Saura.

2 EATING & DRINKING IN ARGENTINA

The recent renaissance in Argentine food has seen appetites move away slightly from the traditional beef, pasta, and pizza-based menu. Strong regional influences are coming to the fore, and the best restaurants are keen to offer local products in tune with the seasons. The Northwest is fond of indigenous recipes with a strong Spanish colonial tradition. *Locro* and *humita* are two maize-based broths often accompanied by tamales and empanadas stuffed with llama meat. In the wetlands of the northeast, the Guarani Indian tradition is evident in dishes made from *manioc,* pumpkin, and fruit such as papaya. The river lifestyle means excellent fish in the form of dorado, *surubí,* and *pejerrey.* Kid goat is popular in the central western provinces; Patagonian cuisine consists of wild boar, venison, and lamb; and plentiful trout and salmon caught fresh from the many rivers and king crab rule the dinner table in the far southern coastal areas such as Tierra del Fuego.

Despite such changes, there is no denying that beef remains the staple of every Argentine household and world-famous Argentine steak is top of every visitors list to try as soon as possible. Sidewalk restaurants and cafes have a multitude of meat-based snacks such as *milanesas* (filet in bread crumbs) and *lomitos* (steak sandwiches). The ultimate cow experience is the epic Argentine *asado,* something the translation "barbecue" does no justice to as there is not a hot dog or hamburger in sight. Instead you get a mouthwatering parade of every meat cut imaginable such as *costillas* (ribs) and *bife de chorizo* (tenderloin). Offal is popular in the form of *mollejas* (sweetbread) and *chimchullinis* (intestine). A weekend invitation to a family *asado* should not be missed, and as you travel around you will see such gatherings in the unlikeliest of places such as freeway curbs, street steps, and high-rise balconies. When Argentines want to celebrate, it is always with an *asado.* If such an invite is not forthcoming, settle for an *asado de tira* in any *parrilla* (grill-house restaurant), with the ubiquitous empanadas for starters.

Regarding drinks, *mate* tea is a national obsession, with groups consuming this bitter, green infusion on street corners, park benches, and even behind the car steering wheel. Service stations have machines dispensing free hot water to those who want to top up their thermos, which in turn tops up their *mate* gourds. Coffee is popular and served strong. Cafe culture is vibrant, with the prework caffeine lift and chat a prerequisite among many. For something different, try a *submarino*—a tall glass of hot milk dunked with a lump of dark chocolate (often in the shape of a submarine). Ice cream is indulged in at all hours, and many parlors remain open until the early morning serving a bewildering choice topped by the national pride *dulce de leche* (caramelized milk).

The Italian *digestif* Fernet has taken on a new life as the alcoholic drink of the young and is phenomenally popular in late-night bars and discos; its sweet cough-medicine taste is tamed with lots of cola and ice. Argentine wine is now some of the best in the world, with the powerful red Malbec from Mendoza the perfect companion with beef and the aromatic white Torrontes from Salta and La Rioja excellent with fish or pasta. Other wine varietals to look out for are the toast-flavored Bonarda and the rich and silky Tempranillo.

Argentine eating habits deserve a book in itself. Just be aware that dinner is late and most restaurants do not get busy until after 10pm.

PLANNING YOUR TRIP TO ARGENTINA

by Charlie O'Malley

3

To be prepared is always good advice. Though you cannot anticipate every situation that may occur on your holiday, a little advance planning can make the difference between a good trip and a great trip. This book should provide you with everything you need to know before you depart. Timing is important, as is the route you choose to get there. Determine your budget and take into account that many places do not accept credit cards and that ATMs set ridiculously low limits on withdrawals. There are also some health and safety precautions that should be taken. This chapter outlines all the basics—the when, why, and how of traveling to and around Argentina.

VISITOR INFORMATION

IN THE U.S. The **Argentina Government Tourist Office** has offices at 12 W. 56th St., New York, NY 10019 (℗ **212/603-0443;** fax 212/315-5545), and 2655 Le Jeune Rd., Penthouse Ste. F, Coral Gables, FL 33134 (℗ **305/442-1366;** fax 305/441-7029). For more details, consult Argentina's Ministry of Tourism website (see "Websites of Note," below).

IN CANADA Basic tourist information can be obtained by the **Consulate General of Argentina,** 2000 Peel St., Ste. 600, Montreal, Quebec H3A 2W5 (℗ **514/842-6582;** fax 514/842-5797; www.consargenmtl.com); for more details, consult Argentina's Ministry of Tourism website (see "Websites of Note," below).

IN THE U.K. For visitor information, contact the **Embassy of Argentina in London** (see "Entry Requirements & Customs," below) or consult Argentina's Ministry of Tourism website (see "Websites of Note," below).

IN BUENOS AIRES The central office of the **City Tourism Secretariat,** Calle Balcarce 360, in Monserrat (℗ **11/4313-0187;** www.turismo.gov.ar), is responsible for all visitor information on Buenos Aires but is not open to the general public. Instead, the city operates kiosks spread throughout various neighborhoods, which have maps and hotel, restaurant, and attraction information. **Tourist Information Office,**

Av. Santa Fe 883 (© **11/4312-2232**), is one of the best located as is the office located at the entrance to Retiro Terminal.

The **Buenos Aires City Tourism Office** runs an information hot line (© **11/4313-0187**) from 7:30am to 6pm Monday to Saturday, and Sunday 11am to 6pm.

Websites of Note

○ **www.embassyofargentina.us:** Up-to-date travel information from the Argentine embassy in Washington, D.C.

○ **www.turismo.gov.ar:** This Ministry of Tourism site has travel information for all of Argentina, including a virtual tour of the country's tourist regions, shopping tips, links to city tourist sites, and general travel facts.

○ **www.mercotour.com:** A travel site focused on adventure and ecological excursions, with information on outdoor activities in both Argentina and Chile.

○ **www.allaboutar.com:** This well-written site is packed with practical information about the country, including skiing, golfing, and *estancia* (ranch) stays.

○ **www.welcomepatagonia.com:** This fantastic website has extensive information about this region of Argentina, including hotels, itineraries, and other details.

○ **www.welcomeargentina.com:** Great information about Argentina, and extensive details on things to do in Buenos Aires. Includes self-guided tour ideas, lists of hotels, and up-to-date information on restaurants and other trends.

○ **www.bue.gov.ar:** A comprehensive tourism website set up by the city of Buenos Aires, with details on neighborhoods and a calendar of events in English and other languages. The website has lots of extremely detailed and useful information, but it can be cumbersome to work through its windows and pop-ups. Be patient with it.

○ **www.wine-republic.com:** This is a lively, irreverent Mendoza-based website explaining Argentine culture and the best destinations, with the focus on good food and wine.

○ **www.palermoviejo.com:** This Spanish-language site fills you in on what's doing in Buenos Aires's trendiest neighborhood, full of the newest restaurants, shops, and boutique hotels.

○ **www.google.com.ar:** If you're good at Spanish, use this Argentina-based division of the popular Google search engine. Clicking on "Páginas de Argentina" will give you the most up-to-date, locally produced information.

○ **www.subte.com.ar:** This website explains in detail the workings of the Buenos Aires subway system and allows you to locate hotels and other sites of interest in relation to subway stops. It also includes downloadable maps and an interactive feature that helps you to calculate travel times between destinations.

ENTRY REQUIREMENTS & CUSTOMS

Entry Requirements

Citizens of the United States, Canada, the United Kingdom, Australia, New Zealand, Ireland, and South Africa require a passport to enter the country. No visa is required for citizens of these countries for tourist stays of up to 90 days. However, citizens of the United States, Canada, and Australia are required to pay a "reciprocity fee" of US$140, US$70, and US$100 respectively. Introduced in 2009, this regulation is only applied at Ezeiza and Jorge Newbery airports in Buenos Aires, but plans are under way to eventually roll it out to all points of entry into the country. The United States fee is valid for 10 years and allows for multiple entries. The Canadian fee applies to one entry only, but for an extra C$75 its use can be extended for 5 years; the Australian fee is for 1 year. For more information concerning fees, longer stays, employment, or other types of visas, contact the embassies or consulates in your home country. Usually, a hop by boat into neighboring Uruguay or crossing into Brazil during an Iguazú Falls excursion will initiate a new 90-day tourist period. With the increasing number of Americans and other foreigners living in Argentina, this has become one of the preferred quick-fix methods of bypassing visa extension bureaucracy. If you are planning to buy property, retire, or establish a business in Argentina, it is highly advisable to take care of the proper paperwork for your stay.

IN THE U.S.   Contact the Consular Section of the Argentine Embassy, 1811 Q St. NW, Washington, DC 20009 (✆ **202/238-6460**). Consulates are also located in Los Angeles (✆ **323/954-9155** or -9156), Miami (✆ **305/373-1889**), Atlanta (✆ **404/880-0805**), Chicago (✆ **312/819-2610**), New York City (✆ **212/603-0400**), and Houston (✆ **713/871-8935**). For more information, try www.embassy ofargentina.us, with links to various consulates in the U.S.

IN CANADA   Contact the Embassy of the Argentine Republic, Ste. 910, Royal Bank Center, 90 Sparks St., Ottawa, Ontario K1P 5B4 (✆ **613/236-2351;** fax 613/235-2659; embargentina@argentina-canada.net).

IN THE U.K.   Contact the Embassy of the Argentine Republic, 65 Brooke St., London W1Y 4AH (✆ **020/7318-1300;** fax 020/7318-1301; www.argentine-embassy-uk.org).

IN NEW ZEALAND   Contact the Embassy of the Argentine Republic, Prime Finance Tower, Level 14, 142 Lambton Quay, PO Box 5430, Wellington (✆ **04/472-8330;** fax 04/472-8331; www.arg.org.nz).

IN AUSTRALIA   Contact the Embassy of the Argentine Republic, John McEwen House, Level 2, 7 National Circuit, Barton, ACT 2600 (✆ **02/6273 9111;** fax 02/6273 0500; www.argentina.org.au).

Customs

WHAT YOU CAN TAKE INTO ARGENTINA

Travelers entering Argentina can bring personal effects—including clothes, jewelry, and professional equipment such as cameras and computers—without paying duty. In addition, they can bring in 2 liters of alcohol, 400 cigarettes, and 50 cigars duty-free. *Note:* In recent times Customs regulations have become very strict regarding brand-new electronic goods; if you cannot prove the item is yours and was bought well before the trip, they can charge a whopping 45% import tariff.

WHAT YOU CAN TAKE HOME FROM ARGENTINA

Returning **U.S. citizens** who have been away for at least 48 hours are allowed to bring back, once every 30 days, $800 worth of merchandise duty-free. You'll be charged a flat rate of duty on the next $1,000 worth of purchases. Any dollar amount beyond that is dutiable at whatever rates apply. On mailed gifts, the duty-free limit is $200. Have your receipts handy to expedite the declaration process. *Note:* If you owe duty, you are required to pay on your arrival in the United States by cash, personal check, government or traveler's check, or money order, and in some locations, a Visa or MasterCard.

In Argentina, this is rarely an issue unless you have a lot of electronics. To avoid having to pay duty on foreign-made personal items you owned before you left on your trip, bring along a bill of sale, insurance policy, jeweler's appraisal, or receipts of purchase. Or you can register items that can be readily identified by a permanently affixed serial number or marking—think laptop computers, cameras, and CD players—with Customs before you leave. Take the items to the nearest Customs office or register them with Customs at the airport from which you're departing. You'll receive, at no cost, a Certificate of Registration, which allows duty-free entry for the life of the item.

You cannot bring fresh fruit and vegetables into the United States, with some exceptions. For specifics on what you can bring back, download the invaluable free pamphlet, *Know Before You Go*, online at **www.cbp.gov** (Click on "Travel," and then on "Know Before You Go! Online Brochure."). Or contact the **U.S. Customs & Border Protection (CBP),** 1300 Pennsylvania Ave. NW, Washington, DC 20229 (© **877/287-8667**), and request the pamphlet.

For **Canadian** rules, write for the booklet *I Declare*, issued by the **Canada Border Services Agency** (© **800/461-9999** in Canada or 204/983-3500; www.cbsa-asfc.gc.ca). Canada allows its citizens a C$750 exemption, and you're allowed to bring back duty-free one carton of cigarettes, one can of tobacco, 40 imperial ounces of liquor, and 50 cigars. In addition, you're allowed to mail gifts to Canada valued at less than C$60 a day, provided they're unsolicited and don't contain alcohol or tobacco (write on the package "Unsolicited gift, under $60 value"). Declare all valuables on the Y-38 form before departure from Canada, including serial numbers of valuables you already own, such as expensive foreign cameras. *Note:* The C$750 exemption can only be used once a year and only after an absence of 7 days.

Citizens of the U.K. who are **returning from a non-E.U. country** have a Customs allowance of 200 cigarettes; 50 cigars; 250 grams of smoking tobacco; 2 liters of still table wine; 1 liter of spirits or strong liqueurs (over 22% volume); 2 liters of fortified wine, sparkling wine, or other liqueurs; 60 cubic centimeters (mL) of perfume; 250 cubic centimeters (mL) of toilet water; and £145 worth of all other goods, including gifts and souvenirs. People 16 and under cannot have the tobacco or alcohol allowance. For more information, contact **HM Customs & Excise** at © **0845/010-9000** (from outside the U.K., 020/8929-0152), or consult their website at www.hmce.gov.uk.

The duty-free allowance in **Australia** is A$400 or, for those 17 and under, A$200. Citizens can bring in 250 cigarettes or 250 grams of loose tobacco, and 1,125 milliliters of alcohol. If you're returning with valuables you already own, such as foreign-made cameras, you should file form B263. A helpful brochure available from Australian consulates or Customs offices is *Know Before You Go.* For more information, call the **Australian Customs Service** (© **1300/363-263;** www.customs. gov.au).

The duty-free allowance for **New Zealand** is NZ$700. Citizens 18 and over can bring in 200 cigarettes, 50 cigars, or 250 grams of tobacco (or a mixture of all three if their combined weight doesn't exceed 250g); plus 4.5 liters of wine and beer, or 1.125 liters of liquor. New Zealand currency does not carry import or export restrictions. Fill out a certificate of export, listing the valuables you are taking out of the country; that way, you can bring them back without paying duty. Most questions are answered in a free pamphlet available at New Zealand consulates and Customs offices: *New Zealand Customs Guide for Travellers, Notice no. 4.* For more information, contact **New Zealand Customs,** The Customhouse, 17–21 Whitmore St., Box 2218, Wellington (☎ **04/473-6099** or 0800/428-786; www.customs.govt.nz).

WHEN TO GO

The seasons in Argentina are the reverse of those in the Northern Hemisphere. Buenos Aires is ideal in fall (Mar–May) and spring (Sept–Nov), when temperatures are mild. The beaches and resort towns are packed with vacationing Argentines in summer (Dec–Mar), while Buenos Aires becomes somewhat deserted of locals, which is not a bad thing regarding traffic. Plan a trip to Patagonia and the southern Andes in summer, when days are longer and warmer. Winter (June–Aug) is the best time to visit Iguazú and the Northwest, when the rains and heat have subsided; but spring (Aug–Oct) is also pleasant, as temperatures are mild and the crowds have cleared out.

CLIMATE   Except for a small tropical area in northern Argentina, the country lies in the Temperate Zone, characterized by cool, dry weather in the south and warmer, humid air in the center. Accordingly, January and February are quite hot—often in the high 90s to more than 100°F (35°C–40°C)—while winter (approximately July–Oct) can be chilly.

HOLIDAYS   Public holidays are January 1 (New Year's Day), Good Friday, March 24 (Truth and Justice Day), April 2 (Veterans Day), May 1 (Labor Day), May 25 (First Argentine Government), June 10 (National Sovereignty Day), June 20 (Flag Day), July 9 (Independence Day), August 17 (Anniversary of the Death of General San Martín), October 12 (Día de la Raza), December 8 (Immaculate Conception Day), and December 25 (Christmas). Christmas, however, is usually celebrated on December 24, and called Noche Buena. Many stores and other services close this day.

FESTIVALS & SPECIAL EVENTS   Several holidays and festivals are worth planning a trip around; the best place to get information for these events is through your local Argentine tourism office (see "Visitor Information," earlier in this chapter). **Carnaval (Mardi Gras),** the week before the start of Lent, is celebrated in many towns in Argentina, although to a much lesser extent than in neighboring Brazil. The main area for this is in Gualeguaychú, about 3 hours north of Buenos Aires in Entre Rios Province. In Salta, citizens throw a large parade, including caricatures of public officials and "water bomb" fights. The **Gaucho Parade** takes place in Salta on June 16, with music by folk artists and gauchos dressed in traditional red ponchos with black stripes, leather chaps, black boots, belts, and knives. For more gaucho madness, visit the city of San Antonio de Areco, about 1½ hours from Buenos Aires. **Día de la Tradición** is generally celebrated around November 10, when gauchos and the tourists who love them flock to the picturesque town.

Inti Raymi (Festival of the Sun) takes place in towns throughout the Northwest the night before the summer solstice (June 20) to give thanks for the year's harvest. **Día de Independencia (Independence Day)** is celebrated in Tucumán on July 9. **Exodo Jujeño (Jujuy Exodus)** takes place August 23 and 24, when locals reenact the exodus of 1812. The **Batalla de Tucumán (Battle of Tucumán)** celebrates Belgrano's victory over the Spanish on September 24. And the **Fiesta Provincial del Turismo (Provincial Tourist Festival)** takes place in December in Puerto Iguazú.

The Buenos Aires version of Carnaval, or Mardi Gras, is called **Fiesta de las Murgas,** and though it's not as colorful as Rio de Janeiro's or even the one in Gualeguaychú, it is celebrated every weekend in February. Various neighborhoods have costumed street-band competitions full of loud music, drums, and dancing. Contact the Buenos Aires tourism office (www.bue.gov.ar) for more information.

The **World Tango Festival** is celebrated in early to mid-October, with various events, many concentrated in the tango neighborhood of San Telmo. See www.worldtangofestival.com.ar for more information and exact dates.

The world's biggest polo event, the **Argentine Open Polo Championships,** is held in the polo grounds in Palermo, near the Las Cañitas neighborhood, generally in late November, attracting moneyed crowds from around the world who get to mingle with visiting British royalty. Visit their website, www.aapolo.com.

The **National Gay Pride** parade is held in November and can switch at the last minute from the first Saturday to the third Saturday of the month, so check Comunidad Homosexual de Argentina's website, at www.cha.org.ar, for updated information.

Some big regional parties include **Octoberfest,** in Villa Belgrano, Córdoba, every second weekend of October and **Mendoza Wine Harvest Festival** every first weekend in March.

Though Argentina has little in the way of Christmas ritual, **midnight Mass on Christmas Eve (Noche Buena),** at the Metropolitan Cathedral in Buenos Aires, is a beautiful spectacle. It is usually held at 10pm on December 24.

GETTING THERE

By Plane

Argentina's main international airport is **Ezeiza Ministro Pistarini** (EZE; © 11/5480-2500/6111), located 42km (26 miles) west of Buenos Aires. Allot at least 45 minutes to an hour for travel between the airport and the city, more in rush hour.

Below are the major airlines that fly into Argentina from North America, Europe, and Australia; see chapter 14, "Fast Facts: Argentina," for complete phone and website details. Argentina's national airline is **Aerolíneas Argentinas** (© 800/333-0276 in the U.S., 0810/222-86527 in Buenos Aires, or 1800/22-22-15 in Australia; www.aerolineas.com.ar). The airline flies a few times a week from New York and daily from Miami. Aerolíneas Argentinas is an interesting introduction to the excitement of Argentina and its culture. The female flight attendants tend to be particularly glamorous, and the staff, mostly natives of Argentina, can offer excellent advice for you to use once you are on the ground. Argentine wine is free and liberally served in coach and all classes. Renationalized in 2008, the company retains its reputation for strikes, delays, and general inefficiency, especially on domestic flights in the summer season.

Other operators include American Airlines, United Airlines, Air Canada, British Airways, Gol, Taca, Tam, and Iberia. LAN also provides connections from Miami and New York, both direct and through Santiago to Buenos Aires. Australia's Qantas Airlines offers service from Sydney to Santiago, with shared service continuing to Buenos Aires on LAN.

Domestic airlines and flights to Uruguay use **Jorge Newbery Airport** (© 11/4514-1515), located only 15 minutes to the north, along the river from downtown.

The easiest way to travel Argentina's vast distances is by air, though flights are expensive and foreigners are charged substantially more than locals. **Aerolíneas Argentinas** (see above) connects most cities and tourist destinations in Argentina, including Córdoba, Jujuy, Iguazú, Salta, and the beach resorts. **LAN** (✆ **866/435-9526** in the U.S. and Canada, or 11/4378-2222 in Buenos Aires; www.lan.com) flies to Córdoba, Mendoza, and Iguazú. **Sol** (✆ **0810/444-4765;** www.sol.com.ar) flies daily to Córdoba. When taking domestic flights, go to the airport well stocked with snacks, water, and reading material as delays are common and airport prices exorbitant.

By Bus

The **Estación Terminal de Omnibus,** Av. Ramos Mejía 1680 (✆ **11/4310-0700**), located near Retiro Station, serves all long-distance buses. You would use this station when connecting to other parts of Argentina, or by long-distance coach from other countries. Due to the high cost of air transport for most South Americans, the continent is served by numerous companies offering comfortable, and at times luxurious, bus services to other capitals, often overnight. This is ideal for student and budget travelers.

Among the major bus companies that operate out of Buenos Aires are **Andesmar** (✆ **261/405-0600**) and **La Veloz del Norte** (✆ **11/4315-2482**), which serve destinations in the Northwest, including Salta and Jujuy; **Singer** (✆ **11/4315-2653**), serving Puerto Iguazú as well as Brazilian destinations; and **T.A. Chevallier** (✆ **11/4313-3297**), serving points throughout the country.

The **Estación Terminal de Omnibus,** sometimes referred to as the Retiro Bus Station, is sprawling, enormous, and confusing. Just walking from one end to another takes about 15 minutes, given the ramps, crowds, and stairs you have to maneuver through. Routes and platform locations rarely make it to the overhead boards also, so don't rely on them. Still, in spite of the chaos, there is an overarching order. A color-coded system used at the ticket counters explains in general which destinations of the country are served by which bus lines. Red, for instance, indicates the center of the country, including the province of Buenos Aires; dark blue, the south; orange, the north; green, the northeast; light blue, the central Atlantic coast; and gray, the international destinations. However, at their sales counters, many bus companies indicate names of cities on their destination lists that they no longer serve, so you may have to stand in a line to ask. Many companies also have more than one name, adding to the visual clutter at the ticket counters. To help you make sense of it all, use **www.tebasa.com. ar**, the terminal's website, while planning your trip. Click on the province where you are traveling, and a list of bus companies and phone numbers will come up. Bus tickets can also be purchased at most travel agencies. This can cost slightly more but can save a lot of confusion if you're short on time. A very handy website is **www. plataforma10.com**, which sells tickets and gives information on bus routes around the country.

By Car

In Buenos Aires, travel by *subte* (subway) or *remises* (radio-dispatched taxis, as opposed to street taxis) is easier and safer than driving yourself. Rush-hour traffic is chaotic, and parking is difficult. If you have rented a car for whatever reason, park it at your hotel or a nearby garage and leave it there. Most daily parking charges do not exceed $8 or $10. Many recently built hotels have parking on the premises; others use nearby garages.

If you're traveling outside of Buenos Aires, it's another story when it comes to having a car. Argentine roads and highways are generally in good condition, with the exception of some rural areas. Most highways have been privatized and charge nominal tolls. In Buenos Aires, drivers are aggressive and don't always obey traffic lanes or lights. Wear your seat belt, as required by Argentine law. U.S. driver's licenses are valid in greater Buenos Aires, but you need an Argentine or international license to drive in most other parts of the country. Fuel (known as NAFTA) is expensive, at about $1 per liter (or $4 per gallon).

The **Automóvil Club Argentino (ACA),** Av. del Libertador 1850 (© **11/4802-6061;** www.aca.org.ar), has working arrangements with international automobile clubs. The ACA offers numerous services, including roadside assistance, road maps, hotel and camping information, and discounts for various tourist activities. Another excellent resource is the website **www.ruta0.com**. Here you can input your planned road trip and the site will display a ready-to-print route map, giving you exact distances, estimated fuel consumption, and projected toll fees.

CAR RENTALS Many international car-rental companies operate in Argentina, with offices at airports and in city centers. The main offices in Buenos Aires for the following agencies are **Hertz,** Paraguay 1122 (© **800/654-3131** in the U.S., or 11/4816-8001 in Buenos Aires; www.hertz.com); **Avis,** Cerrito 1527 (© **800/230-4898** in the U.S., or 11/4300-8201 in Buenos Aires; www.avis.com); **Dollar,** Marcelo T. de Alvear 523 (© **800/800-6000** in the U.S., or 11/4315-8800 in Buenos Aires; www.dollar.com); and **Thrifty,** Av. Leandro N. Alem 699 (© **800/847-4389** in the U.S., or 11/4315-0777 in Buenos Aires; www.thrifty.com). Car rental is expensive in Argentina, with standard rates beginning at about $60 to $70 per day for a subcompact with unlimited mileage (ask for any special promotions, especially on weekly rates). Check to see if your existing automobile insurance policy (or a credit card) covers insurance for car rentals. Watch out for hidden extras such as airport pickups and car wash charges.

MONEY & COSTS

Cash & Currency

The official Argentine currency is the **peso,** made up of 100 **centavos.** Money is denominated in notes of 2, 5, 10, 20, 50, and 100 pesos; and coins of 1, 2, and 5 pesos, and 1, 5, 10, 25, and 50 centavos. At the time of writing, the exchange rate was 4 pesos to the dollar.

Argentina is not the bargain destination it was post-crisis 2001. Thirty percent inflation in 2010 means prices have risen significantly and a good meal in Buenos Aires will match what you pay in North America or Europe, but it is still relatively cheap. However outside the capital and especially in the Northwest, prices are quite reasonable. High-end hotels are now very expensive, but you can still get some great rates, especially for the midrange and budget options. As the dollar is widely quoted in Argentina and is the more stable of both currencies, we have chosen to quote most prices in dollars.

What Things Cost

We categorize our hotels and restaurants according to location and price. As for accommodations, you can expect to pay more than $300 for a double in the **Very**

Expensive category; $200 to $299 in the **Expensive** category; $125 to $199 in the **Moderate** range; and less than $125 in the **Inexpensive** category.

You can expect restaurants in the **Very Expensive** category to cost more than $30 per person for dinner without drinks, while in the **Expensive** category, meals average $20 to $29. **Moderate** restaurants serve dinners ranging mostly from $12 to $19, while **Inexpensive** restaurants offer meals for less than $12. Keep in mind, however, that these are only guidelines.

Exchanging Money

It's a good idea to exchange at least some money—just enough to cover airport incidentals and transportation to your hotel—before you leave home (though don't expect the exchange rate to be ideal), so you can avoid lines at airport ATMs (automated teller machines). You can exchange money at your local American Express or Thomas Cook office or your bank. If you're far away from a bank with currency-exchange services, American Express offers traveler's checks and foreign currency (plus a $15 order fee and additional shipping costs) at www.americanexpress.com or ✆ **800/ 807-6233.**

U.S. dollars are not widely accepted in Buenos Aires. However, you can still use them to pay in some business-class hotels, tourist-popular restaurants, and businesses catering to large numbers of tourists. Such places will often post their own daily exchange rate at the counter, which is always significantly lower. For the vast majority of your purchases, however, you will need pesos. You can convert your currency in hotels, *casas de cambio* (money-exchange houses), some banks, and at the Buenos Aires airport, although exchange rates offered at airports in general are very poor value. Exchange American Express traveler's checks for pesos in Buenos Aires at **American Express,** Arenales 707 (✆ **11/4130-3135**). It is sometimes difficult to exchange traveler's checks outside the center of Buenos Aires, so plan ahead to have a sufficient amount of cash in pesos on day trips.

ATMs

ATMs are maddening in Argentina, as they allow only ridiculously low withdrawals of $150—though you can withdraw several times in 1 day and rack up substantial bank charges. It is best to plan ahead, if you know you need large amounts of cash; or you might test various cash machines, as some will allow $200 and $300 limits. Machines are ubiquitous in Buenos Aires and other urban and tourist areas, but don't depend on finding them off the beaten path. It is a good idea to let your bank know ahead of time that you will be using your ATM card overseas so that they do not block transactions in an effort to prevent fraudulent transactions.

The **Cirrus** (✆ **800/424-7787;** www.mastercard.com) and **PLUS** (✆ **800/843- 7587;** www.visa.com) networks span the globe; look at the back of your bank card to see which network you're on, and then call or check online for ATM locations at your destination. Be sure you know your personal identification number (PIN) before you leave home and be sure to find out your daily withdrawal limit before you depart, though this is slightly irrelevant if the Argentine network imposes its own limits. Also keep in mind that many banks impose a fee every time a card is used at a different bank's ATM, and that fee can be higher for international transactions (up to $5 or more) than for domestic ones. On top of this, the bank from which you withdraw cash may charge its own fee. To compare banks' ATM fees within the U.S., use **www. bankrate.com**. For international withdrawal fees, ask your bank.

Traveler's Checks

Traveler's checks are something of an anachronism from the days before the ATM made cash accessible at any time. Within the Pampas and rural areas of Buenos Aires Province, however, they're still welcomed by many establishments.

You can get traveler's checks at almost any bank. **American Express** offers denominations of $20, $50, $100, $500, and (for cardholders only) $1,000. You'll pay a service charge ranging from 1% to 4%. You can also get American Express traveler's checks over the phone by calling © **800/221-7282;** Amex gold and platinum cardholders who use this number are exempt from the 1% fee.

Visa offers traveler's checks at Citibank locations nationwide, as well as at several other banks. The service charge ranges between 1.5% and 2%; checks come in denominations of $20, $50, $100, $500, and $1,000. Call © **800/732-1322** for information. AAA members can obtain Visa checks for a $9.95 fee (for checks up to $1,500) at most AAA offices or by calling © **866/339-3378. MasterCard** also offers traveler's checks. Call © **800/223-9920** for a location near you.

Foreign-currency traveler's checks are useful if you're traveling to one country; they're accepted at locations, such as bed-and-breakfasts, where US$ checks may not be, and they minimize the amount of math you have to do at your destination. **American Express, Thomas Cook, Visa,** and **MasterCard** offer foreign-currency traveler's checks. You'll pay the rate of exchange at the time of your purchase (so it's a good idea to monitor the rate before you take the plunge), and most companies charge a transaction fee per order (and a shipping fee if you order online).

If you choose to carry traveler's checks, be sure to keep a record of their serial numbers separate from your checks, in the event that they are stolen or lost. You'll get a refund faster if you know the numbers.

Credit Cards

Visa, American Express, MasterCard, and Diners Club are commonly accepted. However some establishments—especially smaller businesses—will give you a better price if you pay cash or may refuse credit cards altogether. Go easy on such vendors. They have reason to be reluctant as the bank charges exorbitant fees for processing card purchases and the vendor does not receive the payment for 6 weeks. If you are really annoyed at the lack of credit card facilities in Argentina, complain to your credit card company. Credit cards are accepted at most hotels and the more expensive restaurants. But note that you cannot use credit cards in many taxis or at most attractions (museums, trams, and so on). Like ATM cards, many credit card companies are also now applying fees to international transactions, often as high as 3%. If you have more than one credit card and expect to charge a lot, call the credit card companies before you leave on your trip to find out which charges the lowest, if any, fee. Using the wrong card can make a bargain not such a bargain anymore.

You can get **cash advances** off your credit card at any bank, and you don't even need to go to a teller; you can get a cash advance at the ATM if you know your PIN. If you've forgotten your PIN, or didn't even know you had one, call the phone number on the back of your credit card before your trip and ask the bank to send it to you. It usually takes 5 to 7 business days, although some banks will do it over the phone.

Another hidden expense to contend with: Interest rates for cash advances are often significantly higher than rates for credit card purchases. More importantly, you start paying interest on the advance *the moment you receive the cash.*

Internet Payments

Many small hotels and tour companies prefer payment by the Internet payment service PayPal.com. To use PayPal you must first set up your own account, which links your debit or credit account to your PayPal account. This may take several days, so it's best done before you leave home. Patronizing PayPal facilities can save some headaches as you can avoid carrying cash and maxing out your cash card to pay for tours and rooms. PayPal can be suspicious of payments made within South America, however, and may reverse the payment. However, it eventually allows the payments if you repeat the process.

3 TRAVEL INSURANCE

Check your existing insurance policies and credit card coverage before you buy travel insurance. You may already be covered for lost luggage, canceled tickets, or medical expenses.

The cost of travel insurance varies widely, depending on the cost and length of your trip, your age and health, and the type of trip you're taking, but expect to pay between 5% and 8% of the vacation itself.

TRIP-CANCELLATION INSURANCE Trip-cancellation insurance helps you get your money back if you have to back out of a trip, if you have to go home early, or if your travel supplier goes bankrupt. Allowed reasons for cancellation can range from sickness to natural disasters to the Department of State declaring your destination unsafe for travel. (Insurers usually won't cover vague fears, though, as many travelers discovered who tried to cancel their trips in Oct 2001 because they were wary of flying.) In this unstable world, trip-cancellation insurance is a good buy if you're getting tickets well in advance—who knows what the state of the world, or of your airline, will be in 9 months? Insurance policy details vary, so read the fine print and make sure that your airline or cruise line is on the list of carriers covered in case of bankruptcy. A good resource is **"Travel Guard Alerts,"** a service that provides a list of companies considered high-risk by Travel Guard International (see website below). Protect yourself further by paying for the insurance with a credit card—by law, consumers can get their money back on goods and services not received, if they report the loss within 60 days after the charge is listed on their credit card statement.

For more information, contact one of the following recommended insurers: **Access America** (© 866/807-3982; www.accessamerica.com); **Travel Guard International** (© 800/826-4919; www.travelguard.com); **Travel Insured International** (© 800/243-3174; www.travelinsured.com); and **Travelex Insurance Services** (© 888/457-4602; www.travelex-insurance.com).

MEDICAL INSURANCE For travel overseas, most health plans (including Medicare and Medicaid) do not provide coverage, and the ones that do often require you to pay for services upfront and reimburse you only after you return home. Even if your plan does cover overseas treatment, most out-of-country hospitals make you pay your bills upfront and send you a refund only after you've returned home and filed the necessary paperwork with your insurance company. As a safety net, you may want to buy travel medical insurance. If you require additional medical insurance, try **MEDEX Assistance** (© 410/453-6300; www.medexassist.com) or **Travel Assistance International** (© 800/821-2828; www.travelassistance.com; for general information call the company's Worldwide Assistance Services, Inc., at ℂ **800/777-8710**).

LOST-LUGGAGE INSURANCE On domestic flights, checked baggage is covered up to $2,500 per ticketed passenger. On international flights (including U.S. portions of international trips), baggage coverage is limited to approximately $9.07 per pound, up to approximately $635 per checked bag. If you plan to check items more valuable than the standard liability, see if your valuables are covered by your homeowner's policy, get baggage insurance as part of your comprehensive travel-insurance package, or buy Travel Guard's "BagTrak" product. Don't buy insurance at the airport, as it's usually overpriced. Be sure to take any valuables or irreplaceable items with you in your carry-on luggage, as many valuables (including books, money, and electronics) aren't covered by airline policies.

If your luggage is lost, immediately file a lost-luggage claim at the airport, detailing the luggage contents. For most airlines, you must report delayed, damaged, or lost baggage within 4 hours of arrival. The airlines are required to deliver luggage, once found, directly to your house or destination free of charge.

HEALTH & SAFETY
Staying Healthy

Argentina requires no vaccinations to enter the country, except for passengers coming from countries where cholera and yellow fever are endemic.

Some people who have allergies can be affected by the **pollution** in Buenos Aires's crowded MicroCentro, where cars and buses remain mired in traffic jams, belching out pollution. The beautiful spring blossoms also bring with them **pollen,** and even people not usually affected by plants might be thrown off seasonally and by species of plants different from those in North America and Europe. It's a good idea to pack a decongestant with you, or asthma medicine if you require it. With the new anti-smoking laws, you will not find indoor smoke to be the hazard it once was.

Because motor vehicle crashes are a leading cause of injury among travelers, walk and drive defensively. Do not expect buses and taxis to stop for you when crossing the street. Always use a seat belt, which is now required by law in Buenos Aires, even in taxis.

Most visitors find that Argentine food and water are generally easy on the stomach. Water and ice are considered safe to drink in Buenos Aires. You should avoid street food and drinks served out of canisters by roving salespeople at the ubiquitous festivals all over the city. Vegetarians should take note that food that seems vegetarian often is not. With all those cows slaughtered for meat, there's plenty of cow fat finding its way as cooking oil for bread and biscuits. Read ingredients carefully and ask if in doubt.

Buenos Aires's streets and sidewalks can be disgustingly unsanitary. While there is a pooper-scooper law on the books, dog owners seem to take delight in letting their pets relieve themselves in the middle of the sidewalk. The rule of thumb also seems to be the better the neighborhood, the more poop there is, making Recoleta an obstacle course. Watch your step!

DRUGS & PRESCRIPTIONS Many drugs requiring a prescription in the United States do not necessarily need one in Argentina. Hence, if you lose or run out of a medicine, it might not be necessary to schedule a doctor's appointment to get your prescription. The same goes if you become ill and are sure you know what you need. Many of the pharmacies in the MicroCentro have staff members who speak English. Not all medicines, however, are a bargain in Argentina.

AUSTRAL SUN   The summer sun is hot and strong in Buenos Aires. It's best to bring sunblock, though it is available in stores and pharmacies throughout the city. There are no beaches within the city proper, but many people go tanning in the Palermo and Recoleta parks or in the Ecological Preserve.

MALARIA & OTHER TROPICAL AILMENTS   Malaria is not an issue in most of Argentina. However, the humid summer months of January and February mean you will sometimes find swarms of mosquitoes wherever you go. Bring repellent to avoid bites. To get shots or advice for various illnesses if you are traveling from Buenos Aires to the jungle for long periods of time, contact **Vacunar,** a chain of clinics specializing in vaccinations and preventing illness, with locations all over Buenos Aires (www.vacunar.com.ar). Keep in mind that many shots require a period of time before they become effective. They will also explain, country by country, what is required if you are traveling to other parts of South America.

WHAT TO DO IF YOU GET SICK AWAY FROM HOME

Any foreign consulate can provide a list of area doctors who speak English. If you get sick, consider asking your hotel concierge to recommend a local doctor—even his or her own. You can also try the emergency room at a local hospital. Many hospitals also have walk-in clinics for emergency cases that are not life-threatening; you may not get immediate attention, but you won't pay the high price of an emergency room visit.

If you suffer from a chronic illness, consult your doctor before your departure. For such conditions as epilepsy, diabetes, or heart problems, wear a **MedicAlert identi-fication tag** (© 888/633-4298; www.medicalert.org), which will immediately alert doctors to your condition and give them access to your records through MedicAlert's 24-hour hot line.

The medical facilities and personnel in Buenos Aires and other urban areas in Argentina are very professional. Argentina has a system of socialized medicine, where basic services are free and doctors are well trained, but the facilities are poorly maintained due to lack of funding. There are many private clinics in every city, and they are inexpensive by Western standards. For an English-speaking hospital, call the **Hospital Británico** (© 11/4304-1081), established over 150 years ago during the British Empire's heyday. If you worry about getting sick away from home, you may want to consider **medical travel insurance** (see the section on travel insurance above). In most cases, however, your existing health plan will provide all the coverage you need, but call to make sure. Be sure to carry your identification card in your wallet. You should also ask for receipts or notes from the doctors, which you might need for your claim.

Safety

Petty crime exists in Buenos Aires but no more so than any major city. Travelers should be especially alert to pickpockets and purse snatchers on the streets and on buses and trains. Tourists should take care not to be overly conspicuous, walking in pairs or groups when possible. Never walk around with your passport, as to lose it is a major headache. In Buenos Aires, do not take taxis off the street; call for a radio-taxi instead. Take similar precautions when traveling in Argentina's other big cities.

SPECIALIZED TRAVEL RESOURCES

Travelers with Disabilities

Buenos Aires is not a very accessible destination for travelers with disabilities. Four- and five-star hotels in Buenos Aires often have a few rooms designed for travelers with disabilities—check with the hotel in advance and ask specific questions. Some hotels claim to be equipped for those with disabilities but still have one or two stairs leading to their elevator bays, making wheelchair access impossible. American-owned chains tend to be better at accessibility. Hotels with recent renovations sometimes will also have a room with limited capabilities and pull bars in the bathrooms. The tiny crowded streets of the MicroCentro can often barely accommodate two people walking together, let alone a wheelchair, and sidewalk cutouts do not exist in all areas. Fortunately, there are several organizations that can help.

Many travel agencies offer customized tours and itineraries for travelers with disabilities. **Flying Wheels Travel** (℗ 507/451-5005; www.flyingwheelstravel.com) offers escorted tours and cruises that emphasize sports and private tours in minivans with lifts. **Access-Able Travel Source** (℗ 303/232-2979; www.access-able.com) offers extensive access information and advice for traveling around the world with disabilities. **Accessible Journeys** (℗ 800/846-4537 or 610/521-0339; www.disabilitytravel.com) caters specifically to slow walkers and wheelchair travelers and their families and friends.

Organizations that offer assistance to travelers with disabilities include **Moss Rehab** (www.mossresourcenet.org), which provides a library of accessible-travel resources online; **SATH** (Society for Accessible Travel & Hospitality; ℗ 212/447-7284; www.sath.org; annual membership fees: $49 adults, $29 seniors and students), which offers a wealth of travel resources for all types of disabilities and informed recommendations on destinations, access guides, travel agents, tour operators, vehicle rentals, and companion services; and the **American Foundation for the Blind** (AFB; ℗ 800/232-5463; www.afb.org), a referral resource for blind or visually impaired individuals that includes information on traveling with Seeing Eye dogs.

For more information specifically targeted to travelers with disabilities, check out the quarterly online magazine *Emerging Horizons* ($16.95 per year; www.emerginghorizons.com).

Senior Travel

Argentines treat seniors with great respect, making travel for them easy. The Argentine term for a senior or retired person is *jubilado* or *jubilada*. There are often discounts at theaters and museums, too, or even free admission. **Aerolíneas Argentinas** (℗ 800/333-0276 in the U.S.; www.aerolineas.com.ar) offers a 10% discount on fares to Buenos Aires from Miami and New York for passengers 62 and older; companion fares are also discounted.

Members of **AARP** (formerly known as the American Association of Retired Persons), 601 E St. NW, Washington, DC 20049 (℗ 888/687-2277; www.aarp.org), get discounts on hotels, airfares, and car rentals. AARP offers members a wide range of benefits, including *AARP The Magazine* and a monthly newsletter. Anyone over 50 can join.

The **Alliance for Retired Americans,** 8403 Colesville Rd., Ste. 1200, Silver Spring, MD 20910 (© 301/578-8422; www.retiredamericans.org), offers a newsletter six times a year and discounts on hotel and auto rentals; annual dues are $10 per person or couple. *Note:* Members of the former National Council of Senior Citizens receive automatic membership in the Alliance.

Many reliable agencies and organizations target the 50-plus market. **Road Scholar,** formerly Elderhostel, Inc. (© 877/426-8056; www.roadscholar.org) arranges study programs for those ages 55 and over (and a spouse or companion of any age) in the U.S. and in more than 80 countries around the world. Most courses last 5 to 7 days in the U.S. (2–4 weeks abroad), and many include airfare, accommodations in university dormitories or modest inns, meals, and tuition. **ElderTreks** (© 800/741-7956; www.eldertreks.com) offers small-group tours to off-the-beaten-path or adventure-travel locations, restricted to travelers 50 and older. Recommended publications offering travel resources and discounts for seniors include the quarterly magazine *Travel 50 & Beyond* (www.travel50andbeyond.com); *Travel Unlimited: Uncommon Adventures for the Mature Traveler* (Avalon); *101 Tips for Mature Travelers,* available from Grand Circle Travel (© 800/221-2610 or 617/350-7500; www.gct.com); and *Unbelievably Good Deals and Great Adventures That You Absolutely Can't Get Unless You're Over 50* (McGraw-Hill), by Joann Rattner Heilman.

Gay & Lesbian Travelers

Though much has recently changed, Argentina remains a very traditional, Catholic society that is fairly closed-minded about homosexuality. Buenos Aires, however, is a more liberal exception to this rule, where gays and lesbians are part of the fabric of city life. Gay and lesbian travelers will find numerous clubs, restaurants, and even tango salons catering to them. Buenos Aires has become a major gay-tourism mecca since gay marriage was legalized in 2010. Maps highlighting gay-friendly establishments are now available from the Buenos Aires Tourism Office, along with standard travel information. Most hotel concierges also easily provide this information, recognizing the importance of the emerging market.

Many Argentine cities have a vibrant gay scene, but for the most part many gays and lesbians remain fairly closeted. Violence is sometimes aimed at the transgendered, even by police.

The **International Gay and Lesbian Travel Association (IGLTA;** © 800/448-8550 or 954/776-2626; www.iglta.org) is the trade association for the gay and lesbian travel industry and offers an online directory of gay- and lesbian-friendly travel businesses.

The **Comunidad Homosexual de Argentina (CHA;** © 11/4361-6382; www.cha.org.ar) is the main gay- and lesbian-rights group in Argentina; the group was the main proponent of the Civil Unions law. They also run the annual Gay Pride March, known as Marcha del Orgullo Gay, in November.

Many agencies offer tours and travel itineraries specifically for gay and lesbian travelers. **Olivia Cruises & Resorts** (© 800/631-6277; www.olivia.com) charters entire resorts and ships for exclusive lesbian vacations and offers smaller group experiences for both gay and lesbian travelers.

BueGay Travel (© 11/4184-8290; www.buegay.com.ar) handles upscale gay tourism within Buenos Aires and other parts of Argentina. Since 1992, **Gay.com**

Travel and its predecessor **Out and About** (© 800/929-2268; www.outandabout. com) have provided gay and lesbian travelers with objective, timely, and trustworthy coverage of gay-owned and gay-friendly lodging, dining, sightseeing, nightlife, and shopping establishments in every important destination worldwide. **Out Traveler** (© 800/792-2760; www.outtraveler.com) is a gay travel magazine published by LPI Media, the owners of the U.S. gay newsmagazine the **Advocate. Spartacus International Gay Guide** (Bruno Gmünder Verlag; www.spartacusworld.com/gayguide) and **Odysseus** (Odysseus Enterprises Ltd.) are good, annual English-language guidebooks focused on gay men, with some information for lesbians. You can get them from most gay and lesbian bookstores, or order them from **Giovanni's Room** bookstore, 1145 Pine St., Philadelphia, PA 19107 (© 215/923-2960; www.giovannisroom. com).

Women Travelers

Despite a female president, Argentina remains at heart a sexist country. There is a glass ceiling for women in many corporations, and female beauty is highly idealized above all other traits. Men are extremely flirtatious, and leering looks are common, owing perhaps to the strong Italian influence in the country. While disconcerting, any looks and calls you might get are rarely more than that. Drunk men in clubs can sometimes be physically harassing, however. If you want to avoid unwanted attention, don't dress skimpily (as many Porteñas, or Buenos Aires natives, do). Women should be cautious when walking alone at night and should take radio-taxis, known as *remises* (p. 32), after dark.

In the rare and unlikely event of an assault or sexual attack, contact the police immediately. More help can also be received from the **Centro de Encuentros Cultura y Mujer (CECYM),** Guatemala 4294 (© 11/4865-9102). It combats sexual violence against women, but not all of the staff members speak English.

Check out the award-winning website **Journeywoman** (www.journeywoman. com), a "real-life" women's travel information network where you can sign up for a free e-mail newsletter and get advice on everything from etiquette and dress to safety; or the travel guide *Safety and Security for Women Who Travel,* by Sheila Swan and Peter Laufer (Travelers' Tales, Inc.), offering common-sense tips on safe travel.

Kids & Teens

Argentines love and pamper their children in every way possible. Argentine kids are also trained from an early age to stay up late like their parents. Don't be surprised to find yourself passing a playground full of kids and their parents on the swing sets at 2am, when you're trying to find your way back to your hotel.

Many hotels have programs for children, especially around the holidays. Most will also provide babysitting, as long as it is requested in advance.

Student Travelers

Student discounts are very common in Argentina, but usually only if one has appropriate ID. **STA Travel** (© 800/781-4040 in the U.S., 020/7361-6144 in the U.K., or 1300/360-960 in Australia; www.statravel.com) specializes in affordable airfares, bus and rail passes, accommodations, insurance, tours, and packages for students and young travelers, and issues the **International Student Identity Card (ISIC).** This is the most widely recognized proof that you really are a student. As well as getting you discounts on a huge range of travel, tours, and attractions, it comes with a 24-hour emergency help line and a global voice/fax/e-mail messaging system with discounted international telephone calls. Available to any full-time student age 13 and over, it costs $22.

Argentina is great for college students on vacation and on a budget. The legal drinking age in Argentina is 18. There are places to drink and socialize all over Argentina. Within Buenos Aires, the bars around Plaza Serrano (see chapter 5) in Palermo Soho offer inexpensive beers on tap and pitchers of sangria. This is often served up with inexpensive snacks and live music, meaning having fun won't break a student budget. Córdoba is another city notable for its sizeable student population, with a wealth of pubs and clubs. Bariloche in the Lake District attracts thousands of Argentine students in the winter and summer looking for a good time.

ESCORTED GENERAL-INTEREST TOURS

These days, so many people plan their trips via websites and e-mail that it's easy to forget that a computer can never replace the knowledge of a good travel agent.

RECOMMENDED U.S.-BASED OPERATORS   The following U.S.-based tour companies offer solid, well-organized tours in various price categories, and they are backed by years of experience. All can arrange tours of Buenos Aires, the surroundings, and other parts of Argentina and South America.

○ **Borello Travel & Tours,** 7 Park Ave., Ste. 21, New York, NY 10016 (© **800/405-3072** or 212/695-3200; www.borellotravel.com), is a New York–based travel firm specializing in upscale travel to South America. The owner, Sandra Borello, has run her company for nearly 20 years and is a native of Buenos Aires. Prices can vary, depending on the season, options, and hotel, but a 1-week package to Buenos Aires can cost about $3,500 per person. They maintain an additional office in Buenos Aires, which can be reached at © **11/5031-1988.**

○ **Travel Dynamics International,** 132 E. 70th St., New York, NY 10021 (© **800/257-5767** or 212/517-0076; www.traveldynamicsinternational.com), is a luxury cruise operator that specializes in educational enrichment programs aboard small cruise ships. TDI voyages include expert guided land tours and onboard lectures by distinguished scholars and guests. They cater to the traveler with an intellectual interest in history, culture, and nature. Operating for almost 40 years, this company offers voyages with destinations in South America and Antarctica. Their journeys to Antarctica usually open with an overnight stay in Buenos Aires and begin at $8,495 for a 14-day program (prices may vary).

RECOMMENDED BUENOS AIRES–BASED OPERATORS   Even if you have arranged things at home, once you're in Buenos Aires, there are always last-minute changes or new things you would like to see. The following companies are all excellent and have English-speaking staff members. All can also provide trips to other cities in Argentina outside of Buenos Aires, as well as South America.

○ **Say Hueque Tourism,** Viamonte 749, Office 601, 1053 Buenos Aires (© **11/5199-2517;** www.sayhueque.com), is a highly recommended small company with knowledgeable, friendly service and attention to personalized client care. The company began by catering to the young and adventurous on a budget, but has begun to deal with a more upscale yet independent-thinking clientele. Various tour themes include Literary Buenos Aires, Biking Buenos Aires, and Tango Buenos Aires, among many others. They also offer adventure tours within the vicinity of Buenos Aires such as to the Tigre Delta. Outside of Buenos Aires, they specialize in Patagonia and Iguazú, finding special out-of-the-way places for their clients. Based on their very personal service, this is among my favorite of the operators within Buenos Aires.

o **Euro Tur,** Viamonte 486, 1053 Buenos Aires (© **11/4312-6077;** www.eurotur. com), is one of the largest and oldest travel companies in Argentina, specializing in inbound travel, but they can also help walk-ins to accommodate travelers' needs directly while in Buenos Aires. They can arrange basic city tours to trips of all kinds throughout Argentina and South America.

o **Les Amis,** Maipú 1270, 1005 Buenos Aires (© **11/4314-0500;** www.lesamis. com.ar), is another large Argentine tour company, with offices throughout Buenos Aires and Argentina. They can arrange trips for Buenos Aires, Argentina, and many other parts of South America. Within the U.S., they are represented by Gina Heilpern, who maintains an office in New York. She can be reached at © **718/857-5567.**

ORGANIZED ADVENTURE TRIPS The advantages of traveling with an organized group are plentiful, especially for travelers who have limited time and resources. Tour operators take the headache out of planning a trip, and they iron out the wrinkles that invariably pop up along the way. Many tours are organized to include guides, transportation, accommodations, meals, and gear (some outfits will even carry gear for you, for example, on trekking adventures).

o **Abercrombie & Kent,** 1520 Kensington Rd., Oak Brook, IL 60521 (© **800/323-7308;** www.abercrombiekent.com), is a luxury tour operator that offers "Patagonia: A Luxury Adventure," a 16-day trip that heads from Buenos Aires to Ushuaia for a 3-day cruise around Tierra del Fuego, followed by visits to Torres del Paine park, Puerto Varas, and Bariloche. Cost is $10,980 per person, double occupancy.

o **Backroads Active Vacations,** 801 Cedar St., Berkeley, CA 94710-1800 (© **800/GO-ACTIVE** [462-2848] or 510/527-1555; www.backroads.com), offers an 8-day biking tour through Northwest Argentina, with stops in Cachi and Cafayate, staying in luxury accommodations such as Estancia Colomé. Costs run from $4,498.

o **Mountain-Travel Sobek,** 6420 Fairmount Ave., El Cerrito, CA 94530 (© **888/MTSOBEK** [6876235] or 510/527-8100; fax 510/525-7718; www.mtsobek.com), are the pioneers of organized adventure travel, and they offer trips that involve a lot of physical activity. One of their more gung-ho journeys traverses part of the Patagonian Ice Cap in FitzRoy National Park for 21 days; a more moderate "Patagonia Explorer" mixes hiking with cruising. Prices start at $4,495 per person. Sobek always comes recommended for their excellent guides.

o **Wilderness Travel,** 1102 Ninth St., Berkeley, CA 94710 (© **800/368-2794** or 510/558-2488; www.wildernesstravel.com), offers a more mellow sightseeing/day-hiking tour around Patagonia, including Los Glaciares, Ushuaia, El Calafate, and Perito Moreno Glacier. Prices start at $4,295, depending on the number of guests (maximum 15).

o **Wildland Adventures,** 3516 NE 155th St., Seattle, WA 98155 (© **800/345-4453** or 206/365-0686; www.wildland.com), offers a few adventure tours of Argentina. The "Salta Trek Through Silent Valleys" tour takes in Salta, Jujuy, and the Andean plain. Two Patagonia tours are offered: "Best of Patagonia," which concentrates on Argentine Patagonia (including Península Valdés, Río Gallegos, Perito Moreno, and Ushuaia), and "Los Glaciares Adventure," which visits El Calafate, FitzRoy National Park, and Perito Moreno Glacier, among others. Accommodations range from hotels to camping to rustic park lodges. Eco-tourism is an integral part of Wildland tours. Prices start at $3,150 for the 8-day Salta tour and continue upwards of $4,125 for the 10-day Patagonia trip.

PRIVATE TOUR GUIDES   It's easy to hire guides through your hotel or any travel agency in Buenos Aires. You may also want to contact **AGUITBA** (Asociación de Guías de Turismo de Buenos Aires), Carlos Pellegrini 833, Sixth Floor C, Buenos Aires (🕿 **11/4322-2557;** www.aguitba.org.ar), a professional society of tour guides that has tried to promote licensing and other credentials legislation to ensure the quality of guides. Its offices are open Monday to Friday from 1 to 6pm.

Private guides I recommend include Buenos Aires–based Marta Pasquali (🕿 **11/15-4421-2486** [mobile]; marpas@uolsinectis.com.ar) and Monica Varela (🕿 **11/15-4407-0268** [mobile]; monyliv@hotmail.com). Both offer high-quality specialized tours on various themes and often work with corporations. I highly recommend them for their specialized knowledge of the city, which goes far beyond what many other tour guides offer.

STAYING CONNECTED
Calling Home

Every street corner in Argentina has a *locutorio*, a small store with phone booths and often Internet desks. As you enter, say *"Una cabina, por favor,"* and the clerk will direct you to a booth. There, a small monitor will display how much your call costs, and you pay the clerk as you leave. International calls can be pricey, so it is best to use a telephone card such as *Teletele* or *Hablemas*. These are available in most corner stores and come in denominations of 5 pesos and 10 pesos. Increasingly popular and much cheaper are computer-based calling systems such as Skype. Most Internet cafes are now fitted with headphones and webcams, and you just need to open a Skype account to call anywhere in the world. When entering an Internet cafe, say *"Una maquina, por favor,"* and the clerk will direct you to a computer. Some Internet cafes use precharged cards that you purchase at the counter before logging on.

Internet Access Abroad

Travelers have any number of ways to check their e-mail and access the Internet on the road. Of course, using your own laptop—or even a PDA (personal digital assistant) or electronic organizer with a modem—gives you the most flexibility, and Wi-Fi is getting more ubiquitous. But even if you don't have a computer, you can still access your e-mail and even your office computer from cybercafes.

WITHOUT YOUR OWN COMPUTER
It's hard nowadays to find a city that *doesn't* have a few cybercafes. Although there's no definitive directory for cybercafes—these are independent businesses, after all—two places to start looking are at **www.cybercaptive.com** and **www.cybercafe. com**.

Aside from formal cybercafes, most **youth hostels** and hotels nowadays have at least one computer you can get to the Internet on. And most **public libraries** across the world offer Internet access free or for a small charge. Avoid **hotel business centers** unless you're willing to pay exorbitant rates.

Most major airports now have **Internet kiosks** scattered throughout their gates. These kiosks, which you'll also see in shopping malls, hotel lobbies, and tourist information offices around the world, give you basic Web access for a per-minute fee that's usually higher than cybercafe prices. The kiosks' clunkiness and high prices mean they should be avoided whenever possible.

To retrieve your e-mail, ask your **Internet Service Provider (ISP)** if it has a Web-based interface tied to your existing e-mail account. If your ISP doesn't have such an interface, you can use the free **mail2web** service (www.mail2web.com) to view and reply to your home e-mail. For more flexibility, you may want to open a free Web-based e-mail account with **Yahoo! Mail** (http://mail.yahoo.com). (Microsoft's Hotmail is another popular option, but Hotmail has severe spam problems.) Your home ISP may be able to forward your e-mail to the Web-based account automatically.

If you need to access files on your office computer, look into a service called **GoToMyPC** (www.gotomypc.com). The service provides a Web-based interface for you to access and manipulate a distant PC from anywhere—even a cybercafe—provided your "target" PC is on and has an always-on connection to the Internet (such as with Road Runner cable). The service offers top-quality security, but if you're worried about hackers, use your own laptop rather than a cybercafe computer to access the GoToMyPC system.

WITH YOUR OWN COMPUTER

Wi-Fi (wireless fidelity) is the buzzword in computer access, and more and more hotels, cafes, and retailers are signing on as wireless "hotspots" from where you can get high-speed connection without cable wires, networking hardware, or a phone line (Certain places provide **free wireless networks** in cities around the world. To locate these free hotspots, go to **www.personaltelco.net/index.cgi/WirelessCommunities**.) You can get Wi-Fi connection one of several ways. Most laptops sold nowadays have built-in Wi-Fi capability (an 802.11b wireless Ethernet connection). Mac owners have their own networking technology, Apple AirPort. Those with older computers can plug an 802.11b/**Wi-Fi card** (around $50) into their laptops. You sign up for wireless access service much as you do cellphone service, through a plan offered by one of several commercial companies that have made wireless service available in airports, hotel lobbies, and coffee shops, primarily in the U.S. (followed by the U.K. and Japan). **T-Mobile Hotspot** (www.t-mobile.com/hotspot) serves up wireless connections at more than 1,000 Starbucks coffee shops nationwide. **Boingo** (www.boingo.com) and **Wayport** (www.wayport.com) have set up networks in airports and high-class hotel lobbies. iPass providers (see below) also give you access to a few hundred wireless hotel-lobby setups. Best of all, you don't need to be staying at the Four Seasons to use the hotel's network; just set yourself up on a nice couch in the lobby. The companies' pricing policies can be Byzantine, with a variety of monthly, per-connection, and per-minute plans, but in general you pay around $30 a month for limited access—and as more and more companies jump on the wireless bandwagon, prices are likely to get even more competitive.

If Wi-Fi is not available at your destination, most business-class hotels throughout the world offer dataports for laptop modems, and a few thousand hotels in the U.S. and Europe now offer free high-speed Internet access using an Ethernet network cable. You can bring your own cables, but most hotels rent them for around $10. **Call your hotel in advance** to see what your options are.

In addition, major ISPs have **local access numbers** around the world, allowing you to go online by simply placing a local call. Check your ISP's website or call its toll-free number and ask how you can use your current account away from home, and how much it will cost.

If you're traveling outside the reach of your ISP, the **iPass** network has dial-up numbers in most of the world's countries. You'll have to sign up with an iPass provider, who will then tell you how to set up your computer for your destination(s). For a list of iPass providers, go to www.ipass.com and click on "Individuals Buy Now." One solid provider is **i2roam** (© **866/811-6209** or 920/235-0475; www.i2roam.com).

Wherever you go, bring a **connection kit** of the right power and phone adapters, a spare phone cord, and a spare Ethernet network cable—or find out whether your hotel supplies them to guests.

Using a Cellphone Abroad

The three letters that define much of the world's **wireless capabilities** are GSM (Global System for Mobiles)—a big, seamless network that makes for easy cross-border cellphone use throughout Europe and dozens of other countries worldwide. In the U.S., T-Mobile, AT&T Wireless, and Cingular use this quasi-universal system; in Canada, Microcell and some Rogers customers are GSM; and all Europeans and most Australians use GSM.

If your cellphone is on a GSM system and you have a world-capable multiband phone, such as many Sony Ericsson, Motorola, or Samsung models, you can make and receive calls across civilized areas on much of the globe, from Andorra to Uganda. Just call your wireless operator and ask for "international roaming" to be activated on your account. Unfortunately, per-minute charges can be high—usually $1 to $1.50 in western Europe, and up to $5 in places such as Russia and Indonesia.

That's why it's important to buy an "unlocked" world phone from the get-go. Many cellphone operators sell "locked" phones that restrict you from using any other removable computer memory phone chip (called a **SIM card**) other than the ones they supply. Having an unlocked phone allows you to install a cheap, prepaid SIM card (found at a local retailer) in your destination country. (Show your phone to the salesperson; not all phones work on all networks.) You'll get a local phone number—and much, much lower calling rates. Getting an already locked phone unlocked can be a complicated process, but it can be done; just call your cellular operator and say you'll be going abroad for several months and want to use the phone with a local provider.

For many, **renting** a phone is a good idea. (Even world-phone owners will have to rent new phones if they're traveling to non-GSM regions, such as Japan or Korea.) While you can rent a phone from any number of overseas sites, including kiosks at airports and at car-rental agencies, I suggest renting the phone before you leave home. That way you can give loved ones and business associates your new number, make sure the phone works, and take the phone wherever you go—especially helpful for overseas trips through several countries, where local phone-rental agencies often bill in local currency and may not let you take the phone to another country.

Phone rental isn't cheap. You'll usually pay $40 to $50 per week, plus airtime fees of at least a dollar a minute. If you're traveling to Europe, though, local rental companies often offer free incoming calls within their home country, which can save you big bucks. The bottom line: Shop around.

Two good wireless rental companies are **InTouch USA** (☎ **800/872-7626;** www. intouchglobal.com) and **RoadPost** (☎ **888/290-1606** or 905/272-5665; www. roadpost.com). Give them your itinerary and they'll tell you what wireless products you need. InTouch will also, for free, advise you on whether your existing phone will work overseas; simply call ☎ **703/222-7161** between 9am and 4pm EST, or go to http://intouchglobal.com/travel.htm. For trips of more than a few weeks spent in one country, **buying a phone** becomes economically attractive, as many nations have cheap, no-questions-asked prepaid phone systems. Once you arrive at your destination, stop by a local cellphone shop and get the cheapest package; you'll probably pay less than $100 for a phone and a starter calling card. Local calls may be as low as 10¢ per minute, and in many countries incoming calls are free.

PLANNING YOUR TRIP ONLINE
Surfing for Airfares

The "big three" online travel agencies, **Expedia, Travelocity,** and **Orbitz,** sell most of the air tickets bought on the Internet. (Canadian travelers should try Expedia.ca and Travelocity.ca; U.K. residents can go to Expedia.co.uk and Opodo.co.uk.). Each has different business deals with the airlines and may offer different fares on the same flights, so it's wise to shop around. Expedia and Travelocity will also send you **e-mail notification** when a cheap fare becomes available to your favorite destination. Of the smaller travel agency websites, **SideStep** (www.sidestep.com) has gotten the best reviews from Frommer's authors. It's a browser add-on that purports to "search 140 sites at once," but in reality only beats competitors' fares as often as other sites do.

Also remember to check **airline websites.** Even with major airlines, you can often shave a few bucks from a fare by booking directly through the airline and avoiding a travel agency's transaction fee. But you'll get these discounts only by **booking online:** Most airlines now offer online-only fares that even their phone agents know nothing about. For the websites of airlines that fly to and from your destination, see "Getting There," earlier in this chapter.

Great **last-minute deals** are available through free weekly e-mail services provided directly by the airlines. Most of these are announced on Tuesday or Wednesday and must be purchased online. Most are only valid for travel that weekend, but some can be booked weeks or months in advance. Sign up for weekly e-mail alerts at airline websites or check metasearch sites that compile comprehensive lists of last-minute specials, such as **SmarterTravel.com.** For last-minute trips, **lastminutetravel.com** in the U.S. and **lastminute.com** in Europe often have better air-and-hotel package deals than the major-label sites. A website listing numerous bargain sites and airlines around the world is **www.itravelnet.com**.

If you're willing to give up some control over your flight details, use what is called an **"opaque" fare service** such as **Priceline** (www.priceline.com; www.priceline. co.uk for Europeans) or its smaller competitor **Hotwire** (www.hotwire.com). Both offer rock-bottom prices in exchange for travel on a "mystery airline" at a mysterious time of day, often with a mysterious change of planes en route. The mystery airlines are all major, well-known carriers, and the possibility of being sent from Philadelphia to Chicago via Tampa is remote; airlines' routing computers have gotten a lot better than they used to be. But your chances of getting a 6am or 11pm flight are pretty high. Hotwire tells you flight prices before you buy; Priceline usually has better deals than Hotwire, but you have to play their "name our price" game. If you're new at this, the helpful folks at **BiddingForTravel** (www.biddingfortravel.com) do a good job of demystifying Priceline's prices and strategies. Priceline and Hotwire are great for flights within North America and between the U.S. and Europe. But for flights to other parts of the world, consolidators will almost always beat their fares. *Note:* Priceline now has a non-opaque service in addition to their opaque service. You now have the option to pick exact flights, times, and airlines from a list of offers.

Surfing for Hotels

Shopping online for hotels is generally done one of two ways: by booking through the hotel's own website or through an independent booking agency (or a fare-service agency, such as Priceline; see below). These Internet hotel agencies have multiplied in mind-boggling numbers of late, competing for the business of millions of consumers surfing for accommodations around the world. This competitiveness can be a boon to consumers who have the patience and time to shop and compare the online sites for good deals—but shop they must, for prices can vary considerably from site to site. And keep in mind that hotels at the top of a site's listing may be there for no other reason than that they paid money to get the placement.

Of the "big three" sites, **Expedia** offers a long list of special deals and "virtual tours" or photos of available rooms so you can see what you're paying for (a feature that helps counter the claims that the best rooms are often held back from bargain-booking websites). **Travelocity** posts unvarnished customer reviews and ranks its properties according to the AAA rating system. Also reliable is **Hotels.com.** An excellent free program, **TravelAxe** (www.travelaxe.com), can help you search multiple hotel sites at once, even ones you may never have heard of—and conveniently lists the total price of the room, including the taxes and service charges. Another booking site, **Travelweb** (www.travelweb.com), is partly owned by the hotels it represents (including the Hilton, Hyatt, and Starwood chains) and is therefore plugged directly into the hotels' reservations systems—unlike independent online agencies, which have to fax or e-mail reservation requests to the hotel, a good portion of which get misplaced in the shuffle. More than once, travelers have arrived at the hotel only to be told that they have no reservation. To be fair, many of the major sites are undergoing improvements in service and ease of use. In the meantime, we suggest you **get a confirmation number** and **make a printout** of any online-booking transaction.

In the opaque-website category, **Priceline** and **Hotwire** are even better for hotels than for airfares; with both, you're allowed to pick the neighborhood and quality level of your hotel before offering up your money. Priceline's hotel product even covers Europe and Asia, though it's much better at getting five-star lodging for three-star prices than at finding anything at the bottom of the scale. On the downside, many hotels stick Priceline guests in their least desirable rooms. Be sure to go to the BiddingForTravel website (see above) before bidding on a hotel room on Priceline; it features a fairly up-to-date list of hotels that Priceline uses in major cities. For both Priceline and Hotwire, you pay upfront and the fee is nonrefundable. *Note:* Some hotels do not provide loyalty program credits or points or other frequent-stay amenities when you book a room through opaque online services.

Surfing for Rental Cars

For booking rental cars online, the best deals are usually found at rental-car company websites, although all the major online travel agencies also offer rental-car reservations services. Priceline and Hotwire work well for rental cars too; the only "mystery" is which major rental company you get, and for most travelers the difference between Hertz, Avis, and Budget is negligible.

ACTIVE VACATION PLANNER

With so many climate zones and such a wide variety of terrain, Argentina is a haven for outdoor activities of all kinds. Locals have a healthy sense of adventure, and recreational outdoor sports are an important part of life here. Activities around Iguazú Falls range from easy hiking along the waterfall circuits and on San Martín Island to speed-rafting along the river and trekking into the jungle. The high plains of the Northwest draw adventurers seeking a little-traveled wilderness that can be explored by bike, on horseback, or in a 4WD vehicle. Near Mendoza are the tallest mountains in the Western Hemisphere, with spectacular rivers and high plains. And of course, Argentine Patagonia has more kayaking, climbing, and trekking opportunities than you could possibly fit in one lifetime.

Here is a brief introduction to the main outdoor activities in Argentina. Many will require you to hire a local guide to help you navigate the local terrain—and the sometimes-confusing local permit process. For more information, visit the website of the Argentine National Parks Service at **www.parquesnacionales.gov.ar**.

Backpacking

Overnight hiking trips will take you even deeper into the mountains and farther away from the hustle and bustle of life. Organized campsites dot most national parks and have rustic facilities. Camping is a popular activity for young Argentines, who flock to the peaks for their summer holidays in droves. There are excellent backpacking trips in the Lake District, where you can connect rustic and friendly mountain huts in Nahuel Huapi National Park. In the El Chaltén area, overnight trekking can take you beneath the granite spires of Mt. FitzRoy and Cerro Torre. Be sure to head out well prepared, with appropriate clothing and safety gear, a good map, and a reliable weather report. Always tell someone where you are going.

Biking

The wide-open spaces and notoriously long distances can make for some adventurous two-wheel trips. With so many seldom-traveled dirt roads, a good suspension bike will certainly come in handy here. The most popular area for recreational mountain biking is the Lake District, where you can cross the Andes to Chile and back, or pedal the stunning (albeit dusty) Seven Lakes Route, camping lakeside each night. Mountain biking is also popular in the Nahuel Huapi National Park area near Bariloche, as well as in the northern province of Salta, where tours take you from the clouds to the jungle. Biking in the wine country near Mendoza is also fun. And such cities as Córdoba have established bike routes. Virtually every town has a local bike shop, where you can rent a bike and ask locals for trail ideas.

Fishing

Argentine Patagonia is one of the world's premier destinations for fishing, particularly for fly-fishing. Trout and salmon populate the picturesque and isolated rivers and lakes from Junín de los Andes south to Esquel. Tierra del Fuego also draws fly-fishing fanatics. The fishing season runs from November through April, generally, and some areas enforce strict catch-and-release policies. Fishing on the Atlantic Coast is popular anywhere there is a dock, and the giant dorado fish in Entre Rios province is legendary.

Horseback Riding

Argentina has one of the world's great horse cultures, from the polo fields of Buenos Aires to the gauchos roaming the Pampas and Patagonia, and the terrain is ideal for horseback riding. Horses are well cared for and very common. Hour-long trail rides are offered at *estancias* throughout the country. In the wilder areas of the Northwest, the Mendozan Andes, and Patagonia, visitors can sign up for multiday pack trips.

Kayaking

Thanks to the steep eastern slopes of the Andes, there are many fun rivers with bubbling rapids to entertain enthusiasts here. The Mendoza and Atuel rivers, in Mendoza Province, and the Juramento River, in Salta, are important spots. In the Lake District, the main river for rafting and kayaking is the Manso, south of Bariloche, although there are dozens of nearby rivers to keep a river rat happy.

Mountaineering & Rock Climbing

Alpine climbers are drawn to a few hot spots in Argentina: to the mighty summit of Mt. Aconcagua in Mendoza, the tallest mountain in the world outside the Himalaya; to glaciated volcanoes, such as Mt. Tronador or Volcán Lanín, in the Lake District; and to the famous granite spires near El Chaltén.

Scuba Diving

The Atlantic Coast of Argentina offers some good scuba diving at Puerto Madryn, where experienced divers can get close up with marine wildlife. There are also a number of places in the Lake District for freshwater diving.

Skiing/Snowboarding

Alpine skiing and snowboarding in Argentina offer plenty of choices for visitors. The biggest resort, Las Leñas, is nestled in a high altitude valley 5 hours south of Mendoza city. Farther south, the biggest ski resort is at Bariloche's Catedral; and such gems as Chapelco in San Martín or Cerro Bayo in Villa La Angostura are nearby, allowing travelers to visit a few different resorts over the period of one visit. Finally, Cerro Castor in Ushuaia is the southernmost ski resort in the world. The Austral ski season runs from late June to September. Nordic or cross-country skiing is not as popular, as it requires a deeper snow base. Backcountry skiing, or ski-touring, is also on the rise.

Surfing

Riding the breaks off the Atlantic Ocean is a growing sport, and there is a healthy beach culture to accompany the local surfing scene. The most popular area is near Mar del Plata, but there are many interesting surfing spots in Buenos Aires province as well.

Trekking/Hiking

With the spine of the Andes as a western backdrop, Argentina offers many options for hikers. The north of the country offers good trails heading out of virtually every town—from the high *altiplano* of the Northwest, and the tallest mountains in the

Western Hemisphere near Mendoza, to the rolling hills of Córdoba. Farther south, the Lake District has dozens of good day hikes that wind through lush valleys and along high ridges. The El Chaltén area of Los Glaciares National Park is one of the world's top trekking destinations. Don't forget Tierra del Fuego, where the national park blends coastal marine life with high mountains.

Windsurfing/Kite Surfing

Another growing sport, the wind- and kite-surfing scene just outside Buenos Aires at Peru Beach is popular. In the notoriously windy expanses of Patagonia, these sports are somewhat challenged by daunting gusts and cold water, although Bariloche hosts an annual Wind Riders Festival each January.

SUGGESTED ARGENTINA ITINERARIES

BUENOS AIRES IN 5 DAYS

by Michael Luongo

4

No length of time ever seems like enough in a city as wonderful as Buenos Aires. This itinerary takes you through 5 days in the capital—ideally a Wednesday to a Sunday. The route guides you through the best features of various neighborhoods—from the MicroCentro and Palermo Viejo to Recoleta and San Telmo. You'll eat several great meals, go shopping, and take in some breathtakingly beautiful sites. I've scheduled in plenty of downtime, too, in case you want to tango all night long and take it easy the following day (Buenos Aires, like New York, is a city that doesn't sleep).

1 Relaxing & Settling In

More than likely, you've arrived early in the morning after an all-night flight. Before you head out for the day, make reservations at **Cabaña las Lilas** ★★★ (p. 103) for dinner tonight. Afterward, head to Calle Florida, checking out the shops at **Galerías Pacífico** (p. 135), and have a snack at **Il Gran Caffe** ★ (p. 102). Wander down to **Plaza de Mayo** (p. 126) and take a look at historic sites such as the **Cabildo** ★ (p. 127), Buenos Aires's original city hall, recently renovated for the 2010 Bicentennial celebrations, the **Metropolitan Cathedral** ★★ (p. 127), and the **Casa Rosada** ★★★ (p. 127), with Evita's famous balcony. Head back to the hotel for a much-needed nap before heading out to Cabaña las Lilas for dinner. Certainly you've admired the view of **Puerto Madero** (p. 128) from your table, so have a wander dockside.

2 Historical Buenos Aires

I highly recommend exploring the historic center of Buenos Aires with a professional guide, through companies like **Borello Travel & Tours** (✆ 800/405-3072 or 212/686-4911; p. 42), **Say Hueque Tourism** (✆ 11/5199-2517; p. 42), or private tour guides **Marta Pasquali** (✆ 11-15/4421-2486) or **Monica Varela** (✆ 11-15/4407-0268). As they lead you through the historic center of Buenos Aires, passing the **Plaza de Mayo** (p. 126) and the turn-of-the-20th-century marvel **Avenida de Mayo** to **Congreso,** they'll explain how architecture, history, and the lost glory of a powerful Argentina is reflected in the streets of Buenos Aires. Ride the **A line subway**'s (p. 71) wooden trains down to station Avenida de Mayo. Have a coffee and *medialunas* at **Café Tortoni ★★★** (p. 101), one of the city's most historic and scenic cafes, and try to catch the conversation of Buenos Aires locals discussing the latest issues. If it's Thursday, at 3:30pm, head back to Plaza de Mayo for the **Madres of Plaza de Mayo,** a weekly protest held by the mothers of the 30,000 young people who disappeared during the military regime between 1976 and 1982. Head back and take a nap at the hotel. In the evening, have dinner at **Palacio Español ★★** (p. 102) in the glorious gilded dining hall of **Club Español.**

3 A Day in Recoleta

Sleep in and have a late breakfast at your hotel. Have your hotel make dinner reservations at **La Bourgogne ★★★** (p. 105), a fine French restaurant in the **Alvear Palace Hotel ★★★** (p. 85). Then head to **Recoleta Cemetery ★★★** (p. 125), in the Recoleta neighborhood. Pay homage to the most famous tomb of all, Evita's. Make sure to wander around and see many of the other tombs, built like mini-mansions for the dead and covered in marble and bronze sculpture. Around the corner from the cemetery, head to the **Centro Cultural Recoleta ★** (p. 126) and check out the newest art exhibit. If you've brought the kids along or you're feeling young at heart, visit the children's section inside, with its interactive science exhibits. Afterward, head across **Plaza Francia** and take a coffee at **La Biela ★★★** (p. 107), one of the most famous cafes in the city. After this much-needed break, it's time to do some shopping along **Avenida Alvear;** be sure to take a peek at least into **Polo Ralph Lauren** (p. 145), built into a grand mansion. If you've been shopping for hours, you're just in time for your reservation at La Bourgogne.

4 Palermo

After breakfast, head to **Plaza Italia** and take a brief walk around, enjoying the contrast of the green trees against the white-marble buildings lining this part of Avenida Santa Fe. Head to the **Zoological Gardens ★** (p. 124) and check out all the animals, after buying special food for them at the entrance. Afterward, stroll down Avenida Libertador and wander among the parks, heading to **Museo Nacional de Bellas Artes ★★** (p. 132). It's a long walk, but beautiful all along the way. Head back to the hotel, freshen up, and head for dinner at **Casa Cruz ★★** (p. 111), in Palermo Viejo, a glamorous nightclublike dining space and one of the city's best places to be seen on a night out. Then visit **Bar Isabel** (p. 156), next door, a watering hole popular with models.

5 San Telmo & Tango

Head to **Plaza Dorrego** (p. 121) for the Sunday **San Telmo antiques fair ★★★** (p. 121), one of the most enjoyable highlights of Buenos Aires. In this open-air bazaar, you can buy small antiques and souvenirs to bring home, and watch live tango performances. (Be careful of pickpockets targeting mesmerized tourists!) Then, grab a late lunch at the atmospheric **Bar El Federal ★★** (p. 108). Head up **Calle Defensa** to take a look at more antiques in the numerous shops lining the street, such as **Galería El Solar de French** (p. 139). Head back to the hotel and freshen up. You're having dinner tonight at

Buenos Aires in 5 Days

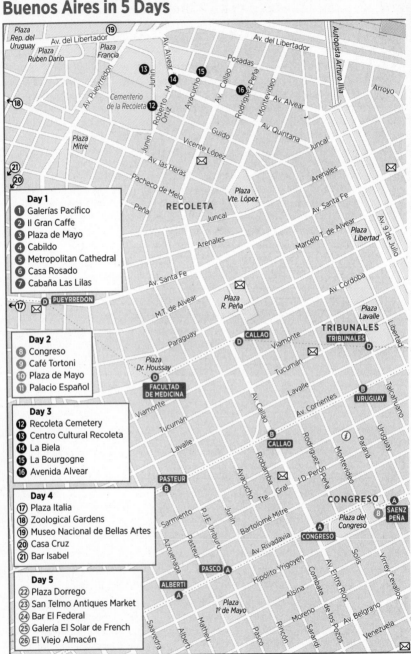

Day 1
1. Galerías Pacífico
2. Il Gran Caffe
3. Plaza de Mayo
4. Cabildo
5. Metropolitan Cathedral
6. Casa Rosado
7. Cabaña Las Lilas

Day 2
8. Congreso
9. Café Tortoni
10. Plaza de Mayo
11. Palacio Español

Day 3
12. Recoleta Cemetery
13. Centro Cultural Recoleta
14. La Biela
15. La Bourgogne
16. Avenida Alvear

Day 4
17. Plaza Italia
18. Zoological Gardens
19. Museo Nacional de Bellas Artes
20. Casa Cruz
21. Bar Isabel

Day 5
22. Plaza Dorrego
23. San Telmo Antiques Market
24. Bar El Federal
25. Galería El Solar de French
26. El Viejo Almacén

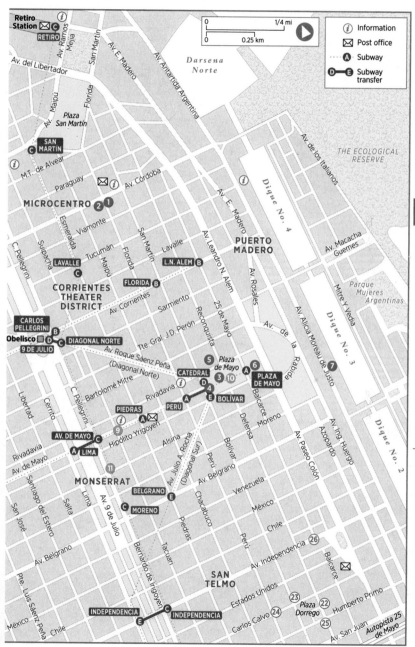

El Viejo Almacén (p. 152). Watching their show is a great way to end your 5-day stay in Buenos Aires.

NORTHERN PATAGONIA: LAKES & VILLAGES

by Christie Pashby

One of the world's great alpine playgrounds, the Argentina Lake District has plenty to discover. Visitors can combine adventure activities with scenic drives and other more chilled-out explorations. In the evenings, enjoy great food and wine, and stay in lovely local inns. While you can move about quite simply on the local buses, having a rental car to get from San Carlos de Bariloche to San Martín de los Andes and back gives you more freedom. Pick one up at the Bariloche airport, but be ready for dirt roads and some aggressive drivers in Bariloche.

The trip starts with some orientation in Bariloche, the area's main city. After exploring there for a few days, you'll continue on to two nearby towns: Villa La Angostura and San Martín de los Andes. The entire driving route is spectacular, with tall forests, expansive mountain lakes, and photo opportunities at every turn.

1 Bariloche

Fly into San Carlos de Bariloche from Buenos Aires. Pick up a rental car at the airport and drive into town along the shores of the spectacular Lago Nahuel Huapi. Check into an inn with a lake view such as **Posada Los Juncos ★★** or **Cacique Inacayal** (p. 317). If you can afford it, head along Avenida Bustillo for 25km (16 miles) to the incredible **Llao Llao Hotel & Resort ★★** (p. 318). After relaxing by the pool, make reservations for dinner at **Butterfly ★★★** (p. 324), near the Llao Llao, or at the hidden **Naan ★★** (p. 321) in town.

2 Bariloche

After a lovely breakfast at your hotel, make a reservation for your next day's activities (see below). Then hop into your car and explore the **Circuito Chico ★★** (p. 312), a leisurely loop that takes you past the many bays of Nahuel Huapi Lake. Take the beautiful sightseeing chairlift to the top of **Cerro Campanario ★**, to get a stunning view of the area before heading west past the Llao Llao Resort. Stop in **Colonia Suiza** for lunch—a traditional *curanto* if it's a Wednesday or Sunday. After a siesta at your hotel room, head out for dinner, Argentine style, sometime after 9pm. Tonight, choose a traditional Argentine *asado* at either **Tarquino** (p. 322) or **El Boliche de Alberto** (p. 322).

3 Bariloche Rafting

There are many active adventures to choose from in Bariloche: sea kayaking, hiking, or fishing, to name a few. My absolute favorite is white-water rafting on the emerald **Manso River,** south of Bariloche. Consider booking with **Patagonia Rafting** (p. 315) or **Extremo Sur** (p. 315). The rafting is intense and adrenaline-packed, for good swimmers only! After lunch, a big barbecue will recharge you before you head back to town. You may be up for a lighter dinner tonight after that big lunch. Try **Kandahar ★** or **Vegetariano ★** (p. 323).

Northern Patagonia Lakes & Villages

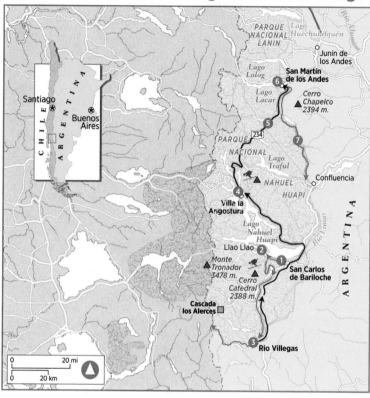

4 Villa La Angostura

Eat breakfast, check out, and give yourself some time to explore the shops and markets of Bariloche. The drive continues along RN 231 along the north shore of Nahuel Huapi Lake to the swanky town of Villa La Angostura. Check into **Las Balsas ★★** (p. 330) or into the more economical **Hostería Le Lac ★** (p. 331). Lunch on the water at the **Correntoso Hotel's Puerto restaurant** (p. 330) and then hike out the Arrayan peninsula, taking a boat back to the port. Enjoy an afternoon of fishing or hiking and then head for dinner at the excellent **Tinto Bistro ★★** (p. 332) or **Delfina ★** (p. 332).

5 Ruta de los Siete Lagos

Eat breakfast, check out, and stop at a supermarket for picnic supplies. Then head north on RN 234, the spectacular Ruta de los Siete Lagos (Seven Lakes Route). It's 110km (68 miles) to San Martín de los Andes, but give yourself most of the day to get there. Plan to stop frequently to explore the lakeshores at Lago

Correntoso and Lago Falkner. The Vuliñaco waterfall is a great picnic spot. You'll arrive in San Martín de los Andes, Bariloche's tidier and smaller sister, in time for an afternoon tea at the historic **Arrayán Tea House** ★ (p. 338). Make your plans for the following day's activities. Check into your inn at **La Casa de Eugenia** ★ or the cozy **La Raclette** ★ (p. 341). San Martín has many good restaurants; try **La Tasca** ★ (p. 343) or **Torino Bistro** ★ (p. 343).

6 San Martín de los Andes

Eat breakfast and leave the car behind. Your hiking guide is here to drive you to the lovely trails of Lanín National Park. In the evening, head to **La Fondue de Betty** ★ (p. 344) for the San Martín classic—a bubbling and scrumptious fondue dinner, with *vino tinto* of course!

7 Bariloche & Home

Check out, fill up the tank, and take the "other" way back to Bariloche. You can either go via the lovely mountain village of **Villa Traful,** or via the marvelous raw canyons of the **Paso Córdoba.** You'll be back in Bariloche in time to catch a midafternoon flight to Buenos Aires.

HIKING SOUTHERN ARGENTINE PATAGONIA IN 1 WEEK

by Christie Pashby

Hikers from all over the world make the long journey to Patagonia for some of the best trekking on the planet. The terrain is simply world-class: stunning granite spires, expansive glaciers, thick forests, and wide-open plains. There is much to see here, enough to keep hard-core hikers and backpackers busy for a month.

This itinerary starts with a day spent visiting the stunning Perito Moreno Glacier and hiking on the ice itself. Then head north to El Chaltén, the "National Capital of Trekking." The hikes are demanding, but easily manageable for fit people with some trekking experience. Each day ends back in town for a good meal and a hot shower.

The best time of year for this trip is either November or March, when the winds are relatively calm, and the trails are less busy than in high season (Jan–Feb).

1 El Calafate

After your trip from Buenos Aires, settle into a nice local inn; try **Kau Yatún** ★ (p. 372) or the economical **Casa de Grillos** (p. 373). Head out for a stroll around town and sign yourself up for the "Big Ice" experience for tomorrow, your tour to Estancia Cristina for the day after. It's also a good idea to book your bus ticket to El Chaltén. Pop in for dinner at the excellent **Casimiro Biguá** ★★ (p. 375), where you can enjoy king crab from Tierra del Fuego or the local specialty, Patagonian lamb. Get a good night's sleep; tomorrow is a big day.

2 Perito Moreno Glacier ★★★

You'll be picked up right after breakfast and driven out to Lago Argentino for the **"Big Ice"** ★★ adventure with outfitter **Hielo y Aventura** (p. 380). Once you spot your first jaw-dropping views of Perito Moreno Glacier, there's no turning back. You'll travel by boat across the lake and then hike up the southern side of

Hiking Southern Patagonia in 1 Week

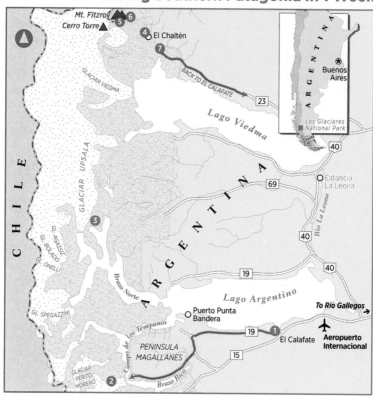

the glacier. Your guides will set you up with crampons and lead you deep onto the seemingly endless mass of ice. You'll skirt crevasses and explore its frozen horizons. After a good siesta back in town, head out for a well-deserved dinner of Argentine classics, such as chorizo and blood sausages, and a big piece of tenderloin with red wine at **Don Pichón ★★** (p. 376).

3 & 4 Estancia Cristina

Another early morning! After boarding the catamaran and heading out on the shores of Lago Argentino, you'll cruise past icebergs and glaciers. Back on ground at the awesome **Estancia Cristina ★★** (p. 374), check into your lovely lodge room and take in the great view of the impressive Cerro Norte. Then, hop into a 4WD truck and drive to a lookout over the massive **Upsala Glacier.** The hiking starts here and heads along the ancient ridges before dropping into a spectacular glacier-carved canyon full of fossils. Keep your eye out for condors and wild horses! The trek ends with enough time to visit the *estancia* museum and learn the heartbreaking but inspiring story of the *estancia*'s pioneers. After dinner, you'll have the place—and all the stars—all to yourself.

Next day, enjoy breakfast in the lodge's main house; it will fuel you for a big morning on the trail, only this time with the *estancia*'s gentle gauchos and beautiful horses. Ride up to a lookout stretching across the Southern Patagonian Icecap, where lunch is served. Head back in time for a warm shower before boarding the boat and heading back to El Calafate. For dinner tonight? How about spaghetti and a few *cervezas* at **La Cocina ★** (p. 375)?

5 El Chaltén & Hiking

The first bus of the day heads to El Chaltén at 7:30am, delivering you there early enough that you'll have time to drop off your luggage at your hotel—**Senderos Hostería ★★** (p. 388) or **Kaulem Hostería** (p. 387)—pick up picnic supplies and hit the trail. Today's trek will take you along the FitzRoy River up to the **Cerro Torre Lookout** (p. 385). It takes about 4 hours. Back in town, stop by **Patagonicus** for a coffee and a sweet treat. After your now-regular siesta, head to the cozy and historic **Ruca Mahuida ★★** (p. 388) for dinner.

6 Hiking

Up early again, you've got a spectacular day ahead of you on the trail. Your inn will give you a good breakfast and pack you a picnic lunch if you ask the previous day. The trail today is **Laguna de los Tres ★★** (p. 385), affording a close-up view of **Mt. FitzRoy.** You'll be on the trail for 10 hours, a good full day. But you'll be home in time for a hot shower, a rest, and then dinner at **Estepa ★** (p. 388), which serves abundant salads and creative pizzas.

7 El Calafate & Home

If your flight leaves El Calafate in the afternoon, you'll need to be on the first bus out of El Chaltén. Back in El Calafate, you may have time for lunch before transferring to the airport and flying to Buenos Aires, exhausted but invigorated from a week of trekking amid fine peaks and grand glaciers.

MENDOZA: MALBEC & MOUNTAINS

by Christie Pashby

You can practically do it all here in Mendoza—live large, indulge your palate, and experience thrilling adventures and marvelous scenery. This journey starts with a few nights based out of Mendoza, a marvelous city with excellent restaurants, charming cafes, and plenty of plazas and parks. Then head out of town to relax in the wine country and explore the three principal wine areas: Luján de Cuyo, Maipú, and the lovely Valle de Uco. You'll also want time to get a good look at the spectacular Andes Mountains, which make a majestic backdrop for the rural countryside here. Good restaurants are another hallmark of the region. Tables are in high demand, so I recommend that you plan ahead by making dinner reservations each morning before you head out. Ask your hotel reception to do so for you, and plan to take a taxi to dinner so you can drink wine. Driving the high mountain roads requires some attention and care. Keep a good map on hand, and don't be afraid to ask for directions. Mendocinos are very friendly, proud, and happy to have you visiting them.

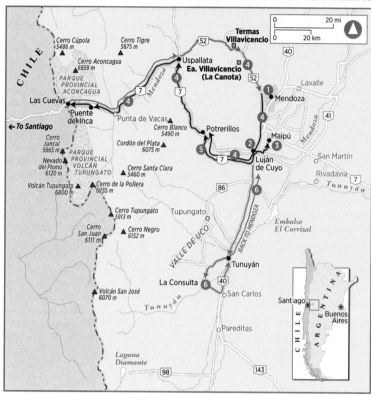

1 Mendoza

A midmorning flight will have you in Mendoza, from either Buenos Aires or Santiago, in time for a leisurely lunch in town. Check into a downtown hotel; the posh **Park Hyatt ★★** (p. 270) has the best location, in front of the Plaza Independencia. Head to the outdoor tables in front of **Azafrán ★★** (p. 273) to acquaint yourself with the local specialties. After an afternoon exploring the parks and plazas of Mendoza, relax by the pool. Then stop by one of the local wine stores for some sampling. The **Vines of Mendoza** (p. 271) runs tastings and offers glasses by the flight. It's a good place to mingle and grab some light dinner. If you've still got room, indulge in some of the continent's best ice cream.

2 Wines of Luján

After a nice breakfast in your hotel, head out for a day exploring the wines of **Luján de Cuyo** (p. 285). This is the "Tierra del Malbec," where Argentina's signature varietal has found its most harmonic home. Because it's your first day in the area, it's worth signing up for an organized tour to help you get the lay of the land. Ask for a tour that includes three vineyard stops and lunch (I highly recommend **Clos de Chacras** ★★ [p. 283] and **Ruca Malen** ★ [p. 287]). In the afternoon, relax in a plaza or by the pool. Then hit the swanky **Grill Q** ★ (p. 273) for dinner, and stroll the sidewalk cafes and bars of Calle Aristides before hitting the sack.

3 Wines of Maipú

Today is a good day to switch to a more rural inn. After breakfast, check out of your hotel and pick up a rental car. Then head south of town and drop your bags off at your inn in either Chacras de Coria, at **Finca Adalgisa** ★★ (p. 283), or farther out of town at the posh **Cavas Wine Lodge** ★ (p. 286). From either one, you can head out on bicycle or in your car to explore more vineyards. Consider lunch at the farm-to-table country restaurant **Almacén del Sur** (p. 289). Don't forget an afternoon by the pool! If you are at Finca Adalgisa, stroll into the charming heart of the village of Chacras de Coria and follow your nose. At Cavas, just stay put. Either way, nighttime amid the vines is romantic and relaxing.

4 Alta Montaña

Eat breakfast, pack a sweater, and pick up supplies for a picnic (olives, jam, cheese, bread—it's all local and right here!), and drive west into the Andes. The road first heads south out of town and then west on RN 7 to Potrerillos and on to the Chilean border. After Uspallata, it's a wild and winding mountain road that takes you to the base of the highest mountain in the world outside the Himalayas, the mighty **Mt. Aconcagua.** Don't miss the photo opportunity at the mystical **Puente de Inca.** If you're a confident driver, return via the winding spiral, cliff-hanging Ruta 52 past the thermal springs at Villavicencio. When you're back in the Mendoza area, it's worth the effort to dine at the **Terruños Restaurant** ★ at Club Tapiz (p. 289). Take a taxi so you can enjoy the excellent wines of the vineyard.

5 Day Off

You'll be tired, perhaps, from driving and indulging. If you're still raring to go, head out for horseback riding or white-water rafting on the Mendoza River. Or rent a bike and explore the rural roads. Be sure to save room for a spectacular dinner at celebrity chef Francis Mallmann's outstanding **1884** ★★★ (p. 272)— another excellent reason to call a taxi.

6 Wines of the Valle de Uco

It may be the most scenic area of Mendoza and well worth the 2-hour drive south of town. After breakfast at your inn, follow the Pan-American Highway RN 40 toward the town of Tunuyán. It's a land of rolling hills, poplar-lined country roads, and in-your-face close-ups of the high Andes. Your first stop should be the impressive **Bodegas Salentein** ★★ (p. 293), which includes an interesting art gallery and one of the spookiest and most fascinating cellars in the country. Either their vineyard cafe or the nearby Posada Salentein makes a good stop for lunch. Drop in at another "it" vineyard such as **Andeluna** or **O. Fournier** in the afternoon. A light dinner may be in order: How about a *tabla de picadas*—a sampling of local cheeses and meats, served with a glass of Malbec on a patio at your inn?

7 Shopping & Home

If this is your only stop in Argentina, it's worth checking out the shops in town for leather goods and other souvenirs. After eating breakfast and checking out of your hotel, stop by the **Palmares Open Mall** (p. 277) and then park in downtown Mendoza for one more stroll down the shop-lined pedestrian mall. Then head to the airport to drop off your car and catch your flight home.

PATAGONIA WILDLIFE: PENINSULA VALDES & LOS GLACIARES NATIONAL PARK

by Christie Pashby

Patagonia is for nature lovers, particularly in November—the one month of the year when you can see whales and penguins on the Atlantic Coast and still see the peaks and glaciers of southern Patagonia without freezing. Start your trip on the coast at Puerto Madryn and spend a full day exploring the Península Valdés. This time should include a whale-watching trip and a visit to sea lion colonies. You will need a second day to see the penguin colony at the northern tip of the peninsula, making it worthwhile to stay on the Península Valdés itself. Then you'll need a full day to travel south to El Calafate. If you are a keen bird-watcher and can afford deluxe lodgings, stay at the spectacular *estancia* Eolo. I saw eight condors at once there in November! From there, you can explore the remote areas of Los Glaciares National Park.

1 Puerto Madryn & Ecocentro

After flying in from Buenos Aires, you have no real choice but to spend the first night on the beachside town of Puerto Madryn. The nicest spot is the **Hotel Territorio ★** (p. 354). A bit more economical, the **Hotel Bahía Nueva ★★** (p. 353) is centrally located. After transferring from the airport at Trelew and checking in, you'll arrive with time to explore the coastal waters and make a visit to the outstanding **Ecocentro** museum **★★** (p. 357), which will orient you to the wonders of the local oceans. Be sure to book tomorrow's full-day tour of Península Valdés, asking the agency to drop you off at your inn the following night. For dinner, indulge in something from the sea at **Mar y Meseta ★★** (p. 355), and stroll back along the beach.

2 Península Valdés

Tours always get an early start; most will have you leaving your hotel in Puerto Madryn at around 8am. Your first stop will likely be the easygoing beach town of **Puerto Pirámides,** from where all the whale-watching tours head out to catch the annual congregation of southern right whales. These are remarkably social mammals, and they'll no doubt get incredibly close to your boat. Later, your guide will head on to the far eastern coast of the peninsula to visit the sea lion and elephant seal colonies. They usually stop at a cafeteria-style restaurant. Keep your eye out for other wildlife, such as ostrich-resembling *choiques* and the strange *mara,* which looks like a mix of a rabbit with a dog. Afterward, they'll drop you off at the outstanding **Faro Punta Delgada ★★** (p. 360) lighthouse

Península Valdés & Los Glaciares

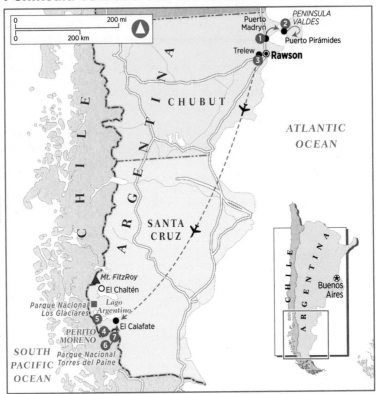

inn, where you can hike along the beach. After a nice dinner in the hotel, climb to the top of the lighthouse for a starry view.

3 Penguins & El Calafate

Eat breakfast at the inn and then ask to be taken to the remote **Estancia San Lorenzo** (p. 360) for a private viewing of their 200,000-strong Magellan penguin colony. From there, head all the way back to Trelew for your flight to El Calafate, and grab lunch en route. You'll arrive in El Calafate in time to be transferred to your *estancia* for dinner. The excellent new rural hotel, **Eolo Patagonia's Spirit** ★★ (p. 374), will take care of it all.

4 Condor-Viewing

Eat breakfast and then head out with your bird-watching guide in search of the majestic condor, with its 3m (10-ft.) wing span. You'll look for shorebirds on the coast of Lago Argentino and the mighty predators amid the high peaks of Cerro Frías. In the afternoon, enjoy a leisurely tea in the ranch's living room, with binoculars nearby. Dinner will also be served in the *estancia*.

5 Perito Moreno Glacier

You can't come to El Calafate without seeing the world-famous Perito Moreno Glacier, a UNESCO World Heritage Site. After breakfast, you'll be driven west to the glacier's lookout point. Plan ahead and sign up for a **"Minitrekking"** (p. 380) tour, where you strap on crampons and go for a short hike on the glacier itself. The tour also includes a short boat trip beneath the southern wall of the glacier. Return to the *estancia* with time to relax, read, and get back to those binoculars. For dinner, don't miss the local specialty, barbecued Patagonian lamb.

6 Torres del Paine

It looks close, and as the crow flies, Chile's **Torres del Paine National Park ★★** (p. 388) is right there on the horizon. Of course, this is Patagonia, and roads are long and dirty. It takes a few hours, in fact, to reach Torres del Paine, but it's well worth the drive, especially if you're looking to see guanacos, the Patagonian cousin of the llama. You'll also see the black rock peaks—known as *torres* and *cuernos* (towers and horns)—of this very popular park and get to do some short hikes. Return for a late dinner at the *estancia*.

7 El Calafate & Home

After breakfast, pack your bags and snap a few more photographs of the incredible emptiness on every horizon. Then stop in the town of El Calafate to stroll the shops along the main tourist drag, Avenida Del Libertador, before heading to the airport for your flight to Buenos Aires.

NORTHWEST ARGENTINA: THE REAL SOUTH AMERICA

by Charlie O'Malley

Argentina is a cultural melting pot, with Buenos Aires having a distinctly European flavor and Patagonia a Scandinavian hue. That is why the Northwest can be so satisfying to visit as it is definitely 100% South American. The following is a 5-day itinerary that ensures that you truly experience the rich indigenous culture of this beautiful region with its strong strain of Spanish colonialism. Grandiose architecture sits well with excellent local food, washed down with delicious wines. The regional handicrafts are as colorful as the landscapes, and the people are Argentina's friendliest. To see the most in the shortest time possible, it is best to hire a car or go with a reliable tour company.

1 Arrival Salta City

Use this charming city as your base for the first few days. Fly in early morning from Buenos Aires and check into the designer chic **Hotel Kkala ★★★** (p. 218), situated in a hilltop residential zone above the city center. Stroll the lovely plaza and visit the gilded **Iglesia San Francisco ★★** (p. 212) and the baroque **Salta Cathedral** (p. 213). Have lunch in the sunny courtyard of **Casa Moderna ★** (p. 220), before doing what the locals do and taking a well-deserved siesta. Early evening is spent in the fascinating **MAAM ★★★**

(p. 212), known locally as the "mummy museum." Enjoy a Torrontes wine at **Café van Gogh** (p. 219) on the plaza before heading to Salta's best restaurant, **José Balcarce ★★★** (p. 220).

2 Shopping in Salta

This special city deserves more than 1 day. Take the **cable car ★** to **San Bernardo Hill** (p. 213) and enjoy panoramic views of the city while sipping a coffee. Then take a taxi to the hilltop village of San Lorenzo, where you can enjoy a lunch at the Tuscan-style **El Castillo de San Lorenzo ★** (p. 219) hotel. After the customary siesta, take a taxi ride to the **Mercado Artesanal** (p. 215), located in a handsome, renovated millhouse. Here you can enjoy afternoon tea amid genuine local products. Back in the city, freshen up before hitting Salta's nightlife street Calle Balcarce. Enjoy a foot-stomping music session at **Café de Tiempo ★** (p. 221) and later join the dancing yourself at the numerous clubs and discos nearby.

3 Wine Tasting in Cafayate

Check out of your hotel and go south in a rented car as far as the wine town of Cafayate. The red rock scenery is gorgeous, and the 3-hour journey goes quickly. Enjoy a light lunch on the plaza of this sleepy village before visiting **El Porvenir ★★** (p. 225) winery for excellent wines and **El Esteco** (p. 224) for palatial architecture. Some of the best wineries are within the town limits, including the new Bodega El Transito with a refreshing, modern design and rich wines. Check into the atmospheric **Killa Cafayate ★★** (p. 226) and dine on llama at **Machacha ★★** (p. 229) restaurant before strolling the lively nighttime plaza alive with musicians playing everything from pan-pipes to saxophones.

4 Cachi

As its name implies, this hilltop village will take a hold of you. Its sparkling white adobe cottages and quaint church take you back in time. Visit the **archaeological museum** (p. 226) to see the area's rich Incan heritage. In the afternoon, check into the luxurious **La Merced del Alto ★★** (p. 223), and stay for dinner.

5 Quebrada de Humahuaca

Jujuy province is the last stop before Bolivia, as seen in its landscape and architecture. Drive north from Salta along the multicolored mountain range **Quebrada de Humahuaca ★** (p. 229), which will make even the most jaded traveler gasp. Go north until you reach **Tilcara ★★** (p. 231), a cobblestoned gem with old-world charm. Lunch at **La Chacana ★★** (p. 233) before visiting the indigenous ruins of **Pucará.** Continue north along the main road before you reach sleepy **Humahuaca** (p. 232) village; stroll through the plaza market before turning south toward Salta. Turn off the main road to visit the quaint village of **Purmamarca ★★★** (p. 229) and its Technicolor backdrop. Pamper yourself at the gorgeous **El Manantial del Silencio ★★** (p. 231) and enjoy Argentine Andean cuisine **Los Morteros ★★** (p. 231) before flying out the next day.

BUENOS AIRES

by Michael Luongo

Before the peso crisis of 2001, Buenos Aires was considered Latin America's most expensive city, with some hotel and restaurant prices rivaling those in New York and Paris. Many on the South American tourist crawl avoided this sophisticated and beautiful metropolis, staying in the cheaper capitals of the countries that surrounded it. For a time, the crisis changed all that, making Argentina and its lovely capital a bargain destination and fueling a legendary tourism boom. While I must report that many of those bargains are gone, don't be discouraged: Buenos Aires still lives up to its reputation as the Paris of South America.

Even though the peso, once on par with the U.S. dollar, is at the time of this writing valued at about four to one, inflation has meant that prices have simply gone up. Hotels, taxi prices, and in many cases, restaurant meals, may now be back to pre–peso crisis prices but they are still reasonable in comparison to vacations in the Unites States, Canada, or Europe.

So while a trip to Buenos Aires is no longer a steal, there are many reasons, old and new, to visit the city. To prepare for Argentina's 2010 Bicentennial, extensive renovations and improvements were made throughout the capital, many of which are ongoing. These range from restoration of buildings to an expansion of the subway system. Yet most of Buenos Aires's delights are eternal. Stroll through the neighborhoods of Recoleta or Palermo, full of buildings with marble neoclassical facades on broad, tree-lined boulevards, or tour the historic Avenida de Mayo, which was designed to rival Paris's Champs-Elysées. European immigrants to Buenos Aires, mostly from Spain and Italy, brought with them the warm ways of Mediterranean culture, wherein friends, family, and conversation were the most important things in life. Whiling away the night over a long meal was the norm, and locals have always packed into cafes, restaurants, and bars until the early morning hours.

Since the peso crisis, Argentines became more self-reflective, examining themselves and the reasons why their country fell into so much trouble. This has led, ironically, to a flourishing of all things Porteño (the word Buenos Aires locals use to describe both themselves and the culture of their city). Unable to import expensive foods from overseas anymore, Buenos Aires's restaurants began concentrating instead on cooking with Argentine staples such as Pampas grass-fed beef, and using locally produced, organic ingredients as seasonings. What has developed is a spectacular array of Argentine nouvelle cuisine of incredible quality and originality. Chefs can't seem to produce it fast enough in the ever-expanding array of restaurants, particularly in the trendy Palermo Viejo district.

Young Argentine designers opened up their own shops and boutiques in the Palermo Hollywood and Palermo Soho neighborhoods. Women, especially, will find fantastic unique fashions, largely at prices lower than in North America and Europe. And when it comes to leather goods, the buck stops here: The greatest variety and quality in the world are available all over town.

Importantly, the most Porteño thing of all, the tango, has witnessed explosive growth. Until recent years, Argentines had worried that the dance would die out as young people bopped instead to American hip-hop and European techno. But now, new varieties of shows for tourists mean you can see a different form of tango every night of your stay. And, more important to residents, traditional, 1930s-style tango salons, called *milongas,* have opened all over town, drawing not only the older, traditional tango dancers but also young Argentines, who have rediscovered their grandparents' favorite dance, as well as young expats from all over the world who are making Buenos Aires the world's new hot city, the way Prague was at the end of the Cold War.

All of this means there is no time like now to visit Buenos Aires, a city rich in culture still available at a price that won't hurt your wallet.

ORIENTATION

Arriving

BY PLANE International flights arrive at **Ezeiza International Airport** (*©* **11/5480-6111** or 5480-2500; www.aa2000.com.ar), located 34km (20 miles) west of downtown Buenos Aires. You can reach the city by shuttle or *remise* (private unmetered taxi); you will see official stands with set fares in the airport once you clear Customs and just outside of the airport exit. Taxis from the airport to the center of town cost about $35. See "Safe Taxi Travel," below. **Manuel Tienda León** (*©* **11/4314-3636;** www.tiendaleon.com.ar) is the most reliable transportation company, offering buses and *remises* to and from the airports, starting at about $12 for bus rides to the city center.

Domestic airlines and flights to Uruguay use **Jorge Newbery Airport** (*©* **11/5480-3000;** www.aa2000.com.ar), located only 15 minutes to the north, along the river from downtown, and it's also called Aeroparque. Taxis and *remises* cost $16 to $25 to the city center.

Note: In 2009, Argentina began charging a "reciprocity fee" for the entrance of United States, Canadian, and Australian citizens who fly into Ezeiza. Though not technically a visa, the fee matches what Argentines pay when applying for visas in these respective countries. As of this writing, the fee is US$140 for Americans, US$100 for Australians, and US$70 for Canadians, and was only charged to people entering Argentina by plane (not by land or sea). Upon payment, a form is placed

---

 Safe Taxi Travel

Buenos Aires has its share of dishonest taxi drivers. At both airports, take only officially sanctioned transportation. Do not accept rides from private individuals. Even if freelance taxi drivers approach you offering cheaper fares, play it safe and use the official *remise* stands. For more details, see "Traveling by Taxi," below.

Great Websites for Your Trip

I have included as many useful websites as possible in this section. The Buenos Aires city government site (www.bue.gov.ar) provides additional tourist information, with links to businesses in town and a calendar of events. For tourist maps, check out www.dediosonline.com. Subway *(subte)* information is available through the interactive website www.subte.com.ar, which offers maps, estimated times, and transfer information between stations. For great self-guided tours of Buenos Aires plus shopping tips, check out www.welcomeargentina.com. If your Spanish is excellent, use the Argentine version of Google, www.google.com.ar, and click on "Páginas de Argentina" for the latest locally produced online information on Buenos Aires. To save money on hotels and car rentals, also check out www.despegar.com.ar, a site for Argentina similar to Priceline.com.

permanently into your passport, which is valid for 10 years. You can pay with cash, Visa, MasterCard, or American Express.

BY BUS The **Estación Terminal de Omnibus de Retiro,** Av. Ramos Mejía 1680 (© **11/4310-0700;** www.tebasa.com.ar), located near the Retiro Train Station complex, serves all long-distance buses connecting Buenos Aires with the suburbs, the coasts and interior of Argentina, and even international destinations. Rates are very affordable. The station is enormous and confusing, however, so give yourself plenty of time to locate your bus company, buy your tickets, and find your bus.

BY CAR In Buenos Aires, it's easier and safer to travel by *subte* (subway), *remise*, or radio-taxi (radio-dispatched taxis, as opposed to street taxis) than by driving yourself. Rush-hour traffic is chaotic, and parking is difficult. If you do rent a car, park it at your hotel or a nearby garage and leave it there.

City Layout

Although Buenos Aires is an expansive city, the main tourist neighborhoods are concentrated in a small, comparatively wealthy part of town that hugs the Río de la Plata. The city's MicroCentro extends from Plaza de Mayo to the south and Plaza San Martín to the north, and from Plaza del Congreso to the west and Puerto Madero to the east. The neighborhoods of San Telmo, La Boca, Puerto Madero, Recoleta, and Palermo surround the MicroCentro. The city layout follows a wobbly grid pattern fanning out from the original Spanish streets in the old core. *Avenidas* are the wide boulevards, where most traffic flows and the subways lines generally run; *calles* are narrower one-way streets; and *diagonales* cut across streets and avenues at 45-degree angles, providing beautiful vistas onto many tourist sites. Each city block extends 100m (328 ft.), within generally each 10 forming a kilometer, and building addresses indicate relative location on the street.

The **MicroCentro** includes Plaza de Mayo (the political and historic center of Buenos Aires), Plaza San Martín, and portions of Avenida 9 de Julio, generally claimed to be the widest street in the world. ***Note:*** Addresses on this thoroughfare generally take on those of its parallel service streets, such as Carlos Pellegrini, Lima, Cerrito, and Bernardo de Irogoyen. Most commercial activity is focused in this busy zone, as are the majority of hotels and restaurants. Next to the

MicroCentro, the recently renovated riverfront area, called **Puerto Madero,** boasts excellent restaurants and nightlife, as well as new commercial and residential zones. Farther south, **Monserrat, San Telmo,** and **La Boca** are the historic neighborhoods where the first immigrants arrived and *milonga* and tango originated. They are beautiful and loaded with areas of interest to tourists, but take caution if exploring them after sunset.

The city's most European neighborhood, **Recoleta,** offers fashionable restaurants, cafes, and evening entertainment on tree-lined streets. It's home to the city's cultural center, built into a former church, as well as the Recoleta Cemetery, the necropolis where key figures such as Evita and many former presidents are buried. Bordering Recoleta, **Barrio Norte** is famous for its Avenida Santa Fe shopping, cafes, and nightlife. The city's trendiest area, **Palermo,** to the northwest, is a sprawling neighborhood of parks, mansions, and cobblestone streets lined with tiny stucco homes. It is vastly wealthy in some parts and gracefully bohemian in others. Palermo is a catchall term for many neighborhoods in Buenos Aires. Today when most people say Palermo, they are not referring to the wealthy European-style section of the city along Avenida Libertador, sometimes also called **Alto Palermo,** but instead to **Palermo Viejo** and its further subdivisions of **Palermo Hollywood** and **Palermo Soho,** hip parts of the city full of chic restaurants and tiny boutiques owned by young up-and-coming designers. When anyone says "meet me in Palermo," it's crucial to clarify exactly which part of the city they mean.

STREET MAPS At the front desk of your hotel, ask for a copy of "The Golden Map" and *QuickGuide Buenos Aires.* To help you plan your trip before you leave home, the Buenos Aires–based publisher **de Dios** (www.dediosonline.com) sells laminated street guides, available from Amazon (www.amazon.com).

Getting Around

The Buenos Aires **metro**—called the *subte*—is the fastest, cheapest way to get around the city. Buses are also convenient, though less commonly used by tourists. Get maps of metro and bus lines from tourist offices and most hotels. (Ask for the *QuickGuide Buenos Aires* or other maps available.) All metro stations are supposed to have maps, but they are rarely in good supply.

BY METRO The efficient *subte* offers six lines that connect commercial, tourist, and residential areas in the city Monday through Saturday from 5am to 11pm, and on Sunday and holidays from 8am to 11pm. These are the official hours, but because of budget cuts, many lines stop running by 10pm. However, they don't always close the stations after the trains have stopped running for the night, so ask if a train is heading in the direction you need during later hours or you could end up waiting for a train that never comes. Service has also been reduced by lengthening the time between trains, even during busy daytime hours, making for extremely crowded trains. A new line, the H or Yellow Line, has been partially built along the Jujuy-Pueyrredón corridor, and existing lines have also been expanded. See the inside front cover of this guide for a map of the system, and be aware that new maps given out or posted at stations might not correctly reflect subway extensions.

The flat fare is 1.10 pesos (30¢). Every station has a staffed ticket window. Some stations have ticket vending machines, but they're unreliable. You can also buy a *subte* pass for 11 pesos ($2.75), valid for 10 trips. The passes are cheap and demagnetize easily, so it is a good idea to buy an extra.

Trains get crowded during rush hours, and cars are not air-conditioned and get unbearably hot in summer. Always be cautious of pickpockets, including tiny pocket-height children who can easily be overlooked.

The A line runs along Avenida de Mayo. Neither Recoleta nor Puerto Madero has *subte* access. Most of Puerto Madero, however, is accessible via the L. N. Alem *subte* stop on the B line. It's a 5- to 20-minute walk, depending on which dock you're going to. (Puerto Madero is a renovated port district that stretches far along the Río de la Plata waterfront downtown.) The D runs through Barrio Norte, which borders Recoleta, so you can save money on taxis by using this line and walking the 15 minutes to that area. Visit www.subte.com.ar for maps before heading to Argentina. The interactive site also gives estimated times and transfer information between stations.

Sightseeing on the *Subte*

Try to ride the A line at least once; it's a tourist attraction in itself. The oldest line, it runs along Avenida de Mayo using some of the original rickety wooden cars. Lima station, in particular, retains most of the original ornamentation and copies of advertisements from the turn of the 20th century.

Be aware that wildcat strikes are common on the system, though workers rarely stop trains between stations.

BY BUS   Buenos Aires has about 140 bus lines that run 24 hours a day. The fare is 1.10 pesos (30¢) and up, depending on distance traveled. Pay your fare inside the bus at the electronic ticket machine, which accepts coins only and provides change. Many bus drivers will tell you the fare for your destination and direct you where to get off, but most speak Spanish only. Locals are just as helpful and sometimes make an almost comical effort to ensure you don't get lost. The *Guia T* is a comprehensive guide to the city bus grid and bus lines. Buy it at bookstores, newspaper kiosks, or on the *subte* or sidewalk from peddlers. The bus system is however also notorious for pickpockets so be very cautious when using. In 2009, a private tour bus system, **Buenos Aires Bus** (© 11/5239-5160; www.buenosairesbus.com), was inaugurated, offering 12 designated stops throughout Buenos Aires, using the hop-on-hop-off method found in most major world cities. Tickets can be purchased aboard the bright yellow and black busses, at the stops, online, and at the Buenos Aires Bus office (10th floor, Av. Roque Sáenz Peña 846, at Florida). Headphones are available onboard, giving passengers recorded tourist information about nearby sites, in English and many other languages. Tickets are available for 24-hour or 48-hour periods and allow unlimited riding; they cost $18 to $23, but various discounts and other pricing options are available.

BY TAXI   The streets of Buenos Aires are swarming with taxis. Fares are generally low, with an initial meter reading of 5.80 pesos increasing 58 centavos every 200m (656 ft.) or each minute, with a 20% higher rate in effect at night. *Remises* and radio-taxis are much safer than street taxis (see "Traveling by Taxi," below). Most of what the average tourist needs to see in the city is accessible for $4 to $10. Radio-taxis, when hailed on the street, are recognizable by the plastic light boxes on their rooftops, though not all will have them. If a cab is available, the word *libre* will flash in red on the windshield. Ordinary taxis, more likely to be run by members of Buenos Aires's infamous taxi mafia, do not have these special lightboxes. I personally have had few problems, but it's always best to err on the side of caution. If you speak English loudly

Traveling by Taxi

At the risk of sounding repetitive, I strongly recommend that if you need a taxi, you call in advance for a *remise* or radio-taxi (see "By Taxi," above, for numbers). Even better: Ask an employee of your hotel, restaurant, or other venue to call on your behalf, as a representative of that establishment, which ensures greater accountability from drivers. If you must hail taxis off the street, use only those with plastic light boxes on their roofs, indicating that they are radio-taxis. Since the economic crisis began, robberies by street taxi drivers have increased sharply. *Remises* are only slightly pricier than street cabs, but far safer. Most hotels have contracts with *remise* companies, and they're accustomed to calling for patrons.

with fellow passengers, identifying yourself as a tourist, expect your ride to take longer than it should, with strange diversions ensuring a higher fare than normal. You can prevent this by being vigilant, having a general idea where you are going, and keeping in mind the one-way street system. Drivers often use traffic problems as their excuse for the runaround. A rarely enforced law means taxi drivers can stop only if their passenger side is facing the curb. If available cabs are ignoring you, cross to the other side of the street and hail again. Though the vast majority of taxi drivers are honest, a substantial number of tourists have been ripped off recently by dishonest drivers. One common scam is saying that you gave a smaller-denomination bill to the driver than you actually have. One way around this is to know in Spanish the value of your bill and announcing it to the driver when requesting change. (Or make sure to have exact change and lots of coins and small bills.) Another scam is to say your bills are counterfeit, and the driver keeps them. Tips are not necessary, but many locals normally round up to the nearest peso for the fare. To request a taxi by phone, consider **Taxi Premium** (© **11/4374-6666**), used by many top hotels.

BY CAR You don't need a car in Buenos Aires, and I don't advise driving yourself unless you're heading out of the city. If you must rent a car, contact one of the international rental companies at either airport, as well as those listed here. Most hotels can also arrange car rentals. Typically, rental cars are manual, and automatic cars are expensive, running at about $100 per day. *Note:* Most local motorists disregard traffic rules except for one—no turn on red.

Rental cars are available from **Hertz**, Paraguay 1138 (© **800/654-3131** in the U.S., or 11/4816-8001); **Avis**, Cerrito 1527 (© **800/230-4898** in the U.S., or 11/4326-5542); **Dollar**, Marcelo T. de Alvear 449 (© **800/800-6000** in the U.S., or 11/4315-8800); and **Thrifty**, Carlos Pellegrini (Nueve de Julio) 1576 (© **800/847-4389** in the U.S., or 11/4326-0418).

ON FOOT You'll probably find yourself walking more than you'd planned in this pedestrian-friendly city. Most of the center is small enough to navigate on foot, and you can connect to adjacent neighborhoods by catching a taxi or using the *subte*. Based on the Spanish colonial plan, the city is a wobbly grid expanding from the Plaza de Mayo, so you are not likely to get too lost. Plazas and parks all over the city supply wonderful spots to rest, people-watch, and meet the locals. Sidewalks are in terrible disrepair, however, throughout the city, not to mention the dog poo—so watch your step as you try to take in all of the local beauty.

Visitor Information

The central office of Buenos Aires's **City Tourism Secretariat,** responsible for all visitor information for Buenos Aires, is located at Calle Balcarce 360 in Monserrat but is not open to the general public; however, they may be reached by phone (*C* **11/4114-5734**), from 10am to 5pm Monday to Friday, if there are specific questions before your trip, though not everyone will speak English. Visit their website, **www.bue.gov.ar,** for more information. While in Buenos Aires, visit one of the City Tourism Secretariat's several information kiosks spread in various neighborhoods; they have maps and hotel, restaurant, and attraction information. You can find them at J.M. Ortiz and Quintana in Recoleta near the cemetery, Puerto Madero, the central bus terminal, Caminito in La Boca, and Calle Florida 100, where it hits Diagonal Norte. Most are open Monday through Friday from 10am to 5pm, although some open and close later, depending on the season. Others are open on weekends as well, including one in San Telmo at Defensa 1250. The center on Caminito in La Boca is open weekends only, usually Saturday and Sunday from 10am to 5pm.

The city also runs free tours, mostly in Spanish, but a few are also in English. For details, call *C* **11/4114-5791** Monday through Friday from 9am to 4pm.

When you arrive in Buenos Aires at Eizeza, there is also a central tourism station just outside of Customs run by the **Tourism Ministry of Argentina** (*C* **0800-555-0016**), with information on Buenos Aires and the rest of Argentina. It's open daily from 8:15am to 8pm.

[FastFACTS] BUENOS AIRES

American Express The huge American Express building is next to Plaza San Martín, at Arenales 707 (*C* **11/4310-3000**). The travel agency is open Monday through Friday from 9am to 6pm; the bank is open Monday through Friday from 9am to 5pm, 10am to 3pm for traveler's check exchange. In addition to card-member services, the bank offers currency exchange (US$ only), money orders, check cashing, and refunds.

Area Code The city area code for Buenos Aires, known locally as a *característica,* is **011.** Drop the 0 when combining numbers from overseas with Argentina's country code, **54.** The

number **15** in front of a local number indicates a mobile/cellular phone, though some phones no longer use this code. This will need the addition of the **011** if you're calling from outside Buenos Aires. Cellphones become complicated when dialing from overseas. Dial whatever international code you need from your country (011 from the U.S. and Canada), then 54 for Argentina, then 9 to indicate a cellphone, then the area code of the cellphone, and then the number. Thus, to call Buenos Aires cellphones from the U.S., you would dial 011-54-9-11 and then the eight-digit number. Be aware that phone numbers in other

areas have anywhere from five to seven digits, but always ask if a number seems strange.

Business Hours Banks are generally open weekdays 10am to 3pm, and ATMs work 24 hours. Shopping hours are Monday through Friday from 9am to 8pm or 10pm, and Saturday from 10am to 8pm or 10pm. Shopping centers are open daily from 10am to 10pm. Most independent stores are closed on Sunday, and some close for lunch. Some kiosks, selling water, candy, and packaged food are open 24 hours. Most neighborhoods have a 24-hour pharmacy, and *locutorios* or phone centers.

Currency Exchange

Although American dollars are often accepted in major hotels and businesses catering to tourists, you will need Argentine pesos for ordinary transactions. Credit cards are widely used, although some businesses charge a small additional fee. It's easiest to exchange money at the airport, your hotel, or an independent exchange house rather than at an Argentine bank. Traveler's checks can be difficult to cash: **American Express** (see above) offers the best rates on its traveler's checks and charges no commission. It offers currency exchange for US$ only. ATMs are plentiful in Buenos Aires, but you should use those only in secure, well-lit locations. At some ATMs, you can withdraw pesos or dollars. Even if your bank allows you to make larger daily withdrawals, Argentine ATMs generally only give out pesos in the value range US$100 to US$250 maximum at a time or on a daily basis, so plan accordingly if you know you will need large amounts of cash while in Buenos Aires. It will be hard to break large bills usually dispensed by ATMs, so withdraw money in uneven amounts so that a portion comes in small bills. You can have money wired to **Western Union,** Carlos Pellegrini 1365 (Nueve de Julio) at Arroyo (© **0800/800-3030** or 11/ 4323-4200).

Embassies & Consulates

See chapter 14, "Fast Facts: Argentina."

Emergencies

For an **ambulance,** call © **107;** in case of **fire,** call © **100;** for **police** assistance, call © **101;** for an English-speaking hospital, call **Clínica Suisso Argentino,** Av. Pueyrredón 1461 at Santa Fe (© **11/5239-6000**); www.cymsa.com.ar, or **Hospital Británico,** Perdriel 74 at Caseros (© **11/4304-1081;** www.hospitalbritanico.org.ar).

Language

Shops, hotels, and restaurants are usually staffed by at least one or two fluent English speakers, and many people speak at least a few words of English. A rule of thumb though is that less-expensive venues will have fewer, if any, English speakers. However, with the massive influx of tourism since the peso crisis, English has become ubiquitous on the streets of the city and many young people know some of the language.

Post Office

You never have to venture more than a few blocks to find a post office, which are open weekdays from 10am to 8pm and Saturday until 1pm. The main post office, or Correo Central, is at Av. Sarmiento 151 (© **11/4891-9191;** www.correoargentino.com.ar). In addition, the post office works with some *locutorios,* which offer limited mailing services. The purple-signed

and ubiquitous **OCA** (© **0800/999-7700;** www.oca.com.ar) is a private postal service that can mail items overseas. UPS has many locations, including Calle Tucumán 300 at 25 de Mayo (© **0800/222-2877;** www.ups.com), plus there's a convenient FedEx location at 25 de Mayo 386 at Corrientes (© **11/4630-0300;** www.fedex.com.ar).

Safety

If former U.S. president George W. Bush's daughters, surrounded by Secret Service and local cops, can still get robbed, as they did in 2006, it says a lot about crime in Buenos Aires. Visitors need to be aware at all times. Crime in Buenos Aires—especially pickpocketing, robberies, and car thefts—has increased sharply in recent years as the economy has collapsed and brought naive tourists. Still it's generally safe to walk around Recoleta, Palermo, and the MicroCentro both day and night. Some tourist areas deemed safe by day, such as La Boca, should be avoided at night. Be careful at night when in San Telmo, especially in outdoor restaurants. Never leave a bag or purse unattended or on the ground. (Though official accounts differ and/or deny the Bush daughters were robbed at all, the method by which they were likely hoodwinked was the "soccer" method: A purse on the ground under a chair is kicked to another thief who then takes it away.) I also would warn tourists against walking around at night in Monserrat, though with increasing gentrification and tourist spillover from San Telmo, the area has become safer. Visitors should walk in pairs or groups when possible and avoid the conspicuous appearance of being a tourist, including speaking loudly in English. Do not flaunt expensive possessions, particularly jewelry. Call for a radio-taxi or *remise* when leaving a place of business. The number-one rule is that thieves take advantage of naiveté and opportunity, but real violence is unlikely. Pickpocketing is likely to be your top problem, so be careful in large crowds, subways, and buses, and especially when watching street performers.

Taxes The 21% sales tax (or VAT) is already included in the sales price of your purchase. Foreign tourists are entitled to a VAT tax return for certain purchases over 70 pesos, but you must request a refund check at the time of purchase from participating shops (the shop should display a "Global Refund" logo). Before departing the country, present these refund checks (invoices) to Customs and then your credit card will be credited for the refund, or you'll receive a check by mail. Be aware when checking into hotels that the posted or spoken price may or may not reflect this tax, so make sure to ask for clarification.

Taxis See "Getting Around," earlier.

Telephone Unless you are calling from your hotel (which will be expensive), the easiest way to place calls in Buenos Aires is by going to a *locutorio* or *tele-centro,* found on nearly every city block. Private glass booths allow you to place as many calls as you like by dialing directly, after which you pay an attendant. A running meter tells you what you'll owe. Most *locutorios* also have fax machines and broadband Internet computers. Calls to the U.S. or Canada run about a peso or less per minute.

Although some coin-operated public phones still exist in Buenos Aires, most require a calling card, available at kiosks, which are specifically branded for the various communication companies. Local calls, like all others, are charged by the minute. Dial ℂ **110** for information and ℂ **000** to reach an international operator. To dial another number in Argentina from Buenos Aires, dial the area code first, and then the local number; this applies to cellular numbers too.

Note: If you call someone's cellular phone in Argentina, the call is also charged to you and can cost significantly more than a standard land-line call. It has also become common for tourists to buy inexpensive cellphones along with a SIM card for use in Buenos Aires. Look for shops on **Calle Florida,** or head to the **Movistar** cellular phone company booth in **Galerías Pacífico,** Calle Florida 750 at Avenida Córdoba (ℂ **11/5555-5287;** daily 10am–9pm).

Tipping A 10% to 15% tip is common at cafes and restaurants. Taxis do not require tips, but many people round up to the nearest peso or 50 centavo figure. If a taxi driver helps you with bags, a small tip might be a nice touch.

WHERE TO STAY

Hotels in Buenos Aires often fill up in high season, so it's important to book ahead. The most convenient hotels are found in Recoleta and the MicroCentro. Recoleta is more scenic and not quite as noisy as the MicroCentro, but you might spend more money on cabs, as it is not near the *subte* lines. Prices listed below are rack rates in high season and include the 21% tax levied on hotel rooms. The prices listed here can differ considerably based on many factors—from type of room, events in the city, views, and the hotel management's discretion, based on overall availability in the city. Do not be surprised if rates vary considerably, up or down, from what I've listed here;

Where to Stay in Buenos Aires

Alvear Palace Hotel **3**
Amerian Buenos Aires
  Park Hotel **20**
Bel Air Hotel **9**
Claridge Hotel **22**
Dazzler Hotel Libertad **10**
Dolmen Hotel **16**
El Lugar Gay **35**
Esplendor **18**
Etoile Hotel **1**
The Faena Hotel and
  Universe **31**
Four Seasons Hotel **5**
Grand Boulevard Hotel **32**
Hilton Buenos Aires **26**
Holiday Inn Express Puerto
  Madero **19**
Hostel Carlos Gardel **34**
Hotel Castelar **28**
Hotel Colón **25**
Hotel de Los Dos
  Congresos **12**
Hotel Emperador **6**
Hotel Ibis **13**
Hotel Ritz **27**
Howard Johnson Florida
  Street **17**
InterContinental **29**
Lafayette Hotel **23**
Lina's Tango GuestHouse **33**
Loi Suites **2**
Marriott Plaza Hotel **15**
NH City Hotel **30**
Palacia Duhua – Park Hyatt
  Buenos Aires **4**
Pan Americano **24**
The Recoleta Hostel **8**
Savoy Hotel **11**
Sheraton Buenos Aires Hotel
  and Convention Center **14**
Sofitel **7**
V&S Hostel **21**

B&B in Buenos Aires = Beautiful & Bargain-Priced

Buenos Aires has a growing number of intimate, chic bed-and-breakfast–type guesthouses for $40 to $100 a night. Unlike American B&Bs—which are so often fusty and cluttered with bric-a-brac and cats—those in Buenos Aires tend to have hip, young owners with very clean, cosmopolitan taste. Many owners are designers who open their homes to the traveling public. Their places tend to be airy and bright, and many have Spanish-style interior gardens and patios. Unless you demand the ultimate in five-star luxury, many private guesthouses are nicer than hotels charging three or four times the price. You can also get to know the owners and other guests. Many offer weekly or monthly rates. I recommend **Che Lulu**, Emilio Zolá 5185 (© 11/4772-0289; www.luluguesthouse.com), between Palermo Soho and Palermo Viejo; the lovely **La Otra Orilla**, Julian Alvarez 1779 (© 11/4863-7426; www.otraorilla.com.ar); or **Cabrera Garden**, J.A. Cabrera 5855 (© 11/4777-7668; www.cabreragarden.com). Check out their websites for rates and more information.

many factors can affect the final price, including whether you book online using the Spanish versus the English version of a hotel's website. Discounts are almost always available in low season, and sometimes even in high season. Web packages and specials are also available on various hotel sites. Most hotels charge about $12 to $24 a night for valet parking or, at the very least, recommend nearby self-parking facilities, but call ahead of time for specifics. Avoid long-term street parking.

Buenos Aires accommodations have improved tremendously in the past few years, following a series of renovations among many of the city's government-rated four- and five-star hotels. Most five- and four-star hotels in Buenos Aires offer in-room safes, cable TV, direct-dial phones with voice mail, and in-room Internet access (in some places for free). Most hotels in this chapter boast four or five stars. Wi-Fi, often free, is standard in the lobbies and public areas of most hotels, including two- and three-star venues.

You love Buenos Aires, and so does everyone else. That means that hotel bargains are hard to find. Exponentially increasing numbers of tourists have made available rooms a scarce commodity, and hotels are trending their rates up in accordance. In fact, many hotel prices are back to their pre-peso-crisis levels. Still, bargains can be had—especially from four-star establishments off the beaten path, and locally owned (rather than international) hotel chains. And, of course, every traveler knows never to accept the first price offered. Always ask for a better rate and whether using your AAA card, student ID, union, or other membership will net additional discounts.

MicroCentro
VERY EXPENSIVE

Marriott Plaza Hotel ★★   This historic property was the grande dame of Buenos Aires for most of the 20th century. The intimate lobby, decorated in Italian marble, crystal, and Persian carpets, is a virtual revolving door of Argentine politicians, foreign diplomats, and business executives. Twenty-six rooms overlook Plaza San Martín, providing dreamlike views of the green canopy of trees in spring and summer. The **Plaza Grill** (p. 98) remains a favorite spot for business lunches and offers a reasonably priced multicourse dinner menu. The **Plaza Bar** (p. 157) is among the most famous in the city. The hotel's enormous health club has a large heated indoor pool and specialized dance and aerobics rooms. Guests whose rooms are not ready can wait in the health club lounge to rest and shower. The hotel lobby has free Wi-Fi access, but in-room Internet access costs about $16 a day, decreasing with additional days. The hotel also offers free high-quality historical tours of Buenos Aires.

Calle Florida 1005 (at Santa Fe overlooking Plaza San Martín), 1005 Buenos Aires. ℂ **11/4318-3000.** Fax 11/4318-3008. www.marriottplazabuenosaires.com. 318 units. $385 double; from $445 suite. Rates include buffet breakfast. AE, DC, MC, V. Valet parking $20. Metro: San Martín. **Amenities:** 2 restaurants; cigar bar; concierge; excellent health club w/outdoor pool; massage; room service; sauna; Wi-Fi in lobby. *In room:* A/C, TV, hair dryer, high-speed Internet, minibar.

Pan Americano ★★★   An enormous hotel, the Pan Americano faces both the Obelisco and the Teatro Colón, offering convenient access to tourist sites as well as the *subte* lines that converge here. The South Tower rooms are a good size, but the North Tower rooms are even larger, and bathrooms have whirlpool tubs and separate shower units. All rooms in both towers come with desks, extra side chairs, and ample closet space. The three-story glass rooftop health club, spa, and sauna give the sense of floating above Avenida 9 de Julio. The health club restaurant, **Kasuga,** becomes a sushi bar at night. Two other restaurants are located in the lobby. **Luciérnaga,** the main lobby bar where breakfast is served, is enormous and **Tomo I** has a modern decor. Both spaces serve international, Argentine, and Italian cuisine. The Pan Americano is sometimes called the Crowne Plaza, though it is no longer part of that chain.

Carlos Pelligrini 551 (at Corrientes), 1009 Buenos Aires. ℂ **11/4348-5000.** Fax 11/4348-5250. www. panamericano.us. 386 units. $346 double; from $550 suite. Rates include buffet breakfast. AE, DC, MC, V. Free valet parking. Metro: Lavalle or Diagonal Norte. **Amenities:** 3 restaurants; babysitting; concierge; enormous health club w/indoor/outdoor pool; massage; room service; sauna; spa. *In room:* A/C, TV, hair dryer, high-speed Internet, minibar.

Sheraton Buenos Aires Hotel and Convention Center ★★   Across from Retiro train station and the British Clock Tower, the Sheraton has an ideal location for business travelers and tourists alike. Rooms are large, and all include the Sheraton trademarked Suite Sleeper bedding. The lobby is very busy, serving as a hub for many activities and stores. The hotel boasts four restaurants that it shares with the Park Tower, including **Crystal Garden,** serving refined international cuisine in an atrium dining room overlooking Alem; **El Aljibe,** cooking Argentine beef from the grill; **Cardinale,** offering Italian specialties; and **Café Express,** a fast-food and pastry shop off the lobby. Its "Neptune" pool and fitness center are among the best in the city. The entire pool and spa complex is set in a garden, giving the sense of being in a resort. One pool has a pressurized current to boost your workout during your swim.

Av. San Martín 1225 (at Leandro N. Alem), 1104 Buenos Aires. ℂ **11/4318-9000.** Fax 11/4318-9346. www. sheraton.com. 742 units. $308 double; from $526 suite. AE, DC, MC, V. Metro: Retiro. **Amenities:** 3 restaurants; snack bar; piano bar; babysitting; concierge; fitness center; massage; room service; 2 pools; putting green; wet and dry saunas; 2 lighted tennis courts. *In room:* A/C, TV, hair dryer, high-speed Internet, minibar.

Sofitel ★★★   The first Sofitel in Argentina opened in late 2002. This classy French hotel near Plaza San Martín joins two seven-story buildings to a 20-story neoclassical tower dating from 1929, linked by a glass atrium lobby. The lobby resembles an enormous gazebo, with ficus trees, a giant iron-and-bronze chandelier, an Art Nouveau clock, and marble filling the space. Adjacent to the lobby, you will find an elegant French restaurant, **Le Sud** (p. 98), and the early-20th-century-style **Buenos Aires Café.** Guest rooms vary in size, mixing modern French decor with traditional Art Deco; ask for one of the "deluxe" rooms or suites if you're looking for more space. Beautiful marble bathrooms have separate showers and bathtubs and feature Roger & Gallet amenities. Rooms above the 8th floor enjoy the best views, and the 17th-floor suite, *L'Appartement,* covers the whole floor. Many of the staff members speak Spanish, English, and French.

Arroyo 841–849 (at Juncal), 1007 Buenos Aires. (C) **11/4131-0000.** Fax 11/4131-0044. www.sofitel.com. 144 units. From $531 double; from $605 suite. AE, DC, MC, V. **Amenities:** Restaurant; cafe; bar; concierge; fitness center; indoor swimming pool; room service. *In room:* A/C, TV, hair dryer, high-speed Internet, minibar.

EXPENSIVE

Claridge Hotel ★ The Claridge is living testimony to the once-close ties between England and Argentina. The grand entrance, with its imposing Ionic columns, mimics a London terrace apartment. The lobby is in a classical style with colored marble. Guest rooms are spacious, tastefully decorated, and equipped with all the amenities expected of a five-star hotel. The restaurant's hunting-themed wood-paneled interior is a registered city landmark, and an inviting breakfast buffet here is included in the room rates. Because it occasionally hosts conventions, the Claridge can become very busy.

Tucumán 535 (at San Martín), 1049 Buenos Aires. (C) **11/4314-7700.** Fax 11/4314-8022. www.claridge. com.ar. 152 units. $229 double; from $339 suite. Rates include buffet breakfast. AE, DC, MC, V. Metro: Florida. **Amenities:** Restaurant; bar; concierge; health club w/heated outdoor pool; massage; room service; sauna. *In room:* A/C, TV, high-speed Internet, minibar.

Holiday Inn Express Puerto Madero ★   This hotel enjoys a convenient location across from Puerto Madero's restaurants and nightlife. The location, within the city's downtown core and bank buildings, is convenient for tourists as well as businesspeople. Guest rooms have large, firm beds; ample desk space; and oversize TVs. Ask for a room facing Puerto Madero for the best views over the Río de la Plata. If you get the city-view side, you can always head to the 24-hour gym on the roof of the building, which has a view to everything.

Av. Leandro N. Alem 770 (at Viamonte), 1057 Buenos Aires. (C) **11/4311-5200.** Fax 11/4311-5757. www. holiday-inn.com. 116 units. From $206 double; $242 suite. Children 17 and under stay free in parent's room. Rates include buffet breakfast. AE, DC, MC, V. Free parking. Metro: L. N. Alem. **Amenities:** Deli; 24-hr. rooftop gym; room service; sauna; whirlpool. *In room:* A/C, TV, high-speed Internet.

MODERATE

Amerian Buenos Aires Park Hotel ★★ 🛅 One of the best four-star hotels in the city, the modern Amerian is a good bet for tourists as well as business travelers. The warm atrium lobby looks more like California than Argentina, and the highly qualified staff offers personalized service. Rooms are elegant and include wood, marble, and granite details. All have comfortable beds, chairs, and work areas. The Argentine-owned hotel is conveniently located just blocks away from Calle Florida, Plaza San Martín, and the Teatro Colón.

Reconquista 699 (at Viamonte), 1003 Buenos Aires. (C) **11/5171-6500.** Fax 11/5171-6501. www.amerian. com. 152 units. $133 double; from $284 suite. Rates include buffet breakfast. AE, DC, MC, V. Parking $16. Metro: Florida. **Amenities:** Restaurant; pub; concierge; exercise room; 24-hr. room service; sauna. *In room:* A/C, TV, high-speed Internet, minibar.

Dolmen Hotel ★   This four-star hotel, centrally located 1 block from Plaza San Martín, offers two things you usually do not find in this price category—quiet and a heated indoor swimming pool. Bathrooms are large, with spacious counters, and well stocked with supplies. A few rooms are suitable for those with special needs. Head upstairs to the pool and gym for great views. The lobby bar, recessed in a space behind the concierge, offers another quiet retreat, with a splashy marble-and-brass decor.

Suipacha 1079 (at Santa Fe), 1003 Buenos Aires. ℗ **11/4315-7117.** Fax 11/4315-5666. www.hoteldolmen. com.ar. 146 units. From $121 double; from $207 suite. Rates include buffet breakfast. AE, MC, V. Free parking. Metro: San Martín. **Amenities:** Restaurant; bar; concierge; small health club; small heated indoor pool; room service; sauna; Wi-Fi. *In room:* A/C, TV, hair dryer, high-speed Internet, minibar.

Esplendor ★★   Esplendor is built into the Galerías Pacífico shopping gallery, in a spectacularly renovated space. If you want a stylish boutique hotel, you don't have to sacrifice a convenient location close to everything. Rooms have a cool decor, mixing neutral tones with splashes of color and interesting fabrics by the Tramando Design House of famed Argentine textile designer Martin Churba. The high ceilings are punctuated by light fixtures, some of which are also made from unique textiles. Beds are very comfortable and the lobby has a restaurant, Rouge, and a gift shop full of design-based items. Double-insulated windows keep out the noise and many rooms also have balconies; bathrooms are very large.

San Martín 780, btw. Viamonte and Córdoba, 1004 Buenos Aires. ℗/fax **11/5256-8800.** www. esplendorbuenosaires.com. 51 units. $156 double; from $167 suite. Rates include breakfast buffet. Parking $12. AE, MC, V. Metro: San Martín. **Amenities:** Restaurant; bar; babysitting; free use of bikes; concierge; health club; room service; sauna; Internet (in business center). *In room:* A/C, TV, Internet, minibar.

Hotel Colón   This hotel is in the heart of the city, on Avenida 9 de Julio overlooking the Obelisco, which gives guests here convenient access to virtually all of the city's *subte* lines. It's a bargain alternative to the Pan Americano next door. Corner rooms are more spacious, and many of the very large suites come with terraces. Bathrooms are quite spacious, and some of the suite bathrooms have Jacuzzis. The restaurant offers international cuisine and a wraparound view overlooking the Obelisco. There is a medium-size heated rooftop pool, but its location in the back of the building means there is no view from up here.

Carlos Pellegrini 507 (at Corrientes), 1009 Buenos Aires. ℗ **11/4320-3500.** Fax 11/4320-3507. www. colon-hotel.com.ar. 173 units. From $139 double; from $209 suite. Rates include buffet breakfast. AE, DC, MC, V. Parking $16. Metro: Carlos Pellegrini or 9 de Julio. **Amenities:** Restaurant; bar; small health club; concierge; pool; 24-hr. room service. *In room:* A/C, TV, hair dryer, high-speed Internet, minibar.

Howard Johnson Florida Street ★★ ⚲   The Howard Johnson has a great location on Calle Florida near Plaza San Martín, with access through a shopping-and-restaurant gallery on the ground level. Guest rooms come equipped with sleeper chairs (in addition to the bed), large desks and dressers, and well-appointed bathrooms. Room size is above average for this category. Each room has two phones, and local calls and Internet use are free. There's a small, airy cafe and bar in the lobby, with additional food served in the gallery below. Four small budget-priced function rooms off the lobby are available for business and social events. There is no pool or health club on the premises, but guests get free access a nearby facility. Wi-Fi is free in the lobby.

Calle Florida 944 (at Alvear), 1005 Buenos Aires. ℂ **11/4891-9200.** Fax 11/4891-1200. www.hojoar.com. 77 units. $169 double. Rates include buffet breakfast. AE, DC, MC, V. Metro: San Martín. **Amenities:** Restaurant; bar; room service; Wi-Fi in lobby. *In room:* A/C, TV, hair dryer, high-speed Internet, minibar.

Lafayette Hotel ★ ☺ Popular with European and Brazilian travelers, the Lafayette Hotel has spacious rooms, with some even large enough to accommodate an entire family. Each has a desk, and all rooms have Wi-Fi. Bathrooms are hit-or-miss—some are large, others seem like jammed-together afterthoughts. Street-side rooms are great for people-watching in the MicroCentro, though you should expect some noise. Back rooms are quieter but offer limited views. The location is ideal for Micro-Centro's Lavalle and Calle Florida shopping, and the subway is only a few blocks away. The buffet breakfast is generous and varied, offering made-to-order omelets on request. The hotel is built in two parts with two different elevator bays, so if you're staying with friends or family, request rooms in the same division of the hotel. A tiny 24-hour gym and sauna are in the building's basement.

Reconquista 546 (at Tucumán), 1003 Buenos Aires. ℂ **11/4393-9081.** Fax 11/4393-2728. www. lafayettehotel.com.ar. 83 units. From $163 double; from $300 suite. Rates include generous buffet breakfast. AE, DC, MC, V. Metro: Florida. **Amenities:** Restaurant; bar; concierge; fitness room; room service; sauna. *In room:* A/C, TV, hair dryer, minibar, Wi-Fi.

INEXPENSIVE

V&S Hostel ★★ 🎒 Privately owned, but part of an Argentine network of hostels, V&S provides exceptionally friendly service in a convenient MicroCentro location. The hostel is inside a gorgeous turn-of-the-20th-century apartment building, with lavish touches such as curved doorway entries, stained-glass ornamentation, and balconies. Six private bedrooms with attached shower-stall bathrooms are also available. Guests can mingle in the quiet library, TV sitting room, or patio; and a kitchen is on hand for making meals. Several computers are available for Internet access. This place is a great value, with air-conditioning throughout the rooms, though they charge an electricity fee of about $1 to $3 a person depending on the room. Except for same-day reservations, the hostel prefers reservation requests by e-mail at reservas@hostelclub.com.

Viamonte 887 (at Suipacha), 1053 Buenos Aires. ℂ **11/4322-0994.** www.hostelclub.com. 60 bed spaces, including some in private room with bathroom. From $13 per bed; $66 private room. Rates include continental breakfast. No credit cards. Metro: Lavalle. **Amenities:** Concierge; high-speed Internet; shared kitchen; lockers; Wi-Fi. *In room:* A/C (for a small fee), hair dryer, Wi-Fi (select rooms).

Monserrat

EXPENSIVE

InterContinental ★★★ This luxurious tower hotel, built in one of the city's oldest districts, is decorated in 1930s style. The marble lobby is beige and apricot, with heavy black and brass accents, and handsome carved-wood furniture and antiques inlaid with agates and other stones. The lobby's small Café de las Luces sometimes offers evening tango performances. The **Restaurante y Bar Mediterráneo** (p. 103) serves healthful, gourmet Mediterranean cuisine on an outdoor patio under a glassed-in trellis. Stop by the Brasco & Duane wine bar for an exclusive selection of Argentine vintages. Guest rooms continue the 1930s theme, with elegant black woodwork, king-size beds, marble-top nightstands, large desks, and black-and-white photographs of the city. Marble bathrooms have separate showers and bathtubs, and extensive amenities.

Moreno 809 (at Piedras), 1091 Buenos Aires. © **11/4340-7100.** Fax 11/4340-7119. www.buenos-aires.
interconti.com. 312 units. $192 double; from $345 suite. AE, DC, MC, V. Parking $20. Metro: Moreno.
Amenities: Restaurant; wine bar; lobby bar; concierge; executive floors; health club w/indoor pool;
massage; room service; sauna; sun deck. *In room:* A/C, TV, hair dryer, high-speed Internet, minibar.

MODERATE

Grand Boulevard Hotel ★ ✦   The Grand Boulevard offers a location similar to
the InterContinental (see above), with easy subway access and a convenient set of
services for both business and leisure travelers, but at a much lower price. Double-
glazed windows lock out noise from Avenida 9 de Julio while offering incredible views
of that street and the river from higher floors. The restaurant/bar is open 24 hours
and features international cuisine, plus a lighter menu. All rooms are outfitted with
desks and large closets. With the *autopista* (highway) nearby, this is also the city's
closest four-star hotel to the airport (parking is free in the hotel's garage). Some of the
rooms here have limited wheelchair accessibility. A small, glassed-in meeting-room
space sits on the roof of the building, with beautiful views of the city.

Bernardo de Irogoyen 432 (at Belgrano), 1072 Buenos Aires. © **11/5222-9000.** www.grandboulevard
hotel.com. 85 units. $151 double; from $266 suite. AE, DC, MC, V. Free parking. Metro: Moreno. **Amenities:** Restaurant; bar; babysitting; concierge; small health club w/personal trainer; massage; room service; rooms for those w/limited mobility; sauna. *In room:* A/C, TV, hair dryer, high-speed Internet or
Wi-Fi, minibar.

Hotel Castelar   The 1929 Hotel Castelar was a stopping point for Spanish literary
stars during Argentina's golden years in the 1930s. Federico García Lorca lived here
in 1934, and his room is preserved as a museum. The lobby retains many original
brass, marble, and heavy plaster elements, including in the dining area, which was
once a *confitería* (cafe) as important as Café Tortoni (p. 101). Mario Palanti, eccentric
architect of nearby Palacio Barolo, designed the Castelar. The Castelar's spa, in the
hotel's basement, is free for guests (men and women are separated), with fees for
various services. Even if you're not a guest, it's worth paying the $15 entrance to see
the Turkish-style, white Carrara marble space. Room renovations occurred in 2005,
but the 1920s wooden touches, speckled glass, and tiled bathroom floors remain. The
rooms are not large, but have a small antechamber adding a sense of privacy. Suites
have an added living area.

Av. de Mayo (at Lima and Av. 9 de Julio), 1152 Buenos Aires. © **11/4383-5000.** Fax 11/4383-8388.
www.castelarhotel.com.ar. 151 units. $127 double; $163 suite. Rates include buffet breakfast. AE,
DC, MC, V. Metro: Lima. **Amenities:** Restaurant; bar; small health club; room service; rooms for those
w/limited mobility (minimal accommodation); extensive spa; Wi-Fi. *In room:* A/C, TV, high-speed
Internet, minibar.

NH City Hotel ★★   The Spanish-owned NH hotel chain opened this property in
the old City Hotel, a Jazz Age masterpiece. Its lobby has been meticulously renovated,
a combination of Art Deco and collegiate Gothic, with earth-tone furnishings offset-
ting the burnished woods, stained-glass ceiling, and honey-colored marble floors.
Rooms are large, some on the dark side, with a masculine combination of red and
black. Others are brighter, with white walls and burnt-sienna offsets. Bathrooms are
spacious. A new building was added to the hotel in 2006. The rooftop, with its small
outdoor heated pool, offers a view all the way to Uruguay on a clear day. A small health
club, with a spa, sauna, and Jacuzzi, is also on this level, as is the executive area. The
downside is many back rooms have no view. There are two restaurants. One is casual,
while the other, **Clue,** is formal, serving Spanish cuisine in a 1930s minimalist space.

Bolívar 160 (at Alsina), 1066 Buenos Aires. © **11/4121-6464.** Fax 11/4121-6450. www.nh-hotels.com. 369 units. From $153 double; from $248 suite. Rates include generous buffet breakfast. AE, DC, MC, V. Parking $13. Metro: Bolívar or Plaza de Mayo. **Amenities:** 2 restaurants; bar; babysitting; concierge; executive floor; small gym facility w/open-air pool; Jacuzzi; room service; sauna; spa. *In room:* TV, hair dryer, high-speed Internet or Wi-Fi, minibar.

INEXPENSIVE

Hotel Ritz ★ One of my favorite bargain Buenos Aires hotels thanks to a great combination of price, warmth of the staff, and location at the juncture of 9 de Julio and Avenida de Mayo. Of the 38 rooms, 30 are large enough for doubles or triples, and 24 have balconies (anyone who saw the awful movie *Testosterone,* starring Antonio Sabato, Jr. and Sonia Braga, will recognize the balconies). High ceilings maintain intricate plaster work, French doors, and brass fixtures. The bathrooms are hit-or-miss—some have only showers with low water pressure. Wi-Fi is free in the breakfast room. The maids are very much like second mothers overseeing your stay in Buenos Aires. There is an elevator, but staircases lead to it, making it hard to access for those with limited mobility. Rooms do not have safes, but front desk staff will guard valuables as well as arrange side trips and city tours.

Av. de Mayo 1111 (at Av. 9 de Julio), 1085 Buenos Aires. ©/fax **11/4383-9001.** www.ritzbuenosaires.com. 38 units. From $50 double. Rates include continental breakfast. AE, DC, MC, V. Off-site parking $12. Metro: Lima. **Amenities:** Concierge; room service; Wi-Fi. *In room:* A/C, TV.

5 Puerto Madero

There are no convenient metro stops to this neighborhood.

VERY EXPENSIVE

The Faena Hotel and Universe ★★★ The Faena opened to much fanfare among fashionistas in 2004, with its Philippe Starck design and handsome owner Alan Faena. The hotel, built into El Porteño, a 1902 grain silo, feels like a resort within the city. In public spaces, decayed Edwardian elegance meets country chic and kitsch—tin metal sheeting, peeling paint, ornamental ceiling molding, and unicorn wall ornaments. In the oversize rooms, midcentury classical meets modern—with white Empire-style furnishings and cut-glass mirrors reminiscent of colonial Mexico, with white and red key color elements. Each room has a home entertainment center. Bathrooms are enormous, completely mirrored, with oversize tubs. Rooms facing the city skyline have incredible vistas; others overlook the nearby Ecological Reserve. The spa is spacious and unique, using the round silos to great effect, with Turkish-style *hammam* baths and a stone Incan-style sauna shaped like an igloo.

Martha Salotti 445 (at Av. Juana Manso), 1107 Buenos Aires. © **11/4010-9000.** Fax 11/4010-9001. www.faenahotelanduniverse.com. 103 units. From $514 double; from $841 suite. Rates include continental breakfast. AE, MC, V. Parking $24. No metro access. **Amenities:** 3 restaurants; 3 bars; large health club; outdoor heated pool; room service; large sauna w/unique elements; spa w/extensive treatments. *In room:* A/C, TV/DVD, hair dryer, high-speed Internet, individualized bath treatments, minibar, Wi-Fi.

EXPENSIVE

Hilton Buenos Aires ★★ The Hilton opened in mid-2000 as the first major hotel and convention center in Puerto Madero. Within easy walking distance of some of the best restaurants in Buenos Aires, it's an excellent choice for steak and seafood connoisseurs. The strikingly contemporary hotel—a sleek silver block hoisted on stilts—features a seven-story atrium with more than 400 well-equipped guest rooms.

These spacious rooms offer multiple phone lines, walk-in closets, and bathrooms with separate showers and tubs. Those staying on the executive floors receive complimentary breakfast and have access to a private concierge. The lobby restaurant, **El Faro,** serves California cuisine with a focus on seafood. The hotel has the largest in-hotel convention center in the city.

Av. Macacha Güemes 351 (at Malecón Pierina Dealessi), 1106 Buenos Aires. © **800/445-8667** in the U.S. or 11/4891-0000. Fax 11/4891-0001. www.buenos.hilton.com. 418 units. From $329 double; from $409 suite. AE, DC, MC, V. Parking $24. No metro access. **Amenities:** Restaurant; bar; babysitting; concierge; modern gym facility w/open-air pool and a service of light snacks and beverages; room service. *In room:* TV, hair dryer, minibar, Wi-Fi.

Recoleta

There are no convenient metro stops to this neighborhood.

VERY EXPENSIVE

Alvear Palace Hotel ★★★   The Alvear Palace is among the world's top hotels. A gilded classical confection of marble and bronze, the Alvear combines Empire- and Louis XV–style furniture with exquisite French decorative arts. Antonio Banderas, Donatella Versace, and the emperor of Japan are some of the Alvear's past guests. A 2008 renovation expanded guest rooms to combine modern conveniences with luxurious comforts, such as chandeliers, Egyptian cotton linens, and silk drapes. All rooms come with personal butler service, cellphones that can be activated on demand, fresh flowers and fruit baskets, and daily newspaper delivery. Large marble bathrooms contain Hermès toiletries, and most have Jacuzzi tubs. The formal hotel provides sharp, professional service, and the excellent concierges go to great lengths to accommodate guest requests. The Alvear Palace is home to one of South America's best French restaurants (**La Bourgogne;** p. 105) and offers an excellent, if expensive, Sunday brunch and afternoon tea in **L'Orangerie.** Kosher dining is also available.

Av. Alvear 1891 (at Ayacucho), 1129 Buenos Aires. © **11/4808-2100.** Fax 11/4804-9243. www.alvear palace.com. 197 units. From $581 double; from $690 suite. Rates include luxurious buffet breakfast. AE, DC, MC, V. Valet parking $23. No metro access. **Amenities:** 2 restaurants; bar; concierge; small health club; massage; room service; private butler service; spa. *In room:* A/C, TV, hair dryer, high-speed Internet, minibar.

Four Seasons Hotel ★★★ ☺   This landmark hotel consists of two parts—the 12-story "Park" tower housing most guest rooms, and the 1916 French-style "La Mansión," with seven elegant suites and private-event rooms. A French-style garden and a pool separate the buildings, and a well-equipped health club contains the spa Pachamama, named for the Incan earth goddess, and offers various treatments including wine massages and facials. The hotel's restaurant, **Le Mistral** (p. 106), serves excellent Mediterranean cuisine in a casual environment. Spacious guest rooms offer amenities such as walk-in closets, wet and dry bars, stereo systems, and cellphones. Large marble bathrooms contain separate water-jet bathtubs and showers. Executive Library Floor guests enjoy exclusive check-in and checkout and additional in-room amenities, including a printer, fax machine, Argentine wine, complimentary breakfast, and evening cocktails; plus a private lounge. Kids receive bedtime milk and cookies. A favorite hotel of many celebrities, it's most famous as Madonna's choice while filming *Evita* and again on her 2008 tour.

Posadas 1086–88 (at Av. 9 de Julio), 1011 Buenos Aires. ✆ **11/4321-1200.** Fax 11/4321-1201. www.fourseasons.com/buenosaires. 165 units. $599 double; from $1,022 suite; $3,500 mansion suite. Prices include breakfast. AE, DC, MC, V. Valet parking $22. No metro access. **Amenities:** Restaurant; lobby bar; babysitting; concierge; executive level; exercise room; health club; massage; heated outdoor pool; room service; sauna. In room: A/C, TV/VCR, hair dryer, high-speed Internet, minibar.

Palacio Duhua–Park Hyatt Buenos Aires ★★★

This hotel combines a modern tower with the Palacio Duhau, the Duhau family mansion. Mansion rooms mix modern and classical details. Tower rooms mix a palette of leather, in browns, charcoals, and silver-grays. Rooms are spacious; suites have extra bathrooms for business meetings. Some tower rooms have breathtaking Río de la Plata views. For eating and drinking, offerings include the **Piano Nobile;** the **Oak Bar,** with panels from a medieval Normandy castle; **Gioia,** offering modern Italian cuisine for breakfast, lunch, and dinner; and **Duhau Restaurant,** featuring an Argentine menu with French touches, for lunch and dinner. The layered garden with gently cascading water lily–filled pools, is a pleasant place for a drink. The underground wine-and-cheese bar stocks about 45 artisanal Argentine cheeses. The spa, called Ahin, offers a broad range of treatments and the gym features a large heated pool. Internet is available all rooms, starting at $12 a day. The multicourse breakfast is not always included in rates and runs about $20.

Av. Alvear 1661 (at Montevideo), 1014 Buenos Aires. ✆ **11/5171-1234.** Fax 11/5171-1235. www.buenosaires.park.hyatt.com. 165 units. $599 double; from $780 suite; from $1,143 select suites. AE, DC, MC, V. Valet parking $24. No metro access. **Amenities:** 3 restaurants; lobby bar; babysitting; concierge; exercise room; health club; massage; heated indoor pool; room service; sauna; Wi-Fi. In room: A/C, TV/VCR, hair dryer, minibar, high-speed Internet, Wi-Fi.

EXPENSIVE

Hotel Emperador ★★

Located on Avenida Libertador, near Patio Bullrich shopping center (p. 135), this hotel is Spanish owned and has a Roman empire theme, which includes a bust of Julius Caesar at the concierge desk. Behind the main restaurant, the lobby opens onto a large overgrown patio with a gazebo and outdoor seating. The lobby bar, in the style of an English hunting lodge, is a draw for ladies who lunch and businesspeople gathering for informal discussions. Guest rooms feature blue carpeting with imperial wreath patterns, and furnishings with rich veneers, brass fittings, and gold velvet upholstery. Spacious suites, with their multiple doors and extra sinks, are ideal for business meetings. Bathrooms are oversize, with cream-and-green marble. Each room comes with a large desk and high-speed Internet and Wi-Fi access, which will cost you about $12 a day. The small gym has a wet and dry sauna, with separate areas for men and women, and a medium-size swimming pool that's surrounded by modern columns.

Av. del Libertador 420 (at Suipacha), 1001 Buenos Aires. ✆ **11/4131-4000.** Fax 11/4131-3900. www.hotel-emperador.com.ar. 265 units. $204 double; from $362 suite; $1,210 nuptial suite. Buffet breakfast $22. AE, DC, MC, V. Valet parking $20. Metro: Retiro. **Amenities:** Restaurant; bar; babysitting; concierge; small fitness center w/indoor heated pool and sauna; massage; room service; garden patio. In room: A/C, TV, hair dryer, high-speed Internet, minibar, Wi-Fi.

Loi Suites ★★

Part of a small local hotel chain, the Loi Suites Recoleta is a contemporary hotel with spacious rooms and personalized service. A palm-filled garden atrium and covered pool adjoin the lobby, which is bathed in various shades of white.

Breakfast and afternoon tea are served in the "winter garden." Management uses the term "suites" rather loosely to describe rooms with microwaves, sinks, and small fridges. But the hotel does offer some traditional suites in addition to its regular studio-style rooms. Loi Suites is just across from the Recoleta Cemetery.

Vicente López 1955 (at Ayacucho), 1128 Buenos Aires. © 11/5777-8950. Fax 11/5777-8999. www. loisuites.com.ar. 112 units. From $121 double; from $260 suite. Rates include buffet breakfast. AE, DC, MC, V. Parking $12. No metro access. **Amenities:** Restaurant; exercise room; indoor pool; room service; sauna. *In room:* A/C, TV, CD players, high-speed Internet (free), fridge, hair dryer, minibar.

MODERATE

Bel Air Hotel   Opened in late 2000, the intimate Bel Air has the ambience of a boutique hotel. Although the lobby and building's exterior are more extravagant than the rooms, guests can still look forward to comfortable, quiet accommodations. Superior rooms are bigger than standards and only slightly more expensive, and suites have separate sitting areas. Certain rooms contain showers only (no tubs). Next to the lobby, **Bis-a-Bis** restaurant and bar features window-side tables, great for people-watching along the fashionable Calle Arenales.

Arenales 1462 (at Paraná), 1061 Buenos Aires. © 11/4021-4000. Fax 11/4816-0016. www.hotelbelair.com. ar. 76 units. $150 double; from $230 suite. Rates include buffet breakfast. AE, DC, MC, V. No parking. Metro: Callao. **Amenities:** Restaurant; bar; gym; room service. *In room:* A/C, TV, high-speed Internet, minibar.

Etoile Hotel ★ 🔥   In the heart of Recoleta, steps from the neighborhood's fashionable restaurants and cafes, the 14-story Etoile is an older hotel with Turkish flair. It's not as luxurious as the area's other five-star venues, but it's not as expensive, either, making it a good value for the neighborhood. Colored in gold and cream, guest rooms are fairly large—although they're not really "suites," as the hotel describes them. Executive rooms have separate sitting areas, large tile-floor bathrooms with whirlpool tubs, and balconies. Rooms facing south have balconies overlooking Plaza Francia and the Recoleta Cemetery.

Roberto M. Ortiz 1835 (at Guido overlooking Recoleta Cemetery), 1113 Buenos Aires. © 11/4805-2626. Fax 11/4805-3613. www.etoile.com.ar. 96 units. $135 double; from $160 suite. AE, DC, MC, V. Free parking. No metro access. **Amenities:** Restaurant; concierge; rooftop health club w/indoor pool; room service. *In room:* A/C, TV, hair dryer, high-speed Internet, minibar.

INEXPENSIVE

The Recoleta Hostel ★ 🏠   This is a great inexpensive choice for young people who want to be in a beautiful neighborhood close to everything, but can't ordinarily afford such a location. Accommodations are simple, with 22 bunk bed–filled rooms for 8 to 12 people each. Two double rooms with private bathrooms can also be rented, but they have bunk beds, too, so couples wishing to cozy up will have to get really cozy. Rooms are simple, with bare floors and walls, beds, and a small wooden desk in the private rooms. The decor is reminiscent of a convent. Public areas have high ceilings, and there is a public kitchen, a TV room, laundry service, lockers, and an outdoor patio. The hostel is also a Wi-Fi hotspot.

Libertad 1216 (at Juncal), 1012 Buenos Aires. © 11/4812-4419. Fax 11/4815-6622. www.trhostel.com.ar. 75 bed spaces, including 4 in 2 bedrooms with private bathroom. From $12 per bed; from $42 per private room. Rates include continental breakfast. No credit cards. Metro: Lavalle. **Amenities:** Concierge; high-speed Internet; shared kitchen; outdoor patio; lockers; Wi-Fi. *In room:* Hair dryer.

San Telmo

INEXPENSIVE

El Lugar Gay ★ This is Buenos Aires's first exclusively gay hotel, but it is open only to men. It's inside a historic turn-of-the-last-century building less than a block from Plaza Dorrego, the heart of San Telmo. It has a homey feeling, with industrial chic well blended into a century-old interior. Ask for the rooms in the back with the beautiful views of the Church of San Telmo, which is beside the building. Rooms are small and sparse. Some share bathrooms with adjacent rooms, but one group has a Jacuzzi. Several flights of narrow stairs leading to the hotel's lobby and rooms might be a problem for people with limited mobility. The hotel becomes a de facto gay community center at times, with its small cafe and Sunday evening tango lessons at 7pm, conducted by the gay tango group La Marshall. These are open to the public, so even if you don't stay here, you can still visit.

Defensa 1120 (at Humberto I), 1102 Buenos Aires. © **11/4300-4747.** www.lugargay.com.ar. 7 rooms, some with shared bathrooms. From $45–$70 double. Rates include continental breakfast. No credit cards. Metro: Independencia. **Amenities:** Restaurant; bar. *In room:* A/C, TV.

Hostel Carlos Gardel ★ If you can't get enough of Gardel in the tango clubs, then stay here, where a red wall full of his pictures is the first thing to greet you. This hostel is built into a renovated old house, and though it has been severely gutted, a few charming elements such as marble staircases, wall sconces, and stained-glass windows remain. Two rooms with private bathrooms are available in this location and are reasonably priced but have few amenities other than a bathroom; a nearby apartment is also available, starting at $43 per day. The staff is friendly, and a large TV room off the concierge area allows for chatting with them and other patrons. A shared kitchen and an *asado* on the rooftop terrace provide more spaces for interacting and sharing stories of your adventures in Buenos Aires. Towels and sheets are provided for guests.

Carlos Calvo 579 (at Perú), 1102 Buenos Aires. © **11/4307-2606.** www.hostelcarlosgardel.com.ar. 45 bed spaces, including some in private room with private bathroom. From $12 per bed; $40 for private room. Rates include continental breakfast. No credit cards. Metro: Independencia. **Amenities:** Concierge; self-service drink station; TV room; free high-speed Internet; shared kitchen. *In room:* Lockers.

Lina's Tango GuestHouse ★★★ 👜 If you want to immerse yourself in the tango scene, this is the place. Owner Lina Acuña, who lives in the hotel, hails from Colombia and is a tango dancer. It's also great for women traveling alone, and Lina often goes with her guests on informal trips to the *milongas*. Although the facade of the hotel dates from the 1960s, it's a turn-of-the-last-century building and some rooms retain original elements, with kitschy colors reminiscent of La Boca. The back garden, overgrown with vines and trees, adds to the authentic Porteño atmosphere. Guests and Lina's friends gather here for conversation, impromptu help with each other's dance techniques, and *asados* on holidays and weekends. Three of the eight guest rooms share bathrooms. Breakfast is included, and guests can use the small kitchen and a washing machine. The TV is in shared living room, and the courtyard can be noisy with people talking and dancing.

Estados Unidos 780 (at Piedras), 1011 Buenos Aires. © **11/4361-6817** or 4300-7367. www.linatango. com. 8 units, 5 with private bathroom. $45–$70 double. 20% added for 1-night stays. Rates include continental breakfast. No credit cards. Metro: Independencia. **Amenities:** Continental breakfast; self-service kitchen; tango tours. *In room:* Wi-Fi.

Palermo

EXPENSIVE

Home ★★★   This is one of Palermo's most popular boutique hotels, thanks to the young couple behind it—Irish-Argentine Patricia O'Shea and her British husband, Tom Rixton. She grew up a few blocks away and he is a former DJ, giving the place both anchor and soul. On Fridays, there's a DJ in the lobby bar, and it's a great place for drinks, even if you're not staying here. There's a real backyard, with grass and an outdoor heated pool, with an ironic suburban edge. Rooms are high design with blonde woods and white linens—modern, but with funky mod accents. Bathrooms are large and some suites come with Jacuzzis and have kitchens. One room is available for travelers with disabilities. A two-level apartment is attached to the property with its own entrance. Home has an excellent spa sunken into its courtyard, which is open to the public; day-rate packages cost about $200 and include breakfast and lunch.

Honduras 5860, btw. Carranza and Ravignani, 1414 Buenos Aires. ✆ **11/4778-1008.** Fax 11/4779-1006. www.homebuenosaires.com. 21 units. From $157 double; from $351 suite; $399 apt. Rates include breakfast buffet. AE, MC, V. Metro: Palermo. **Amenities:** Restaurant; bar; babysitting; free use of bikes; concierge; health club; heated outdoor pool; room service; spa; 1 room for travelers w/limited mobility. *In room:* A/C, TV, hair dryer, kitchen (in some), minibar.

Soho All Suites ★★★   Chic is the word that came to mind when I first stepped into this boutique hotel. The lobby is modern and clean and the staff, clad in all-black uniforms, is immediately attentive. The fashionable lobby bar and its adjacent patio lounge are often the sites of parties and special events for Buenos Aires's young media crowd, and the majority of the hotel's clientele fall within the age range of 25 to 45. All rooms have kitchens and complete apartment accessories, from dishes and microwaves to irons. Guest rooms are in varying sizes and may be outfitted differently, with terraces or extra bedrooms, so ask when booking. They all have a clean, modern feeling, with their large leather sofas, bar stools, and high design. All bathrooms have tub/shower combinations. A rooftop solarium offers lovely views of the neighborhood.

Honduras 4762, btw. Malabia and Armenia, 1414 Buenos Aires. ✆ **11/4832-3000.** www.sohoallsuites. com.ar. 21 units. From $236–$448 suites. Rates include breakfast buffet. AE, DC, MC, V. Parking $8. Metro: Palermo or Ortiz. **Amenities:** Restaurant; bar; concierge; room service; spa. *In room:* A/C, TV, hair dryer, kitchenette, minibar, Wi-Fi.

Congreso

MODERATE

Savoy Hotel   Ever since Dutch Crown Prince William married the beautiful Argentine Maxima in 2002, the Dutch have flocked to Argentina. The Dutch-owned property, formerly known as the Golden Tulip, opened in the historic hotel Savoy and catches that traffic. The original hotel opened in 1910, with largely Art Nouveau elements, part of the glamorous rebuilding of Avenida Callao in the aftermath of the opening of nearby Congreso. Complete hotel renovations finished in 2010, maintaining original details such as gorgeous moldings and stained-glass decoration. Rooms are very large, each entered through its own antechamber. Rooms facing the street have tiny French balconies, but half of the hotel faces an interior courtyard with no views. All rooms are soundproof and have Wi-Fi. Suite bathrooms include a whirlpool bathtub. The hotel's Madrigales restaurant offers Argentine cuisine with interesting Latin American fusion elements. There is no pool, sauna, or gym here, but guests here get free access to a nearby health club.

Where to Stay & Eat in Palermo

PALERMO VIEJO

LAS CAÑITAS

PALERMO

PALERMO HOLLYWOOD

PALERMO SOHO

Plaza Seeber

Jardín Zoológico

Jardín Botánico

MINISTRO CARRANZA

PALERMO

PLAZA ITALIA

Vilanueva
Maure
Jorge Newbery
Benjamin Matienzo
Santos Dumont
Migueletes
J Ortega y Gasset
J Chenaut
Arévalo
Báez
Huergo
Av. Luis María Campos
Av. Dorrego
Freyre
Av. de la Infanta Isabel
Pedro Morti
Av. del Libertador
Segui
Demaría
Cerviño
Juncal
Colombia
Av. Sarmiento
Av. Las Heras
Av. Dorrego
Arevalo
Dr. Emilio Ravignani
Angel Justiniano Carranza
Bonpland
Fitz Roy
Humboldt
Av. Juan B. Justo
Emilio Zola
Godoy Cruz
Fray Justo Santa María de Oro
Av. Santa Fe
Güemes
Darregueira
Uriarte
Thames
Serrano
Gurruchaga
Virasoro
Armenia
Malabia
Charcas
Paraguay
Guatemala
Soler
Nicaragua
Costa Rica
Santa Rosa
El Salvador
Honduras
Gorriti
José Antonio Cabrera
Niceto Vega
Córdoba
Gurruchaga
Jufre
Lerma
Castillo
Loyola
Aguirre
Scalabrini Ortiz
La Valleja
Pringles
José Antonio Cabrera
Gascón
Francisco Acuña de Figueroa
Medrano
Medrano
Honduras
Gorriti
Julián Alvarez
Aráoz
Araoz

1
2
3
4
5
6
7
8
9
10
11
12
13
14
15
16
17
18
19
20
21
22
23
24

⊠ Post office
Ⓓ Subway

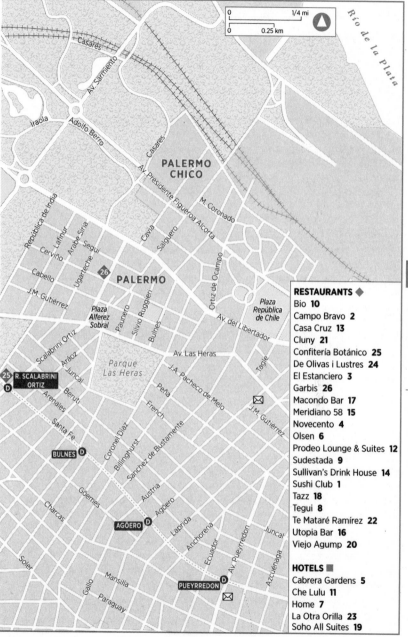

RESTAURANTS ◆
Bio **10**
Campo Bravo **2**
Casa Cruz **13**
Cluny **21**
Confitería Botánico **25**
De Olivas i Lustres **24**
El Estanciero **3**
Garbis **26**
Macondo Bar **17**
Meridiano 58 **15**
Novecento **4**
Olsen **6**
Prodeo Lounge & Suites **12**
Sudestada **9**
Sullivan's Drink House **14**
Sushi Club **1**
Tazz **18**
Tegui **8**
Te Mataré Ramírez **22**
Utopia Bar **16**
Viejo Agump **20**

HOTELS ■
Cabrera Gardens **5**
Che Lulu **11**
Home **7**
La Otra Orilla **23**
Soho All Suites **19**

Av. Callao 181 (at Juan Perón), 1022 Buenos Aires. ☏ **11/4370-8000.** Fax 11/4370-8020. www.savoy hotel.com.ar. 174 units. From $133 double; from $213 suite. Rates include buffet breakfast. AE, DC, MC, V. Parking $18. Metro: Congreso. **Amenities:** Restaurant; bar; concierge; access to nearby health club; room service; spa. *In room:* A/C, TV, hair dryer, minibar, Wi-Fi.

INEXPENSIVE

Hotel de Los Dos Congresos 🏆   This hotel is housed in a historically listed building just across from Congreso. Some units come in odd shapes and arrangements, so ask to see a room before taking it. A few rooms are split-levels, with the bed in lofts; some have very large bathrooms, others small. Some bathrooms have only showers, while others have tub/shower combinations. Suites come with Jacuzzi tubs. Hair dryers are available at the front desk. Rooms facing Congreso have fantastic views, but it can be noisy, especially given the constant protests in front of Congreso. There is no price differential for rooms with or without views. Staff members are exceptionally helpful. Most patrons hail from Europe and South America as part of tour groups.

Rivadavia 1777 (at Callao), 1033 Buenos Aires. ☏ **11/4372-0466** or 4371-0072. Fax 11/4372-0317. www.hoteldoscongresos.com. 50 units. $100 double; from $106 suite. Rates include buffet breakfast. AE, DC, MC, V. Metro: Congreso. **Amenities:** Restaurant; bar; concierge; room service. *In room:* A/C, TV, minibar, Wi-Fi.

Hotel Ibis ★★ ☺ 🏆   Well located on Plaza Congreso, all rooms have street views, many facing the plaza. Rooms are a good size for this price range, and all are identical, with a peach-and-mint color pattern. They are all doubles, with an extra bed available for a few dollars more. Some rooms connect, ideal for families or groups of friends. Bathrooms are bright and clean, all with shower stalls (no tubs). The basic Argentine restaurant is a good value at about $10 for a prix-fixe dinner, and $1 to $3 for most lunch items a la carte. Breakfast is not included in the rates but is about $5 per person. The hotel is popular with French tourists and college-age backpackers. The staff speaks Spanish, English, and French.

Hipólito Yrigoyen 1592 (at Ceballos), 1089 Buenos Aires. ☏ **11/5300-5555.** Fax 11/5300-5566. www. ibishotel.com. 148 units. From $88 double. AE, DC, MC, V. Parking $18 in a nearby garage. Metro: Congreso. **Amenities:** Restaurant; bar; concierge; high-speed Internet; Wi-Fi. *In room:* A/C, TV, Wi-Fi.

Tribunales
EXPENSIVE

Dazzler Hotel Libertad ★   This hotel, built in 1978, is virtually unknown to the North American market. The majority of clients come from South America, though all staff members speak English. The hotel is conveniently situated overlooking Plaza Libertad, set against Avenida 9 de Julio, a few blocks from Teatro Colón (p. 133). Front rooms have excellent views, but they can be noisy. All rooms are on the small side, but they're exceptionally bright, with floor-to-ceiling windows that make the rooms feel larger. Corner rooms offer the most space. Ask about connecting rooms if you're traveling in a group or with family. Large closets and a combination desk and vanity round out the rooms. The small smoke-glass-mirrored lobby has a staircase leading to the large and bright restaurant, where breakfast is served.

Libertad 902 (at Paraguay), 1012 Buenos Aires. ☏ **11/4816-5005.** www.dazzlerhotel.com. 87 units. From $114 double. Rates include buffet breakfast. AE, MC, V. Parking garage across from hotel. Metro: Tribunales. **Amenities:** Restaurant; bar; concierge; small health club; room service; sauna; Wi-Fi. *In room:* A/C, TV, hair dryer, Internet, minibar.

Abasto

MODERATE

Abasto Plaza Hotel ★   A block away from this hotel are both the Abasto Shopping Center and Esquina Carlos Gardel, sites dedicated to the tango crooner. The hotel takes this to heart, with a tango shop for shoes, dresses, and other *milonga* accessories. Free tango lessons and shows take place Thursday evenings at 9pm in the lobby. There's also a free tango show every night at 8pm in the restaurant. Rooms are a good size, with rich dark woods and deep-red carpets, and thematic suites have a tango decor. Superior rooms come with whirlpool bathtubs. The restaurant, **Volver,** is named for a Gardel song. The small heated outdoor pool sits on the rooftop, with access through a small gym. While this hotel does not offer much of interest in itself to Jewish travelers, it is the closest full-service hotel walking distance to Once and Abasto's historic Jewish sites and temples.

Av. Corrientes 3190 (at Anchorena), 1193 Buenos Aires. 🕾 **11/6311-4466.** Fax 11/6311-4465. www. abastoplaza.com. 120 units including 26 suites. From $115 double; from $266 suite. Rates include buffet breakfast. AE, DC, MC, V. Parking $12. Metro: Carlos Gardel. **Amenities:** Restaurant; bar; concierge; small health club; heated outdoor pool; room service; 1 room for those w/limited mobility. *In room:* A/C, TV, hair dryer, high-speed Internet, minibar, Wi-Fi.

WHERE TO EAT

Buenos Aires offers world-class dining with a variety of Argentine and international restaurants and cuisines. Nothing matches the meat from Pampas grass-fed Argentine cows, the focus of the dining experience throughout the city, from the humblest *parrilla* (grill) to the finest business-class restaurant. Empanadas, dough pockets filled with ground beef and other ingredients, are another staple, an Argentine fast food sold almost everywhere.

Buenos Aires's most fashionable neighborhoods for dining are all in Palermo. Las Cañitas provides a row of Argentine and Nouvelle-fusion cuisine concentrated on Calle Báez. Palermo Viejo, in both Palermo Hollywood and Soho, have matched this with even more trendy hot spots combining fine dining with a bohemian atmosphere in small, renovated, turn-of-the-20th-century houses. These restaurants have some of the city's top chefs, many of whom trained in France and Spain. Both Palermo Viejo and Las Cañitas are near the D metro line, but the best restaurants are often a long walk from the stations, which close at 11pm. All things considered, cabs are the best way to reach these restaurants.

Puerto Madero's docks are lined with more top restaurants, many popular as business lunch spots. The MicroCentro and Recoleta offer many outstanding restaurants and cafes, some of which have been on the map for decades. Buenos Aires's cafe life, where friends meet over coffee, is as sacred a ritual to Porteños as it is to Parisians. Favorite local meeting spots include La Biela, in Recoleta, across from the world-famous Recoleta Cemetery, and Café Tortoni, one of the city's most beautiful and traditional cafes, on Avenida de Mayo close to Plaza de Mayo. These places were once evocatively smoke-filled, but an anti-smoking law was enacted in 2006. If you have been here before, you may agree with me that something unique has been lost to Porteño cafes—once smoky, but now somewhat sterile.

Porteños eat breakfast until 10am, lunch between noon and 4pm, and dinner late—usually after 9pm, though some restaurants open as early as 7pm. If you are an early bird diner in the North American and British style, wanting to eat from 5pm on,

Where to Eat in Buenos Aires

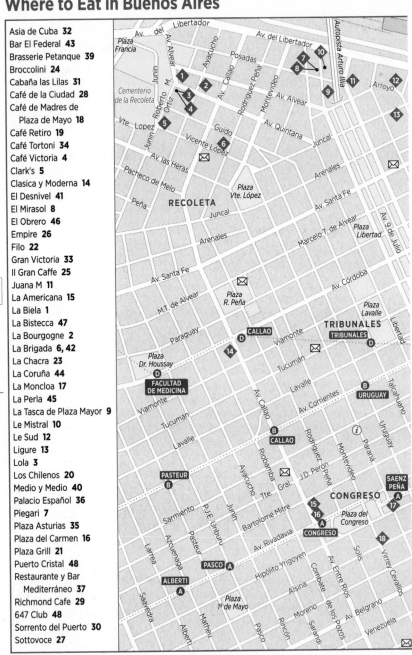

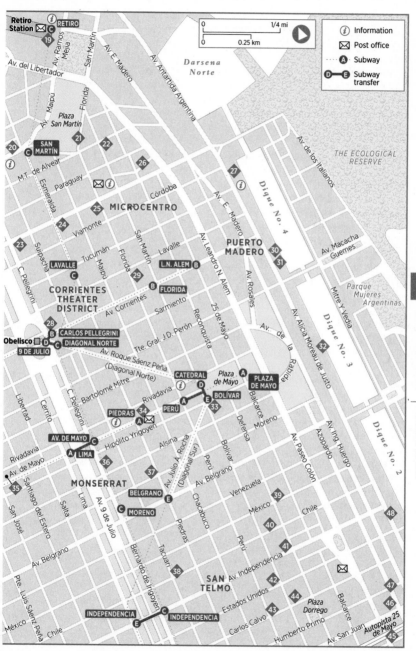

look for restaurants in our listings that remain open between lunch and dinner. If you can make a reservation, I highly recommend doing so. If you do not want to commit, come at 8pm, when most restaurants are empty. However, once the clock hits 9pm, virtually every table at the best restaurants will suddenly be full.

Many restaurants serve executive lunch menus (usually fixed-price, three-course meals) at noon, but most dinner menus are a la carte. There is sometimes a small "cover" charge for bread and other items placed at the table. In restaurants that serve pasta, the pasta and sauce are sometimes priced separately. Standard tipping is 10% in Buenos Aires, more for exceptional service. Even when paying by credit card, leave the *propina* (tip) in cash. Be aware that some restaurants do not accept credit cards, due to fears still resonating from the peso collapse, or they may charge an additional service fee for use. Some restaurants might also have signs indicating they accept credit cards, only to mysteriously have broken machines when you ask to pay this way. Many restaurants close between lunch and dinner, and some close completely on Sunday or Monday, or only offer dinner. In January and February, many restaurants offer very limited hours or close for vacations, because most Porteños flee to the beach this time of year. Call ahead during these months, to avoid disappointment.

Though Buenos Aires is a very cosmopolitan city, it is not very ethnically diverse, at least on the surface. However, a few areas reflect the influences of Middle Eastern and Jewish immigrants who came to this city in the wake of World War I and the Ottoman Empire's collapse. Middle Eastern restaurants are clustered in Palermo Viejo near the *subte* station Scalabrini Ortiz, and also on Calle Armenia. I list several of them below. In Once and Abasto, the traditional neighborhoods for Jewish immigrants, you'll find many kosher restaurants (some traditional, others recently opened by young people trying to bring back the cuisine they remember their grandparents cooking) along Calle Tucumán in particular. Because many were Sephardic or of Middle Eastern descent, you'll also find Arabic influences here along with Ashkenazi, or eastern European Jewish, touches.

With as many local Italian last names as Spanish ones, it's hard to distinguish those of Italian descent as a specific ethnic group within Argentina, as you can in the United States, Canada, or Australia. As such, Buenos Aires's Italian food is Argentine food in essence, and pastas and other Italian dishes are usually folded in with traditional Argentine offerings such as grilled beef. La Boca is Buenos Aires's historic Little Italy, the place where Italian immigrants first settled at the end of the 19th and early 20th centuries. The atmosphere in these restaurants plays on this past and caters to tourists, but this is not where the city's best Italian food is served. Instead, it is usually found in old, simple *parrillas* that have operated for decades and include pastas on their menus. Throughout this chapter, most of these are in the Inexpensive or Moderate categories all over the city. Additionally, though it is on the pricey side, check out Piegari in Recoleta's La Recova restaurant area, which has some of the best northern Italian cuisine in the city.

Asians only make up a tiny portion of Buenos Aires's population, with little effect on local cuisine. Still, in keeping with international trends, sushi bars and other restaurants with Japanese and Chinese influences have cropped up. All over the city, you will find various sushi fast-food-chain restaurants as well. I also describe a few restaurants in Buenos Aires's very tiny and little-known Chinatown district, located in the Belgrano neighborhood.

If you are looking through these listings and still cannot decide what you want to eat, head to one of these four neighborhoods, and you are bound to find something

Part of what makes a meal in Buenos Aires so good is the fine wine selection, specially chosen to complement beef, chicken, fish, and other items on the menu. Most Argentine wine comes from the Mendoza district, bordering the Andean mountains. Malbecs make up most of the best, with cabernets, champagnes, and even grappas on the menus in the humblest restaurants. If you know nothing about wine, you may want to take a wine-tasting class, to make sense of the selections and suggestions offered by the waiter or sommelier. One of the city's best is operated by the **Hotel Alvear's Cave de Vines** (✆ 11/4805-3857; www.alvear palace.com), which is offered Monday to Friday at 7pm and will run you about $78 per person. You'll get about 45 minutes with a sommelier who will explain the grape-growing process, the harvest, and how the wine is actually produced as you sample three different wines and taste them with various appetizers from various regions of Argentina. Like fine diamonds, wine is judged by color and clarity, and you'll learn what to look for in every glass, as well as how to pair wines with food. Other points include discerning taste and scent points as well as how to hold a glass of wine without damaging its contents with your hand's own body heat. The wineshop **Lo De Joaquin Alberdi** in Palermo Viejo, at Borges 1772 at Costa Rica (✆ 11/4832-5329; www.lodejoaquinalberdi.com.ar), also offers tastings by appointment, for about $43 for four wines. In early 2010, the very chic **Experiencia Fin del Mundo** was opened by the Mendoza winery in Palermo Viejo at Honduras 5673 between Fitzroy and Bonpland (✆ 11/4852-6661; www.bodegadel findelmundo.com); it offers a variety of wine tasting options.

that pleases you: **Puerto Madero**'s historic dock buildings are one such place, and many of the restaurants here are a bargain; **Calle Báez,** in the Las Cañitas area of Palermo, is another such area and is also one of the most happening restaurant scenes in the whole city; **Plaza Serrano,** in Palermo Hollywood, and **Calle Chile** in San Telmo, have many a good choice for the young, funky, and bargain-minded. All of these areas also have plenty of places nearby for after-dinner drinks and dancing.

For additional opinions, check out **www.restaurant.com.ar**, which provides information in English and Spanish on restaurants in Buenos Aires and other major cities, and allows you to search by neighborhood as well as cuisine type. Another very helpful restaurant resource online is **www.guiaoleo.com.ar**. You can search by cuisine style and price point, though all listings are in Spanish only. Once in Buenos Aires, look for the excellent restaurant map by **de Dios** in bookstores everywhere, or order it ahead of time at www.guiaoleo.com.ar or www.amazon.com.

Prices at some restaurants have doubled and even tripled since our last edition, in particular at Palermo Viejo restaurants, which now match or exceed prices in Europe and North America. Still, the restaurants listed in the Inexpensive and Moderate categories remain reasonable. Inexpensive restaurants serve main courses from less than $3 to about $10. Moderate restaurants serve entrees from around $5 to about $15. Expensive restaurants' main courses cost about $12 to $25. Very Expensive dishes run from $25 up to almost $50 and higher.

Note: While English is becoming comfortably prevalent in Buenos Aires, less expensive restaurants tend to have fewer English speakers on staff.

Plaza De Mayo Area

MODERATE

Gran Victoria ★ CAFE/ARGENTINE   Watch the political world of Argentina pass by your window at this great cafe overlooking Plaza de Mayo. This cafe sits in the middle of one of the country's most important historic areas, with stunning views of the Cabildo, Plaza de Mayo, Casa Rosada, and the Metropolitan Cathedral, in addition to the excellent people-watching opportunities. Food is basic Argentine, with Italian touches, and a great dessert selection. I'd recommend coming here for a break after sightseeing in the area. What's more, the waitresses have a pleasant sense of humor (I guess they'd have to, dealing with so many politicians).

Hipólito Yrigoyen 500 (at Diagonal Sur). © **11/4345-7703.** Main courses $4–$15. AE, MC, V. Mon–Sat 7am–9pm. Metro: Bolívar.

MicroCentro

EXPENSIVE

Le Sud ★★ FRENCH/MEDITERRANEAN   Executive Chef Thierry Pszonka earned a gold medal from the National Committee of French Gastronomy and gained experience at La Bourgogne (p. 105) before opening this gourmet restaurant in the Sofitel Hotel. His simple, elegant cooking style embraces spices and olive oils from Provence, to create delicious entrees such as stewed rabbit with green pepper and tomatoes, polenta with Parmesan and rosemary, and spinach with lemon ravioli. Le Sud's dining room is as sophisticated as the cuisine: The design is contemporary, with chandeliers and black-marble floors, tables of Brazilian rosewood, and large windows overlooking Calle Arroyo. After dinner, consider a drink in the adjacent wine bar.

Arroyo 841–849 (at Suipacha, in the Sofitel Hotel). © **11/4131-0000.** Reservations recommended. Main courses $15–$25. AE, DC, MC, V. Daily 6:30–11am, 12:30–3pm, and 7:30pm–midnight. Metro: San Martín.

Plaza Grill ★★ INTERNATIONAL   For nearly a century, the Plaza Grill dominated the city's power-lunch scene, and it remains the first choice for government officials and business executives. The dining room is decorated with dark oak furniture, the owners' 90-year-old Dutch porcelain collection, Indian fans from the British Empire, and Villeroy & Boch china place settings. Tables are well spaced, allowing for intimate conversations. Order a la carte from the international menu or off the *parrilla*—the steaks are perfect Argentine cuts. Marinated filet mignon, thinly sliced and served with gratinéed potatoes, is superb. Another interesting choice is venison with crispy applesauce, served during the November and December holiday season, though seemingly incongruous in the heat of Buenos Aires's summer. The "po parisky eggs" form another classic dish dating to the hotel's Belle Epoque opening—two poached eggs in a bread shell topped with a rich mushroom-and-bacon sauce. The kitchen is overseen by Chef Donato Gabriel Mazzeo, and the restaurant's wine list spans seven countries, with the world's best Malbec coming from Mendoza. There is a very reasonable $40 executive lunch menu.

Marriott Plaza Hotel, Calle Florida 1005 (at Santa Fe, overlooking Plaza San Martín). © **11/4318-3070.** Reservations recommended. Main courses $12–$25. AE, DC, MC, V. Daily noon–4pm and 7pm–midnight. Metro: San Martín.

Puertas Cerradas: Closed-Door Dining

In recent years, a trend has developed in Buenos Aires where chefs invite small groups of diners (anywhere from 12–30 people) into their homes. Participants dine together under the guidance of a chef who explains the several-course meal he or she has prepared. In a way, it's a little like a group blind date between you, your travel companion, and whomever else has booked that night. More than 30 operate in Buenos Aires. Some of the best include **Casa SaltShaker** (www.casasaltshaker.com), started by the American chef Dan Perlman and his partner, Henry Tapia; **Cocina Sunae** (http://cocinasunae.blogspot.com), run by the American Christina Sunae Wiseman who uses Asian fusion in her cooking; and **Casa Felix** (www.diegofelix. com), run by the Argentine chef Diego Felix. Most dining sessions are on weekends, but chefs can arrange for private groups, along with cooking classes. Most *Puertas Cerradas* operate on a cash-only basis, but payment can be arranged via PayPal. My experience has been that dining this way allows you to see the interactions among locals, ex-pats, and travelers from various countries; and it often leads to a group night out exploring nightlife after dinner.

MODERATE

Broccolino ★ ITALIAN   The name of this restaurant doesn't mean little broccoli; it's a corruption of Italian immigrant slang for New York's biggest and once most heavily Italian borough (notice the Brooklyn memorabilia filling the walls and the mural of Manhattan's skyline). This casual trattoria near Calle Florida is popular with North Americans. Many of the waiters speak English, and the restaurant has a distinctly New York outer-borough feel. Three small dining rooms are decorated in quintessential red-and-white-checkered tablecloths, and the smell of tomatoes, onions, and garlic fills the air. The restaurant is known for its spicy pizzas, fresh pastas, and, above all, its sauces (*salsas* in Spanish). The restaurant also serves 907 kilograms (2,000 lb.) per month of baby calamari sautéed in wine, onions, parsley, and garlic.

Córdoba 820 (at Esmeralda). © **11/4322-9848.** www.broccolino.com. Reservations recommended. Main courses $5–$15. AE, DC, MC, V. Daily noon–4pm and 7pm–1am. Metro: Lavalle.

Café de la Ciudad CAFE/ARGENTINE   The city's only restaurant with outdoor dining directly overlooking the Obelisco, Café de la Ciudad opened more than 40 years ago on one of the corners around the landmark, on Avenida 9 de Julio. It's like Buenos Aires's Times Square or Piccadilly Circus, where you can watch flashing electronic ads for Japanese and American companies. Sure, it's noisy, and, sure, you're a target for beggars, but you'll be dining under the symbol of the city. The food comes in large portions; sandwiches, pizzas, and specially priced executive menus are made fast, so it's a great stop if you're short on time. The subway station Carlos Pellegrini is right here too. On nights after the Boca Juniors have won a game, it's a great free show, when locals gather to cheer under the Obelisco, as cars and taxis hurtle by, beeping at the crowd. The cafe is open 24 hours, so you can stop by after clubbing or a show at one of the nearby theaters, and watch the parade of Porteños passing by.

5

BUENOS AIRES

Where to Eat

If you want to dine in an atmosphere recalling the glory days of Buenos Aires's past, investigate the list of nearly 40 *bares y cafés notables*—historic restaurants, cafes, and bars specially protected by a law (Law No. 35, to be exact) stating that their interiors cannot be altered. Many of these special establishments appear in this chapter, including **Café Tortoni, La Biela,** and **La Perla.** They tend to be clustered in the city's oldest neighborhoods, such as Monserrat, Congreso, La Boca, and San Telmo. Ask the tourism office for the map *Bares y Cafés Notables de Buenos Aires,* which lists them all, with photographs of the interiors. Many of the venues also sell a coffee-table book with additional photographs, or look for it at bookshops.

Corrientes 999 (at Carlos Pellegrini, Av. 9 de Julio). 🕭 **11/4322-8905** or 4322-6174. Main courses $4–$15. AE, DC, MC, V. Daily 24 hr. Metro: Carlos Pellegrini.

Empire ★ ASIAN/THAI   Empire is in a surprisingly desolate part of the MicroCentro—steps away from the action, on a very small street behind Harrod's that gets little foot traffic. Recently, the street was pedestrianized, making this an ideal outdoor dining and after-work spot. Enter this dark space, with paintings of elephants and mosaic decorations made from broken mirrors on the columns, and you'll feel as though you've stepped into some kind of funky club. For vegetarians seeking a break from the meat offerings everywhere else, it's is an ideal stop, with its many all-vegetable or noodle offerings. Many come for drinks alone and sit at the large bar with shelves of backlit bottles casting a warm glow. Empire's advertising symbol is the Empire State Building, but there's nothing New York about the restaurant. It's also one of the city's most popular restaurants among gay locals.

Tres Sargentos 427 (at San Martín). 🕭 **11/4312-5706.** www.empirethai.net. Main courses $10–$12. AE, MC, V. Mon–Fri noon–1am; Sat 7:30pm–3am. Metro: San Martín.

La Chacra ★ ARGENTINE/PARRILLA   If the stuffed cow outside doesn't lure you in to go and eat some meat, the open-fire spit grill glowing through the window might do the trick. Professional waiters clad in black pants and white dinner jackets welcome you into what is otherwise a casual environment, with deer horns and wrought-iron lamps adorning the walls. Dishes from the grill include sirloin steak, T-bone with red peppers, and tenderloin. Barbecued ribs and suckling pig call out from the open-pit fire, as do a number of hearty brochettes. Steaks are thick and juicy. Get a good beer or an Argentine wine to wash it all down.

Av. Córdoba 941 (at Carlos Pellegrini, on Av. 9 de Julio). 🕭 **11/4322-1409.** Main courses $5–$12. AE, DC, MC, V. Daily noon–1:30am. Metro: San Martín.

Ligure ★★ 🍴 FRENCH/ITALIAN   Painted mirrors look over the long rectangular dining room, which, since 1933, has drawn ambassadors, artists, and business leaders by day and a more romantic crowd at night. A nautical theme prevails, with fishnets, dock ropes, and masts decorating the room; captain's wheels substitute for chandeliers. Portions are huge and meticulously prepared—an unusual combination for French-inspired cuisine. Seafood options include the Patagonian tooth fish sautéed with butter, prawns, and mushrooms, or the trout glazed with an almond sauce. The chateaubriand is outstanding, and the *bife de lomo* (filet mignon) can be prepared seven different ways (pepper sauce with brandy is delightful, made tableside).

Juncal 855 (at Esmeralda). ✆ **11/4393-0644** or 4394-8226. Reservations recommended. Main courses $6–$10. AE, DC, MC, V. Daily noon–3pm and 8pm–midnight. Metro: San Martín.

Los Chilenos ★ SEAFOOD/CHILEAN   A taste of the long country next door is what you'll find here, and because of that, this restaurant is popular with Chileans who live here or are visiting. It's a simple place, with a home-style feeling. The dining room has long tables for communal dining, and it's decorated with posters of Chilean tourist sites and draped with Chilean flags. Fish is one of the restaurant's fortes, and one of the most popular dishes is abalone in mayonnaise.

Suipacha 1024 (at Santa Fe). ✆ **11/4328-3123.** Main courses $3–$10. V. Mon–Sat noon–4pm and 8pm–1am. Metro: San Martín.

Richmond Cafe ★★ CAFE/ARGENTINE   Enter this place and find the pace and atmosphere of an older Buenos Aires. The Richmond Cafe, a *café notable*, is all that is left of the Richmond Hotel, an Argentine-British hybrid that opened in 1917 and once catered to the elite. The cafe sits in the lobby of the former hotel, whose upstairs area has been converted into offices. The menu here is traditionally Argentine, and there is a *confitería* section in the front, serving as a cafe and fast-food eatery. You'll find locals of all kinds, from workers grabbing a quick bite to well-dressed seniors who recall Calle Florida's more elegant heyday. The decor is that of a gentlemen's club, full of wood, brass, and red-leather upholstery. Patrons can still let loose downstairs, in a bar area full of billiard tables. The menu of high-quality pastries is extensive. The restaurant offers hearty basics such as chicken, fish, and beef. A la carte, the food tends to be expensive, but three-course executive menus with a drink included are a good bargain, running about $20, depending on what you choose.

Calle Florida 468 (at Corrientes). ✆ **11/4322-1341** or 4322-1653. http://restaurant.com.ar/richmond. Main courses $6–$10. AE, DC, MC, V. Mon–Sat 7am–10pm. Metro: Florida.

INEXPENSIVE

Café Retiro ★★ 🛍 CAFE/ARGENTINE   This cafe is part of a chain, the Café Café consortium. As such, there is nothing spectacular about the food, but it is high quality, consistent, and inexpensive. The main point of dining here is to enjoy the restored elegance of the original cafe, which was part of Retiro Station when it was built in 1915. The place had been closed for many years but was restored in 2001 and is now one of the *cafés notables,* the interiors of which are considered historically important to the nation. The marble has been cleaned, the bronze chandeliers polished, and the stained-glass windows have been restored, allowing a luminescent light. This cafe is ideal if you are taking a train from here to other parts of Argentina and the province, such as Tigre, or if you came to admire the architecture of Retiro and the other classical stations in this enormous transportation complex. It's worth checking out if you came to see the nearby English Clock Tower. An attached art gallery in the hallway outside also has changing exhibitions.

Ramos Mejía 1348 (at Libertador, in the Retiro Station Lobby). ✆ **11/4516-0902.** Main courses $2–$6. No credit cards. Daily 6:30am–10pm. Metro: Retiro.

Café Tortoni ★★★ 📷 CAFE   You cannot come to Buenos Aires without visiting this Porteño institution. The artistic and intellectual hangout of Buenos Aires since 1858, this historic cafe has served guests such as Jorge Luis Borges, Julio de Caro,

Cátulo Castillo, and José Gobello. Its current location opened in the 1890s, when Avenida de Mayo was created as the main thoroughfare of a rich and powerful emerging Buenos Aires. Wonderfully appointed in woods, stained glass, yellowing marble, and bronzes, the place itself exudes more history than any of the photos and artifacts on its walls. It's the perfect place for a coffee or a small snack after wandering along Avenida de Mayo. Twice-nightly tango shows in a cramped side gallery, where the performers often walk through the crowd, are worth attending, though tight seating means you'll get to know the patron next to you almost too well. Tourists and locals once existed side by side quite comfortably, but tour buses have come filling the venue with gawkers. Try to visit in the morning, or very late at night. However, do not expect great service from the indifferent waiters. And management seems to be limiting who gains entry, disallowing quick peaks inside at the architecture. All told, it's a beautiful, historically important place, but service and treating people well have never been the Tortoni's forte.

Av. de Mayo 825 (at Esmeralda). ℂ **11/4342-4328.** www.cafetortoni.com.ar. Main courses $2–$10. AE, DC, MC, V. Mon–Thurs 8am–2am; Fri–Sat 8am–3am; Sun 8am–1am. Metro: Avenida de Mayo.

Filo ★ 👔 ITALIAN/PIZZA   Popular with young professionals, artists, and anyone looking for cause to celebrate, Filo presents its happy clients with pizzas, more kinds of pasta than you can imagine, salads with an Italian touch, and potent cocktails. The colorfully decorated and crowded bar hosts occasional live music, and tango lessons take place downstairs a few evenings per week. There are also rotating displays of art in the restaurant.

San Martín 975 (at Alvear). ℂ **11/4311-0312.** www.filo-ristorante.com. Main courses $4–$10. AE, MC, V. Daily noon–4pm and 8pm–2am. Metro: San Martín.

Il Gran Caffe ★ CAFE/ITALIAN   As its name implies, this Italian restaurant offers an extensive selection of pastries, pastas, and panini, as well as more traditional Argentine fare. On a busy corner across the street from Galerías Pacífico, it is also one of the best perches to watch crowds passing on Calle Florida. A covered canopy on the Córdoba side also provides further outdoor seating, rain or shine. In fact, the people-watching is so good that the restaurant charges about 10% more for outdoor dining. If that bothers the budget-conscious spy in you, the best compromise is to sit inside on their upper-floor level, with its bird's-eye view of the street and the Naval Academy, one of the city's most beautiful landmarks. Mixed drinks start at about $5 each. They have an excellent Italian pastry menu; the Neapolitan *sfogliatella* is especially good.

Calle Florida 700 (at Córdoba). ℂ **11/4326-5008.** Main courses $4–$15. AE, MC, V. Daily 7am–2am. Metro: Florida.

Monserrat

MODERATE

Palacio Español ★★ SPANISH   This restaurant has one of the most magnificent dining rooms in Buenos Aires. It's located in the Club Español, one of the grandest buildings along Avenida 9 de Julio. An orgy of brass, marble, agate lighting fixtures, carved oak bas-reliefs, and molded plaster ornaments surround you. Interspersed are Spanish paintings of major battles and graceful Art Nouveau maidens who stare down from the tops of pilasters. Despite the restaurant's architectural grandeur, the atmosphere is surprisingly relaxed and often celebratory; don't be surprised to find a table of champagne-clinking Argentines next to you. Tables have beautiful silver place settings, and tuxedo-clad waiters offer friendly but formal service. Although the menu is a tempting sample of Spanish cuisine—including paella and Spanish omelets—the fish dishes are best. Special salads are meals in themselves; a few include calamari. The wine list is pages long, with a large selection of whites to complement the fish offerings. Bills include a table service of about $1.50.

Bernardo de Yrigoyen 180 (at Alsina). © **11/4334-4876.** www.palacioespanol.com.ar. Reservations recommended. Main courses $5–$12. AE, DC, MC, V. Daily noon–4pm and 8pm–midnight (sometimes until 1am Fri–Sat). Metro: Lima.

Restaurante y Bar Mediterráneo ★★ MEDITERRANEAN   The InterContinental hotel's exclusive Mediterranean restaurant and bar were built in colonial style, resembling the city's famous Café Tortoni. The downstairs bar, with its hardwood floor, marble-top tables, and polished Victrola playing tango, takes you back to Buenos Aires of the 1930s. A spiral staircase leads to the elegant restaurant, where subdued lighting and well-spaced tables create an intimate atmosphere. Mediterranean herbs, olive oil, and sun-dried tomatoes are among the chef's usual ingredients. Dishes might include carefully prepared shellfish bouillabaisse; black hake served with ratatouille; chicken casserole with morels, fava beans, and potatoes; or duck breast with cabbage confit, wild mushrooms, and sautéed apples. Express menus (items ready within minutes) are available at lunch.

Moreno 809 (at Piedras in the InterContinental). © **11/4340-7200.** Reservations recommended. Main courses $8–$15. AE, DC, MC, V. Daily 7–11am, 11:30am–3:30pm, and 7pm–midnight. Metro: Moreno.

Puerto Madero

There are no convenient metro stops to this neighborhood.

EXPENSIVE

Asia de Cuba ★ ASIAN/JAPANESE   Though not associated with the other Asia de Cubas around the world, this place offers an exciting environment in which to dine. Renovated in 2008, the space is chic, with carved columns decorated in lotuses, and a golden reclining Buddha over the bar. In the back, there's a sushi bar and a VIP lounge. It's very glamorous at dinnertime; lunch is a more casual affair. A table sushi menu, with 110 different items, is about $180. Dinner comes with all kinds of exotic entertainment, such as Arabian belly dancers. Asia de Cuba is also one of the most important clubs in the Puerto Madero area, ideal for a more mature crowd because a large portion of its clientele is older than 40. Dancing begins at about 1am Tuesday to Saturday, and there is no admission charge if you're already dining. If you do not eat here, admission ranges from $15 to $20, depending on the day. The ideal is to come here late in the evening, dine, and stay around for a night of dancing.

Pierina Dealessi 750 (at Guemes on Dique 3). © **11/4894-1328** or 4894-1329. www.asiadecuba.com.ar. Reservations recommended. Main courses $10–$20. AE, MC, V. Daily 1pm–5am, often later on weekends. No metro access.

Cabaña las Lilas ★★★ ARGENTINE/PARRILLA   Widely considered the best *parrilla* in Buenos Aires, the 400-seat Cabaña las Lilas is always packed. The menu pays homage to Argentine beef, which comes from the restaurant's private *estancia* (ranch). The table "cover"—which includes dried tomatoes, mozzarella, olives, peppers, and delicious garlic bread—nicely whets the appetite. Clearly, you're here to eat steak: The best cuts are the rib-eye, baby beef, and thin skirt steak. Order sautéed vegetables, grilled onions, or Provençal-style fries separately. Service is friendly and professional; ask your waiter to match a fine Argentine wine with your meal. The enormous eatery offers indoor and outdoor seating. In spite of its high prices, it's casual and informal; patrons come in suits or shorts. They also offer a good salad selection, so even vegetarians can share a table with friends.

Alicia Moreau de Justo 516 (at Villaflor in Dique 3). © **11/4313-1336.** www.laslilas.com. Reservations recommended. Main courses $12–$30. AE, DC, V. Sun–Thurs noon–12:30am; Fri–Sat noon–1am. Metro: L. N. Alem.

Sorrento del Puerto ★★ ITALIAN   When the city decided to reinvigorate Puerto Madero in the mid-1990s, this was one of the first 5 restaurants to open (today you'll find more than 50). The sleek modern dining room boasts large windows, modern blue lighting, and tables and booths decorated with white linens and individual roses. The outdoor patio accommodates only 15 tables, but the inside is enormous. People come here for two reasons: great pasta and even better seafood. Choose your pasta and accompanying sauce: seafood, shrimp scampi, pesto, or four cheese. The best seafood dishes include trout stuffed with crabmeat, sole with a Belle Marnier sauce, Galician-style octopus, paella Valenciana, and assorted grilled seafood for two.

Av. Alicia Moreau de Justo 410 (at Guevara on Dique 4). © **11/4319-8730.** www.sorrentorestaurant. com.ar. Reservations recommended. Main courses $10–$25; 3-course lunch with 1 drink $16. AE, DC, MC, V. Mon–Fri noon–4pm and 8pm–1am; Sat 8pm–2am. Metro: L. N. Alem.

Sottovoce ★★ ITALIAN   One of the city's best Italian restaurants, Sottovoce provides great dining with a view to the port. Look for various *lomos* (sirloin cuts), rabbit dishes, saltimbocca, shrimp with a curry red-wine sauce, and nearly 20 different pasta dishes. The wine list, with local, French, and Italian vintages, is more than 10 pages long.

Alicia Moreau De Justo 176 (at Tucumán, on Dique 4). © **11/4313-1199.** www.sottovoceristorante.com. ar. Main courses $12–$25. AE, MC, V. Daily noon–4pm; Mon–Thurs 8pm–midnight; Fri–Sat 8pm–1am. Metro: L. N. Alem.

MODERATE

La Bistecca ★★ 🍴 PARRILLA   Puerto Madero's La Bistecca offers a wide range of meal choices at incredible value for the money. This is an all-you-can-eat establishment, locally called a *tenedor libre*. A three-course lunch is about $12, and dinner ranges from $12 to $20. If you came to Argentina for beef, definitely stop here. The high quality of the meat surprised me, considering the price and bottomless portions. There really was no limit to the number of times I could fill my plate at the various grills in the restaurant. For vegetarians, there is also a diverse salad bar. In spite of the restaurant's large size, the lighting and seating arrangements work to create small intimate spaces. At lunchtime, the place is full of businesspeople, while at night you'll find a mix of couples, friends, and families.

Av. Alicia Moreau de Justo 1890 (at Peñaloza on Dique 1). © **11/4514-4996.** www.labistecca.com. Main courses $8–$12. AE, DC, MC, V. Daily noon–4pm and 8pm–1am. No metro access.

Puerto Cristal ★ INTERNATIONAL/SEAFOOD   The menu here has everything, but fish is why patrons choose this restaurant above all the others in Puerto Madero. The place is enormous, with friendly hostesses and theatrical waiter service; a constant flurry of fresh silverware and dishes will cross your table between courses, befitting a much pricier establishment. Windows overlooking the port and a glassed-in central garden amid the dining area lend tranquillity to the industrial-chic design. Great lunch specials are part of the draw here; their executive menu runs about $15 and usually includes one glass of champagne (other drinks and the table cover are additional).

Av. Alicia Moreau de Justo 1082 (at Villaflor in Dique 3). © **11/4331-3669.** www.puerto-cristal.com.ar. Main courses $6–$20. AE, MC, V. Sun–Fri 6:30am–midnight; Sat 6:30am–2am. No metro access.

Recoleta

There are no convenient metro stops in this neighborhood.

VERY EXPENSIVE

La Bourgogne ★★★ FRENCH   The only Relais Gourmand in Argentina, Chef Jean Paul Bondoux serves the finest French and international food in the city here. *Travel + Leisure* magazine rated La Bourgogne the number-one restaurant in South America, and *Wine Spectator* called it one of the "Best Restaurants in the World for Wine Lovers." Decorated in elegant pastel hues, the formal dining room serves the city's top gourmands. To begin your meal, consider a warm foie gras scallop with honey-wine sauce, or perhaps the succulent *ravioli d'escargots*. Examples of the carefully prepared main courses include *Chateaubriand béarnaise*, roasted salmon, veal steak, and lamb with parsley-and-garlic sauce. The kitchen's fresh vegetables, fruit, herbs, and spices originate from Bondoux's private farm. Downstairs, **La Cave** offers a less formal experience, with a different menu, though the food comes from the same kitchen. Wine tastings are offered Monday through Friday in the restaurant's wine-cellar area, called **Cave de Vines;** contact La Bourgogne directly for details.

Av. Alvear 1891 (at Ayacucho in the Alvear Palace Hotel). ☎ **11/4805-3857.** www.alvearpalace.com. Reservations required. Jacket and tie required for men. Main courses $25–$35. AE, DC, MC, V. Free valet parking. Mon–Fri noon–3pm; Mon–Sat 8pm–midnight. Closed Jan. No metro access.

Piegari ★★ ITALIAN   This is a fine Italian restaurant under the highway overpass in a part of Recoleta dubbed "La Recova," and near the Four Seasons Hotel. Piegari has two restaurants located across the street from each other; the more formal focuses on Italian dishes, while the other, Piegari Vitello e Dolce, is mainly a *parrilla*. Both restaurants are excellent, but visit the formal Piegari for outstanding Italian cuisine, with an emphasis on seafood and pasta. Homemade spaghetti, six kinds of risotto, pan pizza, veal scaloppini, and black-salmon ravioli are just a few of the mouthwatering choices. Huge portions are made for sharing, and an excellent eight-page wine list accompanies the menu. If you decide to try Piegari Vitello e Dolce instead, the best dishes are the short-rib roast and the leg of Patagonian lamb.

Posadas 1042 (at Av. 9 de Julio in La Recova, near the Four Seasons Hotel). ☎ **11/4328-4104.** Reservations recommended. Main courses $25–$45. AE, DC, MC, V. Daily noon–3:30pm and 7:30pm–1am. No metro access.

EXPENSIVE

El Mirasol ★★ PARRILLA   One of the city's best *parrillas,* this restaurant serves thick cuts of fine Argentine beef. Like Piegari (see above), El Mirasol is also located in La Recova, but its glassed-in dining area full of plants and trellises gives the impression of dining outdoors. Your waiter will guide you through the selection of cuts, among which the rib-eye, tenderloin, sirloin, and ribs are most popular. A mammoth 2½-pound serving of tenderloin is a specialty, certainly meant for sharing. El Mirasol is part of a chain that first opened in 1967. The best dessert is an enticing combination of meringue, ice cream, whipped cream, *dulce de leche,* walnuts, and hot chocolate sauce. The wine list pays tribute to Argentine Malbec, Syrah, merlot, and cabernet sauvignon. El Mirasol, frequented by business types and government officials at lunch and a more relaxed crowd at night, remains open throughout the afternoon, ideal for those with North American and British early dining habits.

Posadas 1032 (at Av. 9 de Julio in La Recova, near the Four Seasons Hotel). ☎ **11/4326-7322.** www.elmirasol.com.ar. Reservations recommended. Main courses $8–$40. AE, DC, MC, V. Daily noon–2am. No metro access.

La Tasca de Plaza Mayor ★★ SPANISH   I list the full name of this restaurant, but most people just call it Plaza Mayor, named for Madrid's main square. Decorations on the rough brick walls, such as Spanish fans in glass casements, let you know you have entered into the mother country. The waitstaff in aprons gives old-fashioned service. Highlights of the menu include *pollo Plaza Mayor* (chicken in a wine sauce), several kinds of paella, and lots of steak and pastas as you'd find all over Argentina. There is plenty of exotic fruit of the sea, from octopus to crabs, and an excellent bacalao a la Gallega.

Posadas 1052 (at Av. 9 de Julio in La Recova, near the Four Seasons Hotel). ℂ **11/4393-5671.** www.plaza-mayor.com.ar. Reservations recommended. Main courses $15–$30. AE, MC, V. Daily noon–1am, sometimes later Sat–Sun. No metro access.

Le Mistral ★★ MEDITERRANEAN   This elegant but informal restaurant in the Four Seasons Hotel serves Mediterranean cuisine with Italian and Asian influences and is overseen by chef Matthias Zumstein. The interior pays homage to Argentine materials such as leather and native woods. The executive lunch menu includes an antipasto buffet with seafood, cold cuts, cheese, and salads followed by a main course and dessert. From the dinner menu, the aged Angus New York strip makes an excellent choice. All grilled dishes come with béarnaise sauce or *chimichurri* (a thick herb sauce) and a choice of potatoes or seasonal vegetables. Organic chicken and fresh seafood round out the menu, along with a terrific selection of desserts. Live harp music often accompanies meals, and tables are candlelit at night. Enjoy an after-dinner drink in Le Dôme, the split-level bar adjacent to the lobby featuring live piano music and occasional tango shows. The Sunday brunch, which runs about $35, is one of the best in Buenos Aires.

Posadas 1086 (at Av. 9 de Julio, in the Four Seasons Hotel). ℂ **11/4321-1730.** Reservations recommended. Main courses $13–$25. Sun brunch $35. AE, DC, MC, V. Daily 7–11am, noon–3pm, and 8pm–1am. No metro access.

Lola ★ INTERNATIONAL   Among the best-known international restaurants in Buenos Aires, Lola has a brilliantly lit, contemporary dining room. Caricatures of major personalities adorn the walls, and fresh plants and flowers give Lola's dining room a springlike atmosphere. The menu features dishes such as chicken fricassee with leek sauce, grilled trout with lemon-grass butter and zucchini, and beef tenderloin stuffed with Gruyère cheese and mushrooms. The kitchen is overseen by the Argentine chef Gonzal Vidal, who studied in France's Cordon Bleu school.

Guido 1985 (at Ortiz). ℂ **11/4804-5959.** www.lolarestaurant.com. Reservations recommended. Main courses $10–$20. AE, DC, MC, V. Daily noon–4pm and 7pm–1am. No metro access.

INEXPENSIVE

Café Victoria ★ CAFE   Perfect for a relaxing afternoon in Recoleta, the cafe's outdoor patio is surrounded by flowers and shaded by an enormous tree. Sit and drink a coffee or enjoy a complete meal. The three-course express lunch menu offers a salad, main dish, and dessert, with a drink included. Afternoon tea with pastries and scones is served daily from 4 to 7pm. The cafe remains equally popular in the evening, with excellent people-watching opportunities, when live music enlivens the patio. It's a great value for the area—the Recoleta Cemetery and cultural center are next door.

Roberto M. Ortiz 1865 (at Quintana). ℂ **11/4804-0016.** Main courses $5–$12. AE, DC, MC, V. Daily 7:30am–11:30pm. No metro access.

Clark's ★ INTERNATIONAL   The dining room here is an eclectic mix of oak, yellow lamps, live plants, and deer antlers. A slanted ceiling descends over the English-style bar with a fine selection of spirits; in back, a 3m-high (9¾-ft.) glass case showcases a winter garden. Booths and tables are covered with green-and-white checkered tablecloths and are usually occupied by North Americans. Specialties include tenderloin steak with goat cheese, sautéed shrimp with wild mushrooms, and sole with a sparkling wine, cream, and shrimp sauce. A number of pasta and rice dishes are offered as well. A large terrace attracts a fashionable crowd in summer.

Roberto M. Ortiz 1777 (at Quintana). ✆ **11/4801-9502.** Reservations recommended. Main courses $8–$14. AE, DC, MC, V. Daily noon–3:30pm and 7:30pm–midnight. No metro access.

Juana M ★★ 🍴 PARRILLA   This *parrilla* is hard to find but worth the effort and remains one of my favorite dining spots in the city. A family-owned affair, it takes its name from its chic matriarch owner and is known almost solely to Porteños who want to keep this place all to themselves. Juana Marty and her husband, Enrique, can often be seen floating from table to table, checking in on customers to personally chat with them and make sure all is okay. Located in the basement of a former orphanage, which was once part of the city's Catholic University, this neoclassical building is one of the few saved from the highway demolition that created the nearby La Recova area, where Avenida 9 de Julio intersects with Libertador. This cavernous industrial-chic space can seat over 200 patrons. Art covers one of the walls lining the waiter stations. At night, when the space is lit only by candlelight, trendy young patrons flood in, chattering the night away. The menu is simple, high quality, and inexpensive, with a free unlimited salad bar offered with the *parrilla*.

Carlos Pellegrini 1535 (basement; at Libertador). ✆ **11/4326-0462.** www.juanam.com. Main courses $6–$14. AE, MC, V. Sun–Fri noon–5pm and 7:30pm–1am; Sat 8pm–2am. No metro access.

La Biela ★★★ CAFE   Originally a small sidewalk cafe and grocery opened in 1850, La Biela earned its distinction as the rendezvous choice of race-car champions and early car-owning pioneers. La Biela itself is a Spanish word meaning an engine's connecting rod. Black-and-white photos of early Argentine car enthusiasts and racers decorate the huge dining room. Today artists, politicians, and neighborhood executives (as well as a very large number of tourists) all frequent La Biela, which serves breakfast, informal lunch plates, ice cream, and crepes. The outdoor terrace sits beneath an enormous 19th-century ombu tree, opposite the church of Nuestra Señora del Pinar and the adjoining Recoleta Cemetery. You'll often see live street tango under the tree on weekends. This place ranks among the most important cafes in the city and is a protected *bar notable*. It has some of the best sidewalk viewing anywhere in Recoleta, but I also love looking into La Biela's windows at night, when the place takes on a sepia glow. You might just feel like you're in Paris when you come here.

Av. Quintana 596 (at Alvear). ✆ **11/4804-0449.** www.labiela.com. Main courses $3–$12. V. Daily 7am–3am. No metro access.

San Telmo

EXPENSIVE

Brasserie Petanque ★★ 📷 FRENCH   The Swiss-born owner of this restaurant, Pascal Meyer, made this new brasserie, opened in 2006, look like an old one, with walls painted in soft yellows, old advertising posters, and other decorations such as French flags politely tucked into corners. The stunning tile floor was redone in a turn-of-the-last-century style. The menu is in French and Spanish, and offers such specialties as steak tartare, lemon chicken, trout with almonds, and beef bordelaise. Chef Sebastian Fouillade worked with Alain Ducasse. While on the pricey side for dinner, lunch is very reasonable, especially the three-course menu for $12.

Defensa 596 (at Mexico). ☎ **11/4342-7930.** www.brasseriepetanque.com. Main courses $8–$25. AE, DC, MC, V. Sun–Fri 12:30–3:30pm; Tues–Sun 8:30pm–midnight. Metro: Independencia.

647 Club ★★ 🔲 INTERNATIONAL/MEDITERRANEAN   Tucked away in an obscure part of San Telmo, 647 Club is among the most romantic of restaurants in Buenos Aires. Crystal chandeliers, red walls, and marbleized, gold-flecked mirrors give a retro, nightclub atmosphere. The cuisine is a mix of European influences, heavy on French and Italian touches. Look for such creative starters as the pastry confection duck strudel layered with brie cheese, and smothered in a molasses sauce, or goat sweetbreads drizzled in truffle oil with tomato chimichurri. Main dishes are elaborate, with such ingredients as a risotto made from corn, held together with mascarpone and dotted with sautéed portobello mushrooms, beans, and broccoli; or veal ravioli with toasted almonds. Argentine standbys, such as rib-eye steak, are reinvented as kabobs with a special sauce. You might just come for drinks, however, to check out the atmosphere.

647 Tacuari (at Chile). ☎ **11/4331-3026.** www.club647.com. Reservations recommended. Main courses $15–$20. AE, V. Mon–Sat 8pm–1am, later Fri–Sat. Metro: Independencia.

MODERATE

Bar El Federal ★★ 🔲 ARGENTINE/CAFE   This bar and restaurant, on a quiet corner in San Telmo, presents a beautiful step back in time. Fortunately, as *bar notable,* it will stay that way forever. The first thing that strikes you is the massive, carved-wood and stained-glass ornamental stand over the bar area. Local patrons sit at the old tables whiling away their time, chatting, or sitting with a book and drinking tea or espresso. The original tile floor remains, and old signs, portraits, and small antique machines decorate this space. In business since 1864, Bar El Federal is among the most Porteño of places in San Telmo, a neighborhood with more of these establishments than any other area. Some of the staff has been here for decades on end, and proudly so. Food is a collection of small, simple things, mostly sandwiches, steaks, and *lomos,* with a very large salad selection. Excellent pastries round out the menu.

Corner of Perú and Carlos Calvo. ☎ **11/4300-4313.** Main courses $3–$10. AE, MC, V. Sun–Thurs 7am–2am; Fri–Sat 7am–4am. Metro: Independencia.

El Desnivel ★ PARRILLA   The name of this venue means disorganized in Spanish, and its haphazard layout certainly is. Serving mostly thick, well-cooked, and fatty steaks, this is one of San Telmo's best *parrillas.* Once almost a secret, it has become very popular with tourists. Authenticity abounds, however, on Sunday or when a game is on television, when large local crowds come to watch and eat under the blaring TV screen suspended over the dining area. The decor in this two-level restaurant is unassuming, home style, and full of mismatched wooden chairs, tablecloths, and silverware. Unlike many other local restaurants that have inflated their prices in recent years, this *parrilla* has maintained its reasonably priced menu.

Defensa 855 (at Independencia). ☎ **11/4300-9081.** Main courses $5–$12. No credit cards. Daily noon–4pm and 8pm–1am. Metro: Independencia.

La Brigada ★★★ ARGENTINE   Known as one of the best *parrillas* in San Telmo, La Brigada is reminiscent of the Pampas, with gaucho memorabilia filling the restaurant. White-linen tablecloths and tango music complement the atmosphere. An upstairs dining room faces an excellent walled wine rack. The best choices include the *asado* (short rib roast), *lomo* (sirloin steak, prepared with a mushroom or pepper sauce), baby beef (an enormous 850g/30 oz., served for two), and the *mollejas de chivito al verdero* (young goat sweetbreads in a scallion sauce). The waiters are exceedingly nice and professional. For a period of time, management seemed unhappy that tourists had flooded this venue, driving locals away from this San Telmo favorite. A compromise seems to have been reached, however, with tourists often shunted to the lower floor near the bar, while locals sit in the old portion of the restaurant and upstairs.

Estados Unidos 465 (at Bolívar). ☎ **11/4361-5557.** Reservations recommended. Main courses $4–$25. AE, DC, MC, V. Daily noon–3pm and 8pm–midnight. Metro: Constitución.

La Coruña ★★ 📷 CAFE/ARGENTINE   This extremely authentic old cafe and restaurant bar, another of the *cafés notables* protected by law, is the kind of place where you'd expect your grandfather to have eaten when he was a teenager. This neighborhood hub draws young and old alike, who catch soccer games on television or quietly chat away as they order beer, small snacks, and sandwiches. The TV seems to be the only modern thing in here. Music plays from a wooden tabletop radio that must be from the 1950s, and two wooden refrigerators, dating from who knows when, are still used to store food. José Moreira and Manuela Lopéz, the old couple who own the place, obviously believe that if it ain't broke, there's no reason for a new one.

Bolívar 994 (at Carlos Calvo). ☎ **11/4362-7637.** Main courses $2–$6. No credit cards. Daily 9am–10pm. Metro: Independencia.

INEXPENSIVE

Medio y Medio ★ URUGUAYAN   This place serves Uruguayan *chivitos*, which are *lomo* sandwiches. *Lomo* takes on a different meaning in Uruguay than in Argentina. In Argentina, it is only a cut of beef; in Uruguay, it can be steer, pork, or chicken, cut flat as a filet, served as a hot sandwich with a slice of ham, cheese, and an egg, with a garnish of tomatoes and lettuce. This is a crowded, busy place, especially at night when patrons sit outside under a canopy, at tables painted with *fileteado,* an Italian art of painted filigree borders that has become quintessentially Argentine. Periodically, there are live music and folkloric dance shows, but they are not on a set schedule as they were in our last edition.

Chile 316 (at Defensa). ☎ **11/4300-7007.** Main courses $4–$10. No credit cards. Mon–Tues noon–2am; Wed noon–3am; Thurs noon–4am; Fri noon–8am; Sat 24 hr. Metro: Independencia.

La Boca

There is no convenient subway service to this neighborhood. Wandering at night is not recommended.

MODERATE

El Obrero ★★★ ☺ PARRILLA/ITALIAN/ARGENTINE   Two brothers from Barcelona, Marcelino and Francisco Castro, started this wonderful institution in 1954 in a remote, hard-to-find part of La Boca. Sadly, Francisco died and advanced age has meant that Marcelino no longer is able to work in the place. Fortunately, Marcelino's children, Juan Carlos, Pablo, and Silvia, have taken over and give the place the loving care their relatives once did, personally waiting tables along with the staff. Here, you'll dine on thick, juicy, perfectly cooked steaks. Italian food, including excellent calamari, fish, and chicken are also in the offerings. Ask about half versions of the items on the menu, perfect for kids without letting anything go to waste. Lots of Boca Juniors and other sports memorabilia hanging on the walls remind you that you're in one of the most important *fútbol* (soccer) neighborhoods in the world. This is one of the only places I recommend for serious eating in La Boca, but tables fill up rapidly by 9pm, so reserve or come earlier. Note that you should arrive here by cab and have the restaurant call a cab for you when you leave at night. I cannot stress enough that El Obrero is one of the best restaurants in Buenos Aires based on food and family atmosphere and should not be missed. However, though I have never personally had a problem in La Boca, it is considered a dangerous neighborhood at night and you should not wander around near the restaurant.

Agustin R. Caffarena 64 (at Caboto). ℂ **11/4362-9912.** www.bodegonelobrero.com.ar. Main courses $6-$15. No credit cards. Mon-Sat noon-4pm and 8:30pm-midnight (sometimes later). No metro access.

La Perla CAFE/ARGENTINE   This ancient cafe and bar is one of Buenos Aires's *cafés notables*. It dates from 1899 and has a beautiful interior, loaded with photos of the owners mingling with important visitors from around the world who have come to visit La Boca and this important stop on the tourist circuit. U.S. President Bill Clinton is among the luminaries, and his image is among those most highlighted. Pizzas, *picadas* (cut pieces of meat and cheese), and a range of coffees and drinks are on offer. If you're in La Boca, it's a good place to have a drink and soak up some atmosphere. Ironically, inflationary pressures throughout Buenos Aires mean that this is now a reasonably priced venue, and large numbers of locals often come now in a way they didn't before, adding authenticity to the bar.

Pedro de Mendoza 1899 (at Caminito). ℂ **11/4301-2985.** Main courses $4-$12. No credit cards. Daily 7am-9pm. No metro access.

Barrio Norte
MODERATE
Clásica y Moderna ★★ ▥ARGENTINE   This restaurant helped save an important bookstore from extinction. The bookstore opened in this location in 1938, though the company dates from 1918. Emilio Robert Diaz was the original owner, and now his grandchildren run the place. In 1988, books were relegated to the back to make way for diners, but this is still one of the best bookstores for English-speaking tourists in the city. You'll find Buenos Aires photo and history books, as well as Argentine short-story collections translated into English. While this is a protected *café notable,* the interior has been completely stripped down to the exposed brick, giving the place a dark, industrial feel. Decorations overhead include old bicycles and signs. It is a pleasant relaxed space, where it's easy to chat with the staff as you dine or sit at the bar. There are many light and healthful choices such as salads and soy burgers on the menu. Mixed drinks start at about $6. Events of all kinds are held here too, from literary readings to plays, dance shows, and art exhibitions. Shows are held Wednesday through Saturday starting around 10pm; some nights there are two shows, the second one beginning after midnight.

Callao 892 (at Córdoba). ✆ **11/4812-8707** or 4811-3670. Reservations recommended for shows. Main courses $5-$15. AE, MC, V. Daily 8am-1am, sometimes later Fri-Sat. Bookstore: Mon-Sat 9am-1am; Sun 5pm-1am. Metro: Callao.

Palermo

VERY EXPENSIVE

Casa Cruz ★★ 🏛 ITALIAN/INTERNATIONAL   Casa Cruz is one of the city's chicest restaurants. With its enormous polished-brass doors, you almost feel like you are entering a nightclub, and inside, the dark modern interior maintains the theme. The impressive round bar, always decorated with fresh flower arrangements, is the first thing you'll see before continuing on into the spacious dining area full of polished woods and red upholstery. The place takes its name from its original owner, Juan Santa Cruz. The menu here is eclectic and interesting, overseen by the very creative chef Germán Martitegui, who oversees Olsen and Tegui. Rabbit, sea bass, Parma ham rolls, and other interesting and exotic ingredients go into the many flavorful dishes.

Uriarte 1658 (at Honduras). ✆ **11/4833-1112.** www.casacruz-restaurant.com. Reservations highly recommended. Main courses $25-$45. AE, MC, V. Mon-Sat 8:30pm-3am, later on weekends. No metro access.

Tegui ★★★ 🏛 MEDITERRANEAN/INTERNATIONAL   Tegui is star chef Germán Martitegui's latest venture in Buenos Aires dining, a place he pretends to want to hide. Opened in 2009, there's a virtually unreadable name on a door to a building that's covered in graffiti. Inside, the venue is dimly lit, giving a sense of entering a secret club. The menu is a mix of Mediterranean influences, along with skillfully crafted retakes of Argentine basics, such as veal tenderloin covered in Brazilian manioc (cassava) flour nestling an egg, matched with potatoes and *chimichurri*. Other items are playful combinations of texture and taste, like shrimp ravioli paired with scallop foam and sweet mango. The place is tiny and narrow, seating only 45, the ebony-and-cream vertically striped walls creating an optical illusion leading to the brilliantly lit open kitchen where the staff watches your reaction to the dishes they have created. It's an especially romantic option for couples visiting Buenos Aires. Food may be ordered la carte, or in a tiered system of courses.

Costa Rica 5852 (at Ravignani). ✆ **11/5291-3333.** www.tegui.com.ar. Reservations highly recommended. Main courses $15-$40. AE, MC, V. Tues-Sat 12:30-4pm and 8:30pm-12:30am, later on Fri-Sat. Metro: Ministro Carranza.

EXPENSIVE

Cluny ★★★ INTERNATIONAL/ARGENTINE   Cluny is casual but elegant, looking more like a modernist living room than a dining room, with neutral color patterns and bursts of burnt orange and mauve. A loft space with a filtration system for smoking sits above it all and is excellent for hiding away for private conversations or romance. Others choose to dine outside in the patio garden in the restaurant's front space. Sinatra and bossa nova music from the 1960s add to the soft, casual atmosphere. The food, overseen by chefs Luis Cambre and Juan Manuel Juarez, is the highlight here, with an emphasis on fish and fowl, from prawn risotto to spider crabs and duck magret. There are also many salmon and codfish dishes, and beef, unlike in other Argentine restaurants, seems to be a second thought here, though it is well prepared, especially the veal and risotto. The extensive wine list runs over eight pages, offering the finest Argentine vintages from Catena Zapata to French imports hitting more than $250 a bottle. In the afternoon Cluny offers a fine British tea service, a distinctive feature more associated with the old dowager hotels in the center of the city rather than young and chic Palermo Viejo.

El Salvador 4618 (at Malabia). © **11/4831-7176.** Reservations highly recommended. Main courses $15–$20. AE, MC, V. Mon–Sat 12:30–4pm, 4–7:30pm (teatime), and 8pm–1am (sometimes later). Metro: Plaza Italia.

Meridiano 58 ★★ 🍴ARGENTINE/INTERNATIONAL   This moody Argentine restaurant has an aura of Zen chic. During the day, you'll notice its Argentine touches, such as Salta Indian designs, leather lounge sofas, and tables with dark leather placemats. At night, when the staircase is lit with candles and the water fountain is on, you're in a new romantic world. The restaurant has three levels, plus a torchlit terrace, all overseen by waiters in gauzy outfits with Nehru collars. In spite of these slightly Asian touches, the food is largely Argentine, overseen by Chef Gustavo Soria. It is "elaborado," or ornate Argentine, with many of the meats marinated, such as the beef with mushrooms and herbs. Desserts are worth a trip here, especially the chocolate mousse with passion fruit or the orange flan with ginger and coconut. Prix-fixe lunch and dinner menus run from $15 to $20, Monday to Thursday. The restaurant's name refers Buenos Aires's location on the globe, Meridian 58.

J.L. Borges 1689 (at El Salvador). © **11/4833-3443.** Main courses $10–$20. AE, DC, MC, V. Daily noon–1am, later Sat–Sun. Metro: Plaza Italia.

Olsen ★★ SCANDINAVIAN/SEAFOOD   A bit of Scandinavia has landed in Argentina. Olsen is built into what was once a warehouse, and it soars to churchlike proportions with a mezzanine overlooking the main dining area. The interior, complete with a central round metal fireplace, has a 1960s mod feel to it, decorated in blond woods. The place is set apart from the street by a large wooden fence, which leads into a tranquil patio garden overgrown with vines, complete with a metal sculpture fountain on an adjacent wall and a few chairs and tables. They sink into the grass, giving the feeling of a living room succumbing to nature. Olsen, overseen by Germán Martitegui, who also oversees Casa Cruz and Tegui, is very popular with tourists and locals alike. Starters are fun and meant to be shared, such as an excellent selection of bagels, tiny pancakes, smoked salmon, smoked herring, caviar, and flavored cheeses and butters. Fish is the main point of this place, and a few of the meat dishes, though flavorful, tend to be on the dry side. Many people come just for the bar, with its enormous vodka selection kept in special super-cold freezers. Absolut rules this part of the restaurant and is available by the shot or the bottle. Their Sunday brunch is worth a try.

Gorriti 5870 (at Carranza). © **11/4776-7677.** restaurantolsen@netizon.com.ar. Reservations recommended. Main courses $12–$25. AE, MC, V. Tues–Thurs noon–1am; Fri–Sat 12:30pm–2:30am (sometimes later); Sun 10am–1am. No metro access.

Prodeo Lounge & Suites ★★ INTERNATIONAL/SEAFOOD   Prodeo Lounge & Suites opened in Palermo Soho in mid-2010 by New Jersey native Michael Abridello. Here, you'll find a sleek industrial grey interior, where a lighted glass block pathway leads you to white leather booths, an outdoor poolside dining patio, and a second floor level with an open atrium overlooking the bar. There are cool water elements, from the fountain at the entrance to the carp pond with submerged Buddha. Some weekends there are DJs and the place gets packed for drinks. In fact they also offer a class on bartending if you'd like to try your hand. Dutch chef Jeroen Van den Bos, who has worked throughout Europe and most recently in Aruba, oversees the kitchen. The menu offers creative and playful combinations, such as grilled bass, served on a bed of soba noodles flavored with leeks, sesame, and peanuts, along with pineapple, cilantro, and jalapeño salsa. Homages to beef, lamb, and chicken are also creatively done; many vegetarian options and even a gluten-free menu round out the offerings. On Sunday, try their brunch, noon to 4pm. The Suites portion of the title is a planned hotel above the restaurant, still in the works at the time of this writing.

Gorriti 5374 (btw. Godoy Cruz and Altacalco). ✆ **11/4831-4471.** www.prodeolounge.com. Reservations recommended. Main courses $10–$15. AE, MC, V. Tues–Sat 7pm–3am; Sun noon–4pm. Metro: Palermo.

Sudestada ★ VIETNAMESE/ASIAN/THAI   Inside this simply decorated restaurant, a Zen-like white and black, you'll find some of the best Asian cuisine in Buenos Aires. Sudestada is a mix of Vietnamese, Thai, and other Oriental cuisines. Look for the special wok menu, or choose pork with lemon grass, rabbit with rice and vegetables, or interesting desserts such as lychee pie. Argentine beef is great, but if you're looking for a change, this is a wonderful choice.

Guatemala 5602 (at Fitzroy). ✆ **11/4776-3777.** www.sudestadabuenosaires.com. Main courses $12–$20. AE, MC, V. Mon–Sat noon–3:30pm; Mon–Thurs 8pm–midnight; Fri–Sat 8pm–1am. Metro: Palermo.

Sullivan's Drink House IRISH/ARGENTINE   Sullivan's still retains its green Emerald Isle decor, but has overhauled its menu, bringing it more in line with traditional Argentine fare. That means more beef and other *parrilla* items, and just a smattering of traditional Irish food. Sandwiches and children's meals are also on the menu. Windows to the street give great views, and a VIP lounge decorated in Old English style is upstairs, serving as a cigar bar. On the rooftop there's a covered terrace offering even more dining space. In spite of the change in food, if you have come to drink as the Irish do, well, you're definitely in luck. Sullivan's has one of the most extensive imported whiskey menus in town, beginning at about $5 per serving. The luck of the Irish is indeed evident in the history of this restaurant: They opened on December 20, 2001, just days before the peso crisis, yet they have survived. If you're in Buenos Aires on St. Patrick's Day, this is the place to be.

El Salvador 4919 (at Borges). ✆ **11/4832-6442.** Main courses $7–$12. AE, MC, V. Mon–Thurs 10:30am–2 or 3am; Fri–Sat 10:30am–5am; Sun noon–2:30am. Metro: Scalabrini Ortiz.

Te Mataré Ramírez ★★★ 📖 INTERNATIONAL/FRENCH   This is perhaps the most interesting and creative dining experience in Buenos Aires. Its symbol, an aroused fork with an extended and upright prong, gives you a clue as to the erotic nature of the restaurant. The name of the restaurant literally means "I am going to kill you, Ramírez." It comes from playful arguments the owner would have with a Casanova-esque friend, and this was a threat the friend often heard from husbands with whose wives he was having affairs. It's an erotic restaurant, both in food and decor. The food is an interesting mix of flavors and textures. Sensual combinations include garlic and sun-dried tomatoes mixed with sweet elements and poured over sautéed or marinated meats. The ceilings are decorated with paintings of naked men and women with nothing more than high-heeled shoes, mixed in with naughty cherubs. Erotic art hangs on the walls, all of it for sale. The lighting is boudoir red, and wine is consumed out of antique cut-crystal glasses that cast red sparkles on the tablecloths. Black-clothed actors perform playfully racy shows on a small stage here, using hand-held puppets that do very naughty things. It's hard to describe this place as romantic, but certainly a dinner here might lead to post-meal hanky-panky. Slow, soft music such as jazz and bossa nova plays as you eat, adding to the mood for love.

Gorritti 5054 (btw. Thames and Serrano). *C* **11/4831-9156.** www.tematareramirez.com. Reservations recommended. Main courses $17–$25. AE, MC, V. Daily 8:30pm–1am, sometimes later on weekends. Metro: Scalabrini Ortiz.

MODERATE

Campo Bravo ★★ 🍴 PARRILLA/ARGENTINE   Everyone I know who knows Buenos Aires tests me on this place. Do I know of it, and what do I think? Well, I know it, and I love it! This place serves as the virtual center of the Las Cañitas dining scene. It's relaxed during the day but insane at night. Dining on the sidewalk here, you'll get a great view of the glamorous crowds emerging from taxis to kick off their night in this fun neighborhood. The *parrilla* serves up basic Argentine cuisine, and its enormous slabs of meat are served on wooden boards. A large, efficient waitstaff will take care of you, but they can't do anything about the long wait for an outside table on weekends—sometimes as long as 40 minutes to an hour. There's no way around that, since they don't accept reservations. So do as the locals do on Saturday night: Get a glass of champagne and sip it on the street amid what looks like a well-dressed and over-age frat party. A limited wine selection and imported whiskeys are also part of the drink selection. Can't handle the late nights in Argentina? Well, then you're in luck—they don't close between lunch and dinner, so people used to North American dining schedules can still enjoy a great meal here without a wait.

Báez 292 (at Arévalo). *C* **11/4514-5820.** www.campobravo.com.ar. Main courses $8–$15. AE, MC. Mon 6pm–4am; Tues–Sun 11:30am–4am (often later on weekends). Metro: Ministro Carranza.

De Olivas i Lustres ★★ MEDITERRANEAN/ARGENTINE   This magical restaurant was opened in Palermo Viejo in the 1990s by Miguel Moreno, along with his business partner and chef, Sebastián Tarica, building the foundation for the gastronomic paradise the neighborhood would soon become. The dining room displays eccentric antiques, olive jars, and wine bottles. The reasonably priced menu celebrates Mediterranean cuisine, with light soups, fresh fish, and sautéed vegetables as its focus. The breast of duck with lemon and honey is mouthwatering; there are also a number of *tapeos*—appetizer-size dishes. Best of all: For about $32 per person, you and your partner can share 15 sensational small plates—brought out individually, and building in adventurousness—over the course of a couple of hours. What I find most unique in the restaurant beyond the Mediterranean fare is the use of native and Incan ingredients in various dishes. If you've ever wanted to try alligator or llama, this is the place to do it.

Gorritti 3972 (at Medrano). *C* **11/4867-3388.** www.deolivasilustres.com.ar. Reservations recommended. Main courses $8–$12. AE, MC, V. Mon–Thurs 8:30pm–midnight; Fri–Sat 8:30pm–1am. Metro: Scalabrini Ortiz.

El Estanciero ★ 🍴 PARRILLA   In most of the restaurants in the Las Cañitas section of Palermo, it's all about the glamour. Here, however, in the *parrilla* El Estanciero, it's all about the beef, which I would argue is the best in the neighborhood. The portions are not the largest, but the cuts are amazingly flavorful, with just the right mix of fat to add tenderness. If you order the steak rare (*jugoso*), they know not to serve it nearly raw. The restaurant is in two levels, with sidewalk seating at the entrance and a covered open-air terrace above. The subtle gaucho-accented decor doesn't overwhelm the senses with kitsch. Never as crowded as the other restaurants lining the street, it's a great option when the lines are too long at nearby hot spots.

Báez 202 (at Arguibel). © **11/4899-0951.** Main courses $6–$15. AE, MC, V. Daily noon–4pm and 8pm–1am (until 2am weekends). Metro: Ministro Carranza.

Garbis ★★ ☺ MIDDLE EASTERN If you're looking for great Middle Eastern food at reasonable prices or a spot to entertain the kids, Garbis has the answer. Kabobs, falafel, lamb, and other Middle Eastern mainstays are all on the menu including some as kid-size portions, along with great, friendly service. The desert kitsch—in the form of tiled walls and brilliant colors—makes you think you've wound up far away from Argentina. A children's entertainment center will keep the kids happy while you dine. Tarot card readings on select days add fun for the adults. Call for the mystic's schedule. This is a chain, with additional restaurants in Belgrano and Villa Crespo.

Scalabrini Ortiz 3190 (at Cerviño). © **11/4511-6600.** www.garbis.com.ar. Main courses $6–$15. AE, MC, V. Daily 11am–3pm and 7–11:30pm. Metro: Scalabrini Ortiz.

Novecento ★★★ INTERNATIONAL With a sister restaurant in New York's SoHo, Novecento was a pioneer restaurant in Palermo's Las Cañitas neighborhood. Fashionable Porteños pack the New York–style bistro by 11pm, clinking wineglasses under a Canal Street sign or opting for the busy outdoor terrace. Waiters rush to keep their clients happy, with dishes such as salmon carpaccio and steak salad. The pastas and risotto are mouthwatering, but you may prefer a steak au poivre or a chicken brochette. Other wonderful choices include filet mignon, grilled Pacific salmon, and penne with wild mushrooms. Top it off with an Argentine wine. At night, by candlelight, it makes a romantic choice for couples. A large, separate, slightly sterile side room is available for spillover or to rent for private parties.

Báez 199 (at Arguibel). © **11/4778-1900.** www.novecento.com. Reservations recommended. Main courses $10–$18. AE, DC, MC, V. Daily noon–4pm and 8pm–2am; Sun brunch 8am–noon. Metro: Ministro Carranza.

Sushi Club JAPANESE This restaurant is part of a very popular chain, with many locations throughout the city, but this is one of its nicest outlets. The Sushi Club serves sushi and other Japanese cuisine in a modern clublike interior, with a chic, creamy monotone color and moody lighting. Fish is a highlight of the menu, as is beef with Japanese seasonings. The sushi roll selection is enormous and creative; many of the offerings pay tribute to other international cuisines, using ingredients to match.

Báez 268 (at Arevalo). © **0-810/222-SUSHI** (78744; toll-free) or 11/4772-5270. www.sushiclubweb.com.ar. Main courses $6–$15. AE, DC, MC, V. Sun–Wed noon–1am; Thurs noon–1:30am; Fri–Sat noon–2am. Metro: Carranza.

Utopia Bar ARGENTINE/INTERNATIONAL More cozy and calm than some of the other bars that surround Plaza Serrano, this is an excellent place to grab a drink and a bite in this very trendy and busy neighborhood. Yellow walls and soothing, rustic wooden tables add a sense of calm, though the live music, scheduled on an irregular basis, can be loud at times. There is an emphasis on the drinks here, and breakfast has a large selection of flavored coffees, some prepared with whiskey. At night, pizza and sandwiches make up the bulk of the offerings. The upstairs, open-air terrace on the roof of the bar is one of the best places to sit, but it's small and hard to claim a spot. If a table is open, grab it.

Serrano 1590 (at Plaza Serrano). ℘ **11/4831-8572.** Main courses $2–$8. AE, MC, V. Daily 24 hr. Metro: Plaza Italia.

INEXPENSIVE

Bio ★★ 🍴 VEGETARIAN/MEDITERRANEAN   In a nation where meat reigns supreme, finding an organic vegetarian restaurant is a near impossibility. Bio is the exception, overseen by owner Claudia Carrara. Their "meat" is made on the premises from wheat and then marinated to add more flavor, making for an elevated, tasty variation on a hamburger. All the ingredients are organic, grown or produced in Argentina. Piles of organic cheese line the counters near the chefs, who are happy to explain the processes by which they work. Quinoa, the ancient Incan grain, is also used in many of the dishes, some of which they describe as Mediterranean-Asian fusion, though with the combinations of so many unusual ingredients, anything goes. You have to try the quinoa risotto, one of the restaurant's main specialties, though everything here is simply delicious and fresh. Chairs and tables are painted a spring green, and, on warm days, a few tables are scattered on the sidewalk outside. This is also a great place for veg-heads to go shopping for snacks to bring back to their hotel. They have a small shop inside with organic chips, teas, cheeses, and even organic wine. They also do takeout—a delight if you want to bring something home with you. Perhaps best of all is learning to cook organically: Check the website for class details.

Humboldt 2199 (at Guatemala). ℘ **11/4774-3880.** www.biorestaurant.com.ar. Main courses $8–$10. No credit cards. Mon 9am–5pm; Tues–Sun 9am–1am (often later on weekends). No metro access.

Confitería del Botánico CAFE/ARGENTINE   Stop here after visiting the nearby zoo or Botanical Gardens. It's on a pleasant corner on busy Santa Fe, but the green spaces of the gardens and Plaza Siria give it a more tranquil feel. Enormous windows seem to bring the park inside. Continental breakfast here is inexpensive, and you can also order from the entire menu any time of day (omelets from the dinner menu make a hearty breakfast). Lunch specials run $6 to $10. They also do takeout, which makes a great picnic for the park or zoo.

Av. Santa Fe (at República Siria). ℘ **11/4833-5515.** Main courses $4–$8. AE, MC, V. Sun–Fri 6:30am–midnight; Sat 6:30am–2am. Metro: Plaza Italia.

Macondo Bar ★★ INTERNATIONAL/ARGENTINE   Macondo Bar is one of the stars of Plaza Serrano, with sidewalk seating and lots of levels overlooking the action. Inside, the restaurant twists around several staircases and low ceilings. It's a loud and busy place, for sure, but the setup creates a sense of intimacy if you come here with friends to share conversation over drinks and a meal. Sandwiches, pizzas, salads, and *picadas* make up the menu. DJs blast music of all kinds through the bar, from folkloric to techno to electronica. Technically, there's no live music, but sometimes people come around and play on the street in front of the bar.

Borges 1810 (at Plaza Serrano). ℘ **11/4831-4174.** Main courses $3–$8. No credit cards. Mon–Thurs 6pm–4am; Fri–Sat 5pm–7am; Sun 5pm–3am. Metro: Plaza Italia.

Tazz ★ MEXICAN   In an old house, like so many other restaurants in Palermo Viejo, Tazz is among the best spots for outdoor seating on all of Plaza Serrano. Step inside, however, and you'll think you've entered the dining hall of a spaceship, with blue glowing lights and walls, mod aluminum panels, and billiard table after billiard table. The booths look like little emergency space capsules that can be released if the mother ship gets attacked. The bulk of the menu is Mexican. Pitchers of sangria and margaritas add to the fun. More of a bar than a restaurant, this place is very popular with a young clientele.

Serrano 1556 (at Plaza Serrano). ✆ **11/4833-5164.** www.tazzbars.com. Main courses $6–$12. No credit cards. Sun–Thurs noon–3am; Fri–Sat noon–6am. Metro: Plaza Italia.

Viejo Agump ★ 🏨 MIDDLE EASTERN   In the heart of the old Armenian section of Buenos Aires, owner Elizabeth Hounanjian offers authentic Middle Eastern cuisine and a new hub for her compatriots ("agump" means "club" or "meeting place" in Armenian), in the shadows of the Armenian church and the community center. The exposed-brick interior of the old house adds a touch of comfort to the dining area, where mainstays include kabobs and baklava. Sidewalk seating on this tree-lined street is a delight in warm weather. A special menu is offered for about $14, with appetizer, main dish, and a drink. On weekends, Arabic belly dancing and coffee-bean readings heighten the exotic atmosphere. To schedule a reading, contact the mystic, Roxana Banklian (✆ **11/15-4185-2225** [mobile]; roxanabanklian@arnet.com.ar).

Armenia 1382 (at José Antonio Cabrera). ✆ **11/4773-5081.** www.viejoagump.com.ar. Main courses $6–$12. No credit cards. Mon–Thurs 8am–midnight; Fri 8am–2am; Sat 11am–2am. Metro: Scalabrini Ortiz.

Congreso
MODERATE

La Moncloa ★ 🍴 CAFE   The surrounding trees here give a calming sense to sidewalk eating in what is normally a busy area on a street just off Plaza Congreso. La Moncloa takes its name from a famous Spanish palace. Basic Argentine fare such as empanadas, steaks, and salads is on offer, along with croissant sandwiches and an extensive dessert menu. There is also a large selection of pork dishes, including the tempting pork in white-wine sauce. Still, for the diet conscious, there is also a low-calorie menu with vegetarian offerings. Whatever you order, I recommend taking the time for a break in this restaurant's parklike setting. Flavored and alcoholic coffees, one of their specialties, are about $5. If you don't have time to eat, stop by and grab a menu, as they'll deliver to local hotels.

Av. de Mayo 1500 (at Sáenz Peña). ✆ **11/4381-3357** or 4382-7194. Main courses $4–$12. AE, DC, MC, V. Daily 7:30am–2am. Metro: Sáenz Peña.

Plaza Asturias ★★ 🏨 SPANISH/ITALIAN/ARGENTINE   This decades-old place on Avenida de Mayo is about as authentic as it gets, packed mostly with Porteños who want to keep this place to themselves. Food has touches of Italian, Argentine, and most importantly, authentic Spanish cuisine. They are so busy and have to keep so much food on hand that there are legs of cured ham literally hanging from the rafters over the diners' heads. Steaks are as thick as the crowds waiting to get into this place, and among their specialties are Spanish casseroles and lots of food with various sauces. Fish is also a big highlight.

Av. de Mayo 1199 (at Salta). ✆ **11/4382-7334.** Main courses $6–$12. No credit cards. Daily noon–3am. Metro: Sáenz Peña.

Plaza del Carmen CAFE/ARGENTINE   This is part of a chain, slightly sterile and clean. However, the best part of this cafe is not inside but the view from this corner overlooking Congreso outside. Generally open 24 hours, no matter what time of day it is you can find people having nothing more than croissants and coffee here. Weekdays, the outdoor seating area is a little overwhelming, as there is a huge amount of traffic flowing by this corner. But inside, protected from the noise and the bus and car fumes, everything is just fine. Wait until the weekends, when the sidewalk is less busy and the outdoor area becomes ideal. This restaurant offers standard Argentine cuisine in addition to a healthy choice of salads and other light items. Pizzas, pastas, and other Italian items round out the menu.

Rivadavia 1795 (at Callao). ℰ **11/4374-8477.** Main courses $5–$8. AE, MC, V. Daily 7am–2am. Metro: Congreso.

INEXPENSIVE

Café de Madres de Plaza de Mayo ★★ ☒ CAFE   The official name of this cafe is Çafé Literario Osvaldo Bayer, named for an Argentine political intellectual. This cafe is located inside the lobby of the headquarters and teaching center of the Madres de Plaza de Mayo, just off of Plaza Congreso. What makes the place so special is its location and its left-wing political atmosphere. In few other places in Buenos Aires can you speak so freely with those who had family members disappear during Argentina's military dictatorship, or with young students who have come to study in this building and continue seeking justice in this cause. The Madres bookstore is just to the side of the cafe, and it's full of books and newspapers on liberal causes from throughout Latin America, including the largest collections of books on Che Guevara anywhere in the world. An Argentine native, he is a personal hero to many of the Madres, and his image adorns walls throughout the building. At first just serving snacks and sandwiches, the restaurant now offers light Italian fare, and an outdoor seating area in summer.

Hipólito Yrigoyen 1584 (at Ceballos). ℰ **11/4382-3261.** www.madres.org. Main courses $3–$8. No credit cards. Mon–Fri 8:30am–10:30pm; Sat (and some Sun) 11am–5pm. Metro: Congreso.

La Americana ★★ ARGENTINE/ITALIAN   This place calls itself "La Reina de las Empanadas" (the Queen of Empanadas), and that it is. They offer an enormous range of empanadas, all made with a very light dough and slightly burned edges, never heavy or greasy. The place is busy and loud, with the constant din of conversation bouncing off the tile-and-stone walls and the plate-glass windows looking out over Callao. There are tables here as well as a takeout section and an area for standing and eating—some people just can't be bothered to sit and simply scarf down these delicious creations once they get them. Waiters are frantic, scurrying from table to table as people change their minds after one bite and order extra rounds. You'll have to keep reminding them of what you ordered if you feel it's taking too much time, but don't blame them: It's just too busy for normal humans to keep up with the pace of the place. Italian specialties such as calzones and pizzas round out the menu choices. Deliveries can be made to nearby hotels.

Callao 83 (at Bartolomé Mitre). ℰ **11/4371-0202.** Main courses $1–$7. No credit cards. Sun–Thurs 7am–2am; Fri–Sat 7am–3am. Metro: Congreso.

Abasto & Once

MODERATE

Al Galope ★ ARGENTINE/PARRILLA/MIDDLE EASTERN/KOSHER   This is one of Buenos Aires's most popular kosher restaurants, located in what was once the main area of Buenos Aires's Jewish community. This place is best described as an Argentine *parrilla* with Middle Eastern accents. It serves wonderfully juicy and yet still kosher slabs of beef, made tender through a special marinating process replacing moisture in the meat after the blood has been removed. The interior is simple, wood paneled, and home style. The family that owns the restaurant oversees its operations; sometimes they argue right in front of you. The menu also features a selection of kosher Argentine wines, and you can take a bottle home with you if you'd like. Middle Eastern fare—such as pitas and hummus as starters or sides, and baklava desserts—is also on hand, as well as fast food such as pastrami sandwiches and salads. Service is low-key; unusually quiet waiters almost seem afraid to approach the tables, but the food more than makes up for it.

Tucumán 2633 (at Pueyrredón). ✆ **11/4963-6888.** Main courses $5–$14. AE, D, MC, V. Sun–Fri noon–3pm; Sun–Thurs 8pm–1am; Sat 9pm–midnight, but times will vary seasonally depending on sunset and Jewish holidays. Metro: Pueyrredón.

INEXPENSIVE

Gardel de Buenos Aires ★ ARGENTINE/ITALIAN   You won't see tango here, but this cafe celebrates the famous tango singer Carlos Gardel in other ways. A clock, with his face at the 12 o'clock position, overlooks the dining area, with its brilliant red tablecloths and rich wood trim. Gardel photos adorn red walls like icons in a Russian church. A papier-mâché mannequin of his likeness juts out from one of the walls. On top of that, his songs play nonstop from loudspeakers. It's a cute diversion, and in spite of the overwhelming kitsch, the food is good. The menu offers Argentine standards such as beef and empanadas, salads, pastas, desserts, sandwiches, pizzas, and other Italian specialties. The house specialty is *fugazzata*—a kind of stuffed pizza. Service is fast and friendly, so this is a great place for grabbing a quick coffee or a sandwich. It's open 24 hours Friday and Saturday, so come by and toast Gardel after a night on the town tangoing, with a drink from their extensive menu. Takeout available.

Entre Ríos 796 (at Independencia). ✆ **11/4381-4170.** Main courses $3–$10. AE, MC, V. Sun–Thurs 6am–1am; Fri–Sat 24 hr. Metro: Entre Ríos.

Kosher McDonald's ★★ 🍴AMERICAN/KOSHER   Certainly you didn't come all this way to eat at McDonald's. I wouldn't ordinarily tell a traveler to eat here on vacation, but this franchise is clearly unique: This is the only kosher McDonald's outside of Israel in the world, underscoring Buenos Aires's reputation as one of the world's great Jewish centers. Rabbi supervision makes sure that kosher rules are strictly followed here. It's typical McDonald's fare—burgers, fries, salads, fish sandwiches—except that no dairy at all is served here, and the meat is charcoal grilled, rather than fried.

Abasto Shopping Center Food Court, Av. Corrientes 3247 (at Agüero). ✆ **11/4959-3709** or 0800/777-6236 for McDonald's Argentina information hot line. Main courses $2–$6. No credit cards. Sun–Thurs 10am–midnight; Fri 10am–2pm; Sat 9pm–midnight, but times will vary seasonally depending on sunset and Jewish holidays. Metro: Carlos Gardel.

Belgrano

EXPENSIVE

Buddha BA ★ CHINESE   In the heart of Belgrano's Chinatown, this very elegant, two-level Chinese teahouse and restaurant is built into a house, with an adjacent garden and art gallery selling fine Asian art and antiques. The interesting and creatively named menu includes items such as Dragon Fire, a mix of spicy chicken and curried *lomo*; or Buddha Tears, squid in a soy and chicken broth sauce with seasoned vegetables. The atmosphere is very welcoming and makes a great rest stop if you're exploring this neighborhood in depth.

Arribeños 2288 (at Mendoza). ✆ **11/4706-2382.** www.buddhaba.com.ar. Main courses $8–$15. AE, MC, V. Tues–Sun 12:30–3:30pm, 4–7:30pm (tea service), and 8pm–midnight. Metro: Juramento.

SEEING THE SIGHTS

Buenos Aires is wonderful to explore and fairly easy to navigate. The most impressive historical sites surround Plaza de Mayo, although you will certainly experience Argentine history in neighborhoods such as La Boca and San Telmo, too. Don't miss a walk along the riverfront in Puerto Madero or an afternoon among the plazas and cafes of Recoleta or Palermo. Numerous sidewalk cafes offer respite for weary feet, and good public transportation or a quick cab is available to carry you from neighborhood to neighborhood.

Your first stop should be one of the city tourism centers (see "Visitor Information," earlier in this chapter) to pick up a brochure, city map, and advice. You can also ask at your hotel for a copy of "The Golden Map" and *QuickGuide Buenos Aires,* to help you navigate the city and locate its major attractions.

Neighborhoods to Explore

LA BOCA

La Boca, on the banks of the Río Riachuelo, developed originally as a trading center and shipyard. This was the city's first Little Italy, giving the neighborhood its distinct flavor. La Boca is most famous for giving birth to the tango in the numerous bordellos, once known locally as *quilombos,* which once served the largely male population.

The focus of La Boca is the **Caminito,** a pedestrian walkway, named ironically after a tango song about a rural village. The walkway is lined with humorously sculpted statues and murals explaining its history. Surrounding the cobblestone street are corrugated metal houses painted in a hodgepodge of colors, recalling a time when the poor locals decorated with whatever paint was left over from ship maintenance in the nearby harbor. Today many artists live or set up their studios in these houses. Art and souvenir vendors work side by side with tango performers along the Caminito; this Caminito "Fine Arts Fair" is open daily from 10am to 6pm.

A victim of its own success, La Boca has become an obscene tourist trap. While the area is historically important, most of what you will encounter are overpriced souvenir and T-shirt shops and constant harassment from people trying to hand you flyers for mediocre restaurants. In the summer, the smell from the heavily polluted river becomes almost overbearing. This area is a requisite stop, for at least a quick look, but if you are short on time, don't let the visit take up too much of your day. Ironically, with prices climbing throughout Buenos Aires at restaurants geared toward tourists, prices here, once not reasonable, have stabilized, and even locals are beginning to patronize some of them.

The city of Buenos Aires had wonderful plans to rebuild the La Boca waterfront, replant dead and decaying trees on many thoroughfares, and open new museums throughout the neighborhood, as well as connect a tourist train from the Puerto Madero area. Much of this work was planned for the 2010 Bicentennial celebrations, but the train project has been placed on hold. If this is resolved, how it will impact the neighborhood—including gentrification to push out the poor local residents—remains to be seen. It will certainly reduce crime, however, by bringing more foot traffic through the area at night. Enhanced police presence later in the day aimed at protecting tourists has, however, been implemented.

What remains authentic in La Boca is off the beaten path, such as the art galleries and theaters that cater both to locals and tourists, or the world-famous **Estadio de Boca Juniors,** 4 blocks away in a garbage-strewn lot at the corner of calles Del Valle Iberlucea and Brandsen. This is the home of the *fútbol* club Boca Juniors, the team of Diego Maradona who, like his country, went from glory to fiery collapse and back again all in a Buenos Aires minute. Go on game day, when street parties and general debauchery take over the area. For information on *fútbol* games, see the *Buenos Aires Herald.* Wealthy businessman Mauricio Macri, the former president of the Boca Juniors Fútbol Club and current city mayor, opened a museum in the stadium. He claimed to love soccer, but as a political aspirant who hoped to one day become president of Argentina, the Boca Juniors were a wonderful public relations tool.

Use caution, however, if you stray off the Caminito. Surrounding areas can be unsafe, without police presence. Once the shopkeepers go home, so do police officers. At dusk, away from the Caminito, neighborhood residents quietly reclaim the streets and stroll along the waterfront. Most come not from Italy now, but from the poor interior provinces or neighboring countries. You may have your most interesting interactions with locals at this time, but it's risky and it would in no way be advisable for a naive, non-Spanish speaking tourist. The area is also prone to flooding, so be careful to avoid the neighborhood in intense rainfall.

Caution: After nightfall, avoid La Boca altogether.

SAN TELMO

Buenos Aires's oldest neighborhood, San Telmo originally housed the city's elite. When yellow fever struck in the 1870s—aggravated by substandard hygienic conditions in the area—the aristocrats moved north. Poor European immigrants soon filled the neighborhood, and the houses were converted to tenements, called *conventillos.* In 1970, the city passed regulations to restore some of San Telmo's architectural landmarks. Still, gentrification has been a slow process, and the neighborhood maintains a gently decayed, very authentic atmosphere, reminiscent of Cuba's old Havana. It's a bohemian enclave, attracting tourists, locals, and performers daily. The ups and downs of the peso, and Argentina's economy in general, have also meant that a glut of antiques, sold for ready cash, are available for purchase and export. The best shops and markets line **Calle Defensa.**

After Plaza de Mayo, **Plaza Dorrego** is the oldest square in the city. Originally the site of a Bethlehemite monastery, the plaza is also where Argentines met to reconfirm their Declaration of Independence from Spain. On Sunday from 10am to 5pm (and often even later in summer), the city's best **antiques market ★★★** takes over the square, spilling into the surrounding streets. Here, you can buy leather, silver, handicrafts, and antiques, along with other products, and tango and *milonga* dancers perform on the square. The tall, darkly handsome dancer nicknamed El Indio, whose real name is Pedro Benavente, is the star of the plaza, but there are many others who have made their name here as well.

San Telmo is full of tango clubs and shows; one of the most notable is **El Viejo Almacén ★** (at Independencia and Balcarce). The colonial structure was built in 1798 as a general store and hospital, before its reincarnation as the quintessential Argentine tango club. Make sure to go for a show at night (see "Buenos Aires After Dark," later in this chapter). If you get the urge for a tango course while you're in San Telmo, look for signs advertising lessons in the windows of clubs. If you look foreign or unsure enough, teachers might find their way to you anyway, but use caution when

Buenos Aires Sightseeing

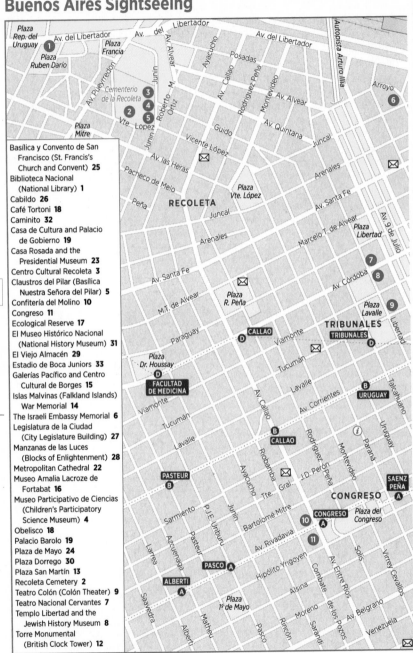

Basílica y Convento de San
  Francisco (St. Francis's
  Church and Convent) **25**
Biblioteca Nacional
  (National Library) **1**
Cabildo **26**
Café Tortoni **18**
Caminito **32**
Casa de Cultura and Palacio
  de Gobierno **19**
Casa Rosada and the
  Presidential Museum **23**
Centro Cultural Recoleta **3**
Claustros del Pilar (Basílica
  Nuestra Señora del Pilar) **5**
Confitería del Molino **10**
Congreso **11**
Ecological Reserve **17**
El Museo Histórico Nacional
  (National History Museum) **31**
El Viejo Almacén **29**
Galerías Pacífico and Centro
  Cultural de Borges **15**
Islas Malvinas (Falkland Islands)
  War Memorial **14**
The Israeli Embassy Memorial **6**
Legislatura de la Ciudad
  (City Legislature Building) **27**
Manzanas de las Luces
  (Blocks of Enlightenment) **28**
Metropolitan Cathedral **22**
Museo Amalia Lacroze de
  Fortabat **16**
Museo Participativo de Ciencias
  (Children's Participatory
  Science Museum) **4**
Obelisco **18**
Palacio Barolo **19**
Plaza de Mayo **24**
Plaza Dorrego **30**
Plaza San Martín **13**
Recoleta Cemetery **2**
Teatro Colón (Colón Theater) **9**
Teatro Nacional Cervantes **7**
Templo Libertad and the
  Jewish History Museum **8**
Torre Monumental
  (British Clock Tower) **12**

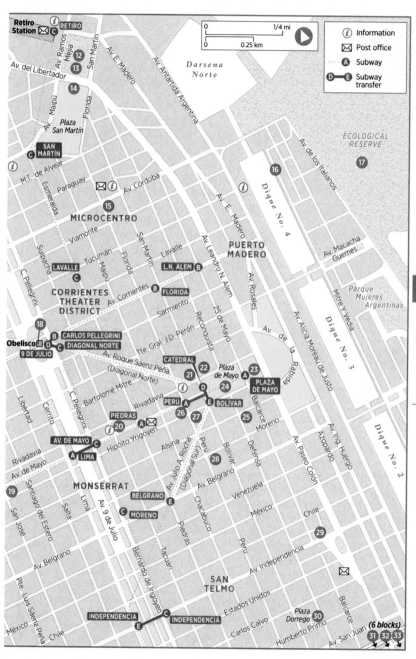

Retiro Station ⊠ Ⓒ RETIRO
Av. Ramos Mejía
12
13
Av. del Libertador
San Martín
Av. E. Madero
Av. Antártida Argentina
14
Florida

Darsena Norte

0 _____ 1/4 mi
0 _____ 0.25 km

ⓘ Information
⊠ Post office
A Subway
Ⓓ━Ⓔ Subway transfer

Plaza San Martín
Ⓒ SAN MARTÍN
ⓘ
M.T. de Alvear
Paraguay
⊠ⓘ
Av. Córdoba
Esmeralda
Maipú
Av. E. Madero
Av. Leandro N. Alem
Av. Rosales

ECOLOGICAL RESERVE
Av. de los Italianos
17
ⓘ
16

MICROCENTRO
15
Viamonte
Tucumán
San Martín
Florida
Lavalle
Suipacha
C. Pellegrini
Ⓒ LAVALLE
Ⓑ L.N. ALEM
PUERTO MADERO

Dique No. 4

CORRIENTES THEATER DISTRICT
Av. Corrientes
Ⓑ FLORIDA
Sarmiento
Reconquista
25 de Mayo
Av. Leandro N. Alem

Av. Macacha Güemes

Parque Mujeres Argentinas

18
Obelisco☐ Ⓑ CARLOS PELLEGRINI
Ⓓ Ⓒ DIAGONAL NORTE
9 DE JULIO
Tte. Gral. J.D. Perón
Av. Roque Sáenz Peña
(Diagonal Norte)
CATEDRAL
21
22
Plaza de Mayo
23 Ⓐ
PLAZA DE MAYO
24
Ⓓ
ⓘ
Bartolomé Mitre
Rivadavia
PERÚ Ⓐ
Ⓔ BOLÍVAR
26
27
Balcarce
25
Moreno
Av. de la Rábida

Dique No. 3

Av. Alicia Moreau de Justo

Libertad
Cerrito
C. Pellegrini
PIEDRAS
ⓘ 20 ⊠
AV. DE MAYO Ⓒ
Ⓐ LIMA
Hipólito Yrigoyen
Alsina
Av. Julio A. Rocha
(Diagonal Sur)
Perú
28
Bolívar
Defensa
Moreno
Av. Paseo Colón

19
Rivadavia
Av. de Mayo
Santiago del Estero
San José
MONSERRAT
Salta
Lima
Av. 9 de Julio
BELGRANO Ⓔ
Ⓒ MORENO
Venezuela
Chacabuco
Av. Belgrano
México
Chile

Dique No. 2

Av. Ing. Huergo
Azopardo

Av. Belgrano
Pte. Luis Sáenz Peña
San José
Piedras
Taclarí
Bernardo de Irigoyen
SAN TELMO
Av. Independencia
Perú
29
⊠

México
Chile
INDEPENDENCIA Ⓒ INDEPENDENCIA
Ⓔ
Estados Unidos
Carlos Calvo
Plaza Dorrego
30
Balcarce
(6 blocks)
Humberto Primo
Av. San Juan
31 32 33

dealing with any stranger who approaches you on the street. Be very wary of pickpockets in this neighborhood.

PALERMO ★★★

"Palermo" is a catchall term for a nebulously defined large chunk of northern Buenos Aires. It encompasses **Palermo** proper, with its park system, also known as **Palermo Alto; Palermo Chico; Palermo Viejo,** which is further divided into **Palermo Soho** and **Palermo Hollywood;** and **Las Cañitas,** next to the city's world-famous polo field.

Palermo Chico is an exclusive neighborhood of elegant mansions off Avenida Libertador, where prices were seemingly unaffected by the peso crisis. This small set of streets, tucked behind the MALBA museum area, has little of interest to tourists besides the beauty of the homes and a few embassy buildings.

Palermo is a neighborhood of parks filled with jacarandas, magnolias, pines, palms, and willows, where families picnic on weekends and couples stroll at sunset. Designed by French architect Charles Thays, the parks take their inspiration from London's Hyde Park and Paris's Bois de Boulogne. Take the metro to Plaza Italia, which lets you out next to the **Jardín Botánico (Botanical Gardens) ★ (© 11/ 4831-2951)** and **Jardín Zoológico (Zoological Gardens) ★ (© 11/4011-9900;** www.zoobuenosaires.com.ar), open dawn to dusk. Stone paths wind their way through the botanical gardens, where locals escape hurried city life reading newspapers on park benches. Flora from throughout South America fills the garden, with over 8,000 plant species from around the world represented. Next door, the city zoo features an impressive diversity of animals, including indigenous birds and monkeys, giant turtles, llamas, elephants, and a polar bear and brown bear habitat. The eclectic kitschy architecture housing the animals, some designed as exotic temples, is as much of a delight as the inhabitants and speaks to the vast wealth and self-conscious architecture from the zoo's turn-of-the-last-century origins. Peacocks and some of the small animals roam free, and feeding is allowed. Kiosks sell special food in the zoo, a wonderful opportunity that children will especially enjoy.

Parque Tres de Febrero ★★, a 400-hectare (1,000-acre) paradise of trees, lakes, and walking trails, begins just past the lovely **Rose Garden ★** off Avenida Sarmiento. In summer, paddleboats are rented by the hour. The **Jardín Botánico,** off Plaza Italia, is another paradise, with many specially labeled South American plants. It is famous for its population of abandoned cats, tended by little old ladies from the neighborhood—a delight for kids to watch. With its small interior fountains and gravel walkways, it has a strong European feel. Nearby, small streams and lakes meander through the **Japanese Garden ★★ (© 11/4804-4922;** daily 10am–6pm; admission is about $2), where children can feed the fish (*alimento para peces* means "fish food") and watch the ducks. Small wood bridges connect classical Japanese gardens surrounding the artificial lake. A simple restaurant offers tea, pastries, sandwiches, and a few Japanese dishes such as sushi and teriyaki chicken. A Japanese cultural center is located on the grounds, and you'll also find notes posted for various Asian events throughout the city.

Previous visitors to the parks within Palermo will notice security changes that impact a visit here. As a result of vandalism and theft, driven both by increased poverty and the high value of metals, many statues and fountains are now surrounded by high gates, and sections of the park are locked at night. You can still look at the statues, of course, but many are impossible to get close to. Many of the statues and other monuments have been cleaned as part of this and are freer of graffiti than in the past.

Palermo Viejo—once a run-down neighborhood of warehouses, factories, and tiny decaying stucco homes (called *chorizo*, or sausage houses, due to their elongated shape), where few cared to live as recently as 15 years ago—has transformed into the city's most chic destination. Railroad tracks and Avenida Juan B. Justo further officially divide the neighborhood into **Palermo Soho** to the south and **Palermo Hollywood** to the north, though many establishments will say they are in one or the other incorrectly. The center of Palermo Soho is Plazaleto Jorge Cortazar, better known by its informal name, Plaza Serrano, a small oval park at the intersection of calles Serrano and Honduras. Take note that Calle Serrano is also called Calle Borges on some maps and street signs. Young people gather here late at night for impromptu singing and guitar sessions, often fueled by drinks at the many funky bars and restaurants around the plaza. A crafts festival runs on weekends spilling into the streets, but you'll always find someone selling bohemian jewelry and leather goods, no matter the day. Palermo Hollywood is better known for boutiques owned by local designers, with some restaurants and hotels mixed in. The neighborhood gained its name because many Argentine film studios were initially attracted to its once cheap rents, large studio spaces, and easy parking. Palermo Hollywood is quieter and less gentrified than Palermo Soho, which, in some ways, has become a victim of its own success, populated during the daytime by lost tourists with maps and guidebooks in hand.

Las Cañitas was once the favored location of the military powers during the dictatorship, and the area remains the safest and most secure of all of the central Buenos Aires neighborhoods. While the military powers no longer control the country, their training base, hospital, high school, and various family housing units still remain and encircle the neighborhood. Today the area is far better known among the hip, trendy, and nouveau riche as the place to dine out, have a drink and party, and be seen along the fashionable venues built into converted low-rise former houses on Calle Báez. Located near the polo grounds, it's a great place for enthusiasts to catch polo stars dining on the sidewalks in season. I place Las Cañitas into Palermo in this guidebook, though some refer to the area as a section of Belgrano or a location independent of any other neighborhood.

RECOLETA

The city's most exclusive neighborhood, La Recoleta wears a distinctly European face. Tree-lined avenues lead past fashionable restaurants, cafes, boutiques, and galleries, many housed in French-style buildings. Much of the activity takes place along the pedestrian walkway Roberto M. Ortiz and in front of the Cultural Center and Recoleta Cemetery. This is a neighborhood of plazas and parks, where tourists and wealthy Argentines spend their leisure time outdoors. Weekends bring street performances, art exhibits, fairs, and informal sports, especially near the entrance to the cemetery.

The **Recoleta Cemetery ★★★** (© **11/4804-7040** or 7803-1594), open daily from 8am to 6pm, pays tribute to some of Argentina's most important historical figures and gives its richest citizens one last chance to show off their wealth. The cemetery was once the garden of the adjoining church. Created in 1822, it's the city's oldest operating grave site—more of a necropolis, with tall mausoleums abutting, lining the paths that run through the walled-in area. You can spend hours wandering the grounds, which cover 4 city blocks, adorned with works by local and international sculptors. More than 6,400 mausoleums form an architectural free-for-all, including Greek temples and pyramids. The most popular site is the tomb of Eva "Evita" Perón, which is always heaped with flowers and notes from adoring fans. To prevent her body from being stolen, as it had been many times, she is buried in a concrete vault 8.1m (27 ft.) underground. In spite of this, people peek through the glass doors and swear they see her. Many other rich or famous Argentines are buried here as well, including a number of Argentine presidents (many names on tombs correspond to names on city street signs). The newest presidential tomb is that of Raúl Ricardo Alfonsín, who died in 2009 and was the first president after the military dictatorship.

Most tourists who come here visit only Evita's tomb and leave, but among the many tombs, two are worth singling out and should not be missed while exploring here. One is the tomb of the Paz family, who owned the newspaper *La Prensa,* as well as the palatial building on Plaza San Martín now known as the Círculo Militar. It is an enormous black stone structure covered with numerous white marble angels in turn-of-the-20th-century dress. The angels seem almost to soar to the heavens, lifting up the spirit of those inside with their massive wings. The sculptures were all made in Paris and shipped here. Masonic symbols such as anchors and pyramid-like shapes adorn this as well as many other Recoleta tombs.

Another tomb I recommend seeing while here is that of Rufina Cambaceres, a young woman who was buried alive in the early 1900s. She had perhaps suffered a coma, and a few days after her interment, workers heard screams from the tomb. Once the tomb was opened, there were scratches on her face and on the coffin from trying to escape. Her mother then built this Art Nouveau masterpiece, which has become a symbol of the cemetery. Her coffin is a Carrara marble slab, carved with a rose on top, and it sits behind a glass wall, as if her mother wanted to make up for her mistake in burying her and make sure to see her coffin if she were ever to come back again. Adorned by a young girl carved of marble who turns her head to those watching her, she looks as if she is about to break into tears, and her right hand is on the door of her own tomb.

The dead are not the only residents of the cemetery—more than 80 cats roam among the tombs. The cats here are plumper than most strays, thanks to a few women from the area who come to feed them at 10am and 4pm. The cats gather in anticipation at the entrance, and this is a good time to bring children who might otherwise be bored in the cemetery. Weather permitting, free English guided tours take place Thursday at 11am from the cemetery's Doric-columned entrance at Calle Junín 1790. These tours are usually run by Marta Granja who works mornings in the cemetery office and can answer English-language questions.

Adjacent to the cemetery, the **Centro Cultural Recoleta** ★ (p. 150) holds permanent and touring art exhibits along with theatrical and musical performances. Designed in the mid–18th century as a Franciscan convent, it was reincarnated as a poorhouse in 1858, serving that function until it became a cultural center in 1979. The first floor houses an interactive children's science museum, where it is "forbidden not to touch." Next door, Buenos Aires Design Center features home decor shops.

PLAZA DE MAYO

Juan de Garay founded the historic core of Buenos Aires, the Plaza de Mayo, in 1580. The plaza's prominent buildings create an architectural timeline: The Cabildo,

Pirámide de Mayo (Pyramid of May), and Metropolitan Cathedral are vestiges of the colonial period (18th and early 19th c.), while the seats of national and local government reflect the styles of the late 19th and early 20th centuries. In the center of the plaza, you'll find palm trees, fountains, and benches. Plaza de Mayo remains the political heart of the city and as such, serves as a forum for protests. In recent years which have seen considerable political and economic turmoil, barriers and a strong police presence have become a fact of life here, making it unpleasant at times. A planned revamp of the park, intended for the 2010 Bicentennial, though largely meant to stop demonstrations from gathering, would remove the benches and further prevent pedestrian flow, making it an even more unpleasant place, but the city has yet to act on the renovation. The mothers of the *desaparecidos,* victims of the military dictatorship's war against leftists, have demonstrated here since 1976. You can see them march, speak, and set up information booths Thursday afternoons at 3:30pm. The circle of head scarves, known as *panuelos,* which surrounds the Pirámide de Mayo marks their demonstration route. The use of the head scarves as a symbol dates from a time when the military finally granted the mothers the right to march in protest, but forbid them speaking to anyone. They wrote the names of their missing children on the scarves, with the hope that someone would see and later, in a safer space, tell them what had happened to their children.

The Argentine president, whose residence is now in Los Olivos, in the suburbs, goes to work at the **Casa Rosada (Pink House)** ★★★. It is from a balcony of this building that Eva Perón addressed adoring crowds of Argentine workers, and former President Carlos Menem allowed Madonna to use it for the 1996 movie. Now, however, many Argentines associate the balcony with military dictator Leopoldo Galtieri's ill-fated declaration of war against the United Kingdom over the Falkland Islands, known here as the Islas Malvinas. You can watch the changing of the guard in front of the palace every hour on the hour. On a side entrance to Casa Rosada is the **Presidential Museum** (© 11/4344-3802), with information on the history of the building and items owned by various presidents over the centuries. It's open Tuesday through Sunday from 10am to 6pm; admission is free. As a result of the 2010 Bicentennial celebrations Casa Rosada is now open on weekends for free tours from 10am to 6pm given every hour on the hour. Visitors see meeting rooms, the presidential office areas, and even can stand on Evita's famous balcony and say "don't cry for me" to the Plaza de Mayo.

The original structure of the **Metropolitan Cathedral** ★★ (© 11/4331-2845) was built in 1745; it was given a new Greek Revival facade with carvings that tell the story of Jacob and his son Joseph, and was designated a cathedral in 1836. From the exterior, only the Spanish colonial tiled dome gives any indication of the building's true age. Inside lies a mausoleum containing the remains of Gen. José de San Martín, the South American liberator regarded as the "Father of the Nation." (San Martín fought successfully for freedom in Argentina, Peru, and Chile.) His body was moved here in 1880 to become a symbol of Argentina's unification and rise to greatness when Buenos Aires became the capital of the country at the end of a civil war. The tomb of the unknown soldier of Argentine independence is also here.

The **Cabildo** ★, Bolívar 65 (© 11/4334-1782), was the original seat of city government established by the Spaniards. Completed in 1751, the colonial building proved significant in the events leading up to Argentina's declaration of independence from Spain in May 1810. Parts of the Cabildo were demolished to create space for

Avenida de Mayo and Diagonal Sur. The remainder of the building was restored in 1939 and is worth a visit. The small informal museum offers paintings and furniture from the colonial period, and its ledges and windows offer some of the best views of the Plaza de Mayo and the opportunity to imagine what the area might have been like in the colonial period (the museum is open to the public Tues–Fri 10:30am–5pm and Sat–Sun 11:30am–6pm; admission is $2, free on Fri). The Cabildo is the only remaining public secular building on the Plaza dating back to colonial times. On Thursday and Friday, the Cabildo's back patio is home to a crafts fair (11am–6pm). The Cabildo underwent an extensive renovation in preparation for the 2010 Bicentennial celebrations, which vastly improved its layout and interpretive historical panels and displays. Many tourists skip visiting inside this building, but its importance to the history of Argentina cannot be overstated.

A striking neoclassical facade covers the **Legislatura de la Ciudad (City Legislature Building),** at Calle Perú and Hipólito Yrigoyen, which houses exhibitions in several of its halls. Ask about tours, offered on an informal basis in English or Spanish. Legend has it that the watchtower was made so high so that the city could keep on eye on the president in the Casa Rosada. In front of the Legislatura, you'll see a bronze statue of Julio A. Roca. He is considered one of Argentina's greatest presidents and generals, but one of his legacies is slaughtering tens of thousands of Indians in the name of racial purity within the province. He is why Argentina, unlike most of Latin America, is a largely white society rather than mestizo, at least within Buenos Aires and the surroundings.

Farther down Calle Perú are the **Manzanas de las Luces (Blocks of Enlightenment)** ★★, Calle Perú 272, which served as the intellectual center of the city in the 17th and 18th centuries. This land was granted in 1616 to the Jesuits, who built **San Ignacio**—the city's oldest church—still standing at the corner of calles Bolívar and Alsina. San Ignacio has a beautiful altar carved in wood with baroque details. It has been recently renovated after years of neglect and was nearly destroyed in the revolution that took Perón out of power in 1955, after he sought to reduce the power of the Catholic Church. The **Colegio Nacional de Buenos Aires (National High School of Buenos Aires)** is also located here. Argentina's best-known intellectuals have gathered and studied here. The name "block of lights" recognizes the contributions of the National School's graduates, especially in achieving Argentina's independence in the 19th century. Tours, usually led on Saturday and Sunday at 3 and 4:30pm, include a visit to the Jesuits' system of underground tunnels, which connected their churches to strategic spots in the city (admission $2). Speculation remains as to whether the tunnels also served a colonial military purpose or funneled pirated goods into the city to avoid taxes under the Spanish, and their full extent is still unknown. Perón and subsequent military regimes had also secretly expanded them. *Ratearse,* the Argentine slang for playing hooky, which literally means becoming a rat, comes from the tunnels, as this is where students hid to skip class. In addition to weekend tours, the Comisión Nacional de la Manzana de las Luces organizes a variety of cultural activities during the week, including folkloric dance lessons, open-air theater performances, art expositions, and music concerts. Call ② 11/4331-9534 for information.

PUERTO MADERO

Puerto Madero became Buenos Aires's second major gateway to trade with Europe when it was built in 1880, replacing in importance the port at La Boca. By 1910, the city had already outgrown it. The Puerto Nuevo (New Port) was established to the north to accommodate growing commercial activity, and Madero was abandoned for almost a century. Urban renewal saved the original port in the 1990s with the construction of a riverfront promenade, apartments, and offices. Bustling and business-like during the day, the area attracts a fashionable, wealthy crowd at night. It's lined with elegant restaurants serving Argentine steaks and fresh seafood specialties, and there is a popular cinema showing Argentine and Hollywood films, as well as dance clubs such as **Asia de Cuba.** The entire area is rapidly expanding, with high-rise luxury residences making this a newly fashionable, if somewhat isolated and artificial, neighborhood to live in. Note that all the streets in Puerto Madero are named for important women in Argentine history. Look for the Buenos Aires City Tourism brochure "Women of Buenos Aires" to learn more about some of them. A plaque also exists on Avenida Alicia Moreau de Justo at Boulevard Villaflor, between Diques 3 and 2, with brief biographies. At sunset, take a walk along the eastern, modern part of the renovated area, and watch the water shimmer in brilliant reds as the city sky-line and older portions of the port form a dramatic, silhouetted backdrop.

As you walk out from the port, you'll also come across the **Ecological Preserve ★★**. This area is an anomaly for a modern city and exists as proof that nature can regenerate from an ecological disaster. In the 1960s and 1970s, demolished buildings and debris were dumped into the Río de la Plata after the construction of the *autopista*, or highway system. Over time, sand and sediment began to build up, plants and grasses grew, and birds now use it as a breeding ground. Ask travel agents about bird-watching tours. In the summer, adventurous Porteños use it as a beach, but the water is too polluted to swim in and you must be careful of jagged debris and the homeless who set up camp here. In spite of official legal protections, Puerto Madero development is slowly creeping onto the preserve. While the Ecological Preserve forms a sort of lung for the city, the height of the buildings in Puerto Madero has been blamed for blocking Río de la Plata winds, further decreasing air quality in downtown Buenos Aires.

PLAZA SAN MARTIN ★★★ & THE MICROCENTRO

Plaza San Martín, a beautiful park at the base of Calle Florida in the Retiro neighborhood, acts as the nucleus of what's called the city's MicroCentro. The large space once housed a long-gone bull fighting arena and was expanded over time as the city rebuilt itself to a European-style plan. In summer months, Argentine businesspeople flock to the park on their lunch hour, loosening their ties, taking off some layers, and sunning for a while amid the plaza's flowering jacaranda trees. A monument to Gen. José de San Martín towers over the scene. The park is busy at all hours; even after midnight, the playground will be teeming with kids and their parents out for a late-night stroll. Plaza San Martín was once the location of choice for the most elite families at the beginning of the 20th century. The San Martín Palace, formerly the home of the Anchorena family, is now used by the Argentine Ministry of Foreign Affairs; the Círculo Militar, once the home of the Paz family who own the *La Prensa* newspaper; and the elegant Plaza Hotel testify to this former grandeur. The change from residential to apartments and commercial structures began in the 1930s with the Depression, when many residents were forced to sell their large mansions. In 1936, the Art Deco Kavanagh Building opened, then the tallest building in South America, and it still dominates the Plaza. Temporary art exhibits, usually with a social purpose, often occur within the Plaza, asking you to stroll and take in each image and think as you consider their connections. The Plaza was also renovated in anticipation of the 2010

Bicentennial with improved sidewalks and paving, as well as brighter lighting and the removal of low growing shrubbery, in theory making the area safer at night.

Plaza San Martín cascades down a hill, at the base of which sits the **Islas Malvinas (Falkland Islands) War Memorial,** a stark circular wall engraved with the names of the nearly 750 dead and an eternal flame, overseen by guards from the various branches of the military. The memorial directly faces the Elizabethan-style **British Clock Tower,** since renamed the **Torre Monumental,** though most locals still use the old name. It was a gift from the British, who built and ran the nearby Retiro train station complex. Oddly, it remained unscathed during the war but was attacked by a mob years later, which also toppled an accompanying statue of George Canning, the British foreign secretary who recognized Argentina's independence from Spain. You can see some of the damage in the ornamental staircase leading up to the tower. The tower is open to the public and provides a view of the city and river.

Calle Florida ★★★ is the city's main pedestrian thoroughfare and a shopper's paradise. The busiest section, extending south from Plaza San Martín to Avenida Corrientes, is lined with boutiques, restaurants, and record stores. It extends all the way through Avenida de Mayo to the south, forming into **Calle Perú** after the intersection with Rivadavia, where many international banks have retail branches. Day and night, street performers walk on glass, tango, and offer comedy acts. Take care when watching the performers to keep an eye out for pickpockets who work the mesmerized crowds. You'll find the upscale Galerías Pacífico fashion center here, near where it intersects Calle Viamonte (see "Shopping," below). Most of the shopping on the street itself, however, is middle-of-the-road, as upper-end retailers have moved into malls and other parts of the city. Leather stores, however, abound, so compare prices and bargain by stopping into a few before finalizing your purchase. Many can also custom-make a special order in a day or two if you can't find exactly what you want. Florida intersects with **Calle Lavalle,** a smaller version of itself. You'll find even more stores, most of lesser quality, and some inexpensive *parrillas* worth visiting. The street is also home to numerous movie theaters and video and electronic game arcades, so it's a good place for teenagers to hang out while you shop around. The city is currently pedestrianizing other streets within the MicroCentro, such as the recently completed Tres Sargentos. **Calle Reconquista,** which parallels Florida and intersects Lavalle, was pedestrianized in 2009. It's a far less busy street, but has several popular bars and restaurants. Buenos Aires plans to pedestrianize more areas within the MicroCentro and also make it more biker friendly, including creating bicycle lanes on **Calle Suipacha.**

Avenida Corrientes ★ is a living diary of Buenos Aires's cultural development. Until the 1930s, Avenida Corrientes was the favored hangout of tango legends. When the avenue was widened in the mid-1930s, it made its debut as the Argentine Broadway, and Evita's first apartment was here as she struggled to make herself famous. Today Corrientes, lined with Art Deco cinemas and theaters, pulses with cultural and commercial activity day and night. It is also home to many bookstores, from the chains that sell bestsellers and offer English-language guidebooks, to independent bargain outlets and rare booksellers. The **Obelisco,** opened in 1936 as Buenos Aires's defining monument to mark the 400th anniversary of the first (unsuccessful) founding of the city, marks the intersection of Corrientes with **Avenida 9 de Julio.** Whenever locals have something to celebrate, they gather here. It's exciting to come here when Argentina wins an international soccer match.

Museums

El Museo Histórico Nacional (National History Museum) ★★ Argentine history from the 16th through the 19th centuries comes to life in the former Lezama family home. The expansive Italian-style mansion houses 30 rooms with items saved from Jesuit missions, paintings illustrating clashes between the Spaniards and Indians, and relics from the War of Independence against Spain. The focal point of the museum's collection is artist Cándido López's series of captivating scenes of the war against Paraguay in the 1870s.

Calle Defensa 1600 (at Caseros). © **11/4307-1182.** Free admission. Tues–Sun noon–6pm. Closed Jan. Metro: Constitución.

MALBA - Fundación Costantini ★★★ The airy and luminescent Museo de Arte Latinoamericano de Buenos Aires (MALBA), located in Palermo Chico, houses the private art collection of Eduardo Costantini, a wealthy Argentine real estate developer. One of the most impressive collections of Latin American art anywhere, its temporary and permanent exhibitions showcase names such as Antonio Berni, Pedro Figari, Frida Kahlo, Cândido Portinari, Diego Rivera, and Antonio Siguí. Many of the works confront social issues and explore questions of national identity. Even the benches are modern pieces of art.

Av. Figueroa Alcorta 3415 (at San Martín de Tours). © **11/4808-6500.** www.malba.org.ar. Admission $5. Free admission Wed. Wed–Mon noon–8pm. No metro access.

Museo Amalia Lacroze de Fortabat ★ One of the newest museums to grace Buenos Aires, this gleaming low-rise structure hugs the banks of Puerto Madero and houses the private collection of Amalia Lacroze de Fortabat. It's best to look at it as the female version of the MALBA, started by a male real estate mogul. This time it's a grande dame, Amalia Lacroze de Fortabat, something of an Argentine Brooke Astor who opened this airy museum in October 2008. The museum contains an enormous collection of Argentine artists, as well as works by Warhol, Dalí, Chagall, the Bruegels, and other well-known painters, as well as a collection of ancient art. Many of the paintings are of Amalia when she was a young, stunning beauty.

Olga Cossettini 141 (at Sanchez de Thompson). © **11/4310-6600.** www.coleccionfortabat.org.ar. Admission $4. Tues–Sun noon–9pm. Metro: Alem.

Museo Evita ★★★ It is almost impossible for non-Argentines to fathom that it took 50 years from the time of her death for Evita, the world's most famous Argentine, to finally get a museum. The Museo Evita opened July 26, 2002, in a mansion where her charity, the Eva Perón Foundation, once housed single mothers with children. While the museum treats her history fairly, looking at both the good and the bad, it is obvious that love is behind the presentation. Indeed, Evita's grandniece Cristina Alvarez Rodríguez is often in the building meeting with the staff. The museum, designed and curated by Gabriel Miremont, divides Evita's life into several parts, looking at her childhood; her arrival in Buenos Aires to become an actress; her assumption as Evita, first lady and unofficial saint to millions; and finally her death and legacy. You will be able to view her clothes, remarkably preserved by the military government, which took power after Perón. Other artifacts of her life include her voting card—significant because only through Evita did Argentine women gain the right to vote. There are also toys and schoolbooks adorned with her image, given to children to indoctrinate them with the Peronist ideology. The most touching artifact of all is a smashed statue of Evita, hidden for decades by a farmer in his barn, despite the possibility of his being jailed for housing it. Scholars of Argentine history should note that one of the largest collections of literature related to the Peróns is in the building, but you will need special permission to visit this section. Whether you hate, love, or remain indifferent to Evita, you shouldn't miss this museum; digesting the exhibitions will help you understand why she remains such a controversial figure within the Argentine psyche.

Calle Lafinur 2988 (at Gutiérrez). ✆ **11/4807-9433** or 4807-0306. www.museoevita.org. Admission $4. Tues–Sun 11am–7:30pm. Metro: Plaza Italia.

Museo Nacional de Arte Decorativo (National Museum of Decorative Art) ★   The building's 18th-century French design by French architect Rene Sergent provides a classical setting for the diverse decorative styles represented within. Breathtaking sculptures, paintings, and furnishings round out the collection, and themed shows rotate seasonally. The **Museo de Arte Oriental (Museum of Eastern Art)** displays art, pottery, and engravings on the first floor of the building. The building is itself a work of art, a representation of the incredible mansions that once lined the avenue, overlooking the extensive Palermo park system.

Av. del Libertador 1902 (at Bustamante). ✆ **11/4801-8248.** www.mnad.org. Admission $2. Tues–Sun 2–7pm; closed Sun Jan–Feb. No metro access.

Museo Nacional de Bellas Artes (National Museum of Fine Arts) ★★
This building, which formerly pumped the city's water supply, metamorphosed into Buenos Aires's most important art museum in 1930. It contains the world's largest collection of Argentine sculptures and paintings from the 19th and 20th centuries and also houses European art dating from the pre-Renaissance period to the present day. Notable pieces include works by Renoir, Monet, Rodin, Toulouse-Lautrec, and van Gogh, as well as a collection of Picasso drawings, many amassed originally by private collectors when Argentina was at its peak of wealth at the end of the 1800s and early 1900s.

Av. del Libertador 1473 (at Pueyrredón). ✆ **11/4803-0802** or 5288-9900. www.mnba.org.ar. Free admission. Tues–Fri 12:30–8:30pm; Sat–Sun 9:30am–8:30pm. No metro access.

Other Attractions

Basílica y Convento de San Francisco (San Francis's Church and Convent) ★   The San Roque parish is one of the oldest in the city. A Jesuit architect designed the church in 1730, but an early-20th-century reconstruction added a German baroque facade, along with statues of Saint Francis of Assisi, Dante, and Christopher Columbus. Within the adjacent museum, you'll find a tapestry by Argentine artist Horacio Butler, along with an extensive library and religious colonial art.

Calle Defensa and Alsina. ✆ **11/4331-0625.** Free admission. Hours vary. Metro: Plaza de Mayo.

Biblioteca Nacional (National Library) ★   Opened in 1992, this modern architectural oddity stands on the land of the former Presidential Residence in which Eva Perón died. With its underground levels, the library's 13 floors can store up to five million volumes. Among its collection, the library stores 21 books printed by one of the earliest printing presses, dating from 1440 to 1500. Visit the reading room—occupying two stories at the top of the building—to enjoy an awe-inspiring view of the city. The library also hosts special events in its exhibition hall and auditorium.

Calle Aguero 2502 (at Libertador). ✆ **11/4808-6000.** www.bn.gov.ar. Free admission. Mon-Fri 9am-9pm; Sat-Sun noon-8pm. No metro access.

Congreso (Congress) ★★★ The National Congress towers over Avenida de Mayo, forming the end of the Avenida de Mayo processional route, which begins at the president's Casa Rosada down the street. The capitol building, built in 1906, combines elements of classical Greek and Roman architecture, topped with an immense central dome modeled after its counterpart in Washington, D.C. Today the building cannot accommodate the entire congressional staff, some of whom had to spill over into neighboring structures. There are daily tours, in English and Spanish, but they are sometimes canceled if there are intense congressional sessions and other activities. Make sure to bring your passport for identification. **Plaza Congreso** was designed in 1910 to frame the congress building and memorialize the centennial of a revolutionary junta that helped overthrow Spanish rule in Argentina. Stroll around the square and its surroundings to see various architectural landmarks, theaters, sidewalk cafes, and bars.

Plaza Congreso, Av. Rivadavia 1850 at Entre Rios and Callao. ✆ **11/6310-7532** or 6310-7100. Free hourly tours daily 11am–4pm, often subject to cancellation. Metro: Congreso.

Teatro Colón (Colón Theater) ★★★ 📷 Buenos Aires's golden age of prosperity gave birth to this luxurious opera house. It's one of the crowning visual delights of Avenida 9 de Julio, though its true entrance faces a park on the opposite side of the building. Over the years, the theater has been graced by the likes of Enrico Caruso, Luciano Pavarotti, Julio Bocca, Maria Callas, Plácido Domingo, Arturo Toscanini, and Igor Stravinsky. Work began in 1889 and took close to 20 years to complete, largely because the first two architects died during the building process, one because of a love affair gone wrong in a deadly manner, a drama worthy of an opera itself. The majestic building opened in 1908 and combines a variety of European styles, from the Ionic and Corinthian capitals and stained-glass pieces in the main entrance to the Italian-marble staircase and French furniture, chandeliers, and vases in the Golden Hall. In the main theater, which seats 3,000 in orchestra seats, stalls, boxes, and four rises, an enormous chandelier hangs from the domed ceiling painted by Raúl Soldi in 1966 during a previous renovation. The theater's acoustics are world-renowned. In addition to hosting visiting performers, the Colón has its own Philharmonic orchestra, choir, and ballet company. Opera and symphony seasons run from February to late December. The building was recently renovated, a process that like its creation, was years behind schedule and full of drama and intrigue with accusations of theft of historical costumes in storage and corrupt use of renovation funds. Officially, the building reopened in May 2010, though at the time of this writing, there were still portions of the building unrenovated; this hasn't impacted performances, but it has put tours on hold (usually offered Mon–Fri 11am–3pm and Sat 9am–noon). Call or visit the website for updates before your visit.

Calle Libertad 621 (or Calle Toscanini 1180 or Cerrito 628) at Tucumán, enter through carriageway portal in middle of building on Tucumán. ✆ **11/4378-7100.** www.teatrocolon.org.ar. Seating at various prices. Metro: Tribunales.

Spectator Sports & Outdoor Activities

GOLF Argentina has more than 200 golf courses. Closest to downtown are **Campo de Golf de la Ciudad de Buenos Aires,** Av. Torquist 1426 (at Olleros; ✆ **11/4772-7261;** www.campogolfpalermo.com), 10 minutes from downtown with great scenery and a 71-par course; and **Jockey Club Argentino,** Av. Márquez 1700 (© **11/4743-1001** or 4815-0561; www.eljockeyclub.com), in San Isidro, which offers two courses (71- and 72-par) designed by Allister McKenzie.

HORSE RACING Throughout much of the 20th century, Argentina was famous for its thoroughbreds. It continues to send prize horses to competitions around the world, although you can watch some of the best right here in Buenos Aires. Races take place at two tracks: **Hipódromo de San Isidro,** Av. Márquez 504 (© **11/4743-4010,** www.hipodromosanisidro.com), and **Hipódromo Argentino de Palermo,** Av. del Libertador 4205 (© **11/4778-2800**), in Palermo. Check the *Buenos Aires Herald* for race information.

POLO Argentina has won more international polo tournaments than any other country, and the **Argentine Open Championship,** held late November through early December, is the world's most important polo event. Argentina has two seasons for polo: March through May and September through December, held at the **Campo Argentino de Polo,** Avenida del Libertador and Avenida Dorrego (© **11/4576-5600**). Tickets can be purchased at the gate. Contact the **Asociación Argentina de Polo,** Hipólito Yrigoyen 636 (© **11/4777-6444;** www.aapolo.com), for information on polo schools and events.

SOCCER One cannot discuss *fútbol* in Argentina without paying homage to Diego Armando Maradona, Argentina's most revered player and one of the sport's great (if fallen) players. Any sense of national unity dissolves when Argentines watch their favorite clubs—River Plate, Boca Juniors, Racing Club, Independiente, and San Lorenzo—battle on Sunday. Passion for soccer could not run hotter, and you can catch a game at the **Estadio Boca Juniors,** Brandsen 805 (© **11/4309-4700;** www.bocajuniors.com.ar), in La Boca, followed by raucous street parties. Ticket prices start at about $7 and can be purchased in advance or at the gate. Adjacent to the stadium is the **El Museo de la Pasión Boquense** (© 11/4362-1100; www.museoboquense.com), which tells about the history of the team and their crazy, passionate fans. It's open daily from 10am to 6pm, and admission is $5.

SHOPPING

Porteños consider their city one of the fashion capitals of the world. Although the wealthiest Argentines still fly to Miami for their wardrobes, Buenos Aires boasts many of the same upscale stores you would find in New York or Paris. Do not expect to find a city full of indigenous textiles and crafts, as you would elsewhere in Latin America; Hermès, Louis Vuitton, Versace, and Ralph Lauren are more on the mark in wealthy districts such as Recoleta or Palermo. Boutiques of local designers, especially in Palermo, are an excellent and unique choice, as are the numerous leather goods stores throughout the city, which offer some of the finest and most interesting products of this type in the world. Look for the **Mapas de Buenos Aires** shopping map series (www.mapasbsas.com), which concentrates on different neighborhoods and shopping themes, and the **GO Palermo** (www.gopalermo.com.ar) shopping booklet at your hotel and tourism kiosks. The **Calle Florida Shopping Association** also puts out a shopping booklet (www.callefloridastreet.com). **De Dios** publishes an excellent laminated shopping map, available at Buenos Aires bookstores and online at www.dediosonline.com and www.amazon.com.

Store Hours & Shipping

Most stores are open weekdays from 9am to 8pm and Saturday from 9am until midnight, with some still closing for a few hours in the afternoon. You might find some shops open Sunday along Avenida Santa Fe, but few will be open on Calle Florida. Shopping centers are open daily from 10am to 10pm. Some stores not catering to tourists will close after Christmas and in early January for their summer holidays.

Certain art and antiques dealers will crate and ship bulky objects for an additional fee; others will tell you it's no problem to take that new sculpture directly on the plane. If you don't want to take any chances, contact **UPS** (© **800/222-2877;** www.ups.com) or **FedEx** (© **810/333-3339;** www.fedex.com). Various stores participate in a tax-refund program for purchases over 70 pesos. In such cases, ask for a special receipt, which can entitle you to a refund of the hefty 21% tax (IVA) when you leave the country.

Great Shopping Areas

MICROCENTRO   Calle Florida, the pedestrian walking street in the MicroCentro, is home to wall-to-wall shops from Plaza San Martín past Avenida Corrientes. The **Galerías Pacífico** mall is on Calle Florida 750 and Avenida Córdoba (© **11/5555-5110;** www.progaleriaspacifico.com.ar), with a magnificent dome and stunning frescoes painted by local artists. Over 180 shops are open Monday through Saturday from 10am to 9pm and Sunday from noon to 9pm, with tango and folk-dancing shows held on Thursday at 8pm in the food court, which is great for a shopping break no matter the time of the day. As you approach Plaza San Martín from Calle Florida, you find a number of well-regarded shoe stores, jewelers, and shops selling leather goods. Sometimes, you'll even find a live tango show here.

RECOLETA   Avenida Alvear is an elegant, Parisian-like strip of European boutiques and cafes. Start your walk from Plaza Francia across from Recoleta Cemetery and continue past the Alvear Palace Hotel to the French Embassy at Cerrito or 9 de Julio for one exclusive shop after another, many in French-style mansions. Avenida Quintana provides a similar atmosphere. **Patio Bullrich,** Av. del Libertador 750 and also entered at Posadas 1245, between Montevideo and Libertad (© **11/4814-7400;** www.shoppingbullrich.com.ar), is one of the city's best malls. Its 68 elegant shops are open daily 10am to 9pm.

AVENIDA SANTA FE   Popular with local shoppers, Avenida Santa Fe, in the Barrio Norte district, runs up through Palermo and offers a wide selection of clothing stores at down-to-earth prices. You will also find bookstores, cafes, ice-cream shops, and cinemas. The **Alto Palermo Shopping Center,** Av. Santa Fe 3253 at Bulnes (© **11/5777-8000;** www.altopalermo.com.ar), is another excellent shopping center, with 155 stores open daily from 10am to 10pm.

SAN TELMO & LA BOCA   These neighborhoods offer excellent antiques, artist studios, and arts and crafts celebrating tango. Street performers and artists are omnipresent, especially on weekends when even locals come to be entertained. Avoid La Boca at night and be aware of pickpockets in both neighborhoods.

Outdoor Markets

The **Feria de San Telmo ★★** (www.feriadesantelmo.com) is a vibrant, colorful experience that will delight even the most jaded traveler and should absolutely not be

Buenos Aires Shopping & Nightlife

SHOPPING

Ashanti Leather Factory **32**
Asunto Impreso **2**
Cándido Silva **58**
Casa López **30**
Clásica y Moderna **22**
Cosentino **44**
Cousiño Jewels **30**
El Ateneo (Grand Splendid) **13**
El Nochero **8**
Escada **10**
Galería El Solar de French **58**
Galería Promenade de Alvear **3**
Galería Ruth Benzacar **33**
Galerías Pacífico **36**
Grand Cru **5**
H.Stern **29, 32**
Jorge Gudiño Antigüedades **56**
La Remera **14**
Marcelo Toledo Gallery **60**
Nora Iniesta **51**
Pallarols **57**
Patio Bullrich **6**
Polo Ralph Lauren **4**
Rossi & Caruso **16, 38**
Tonel Privado **7, 39**
Walrus Books **54**
Winery **28, 34**

AFTER DARK

The Alamo-Shoeless Joe's **15**
Asia de Cuba **46**
Asociación Argentina de Cultura
   Inglesa (British Arts Centre) **11**
Café Tortoni **47**
Central Tango **26**
Centro Cultural de Borges **37**
Centro Cultural Recoleta
   (Recoleta Cultural Center) **1**
El Arranque **27**
El Beso Nightclub **23**
El Niño Bien **50**
El Querandí **49**
El Viejo Almacén **53**
Gran Bar Danzon **17**
Julio Bocca and Ballet
   Argentino **40**
The Kilkenny **34**
La Coruña **55**
Luna Park **45**
Medio y Medio **52**

Milion **19**
Plaza Bar **34**
Plaza Bohemia **41**
Plaza Dorrego Bar **59**
Rey Castro **48**
The Shamrock **12**
Teatro Coliseo **18**
Teatro Colón **21**
Teatro Gran Rex **42**
Teatro Municipal General
   San Martín **27**
Teatro Nacional Cervantes **20**
Teatro Opera **43**
Teatro Presidente Alvear **24**

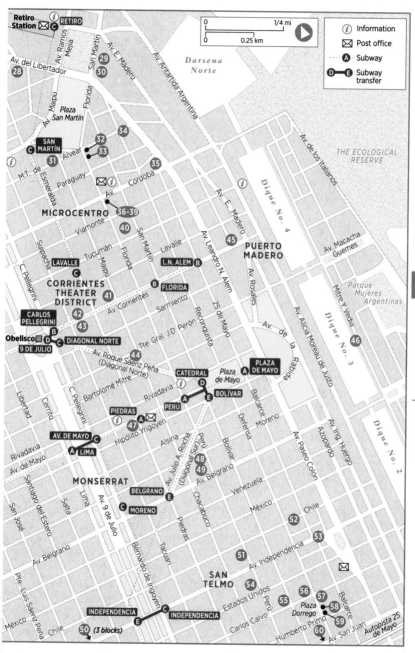

missed—even locals come here for bargains and fun. The market takes place every Sunday from 10am to 5pm at Plaza Dorrego; during the summer, the event ends long after 5pm. As street vendors sell their heirlooms, singers and dancers move though the crowd to tango music. Among the hundreds of vendor stands, you will find antique silver objects, porcelain, crystal, and other antiques along with touristy items to bring home. The Feria has spread well beyond its home on Plaza Dorrego, into adjacent streets and up Calle Defensa towards Plaza de Mayo. It can be insanely crowded, so be aware of pickpockets.

Plaza Serrano Fair is at the small plaza at the intersection of Calle Serrano (Calle Borges on some maps) and Honduras, which forms the heart of Palermo Soho and is also known as Plaza Julio Cortazar. Bohemian arts and crafts are sold here, while dread-headed locals sing and play guitars. Officially, it's held Saturday and Sunday from 10am to 6pm, but impromptu vendors set up at night, too, when the restaurants are crowded. The bars and restaurants surrounding Plaza Serrano are always intensely crowded during the fair, but great for a shopping break.

Recoleta Fair ★★, which takes place Saturday and Sunday in front of Recoleta Cemetery in Plaza Francia from 10am until sunset, offers every imaginable souvenir and craft, as well as food. This has become among the city's largest fair, completely taking over all the walkways in the area—even the Iglesia Pilar gets involved with stands selling religious souvenirs. Live bands sometimes play on whatever part of the hill sloping down to Avenida Libertador is not taken over by vendors.

La Boca Fair is open daily from 10am to 6pm or sundown and concentrates on El Caminito, the colorful pedestrian walkway that is the heart of the neighborhood. It's the most touristy of all the fairs, and most of the items are terribly overpriced. Still, if you need tacky souvenirs in a hurry, you can do all your shopping here. Besides, tango singers and other street performers will keep your mind off the inflated prices. When the vendors start leaving at the end of the day, you should, too, for safety reasons.

Shopping A to Z

Almost all shops in Buenos Aires accept credit cards. However, you will often get a better price if you offer to pay with cash (including U.S. dollars, in certain cases). You won't be able to use credit cards at outdoor markets.

ANTIQUES

Throughout the streets of San Telmo, you will find the city's best antiques shops; don't miss the antiques market that takes place all day Sunday at Plaza Dorrego (see "Outdoor Markets," above). A number of fine antiques stores are scattered along Avenida Alvear in Recoleta, including a collection of boutique shops at **Galería Alvear,** Av. Alvear 1777.

It Pays to Bargain

Most antiques stores will come down 10% to 20% from the listed price if you try to bargain with them.

Calle Antigua ★★ This store sells religious art, chandeliers, furniture, and other decorative objects. The owner, José Manuel Piñeyro, opened his shop more than 20 years ago. He now has two storefronts, both on the same block of Calle Defensa. The stores accept cash and foreign checks, but no credit cards. Both stores are open daily from 10am to 7pm. Calle Defensa 914 and Calle Defensa 974 (at Estados Unidos). ✆ **11/4300-8782** or 15-4472-4158 (mobile). Metro: Independencia.

Galería El Solar de French Built in the early 20th century in a Spanish colonial style, this is where Argentine patriot Domingo French lived. Today it's a gallery, with antiques shops and photography stores depicting the San Telmo of yesteryear. Calle Defensa 1066 (at Carlos Calvo). No phone. Metro: Constitución.

Jorge Gudiño Antigüedades Jorge Gudiño, who has more than 20 years of experience selling antiques, opened this store in 1991. The shop offers beautiful pieces of high-end antique furnishing, which are displayed in interesting ways. This makes the store more visually appealing than many others on the street, and it provides ideas for your own use at home. Only cash and overseas checks are accepted. The store is open Sunday through Friday from 10:30am to 7pm. Calle Defensa 1002 (at Carlos Calvo). ✆ **11/4362-0156.** Metro: Independencia.

Pallarols ★ Located in San Telmo, Pallarols sells an exquisite collection of Argentine silver and other antiques. The Pallarols family represents six generations of silversmithing. Their work is featured in various museums in Buenos Aires, and family members will sometimes conduct silversmith workshops at museum stores. The shop is open Monday to Friday from 10am to 7pm, Saturday 10am to noon. Calle Defensa 1015 (at Carlos Calvo). ✆ **11/4362-5438.** www.pallarols.com.ar. Metro: Independencia.

ART GALLERIES

Cándido Silva ★★★ Filled with antiques and religious objects, this store is a standout in the Galería El Solar de French. Objects come in a range of materials—from wood, to marble, to silver. Many items are centuries-old antiques. Others are tasteful and exquisite reproductions, including a wide selection of canvases painted by indigenous people from throughout South America: Renaissance portraiture comes together with Frida Kahlo's magical realism, in representations of saints, angels, Christ, and numerous renditions on the Virgin Mary. Rural silver and gaucho items are also part of the items on display. Don't worry about fitting it all on the plane—they ship around the world. Calle Defensa 1066 (at Humberto I, in Galería El Solar de French). ✆ **11/4361-5053** or 15-5733-0696 (mobile). www.candidosilva.com.ar. Metro: Independencia.

Galería Ruth Benzacar This avant-garde gallery, in a hidden underground space at the start of Calle Florida, next to Plaza San Martín, hosts art exhibits of local and national interest. Among the best-known Argentines who have appeared here are Alfredo Prior, Miguel Angel Ríos, Daniel García, Graciela Hasper, and Pablo Siguier. Calle Florida 1000 (at Alvear). ✆ **11/4313-8480.** www.ruthbenzacar.com. Metro: San Martín.

Museo Casa—Taller de Celia Chevalier ★★ I don't get excited about much in La Boca, but I highly recommend this place, a boutique and house museum of an artist, located just 2 blocks from El Caminito. Celia Chevalier grew up in Buenos Aires and creates whimsical paintings based on her childhood memories. She is charming and open, though she speaks Spanish only. The house is a restored *conventillo,* the type that Italian immigrants moved into when they came to Buenos Aires before the turn of the 20th century. The house dates from 1885 and was made into her studio museum in 1998. Credit cards are not accepted for art purchases. There is a nominal 5 peso entry fee. Open weekends and holidays from 2 to 7pm; call for an appointment on weekdays. Irala 1162 (at Calle Olavarria). ✆ **11/4302-2337.** celia_chevalier@yahoo.com.ar. No metro access.

Palermo Attractions, Shopping & Nightlife

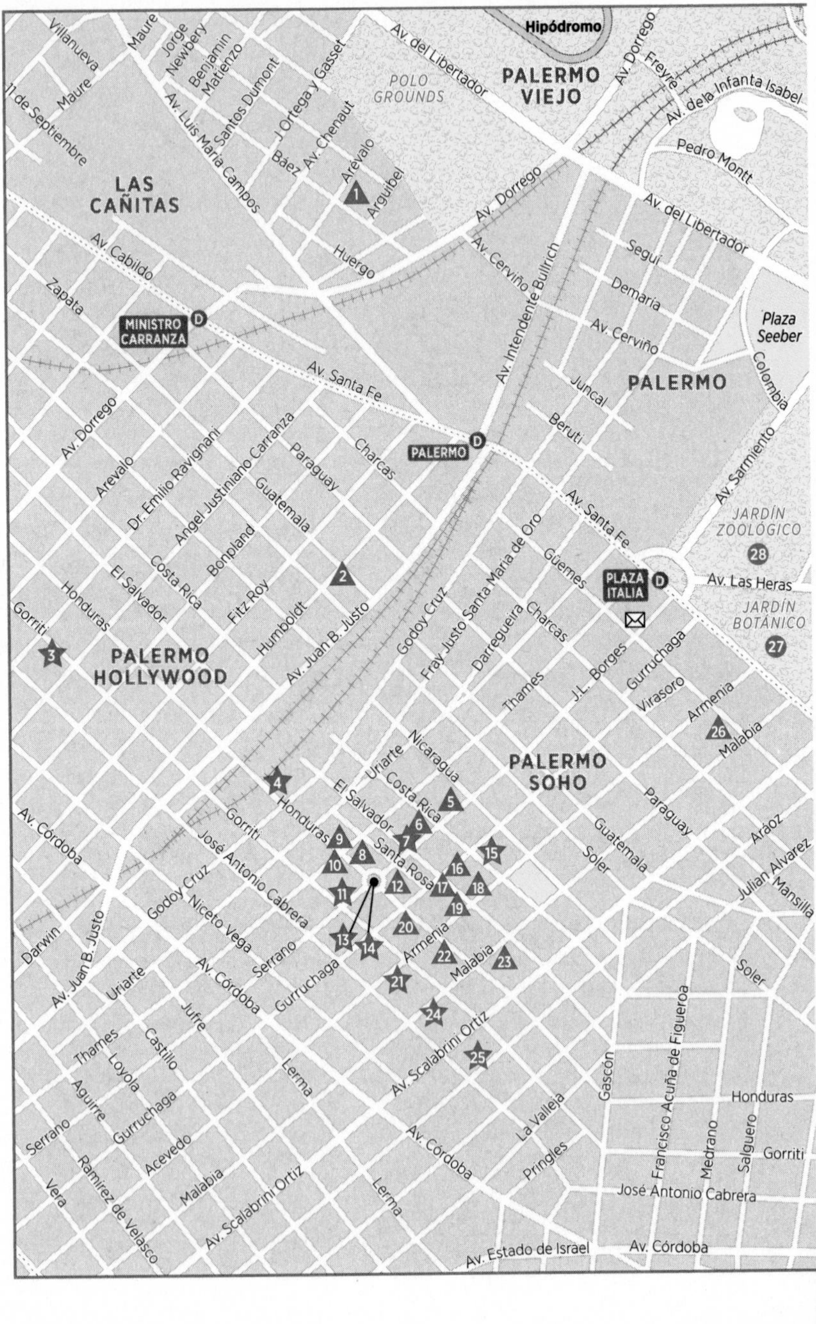

POLO GROUNDS

Hipódromo

PALERMO VIEJO

LAS CAÑITAS

MINISTRO CARRANZA D

PALERMO

Plaza Seeber

PALERMO HOLLYWOOD

PALERMO D

PLAZA ITALIA D

JARDÍN ZOOLÓGICO 28

JARDÍN BOTÁNICO 27

PALERMO SOHO

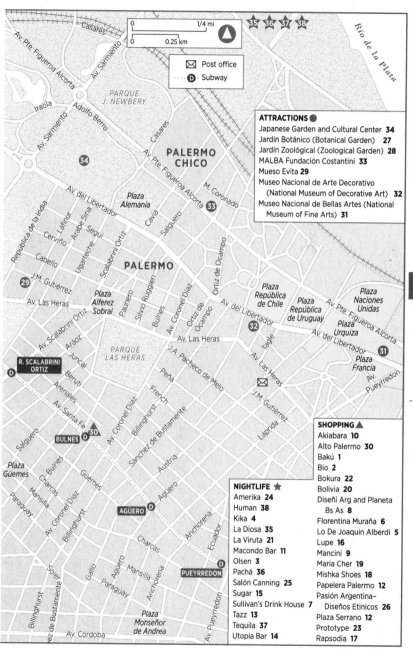

ATTRACTIONS ●
Japanese Garden and Cultural Center **34**
Jardín Botánico (Botanical Garden) **27**
Jardín Zoológico (Zoological Garden) **28**
MALBA Fundación Costantini **33**
Mueso Evita **29**
Museo Nacional de Arte Decorativo
(National Museum of Decorative Art) **32**
Museo Nacional de Bellas Artes (National
Museum of Fine Arts) **31**

SHOPPING ▲
Akiabara **10**
Alto Palermo **30**
Bakú **1**
Bio **2**
Bokura **22**
Bolivia **20**
Diseñi Arg and Planeta
Bs As **8**
Florentina Muraña **6**
Lo De Joaquin Alberdi **5**
Lupe **16**
Mancini **9**
Maria Cher **19**
Mishka Shoes **18**
Papelera Palermo **12**
Pasión Argentina–
Diseños Etinicos **26**
Plaza Serrano **12**
Prototype **23**
Rapsodia **17**

NIGHTLIFE ★
Amerika **24**
Human **38**
Kika **4**
La Diosa **35**
La Viruta **21**
Macondo Bar **11**
Olsen **3**
Pachá **36**
Salón Canning **25**
Sugar **15**
Sullivan's Drink House **7**
Tazz **13**
Tequila **37**
Utopia Bar **14**

☒ Post office
Ⓓ Subway

5

Nora Iniesta ★   Nora made herself famous within Buenos Aires for her kitschy art, incorporating Argentine symbols such as tango or gauchos. With the combination of the tourist boom and the return of the Peronist political movement to power, Evita-inspired art now dominates much of her work. Beyond that, modern shadow boxes, collages, and montages of detritus, dolls, souvenirs, and buttons are some of the mainstays. Some of her work is sold at Museo Evita, or you can come see the much larger selection here. Nora is sometimes in her San Telmo studio during the week from noon to 6pm, but it is best to call for an appointment. Perú 715, Ste. #2 (btw. Independencia and Chile). © **11/4331-5459** or 11/15-5319-1119 (mobile). www.norainiesta.com. Metro: Independencia.

Wussmann Gallery   This beautiful gallery has fantastic works of art, concentrating on contemporary pieces. Among the artists represented is Ral Veroni, a native Argentine who has lived around the world. It's open Monday to Saturday 10am to 6pm. Venezuela 574 (btw. Bolivar and Perú). © **11/4343-4707.** www.wussmann.com. Metro: Belgrano.

BOOKSTORES & STATIONERY

Argentines love to read, and you shouldn't be surprised if you find yourself in literary discussions even with your taxi drivers. Bookstores abound all over the city, with a concentration of stores along Avenida Santa Fe, Calle Florida, and on Avenida Corrientes, west of Nueve de Julio. Many are chains with branches throughout the city. Unlike in North America and the United Kingdom, online bookselling has not made serious inroads on independent and used bookstores, so you'll be able to enjoy old-fashioned browsing and discovery.

Asunto Impreso ★★   This bookstore, part of a small chain, makes a great intellectual pit stop in San Telmo, considering its tag line, "bookstore for the imagination." You'll find very high quality educational and art books here, many of specific interest to the tourist looking to go a little deeper into the history and culture of Buenos Aires. It's open Tuesday through Sunday from 1 to 9pm. Perú 1064 (at Humberto I). © **11/4361-8210.** www.asuntoimpreso.com. No metro access.

El Ateneo (Grand Splendid) ★★ 📷   This is one of Buenos Aires's most magnificent bookstores, for the selection, but most certainly for the location. It's built into a former turn-of-the-20th-century theater and preserves the ornamentation, stage, and even the theater boxes which serve as reading cubbyholes. It's considered to be among the largest bookstores in South America; it certainly qualifies as one of the most beautiful. Open Monday through Saturday from 10am to 10pm, and Sunday from 10am to 9pm. Av. Santa Fe 1860 (at Callao). © **11/4813-6052.** www.tematika.com. Metro: Callao.

Librerías Turísticas   Every and any kind of tourism book on Argentina and the rest of the world can be found here. The company is itself a publisher and seller of books. Open Monday to Friday 9am to 7pm, Saturday from 9am to 1pm. Paraguay 2457 (at Pueyrredón). © **11/4963-2866** or 4962-5547. www.libreriaturistica.com.ar. Metro: Pueyrredón.

Papelera Palermo ★ 🎒   If you're looking for an unusual "only in Argentina" gift, and beautiful paper to wrap it in, this is the place. You'll find small notebooks, bound in leather or with a handcrafted Evita or Che Guevara cover, to write down your thoughts on Buenos Aires. Artistic photo books and other unique leather office goods are also for sale, along with a large selection of colorful specialty papers and notecards. Open Monday to Saturday 10am to 8pm, Sunday 2 to 8pm. Honduras 4945 (at Serrano). © **11/4833-3081.** www.papelerapalermo.com.ar. No metro access.

Walrus Books ★   This unique English-language bookstore was opened by Geoffrey Hickman, an American who moved to Buenos Aires after falling in love and marrying Josefina, his Argentine wife. They stock thousands of used English-language books, and many translations of historical South American texts and literature, as well as collections of new books and travel guides. If you're looking for something literary in English to read on the *subte* or the plane ride home, this is the place to shop. Open Tuesday to Sunday noon to 8pm. Estados Unidos 617 (at Peru). © **11/4300-7135.** www.walrus-books.com.ar. Metro: Moreno.

CAMERAS & ACCESSORIES

Cosentino   If you need something for your camera, are looking for a new one, or need high-quality developing services, Cosentino offers it all and can refer you for camera repairs. It's open Monday through Friday 9am to 7pm and Saturday from 9am to 12:30pm. Av. Roque Sáenz Peña (Diagonal Norte) 738, at Perón. © **11/4328-9120.** www.optica cosentino.com.ar. Metro: Catedral.

FASHION & APPAREL

Palermo Soho is the place for boutiques showcasing both young and well-established designers, though prices are not the bargains they once were here. Women's fashion as a whole is flirty, fun, and, above all, feminine, made for a thin figure. Men's clothing tends toward the conservative, if not drab, in Argentina, but I list a few fashionable choices too. You will find the city's top international fashion stores along Avenida Alvear and Calle Quintana in Recoleta.

Akiabara   This store is part of a chain, with very pretty, feminine creations, many made in Argentina. Prices are moderate to high end. Open daily 10am to 9pm. Honduras 4865 (btw. Serrano and Thames, off Plaza Serrano). © **11/4831-9420.** Metro: Plaza Italia.

Aristocracia   Enter this shop and the first things you'll notice are the red wall treatments and the luxurious, yet casual feel of the place. Lucrecia Gamundi designs most of the items here and has them produced in Argentina. The store also imports clothes from France, Italy, and other countries. This Las Cañitas location is somewhat new, but it was in Recoleta for 10 years before that. The service is excellent in this store that is well known for its interesting window displays. It's open Monday through Saturday from 10am to 9pm. Av. Arguibel 2867 (at Arce). © **11/4772-1144.** Metro: Carranza.

Bakú ★★ 🖋   All the designs in Bakú are the brainchild of Liliana Basili, who opened her own store in 2003 in the Las Cañitas neighborhood of Palermo. She produces unique handbags, leather accessories, belts and belt buckles, and various items of jewelry. All the items are produced in Argentina. Though her shop has a expensive address, the merchandise is quite reasonably priced. Open Monday from 1 to 10pm and Tuesday through Saturday from 10am to 10pm. Av. Arguibel 2890 (at Arce). © **11/4775-5570.** Metro: Carranza.

Bokura ★ 🖋   The amazing decor of this men's store almost takes away attention from the clothes. Built into a soaring former warehouse, the two-level shop is painted black, with Chinese dragons and other Asian decorations throughout. The store concentrates on jeans, designer T-shirts, and other clothing for young men, all produced in Argentina and perfect if you're looking for something to wear to go clubbing. The shop is open Monday through Saturday from 11am to 8:30pm and Sunday from 2 to 8:30pm. El Salvador 4677 (btw. Armenia and Malabia). © **11/4833-3975.** www.bokura.com.ar. No metro access.

Bolivia ★   At one of the city's best casual men's stores, you'll find everything from sportswear and jeans to fashion underwear. The shop is open Monday through Saturday from 11am to 8:30pm. Gurruchaga 1581 (at Honduras). ✆ **11/4832-6284.** www.boliviaparatodos.com.ar. No metro access.

Diseño Arg and Planeta Bs As ★★   More a collection of stores than one store, **Diseño Arg** was started by fashion journalist Claudia Jara. The backstory: Just before the 2001 peso crisis, as Argentina's economy stagnated, young designers she interviewed asked her how they could show their designs when they had no money to open a boutique. Claudia answered their questions by opening this space, where designers were able to rent small booths (it became even more relevant after the crisis ensued). You'll find dozens of designers here with their wares; it's a very personal shopping experience. The shop is primarily for women, with a few men's items thrown in. Nearby, Claudia opened project **Planeta Bs As** (✆ 11/4832-2006), which works on the same principle, at Jorge Luis Borges 1627, just off Plaza Serrano. Planeta Bs As is open Tuesday through Sunday 11am to 8pm. Diseño Arg is open Tuesday to Friday 2 to 8pm, and Saturday and Sunday noon to 8pm. Honduras 5033 off Plaza Serrano. ✆ **11/4832-2006.** www.disenioargshopping.com.ar and www.mujermilenio.com.ar. No metro access.

Escada   This boutique shop sells casual and elegant selections of women's clothing. Clothing from this international brand is slightly less expensive here than in North America and Europe. Av. Alvear 1444 (btw. Parera and Libertad). ✆ **11/4814-0292.** No metro access.

Florentina Muraña ★★ 👜   This wonderful little store in Palermo Soho takes its name from a character in a Borges story that took place in Palermo. You'll find very pretty, feminine clothing made of interesting materials here. Some examples of the offerings include popcorn shag sweaters, handmade in Argentina from Italian wool, crystal jewelry, and an extensive collection of leather clothing and accessories. The owner is Gabriela Sivori; she works in the shop and designs some of the items for sale, all of which are made solely in Argentina. Open daily from 11:30am to 8pm, though hours fluctuate in the summer. Calle Borges 1760, at Pasaje Russel. ✆ **11/4833-4137.** www.florentinamurania.com.ar. No metro access.

La Remera ★★   One of the newer designer shops in Buenos Aires, opened in 2010, La Remera is the creation of Ariel Estanga, an Argentine who had also worked in Spain for Zara and Mango. The clothes are simple and chic, utilitarian, and multifunctional. Ariel calls his clothes "simple and basic pieces you always need, something to use for the day and into the night," things which are great for travelers. Most of the designs are for women, but some are unisex, and a few are for men. Open Monday to Friday 10:30am to 7pm, Saturday from 11am to 2pm. Arenales 1239, the Rue des Artisans Passageway, 1N. ✆ **11/4519-8074.** www.laremera.com. Metro: Callao.

Lupe ★★ 👜   Designer Guadalupe Villar opened this white, airy, and always busy store in 2004. Her designs are young and feminine, with an emphasis on casual sportswear at reasonable prices. Open Monday to Saturday from 11am to 8pm and Sunday 3 to 7pm, though hours will vary in summer. El Salvador 4657 (at Armenia). ✆ **11/4833-9205.** www.lupeba.com.ar. No metro access.

Mancini ★★ 👜   While women can shop 'til they drop with the mind-boggling number of choices in Buenos Aires, most clothing stores in Argentina tend to have a limited selection of interesting men's clothing. Mancini, a chain with men's and women's clothing, is an exception to the rule. This branch, in Palermo Viejo, offers chic clothing, with an emphasis on black. Whether they are unfriendly or simply jaded, the staff generally leaves shoppers in this store on their own, not following them around as in other stores in the city. Open Monday to Saturday from 10am to 8:30pm, Sunday 11am to 7pm. Honduras 5140 (btw. Thames and Uriarte). ✆ **11/4832-7570.** No metro access.

Maria Cher ★   This boutique is a work of art in itself, with its glass-and-steel construction and its own interior bamboo garden. Maria Chernajovky's store has an emphasis on dresses and leather coats and other leather clothing. It's a perfect spot for a woman looking for mature, sophisticated, fashionable clothing. Open Monday to Saturday from 10am to 9pm, and Sunday 2 to 7:30pm, though hours will vary in summer. El Salvador 4724 (at Armenia). ✆ **11/4832-3336.** www.maria-cher.com.ar. No metro access.

Mishka Shoes ★★ 📖   If you're a woman with a shoe fetish, head to this small boutique in Palermo Soho. It's not cheap by any means—prices range up to $500 for Swarovski Crystal beaded sandals and other unique handmade footwear—but it's great for a splurge. All the shoes are made in Argentina, and custom sizes and details can be arranged. If your travel companions get bored, make them wait on the long white settee, while you drool over the selection. Open Monday to Saturday from 11am to 8:30pm. El Salvador 4673 (at Armenia). ✆ **11/4833-6566.** www.mishka shoes.com. No metro access.

Polo Ralph Lauren   This is the Buenos Aires branch of the famous American luxury retailer. You will find slightly lower prices here than in North America or Europe. The building, an old turn-of-the-20th-century Art Nouveau mansion, is also a reason to visit: The ornate wooden trim and balustrades remain, and a stained-glass skylight oversees the whole shop. Open Monday to Saturday 10am to 8pm. Av. Alvear 1780 (at Callao). ✆ **11/4812-3400.** No metro access.

Porto Fem Talles Grandes   While most of the clothes in Buenos Aires seem aimed at top-heavy stick figures, this store has the same styles in plus sizes. A law passed in 2006 states that all stores are supposed to carry large sizes, but in super-skinny Argentina, few stores do; this one, however, focuses on them. Open Monday through Friday 10am to 8pm, Saturday 10am to 2pm. Av. Santa Fe 1129 (btw. Libertad and Cerrito). ✆ **11/4813-6219.** www.portofem.com. Metro: San Martín.

Prototype ★   This store features sleek, well-designed men's clothing that can go from office wear to a night on the town. Focusing on solids and simple patterns, the best way to describe the style is a clean, polished, metrosexual look. All the clothes are Argentine-made, and there is also a great selection of shoes and small leather accessories. Part of a chain, the store has locations throughout Buenos Aires. Some of the stores have furniture sections, with an eye to modern male tastes, concentrating on dark leathers, functional lamps, black-glass knickknacks, and other household goods. Open Monday through Saturday from noon to 9pm. Malabia 1720 (btw. El Salvador and Costa Rica). ✆ **11/4832-8540.** www.prototypeweb.com. Metro: Carranza.

Rapsodia   Clothing in this chain store is often made from exotic fabrics in fantastic color combinations, or ranges to the feminine, frilly, and romantic. Most of the clothing is made in Argentina. Several of the boutiques exist throughout Buenos Aires. This shop is open daily from 10am to 9pm. El Salvador 4757 (btw. Gurruchaga and Armenia). ✆ **11/4832-5363**. www.rapsodia.com.ar. No metro access.

JEWELRY

The city's finest jewelry stores are in Recoleta and inside many five-star hotels. You can find bargains on gold along Calle Libertad, near Avenida Corrientes.

The **Murillo Street Leather Warehouse** district in the Villa Crespo neighborhood lets you compare prices and selection in a hurry. We've listed several individual stores in the area, including the large Murillo 666, one of the street's main outlets. Items are often made above the storefront, or in a factory nearby. Don't be afraid to bargain, or ask for custom orders if you don't find exactly what you like on the shop floor. The densest concentration of stores is on Murillo, between Malabia and Acevedo, but a total of about 50 stores fan out from there, selling everything from leather jackets to purses, luggage, furniture, and more. Many of the smaller stores are owned by Orthodox Jews, so will be closed on Friday evenings and Saturdays, as well as Jewish holidays, so take that into account when planning a visit.

Cousiño Jewels Located along the Sheraton hotel's shopping arcade, this Argentine jeweler features a brilliant collection of art made of the national stone, the rhodochrosite, or Inca Rose. In the Sheraton Buenos Aires Hotel, Av. San Martín. ✆ **11/4318-9000.** Metro: Retiro.

H.Stern This upscale Brazilian jeweler, with branches in major cities around the world, sells an entire selection of South American stones, including emeralds and the unique imperial topaz. It's the top jeweler in Latin America. Branches in the Marriott Plaza, Calle Florida 1005 at Santa Fe, overlooking Plaza San Martín (✆ **11/4318-3083**); Metro: San Martín; and the Sheraton, Av. San Martín 1225 at Leandro N. Alem (✆ **11/4312-6762**); Metro: Retiro.

Marcelo Toledo Gallery ★★★ The jewelry and silver objects made in Marcelo Toledo's gallery are exquisite and represent some of the finest traditional craftsmanship in Argentina. Famous clients include U.S. President Bill Clinton and various royal heads of state. In 2007, Toledo launched a special collection called Evita, based on artifacts of the time of Maria Eva Duarte de Perón, which is also available in his shop here and in various hotel gallery shops throughout Buenos Aires and in the Museo Evita. Open Sunday to Friday, from 10:30am to 5:30pm. Humberto I 462 (btw. Bolívar and Defensa). ✆ **11/4362-0841.** www.marcelotoledo.net. Metro: San Juan.

LEATHER

With all that beef in its restaurants, Argentina could not be anything but one of the world's best leather centers. If you're looking for high-quality, interestingly designed leather goods, especially women's shoes, accessories, and handbags, few places beat Buenos Aires's selection. Many leather stores will also custom-make jackets and other items for interested customers, so do ask if you see something you like in the wrong size or want to combine ideas from pieces. Most can do this in a day or two, but if you are intent on bringing something home from Argentina, you should start checking out stores and prices early on in your trip. Some stores take a week for custom orders, and if something is complicated to make, it might take even longer.

Ashanti Leather Factory ★ This small store on Calle Florida offers a wide selection of leather goods, from men's and women's jackets to funky and interesting women's handbags. Their prices on jackets are not the best, but women's accessories are very competitively priced, and you can always bargain. Best of all, their factory is in the basement of the shop, so they can easily custom-make almost anything for you. Ask them for a tour, through which you can meet the craftspeople Roberto, Victor, and Oscar, who sit surrounded by sewing machines and colorful bolts of leather. Open daily from 10am to 10pm. Calle Florida 585 (at Lavalle). ✆ **11/4394-1310.** Metro: San Martín.

Casa López ★★ Widely considered among the best *marroquinería* (leather-goods shops) in Buenos Aires, Casa López sells an extensive range of Argentine leather products. There is also a shop in the Patio Bullrich Mall (see "Recoleta" under "Great Shopping Areas," earlier). Open Monday to Friday 9am to 9pm, Saturday and Sunday 10am to 6:30pm. Marcelo T. de Alvear 640 (at Maipú, near Plaza San Martín). ✆ **11/4311-3044.** www.casalopez.com.ar. Metro: San Martín.

Chabeli This store offers a wide selection of women's shoes and pocketbooks, and most things cost no more than $150. They also offer an interesting selection of hand-made Argentine jewelry from crystals and semiprecious stones. Designs of leather accessories and jewelry fall into two main categories: native Argentine and very pretty and feminine, with pink and pastel materials. They also have another branch in the Patagonian resort town of Bariloche. Open Monday through Friday from 10am to 6pm, Saturday 10am to 3pm. Calle Venezuela 1454 btw. San Jose and Saenz Pena. ✆ **11/4384-0958.** Metro: Saenz Pena.

El Nochero All the products sold at El Nochero are made with first-rate Argentine leather and manufactured by local workers. Shoes and boots, leather goods and clothes, and decorative silverware (including *mates,* for holding the special herbal tea Argentines love) fill the store. Open Monday through Saturday from 10am to 9pm, Sunday and holidays noon to 9pm. Posadas 1245 (in the Patio Bullrich Mall). ✆ **11/4815-3629.** www.elnochero.com. No metro access.

Murillo 666 ★★ This store is the main outlet in the Murillo Street Leather District in the Villa Crespo neighborhood. They have a large selection of women's coats and accessories, and one of the largest assortments of men's jackets, which they will also custom-make. Plus, they have the largest furniture showroom in the district. Officially, unlike many stores around here, they offer the same prices for cash or for credit, but sometimes you can still bargain a price down slightly with cash only. Open daily 9:30am to 8pm. Murillo 666 (btw. Malabia and Acevedo in Villa Crespo). ✆ **11/4856-4501.** www.murillo666.com.ar. Metro: Malabia.

Outlet ★ The name says it all for this store just off Murillo: This is definitely a place to bargain, and shopping with friends might save you even more money, because they offer group discounts. In addition to large selections of jackets, hand-bags, gloves, and other items, this store also carries a small selection of shoes. Those couches you're sitting on as your friend tries everything on? You can buy those in various colors as well. There is also a small selection of women's fur coats here. Open Monday to Friday 10am to 7:30pm, Saturday 10am to 2pm. Scalabrini Ortiz 5 (at Murillo, in Villa Crespo). ✆ **11/4857-1009.** Metro: Malabia.

Outlet de Cuero Smaller than some of the other stores, this shop still provides great service, though the selection is better for women than men. Items range from jackets to handbags. If you can't find what you want, this is a perfect place to ask about what can be made from their various leather swatches on hand. Open Monday to Saturday 9am to 7pm. Murillo 643 (btw. Malabia and Acevedo, in Villa Crespo). ✆ **11/4854-8436.** Metro: Malabia.

Paseo Del Cuero ★ Along with coats and the usual items for men and women, this factory outlet in the Murillo district also has a great selection of men's and women's small luggage carry-ons and gym bags. Feel free to bargain, as the staff often gives you a slightly lower price if you hesitate or offer to pay in cash. Looking for cowhide throw rugs? They've got those too. Open Monday to Saturday 9:30am to 7:30pm. Murillo 624 (btw. Malabia and Acevedo, in Villa Crespo). ℂ **11/4855-9094.** www.paseodel cuero.com.ar. Metro: Malabia.

Pasión Argentina–Diseños Etnicos ★★ With chain stores overrunning Palermo Viejo, it's good to see this small independent shop thriving in the heart of it all. Owner Amadeo Bozzi concentrates on leather goods primarily for women, accessories for men and women, and the home. All items are produced in Argentina; they are well designed and well made. Some combine leather with other native materials made by members of the Wichi tribe, a native group in the Chaco region. I highly recommend visiting this store, which is technically by appointment only, from Monday through Friday from 10am to 6pm, and at other times. Scalabrini Ortiz 2330 (btw. Charcas and Güemes). ℂ **11/4832-7993.** www.pasion-argentina.com.ar. Metro: Scalabrini Ortiz.

Raffaello by Cesar Franco ★★ Cesar Franco got his start designing for the theater and tango shows and it comes through in the flare of his clothes. His shop has everything from sportswear to wedding dresses, and truly exquisite leather coats for both men and women, many made by combining leather strips with rich fabrics, in designs that recall Renaissance-era clothing. The shop is open Monday to Friday from 10am to 6pm, Saturday 10am to 2pm, and by appointment. Rivadavia 2206, 1st floor, Ste. A (at Uriburu). ℂ **11/4952-5277.** www.raffaellobuenosaires.com. Metro: Congreso.

Rossi & Caruso Offering some of the best leather products in the city since 1868, this store is the first choice for visiting celebrities—the king and queen of Spain and Prince Philip of England among them. Products include luggage, saddles, and accessories as well as leather and chamois clothes, purses, wallets, and belts. There is another branch in the Galerías Pacífico mall (p. 135). Open daily 9:30am to 8:30pm. Av. Santa Fe 1377 (at Uruguay). ℂ **11/4814-4774.** www.rossicaruso.com. Metro: Bulnes.

626 Cueros The blasting disco music here tells you you're in a place with a little edge compared to some of the other leather stores in the Murillo district. Here you'll find interestingly designed men's and women's coats, many slightly less expensive than in the other stores. Pay cash and get a discount. Open Monday to Saturday 10am to 6pm. Murillo 626 (btw. Malabia and Acevedo, in Villa Crespo). ℂ **11/4857-6972.** Metro: Malabia.

WINE SHOPS

Argentine wineries, particularly those in Mendoza and Salta, produce some excellent wines. Stores selling Argentina wines abound, and among the best are **Grand Cru,** Av. Alvear 1718; **Tonel Privado,** in the Patio Bullrich Shopping Mall and in Galerías Pacífico; **Winery,** which has branches at L. N. Alem 880 and Av. Del Libertador 500, both downtown; **Vinos Argentinos** at Tucumán 565 just off Calle Florida; and in Palermo Viejo, **Lo De Joaquin Alberdi** at Borges 1772 at Costa Rica.

BUENOS AIRES AFTER DARK

From the Teatro Colón (Colón Theater) to dimly lit tango salons, Buenos Aires offers an exceptional variety of nightlife. Porteños eat late and play later: Theater performances start around 9pm, bars and nightclubs open around midnight, and no one shows up until after 1am. Thursday, Friday, and Saturday are the big nights for going out, with the bulk of activity in Recoleta, Palermo, and Costanera. Summer is quieter, because most of the town flees to the coast.

Performing arts in Buenos Aires are centered on the highly regarded Teatro Colón, home to the National Opera, National Symphony, and National Ballet. In addition, the city boasts nearly 40 professional theaters (many located along Av. Corrientes, btw. 9 de Julio and Callao, and in the San Telmo and Abasto neighborhoods) showing Broadway- and off-Broadway-style hits, Argentine plays, and music revues, although most are in Spanish. Buy tickets for most productions at the box office or through **Ticketmaster** (© 11/4321-9700). The **British Arts Centre,** Suipacha 1333 (© 11/4393-0275), runs productions in English.

For entertainment listings, check the *Buenos Aires Herald* (in English) or any of the major local publications. The *QuickGuide Buenos Aires* also has information on shows, theaters, and nightclubs. Many of Buenos Aires's nightlife venues also have a presence on Facebook, Twitter, and MySpace, so you can get onto guest lists and find out the very latest about their events.

The Performing Arts
THEATERS, EXHIBITIONS & OTHER VENUES
There is no shortage of exciting theater and art exhibitions in Buenos Aires. It's high quality, varied, and extremely inexpensive considering what you get. Check out the options below, or head to Corrientes, Buenos Aires's answer to Broadway, and look at whatever is currently running in town. Besides the offerings at the British Arts Centre, virtually everything will be in Spanish. I list some ticket prices in this section, particularly on the low end. However, for the larger theaters and for international stars, expect to pay prices only about 20% to 30% less than in North America or Europe. Tickets can be purchased at most theaters listed here by going to the box office, or by visiting **Ticketek.com (www.ticketek.com.ar),** which also lists performance schedules. More programming can also be found under the Culture ribbon on the city's website, www.buenosaires.gov.ar. Many theaters close just before Christmas and early January, following the summer crowds to Mar del Plata, so check to see if a show you want to see is actually running. As in North America and Europe, Monday is usually the dark night in larger theaters, except on national holidays, when there are usually slightly early evening performances.

Asociación Argentina de Cultura Inglesa (British Arts Centre) ★★★
This multifunctional facility was established nearly 80 years ago by a British ambassador who wanted to do more to promote British culture within Argentina. He was highly successful in his efforts, and today the AACI teaches English to tens of thousands of students a year; runs several film, theater, culture, and art programs; and generally provides a very welcoming environment for any homesick English speaker. Events can range from the rarefied (Shakespeare) to the raunchy (*Absolutely Fabulous* TV program showings). The center has a very limited summer schedule from January to March, and be aware that as of this writing recent British austerity measures are likely to also have an impact on programming. You can pick up brochures and event listings at the center, or look up listings in the English-language *Buenos Aires Herald.* Suipacha 1333 (at Arroyo). © **11/4393-2004** or 4393-6941. www.aaci.org.ar and www.britishartscentre. org.ar. Tickets $4–$20. Metro: San Martín.

Centro Cultural de Borges ★★ Not only can you shop all you want in Galerías Pacífico, but, if it's culture you're after, you can find that there too. The shopping mall houses this arts center named for Jorge Luis Borges, Argentina's most important literary figure. You'll find art galleries; lecture halls with various events; an art cinema; art bookstore; the **Escuela Argentina de Tango,** which offers a schedule of lessons tourists can take with ease (ℰ **11/4312-4990;** www.eatango.org); and the ballet star **Julio Bocca's Ballet Argentino** performance space and training school, full of young ballet stars (see below). Enter through Galerías Pacífico or at the corner of Viamonte and San Martín. ℰ **11/5555-5359.** www.ccborges.org.ar. Ticket prices vary. Metro: San Martín.

Centro Cultural Recoleta (Recoleta Cultural Center) ★

To the side of the famous cemetery, this distinctive building—originally designed as a Franciscan convent—hosts Argentine and international art exhibits, experimental theater works, occasional music concerts, and an interactive science museum for children called Museo de Ciencias Participativas, where children are encouraged to touch and play with the displays. Some events within the Centro require tickets, but many exhibitions are free. The Hard Rock Cafe is behind the Cultural Center in the Recoleta Design Shopping Center. It's open Monday through Friday from 2 to 8pm, Saturday and Sunday 10am to 9pm. Junín 1930. ℰ **11/4803-1040.** www.centroculturalrecoleta.org. Tickets $2–$15; many events are free. No metro access.

Grupo de Teatro Catalinas Sur

This theater company presents outdoor weekend performances in different areas of La Boca, as well as in their own theater in a converted warehouse. It's in Spanish, but it's mostly comedy, and both adults and children are likely to enjoy the productions. Av. Benito Pérez Galdós 93 (at Caboto). ℰ **11/4300-5707.** www.catalinasur.com.ar. Tickets $4–$15. No metro access.

Julio Bocca's Ballet Argentino ★★★

Julio Bocca is Argentina's greatest ballet and dance star. Many of his performances combine tango movements with classical dance, creating a style uniquely his own, and uniquely Argentine. He runs a studio in the Centro Cultural de Borges for classical dance and ballet performances, as well as another performance space in Teatro Maipo on Calle Esmeralda, offering a range of events from dance to comedy plays. Mr. Bocca himself has officially retired, but even without him on stage, his Ballet Argentino troupe is a must-see for lovers of ballet and dance, especially the performances featuring Claudia Figaredo and Hernan Piquin. In the Centro Cultural de Borges, at Galerías Pacífico (at the corner of Viamonte and San Martín). ℰ **11/5555-5359.** www.juliobocca.com. Tickets $8–$30. Metro: San Martín. Teatro Maipo: Calle Esmeralda 449 (at Corrientes). ℰ **11/4394-5521.** Metro: Lavalle.

Luna Park

Once the home of international boxing matches, the Luna is the largest indoor stadium in Argentina, hosting some of the biggest shows and concerts in Buenos Aires. Many of these are classical music concerts, and the National Symphonic Orchestra often plays here. Though they had actually met previously, legend has it that a 1944 fundraiser here, for the victims of the San Juan earthquake, was where Juan Perón first met a very young actress named Eva Duarte, changing Argentine history forever. The song "On This Night of a Thousand Stars" in the musical commemorates this fundraising event. Numerous international stars have played here, and seeing them in Argentina costs significantly less than in North America and Europe. Av. Corrientes and Bouchard. ℰ **11/4311-1990** or 5279-5279. www.lunapark.com.ar. Metro: L. N. Alem.

Teatro Colón (Colón Theater) ★★★ 📷

A more detailed description of this venue appears in "Other Attractions," earlier in this chapter. The building itself is a major tourist stop, in addition to being a performance space. This magnificent space, home to the country's finest opera, classical music, and theater performances, recently underwent an extensive renovation, which was more than 2 years behind schedule. As of this writing, portions of the theater are still being renovated, but this does not impact performances. If you're in Buenos Aires, don't miss this venue: The memory of an opera or musical in the Teatro Colón will last a lifetime. Calle Libertad 621 (at Tucumán). ✆ **11/4378-7100.** www.teatrocolon.org.ar. Metro: Tribunales.

Teatro Gran Rex   Within this sleek, imposing Art Deco theater, you can see many national and foreign music concerts. Av. Corrientes 857 (at Suipacha). ✆ **11/4322-8000.** Metro: Carlos Pellegrini.

Teatro Municipal General San Martín   This entertainment complex has three theaters staging drama, comedy, ballet, music, and children's plays. The lobby in itself, which often hosts exhibitions of photography and art, is worth a special visit during the daytime. Lobby exhibitions are usually free. Corrientes 1530 (at Paraná). ✆ **0800/333-5254.** www.teatrosanmartin.com.ar. Metro: Uruguay.

Teatro Nacional Cervantes   Some of the city's best theater takes place here, in this production house originally built by a group of Spanish actors as a thank you to Buenos Aires. The building is sumptuous, in an ornate Spanish Imperial style, using materials brought from Spain. In 2008 and 2009, a restoration program helped the detailed facade gleam anew. Av. Córdoba 1155 (at Libertad). ✆ **11/4815-8883.** www.teatro cervantes.gov.ar. Metro: Tribunales.

Teatro Opera Citi ★   This futuristic, Art Deco theater has been adapted for Broadway-style shows. The building is itself a unique and rare example of Art Deco design in Buenos Aires. The facade has undergone a partial renovation, which has revealed the lightning-bolt glass panels once hidden by advertising signs. Citibank is now the official sponsor of the theater. Many locals complained when Citibank removed the neon Opera sign, replacing it with its own. Now, there is a compromise where the neon reads Opera Citi. It brings up the dilemmas of corporate sponsorship for cultural venues but it's a tossup considering the even more ugly advertising plaques have been removed. Av. Corrientes 860 (at Suipacha). ✆ **11/4326-1335.** Metro: Carlos Pellegrini.

Teatro Presidente Alvear   Tango, classical, and other music shows take place at this theater. Av. Corrientes 1659 (at Montevideo). ✆ **11/4374-6076.** www.unica-cartelera.com.ar/alvear.htm. Metro: Callao.

The Club & Music Scene
TANGO SHOWS

In Buenos Aires, you can watch the tango or dance the tango. You'll have many opportunities to see the dance during your visit: Tango and *milonga* dancers frequent the streets of La Boca and San Telmo, some hotels offer tango shows in their lobbies and bars, and tango salons blanket the city. San Telmo's are the most famous (besides Café Tortoni), and they usually combine dinner and a show. Call a radio-taxi, or *remise,* to get to San Telmo, La Boca, or Barracas at night. For safety's sake, don't take the metro there or walk. Most of the tango shows also offer direct transportation. While I include some general ticket prices as a guide, ask your hotel concierge for special ticket prices, which include transportation from the hotel (usually a shuttle bus). Travel agencies can also sometimes book tickets at group rates.

Café Tortoni   High-quality yet inexpensive tango shows take place in the back room of the Café Tortoni. The prices, generally about $20, do not include dinner as in other tango shows, but you can order off the menu and pay extra. Shows run Wednesday through Monday at 9pm. Av. de Mayo 829. ✆ **11/4342-4328.** www.cafetortoni.com. ar. No cover. Metro: Plaza de Mayo.

El Querandí El Querandí offers the best historically based tango show in the city, tracing the tradition from its early roots in bordellos, when only men danced it, to its current leggy, sexy style. A great slab of beef and glass of wine come with the show. Open Monday through Saturday; dinner begins at 8:30pm, followed by the show at 10:15pm. Perú 302 at Moreno. ✆ **11/5199-1770.** www.querandi.com.ar. Tickets $80–$100. Metro: Moreno or Bolívar.

El Viejo Almacén The most famous of the city's tango salons, the Almacén offers what some consider the city's most authentic performance. Shows involve traditional Argentine-style tango (many other shows feature international-style tango). Sunday through Thursday shows are at 10pm; Friday and Saturday shows are at 9:30 and 11:45pm. Dinner is served each night before the show starts, in the restaurant across the street. Guests may opt for dinner and the show or show only, with standard and VIP pricing for seats closer to the stage. Some hotels offer transportation. Independencia and Balcarce. ✆ **11/4307-6689.** www.viejo-almacen.com.ar. Tickets $60–$137. Metro: Independencia.

Esquina Carlos Gardel ★ In my opinion, this is one of the most elegant tango shows. It's on the former site of the Chanta Cuatro—a restaurant where Carlos Gardel used to dine with his friends—though the building is new. The dining room has a luxurious old-time vibe but it features high-tech acoustics and superb dancers, creating a wonderful environment for this excellent performance. Doors open at 8pm, with standard and VIP pricing for seats closer to the stage. Carlos Gardel 3200 at Anchorena, across from the Abasto Shopping Center. ✆ **11/4867-6363.** www.esquinacarlosgardel.com. ar. Tickets $105–$210. Metro: Carlos Gardel.

Señor Tango This enormous theater is more akin to a Broadway production hall than a traditional tango salon, but the dancers are fantastic. The owner, who clearly loves to perform, is also a good singer. Walls are covered with photos of what appears to be every celebrity who's ever visited Buenos Aires—and all seem to have made it to Señor Tango. Diners choose among steak, chicken, or fish for dinner. Despite the huge crowd, the food quality is commendable. Have dinner (at 8:30pm) or come only for the show (at 10pm); standard and VIP pricing for seats closer to the stage or private alcoves. Vieytes 1655 (at Domingo). ✆ **11/4303-0231.** www.senortango.com.ar. Tickets $47–$213. No metro access.

TANGO DANCE CLUBS (MILONGAS)

Tango palaces and dance performances are wonderful, but nothing compares to the lure of a *milonga* (tango salon), and Buenos Aires seems to have more now than ever. Rather than destroy tango, the peso crisis has heightened its popularity, here and abroad. Just as the early Porteños turned to tango a century ago to alleviate their pain and isolation, now modern residents are dancing their melancholy away. With the increase in tourism and the enormous number of Europeans and North Americans lured here by the dance, the number of *milongas* is unprecedented.

The numbers listed here are not necessarily those of the venues, but rather the dance organizations that organize the events, often with rotating venues. For further details, check the listings in *La Milonguera* or *El Tangauta,* the city's tango magazines. There's usually a $5 to $10 fee to get into a *milonga*. Tango, like most nightlife in Buenos Aires, is a very late affair; most *milongas* don't get busy until 2am—even on weeknights.

Important: Note that this scene is not without its rules and obstacles. Tango is an art form and a unique part of the city's culture. Never enter a *milonga* with the obvious air of a clueless tourist, which might alter the atmosphere of a venue. You might even be refused entry or asked to leave if your behavior or appearance upsets the balance of a place in some of the smaller, more traditional venues. In fact, some of the city's underground *milongas* aren't listed anywhere and require a contact to get in, akin to a 1920s speak-easy. If possible, attend a *milonga* with a local who knows the scene.

El Arranque 👫 El Arranque may look like a Knights of Columbus hall, but it's one of the most authentic venues for *milongas;* it's also one of the few places that hosts afternoon dancing. Tango's late-night schedule could drive even a vampire crazy, but here you can dance and still get a real night's sleep afterward. No matter how old and pot-bellied a man is, he can be with any woman in the crowd as long as he dances well. Even older women, however, tend to keep up appearances here, dressing beautifully and stylishly. This place will be very comfortable for older crowds. They strictly enforce traditional tango rules about separating the sexes, however; couples might not even be allowed to sit together. Open Tuesday through Sunday, dancing starts around 3pm. Bartolomé Mitre 1759 (at Callao). ✆ **11/4371-6767.** Admission $5. Metro: Congreso.

El Beso Nightclub 👫 The way to this club may be a little confusing, but follow my directions and you'll be fine. It's unmarked, so the street address is your only indication that you're in the right spot. Walk upstairs, pay your fee, and squeeze past the crowded bar blocking your view. The small space beyond maintains the air of a 1940s nightclub, updated for the modern era with brilliant reds and modern abstractions painted on some of its walls. Ceiling lamps made from car air filters cast a golden glow on the dancers. Some of the best performers drag their egos with them to the floor, so if you're not so good on your feet, just watch; the last thing you want is to bump into someone. The divisions between the *milongueras* and *milongueros* are not so strong, and the sexes tend to mix informally. Reserve a table ahead of time if you can. Different *milongas* take place on different nights. Check their calendar in advance for details. Snacks, wine, and beer are on sale. Riobamba 416 (at Corrientes). ✆ **11/4953-2794** or 15-4938-8108 (mobile). Admission $5. Metro: Callao.

El Niño Bien ★★ 👫 If you want to travel back in time, to an era when tango ruled Buenos Aires, few places will do you better than El Niño Bien. The beautiful main dance hall is straight from the Belle Epoque; you'll half expect Carlos Gardel himself to show up behind the mic. Dressed in black, men and women tango while patrons at side tables respectfully study their techniques. Don't look too closely at anyone, however, unless you know what you're doing: *Milonga* eyes—staring across a room to attract a partner onto the dance floor—are taken seriously. Food is served, but don't bother unless you're famished; it's only so-so. Unfortunately, Niño Bien is becoming a victim of its own success, and many tour groups are starting to unload here. If you're looking to find a tango teacher, one will probably find you first at this venue; many instructors come here seeking students for private lessons. Centro Región Leonesa, Humberto I no. 1462 (at San José). ✆ **11/4483-2588.** Admission $5–$6. No metro access.

La Viruta 👫 Located in the cellar of the Armenian Community Center, this is one of the most interesting *milongas*. It is authentic, but it attracts a very young crowd of Porteños and expats who have come from all over the world to dance their lives away in Buenos Aires. Many nights it is just a *milonga*. Other nights host shows and competitions, often involving tango and folkloric and modern dance. When decorated with balloons for some events, it looks a little like a high school prom from the 1970s. There is an admission fee, but it is usually free here after 3am, when a throng arrives from other *milongas*. Armenia 1366 (at Cabrera). ✆ **11/4774-6357.** Admission $8. No metro access.

It seems impossible to imagine Argentina without thinking of tango, its greatest export to the world. First danced by working-class men in La Boca, San Telmo, and the port area, tango originated with a guitar and violin toward the end of the 19th century. Combining African rhythms with the *habanera* and *candombe,* it was not the sophisticated dance we now know. It originated in brothels, known locally as *quilombos,* and was considered too obscene for women—even "working" women. Men would actually dance it with each other as they waited their turn in the lounges of brothels.

Increasing waves of immigrants added Italian elements to tango, which helped the dance make its way to Europe. It was eventually internationalized in Paris. With a sense of approval from Europe, Argentine middle and upper classes began to accept the newly refined dance as part of their cultural identity. The form blossomed under the extraordinary voice of Carlos Gardel, who brought tango to Broadway and Hollywood. Astor Piazzola further heightened the international recognition of tango music, increasing its complexity by incorporating classical elements.

Tango music usually involves a piano and *bandoneón*—an instrument akin to an accordion, introduced by German immigrants. If a singer is participating, the lyrics might come from one of Argentina's great poets, such as Jorge Luis Borges, Homero Manzi, or Horacio Ferrer. Themes focus on a downtrodden life or a woman's betrayal, making it akin to American jazz and blues, which developed at the same time. The dance itself is improvised, consisting of a series of long walks and intertwined movements, usually in eight-step. The man and woman glide across the floor, with the man leading the way through early flirtatious movements that give way to dramatic leads and heartfelt turns. These movements—including kicks that simulate knife movements, or the sliding, shuffled feet that mimic a gangster silently stealing up to murder someone—reflect the dance's rough origins, even though tango today is refined and beautiful. The dancing style in salons is much more subtle and subdued than "show tango."

Tango lessons are an excellent way for a visitor to get a sense of what makes the music—and the dance—so alluring. Most respectable dancers would not show up before midnight, giving you the perfect opportunity to sneak in for a group lesson, offered at most of the salons starting around 9pm. They usually cost between $12 and $20 for an hour; you can request private instruction for between $20 and $40 per hour, depending on the instructor. In summer, the city of Buenos Aires promotes tango by offering free classes in many locations. Visit the nearest tourist information center for updated information. Among the most magical days to be in Buenos Aires is December 11, the Dia Nacional de Tango, sometimes also called Milona Nacional, and Carlos Gardel's birthday. Buenos Aires and many other cities in Argentina close off major thoroughfares to allow thousands of couples to dance in the streets.

Plaza Bohemia 🍴 You'll find this place in what seems an isolated part of the MicroCentro by noticing the open door late at night, leading to a staircase. Inside, the interior is plain, highlighted by mirrors and a DJ booth. Here though, it's all about the dancing with various events on different nights, including the Wednesday night gay tango **La Marshall** (www.lamarshall.com.ar). Check local listings for various nightly events, including special tango presentations. Maipú 444 (at Corrientes). ✆ **11/4328-0465** or 15-6657-9867 (mobile). www.plazabohemia.net. Admission $5–$8. Metro: Florida or Lavalle.

Salón Canning ★★ 🎵 This is among the most authentic of all of the *milongas*. At the end of a long hallway, spectators crowd around the main dance floor to watch couples make their way around it. Salón Canning is known for its extremely smooth, high-quality wooden parquet floor, considered one of the best for dancing in all of Buenos Aires. This tango hall is among the few things left in Buenos Aires that still bear the name of George Canning—a British diplomat who opened relations between Argentina and Great Britain after independence from Spain. Many nights are run by the group ParaKultural (www.parakultural.com.ar), and you may hear locals referring to Salon Canning with this name. Many nights incorporate a mix of tango dancing, special guest dancers who are often old tango stars, along with live orchestras. It is a place that should not be missed. Friday is among the best nights, with many young, fashionable tango enthusiasts, many residing in Palermo. Saturday is more traditional. Scalabrini Ortiz 1331 (at Gorriti). ✆ **11/4832-6753.** Admission $8. No metro access.

OTHER DANCE CLUBS

Dancing in Buenos Aires is not just about tango; the majority of the younger population prefers salsa and techno beats. Of course, nothing in life changes quite so fast as the "in" discos, so ask around for the latest hot spots. The biggest nights out are Thursday, Friday, and Saturday. The websites **www.adondevamos.com** and **www.bsasinsomnio.com.ar** are great resources for Buenos Aires nightlife. Club entry will generally run $15 to $25. The city's best salsa dancers head to **Salsón,** Av. Alvarez Thomas 1166, between Loreto and Zabala (✆ **11/4551-6551**), a megaclub that offers lessons on Wednesday and Friday evenings at 9pm. In Palermo Soho, head to **Kika,** Honduras 5339, at Juan B. Justo (✆ **11/4137-5311;** www.kikaclub.com.ar), for rock and techno. Some of the city's largest clubs are in the Costa Salguero riverfront industrial complex, near Palermo but far from where they can wake anybody up. They include **Pachá,** Avenida Costanera Norte at Pampa (✆ **11/4788-4280;** www.pachabuenosaires.com), modeled after the iconic Ibiza original. Call ahead for VIP tables. Nearby, **Tequila,** Costanera Norte and La Pampa (✆ **11/4788-0438**), is packed every night; and **La Diosa,** Rafael Obligado 3731, off Avenida Costanera Norte (✆ **11/4806-9443** or 15-4997-2082 [mobile]; www.ladiosabuenosaires.com.ar), caters to a young, mixed crowd. One of the most popular gay and lesbian clubs is **Amerika,** Gascón 1040, at Córdoba in Barrio Norte (✆ **11/4865-4416**), which has two floors of dance music on Friday and Saturday. Straight Porteños come often too, claiming it has the best music, generally staying on the smaller upstairs level. Saturdays, **Human** (www.humanclub.com.ar), at Avenida Costanera Norte and Sarmiento, is another popular gay night spot.

The Bar Scene

Buenos Aires has no shortage of popular bars, and Porteños need little excuse to party. The following are only a few of the bars and pubs worthy of recommendation. Strolling along, you'll find plenty on your own. Most smoking now takes place outside, though you'll still find plenty of people breaking the ban indoors.

The Alamo-Shoeless Joe's No matter what time of day it is, you'll find something going on at this American-owned 24/7 bar. The Alamo-Shoeless Joe's was originally simply called Shoeless Joe's, but when the Texas-born owner Pete found Argentines could not pronounce it, he added an homage to his home state in the name. The bar is also managed with Dave from Chicago, a friend. It's a great gathering place for football games and other American sports events, but even locals come too. Breakfast specials are a treat after being out all night clubbing, and there's beer of all kinds by the bottle or on tap in huge pitchers, along with student discounts, free pizza during the happy hour from 8 to 10pm during the week, and other bargains. Food is a simple selection, with most mains running about $4 to $12. With the free Internet station, you'll find another reason to come by. Uruguay 1175 and 1177 (btw. Santa Fe and Arenales). ℂ **11/4813-7324.** www.elalamobar.com. Metro: Callao.

Bar Isabel   When this bar opened in Palermo Soho, next to Casa Cruz, it took the city by storm, becoming famous as the place for models. Now it's hit or miss, but if there are models to be found it's on Tuesday. The bar was opened by Juan Santa Cruz, the original force behind Casa Cruz. Drinks are expensive, and they use a system called Isabelitas, 25-peso poker chips. You'll need one for water or soft drinks, two for mixed drinks, meaning a cocktail will set you back about $13 each, a very high price in Buenos Aires. The club is a mix of mod funk and classic styling, with 1940s style veneered nightclub tables, edged with S&M studs, all lit from above by orange glowing mushroom lights. Outside, the fireplace patio is a great place for a smoke and to chat, whether or not your companion has graced the cover of *Vogue*. Uriarte 1664 (at Honduras). ℂ **11/4834-6969.** www.barisabel.com. Metro: Callao.

Cronico Bar   The bar has overlooked Plaza Serrano for over 20 years, and its movie posters outside are probably the first thing you'll notice. Inside, you'll find a busy place where people sit at tables painted with nude women in the style of Picasso. There's typical bar food such as sandwiches and hamburgers, but with a larger menu than most of the surrounding bars. Live rock music sometimes entertains the crowd. It's also open 24 hours daily, so it's also good for an after-hours snack. Borges 1646, at Plaza Serrano. ℂ **11/4833-0708.** www.cronicobar.com. Metro: Plaza Italia.

Gran Bar Danzon   A small, intimate bar, Danzon attracts a fashionable crowd with its small selection of international food and smart, relaxing lounge music. An excellent barman serves exquisite cocktails and a variety of liquors and wines. Libertad 1161 (at Santa Fe). ℂ **11/4811-1108.** www.granbardanzon.com.ar. Metro: San Martín.

The Kilkenny   This trendy cafe/bar is more like a rock house than an Irish pub, although you will still be able to order Guinness, Kilkenny, and Harp on tap. It's packed with locals and foreigners, and you are as likely to find people in suits and ties as in jeans and T-shirts. Happy hour runs nightly from 6 to 8pm and live bands hit the stage every night after midnight; it stays open until 5am. Marcelo T. de Alvear 399, at Reconquista. ℂ **11/4312-9179** or 4312-7291. www.thekilkenny.com.ar. Metro: San Martín.

Milion ★★   A bar and a restaurant, this place really comes alive at night, especially on weekends. It is one of the most stunningly set locales in Buenos Aires, inside a turn-of-the-last-century mansion in Barrio Norte. On the ground floor is the restaurant, but head upstairs to the bar, where a very glamorous set of locals is ordering drinks and getting to know each other. The activity spreads up the French wrought-iron staircase throughout the building's various levels, where rooms are strewn with chairs, couches, and ottomans. There's also an outdoor patio, and drinking and socializing flows down the glamorous marble staircase leading into the garden. If you hear about any of the local art or media parties that sometimes happen here, make sure to go. Parana 1048 (at Santa Fe). ℂ **11/4815-9925.** www.milionargentina.com.ar. Metro: Callao.

Plaza Bar   Nearly every Argentine president and his or her cabinet have come here, in addition to visiting celebs such as the queen of Spain, the emperor of Japan, Luciano Pavarotti, and David Copperfield. A vague mix of Art Deco and English country, the bar features mahogany furniture and velvet upholstery, where guests sip martinis and other high-end drinks. Tuxedo-clad waiters recommend a fine selection of whiskeys and brandies. In 2005, *Forbes* magazine declared it among the world's top nine hotel bars, based on several factors—the clientele, the beverage selection, and the way the staff makes everyone feel welcome, even if they come only once in a lifetime. This was at one time the city's most famous cigar bar, but the 2006 anti-smoking law put an end to that decades-long tradition. Nevertheless, add it to your list of things to do. Inside the Marriott Plaza Hotel, Calle Florida 1005, at Santa Fe (overlooking Plaza San Martín). © **11/4318-3000.** Metro: San Martín.

Plaza Dorrego Bar ★   Representative of a typical 19th-century Porteño bar, Plaza Dorrego displays portraits of Carlos Gardel, antique liquor bottles in cases along the walls, and anonymous writings engraved in the wood. This is one of the specially protected bars and *cafés notables;* stop by on Sunday, when the crowd spills onto the street and you can catch the San Telmo antiques market on the plaza in front. Calle Defensa 1098, at Humberto I (overlooking Plaza Dorrego). © **11/4361-0141.** Metro: Constitución.

Rey Castro ★   A giant statue of Castro greets you as you enter this club and restaurant. They have an excellent Caribbean menu, and hot salsa and Latin dancing on two levels. For happy hour (Mon–Thurs 6–9:30pm) the emphasis is on mojitos and Cuba Libres. Calle Peru 342 (at Moreno). © **11/4342-9998.** www.reycastro.com. Metro: Moreno.

The Shamrock   The city's best-known Irish pub is lacking in authenticity; you're more likely to hear hot Latin rhythms than soft Gaelic music here. That said, it remains hugely popular with Argentines and foreign visitors alike, and it's a great spot to begin the night. There is an enormous game room with pool tables and other attractions in the basement. Rodríguez Peña 1220 (at Juncal). © **11/4812-3584.** Metro: Callao.

Sugar   This Palermo Soho spot has become trendy with English-speaking expats who have decided to make Buenos Aires their home and the Argentines who like to meet them. When major news or sports events happen of interest to the English-speaking world, this is where people gather to watch them. They have an inexpensive bar menu, a daily $2-a-drink happy hour (7pm–midnight), and DJ-accompanied mingling. Costa Rica 4619 (btw. Armenia and Gurruchaga). © **11/4831-3276.** www.sugarbuenosaires.com. No metro access.

5

BUENOS AIRES

Buenos Aires After Dark

SIDE TRIPS FROM BUENOS AIRES

by Michael Luongo

I f you're spending more than 4 or 5 days in Buenos Aires, you might want to consider a side trip—especially if you're visiting in summer, when many Porteños hit the beach resorts. Mar del Plata is the country's most popular stretch of shore, and some of the country's most famous musicians and other entertainers follow the beachgoers there. To describe Mar del Plata as crowded in summer is an understatement, as more than eight million people visit in December, January, and February alone.

Just outside Buenos Aires's suburbs is the **Tigre Delta,** a beautiful complex of islands and marshland full of small bed-and-breakfasts, resorts, and adventure trails. You can make a day trip here on mass transit from Buenos Aires, or you can stay overnight. It is busiest in summer, but most sites and hotels are open year-round.

The Pampas surround Buenos Aires, and here you'll find gauchos and the stuff of Argentine cowboy lore. The region's main town is **San Antonio de Areco,** about 90 minutes north of the capital. Few people stay in town, preferring to lodge at the surrounding *estancias* (19th-c. ranch farms), several of which are detailed here. Across the Río de la Plata from Buenos Aires is Uruguay. Many Argentines will tell you to skip it, but you would be missing out on this tiny country's charms. **Colonia,** 45 minutes away from Buenos Aires by ferry, is a delight for a day trip, or a romantic overnight for couples. Uruguay's capital, **Montevideo,** with its own nightlife, restaurants, and cultural scene, is perfect, and just 3 hours by boat from Buenos Aires.

MAR DEL PLATA

400km (248 miles) S of Buenos Aires

Argentina's most popular beach resort is a sleepy coastal city of about 700,000 long-term residents—that is, until mid-December, when Porteños flock here through March for their summer vacation. Nearly eight million vacationers will pass through in the summer season, the vast majority of them Argentines. Although it's not as luxurious as Uruguay's Punta del Este—the beach favorite of many jet-setting Argentines—Mar del Plata is closer to Buenos Aires and far cheaper. Its long, windy coastline is known for its crowded, tan-bodied beaches and quieter seaside coves, and beautiful landscapes farther inland, leading to the edge of the grassy Pampas. The resort was once very exclusive, but in the Perón era hotels and high-rises were built for labor unions and the middle class, changing the social and physical makeup of the city forever. Some of the magnificent French- and Tudor-style mansions, which housed Argentina's summer elites in the early 20th century, have been meticulously preserved as museums.

Mar del Plata offers excellent nightlife in summer, when independent theater companies from Buenos Aires come to town, and nightclubs open their doors to passionate Latin partygoers. The months of December, January, and February are the most crowded, wild, and expensive for visiting. In March, families with children and retired couples make up the bulk of vacationers, taking advantage of a more relaxed atmosphere and the slight reduction in prices. Many hotels and restaurants remain open year-round; though the weather is chillier, people do vacation here on winter weekends too. While Argentines will tell you stories about family vacations here over the generations, the city only hit the international radar during the November 2005 Summit of the Americas, when massive protests took place against the former U.S. president George W. Bush's presence.

Essentials

GETTING THERE   You can reach Mar del Plata by plane, car, bus, train, or boat. The airport lies 10 minutes from downtown and is served by **Aerolíneas Argentinas** (✆ **800/333-0276** in the U.S., or 0810/222-86527 in Argentina; www.aerolineas. com.ar). Flights are just under an hour, and about three flights depart each day. Cabs will cost about $15 to $20 into the center of town. The RN 2 is the main highway from Buenos Aires to Mar del Plata; it takes about 4 to 5 hours to drive between these cities. More than 50 bus companies link Mar del Plata with the rest of the country. Buses from Buenos Aires, which arrive at the central bus terminal at Alberti 1602 (✆ **223/451-5406**), are comfortable and cost under $30. One company serving Mar del Plata is **Chevallier** (✆ **11/4000-5255** in Buenos Aires and 0223/561-3719 in Mar del Plata; www.nuevachevallier.com). Buses depart Buenos Aires at the Retiro Bus Station. A train run by the company **Ferrobaires** (✆ **223/475-6076** in Mar del Plata, or 11/4304-0028 in Buenos Aires). also connects Mar del Plata with Buenos Aires, and it's only slightly more expensive than the buses. It leaves Buenos Aires from Constitución, in the southern part of the capital, and runs three times a day. In Mar del Plata, purchase tickets at the train station, located at avenidas Luro and Italia Bus; the trip takes about 4 to 5 hours.

VISITOR INFORMATION   The **Centro de Información Turística,** Bd. Marítimo P.P. Ramos 2270, at the Casino building (✆ **223/495-1777;** www.mardel plata.gov.ar or www.turismomardelplata.gov.ar), has a knowledgeable, helpful staff offering maps and suggested itineraries. It is open daily from 8am to 9pm. There is also a branch at the airport. An additional website for tourism information is www. mdp.com.ar.

GETTING AROUND   La Rambla marks the heart of the city, the seaside walk in front of the casino and main city beach. This area is walkable on its own, with restaurants and other businesses clustered here and between the nearby bus station and Plaza San Martín. Farther south, the Los Tronces neighborhood houses the city's most prominent residences as well as Playa Grande (the main beach), the Sheraton hotel, and the Mar del Plata Golf Club. Mar del Plata has 47km (29 miles)

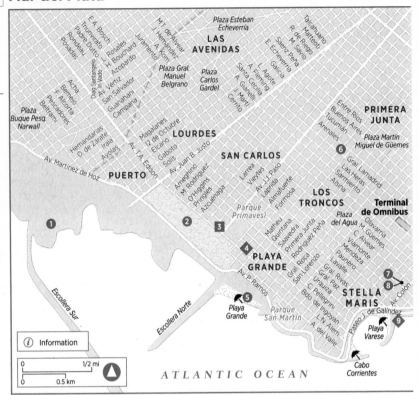

of Atlantic coastline, so if you plan to go to that part of the city, you'll need to take a taxi or rent a car. **Avis** (📞 **0810/9991-AVIS [2847];** www.avis.com.ar) rents cars at the airport.

Seeing the Sights

The main reason to visit Mar del Plata is the beaches, all of which spread out from the city's heart at **Plaza Colón.** Here you'll find the **Mar del Plata Casino,** also known as **Casino Hotel Hermitage** (📞 **223/451-9226;** www.loteria.gba.gov.ar). The red brick–and–granite structure guarded by sea lion sculptures is the social center of the city. Walkways and steps lead from here to the beach, with many people posing in front of the giant granite sea lions for their only-in–Mar del Plata photos. In the early evening, as the crowds head home from the beach, you'll often see street performers and musicians here. (Watch your pockets if you stand and admire.) With long, slow breaks, **Waikiki** is the best spot for surfing. The coastline is nice, but you should not come expecting to find the Caribbean—the Atlantic remains fairly cold, even during summer. Once you've brushed off the sand, visit the **fishing harbor,** where hundreds of red and yellow boats unload their daily catches. The harbor houses a colony of 800 male sea lions that come to bathe on the rocky shores. (Be

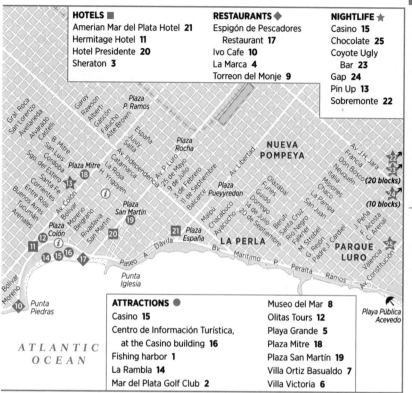

HOTELS ■
Amerian Mar del Plata Hotel **21**
Hermitage Hotel **11**
Hotel Presidente **20**
Sheraton **3**

RESTAURANTS ◆
Espigón de Pescadores
    Restaurant **17**
Ivo Cafe **10**
La Marca **4**
Torreon del Monje **9**

NIGHTLIFE ★
Casino **15**
Chocolate **25**
Coyote Ugly
    Bar **23**
Gap **24**
Pin Up **13**
Sobremonte **22**

ATTRACTIONS ●
Casino **15**
Centro de Información Turística,
    at the Casino building **16**
Fishing harbor **1**
La Rambla **14**
Mar del Plata Golf Club **2**

Museo del Mar **8**
Olitas Tours **12**
Playa Grande **5**
Plaza Mitre **18**
Plaza San Martín **19**
Villa Ortiz Basualdo **7**
Villa Victoria **6**

warned that btw. the sea lions and the fishing boats, it's an olfactory disaster.) Next to the colony, there's an ugly but intriguing boat graveyard where rusty boats have been left to rot away.

In the Los Tronces neighborhood, **Villa Victoria,** at Matheu 1851, at Arenales (© **223/492-0569**), showcases the early-20th-century summerhouse of wealthy Argentine writer Victoria Ocampo, who published the Argentine literary magazine *Sud* and was the first female member of the Argentine Academy of Letters. Some of Argentina's greatest authors have stayed here visiting her writing salons, including Jorge Luis Borges. It is open year-round Thursday to Tuesday from 1 to 8pm, with an admission charge of about $4. In summer, musical and theatrical performances are held in the gardens, with various entry prices depending on the event. **Villa Ortiz Basualdo,** Av. Colón 1189 (© **223/486-1636**), is an English-style Victorian mansion decorated with exquisite Art Nouveau furniture from Belgium. The building is open daily from 10am to 10pm with an entry charge of just over $1. In the same neighborhood, the **Museo del Mar,** Av. Colón 1114, at Viamonte (© **223/451-9779;** www.museodelmar.com), houses a collection of 30,000 seashells. Stop in for a bite at their cafe, surrounded by tanks of sharks eyeing you and your meal. This is an ideal spot for visiting if you're with kids, and the rooftop terrace has an amazing view to the ocean a few blocks away. In summer, it is open Sunday to Friday 9am to 7pm, Saturday 9am to 10pm. During the winter, it's open daily from 9am to 1pm. Admission is about $3 for the museum, and various prices for lectures and other events at the adjacent auditorium.

Twenty minutes from the city center, **De Los Padres Lake and Hills** is a picturesque forest with wide parks surrounding the lake, perfect for an afternoon picnic. Nearby, in the Barrio Sierra de los Padres, is the **Zoo El Paraíso**, Ruta 266, Km 16.5 (© **223/463-0347;** www.zooelparaisoonline.com.ar). The park is open daily 10am to 7pm, with a charge of $8 for adults and $3 for children. It features a wonderful collection of flora and fauna, including plants and trees from all over Argentina as well as lions, pumas, monkeys, llamas, and other animals. For information on surfing, deep-sea fishing, mountain biking, horseback riding, trekking, and other adventure sports, contact the tourism office. The tour company **Olitas Tours** also does half-day city tours, as well as a special tour for children on a bus filled with clowns. Visit their kiosk at Plaza Colón, call © **223/500-2816,** or log on to www.olitas-tours.com.ar.

Where to Stay

EXPENSIVE

Sheraton ★★ ☺   The Sheraton overlooks the golf course and the military port, near Playa Grande. Rooms were renovated in 2007 and include trademark Sheraton Suite Sleeper beds. The hotel has a children's area and a video arcade, making it a great family choice. The Sheraton has two pools (one indoors, one out); a $15 charge applies to use of the indoor pool, connected to the spa and sauna complex. Two restaurants are in the hotel: the informal **La Pampa,** open for breakfast, lunch, and dinner, with an international menu, as well as the formal **Las Barcas,** only open for dinner Wednesday to Sunday. With the gym's view to the sea, it's simply stunning for a workout; updated equipment makes it even better. Rooms are airy and even standards seem oversize; suites have Jacuzzi tubs.

Alem 4221, 7600 Mar del Plata. © **0800/777-7002** or 223/414-0000. Fax 223/499-0009. www.sheraton mardelplata.com.ar. 191 units. From $236 double with city views; $272 double with ocean views; from $405 suites. Rates include buffet breakfast. AE, DC, MC, V. Parking $15. Pets allowed. **Amenities:** 2 restaurants; bar; babysitting; concierge; golf; large health club; massage; 2 pools (fee for use of indoor pool); 24-hr. room service; rooms for those w/limited mobility. *In room:* A/C, TV, hair dryer, high-speed Internet, Jacuzzi (suites only), minibar, Wi-Fi.

MODERATE

The Hermitage Hotel   This is Mar del Plata's grande dame hotel, opened in 1943 and where celebrities often stay. The Louis XV–style lobby has gilded friezes of fishermen, with art and photos of old Mar del Plata. The hotel added a new building, Torre Colón, in 2002 at the same time renovating the old building. The Torre Colón rooms are nicer and pricier, with sea or city views. Formal restaurant Luis Alberto, where breakfast is served along with lunch and dinner, is in a connecting atrium. The hotel has a private casino (open Sun–Thurs 3pm–midnight, Fri–Sat until 4am) and beach with bar and towel service from 8am to 10pm. While the hotel faces the ocean, the Torre Colón lobby is the main entrance. Also on property are a small gym and spa, and a rooftop heated pool with a spectacular sea view.

Bd. P.P. Ramos 2657 and Av. Colón 1643 (overlooking the Casino), 7600 Mar del Plata. www.hermitage hotel.com.ar. © **223/451-9081.** Fax 223/451-7235. 300 units. From $164 double in old building; from $200–$215 double in Torre Colón; from $300–$350 suites. Rates include buffet breakfast. AE, DC, MC, V. Parking $10. **Amenities:** Restaurant; bar; babysitting; casino; concierge; health club; massage; pool; 24-hr. room service; spa; rooms for those w/limited mobility. *In room:* A/C, TV, hair dryer, high-speed Internet, minibar, Wi-Fi.

Hotel Presidente   This small older four-star hotel, owned by Spanish chain Hoteles Alvarez, is about a block from the beach. It's full of dark woods, and some rooms are on the small side, but the pleasant staff more than makes up for any faults. Some amenities, such as the restaurant **Tartufu,** where breakfast is served, and the small gym, are shared with neighboring Hotel Iruña. Breakfast is included, and some side rooms have sea views. Overall this hotel is a good choice for those who want good service on a reasonable budget. Each room comes with a small desk and vanity. A small convention center on the eighth floor hosts meetings, and the lobby bar can be very busy. Here, you'll also find two computer terminals with free Internet access.

Corrientes 1516 at Diagonal J. B. Alberdi, 7600 Mar del Plata. ℰ **223/491-1060.** Fax 223/491-1183. www. hotelpresidente.com. 53 units. From $155 double with city view; $158 double with sea view; from $207–$254 suites. Rates include buffet breakfast. AE, DC, MC, V. Parking $10. **Amenities:** Restaurant; lobby bar; babysitting; concierge; small health club; massage; 24-hr. room service; spa; Internet stations. *In room:* A/C, TV, hair dryer, Wi-Fi.

INEXPENSIVE

Amerian Mar del Plata Hotel   The Amerian is an Argentine chain hotel, and this branch in Mar del Plata overlooks Plaza España and La Perla Beach. The hotel is surrounded by several nightclubs, so it can be noisy at night. Prices may differ depending on view (sea or city). Rooms are spacious, however—especially in this price category. Junior suites, positioned at angles, all have some form of sea view, even if it's not direct. Suites come with Jacuzzi tubs, and all the bathrooms are on the large side no matter the category. Wi-Fi is available in the rooms for a $5 charge and for free in the lobby where a small computer station is available for guest use. There is no gym, though staff will help guests arrange to visit one nearby for $4.

Av. Libertad 2936 (at La Rioja and Yrigoyen), 7600 Mar del Plata. www.amerian.com. ℰ **223/491-2000.** Fax 223/491-2300. 58 units. From $102 double; from $123 suite. Rates include buffet breakfast. AE, DC, MC, V. Free parking. **Amenities:** Restaurant; bar; access to nearby fitness center; Internet station; limited room service; Wi-Fi. *In room:* A/C, TV, hair dryer, minibar, Wi-Fi.

Where to Eat

Espigón de Pescadores Restaurant ★★ SEAFOOD   You'll see this restaurant the moment you pull into Mar del Plata, only because it's under the enormous Quilmes neon billboard sign on the pier. The three-level eatery juts into the ocean and is one of the best seafood restaurants in town. Built into the Fisherman's Club, it's the next best thing to catching the fish yourself. Fish of all kinds—sole, salmon, calamari, lobster, oysters, and everything else local or shipped in—is here. Landlubbers will find pasta, salads, and *parrilla* (grill) offerings too, and some of the same sauces for fish double as pasta sauces. Naturally, there are a lot of white wines on the menu. I list a high top price here, but most main courses run about $12.

Bd. Marítimo and Av. Luro, in the Club de Pesca, on the city pier. ℰ **223/493-1713.** www.espigonde pescadores.com.ar. Main courses $6–$25. AE, DC, MC, V. Daily noon–3pm and 8pm–midnight.

Ivo Cafe ★★ GREEK/ARGENTINE   I can't say enough about this fantastic two-level Greek restaurant at the bottom of a high-rise condo overlooking the ocean with sidewalk seating. The Greek owners serve Greek food—oversize Greek salads, excellent souvlakia, and many other choices—along with Argentine *parrilla*. Chic black tables are set with olive- and eggplant spreads for dipping your bread. They have an English-language menu, but ask for the Spanish one if you can read it; it has more and better choices. From the plate-glass windows, diners have a view of the sweeping arc of lights on the Mar del Plata shoreline. Come for dinner shows each Thursday, beginning at 9pm, with Greek dancing for a charge of about $20, which includes a meal but not the cost of drinks. Or, come in the wee hours on any day, and you'll find that the staff breaks into piano playing, singing, and traditional dancing.

Bd. Marítimo 3027 at Güemes. ☎ **223/486-3160.** www.ivocafe.com. Main courses $8–$13. AE, MC, V. Daily 24 hr. in summer; winter Sun–Thurs 8am–3am, Fri–Sat 24 hr.

La Marca ★★ ARGENTINE   This restaurant became famous for serving a whole cow upon special request, for large groups of 50 or more people. It's not often that they do that anymore, but La Marca remains the town's best *parrilla*, serving thick rump steaks, tenderloins, and barbecued ribs of beef, flanks, and other cuts of beef. The tender filet mignon with mushroom sauce is delicious. The menu includes pork chops, sausages, sweetbreads, black pudding, and other delights as well. The salad bar is extensive. Service is polite and unhurried. Try the *dulce de leche* before you leave.

Almafuerte 253 at Alem, on Playa Grande near the Sheraton. ☎ **223/451-8072.** www.lamarcarestaurant. com.ar. Main courses $8–$12. AE, DC, MC, V. Daily noon–3pm and 8:30pm–1am.

Torreon del Monje ★★ ARGENTINE   It's hard not to notice this restaurant, located inside a castlelike structure dating from 1904 and overlooking the Atlantic. Day or night, the plate-glass windows over the sea and opening onto the street offer a fantastic view. Food runs from simple sandwiches to a *parrilla* with steak, chicken, and, of course, locally caught seafood. Almost each night, dinner shows take place while you dine, beginning at 10pm. Some are tango, others flamenco and folkloric. There is no additional charge for the shows; they're part of the experience of dining here. If you've dined elsewhere, stop in for drinks at the beautiful oak bar. During the day, many people come for the flavored and alcoholic coffee specials in the Esmeralda lounge.

Paseo Jesús de Galíndez, at the Puente del Monje, on the water. ☎ **223/451-9467.** www.torreondel monje.com. Main courses $6–$15. AE, DC, MC, V. Sun–Thurs 8am–2am; Fri–Sat 8am– 4am.

Mar del Plata After Dark

Nightlife follows closely behind beaches as Mar del Plata's biggest draw. In summer, theater companies leave Buenos Aires to perform in this coastal resort; ask the tourism office for a schedule of performance times and places. The city's most popular bars are south of Plaza Mitre, off Calle San Luis. The best dance clubs are along Avenida Constitución, 3km (2 miles) from downtown, including **Chocolate,** Av. Constitución 4445 (☎ **223/479-4848;** www.chocolatemdq.com.ar); **Gap,** Av. Constitución 5780 (☎ **223/479-6666**), featuring live rock music; and **Sobremonte,** Av. Constitución 6690 (☎ **223/479-7930**). **Pin Up,** Santiago del Estero 2265 (no phone; www.pinupweb.com), is one of the most popular gay discos. **Coyote Ugly Bar,** Av. Constitución 6690 (☎ **223/479-2600**), is a favorite Mexican restaurant and bar, which breaks into salsa and merengue dancing as the night goes on.

TIGRE & THE DELTA

36km (22 miles) NE of Buenos Aires

The Tigre River Delta is in essence a wild natural suburb of Buenos Aires, but it seems a world apart from the city. The delta is formed by the confluence of five rivers, where they flow from the Pampas into the Río de la Plata. This marshy complex is full of silt and thousands of tiny islands. Over time, the Delta is continuing to grow down the Río de la Plata and has grown considerably since the Spanish Conquest. In theory, within several hundred years, the Delta will reach the capital. The islands are a mix of grassland, swamp, and true forest, with a variety of animal and plant life. The name Tigre comes from the tigers, actually jaguars, which once roamed here.

The development of the Tigre Delta into a resort area owes to two concurrent historical circumstances in Buenos Aires in the 1870s. One was the construction of railroads from Buenos Aires into the rest of the country. The other was the 1877 outbreak of yellow fever, which caused wealthy Porteños to seek out new parts of the city for new year-round homes as well as summer vacation spots. The English were in charge of much of the construction here, so many of the older neo-Gothic and mock-Tudor mansions and bed-and-breakfasts that line the banks of the river passages look like Victorian London buildings transplanted into the wild marshes of the Pampas.

Today, many Porteños come here on weekends to relax, kayak, ride horseback, hike, fish, swim, or do nothing at all. It's also a convenient destination for tourists, since it's easy to come here just for the day, tour the islands by boat, and return to Buenos Aires in time for dinner. There is a year-round population of residents on these car-free inner islands, and they go to school, work, and shop for groceries using a system of boats and docks. The Delta fell into decline a number of years ago, but has been revived. Very wealthy Argentines are beginning to move and vacation here, buying large homes on remote islands, and frequenting the recently developed spa resorts.

Essentials

GETTING THERE The Tigre Delta is best reached by train from Buenos Aires and then a boat or launch from the train station if continuing on to the islands. Trains from Buenos Aires depart **Estación Retiro** for Estación Tigre, at Avenida Naciones Unidas, every 10 to 20 minutes along the Mitre Line. Tickets run about $1 round-trip. Call © 11/4317-4445 or 0800-3333-822 for schedules and information, or visit www.tbanet.com.ar. **Sturla** (© 11/4731-1300 in Tigre or 4314-8555 in Buenos Aires; www.sturlaviajes.com.ar) also runs a boat from Puerto Madero in Buenos Aires to Tigre, offering sensational waterfront views. Within Tigre, the **Estación Fluvial Tigre,** where the boats depart to head through the various rivers and islands, is on the next block over from the train station, **Estación Tigre,** at Mitre 305. Many companies run launches and services on both banks of the river here; you have to know where you want to go, or simply choose one and go where it takes you. Among the many companies are **Catamaranes Interisleña** (© 11/4731-0261; www.tigreencatamaran.com.ar); **Líneas Delta** (© 11/4749-0537; www.lineasdelta.com.ar); and **Catamaranes Río Tur** (© 11/4731-0280; www.rioturcatamaranes.com.ar). To reach **Martín García Island,** one of the most remote parts of the delta, you have to travel with **Cacciola** (© 11/4749-0329; www.cacciolaviajes.com). Most of these companies service the various islands but allow you to ride on the boat until the end of the trip and then simply return. Ticket prices vary but range from less than $5 and up. I highly recommend that you find out when the last few boats leave from your destination; toward the end of the day, boats can fill up quickly, leaving some passengers to wait for the next boat. Extra boats are dispatched at peak times, but you still may have to wait a few extra hours at the end of the day, especially on Sunday. Build this time into your plans or you may literally get stuck in the mud. Many tour companies in Buenos Aires also provide excursions to the Tigre Delta, and I have included that information below.

VISITOR INFORMATION There are two main **Centros de Información Turística.** One is in Estación Tigre, open daily 9am to 6pm, and another at Estación Fluvial Tigre, at Mitre 305 (© **0800/888-TIGRE** [84473] or 11/4512-4497; www.tigre.gov.ar and www.vivitigre.gov.ar), open daily 8am to 6pm. This very busy office provides information on the islands, hotels, rentable bungalows, and other activities. You may have to wait for help, but most of the staff speaks English. Other useful tourism sites are www.laisladelta.com.ar and www.puntodelta.com.ar. Two excellent tour guides for Tigre are **Susana Neira** (© 11/4992-3780; susananeira159@gmail.com) and **Mariana Jimenez** (© 11/4997-7832; mariana.v.jimenez@gmail.com).

GETTING AROUND Within the town of Tigre itself, where both the train station and the docks are, one can easily walk along both banks. There are restaurants, playgrounds for children, and a few tourist-oriented shops along the waterfront and on the streets heading to the Puerto de Frutos (see below). To get around and see the delta, however, you will need a boat (see "Getting There," above). Of course, if you have the skills and stamina, swimming is another option.

Seeing the Sights

The main thing to see in Tigre is the delta itself and the various islands and resorts that dot the area. Within the town of Tigre, where the train station and boat docks are, there are a few services and various other places of interest. Many people simply stay in this area and dine in the restaurants, sunbathe along the shoreline, or wander the town. Ponies march up and down the eastern shoreline in the city center, near the intersection of calles Lavalle and Fernández (no address or phone); children love riding them. From this area, head along what is called **Paseo Victórica,** a collection of Victorian mansions along the waterfront of Río Lujan, until it intersects with Río Conquista. This is one of the prettiest parts of Tigre, and you will find many people sunbathing along the shore here. In the midst of all this Victorian splendor is the **Naval Museum,** Paseo Victorica 602, at Martínez (© 11/4749-0608). On the opposite bank is the **Parque de la Costa,** Vivanco, at Montes de Oca (© 11/4732-6000; www.parquedelacosta.com.ar), full of rides for kids and grown-ups. Just outside of the center of Tigre is the famous **Puerto de Frutos** (© 11/4512-4493; www.puertodefrutos-arg.com.ar), at Calle Sarmiento 160, along Río Lujan. Fruit farming was integral to the early development of the Tigre Delta, and this market is a holdover from those days. Most people rave about seeing this site, but in general, I have always found it disappointing, with almost no fruit. Besides the traditional basket weavers who create their wares using the reeds growing in the delta, the market is now mostly full of odds and ends and less interesting crafts that can be found in many places. Still, it is worth a quick visit. The **Museo de Arte de Tigre,** Paseo Victorica 972 (© 11/4512-4528; www.mat.gov.ar), however, is definitely worth your time. Built into what had been the Tigre Casino, the building is among the most impressive Argentine Beaux Arts buildings outside of Buenos Aires and took years to restore. The redesign of the casino as a museum was done by Gabriel Miremont, curator of the Museo Evita and numerous museums throughout Argentina. Admission is free and the museum is open Wednesday to Friday 9am to 7pm, and Saturday and Sunday noon to 7pm. This is a must-see in Tigre, and the collection of art will also help you understand when Tigre was a place for wealthy Bohemians to get away from the city and spend their time painting.

A 3-hour boat ride each way from the center of Tigre will take you to **Martín García Island.** It is famous for its upscale political prison, where various Argentine presidents, including Juan Perón, have been incarcerated, but exploring here will take a full day once you account for the round-trip boat ride.

Note: If you are doing any trekking on the islands, even in hot weather, you will need hiking boots, long pants, and long-sleeved shirts. Saw grass and other sharp plants inhabit the area and will rip into unprotected skin. You should also bring mosquito repellent, though malaria is not a problem in the Delta, only painful itching. It's also a good idea to pack binoculars, to view birds and other wildlife. Tigers and jaguars are no longer a concern in Tigre.

EXCURSION COMPANIES SERVING TIGRE DELTA

Various travel companies in Buenos Aires offer day-trip excursions to the Río Tigre delta or will arrange longer stays in the many B&Bs, bungalows, and adventure lodges there. **Say Hueque Tourism,** with two locations (Viamonte 749, Office 601, 1053 Buenos Aires, ✆ 11/5199-2517; Thames St. 2062, Buenos Aires, ✆ 11/5258-8740;** www.sayhueque.com), is one that I highly recommend, especially for longer trips and adventure excursions to see the natural beauty of the area. **Travel Line** (✆ 11/4393-9000; www.travelline.com.ar) offers Tigre Delta day tours, among many other excursions. The full-day Tigre tours are Sundays only (ask for an English-speaking guide) and include lunch, train transportation to Tigre, and a boat ride among the rivers of the Tigre delta for about $65 per person. Additionally, **Borello Travel** (✆ 800/405-3072 in the U.S. and Canada or 11/5031-1988 in Buenos Aires; borellotravel.com) offers luxury trips to the Delta, including stays at the spa resorts.

Where to Stay

Bonanza Deltaventura ★★   Head to this adventure hotel on one of the islands in the Río Tigre delta to get away from it all. There are miles of walkways through the grasslands for bird-watching and horses for riding along the shoreline. Or just swim off the dock out front. Guests can rent four small but comfortable rooms as either singles or doubles, for a total of eight people in the lodge. The living style is communal, with shared bathrooms and kitchen. The price is for 2 days and 1 night and includes meals and excursions, but alcoholic drinks cost extra. The staff also speaks English. You will need to call ahead of time to stay here, to ensure that space is available and that you take the right boat. The hotel is on the Carapachay River islands section of the delta, about a 1-hour boat ride from the center of the town of Tigre.

Carapachay River Islands, 1648 Tigre. ✆ **11/4728-1674** or 15-5603-7176 (mobile). www.deltaventura. com. 4 units. From $140 a person. Rates include meals and trekking. No credit cards. **Amenities:** Shared kitchen; horses; trekking.

Casona La Ruchi ★★   This charming bed-and-breakfast overlooks the waterfront across the bank from the Estación Fluvial. Owners Dora and Jorge Escuariza and their children run the place, treating guests who stay in the 1893 mansion like family. In the back, guests can gather and barbecue at the pool and grill. Rooms are furnished with quaint Victorian antiques, and some have windows looking out onto the waterfront. The place is open year-round, but busiest on summer weekends. Guests have 24-hour access, though the family does not have an actual overnight staff person. Call if you're arriving late in the day to verify that someone can let you in. You will enjoy the warmth and hospitality at this place. Some rooms share a bathroom; all have Wi-Fi.

Lavalle 557 (at Av. Libertador), 1648 Tigre. © **11/4749-2499.** www.casonalaruchi.com.ar. 6 units, some with shared bathroom. $60 double. Rates include continental breakfast. No credit cards. **Amenities:** Outdoor pool; use of kitchen and backyard grill; Wi-Fi.

Delta Eco Spa ★★   This resort hotel and spa complex opened in mid-2010. Portions, including additional bungalows and year-round residences off the main grounds, are still under construction as of this writing. Built on its private island, the complex has the feel of a rustic luxury jungle resort. The large spa has several treatment rooms with a view of the grounds, a wet and dry sauna, and an indoor heated pool. Rooms are large, perfect for couples. Some come with dual sinks and showers, and all have balconies or patios. The complex, including the spa, is open to the public for day trips and dining. Bungalows have cathedral ceilings and line a small inlet. I list daily rates, but rooms are usually booked as 2-night packages, which include scheduled express transport from central Tigre. No children under 10.

Río Carapachay, western delta, 1648 Tigre (20–30 min. boat ride from central Tigre). © **11/5236-0553.** www.deltaecospa.com. 20 units. From $165 double; from $340 suite; from $415 bungalow. Day rate with lunch $96, Spa Day $155 (with lunch, without treatments); $180 (with lunch and 1 treatment). Rates include meals and scheduled transport from central Tigre; spa treatments additional. AE, MC, V. **Amenities:** Restaurant; bar; concierge; massage; indoor pool; outdoor pool, room service; dry and wet sauna; spa; Wi-Fi. In room: A/C, TV, DVD, hair dryer, minibar, Wi-Fi.

Rumbo 90 Delta Lodge and Spa ★★★   This small, romantic spa resort with only seven rooms, all with Jacuzzis and balconies, was opened by the Gezzi family on the Canal del Este. The name is a nautical reference, meaning to turn east. Rooms are oversized, filled with antiques, and the honeymoon suite has an enormous balcony and two-person Jacuzzi. The large private island is divided into sections, with the main lodge grounds and a working farm. The spa, with a heated pool connecting to the outdoor pool, dry and wet sauna, and various treatment and massage rooms is open to the public for day trips on a limited basis so as not to spoil the low-key atmosphere, and the restaurant features its award-winning Menu Tigre, with an emphasis on local fish. I list daily rates, but rooms are usually booked as 2-night packages, which include scheduled express transport from central Tigre. No children under 16.

Canal del Este, eastern delta, 1648 Tigre (30-40 min. boat ride from central Tigre). © **11/4749-2499** or 15-5843-9454. www.rumbo90.com.ar. 7 units. From $220 double; from $300 suite. Day rate with lunch $88; Spa Day is $120 (lunch included; treatments extra). Rates include meals and scheduled transport from central Tigre. AE, MC, V. **Amenities:** Restaurant; bar; concierge; massage; outdoor/indoor pool; room service; dry and wet sauna; spa; Wi-Fi. In room: A/C, TV, DVD, hair dryer, minibar, Wi-Fi.

Where to Eat

Don Emilio Parrilla ARGENTINE/PARRILLA   A rustic interior and a casual atmosphere with tables in bright Provençal yellow await you in this *parrilla* overlooking the waterfront. The food here is great, and a complete meal will run you about $15 a person. Unfortunately, it's only open on weekends.

Lavalle 573, at Av. Libertador. © **11/4631-8804.** Main courses $3–$10. No credit cards. Fri 8pm–1am; Sat–Sun 11:30am–5pm and 8pm–2am.

El Moño Rojo ★ ARGENTINE/INTERNATIONAL   An enormous restaurant complex overlooking the waterfront near the Estación Fluvial, this is one of the best places to come for a meal with entertainment. The atmosphere is brilliantly red, festive, and very kitschy, full of posters of tango stars, pictures of Argentine actors and actresses, and old Peronist memorabilia. On Friday they stage a tango show. The food is a mixture of pizzas, snacks, sandwiches, and traditional *parrilla* grilled meat, so there should be something to please everyone here.

Av. Mitre 345, at Estación Fluvial Tigre. ✆ **11/15-5135-7781** (mobile). Main courses $4–$12. No credit cards. Daily 8am–2am.

La Terraza ★ ARGENTINE/INTERNATIONAL   This two-level restaurant looks like it was dropped in from a tropical island, with its wraparound verandas and palm tree overhangs. A full *parrilla* offers some of the best steak dining in Tigre. You'll also find chicken, salads, and Italian cuisine. Drink in the beautiful view to the Río Lujan.

Paseo Victoria 134, at Colon Tigre. ✆ **11/4731-2916.** www.laterrazatigre.com.ar. Main courses $4–$10. No credit cards. Tues–Sun noon–5pm; Fri–Sat 8pm–1am (sometimes later).

COLONIA DEL SACRAMENTO, URUGUAY

140km (87 miles) W of Buenos Aires

The tiny gem of Colonia del Sacramento, declared a World Heritage Site by UNESCO, appears untouched by time. Dating from 1680, when it was established by Manuel Lobo as a buffer colony by the Portuguese against the Spanish, the old city boasts beautifully preserved colonial artistry down its quiet, bougainvillea-draped, cobblestone streets. A leisurely stroll into the **Barrio Histórico (Historic Neighborhood)** leads you under flower-laden windowsills to churches dating from the 1680s, past simple single-story homes—from Colonia's time as a colonial settlement—and on to local museums detailing the riches of the town's past. The Barrio Histórico contains brilliant examples of colonial architecture and many of Uruguay's oldest structures. A mix of lovely shops, tiny *posadas,* and delicious cafes and restaurants makes the town more than a history lesson.

Most visitors take day trips to Colonia from Buenos Aires. However, staying overnight or exploring the region further has certain advantages. Colonia is surrounded by wineries and *estancias* and some of Uruguay's most beautiful landscapes, as well as spa resorts. Only recently touched by international tourism, many of these sites have a more authentic atmosphere than their Argentine counterparts. Small as it is, an overnight in Colonia allows you to have the town to yourself, after day-trippers have left, to wander the cobblestone streets unencumbered. Photography buffs in particular will find this delightful. For couples, the small town is serenely romantic for watching a sunset together and then heading to candlelit restaurants serving steaks, locally caught fish, and wines from the surrounding vineyards.

Essentials

GETTING THERE   The easiest way to reach Colonia from Buenos Aires is by ferry. **Seacat Colonia,** formerly known as FerryLíneas (✆ **02/915-0202** in

Uruguay and 11/4314-5100 in Argentina; www.seacatcolonia.com), runs a fast boat that takes 45 minutes. **Buquebús** (✆ 02/916-1910 in Montevideo and 11/4316-6500 in Buenos Aires; www.buquebus.com) offers two classes of service, priced from $30 to $95 each way. **Colonia Express** (in Buenos Aires ✆ 54/11-4317-4100 or Montevideo 02/901-9597; www.coloniaexpress.com) has similar prices but makes fewer trips.

Colonia is a good stopping-off point if you're traveling between Buenos Aires and Montevideo. **COT** (✆ 02/409-4949 in Montevideo; www.cot.com.uy) offers bus service from Montevideo and from Punta del Este.

VISITOR INFORMATION The main **Oficina de Turismo,** General Flores and Rivera (✆ 0452/26141) is open daily from 9am to 8pm. Just outside the gates to the Barrio Historico, open daily 9am to 6:30pm, is a smaller **Oficina de Turismo,** Calle Manuel Lobo 224, between Ituzaingó and Paseo San Miguel (✆ 0452/28506). Speak with someone at the tourism office to arrange a guided tour of the town, or contact the **Asociacion de Guias Profesionales de Turismo del Departamento de Colonia** (✆ 0452/22309; www.asociacionguiascolonia.blogspot.com). Visit www.colonia.gub.uy or www.uruguaynatural.com for information about Colonia and the surrounding region. The website www.guiacolonia.com.uy also has useful information. Keep an eye out for the bimonthly booklet **Güear** (www.guear.com), which has shopping, restaurant, hotel, and nightlife listings, as well as profiles of local chefs and other information. A PDF of the booklet can be downloaded. Most locations listed here take Argentine pesos, Uruguayan pesos, euros, and U.S. dollars. At the end of 2010, Colonia's area code changed from 052 to 0452; however, both numbers can still be used for the time being and you will see this reflected on literature and websites. Try either version if having trouble calling the other and remember to drop the 0 when calling from overseas with Uruguay's country code 598.

Seeing the Sights

A WALK THROUGH COLONIA'S BARRIO HISTORICO

Your visit to Colonia will be concentrated in the **Barrio Histórico (Old Neighborhood),** located on the coast, at the far southwestern corner of town. The sites, which are all within a few blocks of each other, can easily be visited on foot within a few hours. Museums and tourist sites are open Thursday through Monday from 11:15am to 4:45pm. For about $3, you can buy a pass at the Portuguese or municipal museums, which will get you into all the sites. Many locations in Colonia don't have real addresses, but often an intersection of two streets is used for direction. Individual museums don't have phone numbers either, so make sure to get a map at the tourist office. While the town is small and convenient for walking, almost nothing in the center of Colonia is handicap accessible. It is a difficult visit for anyone in a wheelchair, except to see the exteriors of important structures.

Start your tour at **Plaza Mayor,** the principal square that served as the center of the colonial establishment. To explore Colonia's Portuguese history, cross the Calle Manuel Lobo on the southeastern side of the plaza and enter the **Museo Portugués (Portuguese Museum),** which exhibits European customs and traditions that influenced the town's beginnings. Its most important holding is the final Portuguese royal medallion to grace the city walls before the city finally fell into Spanish hands. Leading behind the Museo Municipal is the **Street of Sighs,** or the **Calle de Los Suspiros,** so called because it was where the prostitutes worked their trade in olden days, when the military barracks were just off the Plaza Mayor. It remains the most intact colonial street in the city, with its angled cobblestone drain leading to the waterfront. You also see side by side the difference between Portuguese and Spanish colonial construction. If the roof is flat, it is Spanish. If the roof is angled with tiles, it is Portuguese. Nearby are the **Ruinas Convento San Francisco (San Francisco convent ruins).** Dating from 1696, the San Francisco convent was once inhabited by Jesuit and Franciscan monks, two brotherhoods dedicated to preaching the gospel to indigenous people. You can crawl over the ruins, or climb the adjacent 30m (100-ft.) high **Faro** or **Lighthouse** after paying the $1 fee. The wind is strong up there and gives a view to Buenos Aires on a clear day. The lighthouse is open daily from 10am to 8pm and is overseen by the Uruguayan navy, which has a small base just off Plaza Mayor.

Around the corner is the **Casa de Brown (Brown House),** which houses the **Museo Municipal (Municipal Museum).** Here, you will find an impressive collection of colonial documents and artifacts, a must-see for history buffs. For those with a more artistic bent, make sure to check out the **Museo del Azulejo (Tile Museum),** close to the waterfront on Calle Misiones de los Tapes at Paseo de San Gabriel, a unique museum of 19th-century European and Uruguayan tiles housed in a gorgeous 300-year-old country house. Upon exiting the museum, turn right for a walk along the water and then make a right onto Calle de la Playa, enjoying the shops and cafes along the way, heading up to the **Iglesia Matriz,** originally dating from 1680. Fighting meant the church was reconstructed several times, and today's building is a mix of colonial and neoclassical styles. To the side of the church is **Plaza de Lobo,** with its excavated **Ruinas Casa del Gobernador (House of the Viceroy Ruins),** built by the Portuguese and destroyed in 1777 by the Spanish. The House of the Viceroy captures something of the city's 17th- and 18th-century magistrates, when the port was used for imports, exports, and smuggling. Complete your walk by heading back toward the Plaza Mayor. To the left, you'll see the **City Gate** or **Portón de Campo** and what remains of the ramparts that once served to protect the city. Climbing them and contemplating, while looking out to the Río de la Plata and the world beyond, will help you understand that in spite of its tiny size, Colonia played a pivotal role in the global struggle between two European empires to dominate a continent an ocean away.

Where to Stay

COLONIA

Hotel La Misión   This hotel overlooking the Plaza Mayor was partly renovated in 2008, adding new bathrooms and rooms that mix modern and traditional. An antiques-filled lobby leads to a small courtyard dripping with bougainvillea. The original building dates from 1762.

Misiones de los Tapes 171, CP 70000, Colonia. ✆ **0452/26767.** www.lamisionhotel.com. 11 units. From $120 double. Rates include buffet breakfast. AE, MC, V. **Amenities:** Restaurant; concierge; room service. *In room:* A/C, TV, minibar, Wi-Fi.

Posada Plaza Mayor   Among the most charming accommodations in the center, this hotel has several rooms that wrap around a tranquil central courtyard with a fountain. Rooms are a mix of modern and rustic, and the breakfast room has a spectacular view over the Río de la Plata.

Calle de Comercio 111, CP 70000, Colonia. ✆ **0452/23193.** www.posadaplazamayor.com. 15 units. From $110 double. Rates include buffet breakfast. AE, MC, V. **Amenities:** Restaurant; concierge; room service. *In room:* A/C, TV, hair dryer, minibar, Wi-Fi.

OUTSIDE COLONIA

Four Seasons Carmelo ★★   One of the most luxurious and award-winning resorts in South America, the Four Seasons Carmelo is about 90km (54 miles) from the center of Colonia, set on the Río de la Plata. The enormous rooms and suites, about 93 to 120 sq. m (1,000–1,300 sq. ft.), and with fireplaces and cathedral ceilings, are set in individual bungalows in a landscaped garden surrounding the pool, making for a romantic getaway or honeymoon spot. The spa offers extensive treatments in a calming Asian-inspired setting. Also on property are a golf course and polo grounds, among other things; special children's programs are also on offer. It takes about an hour to drive there from Colonia, and the hotel also runs a shuttle service from Colonia's port, for $90 one-way and $132 to $410 round-trip, per person.

Ruta 21, Km 262, CP 70000, Carmelo. © **0542/9000.** Fax 0542/9999. www.fourseasons.com. 44 units with 24 dual-level suites. From $430 double; $465 suite. Rates include buffet breakfast. AE, DC, MC, V. Valet parking. **Amenities:** Restaurant; bar; babysitting; children's center; concierge; golf course; deluxe health club w/fitness center; massage; polo grounds; indoor pool; outdoor pool; room service; sauna; spa. In room: A/C, TV, hair dryer, minibar.

Sheraton Colonia ★★   Opened in 2005, the Sheraton Colonia is a 10-minute cab ride from the center of town. Built on a golf course, with a view to the Río de la Plata, it's a family-friendly, resort-style option if you want to spend more time in the area. The pool cascades over several levels in a landscaped garden and is spectacular at sunset. A lobby restaurant serves breakfast, lunch, and dinner, and dinner is also available at the golf clubhouse, set in the gardens. The gym and health club area is large with enormous glass windows overlooking the river. The large spa has 18 treatment rooms and offers a romantic champagne whirlpool treatment for couples, among many other options. Some suites have kitchens.

Continuación de la Rambla de Las Américas s/n, CP 70000, Carmelo. © **0452/29000.** Fax 0452/29001. www.sheraton.com. 92 units. From $204 double; from $385 suite. Rates include buffet breakfast. AE, DC, MC, V. **Amenities:** Restaurant; bar; babysitting; children's center; concierge; golf course; deluxe health club w/fitness center; massage; indoor pool; outdoor pool; room service; sauna; spa. In room: A/C, TV, hair dryer, kitchen (in some suites), minibar.

Where to Eat

El Drugstore ★ URUGUAYAN/JAPANESE/SEAFOOD   This charming spot has a colorful, kitschy interior with posters, bric-a-brac, and polka-dot tablecloths. An antique car parked outside was converted into a dining area and is often used in Colonia photo shoots. Traditional *chivitos* (traditional Uruguayan meat filet and egg sandwich), fish, steak, pastas, and Japanese food are on the menu. Live music, an Executive Menu for $17, and an open kitchen make this an unique place to dine.

Vasconcellos 179, at Portugal, across from Iglesia Matriz. © **0452/25241.** Main courses $4–$14. No credit cards. Daily noon–midnight.

Mesón de la Plaza ★ URUGUAYAN   Among the most traditional and elegant spots in Colonia, this location serves fine steaks and Uruguayan cuisine. It's located in a large colonial building with high ceilings, across from Iglesia Matriz.

Vasconcellos 153, at Portugal. © **052/24807.** Main courses $6–$15. AE, MC, V. Daily noon–midnight.

Pulpería de los Faroles ★ URUGUAYAN   Waiters with vests add formality to this old institution, with ancient brick walls offset by pastel tablecloths. Traditional food includes locally caught fish, steak, and pasta.

Calle Misiones de los Tapes 101 at Comercio, on the Plaza Mayor. © **052/25399.** Main courses $8–$15. AE, MC, V. Daily noon–midnight.

Colonia After Dark

Believe it or not, there is nightlife in Colonia, whether it's locals partying after work, or tourists staying in the local *posadas* and the surrounding spa-hotels. Bar life begins at 10 or 11pm, but for serious dancing, expect things to get started after 1am. With its white leather lounges and blue-neon backlit bar, **Mar Dulce Resto Pub,** at Virrey Cevallo 232 and General Flores (© **098/500898** [mobile]), looks like it was plucked from Miami Beach and offers live music, DJs, and dancing. **Tresquarto** at Av. Méndez 295 (© **052/29664** or 099/523043 [mobile]; www.trescuarto.com), is the town's mega-disco, a four-level venue with three kinds of music, hence the name. It's open only on Fridays and Saturdays.

MONTEVIDEO, URUGUAY

215km (133 miles) E of Buenos Aires

Montevideo, the southernmost capital on the continent, along with its suburbs, is home to half of Uruguay's population of three million. On the banks of the Río de la Plata, Montevideo first existed as a fortress of the Spanish Empire and developed into a major port city in the mid–18th century. European immigrants—including Spanish, Portuguese, French, and British—have influenced the city's architecture. A walk around the capital reveals architectural styles ranging from colonial to Art Deco.

Although Montevideo has few must-see attractions, its charm lies in wait for the observant traveler. A walk along La Rambla, stretching from the Old City to the neighborhood of Carrasco, takes you along the riverfront, past fishermen and their catch, to parks and gardens where children play and elders sip *mate* (a tealike beverage). Restaurants, cafes, bars, and street performers populate the port area, where you will also discover the flavors of Uruguay at the afternoon and weekend Mercado del Puerto (Port Market). Many of the city's historic sites and museums surround or are close to Plaza Independencia and can be visited in a few hours.

If you're visiting Montevideo as a side trip from Buenos Aires, ignore comments from Porteños that there is nothing here. It's true that Buenos Aires is larger and more active, but Montevideo has its own charms. The best way for English speakers to understand the relationship between Montevideo and Buenos Aires, and by extension the countries themselves, is to think of that of Canada to the United States, New Zealand to Australia and to a degree, Ireland to the United Kingdom. Both Uruguay and Argentina have similar histories and cultures, but the smaller one has always had to live in the other's shadow, dominated politically and denigrated culturally. This has resulted in a self-consciousness for Uruguayans meeting visitors, who come with little to no knowledge of the country. Knowing you're visiting from a place that likes to throw its weight around, Montevideans reach out to welcome visitors and make sure you have a good time in their city to counter whatever Argentines have told you.

Essentials

GETTING THERE International flights and those from Buenos Aires land at **Carrasco International Airport** (© **02/604-0329;** www.aeropuertodecarrasco. com.uy), located 19km (12 miles) from downtown Montevideo. Uruguay's national carrier is **Pluna,** Colonia 1021 at Julio Herrera (© **0800/118-811** or 02/401-5000, or 11/4132-4444 in Buenos Aires; www.pluna.com.uy), which operates several flights daily from Aeroparque. **Aerolíneas Argentinas** (© **02/901-9466** or 000/4054-86527) connects both Aeroparque and Ezeiza with Montevideo; the flight takes 50 minutes. The fare ranges between $150 and $250 round-trip, depending on how far in advance you make reservations. In 2009, **American Airlines** (© **800/433-7300** in the United States and Canada, or 02/916-3929 in Montevideo; www.aa.com) began offering direct service from Miami to Montevideo—with frequency varying by season—in addition to its already existing flights, which connect to Montevideo with stopovers in Buenos Aires. A taxi, or *remise* (private, unmetered taxi), from the airport to downtown is about $17.

The most popular way to get to Montevideo is by ferry. **Buquebús,** Calle Río Negro 1400 (© **02/916-8801** or 916-1910, 11/4316-6500 in Buenos Aires; www.buquebus.com), operates three to four hydrofoils per day from Buenos Aires; the 3-hour trip costs about $200 round-trip. Montevideo's port is about 1.5km (1 mile) from downtown. See p. 169 in Colonia for more ferryboat options.

Terminal Omnibus Tres Cruces, General Artigas 1825 (© **02/409-7399** or 401-8998, www.trescruces.com.uy), is Montevideo's long-distance bus terminal, connecting the capital with cities in Uruguay and throughout South America. Buses to Buenos Aires take about 8 hours. **COT** (© **02/409-4949;** www.cot.com.uy) offers the best service to Punta del Este, Maldonado, and Colonia.

ORIENTATION   Montevideo is surrounded by water on three sides, a testament to its earlier incarnation as an easily defended fortress for the Spanish Empire. The Old City begins near the western edge of Montevideo, found on the skinny portion of a peninsula between the Rambla Gran Bretaña and the city's main artery, Avenida 18 de Julio, named for the date the new constitution was adopted. Look for Plaza Independencia and Plaza Constitución to find the center of the district. Many of the city's museums, theaters, and hotels reside in this historic area, although a trip east on Avenida 18 de Julio reveals the more modern Montevideo, with its own share of hotels, markets, and monuments. Along the city's long southern coastline runs the Rambla Gran Bretaña, traveling 21km (13 miles) from the piers of the Old City, past Parque Rodó, and on to points south and east, passing fish stalls and street performers along the way.

GETTING AROUND   It's easy to navigate around the center of Montevideo on foot or by bus. Safe, convenient buses crisscross Montevideo, making it easy to venture outside the city center, for 15 Uruguayan pesos (about 60¢). Taxis are safe and relatively cheap, but it can be difficult to hail one during rush hour. I recommend calling **Remises Carrasco** (© **09/440-5473** or 02/606-2122; www.remisescarrasco.com.uy). To rent a car, try **Thrifty** (© **02/204-3373** or 682-4495; www.thrifty.com). For roadside emergencies or general information on driving in Uruguay, contact the **Automóvil Club de Uruguay,** Av. Libertador 1532 (© **02/902-4792;** www.acu.com.uy), or the **Centro Automovilista del Uruguay,** E. V. Haedo 2378 (© **02/903-3344**).

VISITOR INFORMATION   Uruguay's **Ministerio de Turismo** is at Av. Libertador 1409, corner of Colonia (© **02/1885**). It assists travelers with countrywide information and is open daily from 8am to 8pm. There are also branches at Carrasco International Airport (© **02/604-0386**); Tres Cruces bus station (© **02/409-7399**) open daily 8am to 10pm; and at the port, to greet Buquebús and cruise-ship visitors (Rambla 25 de Agosto de 1825 and Yacaré; © **02/188-5100**), with hours of

Montevideo

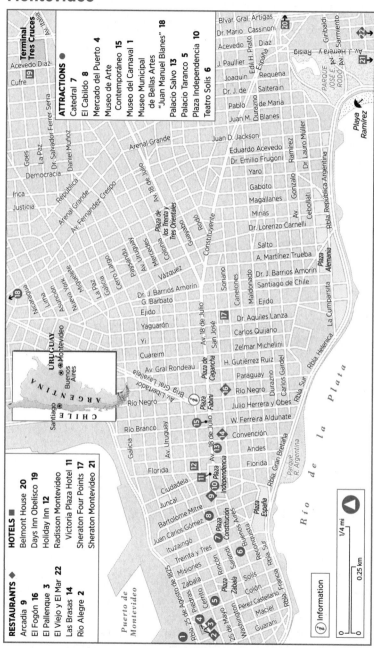

RESTAURANTS ◆
Arcadia **9**
El Fogón **16**
El Pallenque **3**
El Viejo y El Mar **22**
Las Brasas **14**
Río Alegre **2**

HOTELS ■
Belmont House **20**
Days Inn Obelisco **19**
Holiday Inn **12**
Radisson Montevideo
Victoria Plaza Hotel **11**
Sheraton Four Points **17**
Sheraton Montevideo **21**

ATTRACTIONS ●
Catedral **7**
El Cabildo **8**
Mercado del Puerto **4**
Museo de Arte
  Contemporáneo **15**
Museo del Carnaval **1**
Museo Municipal
  de Bellas Artes
  "Juan Manuel Blanes" **18**
Palacio Salvo **13**
Palacio Taranco **5**
Plaza Independencia **10**
Teatro Solís **6**

(i) Information

175

Monday to Friday 8am to 6pm and varied hours on weekends, depending on cruise-ship docking schedules. The **municipal tourist office,** Explanada Municipal, inside of the atrium of the Intendencia (or City Hall), at Avenida 18 de Julio, and Ejido (✆ 02/916-8434 or 1950), offers city maps and brochures of tourist activities. It's open daily from 10am to 4pm. This office also organizes cultural city tours on week-ends. Though not officially open to the public, Montevideo's Tourism Office is on the building's third floor and is reachable at ✆ **02/1950-3171.** The city also has a satel-lite tourism office, usually open Monday to Friday from noon to 7pm, at San Jose 1328 at Ejido (✆ **02/1950-2043**), built into a walkway that is part of the basement of the Sheraton Four Points hotel. In the event of an emergency, the **Tourist Police** can be reached at ✆ **911** or **0800-8226,** and their office is at Colonia 1021. Visit www.presidencia.gub.uy, www.uruguaynatural.com.uy, www.montevideo.gub.uy, or www.turismo.gub.uy for more tourism information. The travel magazine *Pasaporte Uruguay* also provides a wealth of information, in English and Spanish, and is avail-able free in some locations, for sale for about $3 in others. Register for their newslet-ter at www.pasaporteuruguay.com.

TOUR COMPANIES In business for nearly 60 years, **Buemes Travel Services,** Colonia 979 (✆ **02/902-1050;** www.buemes.com.uy), is among the largest full-service tour companies in Uruguay. Much of their business involves planning trips and tours for passengers coming into Montevideo by cruise ship. Contact them for day trips or history tours on various themes or for booking hotels and airline flights. They also arrange trips to other parts of Uruguay, including Colonia, Punta del Este, and the range of *estancias* near Montevideo that foreigners have only recently discov-ered. One of the best private tour guides in Montevideo is **Tamara Levinson** (✆ **02/710-3312** or 099/696-518; tamaral@montevideo.com.uy), who conducts individual custom tours of Montevideo and other parts of Uruguay. She works for Buemes, but visitors can hire her, in her spare time, to lead individualized travel tours.

[FastFACTS] MONTEVIDEO

Area Code & Phone Numbers
The country code for Uruguay is **598;** the city code for Montevi-deo is **02,** and you drop 0 when dialing from overseas. Land line phones have seven digits, but many government offices are now using four-, seven-, or eight-digit systems. Ask for clarification with any phone number that seems unusual. Many times these four- and eight-digit numbers do not work properly, so ask for alternative numbers or even a contact's cellphone when

given them. Cellphones have a three-digit begin-ning code, usually begin-ning with 09 and then six digits, and do not need an area code in front of them. Drop the 0 also when dial-ing from overseas. Informa-tion is ✆ **122,** or the fee service ✆ **0900-2020.**

ATMs
ATMs are plentiful; look for **Bancomat** and **Redbrou** banks. Most have access to the Cirrus net-work. The PLUS system is harder to find. The ATM at the casino in the Radisson takes everything.

Currency Exchange
To exchange money, try **Turisport Limitada** (the local Amex representative), San José 930 (✆ **02/902-0829**); **Gales Servicios Financieros,** Av. 18 de Julio 1046 (✆ **02/902-0229**); or one of the airport exchanges. About 20 Uru-guayan pesos equaled US$1 at the time of this writing.

Hospital
The **British Hos-pital** is located at Av. Italia 2420 (✆ **02/487-1020**) and has emergency-room services.

Internet Access Internet cafes appear and disappear faster than discos, but you won't walk long before coming across one in the city center. Reliable cybercafes include **El Cybercafé,** Calle 25 de Mayo 568; **Arroba del Sur,** Guayabo 1858; and **El Cybercafé Softec,** Santiago de Chile 1286. The average cost is $2 per hour of usage.

Post Office The main post office, Calle Buenos Aires 451 (© **0810/444-CORREO** [267736]), is open weekdays from 9am to 6pm.

Safety Although Montevideo remains very safe by big-city standards, street crime has risen in recent years. Travelers should avoid walking alone, particularly at night, in Ciudad Vieja, Avenida 18 de Julio, Plaza Independencia, and the port vicinity. Take a taxi instead. The city has vastly increased the presence of tourism police, particularly in Ciudad Vieja. Look for the men and women with green fluorescent vests.

Seeing the Sights

Catedral ★ Also known as Iglesia Matriz, the cathedral was the city's first public building; the current structure dates to 1804, but with earlier origins. It houses the remains of some of Uruguay's most important political, religious, and economic figures, and it's distinguished by its domed bell towers.

Calle Sarandí at Ituzaingó, overlooking Plaza Constitución. © **02/915-7018.** Free admission. Mon–Fri 8am–8pm.

El Cabildo (Old Town Hall) ★ Uruguay's constitution was signed in the old town hall, which also served as the city's jailhouse in the 19th century. Now a museum, the Cabildo houses the city's historic archives, as well as maps and photos, antiques, costumes, and artwork.

Juan Carlos Gómez 1362, overlooking Plaza Constitución. © **02/915-9685.** Free admission. Tues–Sun 2:30–7pm.

Museo de Arte Contemporáneo (Museum of Contemporary Art) ★ This museum is dedicated to contemporary Uruguayan art, and it exhibits the country's biggest names. To promote cultural exchange across the region, a section of the museum is set aside for artists who hail from various South American countries.

Av. 18 de Julio 965, 2nd floor. © **02/900-6662.** www.cultura.montevideo.gub.uy. Free admission. Daily noon–8pm.

Museo de Artes Decorativas (Decorative Arts Museum) Palacio Taranco ★ Now the decorative arts museum, Taranco Palace was built in the early 20th century, in the French style popular during that period. The museum displays Uruguayan furniture, draperies, clocks, paintings, and other cultural works.

Calle 25 de Mayo 379. © **02/915-6060.** www.cultura.montevideo.gub.uy. Free admission. Tues–Sat 10am–6pm.

Museo Municipal de Bellas Artes "Juan Manuel Blanes" (Municipal Museum of Fine Arts) ★ The national art-history museum displays Uruguayan artistic styles from the nation's inception to the present day. Works include oils, engravings, drawings, sculptures, and documents. Among the great Uruguayan artists exhibited are Juan Manuel Blanes, Pedro Figari, Rafael Barradas, José Cúneo, and Carlos Gonzales.

Av. Millán 4015. © **02/336-2248.** www.museoblanes.org.uy. Free admission. Tues–Sun 2–7pm.

Palacio Salvo ★ Often referred to as the symbol of Montevideo, the 26-story Salvo Palace was once the tallest building in South America. It was the work of eccentric Italian architect Mario Palanti, who also designed the very similar structure Palacio Barolo on Buenos Aires's Avenida de Mayo. Though you might expect such an iconic building to be open to the public and have a vista station in its tower, there isn't such a thing. The lobby to this residential tower, however, is open, and periodically has free exhibits related to the structure and other themes.

Plaza Independencia and Av. 18 de Julio. www.palaciosalvo.com.

Plaza Independencia ★★ Originally the site of a Spanish citadel, Independence Square marks the beginning of the Old City, and it's a good point from which to begin your tour of Montevideo. Only one gate to the old fortress remains. An enormous statue of Gen. José Gervasio Artigas, father of Uruguay and hero of its independence movement, stands in the center. His ashes are in a mausoleum underground, beneath the monument. It's a severe, modern structure, with eerie lighting reminiscent of a horror movie, but has recently begun to host art exhibitions, cheering the place up at least a little bit. A changing-of-the-guards ceremony takes place every few hours.

Bordered by Av. 18 de Julio, Florida, and Juncal.

Teatro Solís ★★ Montevideo's main theater and opera house, opened in 1852, underwent an extensive renovation in late 1990. It hosts Uruguay's most important cultural events. While the structure on its outside remains historical, the interior is a thoroughly modern contrast.

Calle Buenos Aires 652. © **02/1950-3323** or 1950-3325. www.teatrosolis.org.uy. Guided tours are Tues, Thurs–Fri, and Sun 11am, noon, and 5pm and Sat 1pm for about $1 in Spanish and $2 in English and Portuguese. Wed guided tours at 11am, noon, and 5pm are free. Evening cultural productions vary in price and time. Guided tour schedule changes season to season. Check the website or call.

CELEBRATING CARNAVAL IN MONTEVIDEO

One of the most delightful times to visit Montevideo is during Carnaval season, usually in late January, February, and early March, corresponding to the period before Ash Wednesday in the Catholic calendar and the 40-day Lenten period before Easter, when there are street festivals as well as theatrical competitions. It's at this time that several aspects particular to Uruguayan culture come to the forefront. As Uruguay was established as a border colony between the edges of the Spanish and Portuguese empires, the festival appeals to both sides. You'll see *murgas,* or street dancing bands, similar to those in Argentina, as well as feather-festooned females as you'd see in Rio. It's also a time when the Afro-Uruguayan population, descendants of slaves who represent about 7% of the country, become truly visible and celebrated. *Llamadas,* or African drum bands, are part of the festivities. A highlight of Carnaval season is February 2, the day celebrating the sea-goddess *Yemanga,* in some representations resembling a seafaring Virgin Mary, from the *Candomblé* religion, a fusion of African beliefs brought over by slaves and blended with Catholic ideology. (This is the goddess in the Penelope Cruz movie *Woman on Top.*) Thousands head to Playa Ramirez, across from Parque Rodó and other beaches, to listen to music, worship, and leave offerings in the sea. Year-round, the **Museo del Carnaval,** at Rambla 25 de Agosto de 1825 no. 218 at Maciel (© **02/916-5493** or 915-0802; www.museodelcarnaval.org), in the port area, provides an excellent perspective on the celebrations.

Where to Stay

Parking is included in the rates of most Uruguay hotels. In 2005, Montevideo repealed its 10% hotel tax for foreigners (but it's still paid by locals).

EXPENSIVE

Belmont House ★★ 🎁 A boutique hotel in Montevideo's peaceful Carrasco neighborhood, Belmont House has small elegant spaces with carefully chosen antiques and wood furnishings that give this hotel the feeling of a wealthy private home. Guest rooms feature two- or four-poster beds; rich, colorful linens; and marble bathrooms with small details such as towel warmers and deluxe toiletries. Many rooms have balconies overlooking the courtyard and pool, and two rooms have Jacuzzis. Belmont House is close to the beach, golf, and tennis. Gourmands will find an excellent international restaurant, afternoon tea, and a *paradilla* (Uruguayan version of a *parrilla*) open weekends next to the pool.

Av. Rivera 6512, 11500 Montevideo. ✆ **02/600-0430.** Fax 02/600-8609. www.belmonthouse.com.uy. 28 units. $290 double; from $408 suite. Rates include gourmet breakfast. AE, DC, MC, V. **Amenities:** Restaurant; *paradilla;* bar; tearoom; babysitting; small fitness center; discounts for nearby golf and tennis; beautiful outdoor pool; sauna. *In room:* A/C, TV, hair dryer, minibar.

Radisson Montevideo Victoria Plaza Hotel ★★ The Victoria Plaza has long been one of Montevideo's top hotels. Standing in the heart of the financial district, this European-style hotel makes a good base from which to do business or explore the capital. Its convention center and casino also make it the center of the city's business and social activity. Ask for a room in the new tower, which houses spacious guest rooms and executive suites with classic French-style furnishings and panoramic city or river views. The hotel has a large multilingual staff. Inquire about weekend spa packages. The casino has French roulette tables, blackjack, baccarat, slot machines, horse races, and bingo. There are two lobby bars, in addition to the casino bars. **Arcadia** (p. 180), on the 25th floor, is the city's most elegant dining room.

Plaza Independencia 759, 11100 Montevideo. ✆ **02/902-0111.** Fax 02/902-1628. www.radisson.com/montevideouy. 254 units. $219 double; from $299 suite. Rates include breakfast at rooftop restaurant. AE, DC, MC, V. Free parking. **Amenities:** Restaurant; cafe; 2 bars; concierge; executive floors; fitness center w/aerobics classes; excellent health club w/skylit indoor pool; Jacuzzi; massage; room service; sauna. *In room:* A/C, TV, hair dryer, minibar, Wi-Fi.

Sheraton Montevideo ★★ When it opened in 1999, the Sheraton Montevideo replaced Victoria Plaza as Montevideo's most luxurious hotel. A walkway connects the hotel to the Punta Carretas Shopping Center, one of the city's best malls. Spacious rooms have imported furniture, king-size beds, sleeper chairs, marble bathrooms, wide-panel TVs, and works by Uruguayan artists. Choose views of the Río de la Plata, Uruguay Golf Club, or downtown Montevideo; views from the 20th through 24th floors are the most impressive. Rooms on the top two executive floors feature Jacuzzis and individual sound systems. Hotel service is excellent, particularly for guests with business needs. The main restaurant, Las Carretas, serves Continental cuisine with a Mediterranean flair. Don't miss the dining room's spectacular murals by contemporary Uruguayan artist Carlos Vilaro. Next door, the lobby bar is a popular spot for casual business meetings and afternoon cocktails.

Calle Víctor Soliño 349, 11300 Montevideo. ✆ **02/710-2121.** Fax 02/712-1262. www.sheraton.com. 207 units. From $225 double; from $325 suite. Rates include buffet breakfast. AE, DC, MC, V. Free parking. **Amenities:** Restaurant; bar; babysitting; concierge; executive floors; massage; deluxe health club w/fitness center; indoor pool; room service; sauna; emergency medical service. *In room:* A/C, TV, hair dryer, Internet (fee), minibar.

MODERATE

Holiday Inn ★ This colorful Holiday Inn is actually one of the city's best hotels, popular with tourists and business travelers alike. It's in the heart of downtown, next to Montevideo's main square. Bilingual staff members greet you in the marble lobby, which is attached to a good restaurant and bar. Guest rooms have simple, contemporary furnishings typical of an American chain. Because the hotel doubles as a convention center, it can get very busy.

Colonia 823, 11100 Montevideo. © **02/902-0001.** Fax 02/902-1242. www.holidayinn.com.uy. 137 units. From $118 double; from $168 suite. Rates include buffet breakfast. AE, DC, MC, V. **Amenities:** Restaurant; bar; fitness center; heated indoor pool; room service; sauna; Wi-Fi in public areas. *In room:* A/C, TV, high-speed Internet, minibar.

Sheraton Four Points Montevideo ★★ The Sheraton Four Points is among the newest of Montevideo's international hotels. It's considered a four-star property, but falls somewhere between four and five. The staff is extremely helpful, and whether you are on business or visiting as a tourist, the location across from city hall is convenient. The lobby is stark and modern, with polished black-granite panels over white walls in the soaring atrium. Many rooms have views to the Río de la Plata. Bathrooms are spacious and suite bathrooms have hydro-massage bathtubs. While small, the enclosed rooftop gym and spa has an unparalleled view of the city. There is a $5 charge for using these areas. Breakfast ($16) is available in the lobby restaurant, which is also open for lunch and dinner.

Ejido 1275, at Soriano, across from the Intendencia (City Hall), 11000 Montevideo. © **02/901-7000.** Fax 02/903-2247. www.fourpoints.com/montevideo. 135 units. From $129 double; from $219 suite. AE, DC, MC, V. Free parking. **Amenities:** Restaurant; bar; babysitting; concierge; health club w/fitness center; indoor pool; 24-hr. room service; sauna. *In room:* A/C, TV, hair dryer, high-speed Internet ($16/day), minibar.

INEXPENSIVE

Days Inn Obelisco 🍴 This modern Days Inn caters to business travelers looking for good-value accommodations. The hotel is located next to the Tres Cruces bus station, not far from downtown or the airport. Rooms are comfortable and modern, if not overly spacious. Free local calls are permitted.

Acevedo Díaz 1821, 11800 Montevideo. www.daysinn.com.uy. © **02/400-4840.** Fax 02/402-0229. 60 units. From $100 double; $140 suite. Rates include buffet breakfast. AE, DC, MC, V. **Amenities:** Coffee shop; small health club; room service. *In room:* A/C, TV, hair dryer, minibar.

Where to Eat

Restaurants in Montevideo serve steak that rivals anything in Argentina, and they usually offer stew and seafood selections as well. You'll find the native barbecue, in which beef and lamb are grilled on the fire, in any of the city's *parrilladas* (the name for *parrillas* in Uruguay). Sales tax on dining in Montevideo is a whopping 23%. There's also usually a table cover charge (*cubierto*) of about $2 per person. Check out the Uruguayan restaurant website www.saliracomer.com for more options.

EXPENSIVE

Arcadia ★★ 📷 INTERNATIONAL   While the food is great, the wraparound views from this 26th-floor restaurant outshine the menu. Tables are nestled in semi-private nooks with floor-to-ceiling bay windows. The classic dining room is decorated with Italian curtains and crystal chandeliers; each table has a fresh rose and sterling silver place settings. Creative plates, such as terrine of pheasant marinated in cognac, are followed by grilled rack of lamb glazed with mint and garlic, or duck confit served on a thin strudel pastry with red cabbage. I list general main course prices below, but the Uruguayan caviar menu will set you back about $200.

Plaza Independencia 759. © **02/902-0111.** Reservations recommended. Main courses $6–$25. AE, DC, MC, V. Daily noon–3pm and 7pm–midnight.

MODERATE

El Fogón ★ PARRILLADA/SEAFOOD/URUGUAYAN   This brightly lit *parrillada* and seafood restaurant is popular with Montevideo's late-night crowd. The extensive menu includes calamari, salmon, shrimp, and other fish, as well as generous steak and pasta dishes. Food here is priced well and prepared with care. The express lunch menu comes with steak or chicken, dessert, and a glass of wine.

San José 1080 at Río Negro. ✆ **02/900-0900.** www.elfogon.com.uy. Main courses $7-$15. AE, DC, MC, V. Daily noon-4pm and 7pm-1am.

El Palenque ★ SEAFOOD/PARRILLADA   Located in the Mercado del Puerto, this restaurant has been around since 1958 and is one of the area's most popular restaurants, crowded with locals and tourists alike (though it gets especially crowded when the cruise ships come in). Fish is the highlight, but they also have tapas, pastas, paellas, and lots of grilled meats. A specialty is the Paella Exotica, made with rabbit.

Perez Castellano 1579 (at Rambla 25 de Agosto 400, in the Mercado del Puerto). ✆ **02/917-0190** or 915-4704. www.elpalenque.com.uy. Main courses $8-$17. AE, DC, MC, V. Mon-Sat noon-midnight; Sun noon-5pm.

El Peregrino PARRILLADA/SEAFOOD/ITALIAN   This large, charming spot offers atmospheric dining with rustic tables, brick and yellow walls, and old photographs. They offer several fish dishes, Italian specialties, plus lots of beef, pork and chicken.

Calle Pérez Castellano 1553, at Piedras (at the Mercado del Puerto). ✆ **02/916-4737.** Main courses $5-$8. AE, DC, MC, V. Daily 11am-midnight.

El Viejo y el Mar ★ SEAFOOD   Resembling an old fishing club, El Viejo y el Mar is on the riverfront near the Sheraton. The bar is made from an abandoned boat, and the dining room is decorated with dock lines, sea lamps, and pictures of 19th-century regattas. Every kind of fish and pasta is on the menu, and the restaurant is equally popular for evening cocktails. An outdoor patio is open most of the year.

Rambla Gandhi 400. ✆ **02/710-5704.** Main courses $5-$10. MC, V. Daily noon-4pm and 8pm-1am.

Los Leños ★★ PARRILLADA/SEAFOOD/URUGUAYAN   This casual *parrillada* resembles one you'd find in Buenos Aires—except it also serves an outstanding range of *mariscos* (seafood), such as the Spanish paella or *lenguado las Brasas* (a flathead fish) served with prawns, mushrooms, and mashed potatoes. From the *parrillada,* the *filet de lomo* is the best cut—order it with Roquefort, mustard, or black-pepper sauce. The restaurant's fresh produce is displayed in a case near the kitchen. Hillary Clinton once visited, and a picture of her with staff hangs on the wall.

San José 909, at Convencion. ✆ **02/900-2285.** www.parrilla.com.uy. Main courses $2-$17. AE, DC, MC, V. Daily 11:45am-3:30pm and 8pm-midnight.

Shopping

The **Villa Biarritz fair,** at Parque Zorilla de San Martín-Ellauri, takes place Saturday from 9:30am to 3pm, and features handicrafts, antiques, books, fruit and vegetable vendors, flowers, and other goodies. The **Mercado del Puerto (Port Market) ★** opens afternoons and weekends at Piedras and Yacaré; here, you can sample the flavors of Uruguay, from small empanadas to barbecued meats. Saturday is the best day to visit. Numerous leather and souvenir stores are on Calle Perez Castellano, leading from the port. **Tristán Narvaja,** Avenida 18 de Julio in the Cordón neighborhood, is the city's Sunday flea market (6am–3pm), initiated nearly 60 years ago by Italian immigrants. **De la Abundancia/Artesanos** is a food-and-handicrafts market Monday through Saturday from 10am to 8pm at San José 1312. **Tres Cruces Shopping Mall** is part of the bus terminal complex, with dozens of shops. It's at Avenida Serra with Acevedo Diaz (© **02/408-8710** or 401-8998; www.trescruces.com.uy).

Montevideo After Dark

As in Buenos Aires, nightlife in Montevideo means drinks after 10pm and dancing after midnight. For earlier entertainment, ask at your hotel or call the **Teatro Solís,** Calle Buenos Aires 652 (© 02/1950-3323; www.teatrosolis.org.uy), the city's center for opera, theater, ballets, and symphonies. **SODRE,** Av. 18 de Julio 930 (© 02/901-2850; www.sodre.gub.uy), is the city's "Official Radio Service," which hosts classical music concerts from May to November. Gamblers should head to the **Plaza Victoria Casino,** Plaza Independencia (© 02/902-2155, www.casinos.gub.uy), a fashionable venue with French roulette tables, blackjack, baccarat, slot machine, and bingo. It opens at 2pm and keeps going through most of the night. **Mariachi,** Gabriel Pereira 2964 (© 02/709-1600), is one of the city's top bars and discos, with live bands or DJ music Wednesday to Sunday after 10pm. **Café Misterio,** Costa Rica 1700 (© 02/600-5999), is another popular bar. Montevideo's best tango clubs are **La Casa de Becho,** Nueva York 1415 (© 02/400-2717 or 094-448-525 [mobile]; Fri–Sat after 10:30pm, sometimes closed in summer), where composer Gerardo Mattos Rodríguez wrote the famous "La Cumparsita;" and **Cuareim,** Zelmar Michelini 1079 (no phone; Wed and Fri–Sat after 9pm), which offers both tango and *candombe,* a lively dance indigenous to the area with its roots in early slave culture. The tourist office can give you schedule information for Montevideo's other tango salons.

SAN ANTONIO DE ARECO & PAMPAS ESTANCIAS

111km (69 miles) NW of Buenos Aires

San Antonio de Areco is a quiet little town about 90 minutes north of Buenos Aires, deep in the heart of Argentina's famous Pampas. The city is best known as the center for gaucho culture, Argentina's version of American cowboy tradition. Few people stay in San Antonio, choosing to visit it as a day trip from Buenos Aires, or as a base for exploring the nearby *estancias* that surround the town.

The city is compact, built in 1730 around an old colonial church dedicated to San Antonio of Padua, from which the town takes its name. Colonial and turn-of-the-20th-century buildings abound, all reached on walkable cobblestone streets that radiate from the church and Plaza Ruiz de Arellano, the town's main square. The Río Areco divides the town in two parts. Here along the river is a monument-lined green space called Parque San Martín, crossed by an old pedestrian bridge to Parque Criollo, where the city's most famous site, the Museo Gauchesco Ricardo Güiraldes, sits.

The city's main shopping streets are Alsina and Arellano, heading south from Plaza Arellano. A year-round tourism destination, it lives for the annual **Día de la Tradición,** held around November 10. Gauchos, real and wannabe, fill the town, playing gaucho games of skill such as the *sortija,* where they catch rings from poles while riding horses, giving them as gifts to beautiful women in the audience. San Antonio has only a small number of hotels, which fill up fast at this time of year. (Of course, there's always the gaucho's pad, if he gives you his *sortija* ring.) See also the section on *estancias,* below; all are within a short drive of the center of San Antonio.

Essentials

GETTING THERE   San Antonio de Areco can be reached by car from Buenos Aires by driving north along Ruta 8. The drive takes about 1½ hours. Most people come by bus, however. **Chevallier** (*℃* **2326/453-904** in San Antonio, 11/4000-5255 in Buenos Aires, or 0800/222-6565 toll-free; www.nuevachevallier.com) offers hourly bus service from Buenos Aires's Retiro Bus depot.

VISITOR INFORMATION   The **Dirección de Turismo de San Antonio de Areco** tourism information center (*℃* **2326/453-165;** www.pagosdeareco.com.ar) is in Parque San Martín along the Río Areco waterfront, near the intersection of Avenida Zerboni with Calle Zapiola and Calle Arellano. It is open daily, from 8am to 7pm. The websites www.visiteareco.com and www.sanantoniodeareco.com are worth checking.

GETTING AROUND   Within San Antonio itself, your feet can take you most of the places you need to go. Even the most distant actual attraction, Museo of the Gaucho, is just a 15-minute walk from the center. Because many people use the town as a base for exploring other parts of the Pampas, such as the numerous *estancias, remises* are a must. Contact the 24-hour **Remis Zerboni,** Zerboni 313, near Alsina (*℃* **2326/453-288**). The town is also great for bike riding; most hotels offer free bike loans.

Seeing the Sights

The center of San Antonio de Areco is the leafy **Plaza Arellano,** surrounded by cobblestone streets and overseen by a statue of Juan Hipólito Vieytes, a local involved in the Argentine war for independence from Spain. His memorial sits in an acoustic circle, so talking here is fun, especially if you bring kids. The statue faces south to Mitre Street, staring at the church from which the town draws its name, **San Antonio de Padua,** rebuilt in the late 1800s over the original 1730 colonial version. Colonial on the outside, the interior mixes Gothic and neoclassical styles with frescoes of angels and saints in niches on the walls, all overseen by a coffered ceiling. On the plaza's north side is the Belle Epoque **Municipal Hall,** a long pink building at Lavalle 363 with an attractive central courtyard. Nearby is the **Draghi Museum and Shop,** Lavalle 387, between Alsina and Arellano (*℃* **2326/454-219;** daily approximately 10am–5pm, though technically by appointment only). Opened by the late Juan Jose Draghi, a master silversmith who began his career nearly 50 years ago making ornamental items for gauchos, it is now run by his son Mariano. The museum is itself a work of art, with its exquisite stained-glass ceiling. The museum also has its own hotel (p. 184). A few blocks away, you can watch other silversmiths at work in the small **Artesano Platero,** Alsina at Zerboni, facing the Parque San Martín (*℃* **2326/454-843** or 2325/15-656-995 [mobile]; www.arecoplateria.com.ar; daily 9:30am–12:30pm and 3–9pm).

From here, head to **Parque San Martín,** on the south side of the Río Areco. It's lined with trees and monuments, and full of vine-covered walkways called *glorietas.* It's a place where families picnic and kids play soccer or climb over the small dam constructed in the river. Two bridges cross the park here, but the most picturesque is the **Puente Viejo,** originally constructed in the 1850s as a toll crossing. The other end of the river has Parque Criollo, and here sits the city's most famous site, the **Museum of the Gaucho,** aka **Museo Ricardo Güiraldes,** in honor of the author of *Don Segundo Sombra,* Camino Ricardo Güiraldes, at Sosa (*℃* **2326/455-839;** www.museoguiraldes.com.ar; Wed–Mon 10am–4:30pm). Written in 1926, the novel immortalized the noble gaucho, making him an honored part of Argentine history. The museum combines an authentic

1830 *pulpería,* or country general store, where gauchos gathered, with a museum designed in a colonial style by Argentine architect José María Bustillo in 1936. Here you will find the author's personal effects, photos, books, and other gaucho memorabilia. It's a bit kitschy (think rooms filled with gaucho mannequins), but if you speak Spanish, a conversation with the museum's guide and historian, Omar Tapia, will help you put the gauchos in their proper historical context.

EXCURSIONS TO SAN ANTONIO & ESTANCIAS

Various travel companies in Buenos Aires arrange day trips to San Antonio de Areco, with or without overnight stays on nearby *estancias.* **Borello Travel & Tours** is a travel firm specializing in upscale travel with offices in New York and Buenos Aires (7 Park Ave., Ste. 21, New York, NY 10016; ℂ **800/405-3072** or 212/686-4911) or Perú (359 Ste. 407, Buenos Aires 1067; ℂ **11/5031-1988;** www.borellotravel.com). They can include a visit to San Antonio with stays in the local *estancias.* They maintain an additional office in Buenos Aires (ℂ **11/5031-1988**). Buenos Aires–based **Say Hueque Tourism,** with two locations (at Viamonte 749, Office 601, 1053 Buenos Aires, ℂ **11/5199-2517;** Thames St. 2062, Buenos Aires, ℂ **11/5258-8740;** www.sayhueque.com), also provides trips to this area.

Where to Stay

Draghi Paradores ★ The Draghi Paradores is a small apartment hotel opened in 2006 behind the Draghi museum and store. One of the nicest of San Antonio's hotels, it has a romantic feel. Built in a Spanish colonial style, the entrance is graced by a small pool and fountain in an enclosed courtyard. It looks a little like a miniature of the *Melrose Place* apartment building, minus backstabbing blondes in high heels and miniskirts. The five rooms are clean with a country style to them, with a rich use of woods, frilly white bedding, and terra-cotta tiles. Two rooms come with small kitchens, ideal for families or for longer-term stays in San Antonio.

Lavalle 387 (btw. Alsina and Arellano), 2760 San Antonio de Areco. ℂ **2326/455-583** or 454-515. www.paradoresdraghi.com.ar. 5 units. From $80 double. Rates include breakfast. AE, DC, MC, V. Free parking. **Amenities:** Free use of bikes; concierge; heated outdoor pool; limited room service. *In room:* A/C, TV, hair dryer, kitchen (in some), minibar, Wi-Fi.

Hostal de Areco This small family-style hotel is in a historic turn-of-the-20th-century red house, set back from the street and surrounded by a small garden. There are seven small, spartan, tile-floor rooms, each equipped with a full-size bed and a bathroom. Dark-green curtains and bedspreads give the rooms an even smaller appearance. The accommodations are basic. Only some rooms are air-conditioned, others with fans, but all come with cable TV and Wi-Fi.

Zapioli 25, near the intersection of Zerboni, 2760 San Antonio de Areco. ℂ **2326/456-118.** www.hostaldeareco.com.ar. 7 units. From $45–$55 double. Rates include breakfast. No credit cards. Free parking. **Amenities:** Free use of bikes; concierge. *In room:* Ceiling fan or A/C, TV, Wi-Fi.

Hotel San Carlos ★ Overlooking the Parque San Martín, you'll find a sun deck equipped with a grill, Jacuzzi, and two outdoor heated swimming pools in the courtyard, with a fountain decorated with a mosaic of San Antonio de Padua. (It's one of the few places where you're likely to see bikini-clad women frolicking in front of religious icons, unless you belong to a particularly liberal church.) Some rooms are on the small side, but they're larger in the hotel's new wing. Many come with hydromassage tubs or Jacuzzis in the bathrooms, and a few two-bedroom apartments have kitchens. The hotel added a spa in 2008; ask about special packages.

Avenida Zerboni (on the west corner, at the intersection of Zapiola), 2760 San Antonio de Areco. © **2326/453-106.** www.hotel-sancarlos.com.ar. 30 units. From $60 double; from $85 apt. Rates include breakfast. Higher prices for all-day use of spa. AE, MC, V. Free parking. **Amenities:** Free use of bikes; concierge; health club; high-speed Internet station; Jacuzzi; 2 heated outdoor pools; 24-hr. room service; spa; *asado* (barbecue); Wi-Fi in lobby. *In room:* A/C, TV, hair dryer, minibar, Wi-Fi.

Los Abuelos   Alberto Cesar Reyes is your grandfather at this property overlooking Parque San Martín and the Río Areco—the hotel's name literally means the grand-parents. The hotel is basic, with a lot of white metal and Formica furnishings in the tile-floored room. The beds are covered with sea-foam green chenille bedspreads. Some bathrooms have tub/shower combinations, while others have just stand-alone showers. An aboveground pool is surrounded by a small deck in the back of the property near the parking lot. A nice warm touch is a gas fireplace in the front lobby, which is surrounded by simple pine chairs and tables where breakfast is served.

Avenida Zerboni on the corner at the intersection of Zapiola. 2760 San Antonio de Areco. www.san antoniodeareco.com/losabuelos © **02326/456-390.** 9 units. From $50 double. Rates include break-fast. No credit cards. Free parking. **Amenities:** Free use of bikes; concierge; pool; 24-hr. room service. *In room:* A/C, ceiling fan, hair dryer, TV, Wi-Fi.

Where to Eat

Almacén de Ramos Gerelos ARGENTINE/SPANISH/PARRILLA   This res-taurant, housed in a turn-of-the-20th-century building, is one of the best-known restaurants in San Antonio de Areco. It has a *parrilla* as well as international items on the menu and also offers a broad selection of paellas. Its interior, with rich wooden details, will take you back in time.

Zapiola 143, at Segundo Sombra. No phone. Main courses $4–$10. AE. Daily noon–3pm and 8–11pm.

Corner Pizza ARGENTINE/INTERNATIONAL   This simple place overlooks the Parque San Martín and the Río Areco. You'll find a selection of fast-food items on the menu, from hot dogs and hamburgers to pizza. Many people just come here to down a beer and look at the park. It's ideal if you're on a budget.

Av. Zerboni at Alsina, overlooking Parque San Martín. No phone. Main courses $2–$6. No credit cards. Daily 10am–11pm.

La Esquina de Merti ★ PARRILLA/ARGENTINE   This restaurant has an old-fashioned feel to it, with exposed brick walls, an ancient copper coffeemaker on the bar, wooden tables overlaid with black-and-white-checkered tablecloths, and shelves full of apothecary jars. But it's all a trick: La Esquina de Merti opened in late 2005, in the location of an old *almacén,* or Argentine general store. In any case, the food, concentrating on the beef the region is famous for, is great. You'll find a beef and chicken *parrilla,* and a selection of pastas and empanadas. The house specialty is *mollejas* with cream, lemon, and champagne (*mollejas* are the softly grilled, melt-in-your-mouth pancreas or thymus of a cow, which might be worth trying for an only-in-Argentina experience). A large wine selection complements everything on the menu.

Arellano 147, at Segundo Sombra (overlooking Plaza Arellano). © **2326/456-705.** www.esquinade merti.com.ar. Main courses $4–$10. AE, V. Sun–Thurs 9am–2am; Fri–Sat 9am–3am.

Pampas & Estancias

San Antonio is a popular base for exploring Argentina's famous *estancias,* which dou-bled historically as both farms and fortresses, built throughout the country along trails from Buenos Aires as a means of conquering and stabilizing territory originally controlled by the Indians. The majority of Argentina's *estancias* date from the mid- to late 1800s. After General Roca's Campaign of the Desert in the 1870s, in which he murdered most of the Indian population within 150 miles of Buenos Aires, the land gave rise to *estancias* and their cattle and grain production. Despite the bloody history that gave birth to them, today they're seen as a retreat from the stress of Buenos Aires. They are popular among Porteños on weekends or for day trips. With the increasing boom of tourism to Argentina, many foreigners delight in them as well.

Most *estancias* listed here are a half-hour from San Antonio, and no more than 2 hours from Buenos Aires. You can drive on your own, or use a bus service from Buenos Aires to San Antonio, and catch a taxi from there. For a fee in the range of $80 to $120 or more, most *estancias* provide transportation from your hotel or either Buenos Aires airport. Because many *estancias* are accessed by dirt roads, it is advisable to rent a 4WD vehicle if you drive yourself, especially if rain is predicted during your visit. The *estancias* here have detailed driving maps on their websites.

Services and features vary, but the atmosphere at most *estancias* is a cross between a rustic resort and bed-and-breakfast. Nothing relieves stress like a few days in the country, and horseback riding, trekking, lounging by the pool, and eating and drinking aplenty are all part of a day in the Pampas. In general, the rates for *estancias* include a full board of four meals—breakfast, lunch, afternoon tea, and dinner—and sometimes all drinks, including alcohol. Lunch, the highlight of dining on an *estancia,* is usually an *asado,* or barbecue, where everyone, including the workers, gathers to socialize. Day rates generally include only lunch and limited activities. Most *estancias* are real working farms, with hundreds of acres and cows, horses, and other animals attended by real gauchos (not all of whom dress in the traditional way). If you're in the mood to milk a cow or watch the birth of colt, you just might have the chance.

El Cencerro ★★★   Smaller, cozier, and more rustic than some of the other places listed here, this working *estancia* will make you feel like you're part of the farm's daily goings-on. It's owned by Buenos Aires–based psychologist Liliana Herbstein, who spends her weekends here. The ranch takes its name from the *cencerro,* a bell used by gauchos to tame horses. Rooms and public areas are filled with antiques and odd objects Liliana and her husband, Eduardo, have collected over the years, including antique luggage from Liliana's family's old store in Buenos Aires. Eduardo is an architect and artist, whose work also hangs throughout the main house. Activities include horseback riding, helping with the animals if you want, carriage rides, bicycle rides, and trekking. The main house was renovated in 2008 so that it contains five bedrooms, three as suites with private bathrooms, each large enough for a family of four. A gourmet chef cooks dinner, and a new playroom has a game room, small home theater, and other amenities. The 21-hectare (52-acre) property also has a wooded creek, a relaxing place for a nap, a picnic, or afternoon reading. In 2011, the owners added a *fogón,* or outdoor fireplace, along with a Jacuzzi and a mud oven for more open-air enjoyment. By *remise* from Buenos Aires, 80km (50 miles) away, it's about $75. Only 3km (2 miles) away is historic **Capilla del Señor,** a charming colonial town. You can access the *estancia* by bus from Buenos Aires to Capilla del Señor and then a $6 taxi ride. Similar to San Antonio de Areco in feel, it's virtually unknown to foreigners and walkable from the *estancia.* Real gauchos wander downtown and every second Tuesday of the month, there is an animal auction, which Liliana attends with guests. The area is also a ballooning center, offered as an option for $150 per person.

Buenos Aires Provincial Ruta 39, 2812 Capilla del Señor. ℭ **11/4743-2319** or 15-6093-2319 (mobile) in Buenos Aires. www.estanciaelcencerro.com.ar. 5 units. From $150. Rates include all meals and some drinks. Day rate of $75 includes lunch only. No credit cards. Free parking. **Amenities:** Free use of bikes; outdoor pool; limited room service; bird-watching; carriage riding; horseback riding. *In room:* A/C, ceiling fan, TV, DVD.

El Ombú de Areco ★★★   El Ombú takes its name from the tree that dominates the Pampas. It's among the most historic *estancias* near Buenos Aires. General Pablo Riccheri, an Italian military man who came to Argentina during the unification wars, built the original vine-covered house in 1880. The general atmosphere and overgrown row of trees out front will remind you of a Southern U.S. plantation. The rooms in the old house, with high ceilings, are best. But you really can't go wrong here; all the rooms have romantic appeal, decorated with brass beds, floral linens, and a strong country atmosphere. Some bathrooms have hydro-massage tubs, and others tub/shower combinations. The guest rooms are not air-conditioned but have ceiling fans. The property has two pools, one in a small courtyard, another on the edge of the main garden with a fantastic view of the sun setting over horses in the fields. Several game rooms are on the grounds, with TVs, movies, and other activities, and it's easy to mingle with the very friendly staff. This is a working ranch, with 300 hectares (741 acres) of land and more than 400 cows and other animals. Horseback riding, cattle roundups, sunset carriage riding, bicycling, and many other activities are available, and all four meals and drinks are included in the rate. The *estancia* is about 10km (6 miles) from San Antonio and 120km (74 miles) from Buenos Aires. Their *remise* service costs $90 from Buenos Aires and $115 from Ezeiza airport. Taxis from San Antonio de Areco run about $11.

Buenos Aires Provincial Ruta 31, Cuartel 6, 2760 San Antonio de Areco. ✆ **2326/492-080** or 11/4737-0436 in Buenos Aires. www.estanciaelombu.com. 9 units. From $200 single; $340 double. Rates include all meals and drinks. Day rate of $75 includes lunch only. AE, V. Free parking. Pets allowed. **Amenities:** Babysitting; free use of bikes; concierge; 2 outdoor pools; 24-hr. room service; carriage riding; horseback riding. *In room:* Ceiling fan, hair dryer.

El Rosario de Areco ★★★   Unlike most *estancia* owners, who live in Buenos Aires, Francisco and Florencia de Guevera, distant relatives of Che who only comment that they have a very different political ideology from him, live year-round on their *estancia*, along with some of their nine children. This *estancia* is among the most pleasant to visit, with its barn-red buildings and bougainvilleas scattered among the grounds. The *estancia* dates from 1892, but the rooms, many of which are in former horse stalls, have surprisingly modern interiors. The waitstaff is a little different here, too. Instead of running around in gaucho outfits, they wear chic black uniforms, as if they popped in from Palermo. The owners regularly mingle with guests, and Francisco cooks the lunch *asado*. They have 16 double rooms, all with large private bathrooms. Rooms are not air-conditioned, but have ceiling fans, and some rooms have fireplaces. In early 2011 the owners opened a small luxury hotel with 30 rooms on the 80-hectare (198-acre) grounds. The property offers a small polo field, horseback riding, carriage riding, two swimming pools, several public rooms with TVs, and other recreational activities such as pool and video games. The *estancia* is 7km (4⅓ miles) from San Antonio de Areco and 100km (62 miles) from Buenos Aires. From San Antonio, a taxi is about $11 and the *estancia's remise* service is $112 from Buenos Aires.

Buenos Aires Provincial Ruta 41 (mailing address is Castilla de Correo 85), 2760 San Antonio de Areco. ✆ **2326/451-000.** www.rosariodeareco.com.ar and www.pampasdeareco.com. 16 units. From $380 double in *estancia*. Rates include all meals and drinks. Day rate of $90 includes lunch only (call ahead for day-rate availability). From $300 double in hotel; from $370–$400 suite. No credit cards. Free parking. **Amenities:** Babysitting; free use of bikes; concierge; 2 outdoor pools; limited room service; carriage riding; horseback riding; polo fields; TV lounges; Wi-Fi. *In estancia room:* Ceiling fan, hair dryer, fireplace (in some rooms), Wi-Fi. *In hotel rooms:* TV, A/C, hair dryer, minibar, Wi-Fi.

La Bamba ★★★   This is one of the most gorgeous and romantic *estancias* near Buenos Aires. The original building opened in 1830 as a stagecoach stop along what had once been the old Camino Real, linking Buenos Aires with other colonial cities. The buildings are Pompeian red with white trim, contrasting with the rich green landscape. The Argentine movie *Camila,* about a forbidden romance in the 1840s, was filmed here and nominated for Best Foreign Film in the 1984 Academy Awards. If you are honeymooning in Argentina, this place is ideal—especially the isolated Torre Room in the main house, on the third floor, in what had been a lookout tower with windows on all sides opening onto the expansive Pampas. Swimming, horseback riding, carriage riding, trekking, and other activities are all available. The 150-hectare (371-acre) property has cows, soy, and wheat fields. The *estancia* is 13km (8 miles) from San Antonio and 123km (76 miles) from Buenos Aires. The *estancia* was bought by Frenchman Jean Francois Decaux who vastly renovated the property including new wiring, air-conditioning, pool, and polo ground improvements, all while maintaining the historic nature of the location.

Buenos Aires Provincial Ruta 31, 2760 San Antonio de Areco. www.labambadeareco.com. ✆ **2326/454-895** or 11/15-4444-6560 [mobile]. 11 units. $530–$600 double. Rates include all meals and drinks. Day rate of $140 includes lunch only. AE, DC, MC. Free parking. **Amenities:** Babysitting; free use of bikes; concierge; outdoor pool; limited room service; spa; carriage riding; horseback riding; high-speed Internet. *In room:* A/C, ceiling fan, TV, hair dryer, Wi-Fi.

IGUAZU FALLS & THE NORTHEAST

by Charlie O'Malley

guazú Falls, the mother of all waterfalls, cannot fail to impress even the most jaded traveler. This huge chasm of cascading foam and spray was the location of the opening scene of the epic movie *The Mission,* when the Guarani Indians sent an unwanted priest over the side on a crucifix. Nowadays the locals have a little more trouble keeping visitors away as the Falls is Argentina's top tourist attraction with 1.2 million people a year making their way to eye what is truly one of the world's most spectacular natural wonders. Twenty-three kilometers (14 miles) of deafening waterfalls plummet up to 70m (229 ft.) into a giant gorge in a spectacular subtropical setting. The sheer power is overwhelming. You come face to face with raging sheets of water, with sprays so intense it seems as though geysers have erupted from below. Iguazú is a must-see on any trip to Argentina.

It's shocking that this ecological blockbuster is a 90-minute flight from the civilized, cosmopolitan buzz of Buenos Aires. Many people drop into this humid corner of Misiones province on a day trip or for 2 days max. Yet this fascinating jungle zone of red soil, giant butterflies, and comical toucans has more to offer than jaw-dropping waterfalls. Misiones Province is a heady mix of strong indigenous tribal culture, blond eastern European settlers, and tropical frontier land. Its abundant wildlife and its long-fallen, mysterious Jesuit ruins are worth exploring. With its multitude of isolated national parks and huge swaths of untouched rainforest, it is an eco-tourist's paradise, with several genuine jungle lodges. Civilization has encroached in the form of tea plantations and pine forests, yet it is possible to get off the beaten track and visit isolated wonders such as Esteros del Ibera, a vast marshland teeming with wildlife that is fast becoming one of Argentina's hottest destinations.

IGUAZU FALLS & PUERTO IGUAZU ★★

1,330km (825 miles) NE of Buenos Aires

A dazzling panorama of cascades whose power overwhelms the sounds of the surrounding jungle, **Las Cataratas del Iguazú (Iguazú Falls)** refers to the spectacular canyon of waterfalls fed by the Río Iguazú. Declared a World Heritage Site by UNESCO in 1984, these 275 waterfalls were shaped by 120 million years of geological upheaval, forming one of earth's most unforgettable sights. Iguazú Falls are shared by Argentina and Brazil, and are easily accessible from nearby Paraguay as well. More than one million visitors a year means the park has become somewhat overdeveloped, with too many restaurants and a theme park–style railway. However, the falls are too huge and magnificent to be encroached upon completely by humans, and the excellent walking circuits on both the Argentine and Brazilian sides allow visitors to peek over the tops and almost touch the torrent. Most visitors stay in the towns of Puerto Iguazú, in Argentina, or Foz do Iguaçu, in Brazil, or in some well-appointed hotels on the road to the park.

Worth exploring is the park's subtropical jungle (see "Behind the Falls & into the Jungle," below). Here, cupay trees (South American hardwoods) tower over the various layers of life that compete for light; and the national park is known to contain 200 species of trees, 448 species of birds, 71 species of mammals, 36 species of reptiles, 20 species of amphibians, and more than 250 species of butterflies. Iguazú's climate also provides for the flowering of plants year-round, lending brilliant color to the forest. Because spray from the waterfall keeps humidity levels over 75%, there's a tremendous growth of epiphytes, or plants that grow on other plants without taking nutrients from their hosts.

You can visit the waterfalls on your own, but you will most certainly need a tour operator to explore the jungle. Allow at least 1 full day to explore the waterfalls on the Argentine side, another to visit the Brazilian side, and perhaps half a day for a jungle tour. Many visitors base themselves in the sedate town of Puerto Iguazú, 18km (11 miles) from the park. Though hardly the most memorable place, Puerto Iguazú has a subdued charm, pretty vegetation, and friendly people, and it's not yet ruined by the tourist trade. Accommodations options are improving all the time. If you want something more vibrant, go to the Brazilian town of Foz do Iguaçu, on the other side (see "Border Crossing," later in this chapter).

Essentials

GETTING THERE   Aerolíneas Argentinas (© 0810/222-86527 or 3757/420-194; www.aerolineas.com.ar), and **LAN** (© 3757/424-296; www.lan.com/chile) offer up to nine daily flights from Buenos Aires to **Aeropuerto Internacional Cataratas** (© 3757/422-013); the trip takes 1½ hours. Round-trip fares cost approximately $420, depending on whether any specials are on offer. Aerolíneas Argentinas occasionally offers flights to Iguazú from Ezeiza international airport, usually on Saturday or Sunday. **Andes Lineas Aereas** (© 0810/777-26337; www.andesonline.com) operates twice-weekly flights to and from Salta with onward connections to Mendoza and Bariloche. The flights are on Monday and Wednesday and cost $190 one-way. It's a 20-minute drive from the airport to Puerto Iguazú; catch a taxi (for about $20) or one of the shuttles from the airport to town ($5).

The fastest bus service from Buenos Aires is with **Vía Bariloche** (© 11/4315-4456 in Buenos Aires; www.viabariloche.com.ar), which takes 18 hours and costs $105 to $123 one-way, depending on the seat you choose. (The more expensive fare gets you a fully reclining *cama* [bed] seat.) Cheaper but longer (21 hr.) bus travel is available through **Expreso Singer** (© 11/4313-3927 in Buenos Aires; www.expresosinger.com.ar) and **Expreso Tigre Iguazú** (© 11/4313-3915 in Buenos Aires; www.tigreiguazu.com.ar), which both cost about $92 one-way. **Puerto Iguazú Bus Terminal,** Calle Córdoba and Avenida Misiones (© 3757/423-006), is located in the town center.

The Iguazú Falls Region

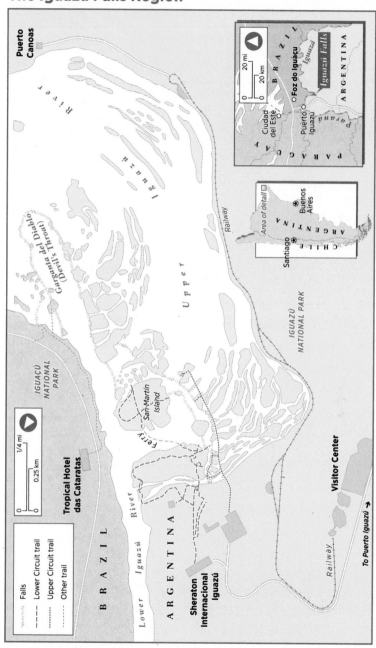

Puerto
Canoas

Iguazú   River

Garganta del Diablo
(Devil's Throat)

IGUAZÚ
NATIONAL
PARK

Upper

Railway

San Martín
Island

Ferry

IGUAZÚ
NATIONAL PARK

Tropical Hotel
das Cataratas

Iguazú   River

Lower

BRAZIL

ARGENTINA

Sheraton
Internacional
Iguazú

Visitor Center

Railway

To Puerto Iguazú →

Falls
Lower Circuit trail
Upper Circuit trail
Other trail

0   1/4 mi
0   0.25 km

Foz do Iguaçu
Iguazú Falls
BRAZIL
ARGENTINA
Ciudad
del Este
Puerto
Iguazú
Paraná
PARAGUAY

0   20 mi
0   20 km

Area of detail
Buenos
Aires
ARGENTINA
CHILE
Santiago

191

VISITOR INFORMATION   In Puerto Iguazú, obtain maps and park information from the **Parque Nacional** office at Victoria Aguirre 66 ((C) **3757/420-722;** www. iguazuargentina.com), open Monday through Friday from 8am to 9pm. For information on the town, contact the municipal tourist office, at Victoria Aguirre and Brañas ((C) **3757/420-800;** www.turismo.misiones.gov.ar). It's open Monday to Friday from 8am to 9pm, Saturday and Sunday from 8am to noon and 3 to 9pm. Visitor information is also available near the national park entrance (see below).

In Buenos Aires, get information about Iguazú from Casa de la Provincia de Misiones, Av. Santa Fe 989 ((C) **11/4322-0686;** www.misiones.gov.ar), open Monday through Friday from 10am to 5pm.

GETTING AROUND   **El Práctico** local buses run every 45 minutes from 7am to 8pm between Puerto Iguazú bus terminal and the national park; the cost is $3.75.

Taxis are unmetered and relatively expensive, with most drivers charging a flat fee of $20 wherever you go, whether it's to the airport or park. **Parada 10** ((C) **3757/421-527**) and **Remisses Falls VIP,** Bompland 185 ((C) **3757/420-805**), provide 24-hour taxi service. Within both Puerto Iguazú and the national park, you can easily walk or, in the former, take the narrow-gauge train.

If you choose to travel by car, the main roads are excellent but be prepared for wretched mud baths if you stray. **Budget,** Paulino Amarante 76, Puerto Iguazú ((C) **3757/421-675;** www.budget.com), offers small cars for $80 a day.

Bike rentals are available for $10 a day from **Internet Yguazu,** Av. Victoria Aguirre 552 ((C) **3757/424-034**).

Visiting the National Park ★★★

Your first stop will likely be the **visitor center** ((C) **3757/491-444**), where you'll find maps and information about the area's flora and fauna. Known as the Centro de Interpretacion, it is .8km (½ mile) from the park entrance, close to the parking lot and footbridges for the waterfall circuits. Adjacent to the visitor center, you will find a restaurant, snack shops, and souvenir stores. A natural-gas train takes visitors to the path entrance for the Upper and Lower circuits and to the footbridge leading to Devil's Throat. (If you'd rather walk, footpaths are available, but note that the walk to Devil's Throat is about 3km/1.75 miles.) The visitor center is staffed with a number of English-speaking guides, available for private tours. You may opt to see the falls on your own or with an experienced local guide. A guide is not really necessary, however, unless your time is limited or you want to ask detailed questions about the region's geography and fauna. The entrance fee for non-Argentines is $21 and includes the cost of the train ride. The park is open daily 8am to 7pm in summer, 8am until 6pm in winter.

The two main paths from which to view the waterfalls are the **Circuito Superior (Upper Circuit)** ★ and the **Circuito Inferior (Lower Circuit)** ★, both of which begin within walking distance (less than .8km/½ mile) from the visitor center. You may want to save your energy, however, and catch the train to the path entrance. There's a small snack shop near the beginning of the trails. The Upper Circuit winds its way along the top of the canyon, allowing you to look down the falls and see the area's rich flora, including cacti, ferns, and orchids. The Lower Circuit offers the best views, as magnificent waterfalls come hurtling down before you in walls of silvery spray. The waterfalls are clearly marked by signs along the way.

The best time to walk the Upper Circuit is early in the morning or late in the afternoon, and rainbows often appear near sunset. This .9km (.5-mile) path takes 1 to 2 hours, starting at the viewing tower and leading past **Dos Hermanas (Two Sisters), Bossetti, Chico (Small), Ramírez,** and **San Martín** (the park's widest) falls. You can come right to the edges of these falls and look over them as they fall as far as 60m (197 ft.) below. Along your walk, you can also look across to San Martín Island and the Brazilian side, and you'll pass a number of small streams and creeks.

The 1.8km (1.25-mile) Lower Circuit takes 2 hours to walk, leading you first past **Lanusse** and **Alvar Núñez** falls, and then along the Lower Iguazú River past the raging **Dos Mosqueteros (Two Musketeers)** and **Tres Mosqueteros (Three Musketeers)** falls. The trail winds its way toward **Ramírez, Chico,** and **Dos Hermanas** falls. Here, you'll find an inspiring view of the **Garganta del Diablo (Devil's Throat)** and **Bossetti** falls. From the Salto Bossetti waterfall, a small pathway leads down to a small pier, where you can catch a free boat to **San Martín Island.**

Once on the island, climb the stairs and walk along the clearly marked trails for remarkable views of the surrounding *cataratas* (falls). To the left, you see the enormous Garganta del Diablo, **Saltos Brasileros (Brazilian Falls),** and **Ventana;** to the right, you overlook the mighty **Salto San Martín,** which sprays 30m (98 ft.) high after hitting the river below. This panoramic view looks out at dozens of falls forming an arch before you. San Martín Island also has a small, idyllic beach perfect for sunbathing and swimming.

Garganta del Diablo is the greatest of all waterfalls in Iguazú, visible from observation points in both the Brazilian and Argentine parks. You'll notice that the water is calm as it makes its way down the Iguazú River and then begins to speed up as it approaches the gorge ahead. Before you, Mother Nature has created a furious avalanche of water and spray that is the highest waterfall in Iguazú and one of the world's greatest natural spectacles. You might want to bring a raincoat, because you will get wet.

OUTDOOR ACTIVITIES

INSIDE THE PARK The park's official tour operator is **Iguazú Jungle Explorer** (© 3757/421-696; www.iguazujunglexplorer.com), located both inside the national park and in the Sheraton Internacional Iguazú. This company offers the Nautical Adventure tour ($30), which visits the falls by inflatable raft; the Ecological Tour ($13), which takes you to Devil's Throat and lets you paddle rubber boats along the Upper Iguazú Delta; and the Gran Aventura (Great Adventure) tour ($55). This last tour begins with an 8km (5-mile) safari ride along the Yacoratia Path, the original dirt road that led through the forest and on to Buenos Aires. During the ride, you'll view the jungle's extensive flora and might catch a glimpse of some of the region's indigenous wildlife (see "Behind the Falls & into the Jungle," below). You will then disembark at Puerto Macuco, where you'll hop into an inflatable boat with your tour group and navigate 6.5km (4 miles) along the lower Iguazú River, braving 1.6km (1 mile) of rapids as you approach the falls in Devil's Throat Canyon. After a thrilling and wet ride, the raft lets you off across from San Martín Island. From there, catch a free boat to this island with excellent hiking trails and a small beach for swimming and sunbathing. You can combine the Ecological Tour and Great Adventure by buying a full-day Pasaporte Verde for $63. An increasingly popular tour is a guided walk around the falls under a full moon, where nighttime rainbows appear.

If you want to arrange a private adventure tour for your specific interests, the best outfit is **Explorador Expediciones,** with offices in the Sheraton Internacional Iguazú and in Puerto Iguazú at Perito Moreno 217 (© **3757/421-632;** www.rainforestevt.com.ar). The guides are experts on life in the Iguazú jungle. A jungle safari costs $45 and an excursion to the waterfall is $36. English guides are available, and tours last 2 hours.

OUTSIDE THE PARK

CANOPY & ROCK CLIMBING **Iguazú Forest,** Mariano Moreno 58, Puerto Iguazú (© **3757/421-140;** www.iguazuforest.com), organizes canopy, hiking, and rappelling excursions. Their guides can also show you how to climb a waterfall in a nature reserve, 7km (4⅓ miles) south of the town.

TREKKING & BIRD-WATCHING **Iguazú Forest** (see "Canopy & Rock Climbing," above) will take you out with trained naturalists, where you can learn more about the birds and butterflies in the area.

HORSEBACK RIDING **Cabalgatas Ecológicas** (© **3757/421-543** or 15-675-539 [mobile]; www.cabalgatasecologicas.com) conducts 2-hour jungle circuits that cost $20.

FISHING **Iguazú Water Sports,** Town Port, Puerto Iguazú (© **3757/556-932** [mobile]; www.iguazuwatersports.com.ar), organizes daylong fishing excursions, which include riverside *asados* (barbecues) and other watersports.

SEEING THE SIGHTS AROUND PUERTO IGUAZU

La Aripuca, RN 12, Km 4.5, Puerto Iguazú (© **3757/423-488;** www.aripuca.com.ar), is a giant house made from fallen tree trunks, its design based on a primitive bird trap. It is located outside the town on the way to the park and worth a morning stroll, with a handicraft store selling everything from *mate*-flavored ice cream to leather goods. It is open every day from 8am to 7pm. Puerto Iguazú also boasts two colorful orchid gardens: **Indio Solitario,** Calle Jangadero 719, Puerto Iguazú (no phone), open Tuesday to Saturday 9am until midday and 3 to 8pm and Sunday from 9am to midday, and **Jardín de Ozain,** Fray Luis Beltran 84, Puerto Iguazú (© **3757/421-302**), which is open daily from 8am to 6pm. Perhaps one of Iguazú's most eccentric sites is the **Plastic Bottle House,** RN 12, Km 5, Puerto Iguazú (© **3757/405-621**). The somewhat ugly bungalow made from recycled materials is just down the road from La Aripuca and worth a 20-minute stop and the $2 admission. **Guïrá Ogá Bird's House ★**, RN 12, Km 5, Puerto Iguazú (© **3757/423-980;** www.guiraoga.fundacionazara.org.ar), is an interesting animal refuge full of parrots, owls, and monkeys. Admission is $7.50. **Fortín M'Bororé** is a Guarani Indian community that now accepts visitors; here, they reveal some of the secrets behind their ancient traditions of hunting, natural medicine, and handicrafts. Two-hour tours ($21) are organized by the agency **Cuenca del Plata,** Tareferos 111, Puerto Iguazú (© **3757/423-300;** www.cuencadelplata.com); a significant share of the costs goes toward social projects and medical assistance.

SHOPPING Feathered Guarani wander the town selling trinkets, and the principal streets are jammed with shops selling all types of tourist tat, from factory-produced *mate* gourds to dreamcatchers. Look hard enough though and you will find genuine, locally produced weavings and handicrafts. **Patria Gaucha,** Victoria Aguirre 222, Puerto Iguazú (© **3757/423-469**), is perfect for those cowboy shoppers who want leather boots, jackets, and ponchos. **Claudia G,** Av. Brasil 154, Puerto Iguazú (© **3757/425-456**), specializes in wool and cotton goods, with a nice line of candles.

BEHIND THE FALLS & INTO THE jungle

Dawn in Iguazú brings the first rays of light through the forest canopy, as orchids, butterflies, frogs, lizards, parrots, and monkeys awaken and spread color and life through the forest. Binoculars in hand, step softly into this wonderland, where most sounds are masked by the roar from the falls.

You'll see parakeets long before entering the jungle. Their green bodies and loud song make them easy to spot; macaws, parrots, and toucans also live here. Look and listen carefully for the great dusky swift, which nests near the waterfalls, and the great yellow-breasted kiskadee, whose family name—Tyrannidae—tells much about its hunting prowess. Look below the canopy to observe an enormous population of butterflies, the other flying wonders of the park. Brilliant blue flyers, known as morpho butterflies, flit between deciduous trees and above lines of leaf-cutter ants, along with beautiful red, black, and yellow butterfly species.

It's close to impossible to walk through the park without running across some local indigenous reptiles. Ubiquitous tropidurus lizards, which feed on bird eggs, scamper everywhere. Colorful tree frogs hop and croak the nights away. Only patient and persistent visitors, however, will discover larger and rarer creatures, such as the 1.5m-long (5-ft.) tegu lizard and the caiman, a crocodile-like reptile.

Warm-blooded creatures share this forest as well. Coatis—aardvarklike mammals that travel in groups searching for insects and fruit—are frequent and fearless visitors to the trails. Swinging above the footpaths are brown capuchin monkeys, whose chatter and gestures make them seem more human than most primates. The predators of this warm-blooded group range from vampire bats to endangered jaguars and pumas. For your safety, stay on the walking paths and, when you're in the jungle, with your tour operator.

An array of subtropical flora surrounds Iguazú's resident animals and insects. Bamboo, ficus, fig, and ancient rosewood trees—up to 1,000 years old—are but a few of the trees that grow near the river and compete for light, along with a proliferation of epiphytes (plants growing on other plants), such as bromeliads, güembés, and orchids. Eighty-five species of orchid thrive in the park, mostly close to the damp and well-lit waterfalls.

SPAS & WELLNESS CENTERS   All that mud and humidity takes its toll, and after a long day in the jungle, your body will appreciate an hour in a sauna or on the massage slab. **Spa de la Selva,** Route 12, Km 5 (© **3757/420-057;** www.spadela selva.com.ar), is a charming garden facility beside the Orquídeas Palace, offering everything from manicures to yoga sessions. For something closer to town, try **Vergel Iguazú Relax,** Bonpland 111, Puerto Iguazú (© **3757/421-733**), a small street clinic with hot stone massage and aromatherapy baths. Most of the high-end hotels have in-house spas that welcome nonguests—the most notable in town being the **Hotel Saint George,** Av. Córdoba 148, Puerto Iguazú (© **3757/420-633;** www. hotelsaintgeorge.com).

Where to Stay

Puerto Iguazú has 90 registered places to stay. Some are five-star complexes located on the road to the park, while others are more budget options in the town that vary between two-star hotels and family-oriented cabins. A complete list can be found at the municipal tourist office, at Victoria Aguirre and Brañas (© **3757/420-800**) but it is always wise to book in advance, no matter what time of year you go. Peak season for hotels in Iguazú extends through January and February (summer holiday) and also includes July (winter break), Semana Santa (Holy Week, the week before Easter), and long weekends. On the Argentine side, the Sheraton Internacional Iguazú is the only hotel inside the national park. Discounts are common in the off season.

EXPENSIVE

Hotel Cataratas ★ ☺   None of the stuffiness you sometimes feel at luxury hotels is evident here. Despite the hotel's unimpressive exterior, rooms are among the most modern and spacious in the area—especially the 30 "master rooms" that feature two double beds, handsome wood furniture, colorful artwork, large bathrooms with separate toilet rooms, in-room safes, and views of the pool or gardens. These rooms are only slightly more than the standard rooms, called "superior." The hotel's many facilities, including an outdoor pool, spa, tennis and volleyball courts, putting green, and game room, make this a great choice for families. The Cataratas Restaurant offers a fine selection of regional and international dishes, and you can dine inside or out. The hotel lies 4km (2½ miles) from the center of Puerto Iguazú and 17km (11 miles) from the national park entrance. A free shuttle service ferries guests between the park and Puerto Iguazú.

RN 12, Km 4, 3370 Misiones. © **3757/421-100.** Fax 3757/421-090. www.hotelcataratas.com. 130 units. $134 double superior; from $164 master room. Rates include buffet breakfast. AE, DC, MC, V. Free parking. **Amenities:** Restaurant; bar; concierge; Jacuzzi; massage; indoor and outdoor pools; putting green; health club; room service; sauna; spa; tennis court; Wi-Fi. *In room:* A/C, TV, hair dryer, minibar.

Hotel Panoramic   All the upscale, modern hotels are located on the road to the park, except this particular five-star gem that is a 10-minute walk from the town center. Hotel Panoramic lives up to its name with gorgeous views of the river valley and the three frontiers of Argentina, Brazil, and Paraguay, giving you an excellent sense of place that most hotels here lack. The modern five-story building is set in extensive grounds with rolling green lawns you might mistake for a golf course. Felt, chrome, and dark tiles adorn a big, businesslike lobby and the subdued tones continue throughout the carpeted corridors into decent-size rooms with minimalist fittings. From your hardwood balcony you can see the red-toned Río Iguazú pour into the green, meandering Río Parana. The wardrobes are all mirrored and the bathrooms particularly slick with tiles made from hardwood inset with marble. On top is a rather large, soulless common room, but with a great view. From here you can also see a rather stark, but large central courtyard adorned with a small waterfall that is used for events. More inviting is the splendidly big pool set at a decent distance from the hotel building and surrounded by ample tilework and deck chairs. I have no problem recommending this hotel, opened in 2007, for comfort, location, and an incredible view.

Paraguay 372, 3370 Puerto Iguazú. © **3757/498-100.** www.panoramic-hoteliguazu.com. 91 units. $270 double. Rates include buffet breakfast. AE, DC, MC, V. **Amenities:** 2 restaurants; babysitter; casino; concierge; health club; massage; outdoor pool; room service. *In room:* A/C, TV, hair dryer, minibar.

Iguazú Grand Hotel Resort & Casino ★ ☺   Some of my pickiest friends have stayed here and could not fault it. The large, red-brick, mansion-style hotel sits on a low slope with lawns running down to an attractive pool area. The lobby is stunning and elegant, with white pillars and sparkling marble floors. What makes this five-star hotel stand out from the rest are its rooms, or should we say suites; they do not do rooms. Even the junior suites have 40 sq. m (431 sq. ft.) worth of impeccable decor, stylish period furniture, and ample light. The immaculate bathrooms have two wash-basins and a separate section for toilet and bidet. A delicious fruit drink awaits you upon arrival, as do a fresh bathrobe and pair of slippers. All the bathtubs have a hydro-massage. The hotel grounds are delightful, and the three pools are immaculate and well maintained. The breakfast buffet is superb, with a large variety of international dishes. A car service is available to all guests, charging a very reasonable $5 flat rate to all the local attractions. It is located on the road to the falls.

RN 12, Km 1640, 3370 Puerto Iguazú. ℂ **3757/498-050.** www.iguazugrand.com. 120 units. $363 junior suite; $397 garden suite. Rates include buffet breakfast. AE, DC, MC, V. **Amenities:** Restaurant; babysit-ter; casino; children's center; concierge; health club; Jacuzzi; massage; 3 outdoor pools; putting green; room service; sauna; spa; tennis court. *In room:* A/C, TV, hair dryer, minibar.

Sheraton Internacional Iguazú 👆 How on earth this typewriter-shaped bun-ker got to be built in a nature reserve is anybody's guess. The Sheraton enjoys a magnificent and exclusive location inside the national park (read: It's the *only* hotel inside the park). Guests have little need to leave the resort, and you have the added advantage of being able to explore the park when the daily crowds have left. The hotel is only steps from the Upper and Lower circuit trails, and half of the guest rooms have direct views of the water (the others have splendid views of the jungle). The only drawback to the rooms is that the decor is fairly standard Sheraton-issue. Service can be patchy, with forgotten wake-up calls not unheard of. Three restau-rants vie for the world's best restaurant view, with the main one, peering over Devil's Throat, serves pricey international dishes.

Parque Nacional Iguazú, 3370 Misiones. ℂ **0800/888-9180** local toll-free, or 3757/491-800. Fax 3757/491-848. www.sheraton.com. 180 units. $683 double with jungle view; $792 double with view of waterfalls; from $1,076 suite. Rates include buffet breakfast. AE, DC, MC, V. Free parking. **Amenities:** 3 restaurants; babysitting; basketball court; concierge; fitness center; outdoor and indoor pools; room service; spa; 2 tennis courts; Wi-Fi. *In room:* A/C, TV, hair dryer, minibar.

MODERATE

Boutique Hotel de la Fonte This hotel is one of the more interesting accom-modations in town, a beautiful garden hotel with ample grounds and excellent food, located on a quiet, residential street just a 5-minute walk from the downtown area. From the street it looks like any well-to-do residential home, and, indeed, staying there feels like a weekend sojourn with your Argentine cousins. The rooms are a little old-fashioned with low beds and heavy curtains, but it's the rambling garden that makes the place and if you are looking for modern opulence ask for one of the two new suites added in 2010. A marble fountain trickles in the shady corners. A red-tiled patio overlooks a medium-size pool with tall palm trees acting as sentries over the hot tub. The Italian owners are talented chefs, evident in the incredible menu that can be enjoyed in intimate corners of the garden.

1 de Mayo and Corrientes s/n, Puerto Iguazú, Misiones. ℂ **3757/420-625.** www.bhfboutiquehotel.com. 10 units. $140 double; $200 suite. Rates include buffet breakfast. AE, DC, MC, V. Free parking. **Ameni-ties:** Restaurant; Jacuzzi; outdoor pool; Wi-Fi. *In room:* A/C, TV, minibar.

Esturión Hotel & Lodge The Esturión is spacious, well equipped, and just a 10-minute walk from the town center. The main building has the look of a modern, tropical schoolhouse, but, in general, the facilities have a pleasing aesthetic. The huge pool and surrounding grounds have a Caribbean feel, though the safari-style staff uniforms are a little over-the-top. Rooms are decent, if a little functional and dated, and some have pleasant balconies. The lobby bar is very stylish and appealing. Service can be patchy, however; some staff members are helpful and efficient, and others are plain rude. Do not expect much English. The grounds are as expansive as the breakfast buffet, which is an excellent spread, and the food in general is good—particularly the *asado* (Argentine barbecue).

Av. Tres Fronteras 650, 3370 Puerto Iguazú. ✆ **3757/420-100.** Fax 3757/421-468. www.hotelesturion. com. 128 units. $148 double; $234 suite. Rates include buffet breakfast. AE, DC, MC, V. Free parking. **Amenities:** Restaurant; bar; outdoor pool; Wi-Fi. *In room:* A/C, TV, minibar.

Hotel Saint George ★★ 🎁 Undoubtedly the finest conventional hotel located in the town center, the Saint George is a modern cream-colored block with delightful bird of paradise plants outside and an inviting, spacious lobby of marble floors and striped furniture inside. Recently renovated, the new master rooms are much larger than the old standard rooms and worth the extra $10. Sleek flatscreen TVs go nicely with the stylish black minibars, while outside you'll find old telephone operators' desks and pianos gracing corridors that lead to a lush, ample courtyard with a large kidney-shaped pool. The bathrooms are big, with glass-enclosed showers and separate tubs. Service can be patchy but is more than made up for with an excellent breakfast buffet. The family-owned hotel has one of the best eateries in town, **La Esquina,** and is located on one of the main streets, a short stroll from restaurants, stores, and the bus terminal.

Av. Córdoba 148, 3370 Puerto Iguazú. ✆ **3757/420-633.** Fax 3757/420-651. www.hotelsaintgeorge. com. 100 units. $129 double; $173 double with dinner included; $169 suite. Rates include buffet breakfast. AE, DC, MC, V. Free parking. **Amenities:** Restaurant; Jacuzzi; outdoor pool; sauna; Wi-Fi. *In room:* A/C, TV, minibar.

La Aldea de la Selva ★ A sleek wooden walkway leads you through the jungle to a stylish and comfortable boutique hotel that is conveniently located 7km (4⅓ miles) from downtown Puerto Iguazú on the way to the falls. A brilliant blue terraced pool with three levels is surrounded by wooden decking and greenery. The rooms have pine walls and teak flooring that lead to wide wraparound balconies with thick wooden rails you can lean on and touch the jungle. The bathrooms are immaculate and luxurious, with tiled walls and gleaming-white wash bowls and tubs. Opened in 2008, La Aldea is Iguazú's latest accommodations offering and adds a modern, stylish choice to the range of options. In tune with the times, there is an on-site organic vegetable and herb garden and two Jacuzzis. It is perfect for romance and pampering.

Selva Iriapú s/n, Puerto Iguazú, Misiones. ✆ **3757/425-777.** www.laaldeadelaselva.com. 8 units. $156 double. Rates include buffet breakfast. AE, DC, MC, V. Free parking. **Amenities:** Restaurant; outdoor pool; Wi-Fi. *In room:* A/C, TV, minibar.

Orquídeas Palace This resort-style hotel with manicured lawns and low modern buildings has a pared-down, functional feel. At the same time, it's pleasant and relaxing. The decor is simple and elegant, if a little worn around the edges. It has a glass-fronted reception area with comfy couches and well-lit, spacious rooms with tiled floors and small window tables. The fixtures and features, however, could use updating. The bathrooms are all ceramic and clean, with showers and tubs. The 5-hectare (12-acre) garden offers lots of greenery with fruit-laden trees, lush shrubbery, and tropical flowers. A cool, lagoon-shaped pool has deck chairs. Set amid the well-trimmed grounds are some very agreeable cottages with white walls and tiled roofs. Some are older than others and priced accordingly. Beds vary from queen-size to double bunk, and the interiors are well presented with attractive drapes and bed covers. The hotel is on the road to the falls. Buses pass frequently in either direction.

RN 12, Km 5, 3370 Puerto Iguazú. © **3757/420-472.** Fax 3757/420-651. www.orquideashotel.com. 80 units. $106 double. Rates include buffet breakfast. AE, DC, MC, V. Free parking. **Amenities:** Restaurant; outdoor pool; Wi-Fi. *In room:* A/C, TV, minibar.

Posada La Sorgente

At Posada La Sorgente you can enjoy a tropical vibe without leaving town. Located 3 blocks north of the bus terminal, La Sorgente is a spacious pink mansion with floral trimmings that may be not to everybody's taste but is luxurious all the same. A vine-covered pergola out front opens up into a gorgeous lobby with white sofas, decorated floor tiles, and a glass-enshrined tree. The greenery continues into a sumptuous lawn garden with a figure-eight-shaped pool complete with a kitschy bridge that's perfect for a honeymoon photo. Well-appointed guest rooms are located in an L-shaped building with a handsome gallery that surrounds the palm tree courtyard. The rooms have hardwood floors, deep blue walls, and high-raftered ceilings. The bathrooms are equally spacious with old-fashioned tiles but fittings that appear brand new. The giant suite is particularly good value and the very decent Italian restaurant next door means you have all your needs within robe-wearing distance.

Av. Córdoba 454, 3370 Puerto Iguazú. © **3757/424-252.** www.lasorgentehotel.com. 27 units. $82 double; $90 suite. Rates include buffet breakfast. AE, MC, V. Free parking. **Amenities:** Restaurant; outdoor pool; Wi-Fi. *In room:* A/C, TV, minibar.

INEXPENSIVE

Garden Stone Hostel

The cramped guest rooms of this hostel are more than compensated for by a spectacular, rambling garden with a bamboo pergola and inviting hammocks. This small, family-run hostel is housed in a pleasant, low-rise building 3 blocks north of the bus station on a quiet residential street. Its seven rooms are basic in amenities and include two dorms that sleep up to eight. All but one double has shared bathrooms that are also on the small side. Its main attraction (besides location and price) is the flower-speckled grounds with shaded hideaways that are perfect for stealing away with a book. The dining area is also rather nice with lots of light and pleasant decor. The owner, Esther, keeps a tight ship and is helpful regarding tips on what to do in the area.

Av. Córdoba 441, 3370 Puerto Iguazú. © **3757/420-425.** www.gardenstonehostel.com. 7 units. $30 double. No credit cards. **Amenities:** Shared kitchen; TV room. *In room:* A/C, lockers.

Hostería Los Helechos

This is the best budget choice located in the heart of town. The pale-yellow building has a simple design but a cozy feel, with wooden window frames looking in on a large lobby complete with a tropical fish tank. The rooms are pretty basic, but some have windows framed in greenery overlooking a plant-filled courtyard. All have air-conditioning but incur an extra charge of $10 if it's used. The breakfast room is somewhat plain, but clean, and the common room is an inviting mix of big sofas, ceiling fans, and red-brick walls.

Paulino Amarante 76, 3370 Puerto Iguazú. ©/fax **3757/420-338.** www.hosterialoshelechos.com.ar. 60 units. $55 with A/C and TV. AE, DC, MC, V. Free parking. **Amenities:** Restaurant; bar; Internet computer in lobby; pool. *In room:* A/C, TV.

Residencial Uno Hostel

This big, rambling building has mismatching tiles and a thrown-together feel, with a water tank precariously perched high atop its roof. The rooms are basic and come in doubles and dorms. The lobby is dark, cool, and spacious, with an excellent collection of 400 movies in the adjoining common room to while away those hot afternoons. Its main attraction, however, is the large garden with a good-size pool. Owners Valeria and Dayan speak good English and are very helpful regarding tips on what to do in the area. The hostel is located on a quiet residential street 5 minutes from the town center.

Beltran 116, Puerto Iguazú. ✆ **3757/420-529.** www.residencialuno.com. 23 units. $15 dorm bed; $45 double with fan; $55 double with A/C. Rates include breakfast. AE, DC, MC, V. Free parking. **Amenities:** Bar; high-speed Internet; pool; Wi-Fi.

Timbó Posada 🎁   This miniature hostel is for those who like a touch of jungle charm. The dinky little street entrance attracts your attention with a brilliant yellow wall lit up with flowers. A tiny lobby leads to a beautiful garden with wooden platforms and a small pool. Hammocks hang amid greenery in front of a lovely wooden veranda. Everything is small, compact, and shady, including the rooms and their tiny, basic bathrooms. It is located on a street several blocks from the downtown area and close to the bars of Avenida Brasil.

Av. Misiones 157, Puerto Iguazú. ✆/fax **3757/422-698.** www.timboiguazu.com.ar. 5 units. $54 double. AE, DC, MC, V. Free parking. **Amenities:** Restaurant; bar; pool; Wi-Fi.

Yretá Apart Hotel   I lucked out when I found this hotel, new in 2010, quite by accident; and I ended up staying longer than I'd planned. Its main draw is its functional design, spaciousness, and practicality with everything where it should be in a modern hotel—no fumbling around for light switches or cursing the low water pressure. Also it is quite easy on the eye in a very modernist way. Who knew that bare concrete, glass, and dark-wood finishings would go quite so well together? The hotel consists of two buildings set on a quiet residential street 2 blocks north of the bus station. The building up front houses the small airy reception and breakfast deck overlooking a tiny but deep pool. The dark wood decking continues to the next building which houses the large, self-contained apartments with long dining room/kitchenettes and separate bedrooms done in white and beige. Sliding doors lead to small balconies with not much of a view. The kitchen and bathrooms have handsome brown tiling with mosaic trimmings and the bathrooms have top-notch fittings and powerful showers. There is even a thoughtfully placed underground garage to hide that rental car. Yretá, which means *waterland* in Guarani, is very cool in design, layout, and price.

El Uru 30, 3370 Puerto Iguazú. ✆ **3757/422-063.** www.yreta.com. 12 rooms. $87 double. Rates include breakfast. No credit cards. Free parking. **Amenities:** Bar; small outdoor pool. *In room:* A/C, TV, kitchenette, Wi-Fi.

OUTSIDE IGUAZU

Posada Puerto Bemberg   Luxury, peace, and nature are what come to mind when I recall my stay at Posada Puerto Bemberg. Set on a steep river bank 35km (22 miles) south of Puerto Iguazú, the Posada is strictly for those who want splendid isolation with a wonderful romantic view—no wonder it attracts its fair share of hand-holding couples. Set in the grounds of an old *estancia* that is now a nature reserve, the lodge itself is modern colonial. Rooms are set along a cream-colored gallery that overlooks and expansive lawn that runs down to a long boardwalk that takes you out over the Río Parana. On the other side is Paraguay. The rooms and bathrooms are huge and tastefully decorated with not the smallest detail left undone, and even a prodigious number of lamps and wall lights to get the exact mood lighting required. I particularly liked the easy chair by the window that was perfect for a siesta. Forget about TV (though you can get a flatscreen on request) and throw your Blackberry away as there is little signal. The huge library in the excellent restaurant is ideal for those with a low boredom threshold but really, you should be out enjoying the amazing pool. Informative tours of the surrounding jungle and river are included in the price and the large staff is bilingual, friendly, and super professional. The lodge is near the sleepy hamlet of Puerta Libertad and its final 2 miles is on a rocky, flint-paved road.

Puerta Libertad. © **3757/496500** or 11/4152-5266 in Buenos Aires. www.puertobemberg.com. 14 units. $340 double. Rates include buffet breakfast. AE, DC, MC, V. Free parking. **Amenities:** Restaurant; outdoor pool; Wi-Fi. *In room:* A/C, TV, minibar.

Yacutinga Lodge This is the ultimate jungle experience. The fact that you have to make the last leg of the journey there by boat makes you anticipate not so much the heart of darkness, but the heart of another world—a world of giant butterflies, dazzling birds, and hidden jaguars. It is a world where five-star comforts do not exist, so be prepared. But the sacrifices you make (hard beds, limited menu, and patchy service) are worth it for a memorable experience. The Yacutinga Lodge is set in 570 hectares (1,410 acres) of *Jungle Book* paradise, run to ensure that its presence has no negative effects on the surrounding environment; you even get to plant a tree before leaving. The decor might look pseudo-Flintstone, but the chunky wood, adobe walls, and tiny colored glass windows are all made from recycled material. Even the coffee table is a repurposed tree trunk. Set amid this Eden-like Utopia are four-room cabins with decent-size rooms and a wood-fueled fireplace (June–Aug mornings can be

Mocaná Falls

Three miles of thundering falls stretch into the distance along a river that separates Argentina from Brazil. No, I am not talking about Iguazú but its younger brother, Moconá, located 300km (186 miles) south on the Río Uruguay. Anywhere else this would be a major attraction but the more famous falls has stolen Moconá's white-foamed thunder and this national park only draws a small number of visitors. All the more reason to visit as its quiet isolation and lack of crowds makes it's a good antidote to the Disneyfied feel of the bigger park. Another reason to go is the journey itself—a beautiful drive through the heart of Misiones province. Green undulating hills are dotted with picturesque shacks on stilts painted in pastel colors. Barefoot children swing there legs on rickety fences, and red dust-covered farmers sell their produce from stalls in front of their farmhouses. When you get to the reserve you must park and pay a $5 entrance fee. Then continue driving for another 2km (1 ¼ miles) until you reach a small parking lot on the right. Walk down to the end where you will reach a riverbank; here, you can catch a small, guided boat ($20 per person) upriver that rides along the falls and into the spray abyss (prompting much screaming). Sandals and shorts are recommended so you dry off quickly afterwards. If you feel like lingering, stay at the very comfortable **Aldea Yaboty Eco Lodge** (© 11/4371-4498 in Buenos Aires; www.aldeayaboty.com). Moconá can be reached on a now fully paved road by heading south from Puerto Iguazú on Route 12; turn left at El Alcazar, and drive east through the small rural town of El Soberbio.

chilly). The decor is basic, and don't expect air-conditioning. The constant mud, humidity, and water (Wellingtons provided) are not for everyone, but the experience is unforgettable. The lodge is 80km (50 miles) from Iguazú Falls.

Iguazú, Missiones. No phone. www.yacutinga.com. 21 units. $450 for 3 days/2 nights. No credit cards. Free parking. **Amenities:** Restaurant; bar; pool; Wi-Fi.

7 Where to Eat

Dining in Puerto Iguazú is casual and not the bargain it used to be, especially if you choose to eat at your hotel. Big, efficient but somewhat cheerless restaurants have popped up around the bus station and in the town center that are designed to accommodate the large crowds. Meat, pasta, and pizza are the standard fare, and it does not change much between venues. Take advantage of the good river fish you find in the area, mainly *surubí*, pacu, and dorada, although availability depends on the season.

EXPENSIVE

Aqva Restaurant INTERNATIONAL   This busy establishment lacks character in appearance given its location in a somewhat cramped two-story building. That said, the great food, powerful air-conditioning, and prompt service vindicate its popularity. The river fish is highly recommended. Particularly good is the *surubí* brochette in saffron sauce. The pacu, garnished with rice and mushrooms, is also very tasty, as is the vegetarian risotto. Book ahead or you may have to wait in line, even at lunchtime.

Córdoba and Carlos Thays. ☎ **3757/422-064.** www.aqvarestaurant.com. Main courses $15–$20. AE, DC, MC, V. Daily noon–midnight.

El Quincho del Tío Querido ★★ PARRILLA   Located in the heart of town, this restaurant serves excellent *parrilla* and fresh river fish such as dorado or *surubí*, along with terrific wines. Open for nearly 20 years, the restaurant also offers live music, including tango and *folklórico*. Shows start every night at 8pm.

Bonpland 110, at Perito Moreno. ☎ **3757/420-151.** Main courses $15–$20. AE, DC, MC, V. Daily noon–3pm and 7pm–midnight.

La Esquina Restaurante 🍴 ARGENTINE   This handsome restaurant, located in the Saint George hotel, has an interesting menu, including dorado fish al Roquefort and boga fish with lemon sauce. There is a grand central buffet with an excellent salad bar, and it can be all washed down with a selection from a very decent wine list. Try the Patagonian pinot noir Humberto Canale, and you'll be pleasantly surprised. It's a pleasant, upscale restaurant that's perfect for a romantic dinner.

Av. Córdoba 148. ☎ **3757/420-633.** www.hotelsaintgeorge.com. Main courses $15–$20. AE, MC, V. Daily noon–1am.

La Toscana 🍴 ITALIAN   I had my best Iguazú meal at this charming little Italian, not least because its quiet, residential location means you can avoid the crowds and not have to wave frantically for a waiter's attention. La Toscana is part of the lush, tropical boutique hotel Posada la Sorgente, though the decor is a little bit more low-key, yet still bright and colorful. Pasta dominates the menu, which is perhaps not a bad thing as river fish dominates every other Iguazú establishment. I started with the provolone garnished with peas, tomato, and oregano. It almost conquered my appetite for the main course which was penne puttanesca, simply done yet delicious. A good Argentine Cabernet Franc such as Trapiche Fond de Cave completed the experience.

Av. Córdoba 454. ☎ **3757/424-252.** Main courses $15–$18. AE, MC, V. Daily 7pm–midnight.

MODERATE

El Charo 🏛️ARGENTINE   Large and somewhat soulless, El Charo produces delicious food and is tremendously popular with tourists and locals alike. Among the main dishes, you'll find breaded veal, sirloin steaks, pork chops, catfish, and items from the *parrilla*. Also available are salads and pastas such as ravioli and cannelloni.

Av. Córdoba 106. ✆ **3757/421-529.** Main courses $12–$16. No credit cards. Daily 11am–1am.

La Rueda ★ 🏛️ARGENTINE   Nothing more than a small A-frame house with an outdoor patio built from local materials, La Rueda is a delight. Despite the casual atmosphere, tables have carefully prepared place settings, waiters are attentive and friendly, and the food—served in large portions—is very good. The diverse menu features pasta, steaks, and fish. Try the *surubí* brochette, a local whitefish prepared with bacon, tomatoes, onions, and peppers, and served with green rice and potatoes.

Av. Córdoba 28. ✆ **3757/422-531.** Main courses $12–$16. AE. Daily noon–midnight.

INEXPENSIVE

Color ARGENTINE   This is one of Iguazú's most popular restaurants and it's jammed at night, mostly with tourists. It's large and airy indoors (with a large tree growing through the roof) and out, with a street-side courtyard with wooden decking. The stage at one end accommodates live bands on weekends, and it can get noisy. Try the Argentine favorite *milanesa*—a thick slab of grilled beef or chicken dipped in bread crumbs. Color is located close to the town center next to the bus terminal.

Av. Córdoba 135. ✆ **3757/420-206.** Main courses $10–$15. AE, DC, MC, V. Daily 11am–11:30pm.

BORDER crossing

There is currently much confusion among American travelers concerning what their visa requirements are to enter the Brazilian side of the falls. They hear they are required to get a $120 visa in advance, yet they get there to find American citizens crossing the border without hindrance. Indeed, the law says that citizens from the United States, Canada, and Australia must obtain a visa to enter Brazil, whether for 1 day or 90 days. On the ground, however, some local officials, hotel concierges, tourist agencies, and taxi companies ignore the rule to make an extra buck. Rules are rules, however, and it is illegal to enter a country without the proper papers. If you want to see the Brazilian side of Iguazú Falls, my advice is to get a visa.

You can obtain one on short notice in Puerto Iguazú. Visit the **Brazilian Consulate,** Av. Córdoba 264 (✆ **3757/421-348;** Mon–Fri 8am–1pm). The process takes 2 hours and requires a passport photo. You can also apply before traveling, which takes 2 weeks. **U.S. citizens** should contact the Brazilian Embassy at 3006 Massachusetts Ave. NW, Washington DC 20008 (✆ **202/238-2700;** www.brasilemb.org). **Canadian citizens** must contact the Brazilian Embassy at 450 Wilbroad St., Ottawa, ON K1N 6M8 (✆ **613/237-1090;** www.brasemb ottawa.org). **Australian citizens** contact their Brazilian Embassy, at 19 Forster Crescent, Yarralumla, ACT 2600 (✆ **02/6237-2375;** http://brazil.org.au).

El Patio 🐷 PARRILLA El Patio looks and feels like you are in an aircraft hangar. It consists of a huge, not-so-pretty shed right in the center of town, with an open grill smoldering to the left as you walk in. Such "open planning" is not off-putting in the slightest and is more than compensated by the giant portions of meat that keep coming until you are full. The *"tenedor libre"* (eat as much as you like) meal is the best deal in town at around $10 per person. Just ask for a *parrilla*, and the traditional *asado* (barbecue) appears on a sizzling minigrill heaped with sausage, blood sausage, steak, and chicken. The lone waiter is friendly, efficient, and eager to push that last rib on you.

Av. Victoria Aguirre 221. ℂ **3757/424-167.** Main courses $10–$13. No credit cards. Daily 11am–1am.

Gustos del Litoral ★ ARGENTINE This tiny sidewalk restaurant has lots of character. There is room for only three tables inside and a little more in the wooden framed veranda outside. Jazz plays in the background as you eat your way through local river dishes such as pacu fish with lemon sauce and saffron-flavored rice. Small but colorful, it makes a pleasant change from the mammoth tourist joints this town specializes in. Portions could be bigger.

Av. Misiones 209. No phone. Main courses $12–$16. AE, DC, MC, V. Wed–Mon 8am–11:30pm.

Il Fratello ARGENTINE With its big windows overlooking a tidy wooden street deck of wine-colored tablecloths and dark furniture, Il Fratello seems a more stylish and compact restaurant than its tacky neighbors. Located in the heart of the downtown, the restaurant has both an informal outside area, with comfy deck-chair seating, and a bit more formal indoors. Still, it is nice to have cloth napkins for a change instead of the shiny, nonabsorbent serviettes that seem the staple of restaurants up and down the country. Il Fratello offers standard fare in giant portions. The *surubí* fish I ordered was easily three times bigger than any I received in other restaurants and quite delicious.

Gustavo Eppens 294. ℂ **3757/424-157.** Main courses $10–$15. AE, DC, MC, V. Daily 11am–11:30pm.

Puerto Iguazú After Dark

Although it has improved somewhat in recent years, Puerto Iguazú's nightlife is nothing to get your disco flares in a twist about. Most of the bigger restaurants stage live traditional music on weekends, while a series of new, youthful bars has popped up along Avenida Brasil, offering late-night alfresco drinking. The slickest of these disco bars is **Jackie Brown,** Av. Brasil 180 (ℂ **3757/421-208**). The designer-white seating inside goes well with the designer-chrome seating outside. This place rocks to techno all weekend until 5am, with a more eclectic mix of pop during the week. Across the street is the more laid-back **La Tribu** ★, Av. Brasil 155 (ℂ **3757/421-794**), with tropical Latin beats reverberating around a stylish deck and inside bar. It is open every day from 6pm to 2am. Even more chilled out is **Puerto Bambu,** Av. Brasil 96 (ℂ **3757/421-900**). This large corner bar has a giant bamboo veranda and a reggae music list that goes well with frequent happy hours; open daily from 5pm to 3am. **Cuba Libre,** at Paraguay and Brazil (no phone; cubalibre_iguazu@yahoo.com. ar), is the town's oldest nightclub and plays tropical beats until late.

esteros DEL IBERA

The locals turn out in style to greet you in Esteros del Ibera. Southern screamers, red crested cardinals, giant wood rails, storks, cormorants, and kingfishers are just some of the 300 feathered creatures that don their finest plumage—red eye patches, crimson collars, yellow-tipped wings, scarlet hats, and orange headbands in what is nature's version of Carnaval, except it takes place year-round. They swoop, scuttle, scamper, and dive in an acrobatic show of nature that demands a camera with telescopic lens and no time delay.

And that is just what happens in the sky. Bathing in this amazing 2m-deep (6½-ft.) marshland are multitudes of the large blunt-headed rodents known as capybaras. They have family picnics at the edge of floating islands watched by grinning caiman and growling howler monkeys. Yellow-backed anaconda slip between the water reeds, while turtles sleep at the feet of graceful marsh deer that trod gently around lily pads the size of large frying pans.

Esteros del Ibera is a 13,000-sq.-km (5,019-sq.-mile) trough of remarkable wildlife running up the middle of Corrientes, the next province south of Misiones. Dominated by two lakes, Laguna de Luna and Laguna Ibera, it is a morass of waterways and vegetation, with wide-open spaces perfect for a spot of nature spotting. Spectacular sunsets are just the opening act to incredible night skies, and the utter peace and tranquillity demand that you stay for at least 2 or 3 days.

Most people choose to stay in the sleepy settlement of **Colonia Carlos Pellegrini.** It is a quiet, unassuming place of baked brick huts surrounded by water and accessible over an old wooden bridge. Here you'll find some well-appointed lodges that offer all-inclusive 3- or 4-day deals, including daily excursions by boat, canoe, horse, or rubber dinghy to explore the area. **Posada de la Laguna** (© 3773/499-413; www.posada delalaguna.com) is a simple, hacienda-style house with beautifully decorated rooms. Doubles start at $340 per night full board. **Hosteria Ñandé Retá** (© 3773/499-411; www.nandereta.com) is a little more old-fashioned but has lots of space. Rooms start at $140 full board. **Posada Aguape** (© 11/4742-3015** in Buenos Aires, or 3773/499-412 in Corrientes; www.iberaesteros.com.ar) is an upscale facility comprised of four houses with a lakeside location. Here you can stay for 3 days and 2 nights, food and excursions included, for $584 per person. **Lodge Irupé** (© 3752/438-312;** www.irupelodge.com.ar) has palm-fronded wood cabins with large decks to enjoy the sunset. Here a double room costs $120.

Like many of Argentina's most fascinating places, getting there can be a problem. There are direct flights from Buenos Aires to Corrientes city and Posadas, but a 5-hour transfer to the park is still required. Colonia Carlos Pellegrini itself is 740km (460 miles) from Buenos Aires. You can catch an overnight 8-hour bus from Buenos Aires to Mercedes, which is the nearest large town. Recommended bus companies are **Aguila Dorada Bis** (© 11/4311-3700) and **El Cometa** (© 11/4313-7872). Tickets cost $40 from Buenos Aires to Mercedes, and the journey takes 8 hours. From Mercedes, you can organize a private transport through your hotel to Colonia Carlos Pellegrini, which is 120km (75 miles) away and takes 3 hours. **El Rayo** (© 3773/420-184) operates a daily minibus service between Colonia Pellegrini and Mercedes costing $18. It is possible to drive there from Puerto Iguazú or Posadas, but the journey is best done in a 4WD vehicle.

A SIDE TRIP TO THE BRAZILIAN SIDE OF IGUAZU FALLS ★★

A visit to the Brazilian side of Iguazú Falls affords a dazzling perspective on the waterfalls. Trails here are not as extensive as on the Argentine side, but the views are no less spectacular. In fact, many people find Brazil's unobstructed panoramic view of Iguazú Falls even more inspiring.

The national park entrance to the **Cataratas do Iguaçu** is at Km 17, Rodovía das Cataratas, and the entrance fee is $22. Park your car or get off the bus here, and pay your entry fee; private vehicles (except for taxis and guests of the Tropical das Cataratas) are not allowed in the park. From here, you board a shuttle bus bound for the falls. The waterfall path begins just in front of the Tropical das Cataratas Hotel and Resort, which is 11km (6¾ miles) from the national park entrance (if you are taking a taxi, have your driver bring you directly to the Tropical das Cataratas hotel and jump onto the trail from here). You will catch your first sight of the falls from a small viewpoint at the foot of the hotel lawn, from which the path begins. The trail zigzags down the side of the gorge and trundles along the cliff face for about 2km (1.25 miles) past **Salto Santa María, Deodoro,** and **Floriano** falls. There are 275 separate waterfalls with an average drop of 60m (197 ft.). The last catwalk plants you directly in front of the awesome **Garganta do Diablo (Devil's Throat),** where, once again, you will get wet (there's a small store in front where you can buy rain gear and film, if you need it). Back on the main trail, a tower beckons visitors to take an elevator to the top for an even broader panoramic view of the falls. This circuit takes about 2 hours. As you are leaving the park, drop into the **Parque das Aves,** Rodovia das Aves Km 18 (© **4535/298-282;** www.parquedasaves.com.br), a fascinating bird park with large walk-through aviaries holding toucans, egrets, and roseate spoonbills. Admission is $12, and the park is open every day from 8:30am to 5:30pm.

Getting There

FROM THE ARGENTINE SIDE   For most nationalities, crossing the border is fairly easy with a passport. Citizens of the United States, Canada, and Australia must obtain a visa to visit Brazil. (The visa costs $120; see "Border Crossing," above). The easiest way to get from the Argentine to the Brazilian side is by taxi (about $35–$40 round-trip). Buses are considerably less expensive, but less convenient, too. **Tres Fronteras** and **El Práctico** buses make the half-hour trip to Foz do Iguaçu 15 times per day ($4) from the Puerto Iguazú bus terminal. To visit the National Park, ask the bus driver to let you off just after the border check and then catch the National Park bus.

BY CAR   To avoid border hassles and international driving issues, it's best to take a bus or taxi to the Brazilian side.

SALTA & THE NORTHWEST

by Charlie O'Malley

The picturesque provinces of Salta, Jujuy, and Tucumán now offer beguiling Andean-style luxury and Inca-flavored cuisine as this seductive corner of Argentina has become a premier destination and a must-see for its utter uniqueness and a true South American indigenous vibe. So if you can't make it to Bolivia or Peru while visiting South America, don't sweat it: The Northwest of Argentina offers all the color and culture of both countries without the chaos and discomfort. Red deserts, dusty adobe villages, and sparkling white churches will have you reaching for your camera all too frequently. Here you'll find the ruins of ancient civilizations—be it the terraced settlements of the Quilmes Indians or the mysterious standing stones of the Tafi tribe. You can gaze upon the wonderful baroque art and colonial splendor of Salta city. You can sip delicious wines in the vine hamlet of Cafayate. You can follow the narrative of the glorious Gaucho Wars that beat off the Spanish and then gave rise to their own strongmen, such as Martín Güemes and Julio A. Roca. And here begins RN 40, that epic Andean roadway that forms the backbone of Argentina. In the Northwest alone it passes by vineyards, cactus hills, rainforests, tobacco fields, sugar-cane country, dinosaur parks, and vast empty salt plains. All this and more make the Northwest of Argentina the very heart of South America.

Exploring the Region

The Northwest is best explored by car. Although there is bus service between most towns, a car allows you to explore at ease the rainbow-colored mountain ranges of **Humahuaca** or the rugged scenery of **Calchaquíes Valley.** Be prepared for long distances and hidden marvels off the beaten track, such as the Indian settlement of **Quilmes,** the breathtaking canyons of **Talampaya,** or the dinosaur remains of **Ischigualasto.** Most towns, such as **Salta** and **Tilcara,** are best explored by foot, and the wineries of **Cafayate** are easily accessed by bicycle. Three days at a minimum to 5 days should allow you enough time to experience the flavor of the region.

Another way to discover the Northwest is aboard the **Tren a las Nubes (Train to the Clouds)** ★★★, a daylong journey that takes you from Salta toward the Chilean border and back. It runs only from April to November. For more, see "Take the Train to the Clouds," below.

SALTA ★

90km (56 miles) S of San Salvador de Jujuy; 1,497km (928 miles) N of Buenos Aires; 1,268km (786 miles) N of Mendoza

With its cloistered nuns and gaucho waiters, gilded churches and mountain mummies, Salta province is a rich mix of all the things that make the Northwest so distinctive. Here the old meets the new, and the old wins. Time trips at a more rhythmic pace, like the hoof-clopping music *chacareras*, which pipes from every cafe and car. The city itself (pop. 500,000) is a sunny mix of colonial architecture; friendly, gracious people; colorful history; and indigenous pride. Conservative by nature, Salteños let their hair down during Carnaval (Mardi Gras), when thousands come out for a parade of floats celebrating the region's history; water balloons are also tossed from balconies with great aplomb. Ringed by green hills and blessed with a cooler, more temperate climate, Salta City should be top of your list when you're visiting the area. (That is not to say it does not get hot. High season here is actually the winter months of Apr–Oct.)

Essentials

GETTING THERE

I don't recommend making the long-distance drive to Argentina's Northwest; it's safer and much easier to fly or take the bus and hire a car when you get there.

BY PLANE In recent years there are more and more flights, and Chilean-owned **LAN** (𝒞 387/424-8881; www.lan.com) offers the best prices as they do not have the annoying policy of differentiating between nationals and non-nationals as do the other state-subsidized airlines (guess who pays more?). Flights land at **Martín Miguel De Güemes International Airport,** RN 51 (𝒞 387/424-2904), 8km (5¼ miles) from the city center, and nonstop flights from Buenos Aires take 2 hours. LAN flies twice daily from Buenos Aires; a round-trip ticket costs on average $270, depending on the season and availability. **Aerolíneas Argentinas** (𝒞 **0810/222-86527** or 387/431-0862; www.aerolineas.com.ar) flies four times daily from Buenos Aires; a round-trip costs $460. Aerolíneas Argentinas also operates very handy direct flights connecting Salta with Iguazú and Salta with Mendoza. At press time, only two flights were being offered a week (Tues and Sat), but there were plans to add more flights in 2011. Flights between Salta and Iguazú cost $206 one-way. The flight from Salta to Mendoza costs $185 one-way; plus, this same flight then connects to Bariloche meaning you can now fly up and down the Andes without having to change in Buenos Aires as before. **Andes Líneas Aéreas** (𝒞 **0810/122-26337** or 387/424-9214; www.andesonline.com) flies from Buenos Aires daily (some flights make a stop in Córdoba) and costs $232 one-way. They also operate twice-weekly flights from Iguazú to Salta for $202 and twice-weekly service from Córdoba to Salta for $167. The Bolivian airline **Aerosur** (𝒞 387/432-0043; www.aerosur.com) operates Salta's only international flight. The service is to the Bolivian city of Santa Cruz and operates three times a week; a round-trip ticket costs $284. A shuttle bus travels between the airport and town for about $3.25 one-way and is scheduled with every flight arrival. A taxi into town will run about $7.50.

BY BUS The **Terminal de Omnibus,** or central bus station, is at Avenida H. Yrigoyen and Abraham Cornejo (𝒞 387/401-1143). Buses arrive from Buenos Aires (18 hr.; $125) and travel to San Salvador de Jujuy (2½ hr.; $9.25) and other cities in

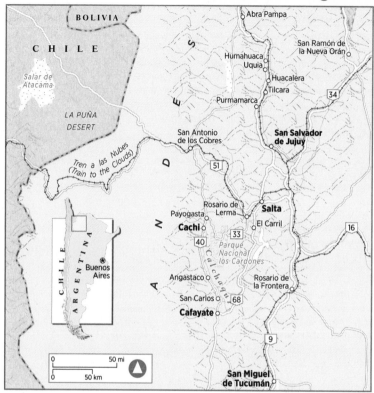

the region. **Andesmar** (📞 387/431-0263; www.andesmar.com), **Chevallier** (📞 387/431-2819; www.nuevachevallier.com), and **La Veloz del Norte** (📞 387/401-2164; www.lavelozcallcenter.com) are the main bus companies.

VISITOR INFORMATION

The tourism office, **Secretaría de Turismo de Salta,** Buenos Aires 93 (📞 387/431-0950 or 431-0640; www.turismosalta.gov.ar), will provide you with maps and information on dining, lodging, and sightseeing in the region. It can also help you arrange individual or group tours. It's open every day from 9am to 9pm. In Buenos Aires, get information about Salta from the **Casa de Salta** in Buenos Aires, Sáenz Pena 933 (📞 11/4326-1314 or 4326-2546). It's open weekdays 10am to 6pm.

[FastFACTS] SALTA

Currency Exchange Exchange money at the airport, at **Dinar Exchange,** Mitre and

España (📞 **387/432-2600;** Mon–Fri 9am–1:30pm and 5–8pm; Sat 10am–3pm), or at **Banco de La Nación,**

Mitre and Belgrano (📞 **387/431-1909;** Mon–Fri 9am–2pm). Traveler's checks can be changed at

209

Masventas, España 666 (℡ 387/431-0298; www.masventasnet.com.ar; Mon–Fri 9am–1:30pm and 5–8pm).

Emergency Dial ℡ **911** for police, ℡ **100** for fire, and ℡ **107** for an ambulance. The tourism police are located on Calle Mitre 23 (℡ **387/437-3199;** poltursalta@gobiernosalta.gov.ar).

Hospital Saint Bernard Hospital is at Dr. M. Boedo 69 (℡ **387/431-8320**).

Laundry Sol de Mayo, 25 de Mayo 755 (℡ **387/431-9718**), provides same-day service with free delivery, as does **Florencia,** Ibazeta 640 (℡ **387/432-2048**).

Spanish Classes Bien Argentina (℡ **387/15-475-0679** [mobile]; www.bien-argentino.com.ar) can hook you up with some local teachers.

Tour Operators Explore the region with **Saltur Turismo,** Caseros 485 (℡ **387/421-2012**). **La**

Vinia, Alberdi 453 (℡ **387/421-9099**), is a conventional agency that will help out with flights and packages all over Argentina. The tourist office also recommends English-speaking guides. **Ferro Turismo,** Buenos Aires 191 (℡ **387/431-5314;** www.ferroturismo.todowebsalta.com.ar), organizes bus excursions along the Tren a las Nubes railway as far as the famous La Polvorilla viaduct.

Getting Around

Salta is small and easy to explore on foot, but be careful: Drivers here are pedestrian-blind, and the summer sun in the afternoon can be stifling. The **Peatonal Florida** is Salta's pedestrian walking street—a smaller version of Calle Florida in Buenos Aires—where most of the city's shops are. The main sites are centered on **Plaza 9 de Julio,** with a monument to General Arenales in the center and a beautiful baroque cathedral at its edge. Built in 1858, the **Catedral** is considered Argentina's best-preserved colonial church. All the other attractions here, except the **Salta Tram** and the **Tren a las Nubes,** are within easy walking distance.

BY BUS ★ A useful service is **Bus Turistico Salta,** 20 de Febrero 798 (℡ 387/422-7798; www.busturisticosalta.com), a shuttle service that takes visitors around the city in high-tech open-top buses with flatscreen displays that act as guides. You can get on and off at any of the 14 stops and get the next bus that comes along (on average, every 25 min.). The service starts at 9:30am and runs until 8pm (with a pause from 1–4pm for siesta). Tickets cost $9 and can be bought on the bus when you board at any of the brightly painted stop signs. The route is as follows: Balcarce Street, Batalla de Salta, Palacio Legislativo, the Cathedral, Convento, Monumento a Quemes, Virrey, Portezuelo, Parque San Martín, La Viña, Paseo de los Poetas, the Mercado Artesanal, and Cabildo.

RENTING A CAR **Noa Rent a Car,** Buenos Aires 1 Local 6 (℡ 387/431-0740; www.noarentacar.com), has subcompacts and 4WDs. **Rentacar Noroeste,** Buenos Aires 88, Local 10 (℡ 387/421-8999; www.rentacarnoroeste.com.ar), is located close by and offers reasonable rates but watch out for hidden extras such as airport drop offs and carwash fees. There are several car-rental offices on Caseros Street and at the airport, most notably: **Hertz,** Caseros 374 (℡ 387/421-6785), and the airport (℡ 387/24-0113; www.hertz.com); **Avis,** Caseros 420 (℡ 387/421-2181); and at the airport (℡ 387/424-2289; www.avis.com.ar); and **Budget,** Caseros 421 (℡ 387/421-1953; www.budget.com.ar). Rates range from $45 to $90 per day but can jump dramatically if you sign up for limited mileage and go over your limit.

Salta

ATTRACTIONS ●
Casa de Cultura **14**
El Cabildo **11**
Iglesia San Francisco **22**
MAAM **9**
Museo Histórico José
   Evaristo Uriburu **12**
Museo Pajarito Velarde **18**
Museo Provincial de
   Bellas Artes de Salta **10**
Salta Cathedral **16**
San Bernardo Convent **24**
Teleférico (Salta cable car) **26**

RESTAURANTS ◆
Café van Gogh **15**
Casa Moderna **8**
Central Market **29**
El Solar del Convento **12**
José Balcarce **3**
Malandrino **2**
Santana **28**

HOTELS ■
Alejandro Primero **7**
Bloomers **19**
Carpe Diem B&B **27**
Casa Real Hotel & Spa **5**
Gran Hotel Presidente **17**
Hotel Almería **20**
Hotel del Antiquo Convento **23**
Hotel Kkala **1**
Hotel Salta **12**
Hotel Solar de la Plaza **6**
Los Cardones Youth Hostel **4**
Posada del Angel **21**
The Sheraton **25**
Victoria Plaza **13**

Seeing the Sights

Most museums in the Northwest don't have formal admission fees; instead, they request small contributions, usually $1 or less.

Casa de la Cultura Salta's cultural center is a hive of activity, staging art exhibitions, dance performances, music recitals, and theatrical plays. The all-glass facade hides an old adobe structure that is a warren of galleries and spaces.

Caseros 460. ⓒ **387/421-5763.** www.culturasalta.gov.ar. Ticket prices vary. Daily 10am–1pm and 3–7:30pm (sometimes later depending on performances).

El Cabildo/Museo Histórico del Norte (Historical Museum of the North) First erected in 1582 when the city was founded, the Cabildo has since reinvented itself a number of times. The latest town hall was completed in 1783; typical of Spanish construction, it has two levels and a tower built around interior patios. The building houses the Museo Histórico del Norte (Historical Museum of the North), with 15 exhibition halls related to the Indian, colonial, and liberal periods of Salteño history. Here you will see religious and popular art, as well as works from the Jesuit period and from upper Peru.

TAKE THE train TO THE CLOUDS

The **Tren a las Nubes (Train to the Clouds)** ★★★ is one of the world's great railroad experiences—a breathtaking ride that climbs to 4,220m (13,842 ft.) without the help of cable tracks. The journey takes you 434km (269 miles), through 21 tunnels and over 13 viaducts and 29 bridges, culminating in the stunning La Polvorilla viaduct. You will cross magnificent landscapes, making your way from the multicolored Lerma valley through the deep canyons and rugged peaks of the Quebrada del Toro and on to the desolate desert plateau of La Puña. The train stops at the peak, where your tour guide (there's one in each car) will describe the region's topography and check that everyone is breathing fine and not suffering from altitude sickness. In the small town of San Antonio de los Cobres, you'll have a chance to buy handicrafts, ponchos, and other textile goods from the indigenous people.

The 15-hour ride includes a small breakfast, lunch, and a folkloric show with regional music and dance. A restaurant, post office, communications center, and infirmary are among the first-class passenger cars. The ride makes for a fascinating experience, but be prepared for a very long day, as departure is at 7am and the train returns at 11pm. Always check ahead, as cancellations are common.

For more information, contact **General Belgrano Train Station,** Ameghino and Balcarce (© **387/422-3033**), or **Tren a las Nubes Buenos Aires Office,** Av. Córdoba 650 (© **11/5246-6666;** www.trenalasnubes.com.ar). The train operates from April to November and departs Salta's General Belgrano Station.

Tickets cost $140, including breakfast and lunch, and can be purchased at any of Salta's conventional travel agencies.

Caseros 549. © **387/421-5340.** www.museonor.gov.ar. Museum Tues–Fri 9am–6.30pm; Sat 9:30am–1:30pm; Sun 9:30am–1pm.

Iglesia San Francisco (San Francisco Church) ★★   Rebuilt in 1759 after a fire destroyed the original building, this is Salta's most prominent postcard image. The terra-cotta facade, with its 53m (174-ft.) tower and tiered white pillars, was designed by architect Luis Giorgi. The belfry—the tallest in the Americas—holds the Campana de la Patria, a bronze bell made from the cannons used in the War of Independence's Battle of Salta. A small museum exhibits 17th- and 18th-century religious images.

Córdoba and Caseros. No phone. Daily 8am–noon and 4–8pm.

Museo de Arqueológia de Alta Montaña (Andean Archaeological Museum) ★★★   A beautifully restored historic building, the MAAM houses a good collection of Andean textiles woven over the years. This museum is also home to a large research library dedicated to Andean culture and anthropology. The main focus of the museum, however, is its three mountain mummies, the perfectly preserved remains of three Inca children sacrificed to the gods. A fascinating film shows the excavations at Mount Llullaillaco, the highest volcanic peak in Argentina, near the Chilean border, which displays the actual extraction of the bodies from their mountain refuge. The Andean mummies (over 500 years old) were found in 1999 by a *National Geographic* team of archaeologists, and MAAM was designed for their display. More than 100 other objects were found with the mummies—gold statues and other objects dating back to the Inca era, which will also slowly be featured over the coming years. Already, the locals are affectionately calling this place the *museo de las momias* (mummy museum). Plan to spend an hour here if you want to watch the 30-minute documentary. There is usually one mummy on display at any one moment.

Mitre 77. ☎ **387/437-0499.** www.maam.org.ar. Admission $7.50. Tues–Sun 11am–7:30pm.

Museo Histórico José Evaristo Uriburu ★ José Evaristo Uriburu's family, which produced two Argentine presidents, bought this simple adobe house with a roof of reeds and curved tiles in 1810. The street entrance leads directly to a courtyard, characteristic of homes of this era. Exhibits include period furniture and costumes, as well as documents and objects belonging to the Uriburus and General Arenales.

Caseros 479. ☎ **387/421-5340.** Admission $1.25. Tues–Sat 9:30am–1:30pm and 3:30–8:30pm.

Museo Pajarito Velarde Guillermo Velarde Mors was one of Salta's most famous bohemians. His little town house was a must-see for any passing writers or artists in 1950s Salta. The quaint little corner cottage is now an interesting museum crammed with musical instruments, Bolivian Carnaval masks, vinyl records, and Independence-era weaponry. The enthusiastic guide, Carol Murgvizur, graciously reveals the literary and cultural legacy of the city and will let you try on a hat once worn by Carlos Gardel.

Pueyrredón 106. ☎ **387/421-2921.** Free admission. Daily 9am–1pm and 3–7:30pm.

Museo Provincial de Bellas Artes de Salta (Museum of Fine Arts) ★ Colorfully decorated tapestries and other regional works fill this 18th-century Spanish house, which features a permanent collection of colonial art upstairs, and religious and contemporary art downstairs. Noteworthy pieces include a portrait of Francisco de Uriburu by Spanish painter Joaquín Sorolla y Bastida, and a painting of Salta by Italian Carlo Penutti.

Florida 20. ☎ **387/421-4714.** Admission $1.25. Mon–Fri 9am–7:30pm; Sat 9am–6pm.

Salta Cathedral The corn-yellow facade of this cathedral dominates the central plaza. Inside you'll find beautiful interiors of ocher, blue, green, and gold with angels and cherubs smiling from the ornate ceiling corners. It holds a pantheon of Salta's luminaries, including local freedom fighter and strongman Martín Miguel de Güemes. There is a lovely side gallery of arches and beautiful floor tiles, and an elaborate pulpit is perched to one side like a tiny gilded balcony.

España 558. No phone. Mon–Fri 6:30am–12:15pm and 4:30–8:15pm; Sat 7:30am–12:15pm and 5–8:15pm; Sun 7:30am–1pm and 5–9:15pm.

San Bernardo Convent ★★ Salta's oldest religious building was declared a Historical National Monument in 1941. It's worthy of a walk by to admire the city's most impressive example of colonial and indigenous art (only Carmelite nuns are allowed to enter). Indigenous craftsmen carved the entrance from a carob tree in 1762.

Caseros near Santa Fe.

Teleférico (Salta Cable Car) ★ ☺ This Swiss-made, well-maintained cable car has been in operation since 1987, ferrying tourists to the top of San Bernardo Hill, 300m (984 ft.) over Salta. It is a pleasant ride up, though the frosted Perspex glass inhibits the view somewhat. At the top there is a set of gardens, artificial waterfalls, and a panoramic view of the Lerma valley. You can grab a snack at the casual restaurant. If you miss the last tram at 7:30pm, a cheap taxi will return you to the city center.

At the intersection of aves. H. Yrigoyen and San Martín. ☎ **387/431-0641.** teleríficosalta@salta.gov.ar. Admission $6.25 adults, $3.75 children. Daily 10am–7pm.

Outdoor Activities & Tour Operators

The bounty of nature around Salta is staggering. Most of the landscape is untouched with plenty of gorges, canyons, and volcanic peaks to negotiate. The city is a good base to go farther and explore the eerie salt plains, known as Salinas, and the multicolored mountain ranges of Humahuaca, in Jujuy province to the north. Tour leaders **Volcan Higueras,** Mendoza 453, Salta (📞 387/431-9175; www.volcanhigueras.com.ar), and **Silvia Magno,** San Juan 2399 (📞 387/434-1468; www.silviamagno.com.ar), conduct 1-day excursions to both places. **Agencia del Peregrino,** Alvarado 351 (📞 **387/422-9440;** www.agenciadelperegrino.com.ar), specializes in tours of the beautiful hilltop villages of Cachi and Purmamarca.

BIRD-WATCHING   Eco-tourism is gaining popularity in the area due to the abundance of wildlife. One- to 4-day safaris and bird-watching expeditions are organized by **Clark Expediciones,** Mariano Moreno, Salta (📞 **387/497-1024;** www.clarkexpediciones.com), an excellent local outfitter. Their bird-watching trips run from half a day to 2 days, and the highlight is usually seeing the immense Andean condor soaring over the mountains.

HORSEBACK RIDING   Finca Lesser (📞 387/155-827-332 [mobile]; www.redsalta.com/fincalesser) is a private nature reserve 15km (9⅓ miles) from the city center. Here you can do half-day or full-day horseback riding along river valleys and lush hills. **Los Amigos,** Quebrado de San Lorenzo (📞 **387/492-7033**), organizes horseback riding in the hills of San Lorenzo overlooking the city. **Sayta** (📞 **387/156-836-565** 📞; www.sayta.com.ar) organizes 1-day excursions to a ranch 40km (25 miles) south of the city, costing $70, including lunch and transfer.

MOUNTAIN BIKING   **Salta Rafting,** Buenos Aires 88, Local 14 (📞 **387/401-0301;** www.saltarafting.com), takes you in 4WD to a mountaintop 3,600m (9,843 ft.) high, where you start an exhilarating 45km (28-mile) descent. **MTB Salta,** Gral. Güemes 569 (📞 **387/421-5971;** www.mtbsalta.com), also organizes mountain bike excursions as well as canoe trips on Campo Alegre dam.

TREKKING   **Adventure Life Journeys,** 1655 S. 3rd St. W., Missoula, MT 59801 (📞 **800/344-6118** or 4065/412677; www.adventure-life.com), offers some of the best-organized treks in the region, usually beginning and ending in Buenos Aires. Their popular 9-day Northwest trek through Salta, Cafayate, and Cachi runs about $2,290 per person, everything included. **Turismo San Lorenzo,** J.C. Dávalos 960, San Lorenzo (📞 **387/492-1757;** www.turismo-sanlorenzo.com), organizes treks through San Lorenzo, starting at $60 per day.

WATERSPORTS   Rafting and windsurfing are popular in the Dique Cabra Corral, 70km (43 miles) south of Salta. For more information, contact **Salta Rafting,** Buenos Aires 88, Local 14 (📞 **387/401-0301;** www.saltarafting.com), and **Active Argentina,** Zuviria 982, Salta (📞 **387/431-1868;** www.active-argentina.com).

Spas & Wellness Centers

All the better hotels have spa facilities. **Touch Relax Urbano,** Lerma 289, Salta (📞 **387/431-7032**), is a city clinic that offers massages and skin care treatments. A 1-hour massage costs $25. **Masaje Terapéutico,** at Reyes Catholicos 1782, Tres Cerritos (📞 **387/425-3775**), is a small massage center that will also send therapists to your hotel. **Don Numas Spa,** Pompilio Guzman 1470 (📞 **387/492-1296;** www.spadonnumas.com.ar), is a small lodge in San Lorenzo with a relaxing spa that is open to day visitors.

Shopping

Salta province's secretary of tourism does a great job controlling their handmade products—from textiles to bamboo and wood ornaments. After certification, they're sold only at the **Mercado Artesanal ★★**, San Martín 2555 (**☏ 387/434-2808**), open from 9am to 9pm daily. Here in a beautifully restored millhouse 23 blocks from the central plaza, you'll find authentic products—from leather goods to candles—made throughout Salta Province by local artisans. The price is controlled, too, so you don't have to worry about bargaining here. You'll also find beautiful jewelry and silver, and you can pause for some sustenance in the coffeehouse with Wi-Fi.

Strangely enough, across the road is a tacky market that draws a larger crowd, partly because the bus tour companies get a commission. Here, like many places in the city, you'll find factory-produced gaucho memorabilia and wall hangings.

Casa de Antigüedades, Caseros 332 (**☏ 387/421-1911**), is a rambling antiques store jammed with everything from period furniture to local art. It's open Monday to Saturday 9am to 1:30pm and 4 to 9:30pm; ring the bell and an owner from the Perez family will happily look after you. **La Casa del Arte,** Buenos Aires 25 (**☏ 387/431-0050**), is a small store crammed with beautiful art and jewelry, as is **Puestos del Marqués,** Buenos Aires 68 (**☏ 387/422-0899**). **Amankay,** Pueblo Chico, Balcarce 999 (**☏ 387/431-0335**), and **Inyás Artisanías,** España 375 (**☏ 387/436-0260;** www.artesaniasinyas.com.ar), both offer original handicrafts and precious stones. For alpaca goods and silverware, try **Ambay,** Caseros 376 (**☏ 387/431-7182**), and **Suay,** Caseros 525 (**☏ 387/431-5961**). For all things leather, try **Torcivia,** Buenos Aires 28 (**☏ 387/422-7097**), or **Decuero,** Mitre 291 (**☏ 387/422-4166**).

Salta does a nice line in regional food products, usually of the sweet variety. Alfajores and Turron Salteños are famous biscuits from the region. You can find both at the family-owned confectionery **La Tía Yola,** Caseros 400 (**☏ 387/422-8418;** www.tiayola.com.ar), as well as homemade fruit preserves. For some of Salta's famous wine, try **Bella Hortencia,** Balcarce 980 (**☏ 387/422-7474**) or **Vinos de Salta,** Caseros 332 (**☏ 387/154-146-063** [mobile]), which conducts tastings and has a selection of the region's best cigars. *Note:* Most stores close for siesta from 1 to 5pm.

Salta's main shopping mall, known as **Alto Noa,** Av. Virrey Toeldo 702 (**☏ 387/431-1000**), is good for some air-conditioned siesta-time shopping. It is located 12 blocks from the central plaza.

Where to Stay

Salta has a wealth of accommodations, and prices are still reasonable in comparison with other parts of the country. Options are good both inside and outside the city center. Staying in the city center gives you a chance to walk everywhere. If you're after some peace and quiet, though, consider staying in the nearby village of San Lorenzo.

CITY CENTER
Very Expensive

Alejandro Primero ★★★ 🍃 Salta's second five-star hotel beats the Sheraton (see below) for color and charm. Two gauchos greet you as you enter an 11-story glass vaulted building of Andean chic. Carpets are adorned with miniature designs of *guanacos* (llamas), ostriches, and cacti. Corridors are enlivened with leather wall hangings, indigenous art, and the occasional ceramic pot. Rooms are spacious with panoramic views; double-glazed windows ensure that the noisy downtown location does not intrude on your *tranquilidad*. The indigenous theme creeps into the room furnishings, with geometric patterns flourishing on armrests, headboards, and curtains. Named after the local owner's son who died in a car crash, Alejandro Primero offers all the luxury of a top hotel without losing a sense of place and a human touch.

Balcarce 252. ☎ **387/400-0000.** www.alejandro1hotel.com.ar. 167 units. $125 double; from $259 suite. Rates include buffet breakfast. AE, DC, MC, V. Free parking. **Amenities:** Restaurant; bar; exercise room; lounge; indoor pool; room service; sauna. *In room:* A/C, TV, hair dryer, minibar.

Hotel Solar de la Plaza ★★★ 🏨 This absolutely charming hotel used to be the residence of one of Salta's well-known families, Patron Costas. The four rooms in the older part of the building were the actual bedrooms of the family members. They have been meticulously transformed into comfortable hotel rooms while retaining their old-world feel—hardwood floors, Jacuzzi tubs, and wrought-iron floor lamps (handmade in Salta). The rooms in the newer wing sport the same decor but with a slightly more modern feel, including marble pedestal sinks in the bathrooms and writing desks made from local wood. Service is gracious and refined, and the public areas are incredibly elegant, from the rooftop pool with its adjoining sun deck to the attractive restaurant serving regional specialties with a nouvelle twist. The English-speaking staff can arrange many outdoor activities, including hiking, horseback riding, and bird-watching at the nearby Patron Costas ranch.

Juan M. Leguizamon 669. ☎/fax **387/431-5111.** www.solardelaplaza.com.ar. 30 units. $105 double; $166 suite. Rates include continental breakfast. AE, DC, MC, V. Free parking. **Amenities:** Restaurant; bar; lounge; exercise room; small outdoor pool; limited room service; sauna; Wi-Fi. *In room:* A/C, TV, minibar.

The Sheraton Salta's first five-star hotel lacks imagination but trumps on location. The design could be described as very Sheraton-esque—bland but luxurious. A plain, cream-colored facade hangs over a dark lobby of stone walls, corduroy seating, and cobbled stones. Bright, terra-cotta hallways lead to an anticlimax, as the spacious rooms are somewhat colorless and sterile. Nevertheless, they have all the creature comforts expected of a Sheraton. What really stands out here is the view. The hotel is a U-shaped, seven-story building cut into the side of a hill overlooking the city (a 10-min. walk from the center). Every room offers a vista of the Andean *precordillera,* and the city's rooftop hodgepodge of terra-cotta tiles, church spires, and bell towers. Guests can admire all this from a large outdoor pool area with wooden decking and a generous-size Jacuzzi.

Av. Ejercito del Norte 330. ☎ **387/432-3000.** www.starwoodhotels.com. 145 units. $125 double; from $245 suite. Rates include buffet breakfast. AE, DC, MC, V. Free parking. **Amenities:** Restaurant; bar; lounge; casino; exercise room; Jacuzzi; outdoor pool; room service; sauna; Wi-Fi. *In room:* A/C, TV, hair dryer, minibar.

Expensive

Casa Real Hotel & Spa ★★ 🍷 Rooms at the Casa Real are very spacious and comfortable, with big picture windows (some overlooking the mountains), large-screen TVs, and firm, comfortable beds. Bathrooms are also large and very clean. The hotel boasts a decent-size exercise room and a good-size indoor pool, as well as an attractive restaurant and bar. The staff is friendly and can help arrange transportation and tours.

Mitre 669. ☎ **387/421-5675.** www.casarealsalta.com.ar. 80 units. $115 double; from $137 suite. Rates include buffet breakfast. AE, DC, MC, V. Free parking. **Amenities:** Restaurant; bar; lounge; exercise room; indoor pool; room service; sauna. *In room:* A/C, TV, hair dryer, minibar.

Gran Hotel Presidente ★ This contemporary hotel has attractive guest rooms splashed in rose and apple green, with sparkling white-tile bathrooms. The chic lobby features black-and-white marble with Art Deco furniture and leopard-skin upholstery. The pleasant international restaurant is located on the upstairs mezzanine, and there's a spa with a heated indoor pool, a sauna, a fitness room, and a solarium.

Av. de Belgrano 353. ©/fax **387/431-2022.** www.granhotelpresidente.com. 96 units. $93 double; $117 suite. Rates include buffet breakfast. AE, DC, MC, V. Free parking. **Amenities:** Restaurant; exercise room; small indoor pool; room service; sauna; Wi-Fi. *In room:* A/C, TV, hair dryer, minibar.

Moderate

Bloomers   Small and quirky, Bloomers is a unique and charming place to stay in the city center. This is not a bed-and-breakfast but a "bed and brunch," indicating the somewhat colorful, bohemian aspect of this boutique hotel. Wacky rugs and arty lamps adorn the five rooms, along with huge ceramic urns and luminous, cube-shaped beanbag-type chairs. One room has a regal flavor, with pink walls, an elegantly hung mosquito net, and silk cushions. The bathrooms are a decent size, with colorful, mosaic-style tiling. Some rooms are bigger than others (ask for one out front), and only two have air-conditioning. Public spaces include a small garden and barbecue terrace.

Vicente Lopez 129. ©/fax **387/422-7449.** www.bloomers-salta.com.ar. 5 units. From $70 double. Rates include breakfast. AE, DC, MC, V. Free parking. **Amenities:** Kitchen. *In room:* A/C (some rooms), TV.

Carpe Diem Bed and Breakfast ★ 📷   This cute little blue house may look unassuming from the street but once inside you realize it is several notches above the average B&B, with thoughtful decor and attentive owners. The communal living room is radiant and inviting with a library that will excite the most demanding bibliophile and colorful, intriguing art. Polished wooden floors, rocking chairs, and striped throws are just some of the cozy features. Out back there is a small charming courtyard with ivy-adorned walls. The rooms are impeccable, bright, and tastefully done and the en suite bathrooms have that all-important powerful shower. The German/Italian owners go out of their way to make sure you get the best out of your stay in Salta, and this warm hotel is right in the thick of it, just several blocks from the main plaza.

Urquiza 329, Salta. © **0387/421-8736.** www.bedandbreakfastsalta.com. 6 units. $100 double. Rates include breakfast. No credit cards. Free parking. **Amenities:** Kitchen. *In room:* A/C.

Hotel Almería ★   This modern hotel has an old-fashioned efficiency about it. The deceptively mediocre white facade, complete with flagpoles, leads to a spacious marble lobby with a gold-trimmed elevator. Plush, upholstered hallways lead to modern, well-fitted rooms that have dark-wood furniture and custom headboards. The spot-lighting and chrome fittings in the all-white bathrooms add to its modern, comfortable feel. Included in the price is use of the marvelous solarium upstairs, with a giant Jacuzzi and splendid view of the city.

Vicente Lopez 146. © **387/431-4848.** www.hotelalmeria.com.ar. 64 units. From $85 double; from $157 suite. Rates include buffet breakfast. AE, DC, MC, V. Free parking. Amenities: Restaurant; bar; Jacuzzi; outdoor pool; room service; solarium. In room: TV, hair dryer, minibar.

Hotel Salta ★ 📷   Popular with Europeans, this neoclassical hotel sits in the heart of Salta—facing Plaza 9 de Julio—and makes an excellent base from which to explore the city. Opened in 1890, these are hardly the most modern accommodations you'll find, but the hotel's wood balconies and arabesque carvings, peaceful courtyard, refreshing pool, and beautiful dining room overlooking the plaza considerably heighten its appeal. At $10 more, "A" rooms are larger than standard rooms and have bathtubs, as opposed to just showers. The friendly staff will arrange horseback riding, golf, and other outdoor activities upon request.

Buenos Aires 1. ✆/fax **387/426-7500.** www.hotelsalta.com. 99 units. From $108 double; from $192 suite. Rates include buffet breakfast. AE, DC, MC, V. Free parking. **Amenities:** Restaurant; bar; massage; pool; room service; sauna. *In room:* A/C, TV, minibar.

Posada del Angel   This is a tidy little boutique hotel located in the heart of the city. It has a homey, villa feel with parquet floors and small courtyard. The brass beds are a little on the small side and the curtains a bit loud, but in general rooms have a very cool ambience. An inviting library is one of its most distinctive charms. Come here if you're laid-back and bookish.

Pueyrredón 25. ✆ **387/431-8223.** www.hotelposadadelangel.com.ar. 7 units. From $62 double. Rates include breakfast. AE, DC, MC, V. Free parking. **Amenities:** Courtyard; library; Wi-Fi. *In room:* A/C, TV.

Inexpensive

Hotel del Antiguo Convento ★★ 🏨   The humble colonial entrance to this budget hotel might make you think it is a little too budget. But you will be pleasantly surprised as the modern reception area opens out into three pretty courtyards and a garden pool. The surrounding rooms are midsize, and the bathrooms are small but sparkling clean and perfectly adequate. Out back is a spacious suite that accommodates three people and is conveniently located in front of the pool. The extremely helpful staff and central location make it the best choice for low-price quality accommodations in the city.

Caseros 113. ✆/fax **387/422-7267.** www.hoteldelconvento.com.ar. 25 units. From $68 double. Rates include breakfast. AE, DC, MC, V. Parking $5. **Amenities:** Outdoor pool; Wi-Fi. *In room:* A/C, TV.

Los Cardones Youth Hostel   Youth is the correct term here when describing one of Salta's better hostels. If you want to meet people and be close to the nightlife action on Balcarce, this pleasant town house is not a bad choice. An attractive common room with comfy sofas leads to clean, simple rooms with bright blue walls and simple beds. The dorms are light and airy with plenty of space, and beds and bunks to choose from.

Entre Rios 454. ✆ **387/431-4026.** www.loscardones.todowebsalta.com.ar. 12 units. From $22 double with shared bathrooms; dorm bed $9 per person. Rates include breakfast. No credit cards. No parking. **Amenities:** Bar; communal TV/DVD player w/DVD library; high-speed Internet.

Victoria Plaza   If you're in Salta to sightsee rather than to loll around in sumptuous hotel rooms, then the Victoria Plaza should do just fine. Rooms are stark and simple, but they're clean, comfortable, and cheerfully maintained. Those on the seventh floor and higher enjoy better views for a few dollars more. The hotel has an excellent location next to the main plaza, the Cabildo (town hall), and the cathedral. The cafeteria-like restaurant is open 24 hours, and the hotel offers free airport transfers.

Zuviría 16. ✆/fax **387/431-8500.** www.hotelvictoriaplaza.com.ar. 96 units. From $75 double. Rates include buffet breakfast. AE, DC, MC, V. Free parking. **Amenities:** Tiny exercise room; sauna; Wi-Fi. *In room:* A/C, TV, fridge.

OUTSIDE THE CITY CENTER
Very Expensive

Hotel Kkala ★★★   This is undoubtedly the best designer boutique hotel in town (or just outside to be exact). The Argentine owners have put an incredible amount of effort into the smallest details and the overall feel is luxurious, intimate, and very indulgent. From the outside it looks like a modernist suburban home with a cube-style design. The front steps made from recycled railway ties set the tone as you enter. Inside is a bewitching arrangement of rooms, steps, decks, balconies, and gardens all tastefully adorned with a mix of old and new. Elaborate wall hangings stretch across wooden chairs, and a mock aviary with dummy parrots adds to the quirky feel. The rooms do not disappoint, with lots of light and space and huge bathrooms. The terraced rooms form an L-shape around a small pool with a deck and rock wall, and the view of the city and mountains from the breakfast sunroom makes the 30-minute uphill walk from town very much worth the effort.

Las Higueras 104, Los Cerritos. ✆ **0387/439-6590.** www.hotelkkala.com.ar. 6 units. $150 double. Rates include continental breakfast. MC, V. Free parking. **Amenities:** Restaurant; lounge; outdoor pool; room service. *In-room:* A/C, TV.

House of Jasmines ★★★ 📷 This pristine farmhouse on 120 hectares (296 acres) was converted into a fantastic inn worthy of a spread in *House & Garden*. There is a beautiful fireplace in the main living room as you enter the house. Each of the seven rooms is different, but all are exquisitely decorated in keeping with the colonial feel of the house—four-poster beds, antique furniture, fluffy duvets. Fresh roses (and jasmines in season) fill your room with a glorious scent. Bathrooms are sparkling and new. Most guests opt to dine in the elegant dining room, and the chef prepares everything from scratch—even the bread is baked on premises. Miles of trails and open fields surround a magnificent swimming pool and a rose garden. You are a guest here, not a customer, and the staff will do everything to help make you feel at home. The farmhouse is close to Salta's airport, about a 15-minute drive from the city center.

Camino al Encon, La Merced Chica. ✆/fax **387/497-2002.** www.houseofjasmines.com. 7 units. $195 double; $340 suite. Rates include continental breakfast. MC, V. Free parking. **Amenities:** Restaurant; lounge; pristine outdoor pool; room service. *In room:* A/C, TV.

Moderate

El Castillo de San Lorenzo ★ One of Salta's most distinctive hotels is a Tuscan-style pile dug into the side of a leafy hill just a 10-minute ride from the city. Italian immigrant Luigi Bartoletti built it in the late 1800s as a summer home in the style of an Italian *castello*. Tall palm trees shade the imposing mansion housing a boutique hotel and slightly ramshackle restaurant that produces excellent regional specialties. The rooms are different but all are comfortable and furnished with antiques. Room no. 3 has a Jacuzzi tub and large windows with views of the lush grounds. The two-story suite comes with a fireplace and a giant candelabrum. There are countless outdoor activities in the area, and the friendly English-speaking staff will be happy to make arrangements for you.

Camino a la Quebrada, Villa San Lorenzo. ✆/fax **387/492-1052.** www.hotelelcastillo.com.ar. 8 units. $65–$75 double; $96 suite. Rates include continental breakfast. MC, V. Free parking. **Amenities:** Restaurant; lounge; beautiful outdoor pool; room service. *In room:* TV.

Where to Eat

The Northwest has its own cuisine influenced by indigenous cooking. *Locro* (a corn-and-bean soup), *humitas* (a sort of corn-and-goat cheese soufflé), tamales (meat and potatoes in a ground corn shell), empanadas (a turnover filled with potatoes, meat, and vegetables), *lechón* (suckling pig), and *cabrito* (goat) occupy most menus. Traditional Argentine steaks and pasta dishes are usually available, too. In addition to the locations listed below, the **Mercado Central,** at Florida and San Martín, has a number of inexpensive eateries serving regional food.

MODERATE

Café van Gogh CAFE "Our mission is to make everyone feel at home, no matter where they're from," says one staff member, who proudly points out a collection of coffee cups from Argentina, Europe, and North America. This cheeky cafe, surrounded by little white lights on the outside and decorated with van Gogh prints inside, serves pizzas, sandwiches, meats, hot dogs, and empanadas. Come evening, the cafe-turned-bar becomes the center of Salta nightlife, with live bands playing Wednesday through Saturday after midnight. Café van Gogh is also a popular spot for breakfast.

España 502. ℭ **387/431-4659.** Main courses $8–$10. AE, DC, MC, V. Daily 7am–2am.

Casa Moderna ★ DELICATESSEN/WINE BAR Casa Moderna is located 2 blocks from the central plaza and has a warm, genuine, old-world feel. You can dine in a lovely small courtyard or the adjacent black-framed sun house. Indoors, ham hangs from the ceiling over shelves crammed with wine, chocolates, cheese, and whiskey, while giant coolers sit behind a long old-fashioned counter that stretches back to a dark salon. The menu includes platters of empanadas and homemade pasta, along with wine and beer, cheese platters, and fondue and fruit salads, the most delicious of which is the roasted pear. A second branch is several blocks away at Viamonte Lopez 423.

España 674. ℭ **387/422-0066.** Main courses $8–$12. AE, DC, MC, V. Mon–Sat 8:30am–2pm and 6–10:30pm.

El Solar del Convento ★★ ARGENTINE Ask locals to point you to Salta's best "typical" restaurant—the word used to describe places serving traditional Argentine fare—and they won't hesitate with their answer. This former Jesuit convent has long been an outstanding *parrilla* (grill), serving quality steaks (the mixed grill for two is a deal at $4) and regional specialties such as empanadas, tamales, and *humitas*. The 10-page menu also includes beef brochettes, grilled salmon, chicken with mushrooms, and large, fresh salads. Two dining rooms are connected by an A-frame thatched roof, and a medieval-style chandelier hangs from the ceiling. The atmosphere is festive, and, even late on a Sunday night, expect the restaurant to be packed.

Caseros 444. ℭ **387/439-3666.** Main courses $10–$15. AE, DC, MC, V. Daily 11am–3pm and 8pm–midnight.

José Balcarce ★★★ 🛎 INTERNATIONAL/REGIONAL José Balcarce is one of the most talked-about dining establishments in northwestern Argentina. Everything here is done right, to make you feel as though you've come to a very special place—from the exposed stone walls to the exquisite lighting and elegant dark-wood tables, to the very efficient service. The luminous blue cattle skulls lined against the wall are an arty touch, and try to figure out what exactly the circular logo on the windows is before the waiter enlightens you. Andean cuisine with a modern flair is the specialty. Here's where you can try roasted llama meat served with Andean potatoes or quinoa, or llama medallions with prickly pear sauce. Local goat cheese is drizzled over a "tower" of grilled eggplant and olive tapenade. You can even have llama carpaccio if you're feeling adventurous, although simpler dishes are always available, such as fresh trout roasted with butter and ginger, or chicken curry with vegetables. The menu changes often and other world cuisines are occasionally featured. Order a well-chilled Torrontes white wine to round out your meal.

Necochea 590. ℭ **387/421-1628.** Reservations recommended. Main courses $10–$14. AE, DC, MC, V. Mon–Thurs 9pm–midnight; Fri–Sat 9pm–1am.

Malandrino REGIONAL This bright arty restaurant is a nice fusion of old and new, traditional and modern, much like the food. Here you can enjoy llama meat stirred in a wok while musing on bright oil paintings above cow-skin seats. The Andean cereal quinoa is in plentiful supply, as is giant *milanesa* (breaded meat cutlet) portions that hang over your plate. The formal waist-coated waiters seem in contrast to the paper napkins, but they are very efficient and helpful. The wine list is decent with the great value Quara Syrah highly recommended. Malandrino is located close to all the nighttime action on Balcarce Street.

Balcarce 892. ☎ **387/154-767653** (mobile). Main courses $8–$12. No credit cards. Tues–Wed 7pm–1am; Thurs–Sun noon–1am.

Santana ★ INTERNATIONAL   This is one of the few international restaurants in Salta with a classic rather than rustic style. The enticing menu features chicken with white-wine cream sauce, lobster with *chimichurri* sauce, and homemade ravioli with various cheeses.

Mendoza 208. ☎ **387/432-0941.** Reservations recommended. Main courses $10–$14. AE, DC, MC, V. Daily noon–3:30pm and 8pm–midnight.

INEXPENSIVE

Viejo Jack II ☺ 🍴 ARGENTINE   An inexpensive local *parrilla* frequented by locals, Viejo Jack II serves succulent steaks and fresh pastas. Kids have access to a play area as well. Viejo Jack I is at Av. Virrey Toledo 145.

Av. Reyes Católicos 1465. ☎ **387/439-2802.** Main courses $4–$6. DC, MC, V. Daily 12:30–3:30pm and 8pm–1am.

Salta After Dark

BARS & NIGHTCLUBS   Night owls will find plenty to occupy themselves, whether it's around the late-night eateries close to the plaza or the pleasant stretch of bars, restaurants, and nightclubs along the nighttime parade known as Calle Balcarce, close to the train station. **Goblin Irish Pub,** Caseros 445 (☎ **387/401-0886**), is a handsome bar that draws an expat crowd eager to speak English. Drinks are pricey, however, compared to other places. **Wasabi,** Balcarce 938 (☎ **387/421-6575**), is a trendy sushi bar and disco, open Tuesday to Sunday 9pm to 2am. **Uno,** Balcarce 926 (☎ **387/422-9120**), is a slick establishment that attracts a young crowd. **Club Nueve,** Balcarce 907 (☎ **387/155-323-009** [mobile]), specializes in electronic music.

CASINOS   Every town and village in Argentina has at least one casino, and Salta is no different. The most upscale is the Sheraton's **Casino Salta,** Ejercito del Norte 330 (☎ **387/437-3022;** www.casinosalta.com). **Boulevard Casino,** Av. Virrey Toledo 702 (no phone), is located in Alto Noa shopping mall and is open 24 hours.

CINEMAS   **Hoyts,** Alto Noa Shopping Mall, Av. Virrey Toledo 702 (☎ **387/421-9666**), offers standard Hollywood fare at its eight-screen theater.

PEÑAS   A trip to Salta would not be complete without a night spent tapping along to a singing gaucho dressed up in billowing pants and knee-high leather boots. Traditional music bars (known as *peñas*) are dotted all around the city, but are particularly numerous on Balcarce Street. **Café de Tiempo ★**, Balcarce 901 (☎ **387/432-0771**), is one of the most famous, with a colorful, old-world interior. **La Vieja Estacion,** Balcarce 885 (☎ **387/421-7727**), and **Los Cardones,** Balcarce 885 (☎ **387/421-7727**), are both big and popular—with handkerchief-waving maidens dancing until late—and serve traditional food. **Peña Gauchos de Güemes,** Av. Uruguay 750 (☎ **387/421-7007;** ww.gauchosdesalta.com.ar), takes it a little more seriously, and the adobe-style venue has been declared a Salta heritage site. It is located 13 blocks from the plaza, close to Alto Noa shopping mall.

A DRIVING TOUR OF THE CALCHAQUIES VALLEY

With green rolling hills, lush jungle, and multicolored rock, the landscape surrounding Salta has it all. Tobacco, tropical fruit, and sugar cane are the main agricultural products here, and you will see tobacco "ovens" off the side of the road. Heading south from Salta on RN 68 for 38km (24 miles), you'll reach **El Carril,** a typical small town of the valley, with a central plaza and botanical garden displaying some 70% of the region's flora.

Although you can reach **Cafayate** more quickly by continuing south on RN 68, it is far more interesting to go west on Ruta 33 for a longer, more rugged circuit that will require you to stop overnight. Travel 2.7km (1¾ miles) after El Carril to **Cabaña de Cabras,** in La Flor del Pago (☏ **387/499-1093**), one of the principal goat farms and cheese factories in Argentina. Ducks, geese, and hundreds of goats roam the scenic property, and you can sample the delicious chivo in the small dining room and cheese shop in the proprietors' home. A bread and jam snack costs only $3; a cheese sandwich is $5; and a glass of local wine is $3. (The kind owners will prepare a multicourse lunch or dinner with advance reservations.) You can also stay over in one of their well-appointed rooms for $70.

Dense vegetation covers the region surrounding El Carril, but the land quickly dries out as you climb RP 33 toward **Piedra del Molino (Mill Rock).** The road narrows from pavement to dirt 10km (6¼ miles) west of El Carril—watch closely for oncoming cars. A small shrine to Saint Raphael (a patron saint of travelers) indicates your arrival at Mill Rock (3,620m/11,874 ft. elevation) and the entrance to **Parque Nacional los Cardones,** a semiarid landscape filled with cacti, sage, and limestone rock formations.

Ten kilometers (6¼ miles) before Cachi lies **Payogasta,** an ancient Indian town on the path of the Inca Road that once connected an empire stretching from Peru to northern Argentina. **Cachi** (see below) is another precolonial village worth a visit for its Indian ruins. From Cachi, take RN 40 south past Brealito to Molinos, a 17th-century town of adobe homes and dusty streets seemingly unchanged from how it must have appeared 350 years ago. Here you will find the increasingly famous winery and wine lodge **Colomé** (see "Colomé—Cactus & Vineyards," later in this chapter). Continuing south, consider stopping 9km (5½ miles) before Angastaco at the **Estancia Carmen** (☏ **387/1568-31322** [mobile]; www.vallesdelcarmen.com.ar), which boasts spectacular views of the Calchaquíes Valley and its long mountain canyon. Between 9am and 6pm, you can visit the ranch's Inca ruins, rent horses, and peek inside the private church in back, where two 300-year-old mummies rest in peace.

Continue south on RN 40 to **Angastaco,** a good place to spend the night. **Hostería Angastaco,** Avenida Libertad (☏ **3868/497-700**), 1km (about ½ mile) west of the village, is popular with European travelers. The simple hotel offers live folkloric music each evening. The staff will help arrange regional excursions and horseback riding. Double rooms start at $25. From Angastaco to San Carlos, you will pass the **Quebrada de las Flechas (Arrows Ravine),** with its stunning rock formations, which appeared in *The Empire Strikes Back*. People often stop their cars by the side of the road and climb a bit. Jesuits settled in **San Carlos,** and the church is a national historic monument. **Cafayate** (see below) marks the southern end of this circuit.

Return to Salta along RN 68 heading north, which takes you through the **Río Calchaquíes Valley** and on to the **Quebrada del Río de las Conchas (Canyon of the River of Shells).** The most interesting crimson rock formations are Garganta del Diablo (Devil's Throat), El Anfiteatro (the Ampitheater), and Los Castillos (the Castles), which are all indicated by road signs. Salta is 194km (120 miles) from Cafayate, along RN 68, and it shouldn't take more than a few hours to drive.

Cachi ★

Home of the Chicoanas Indians before the Spaniards arrived, Cachi is a tiny pueblo of about 5,000 people, interesting for its Indian ruins, colonial church, and archaeological museum. The Spanish colonial **church,** built in the 17th century and located next to the main plaza, has a floor and ceiling made from cactus wood. The **archaeological museum** is the most impressive museum of its kind in the Northwest, capturing the influence of the Incas and Spaniards on the region's indigenous people. Next to the main plaza, its courtyard is filled with Inca stone engravings and pre-Columbian artifacts. Wall rugs, ponchos, and ceramics are sold at the **Centro Artesanal,** next to the tourist office, on the main plaza (the people of Cachi are well respected for their weaving skills, and the ponchos they sell are beautiful). **La Paya,** 10km (6¼ miles) south of Cachi, and **Potrero de Payogasta,** 10km (6¼ miles) north of Cachi, hold the area's most important archaeological sites.

GETTING THERE Cachi is 157km (97 miles) west of Salta on RP 33. **Empresa Marcos Rueda** (☎ 387/421-4447) offers two buses daily from Salta; the trip takes 4 hours and costs $10.

VISITOR INFORMATION You can pick up maps, excursion information, and tips on restaurants and hotels at the **Oficina de Turismo,** Avenida General Güemes (☎ 3868/491902), open Monday through Friday from 8am to 9pm, Saturday and Sunday 9am to 3pm and 5 to 9pm.

WHERE TO STAY

Casa de Campo La Paya ★ Opened in 2000 on a 19th-century *estancia* (ranch), this rustic inn overlooking the Calchaquíes Valley is a quiet place to walk, read, and relax. Guest rooms have adobe walls and wood-beam ceilings, llama-wool rugs, and mattresses laid on stone frames. You can eat your meals here if you like; all the produce (except the meat) comes from this farm. The owners will also arrange excursions to the nearby mountains, valley, and river.

8km (5 miles) from Cachi, on RN 40 to Molinos. ☎/fax **3868/491139.** www.casadecampolapaya.com. ar. 8 units. From $60 double. Rates include breakfast. No credit cards. **Amenities:** Restaurant; pool; outdoor excursions.

La Merced del Alto ★★ Austerity and luxury don't often make good bedfellows, but here they seem to get on just fine. This whitewashed Spanish-style hacienda sits in a fertile valley 1.6km (1 mile) outside Cachi. A domed tower crowns cloistered hallways that lead to ample rooms laid out in the most stylish Andean chic decor. Wrought-iron headboards frame cow-skin pillow cases beneath silver lamps. The varnished floors match the curved bamboo ceilings in what is a tasteful combination of traditional and modern. A spacious gallery invites you to lounge as do the deck chairs beside a gorgeous pool. A treat for those who like to treat themselves, yet beware aware that it is in an isolated spot at the end of a pebbled track, and there is no TV.

Fuerte Alto, Cachi. ℂ/fax **3868/490020.** www.lamerceddelalto.com. 15 units. From $120–$130 double. Rates include breakfast. AE, MC, V. Free parking. **Amenities:** Restaurant; pool; spa; outdoor excursions; free high-speed Internet.

WHERE TO EAT

Confitería y Comedor del Sol REGIONAL   When you walk into this village restaurant, locals are likely to cease their conversations and stare for a minute. Not to worry—they will quickly return to their business once you sit down; many are engaged in the afternoon's current soap opera. The menu is simple, consisting of pastas, *milanesas,* empanadas, and tamales. It's a great lunch stop on your way to Molinos.

Ruiz de los Llanos. ℂ **3868/491222.** Main courses $5–$8. No credit cards. Daily 8am–1am.

Cafayate ★★★

The wine town of Cafayate has its own distinct colors—pink dust, red hills, and olive-green mountains. Corn-yellow sand gathers along the curbstones of this sun-kissed village, while donkeys graze on the central plaza, and heaps of unlocked bicycles stand outside schools and the coffee-colored cathedral. Add to this some pretty, palatial-style wineries, luxury lodges, excellent arts and crafts, and stunning vineyard country producing the aromatic white *torrontes* grape, and you can see why this whole area is becoming known as the Tuscany of Argentina.

GETTING THERE   Cafayate lies 194km (120 miles) southwest of Salta, on RN 68. **Empresa El Indio** (ℂ 387/432-0846) offers three buses daily from Salta; the trip takes 3½ hours and costs about $15. **Empresa Aconquija** (ℂ 0381/422-7620 in Tucumán, or 3867/421025 in Tafí del Valle; www.transporteaconquija.com.ar) offers daily buses; the trip takes 6 hours from Tucumán and costs $18.

VISITOR INFORMATION   The **tourist office** (ℂ 3868/421470) is located on the main plaza and provides maps, bus schedules, and lodging recommendations; it's open Monday through Saturday from 10am to 6pm.

VISITING THE WINERIES ★

There are approximately 25 wineries to visit in the area, some palatial-style villas, others rustic boutique garages. All are within easy reach of the town and can be visited by bicycle or taxi. Some unexpectedly shut down their guided visits, for whatever reasons, so it is always wise to call ahead. The most popular time to visit is from February to early April, during harvest. Most wineries are open Monday to Saturday. **Bodegas Etchart,** Finca La Rosa, 3km (1¾ miles) from Cafayate, on RN 40 (ℂ **3868/421310**), is owned by the French wine giant Pernod-Ricard and is one of the region's most important, producing chardonnay, cabernet sauvignon, Tannat, Torrontes (a Muscatel-like white), and Malbec (a dry red). One-hour guided tours and wine tastings are offered Monday through Friday from 9am to 5pm, Saturday 9am to noon. **Finca Las Nubes,** El Divisadero, Alto Valle de Cafayate, 5km (3 miles) from Cafayate (ℂ **3868/422129**), is one of Argentina's smallest vineyards and is family run, producing some young but excellent wines. The rustic facility is located a few kilometers up a dirt road from the center of town and provides lunch (reservations required). Wine tours and tastings are free of charge Monday to Saturday 9am to 5pm; call for an appointment outside these hours or to arrange for a meal. **Michel Torino,** Finca La Rosa, 3km (1¾ miles) from Cafayate, on RN 40 (ℂ **3868/155-66019** [mobile]; www.micheltorino. com.ar), is a beautiful, hacienda-style complex that also houses the luxury wine lodge Patios de Cafayate. The winery is also known as **Bodega El Esteco** and it produces the

Don David Torrontes, one of the best examples of Argentina's signature white grape. They offer guided tours Monday to Friday from 10am to 6:30pm and Saturday 10am to noon. **Bodegas El Porvenir de los Andes** ★★, Córdoba 32, Cafayate (© 3868/422007; www.bodegaselporvenir.com), is one of my favorite wineries, producing rich concentrated reds. The winery is a handsome town house with courtyard, located 2 blocks from the plaza. While there, pip for the $10 tasting of Laborum, one of the best reds coming out of Salta. **San Pedro de Yacochuya** ★, RP 2, RN 40 (© 3868/421233; www.sanpedrodeyacochuya.com.ar), is a boutique operation started by the Etchart family when they sold their larger winery. It is basically a tidy shed at the end of a dirt road lined by cactus 3km (2 miles) from the town, yet it is producing excellent Torrontes and Malbec from some of the highest vineyards in the world. Visits here are patchy in quality. If you are lucky to meet either Arnaldo or Marcos Etchart you will enjoy their bonhomie, made famous in the documentary *Mondovino*. You can even have lunch in the adjacent family home. Reservations are required, and opening hours can be erratic. **Bodega Nanni,** Silverio Chavarría 151 (© 3868/421527; www.bodegananni.com), is a traditional winery that, in recent years, has concentrated on making organic wine. The old-world industrial-style facility is located in town, 2 blocks from the plaza. **Bodega Domingo Hermanos,** Nuestra Señora del Rosario s/n, Cafayate (© 3868/421225; www.domingohermanos.com), is a famous local producer making decent table wines. It is interesting to visit to see the old-style way of making wine. Located .5km (⅓ mile) from the plaza, it is open every day 9am to 5pm and is popular with tour groups. **Bodega El Transito,** Belgrano 102 (© 3868/422385; www.bodega eltransito.com), is a new modernist winery located close to the town plaza. It is probably the most slick and stylish you'll find in town and the wines are excellent. It's open Monday to Saturday 9am to 1pm and 2:30pm to 7pm, and Sunday from 10am to 1pm and 3 to 6pm. No reservations are required. **Vasija Secreta,** RN 40 (© 3868/421850), is a large *bodega* that also houses a small but interesting museum with winemaking equipment that dates back to 1857. It is located on the outskirts of the town, a short walk from the plaza, and it's open Monday to Saturday 9am to 4pm. **Salvador Figueroa,** Pasaje 20 de Junio (© 3868/421289; gualiama@hotmail.com), located just 2 blocks from the plaza, is as boutique a winery you can get, with a tiny production of 5,600 bottles. It's open to visitors Monday to Friday 9:30am to 12:30pm and 3 to 7pm, but it's best to call ahead and make a reservation.

SEEING THE SIGHTS

Admission to most museums in this area is free or by small donation (usually no more than $1). Even more interesting are the different workshops producing handicrafts from the area.

Arte en Telar   This textile workshop offers a fascinating look into the local tradition of hand weaving. Guests can take a tour (usually in Spanish) and watch women work on hand looms in the garden, converting alpaca and wool into scarves and throws. At the front, there is a small display of all their products.

Colón 71. No phone. arteentelar@hotmail.com. Mon–Sat 10am–2pm and 4–10pm.

Museo de Vitivinicultura (Museum of Grapevines and Wine) ★★   Part of the Bodega Encantada winery, this museum tells the story of grape growing and winemaking in and around Cafayate. The 19th-century building houses old-fashioned machinery and more modern equipment, as well as agricultural implements and documentary photographs.

RN 40, at Av. General Güemes. © **3868/421125.** Mon–Fri 10am–1pm and 5–9pm.

Museo Regional y Arqueológico Rodolfo Bravo (Regional and Archaeological Museum) ★ This small museum displays ceramics, textiles, and metal objects discovered over a 66-year period by Rodolfo Bravo. Covering a period between the 4th and 15th centuries, these archaeological finds celebrate the heritage of Diaguita-Calchaquíes, and Inca tribes in the region.

Colón 191. ☎ **3868/421054.** Mon–Fri 11am–9pm; weekend hours vary.

WHERE TO STAY

Cafayate has seen a surge in luxury accommodations, mostly of the wine lodge variety. Many are within easy walking distance of the village.

Moderate

Killa Cafayate ★★★ With a gorgeous, long, rambling courtyard of whitewashed walls, terra-cotta tiles, wind chimes, and chunky wooden staircases, the Killa Cafayate, 2 blocks from the main plaza, has a bright Mediterranean feel. Its four buildings contain spacious rooms and small immaculate bathrooms with tubs and powerful showers. The 16 rooms are decked out with local stone, windowed wardrobes, and indigenous art. Many have a rooftop view of the village. Little touches such as ceramic-face tiles in the walls, the occasional wicker chair in the courtyard, and white-flower creepers, make this one of the most delightful choices in the area. You will especially enjoy the lovely pool and shaded courtyard out back. Owner Martha Chocobar is constantly on hand to help and offer advice on where to go.

Colón 47, 4427 Cafayate. ☎ **3868/422254.** www.killacafayate.com.ar. 16 units. $97 double; $120 apt for 4. Rates include continental breakfast. MC, V. Free parking. **Amenities:** Small lounge; garden; patio; pool.

Los Sauces 🌶 This is the best modern hotel in town. Its all-glass facade bordered by sleek slate is a refreshing antidote to the quaint, faux colonial overload you get elsewhere. The big, spacious lobby is two stories high with a stairwell leading to generous rooms with low-key but stylish decor and handsome flooring from the local algarroba tree. The queen-size beds come in wrought iron frames and the medium-size bathrooms are clean and well maintained. Some rooms have a patio exit onto what is the hotel's main attraction—a lovely lawn garden and spectacular pool. The master suite is especially luxurious with cactus furniture and a giant bathroom with Jacuzzi. The hotel is located 1 block from the main plaza.

Calchaqui 62, Cafayate. ☎ **3868/421158.** www.hotellossaucessa.com. 24 units. $80 double; $105 suite. Rates include continental breakfast. MC, V. Free parking. **Amenities:** Small lounge; pool; garden; patio.

Portal del Santo This newish hotel (it opened in 2006) harks back to the glory days of Cafayate's classical-style wineries with its impressive white facade festooned with pillars and arches and a huge front door with a relief carving of grapes. Inside however it is all modern with big spacious rooms and bathrooms with attractive fittings. White walls surround queen-size beds and the overall feel is bright and comfortable, helped by the fact that there is lovely big garden out back with a generous-size pool. The balcony at the front has a nice view of the church towers 4 blocks away. Family run, the service is excellent and personal, and the English-speaking host is eager to make sure you are comfortable. The owners even throw the occasional garden *asado* (Argentine barbecue) in the evening.

Silverio Chavarría 250, Cafayate. ☎ **3868/422500.** www.portaldelsanto.com.ar. 13 units. $75 double. Rates include continental breakfast. MC, V. Free parking. **Amenities:** Small lounge; garden; patio; pool.

Villa Vicuña A crazy mural of some local leprechauns stands in the shaded courtyard, surrounded by 12 simple but well-appointed rooms in a modern building with some colonial touches, such as an arched entrance and street balcony. The rooms are very comfortable, with wooden-posted beds, built-in wardrobes, and clean bathrooms of average size (10 have tubs). The decor is somewhat mixed, with plastic chairs in one corner of the courtyard and a traditional loom in the other, not to mention the leprechauns. Nevertheless, if you are looking for a clean, friendly place that's close to the plaza and not too expensive, this one will not disappoint.

Belgrano 76, 4427 Cafayate. © **3868/422145.** www.villavicuna.com.ar. 12 units. $100 double; $130 suite. Rates include continental breakfast. MC, V. Free parking. **Amenities:** Restaurant; lounge; Wi-Fi. *In room:* TV.

Inexpensive
Hotel Gran Real Cafayate   This terribly modest hotel has quiet rooms with very simple furnishings. These rooms, some with pleasant mountain views, are considerably more enticing than the gloomy downstairs lobby and cafe. Popular with Argentine visitors, the Gran Real has an attractive pool and barbecue area, which is its saving grace. Service is friendly.

Av. General Güemes 128, 4427 Cafayate. © **3868/421231.** Fax 3868/421016. www.granrealcafayate. com.ar. 35 units, some with shower only. $47 double. Rates include continental breakfast. MC, V. Free parking. **Amenities:** Restaurant; lounge; nice outdoor pool. *In room:* TV (on request, $3 per night).

WINE LODGES
Expensive
La Casa de la Bodega ★   The 20km (12-mile) drive to this luxury winery lodge is almost as enjoyable as the destination itself. You drive through a desert of pink sand and cactus sentinels until you reach a twisting road that meanders through purple mountains resembling melted Plasticine. The hotel itself is built of sand-colored brick, with lots of tile and wood; the reception desk is a huge trunk of the local tree algarroba. The eight rooms are large with stone headboards and yet more wood. Indigenous designs hang everywhere. The bathrooms are luxurious, with Jacuzzi and hydro-massage. All the rooms have mountain views, and four have balconies. Despite such opulence, there is no mistaking the humble, rural location, with small adobe huts in the distance and the occasional scampering goat and foraging boar to catch your attention. Adjoining the lodge is a small, ultramodern winery producing very decent wine.

RP 68 Km 18, Valle de Cafayate. © **3868/421888.** www.lacasadelabodega.com.ar. 8 units. $127 double. Rates include continental breakfast. MC, V. Free parking. **Amenities:** Restaurant; lounge; outdoor pool; spa; Wi-Fi. *In room:* TV, Jacuzzi.

Patios de Cafayate Hotel & Spa ✋   Patios de Cafayate does not quite get it right but it makes a valiant attempt. Through a series of leafy, flower-adorned courtyards (the patios in the name) you are transported through several eras. First stop: 18th-century colonial splendor. The main building is a palatial-style villa with fountains and even a tiny chapel for private worship. Vaulted corridors lead to suitelike rooms with colonial portraits watching you from the corners. Hand-painted flowers creep over walls and tabletops and into very spacious rooms with Egyptian cotton sheets and generous bathrooms with sunken tubs. You'll feel like Gatsby himself in the high-ceilinged living room, with mellow jazz playing from a gramophone and tall windows overlooking the pool. Then jump ahead several centuries down a jasmine walkway, and you're in the futuristic wine spa—a slate-gray cube of modernist indulgence. Despite such splendor, it must be said the lodge's overall feeling is cold and corporate, and the staff is not very engaging. It has fabulous facilities but lacks a human touch.

colomé–CACTUS & VINEYARDS

Bodega Colomé (Ruta Provincial 53, Molinos, Salta; *©* **3868/494044;** www.bodegacolome.com) is the newest edition to Salta's ever-growing list of wine lodges. Located 4 hours over bumpy, unpaved roads from either Cafayate or Salta, it fits in nicely with owner Donald Hess's penchant for building art-gallery wineries in far-flung, isolated places. The scenery is spectacular, with giant cacti giving three-fingered salutes amid vineyards and multicolored mountains. As you approach the winery, you pass the ancient village Molinos, which has been virtually adopted by the winery, as Hess insists on employing the local population and he has even built a new church and community center. Neat, stoned-lined roads lead to a low cream-colored, colonial-style building with a long gallery of arches. This is the upscale lodge and restaurant that caters to guests who want to get away from it all. In fact, the winery should only be visited if you wish to stay in the area, as it is a long, bumpy, dusty round-trip. There is a helicopter pad for high rollers and talk of a private landing strip for airplanes. The lodge rooms are large and luxurious, with indigenous touches such as the hand-woven rugs that the area is famous for. The restaurant produces some of the best cuisine in Argentina, which is no small achievement considering its remote location. In the past, the lodge has flown in some of the world's best chefs to oversee the kitchen, but they soon tire of the isolation and depart. A former sous-chef from the village now runs the operation, and there are no complaints. Rates start at $390 for a double.

RN 40, at RP 68 (part of El Esteco winery), 4427 Cafayate. *©* **3868/421747.** www.luxurycollection.com/cafayate. 30 units. $280 double. Rates include continental breakfast. MC, V. Free parking. **Amenities:** Restaurant; lounge; outdoor pool; spa. *In room:* TV.

Moderate

Viñas de Cafayate Wine Resort   Situated 3km (2 miles) outside town in the mountain foothills, this beautiful, simply designed wine lodge has a commanding view of the valley. The front facade of pillared arches leads to a large courtyard with a pond and a splash of purple from some lavender bushes; surrounding it are 12 rooms, big with minimal decor. Rooms have traditional cane ceilings, king-size beds, terra-cotta tiles, and the occasional tapestry. The bathrooms are spacious and clean, with a shower and tub. Bordered by vineyards on every side, you can literally pick a grape and eat it while sunbathing by the pool. The restaurant is somewhat hall-like and bare, but it serves good traditional food, such as pork ribs with *choclo* (corn), to guests and visitors alike.

25 de Mayo, Camino al Divisadero, Cafayate. *©* **3868/422272.** www.cafayatewineresort.com. 12 units. $145 double. Rates include continental breakfast. MC, V. Free parking. **Amenities:** Restaurant; lounge; outdoor pool; Wi-Fi.

WHERE TO EAT

When I first visited Cafayate in 2002, there were two very average restaurants on the plaza and little else. Now there are at least 12 restaurants, each offering very much the same standard of decent food with the added extra of live music to help you digest. Howling gauchos compete with saxophone players as you circuit the plaza at night looking for a sidewalk table amid the multitude of diners enjoying the balmy air.

It's an atmosphere more akin to New Orleans than the sleepy wine village I first experienced.

El Rancho ARGENTINE This restaurant is the best one on the main plaza, and it's less touristy than La Carreta (see below); when locals go out to eat, they come here. The expansive dining room has an authentic bamboo roof, and the fans overhead keep things cool in the summer months. Start with freshly made empanadas, *humitas,* or tamales and a salad, and then move on to oven-baked *cabrito* (young goat) with roasted potatoes. Pastas are made on the premises, served with a variety of meat dishes, including tenderloin, for diners after something simple. They stock decent house wines, served in small jugs, and the short wine list features local vintages.

Vicario Toscano 4. ✆ **3868/421256.** Main courses $8–$10. MC, V. Daily noon–3:30pm and 9pm–1am.

La Carreta de Don Olegario REGIONAL Popular with foreign visitors, this restaurant has a pleasant dining room that lacks elegance, but the kitchen serves an authentic selection of regional dishes, including *cabrito.* Service is unhurried, so plan to enjoy a leisurely lunch or dinner if you come here. Folkloric shows take place in the evenings.

Av. General Güemes 20. ✆ **3868/421004.** Main courses $8–$10. MC, V. Daily noon–3pm and 8–11pm.

Machacha ★★ ARGENTINE Cafayate's first gourmet restaurant offers more than steak. The menu of this wine-themed establishment includes exotic dishes such as llama meat and duck. Platters of smoked cheese and cold meats compete with rabbit for your attention. The wine list is all local, with the very rustic Bodega Nanni for example, or the very alcoholic San Pedro de Yacochuya. All this, along with a pebbled courtyard and regional music, make for a very pleasant eating experience.

Av. General Güemes 28. ✆ **3868/422319.** Main courses $20–$30. MC, V. Daily 10am–3pm and 7pm–2am.

HUMAHUACA, JUJUY

1,620km (1,004 miles) NW of Buenos Aires; 90km (56 miles) N of Salta

Quechuan women wearing colorful ponchos walk with babies strapped to their backs, while horses, cows, and goats graze on the surrounding vegetation. Look closely and you might spot a gaucho charging after his herd. Lush fields become increasingly dry and give way to striking rock formations and rainbow-colored mountain ranges so unusual they have been declared a UNESCO World Heritage Site. **Quebrada de Humahuaca** ★ is a 150km (93-mile) strip of land that brings you dangerously close to Bolivia, both in body and spirit. The fiery red ridges and copper-green plateaus hide timeless Indian villages with genuine indigenous charm and picturesque architecture. The area is a must-see, with 1-day excursions possible from Salta or the provincial capital San Salvador de Jujuy. Better still, stay in one of the many charming boutique lodges that are popping up in the area, particularly in Tilcara and Purmamarca.

Purmamarca ★★★

Lying 90km (13 miles) north of Salta City is the small colonial hamlet of **Purmamarca**. Its startling, multicolored mountain backdrop will look vaguely familiar; one of Argentina's most photogenic destinations, you will have undoubtedly spotted it on a website or brochure. The mountain, **Cerro de los Siete Colores (Hill of the Seven Colors),** dominates the village, reflecting its startling red and purple colors onto the pueblo's quiet streets and dusty adobe homes. Try to arrive early—9am is best—when the morning sun shines brightly on the hill's facade and reveals its tapestry of colors. An early start is also wise to miss the busloads of people who throng here at midday. In front of the plaza, you cannot miss the 400-year-old **Iglesia de Santa Rosa,** one of the country's oldest and most beautiful churches. Continue west on the dramatic mountain road RN 16 for 73km (45 miles), and you reach the surreal landscape known as **Salinas Grandes ★**, a dazzling salt plain that stretches for miles.

GETTING THERE   The bus company **Panamericano,** Dorrego, San Salvador de Jujuy (© **3884/237330**), travels each day from Jujuy's provincial capital to Pumamarca, though most buses stop at the main road junction, 2km (1¼ miles) from the town. The journey takes 1½ hours and costs $2.75. There are also regular buses that leave from **Salta Terminal de Omnibus,** at Avenida H. Yrigoyen and Abraham Cornejo, Salta (© **387/401-1143**). The journey takes 3½ hours and costs $7. Travel agencies **Volcan Higueras,** Mendoza 453, Salta (© **387/431-9175;** www. volcanhigueras.com.ar), and **Silvia Magno,** San Juan 2399 (© **387/434-1468;** www. silviamagno.com.ar), offer 1-day excursions from Salta to Purmamarca and beyond.

WHERE TO STAY

The village itself has some very average, down-at-heel *hospedajes.* For a real experience, take the high road out of city toward Susque, which is now dotted with some beautiful, high-end lodges along a wide river valley bordered by towering cliffs.

Casa de Adobe   This modern hotel, opened in 2009, has a gimmicky feel with its stone round tower, concrete amphitheater, and tiny animal pen holding a llama and *choique* (an Andean ostrich). But the decor is pleasant, with warm colors, wooden rafters, and oak finishes. The restaurant upstairs is open to the public; it offers stunning views of the town and the cliff face running along the river valley. You can do a 1-hour spa circuit that includes a sauna and Jacuzzi. Everything is immaculate and new, and the price is not bad considering its excellent facilities and thoughtful, if slightly over-the-top, design.

Ruta 52, Km 4. Purmamarca, Jujuy. © **388/4908003.** www.casadeadobe.com.ar. 15 units. $95 double; $135 cabana. Rates include continental breakfast. MC, V. Free parking. **Amenities:** Restaurant; lounge; outdoor pool; spa. *In room:* TV.

THE FIGHTING spirit OF QUILMES

The Indian community of Quilmes has fought off usurpers since colonial times and is still fighting today. Famous for keeping the Spanish at bay for over 150 years, they have now successfully beat back mining companies and hoteliers through road blockades and pickets. The focal point of such resistance is the fascinating ruins of **Quilmes ★**, located on Route 40, approximately halfway between Tafi del Valle and Cafayate. A field of giant cacti leads to an impressive hillside town with stone foundations—the remains of a thriving settlement built in A.D. 800 that once held 5,000 people. Rock walls make tidy terraces halfway up a hill toward the chief's house. You can climb the southern side to one of two pre-Columbian lookout posts. Below, you'll see the layout of a neatly divided town with the remains of square-shaped houses and circular storage rooms. At the front is a modern stone hotel built in the style of the ruins. Technically, the hotel is open, but the police tape and picketing Indians mean it has very few guests. The ruins are open for visits, however, from 8am to 6pm daily. Admission is $2, with an obligatory Spanish-language guided tour of dubious quality (www.comunidadindiaquilmes.es.tl).

El Manantial del Silencio ★★ This faux colonial villa just outside the town center probably has the best view of Seven Colors Mountain in all its Technicolor glory. The building is stark and simple and reminds me of a very austere 19th-century convent. White vaulted corridors lead to immaculate white rooms that are spacious and simple. Wrought-iron chandeliers have a backdrop of arched windows and ceramic tiling and the overall feel is that this building is very old when in fact it was constructed in 2010 by Salteno owners who have a similar property in Cachi called **La Merced del Alto** (p. 223). The atmospheric communal room would make a great location for a period drama set during the days of Argentine independence. Lush lawns outside lead to a lovely pool with a cliff face view.

Ruta 52, Km 2. Purmamarca, Jujuy. ✆ **388/4908080.** www.hotelmanantial.com.ar. 19 units. $160 double; $258 suite. Rates include continental breakfast. MC, V. Free parking. **Amenities:** Restaurant; lounge; outdoor pool; Wi-Fi. *In room:* A/C.

Luna Daniela ★ Located 2.5km (1½ miles) from the village on the road to Susques, Luna Daniela is an idiosyncratic hotel in an unusual setting. From the road it looks like a low, orange building spread along the riverbank. As you enter you realize the hotel is actually half underground with sweeping views of the valley and river Purmamarca. The owner, Silvia, is in constant attendance and she has given this new hotel, opened in late 2009, her own unique style with pastel colored walls, lots of light, huge balconies, and delightful artwork. The rooms are spacious with king-size beds and well-appointed bathrooms with showers and tubs. An expansive restaurant (open to the public for lunch and dinner) looks over a riverside vegetable patch, and the kitchen prides itself in producing almost everything, especially bread, pasta, and desserts. If you are looking for tranquillity with gorgeous views and a gracious hostess, Luna Daniela is not a bad choice.

Ruta 52, Km 6.5. Purmamarca, Jujuy. ✆ **388/154868007.** www.lunadaniela.com. 7 units. $97 double. Rates include continental breakfast. No credit cards. Free parking. **Amenities:** Restaurant; lounge; outdoor pool; Wi-Fi. *In room:* A/C.

WHERE TO EAT

Los Morteros ★★ REGIONAL When the Buenos Aires glitterati decide to go native and take to the hills to sample some Andean glamour, they invariably end up here at Purmamarca's most famous gourmet restaurant. Its country decor belies its celebrity status with whitewashed walls capped by a cactus roof over a rather large salon dominated by a huge clay fireplace. The menu is decidedly Quechan with quinoa risotto as one of the more unusual dishes and lamb casserole the most satisfying. The wine list is excellent and for the brave and adventurous there is a red from Jujuy's only winery, Bodega Fernando Dupont. The restaurant is 1 block behind the chapel.

Salta s/n, Pumamarca. ✆ **388/4908063.** Main courses $10–$15. No credit cards. Daily noon–3:30pm and 7:30–10:30pm.

Tilcara ★★

Its narrow cobbled streets and low colonial buildings have a dusty yellow hue. If you're lucky enough to find yourself alone, you may feel like you're on the set of an eerie spaghetti western just before the shootout. But chances are you will not be alone. Tilcara is gaining a reputation, becoming a thriving tourist town and the center of operations for those who want to explore the area further. Visitors include artists inspired by the landscape and Carnaval lovers who enjoy a good party (see "Pachamama Parties," below).

GETTING THERE **Panamericano,** Dorrego, San Salvador de Jujuy (© 3884/237330), is one of several local bus companies that travel frequently each day from Jujuy's provincial capital to Tilcara. The journey takes 2 hours and costs $3.25. There are also regular buses that leave from **Salta Terminal de Omnibus,** at Avenida H. Yrigoyen and Abraham Cornejo, Salta (© 387/401-1143). The journey takes 4 hours and costs $8. Travel agencies **Volcan Higueras,** Mendoza 453, Salta (© 387/431-9175; www.volcanhigueras.com.ar), and **Silvia Magno,** San Juan 2399 (© 387/434-1468; www.silviamagno.com.ar), offer 1-day excursions from Salta to Tilcara and the village of Humahuaca farther north.

SEEING THE SIGHTS

Pucará is a reconstructed hilltop fort overlooking the town, first built 900 years ago by the Diaguita tribe. There is a pyramid-shaped monument at the summit and the entire site covers 8 hectares (20 acres), including a high-altitude botanical garden. The site is open daily from 9am to 12:30pm and 2 to 6pm. **Museo Arqueologico Eduardo Casanova,** Belgrano 445 (© 388/495-5006), displays carved standing stones and other pre-Columbian artifacts. It is open daily 9am to 12:30pm and 2 to 6pm. **Museo Regional de Pintura Jose A. Terry,** Rivadavia 459 (© 388/495-5005), displays works by the area's most famous painter. Open Tuesday to Sunday 9am to 7pm.

Beyond Tilcara

Take Route 9 heading north, after Tilcara, and you will notice a trapezoid-shaped monument marking the tropic of Capricorn. Nearby you can visit **La Garganta del Diablo (Devil's Throat)**—a steep gorge with a small walkway leading along the rock's edge. Leave RN 9 and head east of Tilcara for a short distance. Be careful walking here, as there is only a small rope separating you from the depths below.

Continue north along RN 9, where you will pass the small adobe villages of Huacalera and Uquia. About 42km (26 miles) north of Tilcara lies **Humahuaca,** a sleepy yet enchanting village of only a couple thousand Indian residents. Its relaxed pace will make Buenos Aires seem light-years away. Note that at an elevation of 2,700m (8,856 ft.), you will feel a little out of breath here, and nights are quite cold. Although the nearby Inca ruins of **Coctaca** are best explored with a tour guide, you can visit them on your own or with a taxi ($20 round-trip, including driver wait time) by following a dirt road about 10km (6¼ miles) out of Humahuaca. Coctaca is a large Indian settlement that the Spaniards discovered in the 17th century. Although the ruins are hard to distinguish from the rocks and debris, you can make out the outlines of the terraced crop fields for which the Incas were famous. The site is surrounded by cacti and provides excellent photo opportunities.

WHERE TO STAY

New places are popping up all the time and thankfully most retain the earthy character of the village with a hippie, artful twist. The most memorable are listed here. **Quinta La Paceña Posada,** at Padilla and Ambrosetti, Tilcara (© 388/495-5098; www.quintalapacena.com.ar), is a beautiful lodge located 4 blocks from the main plaza. Designed by owner architects Lili and César, the traditional-style building is crammed with heartwarming details such as cactus pillars and a tiny bamboo-covered walkway. The elegant rooms start at $62 for a double. **Rincon de Fuego,** Ambrosetti 445 (© 388/4955130; www.rincondefuego.com), is another traditional-style town house with lots of old-world charm. The all-stone facade on a cobbled street hides luxury rooms with uneven adobe walls and bare rafters. Nothing is spared regarding

pachamama PARTIES

This area is famous for its street parties, and thousands throng to Humahuaca at Carnaval time. For 8 days the entire population dons multicolored costumes and strums on indigenous instruments, known as erkes and charangos. They dress up as clowns and devils and mock politicians with puppets. The festival is a heady mix of Christianity and Indigenous rites, with the last day (known as Temptation Sunday) seeing a shaman burying offerings to Pachamama (Mother Earth) and the devil. Other popular parties are Santa Ana, on the 26th of July, in Tilcara, and the Virgen de Copacabana, in April. Every village has its own *fiesta patronal*, celebrating the local patron saint. One of the most lively and unusual is on the 15th of August in the town of Casabindo. Feathered gauchos steer a bull into an enclosure in front of the village church. Wrapped around the animal's horns is a scarf containing money, which is the prize to whoever is brave enough to grab it.

comfort, with Andean-designed upholstery covering king-size beds. Rooms start at $87 for a double. **Refugio Del Pintor,** at Alvero and Jujuy (© **388/427-1432;** www.elrefugiodelpintor.com), is a modern two-story building done in the traditional style with rock walls and wooden ceilings. The tastefully designed rooms have lots of light and overlook a courtyard with lawn. They start at $68 for a double.

Al Sireno ★★ Cactus wood–paneled doors, marble glass walls that filter the bright mountain light, and puffy cubes covered in llama wool are just some of the features that make this one of the most thoughtfully designed hotels in Tilcara village. Guest rooms surround a small landscaped garden with gravel paths and dark wood decking. Large ceramic jugs sit next to grey rock walls that lead to a bright, all-glass dining area and reception desk in back. The rooms are super chic with king-size beds trimmed with Andean weavings; large, tastefully decorated bathrooms boast powerful showers. Everything is well done and impeccably clean; I could not fault it. Its great location and reasonable price make it my top choice for a stay over in this Indian village.

Padilla 593. © **388/4955568.** www.alsireno.com. 8 units. $65 double. MC, V. Rates include continental breakfast. Free parking. **Amenities:** Lounge; spa; Wi-Fi. *In room:* TV.

WHERE TO EAT

New restaurants are popping up every year, particularly along the principal street, Belgrano. **Los Puestos,** at Padilla and Belgrano (© **388/495-5100**), is a busy tourist stop and deservedly so as it has warm ambience with rock walls and a bamboo roof patio. **Pachamama,** Belgrano 590 (© **388/495-5293**), is a bright red town house serving traditional fare with occasional live music.

La Chacana Bar ★★ REGIONAL This modern restaurant has some old-world touches like cane roofs and bare rafters. The interiors are very pleasant with an ancient stove accompanied by solid wood furniture and cactus sculptures. There is a small, shaded courtyard with wrought-iron tables as you enter from the street. The menu is also a mix of old and new and done surprisingly well. The llama filet wrapped in bacon had me wide-eyed and ravenous. It came with a "volcan" of mushy peas filled with goat cheese and herbs. Other dishes included basil-flavored quesillo (Andean cheese).

Belgrano 472. ☏ **388/1541440833.** www.paseotierraazul.com.ar. Main courses $13–$15. No credit cards. Daily 8am–midnight.

Quinoa Restaurant REGIONAL   This unassuming little restaurant is located in front of the plaza and church. The food is strictly Andean with a gourmet twist such as sorrentinos (ravioli) filled with goat cheese and llama chicharron (rinds) with salsa kollawa (spicy sauce). Old reliables like empanadas, tamales, *locro* (Andean stew), and quinoa casserole reinforce the fact that you are eating in an Indian village high up in the Andes.

Lavalle 660. ☏ **388/155017688.** Main courses $13–$15. No credit cards. Daily 7pm–midnight.

TAFI DEL VALLE, TUCUMAN

1,299km (805 miles) NW of Buenos Aires; 406km (250 miles) S of Salta

"Why aren't the Americans coming to Tafi?" one frustrated hotelier asked me. Another told me that the Tucumanos secretly want to keep this place for themselves, as they have for centuries. Tafi del Valle is a high-altitude oasis of rolling green hills set amid red-rock desert. It is a remarkable place, yet it is not on the radar of many foreign travelers except for a handful of adventurous Europeans. The drive there is fascinating; from the flat plains of sugar-cane country in Tucumán province, you go up a twisting road through cloud forests and lemon groves, an area known as **Selva Tucumana.** You pass the fascinating **Reserva Arqueológica los Menhires,** where you'll find a collection of 50 mysterious standing stones from prehistoric times. If you come from the Salta side, the dry desert changes dramatically and you twist through the misty mountain pass of **La Garganta del Diablo,** at 3,000m (9,480 ft.) above sea level. What was red and dry becomes green and temperate. Tafi del Valle itself is a popular mountain town set by a lake, frequented by Tucumanos, who come to escape the heat of their sweltering capital and take advantage of the excellent opportunities to fish, hike, and sail. Here you can enjoy laid-back country life by staying in some beautiful *estancias* set within the town limits and at half the price you will spend elsewhere.

GETTING THERE   Tafi del Valle lies 107km (66 miles) west of provincial capital San Miguel de Tucumán on RP 307. **Empresa Aconquija** (☏ **0381/422-7620** in Tucumán, or 3867/421025 in Tafi del Valle; www.transporteaconquija.com.ar) offers daily buses; the trip takes 2½ hours and costs $7.50. The same company also runs a daily route between Tafi and Cafayate 120km (75 miles) away that costs $10. The small, modern terminal (☏ **3867/421025**) is on Avenida Gobernador Miguel Critto, close to Estancia Los Cuartos.

VISITOR INFORMATION   The **Oficina de Turismo,** Av. Gobernador Miguel Critto 311 (☏ **3867/421090** or 421880; www.tucumanturismo.gov.ar), has no English-speaking staff and is a little short on flyers and maps. It is also only open in the high season from December to February, but it does offer a comprehensive list of lodgings in the area. One recommended adventure-tourism agency is **La Cumbre,** Av. Presidente Perón 120 (☏ **3867/421768;** www.lacumbretafidelvalle.com).

Seeing the Sights

Jesuítica La Banda Museo, La Banda s/n, Tafi del Valle (☏ **3867/421685**), is a quaint white chapel and colonial house displaying Jesuit furniture, Cuzco art, and Independence-era memorabilia. It is located close to the tourism office and is open

Monday to Saturday 10am to 4pm, Sunday from 9am to noon. Admission is $1. **Los Reserva Arqueológica los Menhires** ★, at Avenida Los Menhires and Calle Nuñorca, El Mollar (no phone), is a fascinating collection of 50 standing stones gathered in a field. The military dictatorship had ripped these stones up from their original locations across the valley and used them to decorate a motorway. With some measuring 4m (13 ft.) in length, much has been lost of their meaning, but it makes for a fascinating 30-minute visit. The reserve is located 10km (6¼ miles) from Tafi del Valle, in the village of El Mollar. It is open daily from 7am to 6pm. Admission is free.

Outdoor Activities

There is a wealth of locations across the valley to explore, and Tafi is a hiker's and horse rider's paradise. **La Cumbre,** Av. Presidente Perón 120 (© 3867/421768; www.lacumbretafidelvalle.com), is the only registered tour operator in town and operates both horseback-riding and trekking excursions. A 2½-hour hiking excursion costs $25 and an all-day horseback-riding excursion, including an *asado* lunch, costs $50.

Shopping

Cheese is the valley's most famous product, and you'll find giant blocks of the cheddar-style local delicacy on every counter. Wool is also in abundance. **Cooperativa Union Diaguita,** Galeria Los Arcos, Avenida Presidente Perón (© 3867/421790), makes sweaters, throws, and tablecloths from local wool using natural dyes. **Artesania Lilen,** Av. Presidente Perón 176 (© 3867/421496), is good for a 20-minute browse through feathered wind chimes and ceramics. Owner Celina Garrido displays local art, including her own colorful landscapes and portraits. **Los Artesanias,** Av. Presidente Perón 252 (© 3867/421758), and **Tinkus Huasi,** Av. Presidente Perón 120 (© 3867/420190), are both crammed with local handicrafts.

Where to Stay

EXPENSIVE

Estancia Jesuítica Las Carreras ★★   Built in 1718 by the Jesuits, this working *estancia* has one of the oldest farmhouses in the province. Everything is maintained true to its original appearance, down to the whitewashed adobe walls and burgundy-colored tin roof. The rooms are sparkling clean and somewhat utilitarian, yet comfortable and pleasing, with terra-cotta tiles and tasseled bed covers. The farm is famous for its cheese-making tradition, which goes back nine generations. They also grow strawberries and raise Jersey cows. Half a mile from the town, it has a stunning mountain backdrop and a countryside feel.

RN 325, Km 13. © **3867/421473.** www.estancialascarreras.com.ar. 6 units. From $140 double. Rates include breakfast. No credit cards. Free parking. **Amenities:** Restaurant; lounge; cheese factory; museum; solarium; Wi-Fi.

Estancia Las Tacanas ★★   Las Tacanas is a genuine Jesuit *estancia* with all the frills. Stone walls, complete with a Virgin Mary grotto, surround a large historic *estancia* right in the heart of the town. The religious theme is continued inside with a bishop's gown displayed in the lobby and paintings hanging on whitewashed walls built by Jesuits 300 years ago. The four-poster bed was once the governor's, and the old saddles and blue ceramics belonged to the town's biggest landowners. That same family has now converted the farmhouse and stables into a luxury lodge with large, spacious rooms and charming period furniture. An old oak tree stands in the ivy

ARGENTINA'S dinosaur PARKS

For an amazing tour into the Triassic Period, consider visiting one the area's unique dinosaur parks:

Parque Nacional Talampaya (Talampaya National Park) ★★, RP 26, Villa Union, La Rioja (☎ 3825/470356; www.talampaya.gov.ar), has captured the 50-million-year-old Triassic period like a perfect geological etching. Multiple layers of sediments have fallen on what used to be a tropical zone, allowing scientists to date and study, indeed discover, what life was like 200 million years ago—the age of dinosaurs, through fossilized remains.

It also makes for some pretty spectacular scenery in a UNESCO World Heritage Site that covers more than 215,000 hectares (a half-million acres) situated in the arid province of La Rioja. The 150m-high (492-ft.) red sandstone walls are as sharp as diamond-cut marble. The park tour bus takes you down this long spectacular gorge that is actually a dry riverbed. The area is one of the driest places on earth, where summer temperatures of 122°F (40°C) are common. You reach a half circle clearing that emits a perfect echo. Nearby 1,800-year-old rock paintings display birdlife and guanacos—a type of llama that still can be seen roaming this scarlet desert. Hard capstones sit precariously on soft pedestals, sculpted by the wind to appear like towers and cathedrals. One geomorphic rock looks like a tortoise. Talampaya is more picturesque than its sister park Ischigualasto, 80km (50 miles) away, which is more famous for its dinosaur fossils. The Talampaya tour is also more fun and informative, as the guide is with you throughout the 3-hour tour; but remember to ask for a tour in English. There is no public transport to either park, so a taxi or tour company must be used from La Rioja city, which is 2½ hours away, or from the small towns Villa Union or Valle Fertil. *Note:* Do not forget a hat, sunblock, and lip balm. The park is open daily (May–Sept 8:30am–5:30pm; Oct–Apr 8am–6pm); admission is $7.50, and you are required to show your passport for entrance.

Parque Triásico Ischigualasto/Valle de la Luna ★★★, in Los Baldecitos, San Juan (☎ 264/422-7372; www.ischigualasto.org), got its start in 1991 when local student Ricardo Martinez tripped across a skull while on a field trip with San Juan University. The glint of teeth encouraged Martinez to dig further until he uncovered an entire

bordered central courtyard, and a line of comfy deck chairs sit among pillars overlooking a field-size garden. And yet, you are a 2-minute walk from main street!

Av. Presidente Perón 372, Tafi del Valle. ☎ **3867/421821.** www.estancialastacanas.com. 9 units. From $100 double. V. Rates include breakfast. Free parking. **Amenities:** Restaurant; garden; patio. *In room:* A/C, TV.

MODERATE

Estancia Los Cuartos ★★ 🗡 To stay in an Argentine *estancia* often requires a car and money. With Los Cuartos you need neither. Located within the town limits means there are no problems with access, and room rates of about $60 per double means you do not have to break the bank to enjoy genuine 19th-century rustic splendor. The lodge sits in a large field surrounded by wood fencing. A low-slung corrugated roof shades a long gallery of dark pillars and white walls. The thick adobe keeps cool the very authentic, cottage-style rooms with green wooden doors and raftered ceilings. The low brass beds face windows overlooking the splendid central courtyard, creature now known as an Eoraptor. The Eoraptor roamed this desolate part of Argentina 225 million years ago, making it one of the oldest dinosaur fossils in the world. Yet it is not quite the oldest; the oldest was discovered 1.6km (1 mile) away and is called a Herrerasaurus.

The park, otherwise known as Valle de la Luna (Moon Valley), is ground zero for dinosaur hunters. The 50,000-hectare (120,000-acre) site of yellow mushroom-shaped rocks and red cliffs is home to the bones of giant reptiles that are constantly surprising paleontologists who, every year, find new species. The entire evolutionary period of these grizzly dragons can be seen here, stretching over 255 million years, up until their extinction, approximately 65 million years ago.

The discoveries can be seen in a purpose-built museum at the park entrance. Curled vertebrate lie in fossilized nests, and giant two-legged monsters are frozen in time. One poignant display shows the remains of three cubs trapped in their lair. A full tour of the park takes 3 hours, a caravan of vehicles following a park ranger around the 40km (25-mile) circuit, stopping at different sites of

interest. You see eerie rock formations and tall pillars of stone standing precariously in the wind. One fascinating place is the *cancha de bochas,* or bowling alley. This is a sandy bunker dotted with smooth black balls belched up from the bowels of the earth.

This UNESCO World Heritage Site takes some effort to see. Located in San Juan province, it is nevertheless a 6-hour drive from the provincial capital. Many people choose to stay in the nearby town of Valle Fertil. However, La Rioja city airport is 2½ hours away by car, and the road passes the equally stunning Talampaya National Park, meaning you can pack in two geological blockbusters in 1 day if you start early enough. *Note:* The routine tours are in Spanish, and the guides are not very inspiring or knowledgeable. Best to call ahead and see if you can reserve an English-speaking guide, preferably one with a background in paleontology or geology. The park also conducts bike tours and full-moon excursions. The park is open daily (Apr–Sept 9am–4pm; Oct–Mar 8am–5pm); admission is $18, and you are required to show your passport for entrance.

and the tiny doors lead to a handsome dining room with an antique table and adjacent library. The small bathrooms with chessboard tiling and bamboo ceilings only add to what is a genuine and good-value experience. The lodge also organizes horseback-riding excursions.

Av. Gobernador Miguel Critto s/n. (C) **3867/155-874230** (mobile). www.estancialoscuartos.com. 7 units. From $62 double. Rates include breakfast. No credit cards. Free parking. **Amenities:** Lounge; Wi-Fi.

Hostería Lunahuana   This is the best modern option in the town, with excellent ambience and top-notch facilities. The modern building is built in the colonial style, with a welcoming lobby of warm earth colors and large windows that give lots of light. Scarlet walls lead to a large bar and tempting fireplace. The rooms are ample and attractive, some with lovely garden views and beautiful furniture. The bathrooms are smallish but clean, with tub/shower combinations. The larger triple rooms have a mezzanine. This *hostería* is for those who like modern luxuries.

Av. Gobernador Miguel Critto 540. ✆ **3867/421330.** www.hosterialunahuana.com. 32 units. From $95 double. Rates include breakfast. AE, DC, V. Free parking. Amenities: Restaurant; solarium; tennis court.

Hotel Tafí   The Hotel Tafí is a very basic hotel with beautiful views that will suit those who are not too fussy. Modern and plain, its deceptively pleasant lobby/breakfast room has tall ceilings and polished wooden floors. The rooms themselves are somewhat of a letdown, with little or no ambience and low, creaking beds. The furniture is monkish and decor nonexistent. However, the view in the morning is spectacular, with large windows revealing a pleasant garden and panoramic view of the valley and fields. Despite its pastoral surroundings, the hotel is located in the heart of the town. It's a decent budget option but with little atmosphere compared to the similarly priced Estancia Los Cuartos.

Av. Belgrano 177. ✆ **3867/421007.** www.hoteltafiweb.com.ar. 30 units. From $70 double. Rates include breakfast. No credit cards. Free parking. **Amenities:** Lounge; garden.

La Guadalupe   This orange adobe lodge does not lack color: Multicolored sombreros hang on corn-yellow walls, and lamps hang from a ceiling of wooden beams. The rooms are welcoming, with private bathrooms and floral murals. Out front is a large pond, and behind are green rolling hills. A popular restaurant serves regional and international fare, and the delightful tearoom dishes out quality cakes and pastries.

Camino de la Costa 650. ✆ **3867/421329.** www.posadalaguadalupe.com.ar. 9 units. From $90 double. Rates include breakfast. No credit cards. Free parking. **Amenities:** Restaurant; pool; solarium.

Where to Eat

There are no fine-dining restaurants in town, with most places serving grilled beef and the local delicacy, kid goat. Main courses cost on average $10 without wine. **El Mangrullo Parrillada,** RN 307, Km 62 (✆ **3867/421554;** www.elmangrullo.8m. com), is a traditional *parrilla* with a folkloric theme. The building is made from traditional adobe and stone, with large windows that give a commanding view of the valley. **Rancho de Félix,** at avenidas Belgrano and Presidente Perón (✆ **3867/421022**), is a cavernous building with cane ceilings. The menu includes *locros, humitas,* and empanadas. **Parrilla Don Pepito,** Av. Presidente Perón 193 (✆ **3867/421764;** www.donpepitodetafi.com.ar), has llama casserole on the board, as well as such fish as pejerrey and dorada. **Bar El Almacen,** at avenidas Presidente Perón and Gobernador Miguel Critto (✆ **3867/420129**), is a pleasant cream-colored bar and restaurant, serving kid goat and pastas.

CORDOBA & THE CENTRAL SIERRAS

by Charlie O'Malley

Colorful nightlife, fascinating history, Jesuit architecture, and cutting-edge art are just some of the attractions Córdoba province has to offer. For lovers of the great outdoors, the fresh air, pastoral estancias, and some of Argentina's best horseback riding and paragliding excursions should satisfy. This central province with a boisterous modern city and bracing rural hinterland attracts 350,000 visitors each year. Neat, tidy towns with majestic Jesuit ruins contrast with vast agricultural flatlands of rusting cereal silos and wind-battered billboards or the rolling green hills of the Punilla Valley. Villa Carlos Paz is a well-polished tourist trap with slick resorts offering watersports and golf. In La Cumbre, you can stay on a luxury estancia and partake in first-class hiking, horseback riding, and paragliding.

9

The industrious Jesuits made Córdoba their South American headquarters in colonial times. Their legacy is still reflected in a famous university tradition and a busy, prolific province that produces everything from soybeans and cars to the country's best graduates.

Córdobeses are Argentina's best-loved citizens, noted for their lilting accents and sharp sense of humor. They also have a talent for partying, with some notable get-togethers such as Oktoberfest in Villa General Belgrano and a famous traditional music festival in Cosquín every January.

CORDOBA

713km (442 miles) NW of Buenos Aires; 721km (447 miles) NE of Mendoza

Stand on the corner of Yrigoyen and Buenos Aires streets and you'll see firsthand Córdoba's heady mix of religion, education, and modern industry. Argentina's second city has a bland backdrop of red-brick high-rises and boxed balconies punctuated with the occasional Gothic spire or colonial facade. Don't be deceived by these first impressions of a dull Legoland. Beneath it all lies a young, vibrant city with lots of heritage, great bars and restaurants, and a considerable student population of 120,000 undergraduates intent on having a good time.

This city of 1.3 million inhabitants was created as a stop for Spaniards traveling between Peru and the Atlantic coast. It was founded in 1573 by Jerónimo Luis de Cabrera. The Jesuits arrived at the end of the 16th century, opening Córdoba's university in 1613 and financing their projects by establishing six large *estancias* throughout the region. Today you can follow the "road of the Jesuit *estancias*" by arranging a tour with a local travel agent.

La Cañada, a waterway created to prevent flooding, is one of the city's symbols. Córdoba's most important historical sights line up around Plaza San Martín, including the Cabildo, cathedral, Marqués de Sobre Monte's residence, and the Jesuit Block. The Manzana Jesuítica, as the Jesuit Block is called in Spanish, developed not just as a place of worship, but also as an intellectual and cultural center that produced Argentina's top doctors and lawyers. It includes the Jesuit churches, the university, and a prestigious secondary school. In 2000, it was declared a UNESCO World Heritage Site and became a historic museum. The city still serves as an intellectual center, increasingly popular to foreign students who wish to study Spanish outside Buenos Aires.

Essentials

GETTING THERE   Córdoba is most easily reached by air, and 15 daily flights depart from Buenos Aires. **Aeropuerto Internacional Ing. Ambrosio Taravella,** also called Pajas Blancas (© 351/475-0871 or 475-0874), is 11km (6¾ miles) outside town. **Aerolíneas Argentinas** (© 0810/222-86527; www.aerolineas.com.ar), **Sol** (© 0810/444-4765; www.sol.com.ar), and **LAN** (© 0810/999-9526; www.lan.com) operate flights here, traveling from Buenos Aires, Mendoza, Salta, Rosario, and Santiago de Chile. Buenos Aires flights cost approximately $160 one-way. **Gol** (© 0810/266-3131; www.voegol.com.br) also flies four times a week from Rio de Janeiro and São Paulo, Brazil. **Iberia** (© 351/422-2793; www.iberia.com) provides direct service from Madrid three times a week while **Copa** (© 0810/222-2672; www.copaair.com) operates a daily flight to Panama City. A **taxi** from the airport to downtown costs $11.

The **Terminal de Omnibus,** or central bus station, is located at Bd. Perón 380 (© **351/433-1982** or 433-1987; www.terminalcordoba.com), 7 blocks east of the city center. It is currently undergoing a messy refurbishment; the expansion is not set for completion until 2012 but the station will remain in operation throughout. Numerous companies serve destinations throughout Argentina. Travel times are approximately 10 hours to Buenos Aires, 12 hours to Mendoza, 30 minutes to Villa Carlos Paz, and 2 hours to La Falda. A one-way ticket from Buenos Aires should cost no more than $55; companies constantly offer promotions and change their prices frequently. I recommend you check with the tourism office or the bus station before booking your ticket. A tourism information office is situated in the bus station (© **351/433-1987**). **Rede Ticket,** Obispo Trejo 325 (© **351/428-0800;** www.redeticket.com.ar), is a booking agency located 4 blocks from the central plaza that charges the same as the bus companies in the station.

If you choose to drive from Buenos Aires, the trip takes approximately 10 hours on RN 9, which is a good road.

CAR RENTAL   To rent a small car costs $60 to $70 per day. Try **Annie Millet-Hertz** (© **351/475-0581** or 475-0587; www.milletrentacar.com.ar) or **Avis** (© **351/475-0815** or 475-0785; www.avis.com.ar) at the airport, or **Europe Rent**

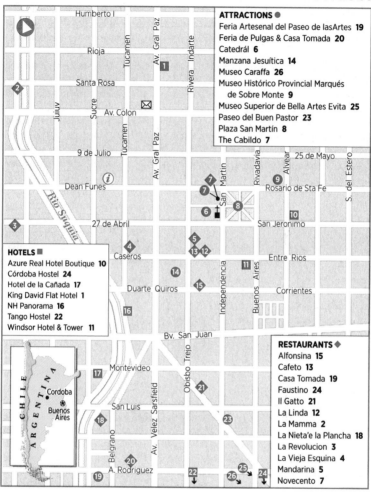

ATTRACTIONS ●
Feria Artesenal del Paseo de lasArtes **19**
Feria de Pulgas & Casa Tomada **20**
Catedrál **6**
Manzana Jesuítica **14**
Museo Caraffa **26**
Museo Histórico Provincial Marqués
   de Sobre Monte **9**
Museo Superior de Bella Artes Evita **25**
Paseo del Buen Pastor **23**
Plaza San Martín **8**
The Cabildo **7**

HOTELS ■
Azure Real Hotel Boutique **10**
Córdoba Hostel **24**
Hotel de la Cañada **17**
King David Flat Hotel **1**
NH Panorama **16**
Tango Hostel **22**
Windsor Hotel & Tower **11**

RESTAURANTS ◆
Alfonsina **15**
Cafeto **13**
Casa Tomada **19**
Faustino **24**
Il Gatto **21**
La Linda **12**
La Mamma **2**
La Nieta'e la Plancha **18**
La Revolucion **3**
La Vieja Esquina **4**
Mandarina **5**
Novecento **7**

9

CORDOBA & THE CENTRAL SIERRAS | Córdoba

a Car, Entre Ríos 70 (℡ **351/422-4867**). **Budget,** San Jerónimo 131 (℡ **351/421-1240;** www.budget.com), is located 1 block from Plaza San Martín.

VISITOR INFORMATION   Córdoba's **Centro de Información Turística,** in the Cabildo (℡ **351/434-1200;** www.cordobaturismo.gov.ar), offers hotel and restaurant information, distributes small city maps, and also provides information and maps on the entire region, such as La Falda or La Cumbre. It's open daily from 8am to 8pm in summer, with shorter hours in winter. There are also branches at the airport (℡ **351/434-8390**) and at the bus station (℡ **351/433-1987** or 433-1982).

GETTING AROUND   The old city of Córdoba is easy to explore on foot, with 24 blocks of pedestrian walking streets near the Cabildo. The heart of the old city spreads out around Plaza San Martín, in the southeast quadrant of Córdoba. Most of the historical sights lie in this area. Avenida Colón, which becomes Avenida Olmos, is the city's main street. **Centro de Información Turística,** in the Cabildo (✆ **351/434-1200**), organizes walking tours of the city in English. As a general rule, you should not walk alone in big cities at night. In Córdoba, this is especially true anywhere along the river.

City buses are cheap and abundant, but only *cospeles*—57¢ tokens, available at kiosks around town—are accepted. **Córdoba City Tour** (✆ **351/424-6605**) is a double-decker bus that offers English-language tours of the city, starting at Plaza San Martín. On Monday, Tuesday, and Thursday the tour starts at 6pm; Friday through Sunday tours start at 10am and 6pm. No tours are offered Wednesday. The whole circuit takes 90 minutes and costs $9.

Driving is difficult in the city, and parking is almost impossible downtown. In Córdoba, taxis are bright yellow, while the safer and similarly priced *remises* (private, unmetered taxis) are light green. As is the case throughout Argentina, it is always safer to hire a *remise* rather than flag a taxi on the streets. This is just an extra measure of security for the visitor—locals have no problems flagging taxis on the street.

Like any big city, cyclists should be aware of heedless drivers. That said, touring by bike is a lovely way to explore the park and plazas. **Córdoba Renta Bike,** San Martín 5 (✆ **351/421-8012**), charges $5.50 for 12 hours; the price includes helmets and maps. You must leave a deposit of $50 and passport.

WHEN TO GO Córdoba can be visited any time of year, although you should expect hot temperatures, stormy weather, and big crowds in January and February, and fairly cold temperatures June through August. In addition to peak summer season, tourist destinations also fill up during Easter week.

[FastFACTS] CORDOBA

Area Code The area code for Córdoba is **351.**

ATMs & Currency Exchange Two reliable exchange houses are **Maguitur,** 25 de Mayo 122, and **Barujel,** Rivadavia 97. There is also an exchange booth at the airport called **Global Exchange** (✆ **351/475-9038**). ATMs are commonplace in the city center, while the main Citibank is located at 25 de Mayo and Rivadavia.

Emergency For a medical emergency, dial ✆ **107;** for police, dial ✆ **100** or

351/428-7000; in case of fire, dial ✆ **101.**

Hospital The **Hospital de Urgencias** (emergency hospital; ✆ **351/427-6200**) is located at Catamarca and Salta.

Internet Access Telecom, with a branch on almost every corner downtown, provides Internet access for less than $1 per hour.

Pharmacy **Farmacia Virtual,** 27 de Abril 99 (✆ **351/411-1101**), is open daily 9am until midnight.

Post Office The main post office, **Correo**

Argentino, is at Av. General Paz 201.

Spanish Classes The city is increasingly popular with study-abroad students who want to catch up on their Spanish, and longterm travelers who want to learn some vocabulary before going farther afield. **Able Spanish,** Caseros 45 (✆ **351/423-3300;** www.ablespanish.com), and **Espanex,** Av. General Paz 55 (✆ **351/421-8954;** www.espanex.org), are two private institutions that can also organize volunteer work and internships.

Where to Stay

Córdoba offers a wide variety of hotels. No stellar choices are available directly downtown, but better facilities can be found in the satellite towns. Parking is usually free for hotel guests.

EXPENSIVE

Azur Real Hotel Boutique ★★   Located above a bank on a busy street, the Azur Real is a surprising oasis of Zen-like calm and minimalist decor. A street elevator takes you to the first-floor lobby with loftlike decor complete with bare brick walls and an open fireplace. Antique doors and high ceilings are combined with all the mod conveniences you'd expect from Córdoba's only upscale boutique hotel. The 15 rooms are ample and tastefully designed with dark wood trimmings, light-colored fabric, and soft lighting; in general the whole setup has a warm, welcoming ambience that makes for a welcome retreat from the chaotic city. The lift continues upwards to an attractive rooftop deck with small dip pool. When booking, insist on a back room away from the noisy entrance. Room nos. 1 to 3 are best avoided.

San Jerónimo 243, Córdoba. © 351/424-7133. www.azurrealhotel.com. 15 units. From $165 double. Rates include buffet breakfast. AE, DC, MC, V. Free parking. **Amenities:** Small outdoor pool; room service; Wi-Fi; roof terrace. *In room:* A/C, TV.

Holiday Inn Córdoba ★ 🗝   One of the city's favorite hotels is situated between the airport and downtown, next to a large shopping complex and near the posh neighborhood of Cerro de las Rosas. Standard rooms are colorful, bright, and airy, with slightly larger rooms on the executive floor. The gorgeous pool is complemented by a fitness center, sauna, and state-of-the-art massage facility. The helpful staff will arrange airport transfers, regional excursions, and sports activities upon request. You'll need to take a taxi or remise to the city center, about 10 minutes away. The hotel also functions as a convention center.

Centro Comercial Libertad, at Fray Luis Beltrán and M. Cardeñosa, 5008 Córdoba. © **351/477-9100.** Fax 351/477-9156/00. www.holidayinncba.com.ar. 144 units. From $105 double. Weekend promotions available. Rates include buffet breakfast. AE, DC, MC, V. Free parking. **Amenities:** Restaurant; bar; poolside bar; babysitting; fitness center; heated outdoor pool; room service; sauna; Wi-Fi. *In room:* A/C, TV, hair dryer, minibar.

King David Flat Hotel ★★ 🗝   In the heart of downtown, just a short walk from all the main attractions, the King David offers 110 modern and comfortable apartment-suites. Every unit has a separate living area with TV and sofa, a small but fully equipped kitchen with microwave and stove, and a spacious marble bathroom next to the smallish bedroom. The decor is contemporary, with light wood and large windows overlooking the city. The staff can be a little cold and unhelpful but will arrange transportation and tours if requested. When making reservations, be sure to ask for promotional rates, as the hotel often offers weekday discounts.

General Paz 386, 5000 Córdoba. © **351/570-3528.** Fax 351/570-3535. www.kingdavid.com.ar. 110 units. From $85 apt for 2; $98 apt for 3; $117 apt for 4. From $82 double. Rates include buffet breakfast. AE, DC, MC, V. Parking $8. **Amenities:** Restaurant; bar; exercise room; tiny outdoor pool; room service; Wi-Fi. *In room:* A/C, TV, minibar.

Sheraton Córdoba Hotel   Just outside the city center, next to a fashionable shopping mall, this five-star Sheraton is an old reliable, if a slightly tired one. Elevators shoot up the center of the 16-floor atrium lobby, which is decorated with rose-colored marble, California palms, and paintings by national artists. The rooms are spacious, though not huge, and well appointed with marble tables and desks, large bathtubs, and views of either the city or mountains. Service is first-rate, although the hotel gets crowded when its convention center is booked. The restaurant is fairly standard, offering a la carte or buffet dining. The breakfast buffet is spectacular, with local and international fare. The piano bar is good evening fun. The Sheraton offers the most extensive list of amenities of any hotel in Córdoba.

Av. Duarte Quirós 1300, 5000 Córdoba. © **351/526-9000.** Fax 351/526-9150. www.sheraton.com/cordoba. 188 units. From $122 double; from $552 suite. Rates include buffet breakfast. AE, DC, MC, V. Free parking. **Amenities:** Restaurant; piano bar; fitness center; heated outdoor pool; room service; sauna; tennis court; Wi-Fi. *In room:* A/C, TV, hair dryer, minibar.

MODERATE

Hotel de la Cañada Spacious rooms with king-size beds and muted lighting make for a comfortable stay at the Hotel de la Cañada, a good, midrange choice. The 11-story red-brick high-rise has an excellent location, and the staff is super friendly. One of its most pleasant features is the reading room and lounge, with old-world decor and comfy armchairs that invite you to sit back, relax, and escape the bustling city.

Marcelo T. de Alvear 580, 5000 Córdoba. © **351/421-4649.** www.hoteldelacaniada.com.ar. 113 units. $95 double. Rates include buffet breakfast. AE, DC, MC, V. Free parking. **Amenities:** Restaurant bar; small outdoor pool; room service; sauna; Wi-Fi. *In room:* A/C, TV, hair dryer, minibar.

NH Panorama The NH Panorama is a 14-story brick box typical of the dreary architecture that has swamped Córdoba in recent years. Inside you'll find the marble countertops, sleek wood paneling, and minimalist furniture typical of this Spanish-owned hotel chain. The panorama of the title is a lovely view of the city plaza and distant hills, but be sure you get a high, west-facing room as otherwise you might just see more red-brick boxes. The location is perfect and the rooftop pool a welcome respite in summer. The restaurant could be better and the elevators faster, but, in general, the NH is a very efficient and businesslike hotel, much like its clientele.

Marcelo T. de Alvear 251, 5000 Córdoba. © **351/410-3900.** www.nh-hoteles.es. 130 units. From $120 double. Rates include buffet breakfast. AE, DC, MC, V. Free parking. **Amenities:** Restaurant; bar; fitness center; small outdoor pool; room service; sauna; Wi-Fi. *In room:* A/C, TV, hair dryer, minibar.

Windsor Hotel & Tower ★ This centrally located hotel is the best choice near Plaza San Martín. Ask for a room in the more modern tower, built in 1999, rather than in the "Classic" section, where the rooms are ridiculously small. Rooms with king-size beds are larger than those with two twins. Also new are the rooftop pool, fitness room, and sauna. The fifth-floor Oxford restaurant enjoys an impressive view of the city, with good international cuisine. Piano music fills the lobby after 9pm, and the hotel staff will organize city tours and mountain excursions.

Buenos Aires 214, 5000 Córdoba. ©/fax **351/422-4012.** www.windsortower.com. 82 units. From $82 double. Rates include buffet breakfast. AE, DC, MC, V. Free parking. **Amenities:** 2 restaurants; piano bar; fitness center; small outdoor pool; room service; sauna; Wi-Fi. *In room:* A/C, TV, hair dryer, minibar.

INEXPENSIVE

Córdoba Hostel The view of red-brick high-rises from the roof terrace may not be the most inspiring sight, but within this bright, three-story building you will find a warren of dorms and double rooms with bright, airy decor and the cheapest beds in town. Rainbow-colored walls with a '70s stucco effect may not be to everybody's taste but style is sacrificed for price and comfort, with a backyard pool and small bar to soothe any aesthetic misgivings and occupy those lazy afternoons. Definitely for the young and sociable.

Ituzaingó 1070, 5000 Córdoba. ℗ **351/468-7359.** www.cordobahostel.com.ar. 20 units, including 5 doubles. $11 dorm beds; from $38 double. No credit cards. **Amenities:** Bar; TV room; Internet stations w/free access; Wi-Fi; roof garden.

Tango Hostel The first hostel to establish itself as the place to throw your gear down is the Tango Hostel. This small, modern town house has a worn but homey feel, and its main asset is two extremely helpful owners. The four-bed dorms are not too claustrophobic, and the series of rambling communal rooms—TV salon, dining area, small bar, and little courtyard—means that there is always some corner to hide away in and read your book, or, if the mood suits, to share a drink with a fellow traveler. The decor is somewhat plain except for the occasional splash of wall color, and the bathrooms are very basic. Perfect for those on a long trip and short budget.

Fructuoso Rivera 70, 5000 Córdoba. ℗ **351/425-6023.** 8 units, including 2 doubles. $11 dorm beds; from $30 double. Rates include breakfast. No credit cards. **Amenities:** Dining area; bar; TV room; Wi-Fi.

A SPLURGE OUTSIDE THE CITY

Estancia El Colibri ★★★ This 170-hectare (420-acre) pocket of pastoral bliss is a 45-minute drive from Córdoba airport. Crisscrossed with rivers, woods, and meadows, the luxury property is traversed by a lavender path that leads to a plush villa and gorgeous pool. The decor is elegant and comfortable, with flower-bedecked walls and red velvet seating. Four-poster beds take pride of place in ample-size rooms with period furniture and silver-framed mirrors. Bathrooms are startling white, with immaculate fittings. The friendly owners ensure that guests are more than occupied with polo demonstrations, gaucho outings, and feastlike picnics beneath the trees. There are excellent wine-tasting sessions in the well-stocked and atmospheric cellar, or you can just join the hummingbirds on the patio and enjoy this laid-back, rural paradise.

Camino a Santa Catalina Km 7, Santa Catalina, Córdoba. ℗ **352/546-5888.** www.estanciaelcolibri.com. 9 units. From $694 double; from $847 junior suite; from $1,089 suite. Rates include full board. AE, DC, MC, V. Free parking. **Amenities:** Restaurant; bar; fitness center; heated outdoor pool; room service; sauna; Wi-Fi. *In room:* A/C, TV, hair dryer, minibar.

Where to Eat

In addition to the restaurants listed below, the most elegant *parrilla* in town is **Alcorta,** Figueroa Alcorta 330 (℗ **351/424-7452;** www.alcortacarnes.com.ar), serving the best cuts of beef in the city, with lunch averaging $30 with wine. The best Italian restaurant is **La Mamma,** at Santa Rosa and La Cañada (℗ **351/421-2212**), with homemade pastas, veal scaloppini, and an incredible lasagna; main dishes cost about $20. **La Nieta'e La Pancha,** on Belgrano 783 (℗ **351/468-1920**), offers typical food such as *locro* (Andean stew), *humitas* (corn cakes), and homemade pastas and empanadas, and here you can also try the ubiquitous *mate* tea so loved by locals. Meals cost around $15.

EXPENSIVE

San Honorato INTERNATIONAL Named after the patron saint of bread bakers, Saint Honorato, this cool Mediterranean-style restaurant used to be a bakery. Needless to say, all the bread is homemade and fresh. The specialty is homemade ravioli with salmon filling. The restaurant is an old-fashioned town house with lots of atmosphere and well-stocked wine cellar with such exclusive wines as Achaval Ferrer and

Terrazas de los Andes. It is 10 minutes by taxi from the city center, in the upscale district of General Paz.

Corner of Pringues and 25 de Mayo. ℂ **351/453-5252.** Main courses $25. AE, MC, V. Tues–Fri 12:30–3pm; Mon–Thurs 8:30pm–midnight; Fri–Sat 8:30pm–12:30am.

MODERATE

Alfonsina ★ ARGENTINE   Fancy a traditional *mate* while surrounded by gaucho paraphernalia such as saddles and horseshoes? Alfonsina is one of the few places that serve hot pots of Argentina's herbal obsession *mate* (usually enjoyed at home or in the open air). Despite the old-world decor of tall ceilings and bare brick walls, this restaurant bar has a youthful, arty clientele that dines on typical student cuisine such as *lomitos* (steak sandwiches) and *milanesa* (grilled, breaded meat cutlet). The 22 varieties of pizza include fugazza, a deliciously simple combination of onion, olives, and oregano. Alfonsina has a second location on the bustling Casa Tomada courtyard, shared with other bars; the entrance is at Belgrano 763.

Duarte Quiros 66. ℂ **351/427-2847.** Main courses $12. No credit cards. Tues–Sun 6pm–1am.

Cafeto ◢ INTERNATIONAL   A small ivy-covered courtyard with tall doors and cream-colored walls leads to an attractive bar with white globe lamps and red shelves. The menu includes a Nordic-style salad heavy with cured ham and beet root. Main courses include pink salmon and chicken stuffed with prawns. Wednesday to Friday, there are special gourmet dinners with wines selected from the in-house cellar. This pleasant eatery also has a nice relaxed vibe for casual morning-coffee drinkers. It also has Wi-Fi.

Caseros 88. ℂ **351/422-4579.** Main courses $12. AE, DC, MC, V. Sun–Tues 8:30am–9pm; Wed–Sat 8:30am–12:30am.

El Rancho Viejo ARGENTINE   A beautiful, traditional *parrilla* situated in the university city, the building is made entirely of stone, with a traditional roof and plenty of greenery surrounding it. Their specialty is kid goat.

Av. Rogelio N. Martínez 1900. ℂ **351/468-3685.** Main courses $15. AE, MC, V. Mon–Sat noon–3:30pm and 8:30pm–midnight; Sun 8:30pm–midnight.

Il Gatto ARGENTINE   This slick, diner-style restaurant has black-and-white photos on red walls, arty square lamps, and giant golden balls to distract your attention from a very pedestrian menu of pizza, pasta, cake, and coffee. Out front is a wooden platform patio to perch upon and watch the busy street traffic go by.

H. Yrigoyen 181. ℂ **351/568-0090.** www.ilgatto.com.ar. Main courses $18. AE, MC, V. Daily 7:30am–1am.

La Linda COFFEEHOUSE   Big and popular, La Linda has gaucho pictures on the walls that match the regional dishes on the menu such as empanadas and *locro*. Its overall ambience is bright and airy, if a little sterile and workaday. It is a popular coffee stop for locals who hang around to talk politics and the economy beneath attractive tapestries hanging on corn-yellow walls. Friday nights see the occasional live-music folklore band.

Paseo Caseros. No phone. Main courses $15. No credit cards. Mon–Fri noon–3:30pm and 8pm–12:30am.

La Revolucion ARGENTINE   Here you step into one of the hippest restaurant bars in the city, popular with students who like to muse over their beers on metal tables amid pink-striped walls holding frames of old-world labels. The place mats celebrate the Argentine Declaration of Independence and bear regular fare such as chicken dishes and pizza. The small zinc bar and the old town-house feel mean La Revolucion is a nice mix of old and new, with lots of atmosphere.

27 de Abril 633. ☎ **351/428-0190.** larevolucion@arnet.com.ar. Main courses $20. No credit cards. Mon–Tues noon–3:30pm; Wed–Sat noon 3:30pm and 9pm–12:30am.

Mandarina ★ ITALIAN   This eclectic restaurant, along the pedestrian walkway Obispo Trejo, is a cornucopia of surreal and occasionally sexual artwork. The city's cultural crowd comes for salads, pizzas, and pastas and later for wines, whiskeys, and wacky cocktails. Freshly baked breads and jams prepared with fresh fruit add to Mandarina's appeal. The best wines on the wine list are Zuccardi, Terrazzas, and Chandon.

Obispo Trejo 171. ☎ **351/426-4909.** Main courses lunch $12, dinner $16. AE, MC, V. Daily 8am–2am.

Novecento ★★ ARGENTINE   This attractive, somewhat trendy restaurant is part of the city museum complex and offers the perfect pit stop while doing the city's Jesuit circuit. Bronze statues of hounds, peasants, and gods circle a tiled courtyard with plants and an arched gallery. A balcony looks down on deck chair–style seating. Inside you'll find a tall glass ceiling and traditional bar with old-style furniture. Provoleta (grilled provolone cheese), risotto, and pasta are all on the menu, as well as salmon and the fish of the day.

Cabildo, Dean Funes 33. ☎ **351/423-0660.** Main courses $20. No credit cards. Daily 11:30am–4pm and 8pm–1am.

INEXPENSIVE

La Vieja Esquina 🍴 ARGENTINE   This is a tiny corner diner that any Córdobesa will tell you does the best empanadas in town. It does a thriving business in home delivery; and no wonder, as this atmospheric little place has room for a small counter bar and little else except brick walls framed with wood and old baskets hanging overhead. Perfect for a quick snack on the go, or a handy number to have if you get peckish in your hotel room early evening.

Corner of Caseros and Belgrano. ☎ **351/424-7940.** Empanadas 30¢. No credit cards. Mon–Sat 11am– 3pm and 7:30pm–midnight.

Seeing the Sights

Córdoba City Tour (☎ 351/424-6605) buses explore the main tourist spots in town. The tour lasts 1½ hours, visiting 40 sights, so it is especially good if you're spending only a short time in Córdoba; you'll see a lot in under 2 hours, and it's just $9 a person. The double-decker red buses leave from Plaza San Martín daily Thursday to Tuesday at 6pm with an extra tour at 10am on Friday, Saturday, and Sunday. The tourism office also arranges 2-hour English-speaking walking tours of the city for $15. Call in advance the **Tourism Information Office,** Rosario de Santa Fe 39 (☎ 351/428-5600; guiasdecordoba@hotmail.com).

Catedrál ★   Construction of the cathedral, situated next to the Cabildo, began in 1577 and took nearly 200 years to complete. No wonder, then, that the structure incorporates such an eclectic mix of styles, heavily influenced by baroque. On each of the towers, next to the bells, you will see Indian angels created by—and in the image of—indigenous people of this region. The dome was painted by Emilio Carrafa, one of Córdoba's best-remembered artists. Visitors are free to enter the church but should respect the Masses that take place at various times during the day.

Independencia 72, at Plaza San Martín. ☎ **351/422-3446.** Free admission. Daily 8am–noon and 4–7pm.

Manzana Jesuítica ★★★   The Jesuit Block, which includes the Society of Jesus' Church, the Domestic Chapel, the National University of Córdoba, and the National School of Monserrat, has been the nation's intellectual center since the early 17th century. Today the entire complex is a historic museum, although the churches still hold Masses, the cloisters still house priests, and the schools still enroll students.

The **Domestic Chapel,** completed in 1668, was used throughout much of its history for private Masses and religious studies of the Jesuits. Having practiced their building skills on the Domestic Chapel, the Jesuits finished the main church, called the **Compañía de Jesús,** in much the same style in 1676. Built in the shape of a Latin cross, the Compañía de Jesús is the oldest church in Argentina. Its nave was designed by a Belgian shipbuilder in the shape of an inverted hull, which was the best way to make use of the short wood beams available for construction at the time. The dome is all wood—no iron is found anywhere—and the beams remain fastened with raw cowhide. The gilded altarpiece was carved in Paraguayan cedar, indicative of baroque design. At each of the church's wings stands a chapel, one of which has often been used for university graduation ceremonies.

In 1613, the Jesuits founded the **National University of Córdoba,** the oldest university in Argentina and one of the continent's longtime academic centers. With most of the university (including the medical and law schools) having moved elsewhere in the city, the majority of rooms here now form part of the historic museum. You can visit the Hall of Graduates, the main university library, and the exquisite Jesuit library holding roughly 1,000 books dating back to the 17th century; the books are primarily in Latin, Greek, and Spanish, with the exception of a complete Bible from 1645 written in seven languages. Many of the original books in the library were secreted to Buenos Aires when the Jesuits were first expelled from the Americas, but some are slowly being returned.

The Jesuit library leads to the **Colegio Nacional de Monserrat (National College of Monserrat),** which opened in 1687 and quickly became one of the country's top public secondary schools. Walking around the cloisters, you can see the classrooms as well as exhibits of early science machines used for mechanics, electronics, magnetics, color, and sound. During the academic year, you will also find students at work here. You can enter the Compañía de Jesús, the university patio, and the Colegio Nacional de Monserrat free of charge. For $1, you can also visit the Domestic Chapel and the Hall of Graduates.

Obispo Trejo 242. ℗ **351/433-2075.** Free admission; tours $2.50. Tues–Fri 10am-12:30pm and 2-4:30pm; Sat 10am-1pm. 40-min. guided tours in English Tues and Thurs 3pm; in Spanish Tues and Thurs 11am. Call in advance to arrange an English-language tour.

Museo Caraffa ★   Raw concrete walls and all glass walkways are the main features in this modern art gallery, with somewhat brutalist architecture contrasting with its original classical-style facade. The multimedia exhibits are surreal and arresting, such as a photomontage of a gaucho arguing with a priest as he hoses water on an injured football player or video loops of children playing in a backyard. Some of the art is hit-and-miss, with frequent exhibitions by local students and art graduates. Named after a famous local painter, the Caraffa is worth an hour of your time to experience the vibrant local art scene.

Av. Poeta Lugones 411, Plaza España. ℗ **351/433-3414.** museocaraffa@gmail.com. Admission $5; free on Wed. Tues–Sun 10am-8pm. Guided tours in English Tues–Fri 11:30am; Sat–Sun 4:30pm.

Museo Histórico Próvincial Marqués de Sobre Monte ★★ The largest colonial house to survive intact in Argentina, this historical museum was used as the 18th-century home and office of the first Spanish governor of Córdoba. Completed in 1772, the house showcases the town's early colonial history. The governor's commercial and office rooms were downstairs, with the more intimate family rooms upstairs. An amazing collection of period furniture fills the bedrooms; public spaces display religious paintings, military uniforms, a rifle collection, early saddles and leatherwear, and an 18th-century chamber organ.

Rosario de Santa Fe 218. ☏ **351/433-1661.** Admission 60¢. Mon–Fri 9:30am–3pm.

Museo Superior de Bella Artes Evita ★★★ Sumptuous, stylish, and modish are just some of the words I would use to describe this Córdoba gallery, opened in 2007. It is located in the fabulous Palacio Ferreyra, a gorgeous French-style mansion once owned by one of the province's richest and best-established families. Gilded baroque collides with 20th-century brashness, and the result is a charming afternoon of smiles and surprises. One such shock is the modern, pitch-black staircase. As you ascend, you realize it is covered entirely in hairy cow skin. Other contrasts include the high, ornate ceiling covings and the futuristic Perspex furniture in the airy cafe with ample balcony. Mosaic floors, golden wallpaper, and glass-draped walls mean this architectural gem has been renovated with a modernist flourish. The excellent exhibits range from 18th-century Cuzco art to 1960s Argentine pop. One giant room is dedicated to the Mendocinean artist Carlos Alonso and his dark, disturbing commentaries on the Dirty War. A must-see.

Hipólito Yrigoyen 511. ☏ **351/434-3636.** vguiadas.palacioferreyra@gmail.com. Admission $1; free on Wed. Tues–Sun 10am–8pm. Guided tours in English Tues–Fri 3pm; in Spanish Sat–Sun 11am and 3 and 5pm.

Paseo del Buen Pastor ★★ ☺ Occupying a triangular city block, El Paseo del Buen Pastor is a modernist maze of cafes, restaurants, exhibition rooms, and art gardens. Located in a former women's prison that is now dedicated to those who suffered under the dictatorship, the complex is a bewildering display of surreal art, glass-framed walkways, and rust-colored flagstones. Stark metal pillars and driftwood installations contrast with a convent-style chapel. Green molded seating and psychedelic cowhide restaurant menus give a futuristic nod, as does the over-the-top light-and-water show featuring a fountain display to a Freddie Mercury soundtrack. The fountain show takes place every day at 7 and 11pm. There is a small cinema, a supervised children's area, and a selection of stores and cafes.

Av. Hipólito Yrigoyen 325. ☏ **351/411-1312** or 411-1213. Free admission. Daily 10am–10pm. Daily guided tours in Spanish 10:20am and 12:20, 2:20, and 4:20pm; English noon Sat.

Plaza San Martín and the Cabildo ★ The 400-year-old plaza orients the city, with General San Martín facing the direction of Mendoza (from which his army crossed into Chile and later Peru to liberate them from Spanish rule). Exhibitions, fairs, and impromptu markets are frequent events on the plaza. The **Cabildo** stands on the plaza's west side. During the military dictatorship of the late 1970s and early 1980s, the Cabildo functioned as police headquarters and was used, as acknowledged by a small sign along Pasaje Santa Catalina, as a clandestine center for detention, torture, and execution. Today the Cabildo is a friendlier place, used mainly for cultural exhibitions and events.

At Deán Funes and Independencia. ☏ **351/428-5856.** Tues–Sun 9am–1pm; daily 4–9pm.

TOURING THE JESUIT estancias

The next time you sip a satisfying glass of Argentine wine, thank the Jesuits of Córdoba. These resourceful monks planted South America's first vineyards in Córdoba in the 16th century, as they required wine to celebrate the Eucharist. They also needed priests, and, for this reason, they established a college in the city, one of the earliest on the continent. Córdoba soon became the headquarters of the entire South American arm of the Jesuits. In 1621, the college was renamed the University of San Carlos. By the 18th century, the city was known as Córdoba Docta, or Learned Córdoba, the undisputed cultural capital of the Vice Regency of La Plata.

To fund such expansion, the Jesuits operated six flourishing *estancias* around the province—three near the town of Jesús María. Produce from their orchards, farms, and vineyards not only paid for students' tuition but funded a massive construction project of beautiful churches and residences. You can still view five of these today, which is a delightful way to get off-road and step back in time.

To visit a provincial Jesuit *estancia,* contact the tourist office, hire a car, or sign up with a local travel agent, such as

Stylo Viajes, Chacabuco 325 (✆ **351/424-6605** or 421-8012; stylo@ arnet.com.ar), or **Córdoba Nativo,** 27 de Abril 11 (✆ **351/424-5341;** www.cordoba nativoviajes.com.ar). A 1-day tour to the three *estancias* at Alta Gracia, Caroya, and Jesús María costs $45.

Estancia de Alta Gracia. A UNESCO World Heritage Site, Estancia de Alta Gracia is now the town center of a sleepy municipality by the same name, 25km (16 miles) southwest of Córdoba city. The *estancia*'s beautiful buildings are situated around the central plaza. On-site is an interesting museum, known as La Casa del Virrey, named after an ex-resident, Santiago de Liniers, Viceroy of the River Plate.

Av. Del Tajamar and Solares. ✆ **3547/421-303.** www.museoliniers.org.ar. Admission 60¢; free on Wed. English guides available. Apr-Nov Tues-Fri 9am-1pm and 3-7pm, Sat-Sun and holidays 9:30am-12:30pm and 3:30-6:30pm; Dec-Mar Tues-Fri 9am-8pm.

Estancia de Caroya. Less grand than Estancia Jesús María nearby (see below), this quaint building with a pretty courtyard and a small Spanish-style chapel is the oldest of all the *estancias.* Built in 1616, it was used as a holiday home for foreign scholars, and an arms factory during the

SHOPPING

Feria Artesanal del Paseo de las Artes is an excellent antiques and handicrafts fair on Achaval Rodríguez and La Cañada on Saturday and Sunday (3–10pm in winter, 6–11pm in summer). Close by is an indoor market known as **Casa Tomada,** Achaval Rodríguez 260. This former 1940s bakery now houses a dozen design stores selling leather goods, jewelry, antiques, and clothes. Out back is a pleasant courtyard with restaurants. It is open Tuesday to Sunday from 5 to 10pm. **Mazamorra,** Rivadavia 153 (✆ **351/423-0513**), is an artisans' cooperative specializing in locally made handicrafts. It is open Monday to Friday from 9am to 7pm. **Utopia,** Rosario de Santa Fe 35 (✆ **351/411-4197**), has traditional and modern handicrafts, including weavings and silverware. It is open Monday through Friday from 9:30am to 8pm and Saturday from 9:30am to 2pm. **Varietal Vinoteca,** Av. Vélez Sarsfield 801 (✆ **351/428-1887;** www.varietalvinoteca.com.ar), is a lavish wine store dispensing Argentina's top brands, including Catena Zapata and Achaval Ferrer. **SBS,** Caseros 79 (✆ **351/423-6448;** www.sbs.com.ar), is one of the best bookstores in town with independence wars. It still boasts the ruins of an abandoned mill and dam. It is a 20-minute walk from Jesús María town center.

Av. 28 de Julio. *C* **3525/426-781.** Admission $2. Tues–Fri 8am–6pm; Sat–Sun 9am–3pm.

Estancia de Jesús María. Close to the laid-back town of Jesús María, 19km (31 miles) north of Córdoba City, this is one of the best-conserved and most visited Jesuit *estancias.* The 17th-century church and residence form a U-shape around a well-tended garden. A pond, woods, and small graveyard give the place an idyllic feel. Its history is fascinating; wine made here was the first American wine served to the Spanish royal family. In the Museo Jesuítico, you'll find colonial objects and paintings, as well as old winemaking equipment. The *estancia* is a 300m (984-ft.) walk from the town. Follow Avenida Juan B. Justo north, turn left onto Cleto Peña, and follow a dirt track until you reach the entrance.

Pedro Oñarte s/n. *C* **3525/420-126.** mjn.jm@ coop5.com.ar. Admission $1.25. Tues–Fri 8am–7pm; Sat–Sun 10am–noon and 3–7pm. Guided visits in Spanish at 9, 10, and 11am.

Estancia de Santa Catalina. This was the biggest and most important of all the *estancias.* Now in private hands, the property is largely closed to the public but still worth visiting for its beautiful location and the magnificent church on the premises, which is open for visits. The amazing baroque-style interior, funded by cattle raising, is one of the most valued works of colonial architecture in the country. It is approximately 19km (12 miles) west of Jesús María, on an unpaved road.

Road north of Ascochinga on Rte. E-66. *C* **3525/421-600.** Church admission 75¢. No English-speaking guides. Tues–Sun 10am–1pm and 3–7pm.

Estancia la Candelaria. To reach this lonely UNESCO World Heritage Site 120km (73 miles) northwest of Córdoba, you must drive across a high-altitude plateau of mountain grass and follow a route through charming rivers and waterfalls. Because of its isolation, it's not as elaborate as its sister establishments. Serving as both a sanctuary for Christians and a fort against hostile indigenous tribes, it has a more austere feel, yet it's nonetheless charming and majestic. One of its main functions was to provide mules for the long trip to the silver mines of Bolivia.

Cruz del Eje, Valle del Norte and Sierras Grandes. *C* **351/433-3425.** Admission 75¢. No English-speaking guides. Wed–Sun 10am–6pm.

a better-than-average English-language section. **Patio Olmos,** avenidas San Juan and Velez Sarsfield (*C* **351/570-4100;** www.patioolmos.com), is the city's plushest shopping mall, located in an old renovated college in the downtown area. It houses a wide variety of designer stores and a multiscreen cinema.

OUTDOOR ACTIVITIES

A number of tour and adventure companies offer excursions into the Sierras de Córdoba, where it is possible to climb a mountain, hike, mountain bike, horseback ride, hang glide, and fish. **Explorando Sierras de Córdoba** (*C* **3543/437-901;** www. explorandosierras.com.ar), offers discovery tours into the mountains, including birdwatching, horseback riding, and overnight camping trips.

Golf is big in Córdoba. Six world-class 18-hole courses are scattered around the city, and two more are just a half-hour drive away. The **Jockey Club** and the **Córdoba Golf Club** are the most popular. Log on to **www.golfencordoba.com** for detailed information about the clubs; the site is available in both English and Spanish.

ATMOSPHERIC street life: FERIA DE PULGAS AND CASA TOMADA ★

A warren of stalls and tiny stores have popped up around a large, rickety building on Achaval Rodriguez and Belgrano. Known as Feria de Pulgas (the flea market), it is great for a weekend stroll and has much the same color and atmosphere as San Telmo market in Buenos Aires (without the tango dancers, it must be said). As well as street stalls, if you follow the chessboard floor tiles inside to the back of the building known as Casa Tomada, it opens up into a large courtyard that is packed with laughing locals enjoying a beer and haggling over tie-dyed shirts. Here you'll find a bar called Alfonsina (see earlier) that spills out onto Belgrano Street, on the other side of the block. The whole complex has a lively underground feel and is perfect for a little shopping or a quick drink as a startup to a lengthy night on the tiles.

Córdoba After Dark

The **Cabildo** serves as a cultural center, with occasional evening events including tango on Friday evenings. For $2, you can get a crash lesson in tango at 9:30pm every Friday, and then try to dance the rest of the night away. **Teatro Libertador San Martín,** Vélez Sársfield 366 (© 351/433-2319), is the city's biggest theater, hosting mostly musicals and concerts. The smaller **Teatro Real,** San Jerónimo 66 (© 351/433-167071), presents more traditional theater. You can pick up current theater, comedy, and special events information in the "Espectáculos" section of the daily paper, *La Voz del Interior.* **El Arrabal,** Belgrano 899, at Fructuoso Rivera (© 351/460-2990), is a bar that hosts excellent tango, *milonga,* salsa, and folkloric shows most nights, open daily from 10am to 2am. A tango dinner show costs $21.

Culture aside, the next best thing to do in Córdoba at night is do as the locals do and party until sunrise. One of the best bars is **Johnny B. Good,** Av. Hipólito Yrigoyen 320 (© 351/424-3960). Giant cardboard cutouts of Paul McCartney, Bono, and the Edge may unsettle your appetite as you munch through typical American food. Amid all this star power is a very nice cake display. It's pure rock 'n' roll. Happy hour takes place weekdays from 7 to 9pm. La Canada is a popular area for bars and open-air drinking. **Bar X** is one of the most famous establishments. A number of upscale discos are located in the Chateau Carreras neighborhood; the most popular is **Carreras,** at Avenida Cárcano and Piamonte. The rest of the city's nightlife is concentrated along Bulevar Guzmán, in the north of the city, and in Nueva Córdoba along Avenida Hipólito Yrigoyen. One of the best disco bars in this area is **Mitre,** Marcelo T. de Alvear 635 (no phone). The El Abasto neighborhood has a more alternative music scene, with live performances of rock, reggae, jazz, and folklore. **Dorian Grey,** Las Heras and Roque Saenz Peña (© 351/15-403-1626 [mobile]), and **Eras Groove House,** Las Heras 218 (no phone), are two of the best known venues, hosting everything from punk to techno. The district of Cerro de las Rosas is another haunt for night owls. It is famous for good restaurants, such as *parrilla*-style **Rancho Grande,** Av. Rafael Núñez 4142 (© 351/481-1529), and Italian restaurant **Restorante Italiano,** Av. Rafael Núñez 3803 (© 351/482-7730). Another decent eatery is **Il Gatto,** Av. Rafael Núñez 3856 (© 351/482-7780). At night, the area is bustling with people frequenting pubs and disco bars all centered around the main drag Avenida Rafael Núñez. **Villa Agur,** Tristán Malbrán 4355 (② **351/481-7520**), is a trendy nightclub in an old and beautiful English-style house, near the Mirador del Cerro, where you can enjoy a great view of the city while you sip on the local brew, Fernet with cola. There is also a restaurant and a bar with live music.

Córdoba is famous for its own type of music called *cuarteto*. Panned by the critics and looked down on by rock aficionados, it is nevertheless a catchy blend of violin, piano, accordion, and bass. It is a foot-tapping alternative to the sometimes bland *rock nacional* you hear everywhere else. You can catch it live at several venues in the city, but beware: It attracts hysterical crowds and it's definitely down-market, for slummers only. For more information, call the **Asociación Deportiva Atenas,** Aguado 775 (② **351/471-5658;** www.atenas.com.ar), the **Estadio del Centro,** Santa Fe 480, or **La Vieja Usina,** Avenida Costanera and Coronel Olmedo (② **351/424-5743**).

VILLA CARLOS PAZ ★

36km (22 miles) W of Córdoba

A quick getaway from Córdoba, Villa Carlos Paz surrounds the picturesque Embalse San Roque. It's actually a reservoir, but vacationing Cordobés and Porteño families treat it like a lake and swim, sail, jet ski, and windsurf in its gentle waters. Year-round, people come here to play outdoors by day and party by night, with disco-bound buses transporting the youth of Córdoba back and forth. The city of 44,500 inhabitants really comes alive in January and February, when more than 200,000 tourists a month pay a visit. Live theater, comedy shows, music, and dancing fill the night air, and no one seems to sleep. Yet you don't have to be a nocturnal animal to enjoy Villa Carlos Paz—the area's quiet lakeside resorts are a more serene alternative.

Essentials

GETTING THERE The N20 is a fast highway (toll 70¢) that goes directly from Córdoba to Villa Carlos Paz. The drive takes no more than 40 minutes, except on Sunday evenings, when Córdobeses vacationers return home from the mountains. Bus transportation to Villa Carlos Paz is frequent and reliable and leaves from the city bus station and Mercado Sur (Bd. Illia 175, at Ituzaingo). The fare is $1.50. **Chevallier** buses to Buenos Aires take about 10 hours.

VISITOR INFORMATION There are two **tourism offices,** at San Martín 600 and San Martín 400 (② **3541/436-688** or 421-624). Both are open daily from 7am to 9pm. The staff provides information on hotels, restaurants, and tourist circuits around the city.

GETTING AROUND Villa Carlos Paz is small and easy to explore on foot. The city is safe to walk in, but it can get extremely crowded in the high season (Dec–Jan).

Seeing the Sights

There are no special sights in the city, save a 7m-high (23-ft.) cuckoo clock that, for no good reason, has become the city's symbol. Daytime activities focus on the lake and excursions into the surrounding hills. It's not clear why the city allows so many water activities in a reservoir. In any case, swimming, sailing, windsurfing, trout fishing, and—at least, for the time being—jet-skiing are all possible. Villa Carlos Paz is also well positioned for the many driving circuits through the Punilla Valley and into the mountains. These include treks to waterfalls, Jesuit ruins, and mountain *estancias*. In summer, buses disguised as trains run city tours. **Bus Panorámico** (📞 **3541/434-587**) costs $4 and lasts 90 minutes. You can call directly for departure times or take them from Avenida San Martín and Belgrano, in front of the bus station, or ask at the tourism office. City tours are worthwhile if you don't have time to meander on your own; they're also a good way to get to know the lay of the land before venturing out on your own.

Where to Stay

The area is very well furnished in terms of accommodations. Choices vary from well-run resorts to simple roadside cabins. If you have been overdoing it on Argentine steak and wine, check into **La Posada del Qenti Health Resort,** RN 14, Km 7.5, 5152 Villa Carlos Paz (📞 **3541/495-715;** www.qenti.com). This plush villa surrounded by hills is brimming with enthusiastic staff intent on restoring you to your former glory.

Hipocampus Resort & Spa ☺ A bumpy back road leads to this hidden retreat, a white colonial house resembling an old Spanish mission. Its two pools sit on a cliff overlooking the lake, and each of the guest rooms has a balcony with a beautiful water view. Rooms are uniquely decorated, and many have hardwood floors and colorful linens. Bathrooms are small, however, with showers only. The hotel offers a cozy fireside sitting room, as well as a small library and TV area. The restaurant serves regional dishes as well as afternoon tea, and the gracious staff makes this feel more like a B&B than a hotel. Excursions, horseback riding, and hiking trips can all be arranged at the reception desk.

Calle Brown 240, 5152 Villa Carlos Paz. 📞 **3541/421-653.** www.hipocampusresort.com.ar. 46 units. $150 double. Rates include buffet breakfast. AE, DC, MC, V. Free parking. **Amenities:** Restaurant; gym; hiking, horseback riding; hydro-massage; 2 outdoor pools (1 heated, 1 for kids); sauna; spa; tennis courts; Wi-Fi. *In room:* A/C, TV, fridge, hair dryer.

Lake Buena Vista Resort & Spa ★ ☺ On the shore of San Roque Lake, this modern resort of giant lagoon-type pools and terra-cotta walls is a great place in which to relax and soak up the sun. The apartment-style rooms are light and airy, with large balcony windows, blue-tile floors, and the occasional ceramic urn. The bedrooms are adequate, and kitchenettes are well equipped.

Enrique Zárate 83, 5152 Villa Carlos Paz. 📞 **3541/435-892.** www.lakebuenavistaresort.com. $187 double. Rates include breakfast. AE, DC, MC, V. Free parking. **Amenities:** Restaurant; poolside bar; airport transfers; babysitting; gym; heated pool; solarium; spa; Wi-Fi. *In room:* Kitchenettes.

Portal del Lago Hotel ★ The striking wood-frame lobby here leads directly out to the main pool and spacious grounds bordering the lake. The hotel forms a half-moon shape along the banks of the lake, and most of the rooms have water views. Brick walls and dark woods give you the sense of being deep in the mountains, and there are many sitting areas for relaxing. Guest rooms vary in size, although all bathrooms are small; some rooms have two levels and multiple beds to accommodate families. A warm therapeutic pool, sauna, and gym are on the top floor, and a lakeview restaurant extends along the mezzanine of the lobby. The hotel also houses a

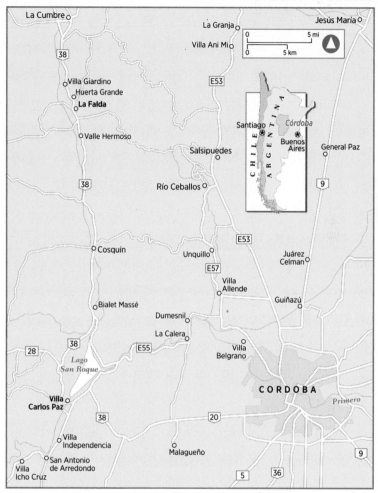

La Cumbre • La Granja • Jesús María • Villa Ani Mi • 5 mi / 5 km • Villa Giardino • Huerta Grande • **La Falda** • Valle Hermoso • Salsipuedes • Santiago • ARGENTINA • Córdoba • CHILE • Buenos Aires • General Paz • 38 • E53 • Río Ceballos • E53 • Cosquín • Unquillo • Juárez Celman • E57 • Villa Allende • Guiñazú • Bialet Massé • Dumesnil • La Calera • Villa Belgrano • 28 • 38 • E55 • Lago San Roque • **CORDOBA** • Primero • **Villa Carlos Paz** • 38 • 20 • Villa Independencia • Malagueño • San Antonio de Arredondo • Villa Icho Cruz • 5 • 36 • 9

convention center. The place can be crowded in summer months; try to make reservations in advance. The hotel's many stairs prevent access to those with disabilities.

Gobernador Alvarez, at J. L. Cabrera, 5152 Villa Carlos Paz. ✆ **3541/424-931.** Fax 3541/424-932. www. portal-del-lago.com. 110 units. $150 double. Rates include buffet breakfast. AE, DC, MC, V. Free parking. **Amenities:** Restaurant; bar; gym; 3 outdoor pools; room service; sauna; Wi-Fi. In room: A/C, TV.

Where to Eat

Villa Carlos Paz lacks gourmet restaurants, with the dining-out emphasis firmly on steakhouses (this is Argentina, after all). Still, there are plenty of good, casual eateries in the city's center. The two best *parrillas* in town are **Carilo,** Yrigoyen 44

CONDOR vantage point: PARQUE NACIONAL QUEBRADA DEL CONDORITO

The spectacular **Quebrada del Condorito** (www.quebradacondorito.com.ar) is a 800m (2,624-ft.) ravine and popular haunt for condors and their fledgling offspring learning to fly. It is the most eastern habitat in South America for this giant bird, and the area is littered with waterfalls, sierra grassland, and sloping hills. In 1995, the Quebrada and 40,000 hectares (98,900 acres) of the surrounding Pampa de Achala (a high-altitude plateau) became a national park.

The park's infrastructure is minimal, to say the least. There are three campsites, but they offer little in the way of facilities. Visitors enter the park from La Pampilla, 55km (34 miles) of stunning scenery southeast of Villa Carlos Paz. From two lookout posts, you can sometimes spy the birds bathing beneath waterfalls. The first is called *balcón norte,* and it's a 3-hour walk from the park entrance. The next vantage point is called *balcón sur,* which is another 2 hours into the park. Condors are shy birds, and sightings are not guaranteed, yet the area itself is a very special hiker's paradise. The park is home to 20 animal species unique to the area. **Nativo Viajes,** 27 de Abril 11, Córdoba (☎ **351/424-5341;** www.cordoba nativoviajes.com.ar) runs an 8-hour trek through the park. **Itati Viajes,** 27 de Abril 220, Córdoba (☎ **351/422-5020;** www. itati.com.ar), staffs English-speaking guides who conduct different kinds of tours, all involving trekking and birdwatching. One-day tours start at $50.

(☎ **3541/431-346**), and **La Volanta,** San Martín 1262 (☎ **3541/422-954**). The latter is easy to spot—look for loud green-and-yellow paint and the carriage sitting on the roof. For excellent Italian dishes, try **Il Gato Trattoria,** at Libertad and Belgrano (☎ **3541/439-500**), and **Parrilla Los Gauchos,** Bd. Sarmiento 1007 (☎ **3541/432-814**), both of which offer fish and meat dishes, too. The latter one has got a beautiful view of the lake. If Mexican is your thing, try **Oaxaca,** Uruguay 93 (☎ **3541/437-550**). **Junior B,** Av. Libertad 200 (☎ **3541/433-559;** www. juniorb.com.ar), dispenses decent pizza and pasta. Ask for *lomito de mollejas,* a sweetbreads sandwich.

Villa Carlos Paz After Dark

Many young—and even not-so-young—people come to Villa Carlos Paz from Córdoba to drink and dance, and some of the discos arrange private caravans from the city. Expect a late night out—dancing begins after 2am and continues past dawn. By far, the most famous disco is **Keop's,** R.S. Peña and Seneca (☎ **3541/433-553**), with **Zebra Restobar Disco,** Bernardo D'Elia 150 (☎ **3541/427-130**), placing second. **Terrazzo,** Av. Atlántica 400 (no phone), is a trendy disco open only in summertime. For something tamer, visit the **Punta Hidalgo** piano bar, at the corner of Uruguay and Hidalgo (☎ **3541/421-127**). **Casino Carlos Paz** is located at Liniers and Uruguay (☎ **3541/425-772**).

Carlos Paz, in summer, is famous for its theatrical cabaret acts; well-known actors from Buenos Aires transplant themselves here for the season. The best-known venues are **Teatro del Sol,** Calle Gral Paz 250 (☎ **3541/422-393**), and **Teatro Candilejas II,** Pasaje Nini Marshal (☎ **3541/422-314**).

LA FALDA ★

70km (50 miles) NW of Córdoba

An excellent base from which to explore the Punilla Valley, La Falda (literally, "lap of the mountain") lies between the Valle Hermoso (Beautiful Valley) and the Sierras Chicas. Argentines come here for rest and relaxation, not wild entertainment. Crisp, clean air; wonderful hikes; and quiet hotels are the draw. The city's main tourist site is the once-prestigious (but now decrepit) Hotel Edén, which entertained international celebrities in the early 20th century.

Essentials

GETTING THERE   Frequent buses travel from both Córdoba and Villa Carlos Paz. The most comfortable is **TranSierras** (© **3548/424-666**), costing about $5. If you are driving, you have the option of going first to Villa Carlos Paz and then to La Falda via the N38. Or you can bypass Carlos Paz by taking the new A73, which branches off from the N20 a few miles before Carlos Paz. The trip takes 2 hours from Córdoba.

VISITOR INFORMATION   The **tourist office** is inside the old train station at Av. España 50 (© **3548/423-007**). Open Monday to Saturday from 8am to 9pm, Sunday 10am to 5pm. It provides city and regional maps as well as hotel, restaurant, and tourist information.

GETTING AROUND   You can walk around the small center, but you will probably want to hire a driver, rent a car, or sign up with a tour operator to explore the Sierras Chicas (although you can always hike as well). La Falda's main road is Avenida Edén, which extends from the town center to the old Hotel Edén.

Seeing the Sights

You come here first and foremost to relax. Once that's accomplished, visit the once prestigious **Hotel Edén** (east end of Av. Edén). During the first half of the 20th century, it hosted the likes of Albert Einstein, the Duke of Savoy, two presidents of Argentina, and other members of Argentine high society. The hotel fell out of favor after World War II, because its owners had been Nazi sympathizers. Boarded up by 1960, the castlelike hotel was left to ruin. The insides have been completely gutted, but, amazingly, the entrance fountain still operates. Ninety-minute guided tours run daily between 9am and 6pm. Admission is $5. There's a bar adjacent to the ghost lobby with pictures of the grand old dame in its day. Outside the city, various adventure agencies offer horseback riding, trekking, mountain biking, hang gliding, and 4WD excursions into the Sierras Chicas. Contact **Polo Tour,** Av. Edén 444 (© **3548/426-101;** www.polotours.com.ar), for details. You might also consider taking a taxi, which is inexpensive, toward La Cumbre, where numerous handicrafts shops and stands dot the road.

Where to Stay

EXPENSIVE

Estancia Los Potreros ★★   The Begg family has been farming in this emerald pocket of Argentina for four generations. Their pastoral paradise of 2,000 hectares (4,940 acres), 600 cows, and 140 horses offers the ultimate gaucho experience with a refined, Anglo-Argentine twist. Set high in the Sierras Chicas, the gleaming, white-washed cottage buildings feature old polished stoves, clunky wooden trunks, cozy raftered ceilings, and big welcoming brass beds. What the *estancia* lacks in opulence (it is a genuine *estancia* after all), it makes up for in sparkling cleanliness, well-equipped attention to detail, and superb personal service. At least one member of the family is on hand at all times, and dinner is a heartwarming and gregarious affair in the family dining room. Boasting some of the best horses in Argentina, Los Potreros is a riders' paradise. Guests here are generally the sort who prefer to spend more time in the saddle than in the pool. The six rooms include a cute honeymooners' cottage straight out of a Hans Christian Andersen story. The *estancia*'s address is La Cumbre, but it is actually accessed from a mountain road behind the Hotel Edén in La Falda. With that said, it is much easier to get there from the eastern side, via Río Ceballos.

Casilla de Correo 4, La Cumbre. © **011/6091-2692.** www.ride-americas.com. 6 units. From $320–$400 per person. Rates are all-inclusive, including airport pickup. Minimum 3-night stay. AE, DC, MC, V. Free parking. **Amenities:** Restaurant; horseback riding; outdoor pool; Wi-Fi.

MODERATE

Hostal L'Hirondelle ★　Never mind the term *"hostal"*; in this case, it's an architectural distinction, rather than a reference to a budget traveler's dormitory. The house looks like a French chalet, surrounded by gardens and the Sierras Chicas. In a tribute to his poet son, the owner has given each individually decorated room a poet's name. On the second floor, Walt Whitman enjoys a corner view of the pool, court-yard, and nearby mountains. French prints and old bottles and spices decorate the long wood dining room, where guests enjoy half-board (breakfast and dinner) in summer months. Breakfast includes tea, croissants, fruit, cereal, homemade sweets, and fresh juice. For city folks unaccustomed to clear, starry nights, the owner has set up a telescope for celestial viewing. The staff will help you arrange outdoor activities, including hiking and horseback riding, as well as airport transfer upon request.

Av. Edén 861, 5172 La Falda. © **3548/422-825.** www.lhirondellehostal.com. 21 units. Summer $85–$94 double; $120 triple. Winter $55–$62 double; $90 triple. Summer rates include half-board; winter rates include breakfast. AE, DC, MC, V. Free parking. **Amenities:** Restaurant; babysitting; outdoor pool; TV room w/video library; Wi-Fi. *In room:* TV.

Posada Las Perdices　Córdoba province is famous for its farming tradition, and such a legacy is in full display at this charming little farmhouse lodge located in a green valley 1 hour north of Córdoba city. Goats, horses, sheep, and ducks traipse across this pastoral property, which consists of a farmhouse and four stone guest-houses located along a gurgling creek. The cottage-like accommodations are a spot-less mix of old and new with antique stoves and intermittent electricity that is powered by a water turbine (and can be temperamental in the summer months). Besides the beautiful location, the lodge's main draw is excellent homemade food made from local produce. There aren't many hotels in the world that make their own butter on-site. The amiable hosts Suzanna and Fernando go out of the way to make your stay as comfortable as possible, but be prepared to practice your Spanish as their English is limited. Posada Las Perdices may not be for everyone—the 10-mile dirt track and rustic setting makes it strictly for those with an adventurous streak who love fresh air, bracing horse rides, and, of course, farm animals. The lodge is located geo-graphically close to La Falda but best accessed via the eastern town of Rio Ceballos.

Candonga. ☏ **3543/493-999.** www.posadalasperdices.com.ar. 6 units. From $175 double. Rates include full board. No credit cards. **Amenities:** Restaurant; outdoor pool; horseback riding.

Where to Eat

La Parrilla de Raúl ★ ARGENTINE   A popular *parrilla* with a distinctive family atmosphere, Raúl's menuless system works like this: First, help yourself to the salad bar, an assortment of mixed vegetable dishes, cabbages, stuffed eggs, candied sweet potatoes, and other delights. As you finish your salad, the first meat course will land on your plate, likely a tender slice of pork with a *cerveza* sauce (yes, beer sauce). Next comes thick chorizo and a rich piece of *morcilla* (blood pudding). No stopping here— *costilla* (a beef rib) is next. Ready for more? Following the rib is *matambre,* another delicious morsel of beef. At this point, you can politely request that they stop bringing you meat, or you can wave on more. Request a large soda, and they will bring you a 1.25-liter bottle to help wash it all down. Finish your meal with a trip to the dessert bar, an enticing table of flans, fruit, creams, and the obligatory *dulce de leche.* Then go hit the gym.

Av. Buenos Aires 111. ☏ **3548/423-181.** Main courses $9–$13. No credit cards. Daily noon–3pm and 8:30pm–midnight.

LA CUMBRE ★

93km (57 miles) NW of Córdoba

La Cumbre could best be described as Little England, with its cottage-style bunga- lows, rose gardens, and rolling golf courses. The colony of Anglo-Argentines who settled here were intent on creating their own corner of "that green and pleasant land," and they have done so with considerable success. It must be one of the few towns in South America where the town plaza is quietly forgotten, and the commer- cial center is situated several blocks away. Famous for its boarding schools and retire- ment homes, this sleepy town is not for thrill seekers, unless, of course, you are into first-class paragliding. Other activities include great trekking, horseback riding, and golf.

Essentials

GETTING THERE   The bus station is on General Juan José Valle 50, in the town center. Frequent buses travel from Córdoba. **TranSierras** (☏ **351/424-3810**) oper- ates from the Córdoba bus station. The trip costs about $7 and takes around 2 hours. **El Práctico** (☏ **011/4312-9551**) and **General Urquiza** (☏ **011/4313-2771**) are two companies that come from Buenos Aires, a 12-hour trip.

If you are driving, you have the option of going first to Villa Carlos Paz and then on to La Falda via the N38. Other towns you'll pass are Huerta Grande and then Villa Giardino. This is a pleasant trip through the valley, but beware of flash floods in the summer.

VISITOR INFORMATION   The **tourist office** is inside the old train station at Av. Caraffa 300 (☏ **3548/452-966**). Open daily from 8am to 10pm, it provides city and regional maps as well as hotel, restaurant, and tourist information. A respected agency specializing in outdoor pursuits in the area is **Sendas Travel,** Calle Dumas 110, La Cumbre (☏ **3548/53-2177;** www.sendastravel.com). **Cuchi Corral**

(📞 **3548/15-570955;** www.cuchicorral.com) specializes in paragliding from the mountain cliff of the same name.

GETTING AROUND You can easily walk around the small town center but you may soon get bored. Most of La Cumbre's attractions are outside the town, usually up a dirt track, so it is advisable to rent a car or sign up with a tour operator. There is no public transport going east or west.

Seeing the Sights

La Cumbre is becoming increasingly famous for adventure sports, particularly **paragliding** ★. A beauty spot called **Cuchi Corral** ★ is a 300m (984-ft.) cliff that overlooks the Rio Pintos valley. Here you'll find a variety of amateurs and professionals hurling themselves into the air and soaring with condors. In 1999, the town hosted the World Paragliding Championship. Other sights worth seeing include **Estancia El Rosario,** 6km (3¾ miles) southeast (📞 **3548/451-257**), home of the ubiquitous *alfajores*—a *dulce de leche* biscuit sandwich popular all over Argentina, and a must-buy souvenir for visiting tourists. In the nearby village of Cruz Chica, you'll find **El Paraíso** (📞 **3548/491-596**), the home of famous Argentine writer Manuel Mujica Lainez and now a museum dedicated to this fascinating character's life. To the north of La Cumbre, near the village of Capilla del Monte, is a mountain known as **Mount Uritorco,** popular with trekkers. The mountain is also a mecca for fans of the supernatural, with a reputedly unique energy source and powerful healing properties. The area is famous for UFO sightings as well. You can investigate this phenomenon at a specially built UFO center called OVNI Center, Intendente Cabus 237, Capilla del Monte (no phone). Farther east, along a dirt track, you'll find **Parque Natural Ongamira,** a weird and wonderful moonscape of pink rock amid green rolling hills.

Where to Stay

EXPENSIVE

Dos Lunas ★★ Sheep graze on the expansive lawn like silent lawn mowers, while a giant circular swimming pool reflects the second moon in the *estancia's* title. Dos Lunas offers the best of both worlds—a lodge that affords the countryside experience without sacrificing luxury. The century-old building is genuinely pioneer-built, with Prussian blue window shutters, tin roofs, and wrought-iron lamps. Yet the interior design is pure urban, boutique chic. Giant, modern rooms have striped sheets, subtle lighting, and wicker toilette kits at the end of each king-size bed. Bathrooms are also generously sized, with showers and tubs. The dining room is a fabulous salon of red lamps, darkly polished oak furniture, and black roof rafters. The two living rooms are decked out with DirecTV, board games, an honor bar (no barman, just a book to note your liquor consumption), and a library collection that includes the diary of the original owner—an English lady who mostly complained about water problems. The tidy stables exude country glamour, and the horse treks across the 3,000-hectare (7,410-acre) property are both scenic and invigorating. A young Porteño couple named Gonzalo and Lorena runs the place with efficient attention to detail and bilingual charm. The *estancia* is situated on a country lane, a 45-minute drive north of La Cumbre.

Alto Ongamira, Todos los Santos, Ischillin. 📞 **11/5032-3410** or 15-6219-5390 (mobile). www.doslunas.com.ar. 8 units. $400 double. Rates include breakfast. AE, DC, MC, V. Free parking. **Amenities:** Restaurant; honor bar; outdoor pool; TV room; library; board games; Wi-Fi.

MODERATE

Hotel La Viña   This charming, ivy-covered, red-brick house is a good budget choice. Its leafy location is close to the town center, affording good views of the mountains. The old-style furnishings and cavernous dining room make you feel like you are on a school outing to your grandmother's. The owners, the Zampieri family, make you feel at home, right down to the homemade scones and jam. Some rooms are spacious and pleasant, while others are monastically bare. Everything is perfectly clean and respectable, and the garden pool beckons.

Caraffa 48, La Cumbre. ℂ **3548/451-388.** www.hotellavina.com.ar. 19 units. $62 double. AE, DC, MC, V. Free parking. **Amenities:** Restaurant; outdoor pool; TV room.

Los Cedros Posada ☺   A long driveway takes you up to a well-endowed mansion of red tiles and white walls, with a glorious pool out front. Family-run Los Cedros consists of three buildings, the oldest of which was built in 1929. Here you will find a well-furnished interior of bright yellow walls, floral curtains, purple sofas, and brick walls. The rooms are of a good size, with built-in wardrobes and large bathrooms (most of which have tubs). A sunroom with wicker chairs overlooks the swimming pool, and the dining room in the back has an unhindered view of the Sierra. In the basement, you will find a large activity room with Ping-Pong tables. Staff members are extremely helpful, and the chef is the most famous in La Cumbre.

Av. Argentina 837, La Cumbre. ℂ **3548/451-028.** www.posadaloscedros.com. 25 units. $95 double; $118 suite. AE, DC, MC, V. Free parking. **Amenities:** Restaurant; outdoor pool; Wi-Fi.

Where to Eat

La Cumbre has the usual variety of *parrillas*, and many specialize in kid goat, a local delicacy. **La Casona del Toboso,** Belgrano 349 (ℂ **3548/451-436**), is one such place, with a nice cottage-house feel and fresh trout on the menu.

La Fontana ★ INTERNATIONAL   La Fontana is a bright, cheerful restaurant with excellent food and service. As you wait for your order, the waitress brings a thirst-quenching aperitif of white wine and fruit juice, accompanied by delicious hors d'oeuvres of cheese and sweet corn in tiny cupcakes. The bread is so fresh, it is hot, and one variety comes with melted cheese. The menu is a refreshingly eclectic mix, including a zesty Waldorf salad, *parrilla*, homemade pasta, and seafood, including octopus and paella. While this white-walled corner restaurant might have a few too many tables, the atmosphere is very welcoming, the bathrooms immaculate, and the prices very reasonable.

Belgrano and Peperina, Villa Giardino (btw. La Falda and La Cumbre). ℂ **3548/491-455.** Main courses $15–$18. AE, MC, V. Daily noon–3:30pm and 8pm–midnight.

ALTA GRACIA ★

35km (21 miles) SW of Córdoba

Calamuchita Valley, south of Córdoba, is a booming agricultural zone dotted with large reservoirs. Alta Gracia is one of the main towns, situated in the foothills of the Sierra Chica, 35km (21 miles) south of Córdoba. It is famous for its Jesuit-built town center (p. 250), but its commercial center is not so pretty. Once a popular haunt for wealthy Porteños escaping the summer heat, it still boasts some impressive summer villas in the residential zone. The town itself is a good base for hiking, fishing, or several lazy rounds of golf.

Essentials

GETTING THERE   The **bus station** (no phone) is located at C. Paravachasca and Nieto. Every 15 minutes, from 6am to 8pm, buses arrive from Córdoba. The journey takes 1 hour and costs $2. **Sarmiento** (② **351/425-5541**) and **Sierras de Calamuchita** (② **351/422-6080**) are two companies worth investigating. The latter runs service farther south to Villa General Belgrano.

VISITOR INFORMATION   The **tourist office** is located at the clock tower, Calle Padre Vieryra and Calle Del Molino (② **3547/428-128;** www.altagracia. gov.ar). It's open daily from 8am until 9pm.

Seeing the Sights

Alta Gracia's main attraction is the Jesuit *estancia* at its center (p. 250). Although the town has attracted its fair share of the rich and famous over the years, none became quite as well known as a shy school boy with asthma known as Che. **Museo Casa de Ernesto Che Guevara ★**, Villa Nydia, Avellaneda 501 (② **3547/428-579** or 0810-555-2582; museochiguevara@altagracia.gov.ar), is a suburban home where the legendary revolutionary spent much of his childhood. There you can see some of his personal possessions and correspondence—some addressed to his old buddy-in-arms, Fidel Castro. Admission is $1.25 and it is open Monday 2 to 7pm and Tuesday to Sunday 9am to 8pm. For a good 5km (3-mile) walk, make for the Jesuit ruins of **Los Paredones,** past the poetic Park García Lorca. The walk includes a view of the **Gruta de Lourdes,** a shrine popular with pilgrims in February, and a replica of the famous French grotto. There is a large reservoir known as **Los Molinos,** 37km (23 miles) south of town. It is popular for watersports and angling for trout and the local pejerrey.

HEADING OUT OF TOWN

One of the province's biggest festivals is the Oktoberfest in **Villa General Belgrano,** 52km (32 miles) south of Alta Gracia and 88km (55 miles) from the capital. This German settlement's population was boosted by interned sailors from the Graf Spee in the war years. A quiet, leafy resort town most of the time, it comes alive the first half of every October with a beer jamboree spiced up with a generous helping of genuine German sausage. For more information, try the village **tourist office,** Av. Roca 168 (② **3546/461-215;** www.vgb.gov.ar), open daily from 8:30am to 8:30pm.

Where to Stay

During high season—in summer, July, and Easter—rooms fill up and prices jump accordingly. **Hostal Hispania,** Vélez Sarsfield 57, Alta Gracia (② **3547/426-555;** $56), is an old residence with large, comfortable rooms and a fine veranda overlooking the sierras. The Spanish owners serve delicious tapas. For something more modern and plush, try **Solares del Alto Hotel,** Bd. Pellegrini 797, Alta Gracia (② **3547/429-086;** www.gruposolares.com; $90 double, including breakfast, heated pool, gym facilities, and Internet). **El Potrerillo de Larreta,** Los Paredones, Km 3, Alta Gracia (② **3547/439-033** or 439-034; www.potrerillodelarreta.com; $172 double), is a swanky country club with beautiful wood-paneled bedrooms and a rolling green golf course. Farther south, in Villa General Belgrano, you'll find a charming Swiss-style hotel: **Berna Hotel,** Vélez Sarsfield 86 (② **3546/461-097;** www.berna hotel.com.ar; from $116 double), is an attractive, efficient hotel with a large garden and pool.

Where to Eat

Hispania, Urquiza 90, Alta Gracia (© **3547/426-772**), serves delicious paella, washed down with sangria. Highly recommended for dessert is the *crema catalana*. Another restaurant with an international menu, **Morena,** Av. Sarmiento 413, Alta Gracia (© **3547/426-365**), is in a lovely old house. **Brunnen,** Av. Roca 73, Villa General Belgrano (© **3546/461-832**), serves German fare and brews a very decent house beer. Visitors can tour the microbrewery out back. **Choperia Blumen,** Av. Roca 356, Villa General Belgrano (© **3546/462-568**), is another good source for reliable German food and draft beer.

MENDOZA, THE WINE COUNTRY & THE CENTRAL ANDES

by Christie Pashby

Here, in the land of sunshine and good wine, life is lovely. With the gorgeous, high Andes mountains forming a dramatic backdrop, and rows upon rows of Malbec vines in the foreground, Mendoza is a very pretty place, one where you'll want to linger and relax. The ultimate Mendoza moment is at a country lodge, with a copa in hand, vines at your side, and the mountains in front. Deeply connected to the land, Mendocinos, the smiling residents of this delightful city and vast province, are relaxed, creative, and so very friendly. They feel lucky to live in the "land of sol y buen vino."

Capital of the province of Mendoza, the city of Mendoza is an oasis amid an almost desertlike high plain, somewhat of a miracle, and a testament to the hard work and determination of local pioneers. If you consider that only 5% of the entire province is cultivated, and that the area receives around 15 centimeters (6 in.) of rain per year, you'll realize the achievement of the simple shade cast by the many giant sycamore trees that line the towns. Thanks to a vast network of aqueducts and dikes, which run through the rural vineyards and even through the heart of Mendoza city, grapes and olives have been harvested to international standards. The most famous grape here is Malbec; it's of French origin, but since storming to global attention in the early 2000s, it has put Argentine wine on the map.

In the past decade, wine exports have jumped 30%, helped significantly by investors and experts from Europe. Tourism has followed suit and experienced a boom throughout the late 2000s. Fortunately, it is growing from the ground up. Locals continue to live as always, but now they welcome visitors into their lives—into their homes, their family farms, and their vineyards.

There is a lot to see and do here. The first decision to be made is whether to stay in the city or out in the wine country. Downtown makes a good base for people who like nightlife, cafes, and strolling on their own.

Mendoza

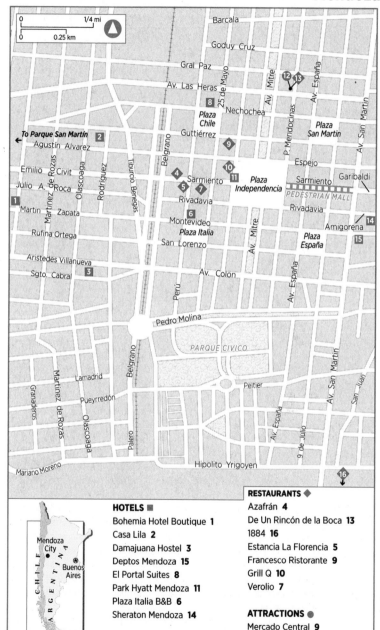

HOTELS ■
Bohemia Hotel Boutique **1**
Casa Lila **2**
Damajuana Hostel **3**
Deptos Mendoza **15**
El Portal Suites **8**
Park Hyatt Mendoza **11**
Plaza Italia B&B **6**
Sheraton Mendoza **14**

RESTAURANTS ◆
Azafrán **4**
De Un Rincón de la Boca **13**
1884 **16**
Estancia La Florencia **5**
Francesco Ristorante **9**
Grill Q **10**
Verolio **7**

ATTRACTIONS ●
Mercado Central **9**

10

MENDOZA & THE WINE COUNTRY | Introduction

265

when to visit MENDOZA

Mendoza is alive four seasons of the year. In winter (June–Aug), you can combine very quiet wine touring with great skiing at Las Leñas (see "Hitting the Slopes in Las Leñas," later in this chapter). In spring (Sept–Nov), the whole area is in bloom. Days are warm, and the air is remarkably aromatic. The hot summer months from December through February require a good sun hat and access to a pool. My personal favorite time to visit is the fall (Mar–May), when the *vendimia* wine harvesting is wrapping up, the alamo and poplar trees glow golden, and the nights are fresh.

Country inns (and there are some outstanding ones) will be better for those who want to relax and soak up as much of the wine scene as possible. Either way, after spending a few days exploring the *bodegas* (wineries) close to the city, don't miss a day of adventure in the *alta montaña*, or high mountains—rafting, horseback riding, or trekking. If you are staying in the country, take a *remise* or taxi into town for a leisurely day visiting museums and enjoying restaurants and the lovely plazas of downtown Mendoza. Blending time in the lovely city of Mendoza with time along the quiet wine routes is ideal.

You should spend at least a day exploring Mendoza's old city—visiting the plazas, and wandering about Parque General San Martín—before heading for the wine routes that wind through the most important wine-producing zones of Mendoza. Choose your own pace when touring the *bodegas;* two or three visits are possible in half a day. Five would be the absolute most doable in a full day. Make a reservation for lunch either at one of the many excellent restaurants in the wine country—or, better yet, a *bodega* itself. Some have truly outstanding restaurants (see recommendations later in this chapter). More and more wineries are now charging for tours, although if you purchase wine at the end of a tour, the entry fee is usually waived. Some are closed on Sundays. Reservations are generally required—don't count on being able to just show up at a vineyard. Another important factor is that the roads in Mendoza can be very hard to navigate, and drivers are particularly aggressive. Only the most confident should rent a car.

A journey into the magnificent mountains, however, is possible anytime and can be easily done on your own. The best circuit is Alta Montaña, which follows parts of the old Inca trail and Andes railroad through the tall Andes to the border with Chile and a lookout over Mt. Aconcagua, the tallest mountain in the world outside Asia.

Mendoza also offers a wealth of outdoor activities, ranging from Class III, IV, and V white-water rafting on the Mendoza River to horseback riding, mountain biking, and trekking in the Andes. Tour operators in Mendoza will arrange an itinerary according to your preferences, from part-day outings to multiday excursions.

Two-and-a-half hours south of Mendoza is the province's second-largest city, San Rafael. More the size of a large town, it's a laid-back, rural place that has some great outdoor activities nearby, as well as its own share of important *bodegas,* although it has little of the chic pizzazz that may appeal to certain foreigners.

Even farther south, Las Leñas is a world-class ski resort that is a winter playground of Porteños escaping the capital for a snowy retreat. Los Penitentes offers decent runs closer to Mendoza. For the bold and the brave, Mount Aconcagua provides an irresistible challenge, and at 6,960m (22,829 ft.) it towers above all other peaks in the

Introduction

MENDOZA & THE WINE COUNTRY

Western Hemisphere. With a good bit of endurance, money, and time on your hands, the mountain can be conquered.

MENDOZA ★★★

This picturesque city lies at the heart of the Cuyo, the name of the region that comprises the provinces of Mendoza, San Juan, and San Luis. It was founded in 1561 by Spanish colonialists and retains an idyllic serenity that has carried over from centuries past.

Mendoza locals may be complaining these days about too much traffic, too much development, and too much change, as their little country *pueblo* starts looking more and more like a big city, but there is still much *tranquilidad* here. It's still Argentina's loveliest, most livable, city, with a unique vibe blending cosmopolitan shopping and dining with rural country life. An artificial oasis, Mendoza receives no more than 5 days of rain per year. A scarce commodity, water is celebrated in the trickling fountains of the city's many lovely plazas, and in the shade of the dike-supported trees that line the boulevards. Give yourself time to linger in Mendoza's cafes, plazas, and many fantastic restaurants, which bustle at noon and midnight (although most are closed during the daily siesta from around 2:30–5:30pm).

Essentials

GETTING THERE Mendoza's international airport, **Francisco Gabrielli** (✆ **261/520-6000**), lies 8km (5 miles) north of town on RN 40. **Aerolíneas Argentinas** (✆ **0810/222-86527;** www.aerolineas.com.ar) offers six daily arrivals from Buenos Aires. Their new tourist-friendly route now links Mendoza with Bariloche to the south and Salta to the north on 2 weekly flights, Wednesday and Saturday. **LAN** (✆ **0810/999-9526;** www.lan.com) flies to Mendoza from both Buenos Aires (three times a day) and from Santiago, Chile, once in midmorning and once in the early evening, making a quick day trip from Santiago possible. Because Buenos Aires has both an international and a domestic airport (which are a minimum of 45 min. apart), it's both faster and easier to get to Mendoza in 1 day via Santiago, which has only one airport.

The **Terminal del Sol** (✆ **261/431-3001**), or central bus station, lies just east of central Mendoza. Buses travel to Buenos Aires (12–14 hr.; $64–$78); Córdoba (12 hr.; $42); Santiago, Chile (7 hr.; $38); Las Leñas (7 hr.; $25); and other cities

staying safe IN MENDOZA

Safety in Mendoza isn't what it used to be. The city has been the scene of some pretty intense thefts and robberies of late, and more than a few have specifically targeted the upscale inns and restaurants frequented by foreign travelers. Snatch-and-run grabs have also been reported. There is no real reason to be alarmed since few have been injured.

There is little one can do except keep only small amounts of cash on you, leave your passport at your hotel, avoid walking in the city late at night, and keep an eye out for pickpockets. Most wineries and hotels now have very strict security measures mainly because the local police aren't effective. Ask when you book.

throughout the region. **Chevallier** (📞 **261/431-0235;** www.nuevachevallier.com.
ar), **Expreso Uspallata** (📞 **261/421-3309;** www.turismouspallata.com), and
Andesmar (📞 **261/431-0585;** www.andesmar.com) are the main bus companies.
Note: Buses from Buenos Aires and elsewhere in Argentina generally arrive in the
early morning—book an early check-in with your hotel to avoid being stranded!

The route from Buenos Aires is a long (10 hr.) but easy drive on either the RN 7
or the RN 8. Mendoza is more easily reached by car from Santiago, Chile, along the
RN 7, although the 250km (155-mile) trek through the Andes can be treacherous in
winter, when chains are required. Give yourself 4 to 6 hours to make the journey from
Santiago.

VISITOR INFORMATION Mendoza's **Subsecretaría Provincial de Turismo,** on Av. San Martín 1143 (📞 **261/420-2800;** www.turismo.mendoza.gov.ar), is
open daily from 9am to 9pm. The helpful staff will provide you with tourist information on the entire province, including maps of the wine roads and regional driving
circuits. **Municipal tourist offices,** called Centros de Información, are located at
Garibaldi near San Martín (📞 **261/420-1333;** daily 9am–9pm), 9 de Julio 500
(📞 **261/429-5185;** Mon–Fri 9am–1:30pm), and Las Heras 340 (📞 **261/429-
6298;** Mon–Fri 9am–1:30pm and 4–8pm). They provide city maps, hotel information, and brochures of tourist activities. You will find small visitor-information booths
at the airport and bus station as well. Information and permits for Aconcagua Provincial Park are available at the **Centro de Informes del Parques,** in Mendoza's
Parque San Martín (📞 **261/420-5052**). The office is only open during the climbing
season, from December through March. During the rest of the year, you must contact
the **Subsecretaría Provincial de Recursos Naturales** (📞 **261/425-2090**).
Permits to climb the summit cost $450, and you must go in person to obtain one. In
addition to the Subsecretaría Provincial de Turismo's website mentioned above, other
useful tourism sites include www.aconcagua.mendoza.gov.ar, www.welcome
argentina.com/mendoza, and www.mendoza.com.ar.

GETTING AROUND You can easily explore central Mendoza on foot, although
you will want to hire a driver or rent a car to visit the wine roads and tour the mountains. Taxis and *remises* (private, unmetered taxis) are inexpensive: Drivers cost no
more than $20 per hour. Travelers should be wary of walking alone both in the heart
of downtown and outside the main center of town, especially at night. Traditionally
Mendoza is one of Argentina's safest cities, but it has experienced an increase in
crime, part of its growing pains. Ask your hotel to call a *remise* or radio-taxi, rather
than flagging down a taxi on your own. For a *remise,* try **Remises Prestige**
(📞 **261/440-1440**) or **Brisas** (📞 **261/437-8080**). For a taxi, call **Radiotaxi**
(📞 **261/430-3300**).

If you do rent a car, parking is easy and inexpensive inside the city, with paid parking meters and private lots (called *playas*) clearly marked. Easy to navigate, the city
spreads out in a clear grid pattern around Plaza Independencia. Avenida San Martín
is the city's main thoroughfare, Paseo Sarmiento is the pedestrian walking street that
extends from Plaza Independencia to Avenida San Martín, and Avenida Emilio Civit
is the posh residential avenue leading to the entrance of Parque San Martín. Outside
the city, road signs are sometimes missing or misleading, and you should pay careful
attention to road maps. The main highways are Hwy. 40, which runs north-south and
will take you to Maipú and Luján de Cuyo; and Hwy. 7, which runs east-west and
will take you to the Alta Montaña Route.

Both **Budget** (© **261/425-3114;** www.budget.com) and **Hertz Annie Millet** (© **261/448-2327;** www.hertz.com) rent cars at Mendoza's airport. Expect to pay about $65 per day for a compact car with insurance and 200km (124 miles) included. If you reserve the car before arriving in Argentina, you can usually negotiate a similar rate, but with unlimited mileage. **AutoMendoza** ★ (© **261/420-0022;** www. automendoza.com), a locally run company, has flexible rates, and will drop a car off wherever you need it. Rates start at $60 per day. You'll get a better deal if you pay in cash.

Mendoza's public bus system is one of the best in the country. Regular buses depart from various stops in town to the outlying wine areas. El Troli, a trolley that follows the main roads in the city, is fun and cheap, at 80¢ per ride. It's an easy way to get up to Parque San Martín and back.

[FastFACTS] MENDOZA

Area Code The area code for the city is **261.** The country code for Argentina is **54.**

ATMs & Currency Exchange ATMs are ubiquitous in Mendoza; currency-exchange houses, however, are harder to find. Two reliable exchange houses, both at the corner of San Martín and Catamarca, are **Magnitur** (© **261/438-0396**) and **Cambio Santiago** (© **261/420-0207**). They are open Monday through Friday from 8:30am to 1pm and from 5 to 8:30pm, and Saturday from 9:30am to 1pm. Major banks, with

ATMs that have Cirrus and PLUS access, are located around the Plaza San Martín and along Avenida Sarmiento, including **Citibank,** Av. Sarmiento 20 (© **261/449-6519**).

Emergency For an **ambulance,** dial © **107** or 261/424-8000; for **police,** dial © **101** or 261/429-4444; in case of **fire,** dial © **100.**

Hospital Hospital Central (© **261/420-0600**) is near the bus station at Salta and Alem.

Internet Access Internet access in most places costs a meager 2.5 pesos (60¢) per hour. A number

of cybercafes run along Avenida Sarmiento; try **WH Webhouse,** Sarmiento 219 (© **261/423-3398**), open daily from 8:30am to 1am. **Telefónica** and **Telecentro** offices, located all over town, also offer Internet use.

Pharmacy Farmacia del Puente, Av. Las Heras 201 (© **261/423-8800**), operates 24 hours.

Post Office The main post office, **Correo Argentino** (© **261/429-0848**), located at the corner of Avenida San Martín and Colón, is open weekdays from 8am to 8pm.

Where to Stay

Mendoza has many new hotels opening, from new five-star chains, such as Sheraton and Diplomatico, to apart-hotels. For those wanting to stay longer than a few nights, your best bet will be out of town in Chacras de Coria (see later in this chapter). I recommend spending a few nights in town and then staying at a rural inn amid the vineyards for a change of pace (see "Touring the Wineries," later in this chapter). More and more *bodegas* are opening up guesthouses, where relaxation and wine are the top draws. Prices quoted are for high season, which in Mendoza is November through March and July. Hotel rates are often discounted 15% to 20% in the off season. Prices listed below do not include the 21% tax.

VERY EXPENSIVE

Park Hyatt Mendoza ★★   Peering majestically over the Plaza de la Independencia, the Park Hyatt is in the restored 19th-century Plaza Hotel and includes a modern seven-story tower of guest rooms out back. It's still, without a doubt, the premier place to stay in town. Sweeping columns of granite and stone showcase the lobby, and an impressive collection of Mendocino art pays tribute to local culture. There's a warm, inviting pool and a casual wine bar in the interior outdoor patio. Guest rooms, in general, are spacious and contemporary, and the huge white-marble bathrooms are the real stars. The spa is only adequate, but it incorporates Mendocino wines in a variety of treatments. A well-equipped fitness room, Jacuzzi, sauna, and steam bath are here, too. Serving as a cultural heart of Mendoza, the hotel hosts frequent events, ranging from jazz and music shows to wine fairs and corporate conferences. Next door, the Regency Casino is Mendoza's nod to Las Vegas. Be sure to check the hotel website for Internet-only rates with a 10% discount. Request a nonsmoking room if that's your preference.

Chile 1124 (Sarmiento and Espejo), 5500 Mendoza. ✆ **261/441-1234.** Fax 261/441-1235. www.mendoza. park.hyatt.com. 186 units. From $215 double; from $275 suite. AE, DC, MC, V. **Amenities:** Restaurant; wine bar; babysitting; concierge; health club; Jacuzzi; heated outdoor pool; room service; sauna; spa; steam bath; nonsmoking rooms. *In room:* A/C, TV, hair dryer, minibar.

Sheraton Mendoza   This high-rise hotel, which opened in 2008, is the tallest building in the city. Inside, it's a straight-up five-star convention center and hotel, with nary a nod to the fabulous surroundings or the wine/food vibe so important to Mendoza. Still, rooms are very comfortable, as to be expected from a Sheraton. And the rooftop lounge has unbeatable views of the city, not to mention a great wine list. There's also a casino attached. Be sure to request a mountain view, even if they won't guarantee it (and it's worth double-checking at check-in). It's best for business travelers and bigger groups. For a real feel of life in Mendoza, choose another option.

Primitivo de la Reta 989 (at the corner of Amigorena), 5500 Mendoza. ✆ **261/441-5500.** www. sheraton.com/mendoza. 180 units. AE, DC, MC, V. $170 standard double; $200 club-level double; from $300 suites. **Amenities:** Restaurant; lounge; babysitting; concierge; fitness center; heated indoor pool; room service. *In room:* A/C, TV, hair dryer, minibar.

EXPENSIVE

El Portal Suites ☺   These comfortable suites have a clean and modern style. They can sleep from two to five people in a variety of bed setups and offer a sense of freedom to travelers who want to make themselves at home. They're an especially good option for families. The staff is friendly and helpful, and will deliver local newspapers to your door each morning. Ask for one of the Grand Suites overlooking the Plaza de Chile. These have Jacuzzis, a large patio, and room for up to five people. Bathrooms are large, while kitchenettes range in size. Upstairs, a terrace with an outdoor Jacuzzi offers glorious views, as well as a small gym and a deck for relaxing.

Necochea 661 (Peru and 25 de Mayo), 5500 Mendoza. ✆/fax **261/438-2038.** www.elportalsuites.com. ar. 26 units. AE, DC, MC, V. $107 double; $145 triple; $190 grand suite (sleeps 4–5). Rates include breakfast and parking. **Amenities:** Restaurant; exercise room; outdoor Jacuzzi; room service. *In room:* A/C, TV, hair dryer, high-speed Internet, kitchenette.

MODERATE

Bohemia Hotel Boutique   There's just enough funkiness and fabulousness to this B&B to take it out of the hostel category and into the boutique hotel one. It's in the quiet and upscale La Quinta neighborhood between downtown and the Parque

If you're visiting Mendoza and want to sample a variety of wines from as many wineries as possible, then take a flight! A flight of wines, that is. The **Vines of Mendoza**, Espejo 567 (📞 **261/438-1031;** www.vinesofmendoza.com), was the first collective tasting room in the region. Led by charming and bilingual wine experts, tastings include daily samples of some of Argentina's finest—and hardest to find—boutique wines. It's open Monday to Saturday 3 to 10pm. On Wednesday nights from October through April (7–9pm; $10), a local winemaker presents his best *vino,* with a bilingual guided tasting and a chance to meet some of the best in the business. A "blending lab" teaches visitors the art of winemaking (by reservation only). The indoor terrace is cozy. They've also opened the Vines Wine Bar & Vinoteca inside the Park Hyatt, where more than 100 of the best local wines are available by the glass. It's also open Monday through Saturday from 3 to 10pm. These are both great places to meet and mingle with expats, other travelers, and local wine lovers.

San Martín. Rooms are small, and decorated in an Art Nouveau style. The quietest and most spacious room is next to the pool. Staff is helpful, friendly, and will even cook you dinner upon request! Expect a 10% surcharge for paying with a credit card.

Granaderos 954 (at Julio A Roca and Martin Zapata), 5500 Mendoza. 📞 **261/423-0575.** www.bohemiahotelboutique.com. 9 units. $85 double; $100 triple. Rates include breakfast. MC, V. **Amenities:** Concierge; lounge; pool. *In room:* A/C, hair dryer, Wi-Fi.

Casa Lila ★★ 🎁 This small guesthouse, rich with warmth and style, is owned by a friendly Mendocina with a wealth of experience working in the area's top hotels. It's close enough to downtown that you can walk (or use one of their bikes). Each room is large and spacious with a private bathroom; the inn's shared large living room has the only TV. This is my choice for the best B&B–style inn in central Mendoza.

Avellaneda 262, 5500 Mendoza. 📞 **261/429-6349.** www.casalila.com.ar. 4 units. $100 double. Rates include breakfast. MC, V. **Amenities:** Free use of bikes; concierge; garden. *In room:* A/C, Wi-Fi.

Deptos Mendoza 🎁 This sleek building of steel and brick offers plenty of great value. ("Depto" is short for *departamento,* which is Spanish for "apartment.") Rent a funky studio and slip into a hip and urban way of life; it seems that easy here. On the top floor of this downtown building is the reception area, which doubles as a lively art gallery. The apartments are decorated with local art, with a focus on function and lighting. Ceramic tiles, aluminum, concrete, and wood dominate the look. Bathrooms are quite small, with showers only. Apartment no. 9 is the largest, with a big, sunny terrace, but the street below is quite noisy at night. If you're coming with a group of friends and you love design, this is a great choice.

Leandro N. Alem 41, 5500 Mendoza. 📞 **261/429-9222.** www.deptosmendoza.com.ar. 12 units. $65–$220 apt. No credit cards. Parking nearby $12. *In room:* A/C, TV, kitchenette, Wi-Fi.

INEXPENSIVE

Damajuana Hostel 🏄 Like a five-star resort at rock-bottom prices, this hostel is located in the heart of the happening Arístides district, in a renovated old family home. It has a huge pool, garden, and barbecue in the backyard, friendly staff and information desk, and a funky bar. It's popular with young travelers and backpackers,

10

MENDOZA & THE WINE COUNTRY | Mendoza

and there's always something going on here. Quiet, peaceful sleeps are not guaranteed! Private double rooms are also available for guests who don't feel up to sharing.

Aristides Villanueva 282 (at Olascoaga and Rodríguez), 5500 Mendoza. ✆ **261/425-5858.** www.damajuanahostel.com.ar. 8 units, all with shared bathrooms. $18 per person in dorm; $50 double. Rates include buffet breakfast. No credit cards. **Amenities:** Bar; Internet; outdoor pool.

Plaza Italia B&B This tiny spot inside a traditional Mendoza family's home has been getting rave reviews for its warm hospitality. The owners love to chat with foreigners. All rooms have air-conditioning and private bathrooms, although one room's bathroom is not en suite. The room inside a renovated garage is the most modern, although it fronts on a busy street. Still, the location is superb, the service very sociable, and the price remains a bargain.

Montevidea 685 (at Peru and 25 de Mayo), 5500 Mendoza. ✆ **261/423-4219.** www.plazaitalia.net. 5 units. $98 double. Rates include breakfast. No credit cards. Free parking. **Amenities:** Concierge; luggage storage; Wi-Fi. *In room:* A/C.

Where to Eat

Mendoza is Argentina's top destination for food lovers. Restaurants here are known around the world, and the food—fresh, local, creative, and very tasty—will certainly be a highlight of your trip. As in the rest of Argentina, Mendocinos dine late. Breakfasts of coffee and pastries are served from around 7:30 to 10:30am. Lunch is generally a leisurely meal, running from 1 to 3pm. Restaurants don't usually open for dinner until 8:30pm, and they don't get busy until 10pm. How can you survive? If you must dine before 9pm, stick to hotel-lobby restaurants, which usually open earlier. Or, do as the locals do: Indulge in an afternoon siesta and then satiate your 6pm hunger with a coffee and snack at one of the city's many lovely outdoor cafes. I highly recommend that you soak up the atmosphere at a Mendoza cafe. There are dozens of cafes with outdoor patios along the Sarmiento Peatonal pedestrian street, where the people-watching is world-class. Don't miss the pastries at **DunKen,** Sarmiento 250 (✆ **261/423-6668**). At Arístides Villanueva 209, try **La Dulcería de la Abuela** (✆ **261/423-5885**) for delicious sweets. For something funky, **Kato Café** ★, Emilio Civit 556 (✆ **261/425-7000**), is artsy and hip. And for the classically elegant Mendocino cafe, nothing comes close to **Vía Civit** ★, Emilio Civit 277 (✆ **261/429-8529**). That can be followed by a stroll through the plazas and maybe a stop at a wine bar. Come 9:30 or 10pm, you'll be ready to head out for dinner.

Even if you are staying in the center of town, make at least one trip out to a restaurant in the suburb of Godoy Cruz or in the wine areas (see "Touring the Wineries," later in this chapter), where some of the best cuisine is to be had at restaurants such as **La Bourgogne** (p. 286) and **Terruños** (p. 289).

EXPENSIVE

1884 ★★★ INTERNATIONAL Some people come to Mendoza just to eat at celebrity chef/philosopher/food guru Francis Mallmann's restaurant, inside the Romanesque Bodega Escorihuela. With fine Argentine meats and fresh local produce, his carefully presented cuisine combines his Patagonian roots with his French culinary training. Local go-tos, such as *lechón* (young pork) and *chivito* (baby goat), are classics, and the huge outdoor wooden stove produces an incredible salted chicken. This is simple food prepared in a rustic, stripped-down style that somehow manages to maintain the poetic flare typical for Mallmann. Dishes are prepared with matching local wine selections, with Malbec and Syrah topping the list. In the

Mendocinos love ice cream, and they have some of the best in a country passionate for the stuff. There are *heladerías* on most every street. The best in town is **Helados Ferruccio Soppelsa** (🕿 **261/422-9000**), run by a family of immigrants from the Italian Dolomites. The classics are *dulce de leche,* tiramisu, and strawberry and cream. And check out the vino-inspired flavors such as pineapple with Voignier, vanilla with Malbec, and peach with Syrah. They have more than a dozen locations in the Mendoza area, but it's fun to join the local families who gather in the evening at the busy shop on the corner of Belgrano and Sarmiento/Civit. There's also one on the northwest corner of the Plaza Independencia, another at the Palmares Mall, and a new one in Chacras de Coria's main square. All shops open at 10am and are scooping until 12:30am in winter, until 1:30am in summertime.

summer, request a coveted garden table. For dessert, the *chocolate fanático* will blow your hat off. Compared to something similar in New York or London, say, this is world-class dining at a true bargain.

Belgrano 1188, Godoy Cruz (at Presidente Alvear). 🕿 **261/424-2698.** www.1884restaurante.com.ar. Reservations highly recommended. Main courses $22–$37. AE, MC, V. Daily 8:30pm–midnight.

Francesco Ristorante ★ ITALIAN   Mendoza is populated by Italians and has many fine Italian restaurants, but Francesco is the most elegant and refined. In the kitchen, María Theresa oversees a menu that has impressed for decades. The meat and homemade pasta dishes are equally excellent. The option of combining three stuffed pastas lets you try some of the highlights. Don't miss the tiramisu for dessert. Service is seriously professional here, including a doting sommelier. The outdoor garden is romantic and lovely on a summer's evening.

Chile 1268 (at Espejo and Guttiérez), Mendoza. 🕿 **261/425-3912.** www.francescoristorante.com.ar. Reservations recommended. Main courses $12–$22. AE, MC, V. Daily 7:30pm–12:30am.

Grill Q ★ PARRILLA   At last, a sophisticated and upscale *parrilla* in downtown Mendoza that showcases the finest of traditional Argentine cuisine. With a super location inside the Park Hyatt hotel, Grill Q has a purely regional menu, from classic cuts of beef (tenderloin, rib-eye, skirt, flank, or rump steaks) to local specialties such as *locro* stew and empanadas. Start with a *matambre* beef roll, then choose a cut of beef, pick a side dish (simple salad or grilled vegetables), and get your knife ready. It's a crisp, bright room, with wooden ceilings and chairs, and a patio that's in the hotel's outdoor atrium. Definitely upscale. Next door is the snazzy Vines Wine Bar & Vinoteca, meaning the wine list at Q is one of the best in the country.

Park Hyatt Hotel, Chile 112 (at Sarmiento and Espejo). 🕿 **261/441-1234.** Reservations recommended. Main courses $14–$22. AE, DC, MC, V. Daily 12:30–3:30pm and 8:30pm–midnight.

MODERATE

Azafrán ★★ 🍴 INTERNATIONAL   This charming restaurant, named after the highly prized and rare saffron spice, is set behind an attractively decorated all-wood wine store/cellar. Needless to say, wines are big here, and they have more than 450 different labels for you to choose from. Before you peruse the menu, step into the cellar to discuss your tastes with the friendly on-site sommelier, who'll encourage you to match your food to your wine (not the other way around). Regardless, the food is imaginative, fresh, relaxed, and eclectic. You may start with the house specialty—a platter of smoked meats and cheeses. For entrees, the rabbit ravioli in champagne sauce is delicate and unusual, and the vegetables and tofu baked in a puff pastry will please any vegetarian. Even the steak here is served with a twist—in this case, with sweet potato puréed in a light cream sauce. Given how busy this place almost always is, the service is convivial, and the wood tables and vintage checkered floors give you a sense of dining in an old farmhouse. In warm months, there are a few lovely tables on the sidewalk for alfresco dining.

Sarmiento 765 (at Belgrano and Perú). ✆ **261/429-4200.** Reservations recommended. Main courses $11–$15. AE, MC, V. Mon–Sat 12:30–2:30pm and 8pm–1am.

INEXPENSIVE

De Un Rincón de la Boca ★ 🍴 PIZZA After digging hard to find the best pizza in Mendoza, the locals point in unison to this joint on Las Heras, about a dozen blocks east of Plaza Independencia. With decades of proven consistency, it's named in honor of a certain blue-and-yellow iconic *fútbol* team and continues to be a great place to watch a soccer match with real fans on the TV screens. The crust is thick and topped with *clásico* toppings like four cheeses, garlic, ham, and fresh tomatoes. It's lively and cheap—plus there's no corkage fee, so pick up a bottle of something interesting at the nearby supermarket and avoid their limited wine list. They also have a second location inside the Mercado Central and a menu that includes local specialties like *milanesas* (breaded veal cutlets). Expect to wait in line for a table during peak hours of 9 to 11pm.

Las Heras 483. ✆ **261/425-1489.** Pizza $4–$8. AE, MC, V. Daily 8pm–2am.

Estancia La Florencia 🍴 ARGENTINE This casual family eatery pays homage to the legendary gaucho, and its two levels mimic a traditional *estancia*. Ask one of the waiters, not one of whom is under 50, for a recommended plate, and he will likely tell you, *"Una comida sin carne no es comida"* (a meal without meat isn't a meal). So choose one of the many varieties of steaks, the *lomo* being the most tender; or order a half-grilled chicken served with a lemon slice. Just remember that a plate of meat is a plate of meat, uncorrupted by vegetables or anything but potatoes (usually fries). Everything else must be ordered a la carte. Food is served promptly and without fanfare.

Sarmiento 698 and Perú. ✆ **261/429-3008.** Main courses $10–$18. AE, MC, V. Mon–Wed noon–5pm and 8pm–2am; Thurs–Sun noon–2am.

Verolio ★ ARGENTINE Mendoza's bounties aren't limited to wine and sunshine. Usually, next to the vines are olive trees, and so some of the finest olive oils in the world are made here as well. This restaurant and gourmet shop downtown is a celebration of olive oil. Founded by a passionate local, you'll want to come by either for a fresh breakfast of homemade pastries, or better yet, for a lunch combining cold (fresh salads and locally sourced cold cuts) and warm plates (traditional pastas and daily quiches) paired with olive oils. You'll likely be surprised by just how much there is to learn and love about olives! Another option is to swing by for pre-dinner tapas, which involves a three-step olive oil tasting, snacks, and a glass of wine for $10. Coming here is sensual experience that's really all about sampling and discovery. Two-hour olive oil appreciation classes are also offered.

Sarmiento 720, Mendoza. ✆ **261/425-5600.** www.verolio.com.ar. Breakfast $4–$6; lunch and dinners $6–$12. AE, MC, V. Tues–Sun 11am–midnight.

Seeing the Sights

Mercado Central ★   If you've come to Mendoza to explore food and wine, don't miss the place where locals shop for it. El Mercado Central, the central market, has been in the same location on busy Las Heras street for 120 years and has plenty of atmosphere and lively characters. Stalls offer up fresh produce, and the butchers are the real deal. It's a great place for people-watching. You can also grab quick, cheap snacks such as empanadas, pizzas, and sandwiches, and the ingredients for a great picnic.

Corner of Av. Las Heras and Patricias Mendocinas. No phone. Free admission. Mon-Sat 8am-1pm and 4-7pm.

Museo Fundacional ★★   This museum, 3km (1¾ miles) from downtown, displays what remains of the old city, which was ravaged by an 1861 earthquake. Chronicling the early history of Mendoza, the museum begins by looking at the culture of the indigenous Huarpes and continues with an examination of the city's development through Spanish colonization to independence. An underground chamber holds the ruins of the aqueduct and fountain that once provided Mendoza's water supply. Near the museum, the **Ruinas de San Francisco** represent a Jesuit church and school that were used until the Jesuits were expelled from the continent in 1767 and later occupied by the Franciscan Order.

Videla Castillo, btw. Beltrán and Alberdi. ℂ **261/425-6927.** Admission 75¢. Tues-Sat 8am-8pm; Sun 3-8pm.

Museo Histórico General San Martín ★   Adjacent to the "Alameda," a beautiful promenade under white poplars, the San Martín Library and Museum stands in the spot where General San Martín—the legendary liberator who freed Argentina, Chile, and Peru from Spain—had hoped to make his home. The museum's small collection of artifacts pays homage to Argentina's beloved hero, who prepared his liberation campaigns from Mendoza.

Remedios Escalada de San Martín 1843. ℂ **261/428-7947.** Admission 75¢. Mon-Fri 9:30am-5:30pm; Sat 9:30am-1:30pm.

Parque General San Martín ★★★   Almost as big as the city itself, this wonderful park, designed in 1896 by Carlos Thays (who also designed the Palermo parks in Buenos Aires), extends over 350 hectares (865 acres) with 17km (11 miles) of idyllic pathways and 300 species of plants and trees. A tourist office, near the park's main entrance, provides information on all park activities, which include walking, jogging, bicycling, boating, horseback riding (outside the park's perimeters), and hang gliding. The stunning entrance gates were originally made for the Turkish Sultan Hamid II but ended up as a gift to Mendoza from England. Don't miss the rose garden, the Islas Malvinas soccer stadium (which was built for the 1978 soccer World Cup), or the hustle and bustle at the Club de Regattas. There's even a golf course (see below). The best hike leads to the top of Cerro de la Gloria, which, at 960m (3,149 ft.) above sea level, offers a panoramic view of the city and surrounding valley, as well as a bronze monument to the men who liberated Argentina, Chile, and Peru. You can hang glide from the top of the other hill, Cerro Arco.

Main entrance at Av. Emilio Civit and Bologne sur Mer. Free admission. Daily 24 hr.

Plaza Independencia ★★   The plaza marks the city center, a beautiful square with pergolas, fountains, frequent artisan fairs, and cultural events. Following the

1861 earthquake, the new city was rebuilt around this area. From Tuesday through Sunday, an extensive craft fair gets going about 4pm. On weekend evenings free live concerts and puppet shows take place here. Four additional plazas—San Martín, Chile, Italia, and España—are located 2 blocks off each corner of Independence Square. Each has its own charms, and they're all worth getting to know. Surrounding the square you will find the Julio Quintanilla Theater, the National School, the Independencia Theater, the Provincial Legislature, the Park Hyatt Hotel, and the small Modern Art Museum. During the annual Vendimia Wine Harvest Festival, all major events are staged here.

Squared in by Patricias Mendocinas, Espejo, Chile, and Rivadavia, and intersected by Av. Mitre y Sarmiento. Modern Art Museum: Underground level of plaza. © **261/425-7279.** Free admission. Mon-Sat 9am–1pm and 4–9pm; Sun 5–9pm.

TOUR OPERATORS & OUTDOOR ACTIVITIES
Turismo Uspallata, Las Heras 699 (© **261/438-1092;** www.turismouspallata.com), runs trips to rural *estancias* and sells bus transfers to all the surrounding areas, including San Rafael and Valle de Uco.

Art lovers can spend the day with local art guide **Cecilia Romera** (© **261/15-541-88800;** www.mendozaarttours.com.ar), who has an insider's access to the top galleries, workshops, studios, and unique exhibits. It's a chance to meet artists face to face, and to explore a blossoming visual arts culture. Customized tours run between $40 and $80, depending on length.

GOLF Three golf courses are located in the Mendoza area and a few more are in the outskirts. The **Club de Campo,** considered the best, has great views of the Andes and opens to the public from Tuesday through Friday. Guest fees are $60 for weekdays, $100 on weekends for 18 holes. **Club Andino** is a course in the middle of the Parque San Martín. Green fees are $60 for foreigners. The club is open daily 8am to 8pm.

HIKING Serious hikers will want to head into the hills with a private local mountain guide like **Pedro Rossell** from **Discover the Andes Expeditions** (© **261/424-5142;** www.discovertheandes.com). Two-hour treks offered by **Argentina Rafting Expediciones** (see "White-Water Rafting," below) extend from Potrerillos to the waterfall at la Quebrada del Salto, where rappelling is possible. The 2-hour trek costs $30, including transfer from Mendoza, which adds another 2 to 3 hours to the outing. A full-day hike, with transfer and lunch, is $63. Another local agency, **Cordón del Plata** (© **261/423-7423;** www.cordondelplata.com), has a lovely *estancia* near Potrerillos where they run great hiking and horseback riding outings.

HORSEBACK RIDING For those looking to release their inner gaucho, **Cabalgata Mendoza** (© **261/15-536-2033** [mobile]; www.cabalgatamendoza.com.ar) specializes in trips from 2 hours to a 12-day crossing of the Andes. **La Guatana** (© **261/15-668-6801;** www.criolloslaguatana.com.ar) leads rides out of the wine country on beautiful horses.

MOUNTAIN BIKING In February, cyclists from around the world participate in **La Vuelta Ciclista de Mendoza,** a mini Andean Tour de France, around Mendoza province. **Argentina Rafting Expediciones** (see "White-Water Rafting," below) runs 2-hour mountain-bike adventures in the rugged Potrerillos area for $32 and full-day rides for $48.

SKIING Perhaps the best place to ski, not just in Argentina but also in South America, is **Las Leñas** (see "Hitting the Slopes in Las Leñas," later in this chapter). Closer to Mendoza, the small resort of **Los Penitentes** (see "The Alta Montaña Driving Circuit," later in this chapter) offers 23 downhill slopes as well as cross-country skiing. **Portillo** is a much larger and better-equipped ski resort just on the other side of the Chilean border. Eighty kilometers (50 miles) south, **Vallecitos** is the smallest and closest ski resort to Mendoza, but it can be difficult to reach in heavy snow conditions. Obtain information on the province's ski areas from Mendoza's **Subsecretaría Provincial de Turismo** (see "Essentials," earlier in this chapter).

WHITE-WATER RAFTING ★ Mendoza affords some of the best white-water rafting in Argentina. During the summer months, when the snow melts in the Andes and fills the Mendoza River, rafters enjoy up to Class IV and V rapids. Rafting is possible year-round, but the river is colder and calmer in winter months. Potrerillos, 53km (33 miles) west of Mendoza, has two professional tour operators offering half-day, whole-day, and 2-day trips on the Mendoza River, including direct transfers from Mendoza. These are **Argentina Rafting Expediciones,** Primitivo de la Reta 992, Office 4 (✆ **261/429-6325**), and **Ríos Andinos,** RN 7, Km64, 5549 Potrerillos (✆ **261/431-6074**). Be sure to bring an extra pair of clothes and a towel because you are guaranteed to get soaked. Children 11 and under are not allowed to raft. Argentina Rafting has a small restaurant and bar where you can eat and defrost after soaking in the river. Rafting starts at $40 for 1 hour on the river, and both agencies also offer kayaking ($85 for a full-day kayaking course), horseback riding, trekking, and mountain biking. Farther south in San Rafael (see "San Rafael," later in this chapter), there is Class II/III rafting on the Atuel River and perhaps the most extreme rafting in all of Argentina on the wild Río Diamante.

Shopping

On Friday, Saturday, and Sunday, an outdoor **handicrafts market** takes place during the day on Plaza Independencia, as do smaller fairs in Plaza España and along Calle Mitre. Thursday through Saturday, don't miss the excellent outdoor **antiques market** held in Plaza Pellegrini. Regional shops selling handicrafts, leather goods, gaucho paraphernalia, and *mate* tea gourds line Avenida Las Heras. Two of the best are **Las Viñas,** Av. Las Heras 399 (✆ 261/425-1520), and **Los Andes,** Av. Las Heras 445 (✆ 261/425-6688). A classier version of the Argentine souvenir shop is **Raíces,** España 1092 (✆ 261/425-4118). For high-quality leather, visit **Alain de France,** Andrade 101 (✆ 261/428-5065), or **CuerPiel,** Rioja 601 (✆ 261/423-7405). More mainstream upscale chain stores line Avenida Rivadavia, and Calle Arístides Villanueva is home to expensive fashion boutiques. The city's best shopping mall is **Palmares Open Mall,** on Ruta Panamericana 2650 in Godoy Cruz (✆ 261/413-9100). Most shops close from 1 to 5pm each day for siesta. You can also buy Mendocine wines at many shops. The least expensive cost a few dollars a bottle, and premiums go for $25 to $80. Some of the best wine boutiques in town include **Terra Viva,** Espejo 415 (✆ 261/420-4810), the stunning **Winery** ★, Calle Chile 898 (✆ 261/420-2840), and **Sol y Vino,** Sarmiento 664 (✆ 261/425-6005).

Mendoza After Dark

Mendoza nightlife is substantially more subdued than Buenos Aires or Córdoba after hours, but a fair selection of bars and nightclubs will capture the attention of night owls. Thursday through Sunday are the biggest nights, when people get started

TAKING wine HOME

Argentine wines are becoming more and more popular in North America and Europe, but you won't find many of the best vintages at home yet. Here are some tips for bringing a few bottles home with you.

○ Although Customs rules depend on your home country, in general you can take as many bottles back as you can carry, provided they are for personal use. Legally, you are usually allowed to bring three bottles duty-free, but if you bring more (say, up to six), just declare them at Customs. If the charge isn't waived completely, it's usually small, based either on the alcohol-per-liter ratio or on the price of the bottle. More than six bottles and you're likely to be paying a visit to Customs officers, who will tax you.

○ Exporting more than a dozen bottles is more complicated. You should discuss the logistics thoroughly with authorities in your country before your trip.

○ Due to recent changes in airline security, you need to limit the amount of liquid you take with you as a carry-on. Therefore, I recommend you put the wine bottles in your checked luggage, keeping weight limits in mind. Pack them well! You can buy wine bags and Styrofoam spacers from wine stores in Mendoza. Try **Terra Viva,** San Martín 107 (☎ **261/425-4555**). They run about $15 each. Many *bodegas* will also help you package special bottles for international travel, and they can help arrange for larger purchases as well. The best option is to buy special boxes with foam hollows for 6 or 12 bottles. These boxes come with handles for comfortable traveling.

○ Another option is to send bottles directly home via a courier service. Ask at the *bodega* or wine store for more information. It runs about $15 a bottle.

○ Know that your home state or province determines the regulations you must follow. To be 100% certain you're not treading into dark waters, consult local authorities before your trip.

around midnight. It's not San Telmo, but there are also some great spots to take in tango. On weekend evenings, locals gather at Plaza Pellegrini for a totally authentic, natural tango dancing session, which is not to be missed. Also check out the *milonga* shows at **Teatro Las Sillas,** San Juan 1436 (☎ **261/429-7742**). There are a few tango bars in Mendoza, including **Café Soul,** San Juan 456 (☎ **261/425-7489**), **C'Gastón,** Lavalle 35 (☎ **261/423-0986**), and **Abril Café,** Las Heras 346 (☎ **261/420-4224**).

Start the night at a local wine bar such as the Vines of Mendoza's wine bar in the Park Hyatt hotel, the **Vines Wine Bar & Vinoteca** (☎ **261/441-1232**) or at a cafe such as **Kato Café,** Emilio Civit 556 (☎ **261/425-7000**). The city's best bars line Aristides Villanueva street close to the center of town. The chic set is keen on **PH,** A. Villanueva 282 (☎ **261/425-5858**). Try **Antares,** A. Villanueva 153 (☎ **261/436-101**), for microbrewed beers; or **Por Acá,** A. Villanueva 557 (no phone), for pizza and microbrewed beers. Most of the serious nightclubs and discos are 10km (6¼ miles) out of town along Ruta Panamericana near Chacras de Coria. **Kamikaze Bar,**

Mendoza Province

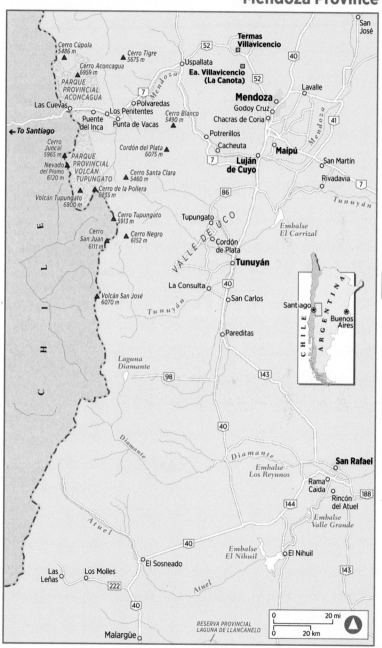

Cerro Cúpola
5486 m

Cerro Tigre
5675 m

Cerro Aconcagua
6959 m

PARQUE
PROVINCIAL
ACONCAGUA

Las Cuevas

Polvaredas

Los Penitentes

Puente
del Inca

Punta de Vacas

Cerro Blanco
5490 m

← To Santiago

Cerro
Juncal
5965 m

Nevado
del Plomo
6120 m

PARQUE
PROVINCIAL
VOLCÁN
TUPUNGATO

Cordón del Plata
6075 m

Cerro Santa Clara
5460 m

Volcán Tupungato
6800 m

Cerro de la Pollera
6235 m

Cerro Tupungato
5913 m

Cerro
San Juan
6111 m

Cerro Negro
6152 m

Volcán San José
6070 m

Laguna
Diamante

Tupungato

Cordón
de Plata

Tunuyán

VALLE DE UCO

La Consulta

San Carlos

Pareditas

Diamante

Diamante

Atuel

Las
Leñas

Los Molles

El Sosneado

Malargüe

RESERVA PROVINCIAL
LAGUNA DE LLANCANELO

Termas
Villavicencio

Uspallata

Ea. Villavicencio
(La Canota)

Mendoza

Godoy Cruz

Chacras de Coria

Potrerillos

Cacheuta

**Luján
de Cuyo**

Lavalle

Maipú

San Martín

Rivadavia

Tunuyán

Embalse
El Carrizal

Santiago

San Rafael

Rama
Caída

Rincón
del Atuel

Embalse
Los Reyunos

Embalse
Valle Grande

Embalse
El Nihuil

El Nihuil

Mendoza

52

40

52

41

7

86

40

98

143

40

144

40

222

40

143

188

CHILE

CHILE

ARGENTINA

Buenos
Aires

0   20 mi
0   20 km

- Schedule three or four *bodegas* to visit per day at the most. Select a variety of sizes (large, medium, small) and styles (modern, traditional, boutique). Stop for lunch at the middle *bodega* or at a restaurant in the wine areas.
- Rest well the night before you hit the *bodegas.* Tours provide plenty of information and sampling, and you will want to be alert enough to soak it all in.
- The sun is hot in Mendoza, and weather can be dry, given the high altitude. The wineries and cellars can be chilly, however, so bring a sweater, even if it's hot outside. Dress appropriately in casual business style; no shorts, rowdy T-shirts, or sneakers.
- Hire a *remise* driver or guide for most days, but treat yourself to 1 day spent roaming the vineyards on bicycle. You will be forced to go at a slower pace and to ride the back roads of the rolling countryside. The best places to do this are the Pedriel area of Luján de Cuyo and the Uco Valley.
* More and more wineries are now offering gourmet lunches. The prices range from $38 at places such as Clos de Chacras to $65 at Andeluna in the Uco Valley and they include various levels of wine pairing. Some of my favorites are Ruca Malen, O. Fournier, and Andeluna. All require reservations and are typically long, leisurely meals in places loaded with ambience; give yourself at least 2 hours.
- Don't wear perfume or lipstick, which distract from the aroma of the wines.
- Note that many bodegas accept only cash for wine purchases, so be sure to stop by an ATM before heading out.

Ruta Panamerica and Corredor del Oest (✆ **261/155-419-210** [mobile]) has four bars and a 3-D light show. **Cacano,** on Aguinaga 1120 (✆ **261/496-2018**), is a classic. Locals flock to **La Reserva,** Rivadavia 32 (✆ **261/420-3531**), on weekend nights for the drag show at midnight. The **Blah Blah Bar,** Paseo Peatonal Alameda, Escalada 2301 Maipú (✆ **261/429-7253**), is great for a late-night drink if you're not heading out to the discos. Hip nightclubs do swap places quickly as the hot spot of the moment, and many have unpublished phone numbers. But in general, most of them don't get going until after 1am.

For you gamblers, the **Regency Casino** at the Park Hyatt, Chile 1124 (✆ **261/441-1234**), is substantially better than the Casino Provincial, offering blackjack, roulette, poker, and slots. Table bets are $1 to $50.

TOURING THE WINERIES ★★★

Traditional and rapidly modernizing in the same breath, Mendoza's wineries have embraced tourism over the past few years. Many now have English-speaking guides and extensive barrel tastings, and have begun to charge for visits. They are generally easily accessible along wine roads, known locally as *los Caminos del Vino.* These roads are as enticing as the wine itself, weaving and winding through tunnels of trees to vast dry valleys dominated by breathtaking views of the snowcapped Andes. Some roads climb as high as 1,524m (4,999 ft.) in the High Zone surrounding the Mendoza River, while others lead to lower-level vineyards in the south. Mendoza's wine region is divided into four zones: the High Zone, Mendoza South, Uco Valley, and Mendoza East. I cover the first three: Mendoza East is mostly large industrial vineyards that make Argentine "table wine" (low in both quality and price) and aren't set up for tourists. To the south, San Rafael is a somewhat distant and off-the-beaten track fourth area covered here (see "San Rafael," later in this chapter). Be sure to pick up the essential collection of maps, "Caminos del Vino." At $8, they're the best investment you'll make in Mendoza. They're available at most hotels and at the wine shops in Mendoza. The mapmaker's website, www.caminosdelvino.com, is an excellent place to get a head start on your planning.

How to See the Vineyards

The list of vineyards is enormous, the road maps unfamiliar, and the options endless. How exactly should you plan to make the most of your time in Mendoza? Consider your options. First, you can sign up for a fully organized multiday trip led by a local guide, who takes care of all the logistics and leads you into the heart of the wine land. (See below for details on guides.) This is the easiest way to do it. You can also just join an organized tour for a day or two. Going on your own is another option. You can hire a *remise* for the day (see "Getting Around," earlier), call in advance to book your reservations, and head out. Renting a car is another alternative, but beware of drinking and driving, poor signage, and aggressive local drivers! Finally, renting a bike gives the day a leisurely pace, but, again, be weary of Mendocino drivers!

Practically all local *bodegas* now open their doors to tourists; some even offer guest rooms—a fabulous trend that is definitely on the rise. If you fall in love with a particular vineyard, ask if they have guest rooms and see if you can stay the night. What makes a good *bodega* tour is a bilingual, educated, and charming guide, and an opportunity to taste some of their best wines at the end.

The **High Zone ★★★** that surrounds the Mendoza River includes Luján de Cuyo and Maipú. This first zone is best regarded for its production of Malbec, although cabernet sauvignon, chenin, merlot, chardonnay, and Syrah are all bottled here as well. Many of the *bodegas* in this zone lie within 1 hour's drive of Mendoza, making tours very convenient. I suggest you begin your touring here, where there is great variety and many visitor-friendly *bodegas* to choose from. South of Mendoza, the beautiful and rural **Uco Valley Region ★★**, including Tunuyán, Tupungato, and San Carlos, produces excellent Malbec, pinot noir, Semillon (a white), and Torrontés (another white, very floral, like a Muscadet, and more common in Salta). Allow at least 2 hours to reach this area. It's a long drive but certainly worth the effort. Farthest away, the **South Region,** between San Rafael and General Alvear, is fed by the Atuel and Diamante rivers. Its best varieties are Malbec, Bonarda, and cabernet sauvignon. Off the tourist track, you will need at least a day to visit this region.

The **Mendoza East Region** is the province's largest wine-producing area in terms of quantity (not necessarily quality). There is little tourism infrastructure here.

With so many wineries (more than 650 at last count), it can be difficult to figure out which to visit. Some are massive, modern industrial complexes funded by foreign investors. Others are traditional "boutique" wineries run by the same family for

---

Sunday Hours

Sunday is a day for Argentines to be with family and have an *asado* barbecue. In Mendoza, as in most of the country, most shops, restaurants, and wineries are closed, with the exception of a handful of *bodegas* and the local mall (Mendoza Shopping Plaza).

generations. Most are open from Monday to Friday from 9am to 5pm, and Saturday from 10am to 3pm; some are now also open on Sunday from noon to 3pm, although the Sunday visit slots are usually booked up early. Reservations are usually required for visits. Wineries are increasingly charging for visits, partly to offset the fact that visitors are buying less wine in-house due to luggage restrictions. Still, compared to elsewhere in the world, a $7 tasting remains a bargain.

Tour Operators

Local tour operators have the inside scoop on everything from booking rural inns to in-depth presentations on the local wine scene. They can make your time in Mendoza more carefree, helping you navigate the rural roads of Mendoza, and narrowing down the hundreds of *bodegas* to choose from. All you have to do is relax, soak up the gorgeous views, and indulge in some fabulous food and wine.

Ampora Wine Tours ★ (*©* 261/429-2931; www.mendozawinetours.com) offers small-group wine tours that visit some of the most interesting wineries in the area. Group size runs from two to eight, and trips to either Luján-Maipú or the Valle de Uco, go out just about every day. Their guides are friendly and trips include a big lunch, with wine of course.

Bikes and Wines (*©* 261/410-6686; www.bikesandwines.com) rents bikes from a handful of spots in the wine country (you can take a local bus to get their hubs), provides an easy-to-follow self-guided route map that includes a handful of close-by *bodega* visits, and books you for lunch. The first winery visit is "free," and then the rest have a charge. While the concept of bike tours in wine country may be successful in other parts of the world, it's still problematic here. Mendocinos are notoriously aggressive drivers, and bike lanes are either ignored or nonexistent! This is the most budget-conscious (if adrenaline-charging) way to see the wineries.

Mendoza Holidays (*©* 261/429-7730; www.mendozaholidays.com) offers private 1-day tours in the wine country starting at $195 per person (two-person minimum) and multiday tours in wine country that include lodging; half-day tours are also available. It also organizes ski trips to Las Leñas, starting at $1,000 a week.

Trout & Wine ★ (*©* 261/429-8302; www.troutandwine.com) runs in-depth and personalized wine tours in Maipú, Uco Valley, and Luján de Cuyo. They know the people behind almost every vineyard in the area, offering a chance to get a more personalized, close-up experience. Tours are limited to six people, and special tastings are arranged. Rates start at $150 a person. Guests also get a gift pack of wine. As their name suggests, they also run fly-fishing tours.

Uncorking Argentina (*©* 866/529-2861 or 261/429-3830; www.uncorking argentina.com) is run by a transplanted Californian who has a deep knowledge of wine and has friends throughout the local wine country—a "wine educator" whose trips are informative, in-depth, and fun. They arrange custom-designed private tours of the Mendoza wine country, offering guided and self-guided adventures from 1 day to multiple days that celebrate the local wine, food, adventure, and art. Prices for 1-day tour start at $140 (four-person minimum).

Chacras de Coria ★★

14km (8½ miles) S of Mendoza

Many travelers use this lovely, leafy suburb of Mendoza as a base for trips to the region. And it's easy to see why: It's convenient to both the city center (20 min. away) and to the *bodegas* area; it has a rich heritage, great restaurants, and a handful of excellent inns; and it's fun and relaxing. This is my first choice for those looking to base their visit away from the hustle of downtown Mendoza.

GETTING THERE

Chacras is accessible via local bus no. 10, which stops on Calle La Rioja in downtown Mendoza and takes about 45 minutes, or via taxi, which takes about 15 minutes ($30–$35) from downtown. It is feasible to tour the area on a day outing from the city, combining a few *bodegas* and a stroll through the town center—either via the bus, with a driver, in a rented car, or on an organized tour. If you are driving, take the Corredor del Oeste south of Mendoza and follow the signs into the heart of town.

GETTING AROUND

Once you're in Chacras, you can walk virtually everywhere, including some *bodegas* and some great restaurants.

WHERE TO STAY

Casa Glebinias This quiet inn is a gardener's delight, nestled amid what may be Chacras's greatest botanical display. Rooms are actually separate houses, each with lovely views of the garden outside each window. Interiors are decorated with an eclectic mix of treasures in a wide range of styles, from Art Deco mirrors and antique window frames, to natural history sketches. All units have a kitchenette, and the staff brings breakfast to your door each morning. This is not a good choice for those who don't like dogs.

Medrano 2272, Chacras de Coria. © **261/496-2116.** www.casaglebinias.com. From $170 suite. MC, V. **Amenities:** Garden; Internet; library; pool. *In room:* A/C, TV, kitchen.

Finca Adalgisa ★★ This is authentic Mendoza: an old family *bodega*, converted into a tranquil and fully authentic inn. Run by the pioneering *hotelera* Gabriela Furlotti, the inn blends old and new, from the slick, modern lounge where you can sample from the *bodega's* limited production of annual Malbecs and olive oils, to a century-old *casa vieja*, or traditional private residence. In the lush backyard, facing the pool, a stone house has six spacious suites and two doubles. The middle rooms have two stories. Friendly and helpful staff members make you feel at home and will help you make reservations at other vineyards or restaurants. Guests can enjoy a complimentary bottle of wine and cheese plate, lemonade by the pool, or *café con leche* anytime.

Pueyrredon 2222, Chacras de Coria. © **261/496-0713.** www.fincaadalgisa.com.ar. 11 rooms. $260 double; $340 suite. MC, V. **Amenities:** Lounge; wine cellar; free use of bikes; high-speed Internet; pool. *In room:* A/C, TV, kitchenettes, Wi-Fi.

Parrador del Angel ★🔑 Run by a mountaineer with a passion for art, this simple bed-and-breakfast is close to Chacras' plaza. Inside an impeccably restored adobe house built in 1907, the six rooms are basic, with funky wooden architecture and colorful woolen blankets. They all look out at the leafy garden that has a small pool. No other inn outside downtown Mendoza offers rates this low.

Jorge Newbery 5418, Chacras de Coria. © **261/496-2201.** www.paradordelangel.com.ar. 6 rooms. $140 standard, $160 superior. MC, V. **Amenities:** Lounge; luggage storage; Wi-Fi. *In room:* A/C.

WHERE TO EAT

Clos de Chacras ★★ ARGENTINE/ITALIAN Set inside a historic *bodega* only a block from Chacras' main drag, there's old-world charm and a relaxed feeling at this garden-side restaurant. Warm, friendly, and proud, the owners have created an intimate and authentic local highlight. A tasting menu, paired with five of their premium wines, starts with a beet salad with toasted seeds and a grilled proveleta (Argentine provolone), followed by chicken and wild mushroom risotto and a slow-roasted beef rib stew with Malbec reduction. For dessert, there's almost always a dulce de leche crème brûlée. Otherwise, you can choose from a strong selection of risottos, pastas, and meat dishes a la carte. It can be tricky to find, so be sure to call ahead.

Monte Libano 1025, Chacras de Coria. ✆ 261/496-0321. www.closdechacras.com.ar. Tasting menu from $35; entrees $14–$18. MC, V. Daily noon–3pm and 8–11pm.

La Piadina ★ 🍴 ITALIAN This traditional Italian cantina serves outstanding homemade pastas and pizzas on rustic northern Italian crusts. Low-key and unassuming, it's a place in which to mingle with the locals and to indulge. The pumpkin-stuffed ravioli with mushroom sauce is delicious. Also worth trying are the carrot pappardelle and the tortellini with ricotta, ham, and walnuts.

Italia 5723, Chacras de Coria. ✆ 261/496-4068. Main courses $9–$15. MC, V. Daily 8:30pm–1am.

Nadia OF ★ ARGENTINE Nadia Heron, wife of the owner and an award-winning head chef at the futuristic O. Fournier winery in the Uco Valley (see p. 295), now has her own small bistro in Chacras. Perhaps due to her origins in Spain, Heron's food is rich in flavor. The menu changes each week, both to highlight seasonal ingredients and to give locals a reason to return. Relying heavily on vegetables, the starters include potato quenelles and cheese crisps. There's always a steak on offer too, often served with blue cheese–stuffed onions and portobello mushrooms. It's also one of the few places around open to BYO. Book a table on the patio, and request privacy if you don't want to sit crammed next to your neighbors.

Italia 6055, Chacras de Coria. ✆ 261/553-1510. Main courses $12–$18. Reservations recommended. MC, V. Wed–Mon 8pm–midnight.

SEEING THE SIGHTS

An authentic mix of traditional rural life and upscale modern infrastructure characterizes the heart of Chacras, founded in 1600. **Plaza General Espejo,** the delightful town square, hosts an **antiques fair ★** on Sunday afternoons. The whitewashed neocolonial parish church, Our Lady of Perpetual Help, faces the plaza. Very good restaurants are within a few blocks from the center.

The most interesting winery in Chacras is **Bodega y Cavas de Weinert,** San Martín 5923 (✆ **261/496-4676;** www.bodegaweinert.com), a large operation that exports high-quality wines around the world and continues using large oak barrels. It's in a quintessential old Spanish-style villa, and the downstairs tasting room is musky and dark, just as a cellar should be. Just steps from the main drag, **Bodega Clos de Chacras ★★**, Monte Libano s/n (✆ **261/496-1285;** www.closdechacras.com.ar), is a boutique winery inside a historic building. Their wines have been receiving many international awards, and their bilingual guides are excellent; plus, they have one of the best restaurants in Mendoza (see above).

To the south of Chacras is the **Museo de Bellas Artes de Mendoza,** San Martín 3651 (✆ **261/496-0224;** admission $1), also known as the Museo Fader, after its chief painter, Fernando Fader. Housed in a brick mansion surrounded by a lovely garden, rooms are dedicated to national and international artists.

Farther down the same road is **Bodega Lagarde,** San Martín 1745 (✆ **261/498-0011;** www.lagarde.com.ar), one of the oldest and most traditional wineries in

Mendoza, with the credo that wines should reflect the vineyards. It is a relaxed, friendly winery that hasn't been slicked up for tourists, so it's a bit untidy. The tour includes a fun lesson in champagne bottling, and they also offer an extensive five-course country-style lunch for $45.

CHACRAS DE CORIA AFTER DARK
Some of Mendoza's top nightclubs are in Chacras de Coria, side by side along the Panamericano Highway. Some of the names are ever-changing, but look for La Guanaca, Pasión, or Cemento.

Luján de Cuyo
17km (11 miles) S of Mendoza

Just south of Chacras de Coria, Luján de Cuyo proudly proclaims itself *"La Tierra del Malbec,"* the land of Malbec. The area's dry, hot weather and high altitudes make it an ideal growing place for the full-bodied wines. In the distance, the eternally snow-capped Cordón del Plata mountain range dominates the views. A large area made up of a few sprawling towns, this is the place to explore the success and allure of Argentina's most hyped *vino tinto*. The town of Luján de Cuyo, at the center of the region, offers little to visitors except for a few great ice-cream shops.

GETTING THERE
Luján de Cuyo is a vast area. The main *bodegas*, in and around Agrelo and Pedriel, can be accessed by public bus no. 10 from downtown Mendoza, which takes you into the center of Luján. From there, you need to take a taxi to outlying areas. If you are driving, take Hwy. 40 south of Mendoza.

GETTING AROUND
If you've arrived by bus, grab a taxi from the center of town to reach the *bodegas*. If you are driving, stick to main roads and follow signs to each *bodega*. None are too far from a main national or provincial highway, and most are well marked.

VISITOR INFORMATION
The **Visitor Information Center,** Saenz Peña 1000 (© **261/498-1912**), is open Monday through Friday from 8:30am to 6pm and on weekends from 10am to 4pm.

WHERE TO STAY & EAT
In addition to the restaurants in this section, many of the *bodegas* listed below in "Seeing the Sights" also serve lunch.

10

MENDOZA & THE WINE COUNTRY

Touring the Wineries

Cavas Wine Lodge ★ This lodge, now part of the Relais & Châteaux chain, is an oasis of luxury amid a vast vineyard, with the High Andes serving as a stunning backdrop. Everything here is private, high-end, and the feeling is definitively exclusive. Suites are scattered two-by-two in spacious adobe bungalows throughout the vineyard, all facing west to the mountains. Inside, rooms are impeccably detailed, with big beds. The ceilings and walls are curved, and bathrooms include soaker tubs. Each unit has a private outdoor hot tub and a stunning upstairs terrace—it's impossible to say which offers a better view of the sun setting behind the Andes. A peaceful spa, a stocked wine cellar, and a first-rate restaurant are on-site as well. Though it is far from town and inconvenient if your goal is to tour a lot, Cavas is ideal, however, for those seeking seclusion and romance. Ask about packages for multinight stays.

Costa Flores s/n, Alto Agrelo. ② **261/15-454-4118** (mobile). www.cavaswinelodge.com. 14 units. $560 double; $710 suite. AE, MC, V. **Amenities:** Restaurant; wine cellar; bicycles; gym; pool; spa. *In room:* A/C, TV, CD players, fireplace, high-speed Internet, private Jacuzzi, minibar, private deck.

La Bourgogne ★★★ FRENCH This restaurant may be the best one in Mendoza, and it certainly rivals any other in the country. Famed chef Jean Paul Bondoux's signature blend of French techniques and natural local ingredients shine. Set inside Carlos Pulenta's modern and serene Vistalba winery, the menu is incredibly creative (cold avocado soup with fennel and onions) and surprising (pumpkin and grapefruit ravioli in prawn broth). Fish of the day is served with watercress, couscous, and wasabi crisps; duck breast is prepared with chestnuts in a Malbec sauce. The wine list is exceptional—don't miss the Vistalba Corte B blends, and don't be shy about asking your waiter or the friendly sommelier for suggestions. Open for lunch only.

R Saenz Peña 3531. ② **261/498-9421.** www.carlospulentawines.com. Reservations strongly recommended. Main courses $12–$18. AE, MC, V. Tues–Sat 12:30–3pm.

SEEING THE SIGHTS

Luján de Cuyo is home to many, many *bodegas*. We've selected the most visitor-friendly and unique ones, to give you a taste of what is out there. Also worth considering are **Alta Vista** (② **261/496-4684;** www.altavistawines.com); **Terrazas de Los Andes** (② **261/488-0058;** www.terrazasdelosandes.com); and **Familia Belasco** (② **261/524-7864;** www.familiabelasco.com), which has a fun and interesting scent-discovery room.

Bodegas

Achaval Ferrer ★★ This is a place to come to sample superb wine. The winery itself impresses little; it's small and a bit messy. But the wines, mostly single-vineyard Malbec produced in small quantities, are simply the absolute best.

Calle Cobos 2601, Pedriel. ② **261/488-1131.** www.achaval-ferrer.com. Reservations required. Tastings $10. Mon–Fri 9am–4pm; Sat 9–11:30am.

Bodega Catena Zapata This strange Mayan temple is the showcase for one of Argentina's most respected and influential winemakers, Nicolás Catena. His journey from California to the top of the crop in Argentina is legendary, and he is usually credited for giving birth to the Malbec boom. The microclimate here is exemplary of the Luján *terroir*. It's not a very personalized or informative tour, but there is a short film that provides a good background and a tour gives an insight into one of the most important families in Mendoza.

Cobos, Agrelo. © **261/490-0214.** www.catenawines.com. Reservations required. Free tours with standard tasting Mon–Fri 9:30am, 11am, 2pm, and 3:30pm; Sat 9:30 and 11am.

Bodega Ruca Malen ★   This is one of many French-owned *bodegas* in the Luján area. The state-of-the-art orange brick building is known for its outstanding four-course *bodega* lunches that highlight pairings from the winery's top two lines: Ruca Malen and Kinien. The guides are entertaining, and the atmosphere is posh and generous. Tour costs are discounted if you purchase wine.

RN 7, Km 1059. © **261/410-6214.** www.bodegarucamalen.com. Reservations required. English-language tours Mon–Fri 10am and 3pm, Sat 10am; tours with lunch Mon–Sat noon and 2pm. Tours $10. Mon–Fri 10am–5pm; Sat 10am–12:30pm.

El Lagar Carmelo Patti 🏠   Patti is the real deal—a winemaker who welcomes each visitor like a family member, while maintaining traditions that date back centuries. A bohemian artist and wine scholar, he'll offer you a tasting straight from the barrel, which is a rarity. Señor Patti's English isn't great, so it's a good idea to bring along a guide if you don't speak Spanish well, to help you appreciate him fully (see "Tour Operators," earlier in this chapter). When it's time for a tasting, see if you can convince him to uncork a bottle of the 2002 Gran Assemblage blend.

San Martín 2614. © **261/498-1379.** Tour reservations required. Free tours Mon–Fri 10am–4pm.

Finca Decero   A brand-new single-vineyard winery (they make all their wine from one single piece of land) that's making high-quality wines in their trademark "by hand" style, it's worth visiting Decero to see their modern and incredibly gentle basket press. They have a very good sit-down "tasting pairing" tour that includes a deli plate.

Bajo las Cumbres 9003, Agrelo. © **261/524-4747.** Reservations required. Tours $8, available on request. Mon–Fri 9:30am–3pm; Sat–Sun 10am–2pm.

Tapiz ★   This winemaker is the creator of the label known as Zolo in the U.S. and Tapiz in Canada. Your tour begins with a horse-drawn carriage ride through the property. After a chance to touch and feel the vines, head in for a taste of whatever wine they're featuring that day. All tours are private. The guide, Carolina Fuller, is an unpretentious professional who makes you feel like you are the only visitor. They also have a fabulous lodge and restaurant in Maipú (p. 288).

RP 15, Km 32. Agrelo. © **261/490-0202.** www.tapiz.com.ar. Reservations required. Tour cost of $7 (or $10 with carriage ride) waived with purchase of wine or lunch at Terruños. Free tour with standard tasting Mon–Fri 10am, noon, 2, and 4pm; Sat 10am and noon.

Vistalba   Carlos Pulenta, the man behind Vistalba, is a star here for his dedication to quality and terroir. The winery is a vision of technological wonder, while the downstairs tasting room is stunning, with its natural wall.

R. Saenz Peña 3531. © **261/498-9400.** www.carlospulentawines.com. Reservations required. Tastings $8–$16 per person, depending on the label. Free tours Mon–Sat 10:30am, noon, 3, and 4:30pm.

Other Attractions

It's not all about wine here in the Land of Malbec. There are also engineering and religious wonders, as well as the chance to explore the mountains around Luján.

The **Cipolletti Dike,** for instance, is a study of Mendoza's intricate system of aqueducts. Known as *el dique Cipoletti* in Spanish, it's in the Vistalba area of Luján. Built by Cesare Cipolletti in 1895, this dike or diversion dam regulates the flow of the Mendoza River and directs its water into various channels, some heading through the fertile vineyards and others forming the Guaymallén Channel, which moves water through the heart of downtown Mendoza and into all those lovely fountains. The Italian hydraulic engineer who organized the irrigation infrastructure here, as well as aqueducts in Florence and on the Tiber River, is a true Mendozan hero, buried nearby. In the near distance is a major oil refinery run by YPF. You'll likely see this dike if you take a standard 1-day tour of the Mendoza area with one of the operators listed earlier in this chapter. Wine tours also drive nearby and would take a detour if you requested it. You'll also pass nearby if you are on a tour of the Alta Montaña on your way to Potrerillos. If you're in possession of a rental car, this engineering marvel is worth a visit on its own. The dike is situated just south of the Mendoza River and west of the Panamerican Hwy. 40. Take RP Hwy. 87.

If you have a spare day and just want to relax, head to the bubbly **Termas Cacheuta,** RP 82, Km 38, Thermas de Cacheuta (𝒞 262/449-0152; www.termas cacheuta.com), for some thermal soaking. There is a natural cave, hydro-massage therapy, and a beautiful garden. You can visit for the entire day and have a gourmet lunch for $38, including transfers from Mendoza. A cheaper option is to bring a picnic and enjoy the nine thermal pools only. With transfers, that runs you $15.

The **Iglesia de la Virgen de Carrodilla ★**, corner of San Martín and Carrodilla, Luján de Cuyo (𝒞 261/435-1667), the home of the patron saint of Mendozan wine, is also worth a visit. The Virgin is depicted in a painting brought from Spain in 1811 that shows Mary pushing a cart, with a child in one arm and grapes in the other. The Spaniard believer built a chapel close to his house to house the painting, which is now a popular historic monument. In 1938, she was consecrated the patron saint of vineyards. The adobe-walled church includes wonderful wine-themed murals. The church museum next door has an interesting collection of Catholic artwork. It's open Monday through Saturday from 9am to noon and 4:30 to 7:30pm. The Virgen de Carrodilla is venerated annually during the Vendimia Festival in March. Across the street is an empanada stand where you can grab a snack.

Maipú

14km (8½ miles) NW of Mendoza

The Maipú region includes vast fields of olives and fruit as well as grape vines. In fact, locals cherish olives every bit as much as grapes here—evinced by the annual National Festival of Olives held in the second half of February each year. If you feel like you are in Tuscany as you roam the shade-lined streets and rural roads, you're not far off the mark: Peek inside any home, and you'll notice that most inhabitants are of Italian descent—which explains their love of good food, good wine, and the good life. Like Luján de Cuyo, Maipú is both a sprawling rural region and a town with the same name.

GETTING THERE

Take a 15- to 25-minute taxi ride from downtown Mendoza, or 30 minutes from the Mendoza airport. Or catch the local bus no. 151 or 160 from the stop on Calle La Rioja—it'll take you into the center of the town of Maipú. Drivers should head south on Hwy. 40 and turn east at Juan J. Paso to get to the center. Other turnoffs will take you to outlying vineyards.

GETTING AROUND

Flat and leafy, Maipú is a good, if busy, place for biking (see "Tour Operators," earlier in this chapter). Alternately, taxis can take you from the bus stop to wherever you need to go.

VISITOR INFORMATION

There is a visitor information center at Ozamis 19 (📞 **261/492-2448**).

WHERE TO STAY & EAT

Almacén del Sur DELICATESSEN   The journey from garden to table is incredibly short at Almacén del Sur. Before seating you, staff members guide you through the herb and vegetable gardens, to demonstrate how fresh the ingredients are. Then you head inside a refurbished farmhouse for your meal. The dishes highlight their gourmet line of deli products sold across the country, including green tomato chutney, cipollino onions in balsamic vinegar, and rose petal preserve. The six-course lunch is definitely not cheap, and wine is extra, though you can opt for a three-course option.

Zanichelli 709, Coquimbito. 📞 **261/497-5802.** www.almacendelsur.com. Reservations highly recommended. Lunch menu $44 for 6 courses; $35 for 3 courses. AE, MC, V. Mon–Sat noon–4:30pm.

Club Tapiz   One of the top lodges in the area is built in an old home dating to the 1890s, tucked inside a 10-hectare (25-acre) vineyard, which you can explore on bike or on foot without having to cross a road. The seven guest rooms are simple and tidy, with modern touches, king-size beds, and bright, if simple, bathrooms. Ask for a room with a window onto the back garden, and be sure to save time for a few hours in the peaceful spa. It's close enough to other *bodegas* to keep you busy for a few days.

Pedro Molina s/n. 📞 **261/496-4815.** www.tapiz.com.ar. 7 units. From $125 double. Rates include breakfast and nightly wine tasting. AE. **Amenities:** Restaurant; lounge; wine cellar; high-speed Internet; pool; spa. *In room:* A/C, TV.

Terruños Restaurant ★ FUSION   Inside the Club Tapiz lodge complex, Terruños is elegant yet funky, with a menu that blends French, Italian, and Asian flavors without distracting too much from the sensational wine list. Pork stuffed with dates in a Malbec sauce is divine, and the young goat cooked in white wine is pure Mendoza. Try the Malbec parfait for dessert. The tea menu is also impressive. On summer nights, ask for an upstairs table on the west side, for killer views.

Pedro Molina s/n, Russel. 📞 **261/496-0131.** Reservations required. Main courses $16–$23. AE. Daily noon–3pm and 8:30pm–1am.

EXPLORING BODEGAS

In addition to the *bodegas* described here, also worth exploring are **San Telmo** (📞 261/499-0050), **Finca Flichman** (📞 261/497-2039; www.flichman.com.ar), and the quaint, tiny **Baquero 1886** (📞 261/429-3915; www.baquerowines.com/winery.htm).

Bodega Benegas   A *bodega* that's as much a museum as a wine cellar, this winery is part of Mendoza's history. Built in 1901 by a former governor, the excellent Andean *poncho* collection is as interesting as the wine.

Accesso Sur and Ruta 60 (Carril Araoz s/n), Cruz de Piedra. 📞 **261/496-0794.** www.bodegabenegas. com. $9.50 visit includes tastings. Mon–Sat 9am–6pm.

Bodega La Rural ★   Founded by Don Felipe Rutini in 1885, this traditional *bodega* maintains an excellent reputation. It's best known for its Trumpeter, San Felipe, and Rutini labels. Next door, the excellent **Museo de Vino** (same contact information), is Latin America's most prestigious wine museum. A great place to start your exploration of Mendoza's wines, it pays tribute to the pioneers of Mendozan wine and provides information on local geology.

Montecaseros 2625, Coquimbito. ℂ **261/497-2013.** www.bodegalarural.com.ar. Reservations are not necessary. Free tour with standard tasting. Rutini and Felipe Rutini tastings require a reservation and fees are charged ($18–$47). Mon–Sat 9am–1pm and 2–5pm.

Carinae Viñedos & Bodega   This *bodega* is receiving a lot of buzz. Owned and run by a very friendly and low-key French couple, Brigitte and Philippe Subra, it's a true boutique *bodega*. Their latest vintages—mostly Malbec, with smaller quantities of Syrah and cabernet sauvignon—have far exceeded any expectations for what was considered a small, unpretentious family project. For an extra $3 a glass, you can sample their award-winning 2004 Carinae Prestige.

Videla Aranda 2899, Cruz de Piedra. ℂ **261/499-0470.** www.carinaevinos.com. Tour with tasting $5 per person; reserve tastings $10–$25. Daily 10am–6pm.

Familia Zuccardi   Familia Zuccardi is perhaps the most savvy and tourist-friendly *bodega* in the area. They serve lunch, dinner, and even high tea. Their multiday programs give you a deeper understanding of Mendoza's wines and cuisine. This authentic family winery is known for its high production. It's located to the east of Mendoza, making it a bit tricky to combine with other winery visits.

RP 33, Km 7.5. ℂ **261/441-0000.** www.familiazuccardi.com. Free tour and tastings. Mon–Sat 9am–5pm; Sun 10am–4pm.

Mendel   Given how highbrow the owners of this boutique winery are, it's surprising to see the historic, unpretentious nature of their rural vineyard. Famed winemaker Roberto de la Mota uses old-vine grapes for award-winning blends like Unus and straight-up Malbecs. Tastings are in a truly charming corner of a sleepy country with gracious hosts.

Terrada 1863, Mayor Drummond. ℂ **261/524-1621.** www.mendel.com.ar. Reservations required. Tastings $9. Mon–Fri 9:30am–1pm.

Tapaus Distillery   This distillery provides a welcome break from grapes. The focus here is on liquor—more precisely, liqueur: brandy, grappa (okay, they use some grapes), and fruit liqueurs. The architecture and design may have your head spinning—if it isn't already.

F. Villanueva 3826. ℂ **261/524-1274.** www.tapaus.com.ar. Free tour with standard tasting. Mon–Fri noon–5pm; Sat 11am–5pm; Sun by appointment only.

Tempus Alba   This is another family establishment dedicated to maintaining a noble, hands-on approach to winemaking. Tours are in-depth and detailed. Come in the afternoon and combine a casual visit with a leisurely bite to eat on their patio.

Carril P. Moreno 572, Coquimbito. ℂ **261/481-3501.** www.tempusalba.com. Free tour; tastings $4 per glass, or 3 glasses for $7. Mon–Fri 10am–5pm.

Trapiche   Founded in 1883, Trapiche is definitely a historic landmark; plus, it's one of the largest wineries in South America. The gorgeous Florentine-style winery in Godoy Cruz has been completely renovated and turned into a visitor center. Situated right next to the old train tracks, where wine was once shipped straight to Buenos Aires, it's a slightly eerie but unique place to visit.

Calle Nueva Mayorga. ℂ **261/520-7666.** www.trapiche.com.ar. Tours $5 include tasting. Mon–Fri 9am–5pm; Sat 9am–1pm.

OTHER LOCAL FARMS

In Maipú, numerous farms allow visitors to explore the production of olive oil and indulge in sensual tastings and appreciation courses. **Quinta Generación,** Ozamis

Sur 2718 (☎ **261/499-0472**), is a boutique olive oil factory that runs guided tours and tastings. Nearby, **Isabel Agrovivero,** Ceferino 544, Cruz de Piedra (☎ **261/410-6325**), also produces figs, walnuts, and grapes. Their tours are very good, and the shop is stocked with goodies. An old olive oil factory, **Laur Olivicola ★**, Videla Aranda 2850, Cruz del Piedra (☎ **261/499-0052**), puts on a show for gourmands—including a presentation on the health benefits of olive oil.

Valle de Uco ★★

90km (56 miles) S of Mendoza

Everything seems to stand still in the remote, high-altitude Valle de Uco, where wild mountains and country towns seem to hide what is one of the world's most fascinating winegrowing areas, full of incredible characters and big dreamers. The scenery is divine, and the towns are sleepy and rural, with an Old West feel. The current "it spot" for groundbreaking wines, La Consulta, has attracted luminaries such as Michel Rolland, Paul Hobbs, and the Lurton brothers. Altitude varies from 800m (262 ft.) in Tunuyán to 1,200m (3,936 ft.) in Tupungato, some of the highest-altitude wineries in the world. Winters here can be very cold, and summers are warm with cooler nights, which help produce superior color and tannins. This area makes an excellent day trip from Mendoza.

GETTING THERE

The main towns of Tupungato and Tunuyán can be reached by local bus from the Mendoza bus terminal. If you are driving, take Hwy. 40 south from Mendoza city. Well-placed signs point you to the major vineyards.

GETTING AROUND

You'll need a car or a hired driver to tour this area. Most distances are too great for biking, and local buses are few and far between.

WHERE TO STAY & EAT

Numerous hotel plans are in the works for the Valle de Uco, including an inn at the O. Fournier *bodega* (see below), and a hotel/spa in Vista Flores, run by the Vines of Mendoza. In the meantime, there are fantastically good lunches at such wineries as O. Fournier and Andeluna (see below).

Finca Ogawa A small, family-run inn rich in rural tranquillity, this is a reasonably priced option. Guests stay in a series of small rustic cabins, or *casitas*, each of which sleeps four and includes kitchen, living room, and a garden with barbecue. For a place so serene, there's still plenty to do here—roam the country roads, visit wineries, indulge in a siesta in the shade, or pitch in with work on the 11-hectare (27-acre) farm.

Bascuñan s/n, Tunuyán. ☎ **877/773-3403** in North America or 261-15-570-7646 (mobile) from within Argentina. www.fincaogawa.com. 2 units. Cabins $125 per night. Rates include breakfast. AE, MC, V. **Amenities:** Free use of bikes; concierge; garden; Wi-Fi. *In room:* Kitchen.

La Posada del Jamón 🍖 CHARCUTERIE This "ham inn," which started as a sandwich and cold cuts shop, is not what you'd expect to find in this region. Despite its kitschy all-pig theme, it's honest, humble, and a rare find. Come for the sausages, cured meats, head cheese, or pork tenderloin with homemade applesauce (some say it's the best pork in the country). The vegetarian lasagna is also good. The family-run service here is great. In summer, ask for an outdoor table for beautiful views.

RP 92, Km 14, Vista Flores, Tunuyán. ☎ **262/249-2053.** www.laposadadeljamon.com.ar. Main courses $8–$14. V. Daily noon–5pm.

Posada Salentein ★   Tucked behind the massive Salentein winery complex, this rural *posada* has an old-time, secluded ranch feel that doesn't overdo the wine theme. Sixteen comfortable rooms are set in three buildings—two older mansion-style houses and a brighter new one. Rooms in the older houses have kitchenettes, but you won't need them—the Argentine-style menu at the restaurant is very personalized and fresh, for lunch and dinner. Packages including half-board are practical, especially those including dinner. You could pop by a nearby winery for lunch, but there's nowhere else to get dinner for miles. This area is particularly gorgeous in the fall when the alamo trees are golden. It's quiet out here amid the vines, making this is a fine place in which to get away from it all.

Ruta 89 and Videla, Los Arboles, Tunuyán. ✆ 262/242-9000. www.bodegasalentein.com. 16 units. $180–$300 double. Rates include breakfast. AE, MC, V. **Amenities:** Restaurant; pool; TV lounge; Wi-Fi.

Postales Valle de Uco   This classic Jesuit-style lodge is in the middle of the Valle de Uco, 10 minutes west of Tunuyán. A rustic but upscale country retreat, it encompasses tree-lined paths, expansive gardens, and breathtaking views of the Andes. The nine double and triple rooms are laid out in two buildings in a U-shape around a pool, garden, and Malbec vines that stretch to the mountains. The location is good, close to lots of wineries, and this is a good base for bike tours. There's a concierge on staff who'll help you with logistics. However, you really need a car to come here. The restaurant/lounge is a cozy, familiar spot.

Calle Tabanera s/n, Colonia de Las Rosas, Tunuyán. ✆ 262/249-0102. www.postalesarg.com. 9 units. $200 double. Rates include breakfast and dinner. AE, MC, V. **Amenities:** Restaurant; wine bar; high-speed Internet; pool. *In room:* A/C.

Rancho 'e Cuero ★★   This remote Argentine mountain *estancia* has no frills, no spa, no TVs in rooms, and no five-star restaurant. What it does have is seemingly endless acreage, great hospitality, and plenty of opportunities for adventure—including horseback riding, hikes to glaciers, and fly-fishing. Deep in the mountains and far from the wineries, the lodge is remarkably comfortable. Watch for foxes and guanacos (cousins of the llama) in the hills, and condors in the skies. You need a good vehicle to get here on your own or need to arrange a transfer with the lodge directly. They also offer lovely day excursions, a spectacular break from the wine touring and a unique chance to hike, horseback ride, dine on a superb traditional *asado* with great wine, and enjoy the mountains all in 1 day.

RP 86, Ugarteche, Tupungato. ✆ 261/15-569-2364 (mobile). www.ranchoecuero.com.ar. 6 units. $350 per person per day. Rates include full board and activities. V. **Amenities:** Restaurant; stable; transfers; living room. *In room:* No phone.

Tupungato Divino   Rustic and remote, this small inn and restaurant brings a bit of elegance to the Uco Valley. Rooms are large and cozy, with fireplaces and are built in a traditional style, with adobe walls and cane roofs. The views are superb. The restaurant is open to the public for lunch, with three-course meals for $25. The hands-on owners are almost always around.

Ruta 89 and Calle Los Europeos, Tupungato. ✆ 2622/15-448-948 (mobile; dial 9 first if calling outside Argentina). www.tupungatodivino.com.ar. 4 units. $150 double. Rates include breakfast. No credit cards. **Amenities:** Restaurant; pool. *In room:* A/C, TV, fireplace, hair dryer, minibar.

SEEING THE SIGHTS

Wineries flourish in all corners of the Valle de Uco. This "New Napa"—the Mendoza region's "it spot"—is specifically near the village of La Consulta, where vineyards such as Clos de La Siete, San Polo, and O. Fournier are making a big name for themselves. Wineries here are part of a rural countryside that differs from the more urban areas of Maipú and Luján de Cuyo. The colder temperatures make for strong production of merlot and pinot noir wines.

If you are looking for a break from the wine-haze, head to the hills. To the south of the Valle de Uco is the spectacular **Laguna del Diamante ★★**, well worth a day trip from either San Rafael or Mendoza city itself. At 3,230m (1,059 ft.), this natural reservoir is backed by the gorgeous Maipú Volcano. The scenery is otherworldly. Take a driver and a good truck. It's open for 4 months in the summer only. **TosoBoehler** (✆ **261/15-454-9005** [mobile]) organizes tours in first-rate 4WD vehicles; including a barbecue lunch at the lake, it's $75 per person. Or, you might opt to play a round of golf at the new **Tupungato Winelands golf course** (✆ **261/429-7407**; www.tupungatowinelands.com). The more adventurous can try biking, rafting, or horseback riding with **Rio Extremo** (✆ **261/15-571-154** [mobile phone; dial 9 first if calling outside Argentina]; www.rioextremo.com.ar) in Tunuyán.

Andeluna ★   This absolutely beautiful, modern winery owned by Texan (and lover of all things Argentine) Ward Lay has a lovely old-world feel. Gourmet lunches are also served, by reservations only. Lay's brought together a top-notch team of winemakers. Tastings are held in a sumptuous "living room" with a stellar mountain view. Their six-course midday meal is superb; along with O. Fournier (see below), it is one of the best in the Uco Valley.

RP 89, Km 11, Gualtallary, Tupungato. ✆ **262/242-3226.** www.andeluna.com. Reservations required. Tour only $5; tastings $10–$27; lunch $56 by reservation only. Tours Tues–Sat 10am–4pm.

Bodega J & F Lurton   Two sons of a Bordeaux wine legend, Jacques and François have wineries around the world. Here in the Valle de Uco, their *bodega* is a wood, concrete, and stainless-steel beauty that fits naturally into the environment. Their Pinot Gris is among the best in South America.

RP 94 Km 21, Vista Flores, Tunuyán. ✆ **262/249-2067.** www.bodegalurton.com. Reservations required. Tastings start at $10. Mon–Fri 10am–5pm.

Bodega La Azul ★★   For a very personalized look at a small boutique winery, visit La Azul. The grapes have to be very, very good to make it into their exclusive, high-quality selection of wines. You'll be especially lucky if the passionate and hands-on owner Shirley Hinojosa is there during your visit.

RP 89, Agua Amarga, Tupungato. ✆ **262/242-3593.** www.bodegalaazul.com. Reservations required. Free tours; tastings $10 per person. Daily 10am–5pm.

Bodegas Salentein ★★   This complex is practically a planet of its own. It includes a modern chapel, a hotel (the Posada Salentein; see above), the much-heralded **Killka Gallery ★**, a restaurant and gift shop, and, of course, the *bodega* itself. Killka blends mostly contemporary Argentine art with a bit of the (unnamed) owner's collection of Dutch classics. The exhibition room is ever-changing. Visits to the *bodega* start with a 15-minute film. Guests then walk across to the cross-shaped *bodega*, which eerily resembles a temple. You wouldn't be the only one who thought of *The Da Vinci Code* or James Bond while touring the underground. Tastings, like everything here, are dramatic. Come to Salentein for the day and include lunch at the Posada.

THE STORY OF MENDOZA'S wine

Blessed by rich sunlight and a panorama of snow-filled mountains, Mendoza dominates Argentina's winemaking industry, and it's one of the most successful wine regions on earth. Surrounding the beautiful city of Mendoza, just to the east of the towering Andes, the province accounts for more than 70% of the nation's wine production, and it's the world's sixth-largest producer of grapes.

The Spanish began cultivating Mendoza's wild American vines in the 16th century as well as grapes they'd brought with them from the Old Continent, and wine production soon dominated the region's economy. They were able to harvest this semiarid land—which receives little natural rainfall—by using a vast irrigation system originally developed by the Incas and extended by the Huarpes, indigenous people from the region. A series of artificial irrigation ditches and canals divert water from the Mendoza, Diamante, Tunuyán, and Atuel rivers, which fill as snow melts in the Andes to nourish the land.

The development of Mendoza's wine industry ebbed and flowed. Wine production stalled in the late 18th century as Spain restricted grape growing to prevent competition with its colonies. The industry was renewed following national independence, as European experts introduced French grapevine stocks and wineries to the region. However, the earthquake of 1861 destroyed most of the existing wineries, and it was not until the opening of a railroad in 1884 that wine production resumed on a significant scale. The railway brought with it many of the founding families of today's wineries, who carried new winemaking techniques and varietals from Italy, France, and Spain. A series of economic crises plagued the industry in the first half of the 19th century, and Mendoza's wines seldom made it farther than the common Argentine table. Some of the wines were so low in quality that soda water was needed to help wash them down, a tradition that continues in some places today, though not because the wine is of poor quality.

In the past decade, wine from Mendoza has reached well beyond the common table to the international stage. Argentina's National Wine Growing Institute has regulated the country's wine industry and spearheaded quality improvements, with increased focus on the international market. New production techniques, state-of-the-art machinery, foreign investment and expertise, advanced irrigation processes, and better grape varieties have combined to bring Mendoza international acclaim. The region's dry, sandy soil; low humidity; and rich sun combine to create wines of high alcohol content and rich fruity character, the most important of which is Malbec, characterized by a powerful fruit bouquet with sweet, dense tannins. Mendocine vineyards grow many other varietals, including cabernet sauvignon, tempranillo, bonarda, Syrah, Barbera, chardonnay, and sauvignon blanc.

RN 89 and Videla, Los Arboles, Tunuyán. © **262/242-9000.** www.bodegasalentein.com. Reservations recommended. Tour with tasting $5 per person, includes entrance to gallery. Mon–Sat 10am–4pm.

Clos de los Siete/Monteviejo   Led by the infamous and influential "flying winemaker" Michel Rolland, seven French wine investors, excited by the limitless possibilities to plant without restriction, make up the **Le Clos de los Siete.** Their property in Valle de Uco is divided into seven wine cellars. They'll help you appreciate the freedom that Mendoza affords the world's great winemakers, who elsewhere feel restricted and left to nature's mercy. A visit here will help you put Mendoza in perspective. For a splurge, ask them to uncork a bottle of the award-winning Clos de los Siete 2003 blend. If you have time, visit two of the other nearby "Clos" cellars, Flechas de los Andes and Cuvelier.

Clodomiro Silva s/n, Vista Flores. ✆ **262/242-2054.** www.monteviejo.com. Reservations required. Free tours; tasting prices range from $17–$47. Daily 10am–5pm.

O. Fournier ★   This Spanish-owned company has a remarkable "concept *bodega*" that shows the power of gravity. It's this natural law that makes for outstanding, natural wine. Opened in 2006, the winery has stunned critics with its modern architecture and new twist on technology. Given their Iberian roots, it's no surprise they have excellent Tempranillos. Their restaurant, **Urban,** is also getting its fair share of praise and has perhaps the best *bodega* lunch in Mendoza.

Los Indios, La Consulta, Tunuyán. ✆ **262/245-1579.** www.ofournier.com. Reservations required. Tour $5; tasting $2.50–$8. Tour fee waived with purchase of wine or tasting. Daily 9:30am–5:30pm.

SAN RAFAEL

234km (145 miles) S of Mendoza

Sleepy and rural, San Rafael is a mini-Mendoza minus the hipsters. The main daily activities here include working in a winery, eating ice cream, and riding a bicycle. It's definitely off the beaten track; very, very few visitors to Mendoza actually make the journey. You'll need a car and a spirit of adventure to explore the area.

Getting There

San Rafael is a 1½-hour drive south of Mendoza down Hwy. 40. The first half of the trip goes through lovely rural towns. The second half crosses a desert wasteland. Many buses leave Mendoza's main terminal heading for San Rafael. **Nueva Chevallier** (✆ 2627/446697) and **Andesmar** (✆ 2627/427720) are the main bus companies. **Aerolíneas Argentinas** (✆ 0810/222-86527; www.aerolineas.com.ar) flies five times a week (currently Mon–Fri only) from Buenos Aires to San Rafael.

Getting Around

The town center is compact and easy to explore on foot. Rural areas will require either a *remise* (call **Remises Del Sur,** ✆ 2627/430646), rental car, or bicycle. For rental cars, try **Hertz** (✆ 2627/436959; www.hertz.com) or **Rent A Car San Rafael** (✆ 2627/437447; www.rentacarsanrafael.com.ar).

San Rafael is flat, so biking is a great way to explore. To rent a bike, try **Bicicletas Rosales** (✆ 2627/430147) or **Bicicleteria Dapratto** (✆ 2627/427738). Rates in San Rafael generally run about $10 for a day's rental.

Many companies offer transfers out to the fertile Valle Grande and Atuel River, including **Transportes Iselin** (✆ 2627/446463), which departs from the bus terminal, and **Atuel Travel** (✆ 2627/429282), which also organizes sightseeing and wine tours.

Visitor Information

The municipal **Tourism Information Office** is at Av. H. Yrigoyen 745 (✆ 2627/424217; www.sanrafaelturismo.gov.ar). It's open daily 8am to 9pm.

Where to Stay & Eat

In addition to the establishments listed below, don't miss **La Delicia Helados** (Yrigoyen and 3 de Febrero; *©* **2627/436333**), which is great for people-watching and ice cream. A slightly hipper joint is **Sin Fondo,** Yrigoyen 1710 (*©* **2627/15-545553** [mobile]), with a relatively broad menu for this town; pastas and seafood are the top draws. A classic neighborhood joint, **Tienda Del Sol,** Yrigoyen 1663 (*©* **2627/425022**), serves pizzas, homemade pastas, huge sandwiches, and *minutas*—breaded veal or chicken topped with a choice of ham, cheese, tomato, or all the above.

Algodon Wine Estates This sprawling resort, about 20km (12 miles) from town, includes a wine cellar, golf course (though hard-core golfers will find it substandard), tennis complex, and private homes. It's putting San Rafael on the map for luxury travelers. Lodge rooms (some with fireplaces) open onto patios overlooking the expansive grounds and pool. Ask for breakfast delivered to your patio. There is a good on-site restaurant, so there's really no need to go anywhere, but this may leave you feeling cut off from the local scene and missing out on the lovely surrounding area. Numerous packages are available and may include meals, horseback riding, and wine tastings. The staff speaks English (a rarity in these parts).

RN 144, Km 675, Cuadro Benegas, San Rafael. *©* **2627/429020.** www.algodonwineestates.com. From $266 double. AE, MC, V. **Amenities:** Restaurant; golf course; outdoor pool; room service; tennis courts; Wi-Fi. *In room:* A/C, fireplace, hair dryer.

Casafuerte Posada Rural 🎁 This romantic, secluded simple little inn outside San Rafael is the kind of get-away where time slows down. It's close to the waters of the nearby dikes. The rooms are all decorated simply with natural and clear colors, giving a warm feeling. The price is a great bargain. No children under 12 years old.

Las Heras 252 (corner of Chacabuco), Villa 25 de Mayo, San Rafael. *©* **2627/495020.** www.posada casafuerte.com.ar. 5 units. $60. No credit cards. **Amenities:** Lounge; wine cellar; library; outdoor pool. *In room:* No phone.

Seeing the Sights

San Rafael is an oasis irrigated by the Atuel and Diamante rivers. Your explorations will combine both the rivers themselves and the productive oasis they give life to— not to mention the local wineries, which make the most of a shallow mineral soil and a warm climate.

BODEGAS

Bodega Jean Rivier This renovated winery blends old and new. The yield is small and strictly controlled and the owner considers himself a rare classic "grower-winemaker," who straddles what are generally considered separate tasks.

Yrigoyen 2385. *©* **2627/432676.** www.jeanrivier.com. Free tour and tasting. Mon–Fri 8–11am and 3–5pm; Sat 8–11am.

Casa Bianchi ★ This traditional family winery is beloved by Argentines throughout the country and is very much at the heart of San Rafael. Their modern *bodega* bears the fruit of grapes brought from Italy in 1910 by Mr. Bianchi himself. If you're lucky, you'll get a taste of the exquisite Enzo Bianchi Malbec. They also have a separate cellar that gives champagne-focused tours.

Comandante Torres 500. *©* **2627/433046.** www.vbianchi.com. Free tour with standard tastings; $9 deluxe tasting. Tours depart every 30 min. Mon–Sat 9am–noon and 2–5pm.

ARGENTINA'S ROADSIDE shrines

At first they seem random. But take a closer look, and you'll discover that the roadside shrines created for the country's folk saints and dotted along this high mountain road (and along most rural roads in Argentina) are of two kinds: piles of clear water bottles and mazes of red ribbons. In fact, they are intriguing cultural phenomena worshiped by devoted cults, yet still unrecognized by the Catholic Church. The water bottles honor the **Difunta Correa,** considered by many to be worthy of sainthood and capable of performing miracles. During the civil wars of the 1840s, Señora Deolinda Correa followed her husband's battalion through the desert. Carrying water, food, and their baby son in her arms, she died en route of exhaustion, thirst, and hunger; but her baby survived by nursing on his dead mother's breasts. Believers, in particular truck drivers, leave bottles full of water to quench her thirst and ask for her protection, which she has been known to offer in abundance to those in need. There is an elaborate shrine in her honor in the town of Vallecito, in San Juan province. Meanwhile, the red ribbons pay tribute to one man: **El Gaucho Gil,** a mythical outlaw cowboy who was said to be a Robin Hood–type character and a conscientious objector to civil wars. In 1878, he was hung for his acts of defiance. Just before his last breath, he pledged that he'd become a miracle worker in the afterlife. Hundreds of thousands of Argentines pray to him for miracles, and he keeps them coming back, always leaving offerings in the color of blood. Just exactly why a Gaucho Gil shrine is located where it is remains a bit of a puzzle to nonfollowers, but many believe they are positioned where miracles have occurred—including narrowly avoided traffic accidents.

OUTDOOR ADVENTURES

San Rafael's bounty stems from the waters of the Atuel River, which local residents have long used as a playground. The road south from town leads through the scenic walls of the **Atuel Canyon.** The adventure scene is headquartered in the tranquil community of **Valle Grande ★,** which stretches along the river itself. Along the way, you'll find cabins for rent, horseback riding trips, rock climbing, and small restaurants. Many cater to large groups of students. For half-day rafting trips, try **Raffeish** (② 2627/436996) or **Antu Aventuras ★** (② 2627/439069). Upriver from Valle Grande are four imposing hydroelectric dams, and beyond that a massive reservoir called El Nihuil where there are boat rentals, restaurants, and beaches.

THE ALTA MONTAÑA DRIVING CIRCUIT

Climbing the mountains on the way to the Chilean border, this excellent driving circuit leads past the magnificent vineyards of Mendoza to breathtaking vistas of the Andes. It is an all-day excursion (at least 5 hr. with no stops) that leads past the Uspallata Valley up to nearly 3,000m (9,840 ft.) at Las Cuevas and the entrance of Aconcagua Park. You can take one of two routes: The easier drive takes you past Potrerillos on the RN 7—a small area along the Mendoza River popular for its whitewater rafting. The more challenging drive (due to winding dirt roads) takes you

CROSSING INTO chile

Trans-Andean neighbors, sometime rivals, colleagues, and "cousins," Chile and Argentina are intricately linked as nations. They share a 5,150km-long (3,193-mile) border from the high deserts of the north to the wilderness of Tierra del Fuego. The busiest border crossing is here at the Paso de Los Libertadores; these border posts are open 24 hours a day for most of the year. In winter, from May 15 to September 1, it's open from 8am to 8pm, or only when the road is open. From here, it's a steep and scenic 3-hour descent to the Chilean capital of Santiago.

through the gorgeous natural-springs town of Villavicencio. (I recommend you go Villavicencio on the way and return via Potrerillos on the RN 7, since you don't want to be stuck above Villavicencio at night.) Whichever route you choose, the roads come together in Uspallata, where the circuit continues to Las Cuevas on the RN 7. You can do this tour on your own, but it is easier with a driver who knows the roads. Note that a 4WD is preferable, although not a necessity, for the route to Villavicencio. Expect temperatures to drop significantly as you climb the mountain; bring a sweater! It's also a nice idea to bring a picnic. In absence of any lovely restaurant for lunch on a terrace with a view of the peaks, a roadside pullout may be the better option.

Heading to Uspallata via Villavicencio

Although it takes a couple hours longer than heading straight north on RN 7, driving the RN 52 takes you to the natural springs of Villavicencio, the source of Argentina's well-known mineral water. If you've ordered bottled water in Argentina, chances are it's Villavicencio. Leaving Mendoza to the north through Las Heras, you'll be driving on the old international road to Chile. After 34km (21 miles), you'll pass the **Monumento Canota,** the spot where generals San Martín and Las Heras split to confront the Spanish at different fronts in 1817. After Canota, you will begin to climb the Villavicencio Valley, and by 40km (25 miles), the road turns to gravel and becomes winding (the road here is known locally as the Caracoles de Villavicencio, or "the snails of Villavicencio"). A small **ranger station** at 50km (31 miles) offers information on the Villavicencio natural reserve, including sources of the mineral water and the region's flora and fauna. Eagles, condors, pumas, mountain cats, foxes, ostriches, guanacos, flowering cacti, and many plants and trees occupy the area.

Villavicencio

45km (28 miles) N of Mendoza

French-owned Danone purchased the rights to this land and its mineral water, and it is working hard to preserve the integrity of the springs. This explains why the **Hotel Termas Villavicencio,** frequented by Argentina's high society until its closing in 1980, has not reopened. The lush gardens of the Normandy-style hotel, seen on the label of Villavicencio bottles on tables up and down the country, are off-limits. Perched against the dusty foothills with oaks and poplars, trickling streams, and wildflowers surrounding it, the hotel's location represents a lush little paradise in the Andes. A small chapel, opened in 1941, lies just behind it. Next to the hotel, you can stop at the Hostería Villavicencio for lunch or a drink.

The Uspallata Valley

Continuing along RN 52, you will follow the path that San Martín used for his liberation campaign. The dirt road zigzags its way up the canyon, dotted with silver mines exploited by the Spaniards in the 18th century. When you get 74km (46 miles) from Mendoza, you will have climbed to the 3,000m (9,840-ft.) summit. From here, you'll have a magnificent view of Aconcagua and the mountains, and the road begins to improve.

The road from the summit to Uspallata is a breathtaking 28km (17-mile) drive through the **Uspallata Valley.** You will descend into the valley through a small canyon, and when the valley emerges, you'll be treated to one of the most beautiful sights in Argentina. The polychromatic mountains splash light off Aconcagua to your left and the "Tiger Chain" ahead, with occasional clouds painting shadows on some mountains and allowing sun to pour light on others. The curious rock formations surrounding you were filmed for the dramatic setting of *Seven Years in Tibet,* starring Brad Pitt. Just before you arrive in Uspallata, 2km (1¼ miles) north of town, you will see **Las Bovedas**—peculiar egg-shaped mud domes built in the 18th century to process gold and silver for the Spaniards.

Heading to Uspallata Via Potrerillos

This drive is significantly easier than the route through Villavicencio, taking you along the RN 7 through the Precordillera mountains. Follow the signs from downtown Mendoza that point to the REPUBLICA DE CHILE. Potrerillos is a bit of a ghost town along the Río Mendoza, where tour companies arrange white-water rafting, horseback riding, and trekking. There is a gas station here. **Argentina Rafting Expediciones** (see "Tour Operators & Outdoor Activities," on p. 276) has its adventure park off the RN 7. It's a great recharger. There is also a small restaurant. A few kilometers upriver, the new **Pueblo del Río Mountain Resort ★** (© **261/424-6745;** www.pueblodelrio.com.ar) has rustic cabins built with stone and wood that sleep up to eight people each. They have fully equipped kitchens and outdoor grills, and cost $90 for two people. There's also a good restaurant. This is a great place to clear your head after trolling around the wineries, and its **Aires de Montaña Spa** offers all the classic treatments to rejuvenate you. It is the nicest place to stay en route to Aconcagua. The drive continues 41km (25 miles) alongside the Mendoza River to Uspallata. Hikers and horseback riders, especially those with kids, will want to make a detour to **El Rincón de los Oscuros** (© **2624/483030;** www.rincondelososcuros.com) where charming gauchos will lead you through spectacular terrain. Simple accommodations are available at the traditional **Estancia La Alejandra,** run by the Cordón del Plata agency (© **261/423-7423;** www.cordondelplata.com). Doubles are $150 per night, dinner and breakfast included.

Uspallata

58km (36 miles) N of Mendoza

With only 3,500 inhabitants (many of them members of the military), Uspallata is a pretty sleepy place. But this small Andean town surrounded by lovely poplar trees and the biggest mountains in the Americas offers a variety of outdoor activities and makes an excellent base from which to explore the mountains. You can obtain limited visitor information from the **tourist information booth,** open daily from 9:30am to 8:30pm, at the corner of RN 7 and RN 52. Gustavo Pizarro is the area's best tour

HITTING THE slopes IN LAS LEÑAS

One of South America's top ski destinations, **Las Leñas** ★ boasts 64km (40 miles) of runs, excellent snow, and typically small crowds. The summit reaches 3,430m (11,250 ft.), with a 1,230m (4,034-ft.) vertical drop. There are 30 runs, with approximately 8% set aside for beginners, 22% for intermediates, and 70% for advanced skiers. The resort's 11 lifts are getting seriously outdated, and there are loud calls for some infrastructure improvements. When the top lift shuts down (as it did for 2 of the season's 4 months in 2006, due to an avalanche), options for experts are limited. When all is running smooth, the lifts here can transport up to 9,200 skiers per hour, which is far more capacity than the town has in accommodations. Consequently, you seldom have to wait in line to get to the top, except during the crazy-busy weeks of Argentine national winter holidays, at the start of August.

Las Leñas is a destination resort—everyone comes on a package that usually includes 1 week of hotel accommodations, lessons, and lift tickets. It has one small grocery store, an interesting little museum, and no nearby town to speak of. Essentially, you must eat all your meals out. It definitely has the feel of a winter wonderland, with no car traffic or high-rises, and hardly any trees. Because the climate is so dry, the powder snow is terrific. In season, it attracts wealthy Porteños and Argentine celebrities, as well as international skiers looking for extreme and challenging off-*piste* terrain, and it has an active nightlife in winter. Local ski instructors are excellent. The majority of people on the slopes are beginner/intermediates, which has historically left the advance terrain virtually untouched and ready for exploration. Today, the numbers of foreigners chasing extreme powder this way each year has grown substantially. Snow season runs from late June to mid-October. In summer (Dec–Feb), Las Leñas offers mountain biking, trekking, rafting, and fishing, and hotel prices drop significantly. The resort is most easily reached via a 90-minute flight from Buenos Aires to Malargüe, followed by a 1-hour bus to Las Leñas (68km/42 miles). Alternatively, you can travel by car or bus from Mendoza, which is a 4- to 5-hour drive (399km/247 miles).

The stylish **Virgo Hotel and Spa** ★★ is a 105-room minimalist resort that has taken the lead as Las Leñas' best hotel,

guide, and his **Pizarro Expediciones**, RN 7 (© **2624/420003**; www.pizarroexpediciones.com.ar), organizes horseback riding, mountain biking, climbing, and white-water rafting tours. If you need gas or any supplies, get them in Uspallata, which is the last real town before the Chilean border.

WHERE TO STAY & EAT

Hostería Los Condores Given the town's limited selection of lodgings, Los Condores is probably your best bet. This traditional small-town hotel's location, steps away from the main intersection and the heart of town, is its best perk. Rooms come in a variety of setups, from simple singles to large triples. All are bright and spacious, with large bathrooms. There's a pool outside, a big breakfast, and a friendly staff.

Las Heras s/n, Uspallata. © **2624/420002**. www.loscondoreshotel.com.ar. 23 units. $60 double. Rates include breakfast. AE, MC, V. **Amenities:** Restaurant; outdoor pool.

which definitely gives the resort something to celebrate. Rooms are spacious and bright. Their quadruple rooms are a great value for larger groups. Bathrooms have a Zen-like simplicity with all natural elements and large showers. The spa is so nice you may not even want to hit the slopes, although with a lift just 15m (49 ft.) from the lobby, it's easy to start linking your turns.

In addition to housing the resort's casino, the 90-bedroom **Piscis Club Hotel** has well-equipped rooms that accommodate up to three people, though it's not quite the five-star hotel the sign proclaims. A stay here includes breakfast and dinner. Like most of the lodgings here, it is ski-in, ski-out. Following a day of skiing, the hotel provides hot drinks and warming by the fireplace, and the indoor pool, Jacuzzi, and sauna should reinvigorate the remaining cold parts of your body. The restaurant, **Las Cuatros Estaciones,** is the best around. All the hotels offer ski instruction and children's activities, as well as adult activities in the casino and nightclub. After a siesta and then a late dinner, swing by **La Cueva del Esquiador** wine bar and sample from a long and impressive wine list. They have

special tastings of Mendozan wine throughout the ski season. As vibrant in the evening as it is on snowy winter days, the place hosts night skiing three times a week and regular concerts, parties, and events.

Las Leñas lies in the southwest of Mendoza province, near the city of Malargüe and close to the Chilean border. To drive from Mendoza, take the RN 40 to the PR 222. Most bookings are done online at www.laslenas.com. **Las Leñas Holidays** (www.laslenasholidays. com) offers packages popular with North Americans and Europeans. A 7-night package starts at $1,700 per person includes accommodations, lift tickets, and breakfasts and lunches daily. They'll also include a few days of wine touring in Mendoza before or after.

Lift tickets run about $55 per day, with multiday passes available. A weekly pass, for example, will run you $275. Prices for lifts, as well as those for accommodations, depend on the time of the season. September is generally a great time to come—fewer crowds, cheaper prices, and longer days. Great last-minute end-of-season promotions are available as well.

Parrillada San Cayetano ARGENTINE   This *parrilla* is widely considered the best Argentine grill in town, serving large portions of standard classics such as young goat, chicken, and beef. Behind the YPF gas station, it's a favorite among truckers crossing the border. For $14, you get a small steaming grill loaded with a variety of cuts. Homemade empanadas and pastas round out the options. The wine list isn't bad, either.

RN 7, Km 1105. © **2624/420149.** Main courses $8–$13. No credit cards. Daily noon–2am.

Heading to Aconcagua from Uspallata

Continuing along the RN 7, you'll drive through the wide U-shaped valley carved from ancient glaciers and loaded with minerals such as iron, sulfur, talc, and copper. As you climb the canyon, you will see on your left the first signs of the atrophying **Andes railway**—an old, narrow track from 1902 that lifted an early-20th-century steam train up the mountains. The railroad was abandoned in 1980, due to a political dispute between Chile and Argentina, but it received new vigor in 2006, when presidents Kirchner, of Argentina, and Bachelet, of Chile, agreed to get it running again. The goal is to build a weatherproof line that won't be snowed out, as are hundreds of cargo trucks on this road each winter. (No word if they will also implement a tourist service, as this would no doubt be one of the world's most beautiful train tours.) As of early 2011, however, the $436-million project—necessitated by increased Argentine exportation and increased Chilean demand for imports—still hadn't broken ground.

When you get 20km (12 miles) from Uspallata, you'll come to **Puente Pichueta,** a stone bridge over the Pichueta River commissioned by Fernando VII in 1770 to allow messengers to cross from Argentina to Chile. The road leading to the bridge forms part of the old Inca trail. The lone tree beside the bridge is a nice picnic spot.

Los Penitentes

165km (102 miles) W of Mendoza

Los Penitentes is a small resort known for downhill and cross-country skiing. Twenty-three slopes accommodate skiers of all levels, and a ski school instructs novices. Skiing is pricier but much better in Portillo, Chile (see note below), but if you decide to stay in Los Penitentes, consider lodging at **Ayelan,** RN 7, Km 165 (© **261/427-1123**), across the street from the ski resort, with basic rooms looking toward the mountains. Doubles cost roughly $75 and include breakfast; the rustic dining room serves a limited selection of high-quality regional dishes. If you are in Mendoza in winter and like to ski, this makes a good day trip.

Note: Serious skiers with more time to ski or snowboard should make the trip to **Portillo** (www.skiportillo.com), a much larger and better-equipped resort across the Chilean border. Or head south of Mendoza to Las Leñas (see below).

Puente del Inca

6km (3¾ miles) W of Los Penitentes

Although it's become somewhat of a tacky tourist trap, the remarkable bridge **Puente del Inca** is nonetheless beautiful. First described in 1646 by the Spanish conquistadores, it's a natural stone bridge used by the Incas to cross the Río de las Cuevas, about 6km (3¾ miles) past Los Penitentes. With its beautiful display of natural colors, it is believed to have once been a bridge made of ice that was hardened by the thermal springs. Now it's holding a fragile balance between natural cementation and erosion. So it's off-limits to visitors—you can look at it, but you can't walk on it. Under the bridge, you will see the remains of an old spa that once belonged to a hotel, built in 1917 to capitalize on the thermal springs. That hotel was destroyed in an avalanche in 1965, but, in what many consider a miracle, the adjacent church went unscathed. Natural hot springs still flow underground here, but access is closed to the public. Near the spa, vendors sell handicrafts. **Hostería Puente del Inca** (© **261/429-9953**) is the best place to eat here. It's a bit stuffy and seems to be trapped in the 1950s, but the set menu is reliable and well priced at $12.

Parque Provincial Aconcagua

Just after Puente del Inca, you will come to the entrance of **Aconcagua Provincial Park.** At 6,960m (22,829 ft.), Cerro Aconcagua is the "Roof of the Americas"—the highest peak not just in South America, but also in the entire Western Hemisphere.

From RN 7, you can see the summit on clear days. For a great look at it, get out of the car at the parking lot on the north side of the highway and hike the 15 minutes to Laguna Los Horcones (there is another stellar view from Km 34 on the road btw. Uspallata and Villavicencio). First climbed in 1897, it is a challenging, although not overly technical, climb, where your body battles the stresses of high altitude in an extreme environment. Only highly experienced climbers should even think about this as a goal—it requires fitness, strength, and endurance, as well as a certified local guide. Most people take over 2 weeks to climb, giving themselves at least 1 week to acclimatize to the altitude before pushing for the top. The south face, which gets little sun, is the most treacherous climb. The normal route is along the west side. The main climbing season is in January and February, when dozens of expeditions from around the world converge to tackle one of the prized Seven Summits. The rest of the year, the park is virtually deserted.

The provincial park includes 71,000 hectares (175,441 acres) of stunning high-mountain country tucked on the eastern side of the border between Chile and Argentina. To enter the park, however, you must first obtain a permit and pay an entrance fee from the park's "attention center," called Edificio Cuba (© **261/425-2031;** www.aconcagua.mendoza.gov.ar), inside Mendoza's Parque San Martín. The location where you can buy permits changes periodically, so check with Mendoza's tourism office for additional details. Permits for 2, 7, and 20 days are available. With one of the shorter-duration permits, you can hike to the base camps without climbing to the summit. Those hoping to reach the top must buy a 20-day permit, the cost of which changes annually but is somewhere above $800 (including emergency medical insurance) in high season. The top guiding company in the park is **Fernando Grajales Expediciones** (© **800/516-6962** or 261/15-500-7718 [mobile]; www.grajales.net), which offers 3-day hikes as well as 19-day summit attempts. Another recommended outfitter is **Aconcagua Trek** (© **261/431-2000;** www.rudyparra.com). Also try **Aymara Adventures & Expeditions** (© **261/420-2064;** www.aymara.com.ar), which has horseback-riding trips in the provincial park.

At the peak's base, across from Puente del Inca, there is a new interpretive trail that takes about 1 hour. A small interpretive center (with bathrooms) is at the trail head. There's also a $2.50 entrance fee charged here if you only want to walk the trail.

After visiting the park, if you have time to go a bit farther and still make it back to Mendoza before too late, continue on to the official border point. At 4,000m (13,120 ft.) above sea level, it's a wild and woolly place. The famous towering bronze monument Cristo Redentor was erected by the neighboring nations in 1902 after they resolved a territorial dispute. Then return to Mendoza via Potrerillos on the RN 7.

MENDOZA & THE WINE COUNTRY

The Alta Montaña Driving Circuit

THE ARGENTINE LAKE DISTRICT

by Christie Pashby

With its tall peaks and crystalline waters, the Argentine Lake District is one of the world's most spectacular mountain playgrounds, yet it is remarkably unknown and unexplored by foreigners. The region stretches from the rugged, Wild West town of Junín de los Andes in the north to the emerald waters of Cholila in the south. In between, cottage-lined towns are scattered about, affording plenty of options for overnight stops. A range of travelers will find something of interest here—alpine adventures, aquatic sports, fabulous wine and cuisine, and cozy chalets and hotels.

Argentines flock here during their twice-annual holidays—to ski in July and August, and to raft in the lakes and hike the mountains in January and February. The rest of the year, it's *tranquilísimo*. I suggest you schedule your visit when the locals are back at work, during the shoulder-season months of November (spring) and March (autumn)—my favorite time to visit here.

For more information about the region, see **www.interpatagonia.com**.

Exploring the Region

In this chapter, I focus both on the Lake District's principal destinations—San Carlos de Bariloche (known here simply as Bariloche), Villa La Angostura, and San Martín de los Andes—as well as stops off the beaten path, such as El Bolsón and Junín de los Andes. This coverage includes numerous national parks, as well as driving tours and boat trips that take in the best of the stunning lakeside scenery. I recommend basing yourself in one of these towns and striking out from there to explore the surrounding wilderness. Or pick two spots and spread your nights out. All the towns described in this chapter offer enough outdoor and sightseeing excursions to fill 1 or even 2 weeks, but 4 to 5 days in one location is ample time for a visit. Based in Bariloche, you can take a day trip south to the crafts fair and lakes at El Bolsón, and then head out for daytime adventures in Nahuel Huapi National Park. Then, take 2 nights to visit San Martín de los Andes and Villa La Angostura. If you're up for it, don't

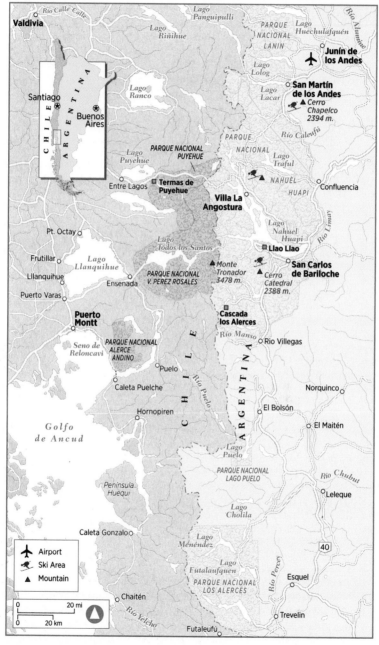

Río Calle Calle

Valdivia

Lago Panguipulli

Lago Riñihue

PARQUE NACIONAL LANÍN

Lago Huechulafquén

Río Aluminé

✈ **Junín de los Andes**

CHILE

ARGENTINA

Santiago ✪

Buenos Aires ✪

Lago Ranco

Lago Lolog

San Martín de los Andes

Lago Lacar

▲ Cerro Chapelco 2394 m.

Río Caleufú

Lago Puyehue

PARQUE NACIONAL PUYEHUE

PARQUE NACIONAL

Lago Traful

Entre Lagos

⬛ **Termas de Puyehue**

NAHUEL

Villa La Angostura

HUAPI

Confluencia

Pt. Octay

Lago Todos los Santos

Lago Nahuel Huapi

Río Limay

Frustillar

Lago Llanquihue

⬛ **Llao Llao**

Llanquihue

Ensenada

▲ Monte Tronador 3478 m.

San Carlos de Bariloche

Puerto Varas

PARQUE NACIONAL V. PEREZ ROSALES

▲ Cerro Catedral 2388 m.

Puerto Montt

⬛ **Cascada los Alerces**

Río Manso

Río Villegas

Seno de Reloncaví

PARQUE NACIONAL ALERCE ANDINO

C H I L E

Puelo

Caleta Puelche

Río Puelo

A R G E N T I N A

Norquinco

El Bolsón

Hornopiren

El Maitén

Golfo de Ancud

Lago Puelo

PARQUE NACIONAL LAGO PUELO

Río Chubut

Leleque

Península Huequi

Lago Cholila

Caleta Gonzalo

Lago Menéndez

40

Lago Futalaufquen

✈ Airport

🎿 Ski Area

▲ Mountain

PARQUE NACIONAL LOS ALERCES

Río Percey

Esquel

0 ___ 20 mi
0 ___ 20 km

Chaitén

Río Yelcho

Trevelin

Futaleufú

miss the chance to sleep in the backcountry—in either a rustic high-mountain hut, a fly-fishing lodge, or a simple tent, after you've taken in the scenery on horseback. Another interesting route is to make a detour into Chile via the lake crossing from Bariloche or to organize a boat-bus combination that loops from Bariloche and Villa La Angostura in Argentina, then crosses the border into Chile, stops in Puyehue, continuing south to Puerto Varas or Puerto Montt, and finally crosses back into Argentina and Bariloche via the Lake Crossing. No vehicles are permitted on the Puerto Montt–Bariloche crossing. Another option is to cross from San Martín de los Andes to Pucón, Chile, which is open to all vehicles.

SAN CARLOS DE BARILOCHE ★★

1,621km (1,005 miles) SW of Buenos Aires; 180km (112 miles) S of San Martín de los Andes

Just mention Bariloche to an Argentine, and you'll inspire a whimsical sigh. Officially known as San Carlos de Bariloche, this city represents the good life in the national consciousness. With stunning natural scenery and fine cuisine, it's a winter and summer playground for vacationing Argentines, and it's practically a rite of passage for Argentine youth to grab a backpack, leave the big city and explore nature in the Nahuel Huapi National Park here, with Bariloche in the middle.

Bariloche is blessed with a strategic geographic position. With the rugged plains of the Patagonian Steppe to the east, the towering snowy peaks of the Andes to the west, and the glistening and grand Nahuel Huapi Lake in front, opportunities for adventure are abundant. Even if you're not much of an adventurer, you'll still find plenty of pleasant sightseeing tours, boat trips, boutiques, driving excursions, and fine dining to keep you busy. Or just park yourself wherever the view is good and soak it all in.

The city itself embodies a strange juxtaposition: an urban city plopped down in the middle of beautiful wilderness. Unfortunately, Argentine migrants fleeing Buenos Aires, an ever-growing tourism industry, and 2 decades of unchecked development have left a cluttered mess in what was once an idyllic mountain town. Bits and pieces of the charming architecture influenced by German, Swiss, and English immigration are still in evidence, but *"el centro"* of Bariloche can be tacky and chaotic. Roads are in bad shape and parking horrendous. Visitors to Bariloche are sometimes overwhelmed by its hodgepodge of ugly apartment buildings and clamorous discos, and the crowds that descend on this area from mid-December until the end of January and again during ski season in July. A visit to Bariloche, however, does not necessarily mean staying in (or spending hardly any time) in the city's core. Your best bet is to spend less time in town, and more on the lake or in the mountains. Drive 10 minutes outside town, and you'll be surrounded again by thick forests, rippling lakes, and snowcapped peaks that rival the Alps. If you're looking for a quiet vacation, you'd be better off lodging outside the city center, on the road to the Llao Llao Peninsula or in the town of Villa La Angostura (p. 328). On the flip side, Bariloche offers a wealth of services, including the area's largest and best-serviced airport.

Essentials

GETTING THERE The **Aeropuerto Bariloche** (© **02944/426162**) is 13km (8 miles) from downtown. Buses to the city center line up outside the arrival area; they're roughly scheduled to coordinate with flight arrivals. A taxi to the center costs about $13. **Aerolíneas Argentinas,** Mitre 185 (© **02944/422548;** www.

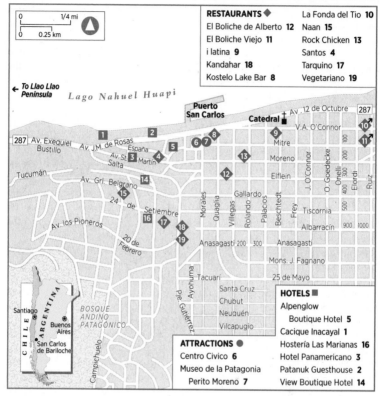

RESTAURANTS ◆
El Boliche de Alberto 12
El Boliche Viejo 11
i latina 9
Kandahar 18
Kostelo Lake Bar 8

La Fonda del Tio 10
Naan 15
Rock Chicken 13
Santos 4
Tarquino 17
Vegetariano 19

HOTELS ■
Alpenglow
Boutique Hotel 5
Cacique Inacayal 1
Hostería Las Marianas 16
Hotel Panamericano 3
Patanuk Guesthouse 2
View Boutique Hotel 14

ATTRACTIONS ●
Centro Civico 6
Museo de la Patagonia
Perito Moreno 7

aerolineas.com.ar), runs at least three daily flights from Buenos Aires; in summer, it also operates two daily flights from El Calafate. They now offer a direct route to and from Mendoza twice a week. **LAN,** Mitre 534 (✆ **800/999-9526;** www.lan.com), runs two or three flights a day from Buenos Aires. **Lineas Aéreas del Estado,** Quaglia 238, #8 (✆ **02944/423562;** www.lade.com.ar), serves small destinations in the area such as Neuquén and Esquel. It's nearly impossible to make it to Bariloche from North America or Europe in a day, as you must change airlines in Buenos Aires. **Andes Aerolíneas** (✆ **810/777-26337;** www.andesonline.com) offers three weekly flights from Buenos Aires, connecting on to Esquel.

The **Terminal de Omnibus** (✆ **02944/432860**) is at Av. 12 de Octubre 2400; a dozen companies serve most major destinations in Argentina and Chile. **Via TAC** (✆ **02944/423552**) schedules three daily arrivals from Buenos Aires ($104–$140) and daily service from El Bolsón, Esquel, Mendoza, and Córdoba. **Vía Bariloche** (✆ **02944/432444**) has eight daily arrivals from Buenos Aires (the trip lasts about 20 hr.) and one daily trip from Mar del Plata. **Andesmar** (✆ **02944/430211**) has service from Mendoza, Río Gallegos, and Neuquén, and service from Osorno, Valdivia, and Puerto Montt in Chile. For long trips, opt for the slightly more expensive

TRAVELING BY boat TO CHILE

Cruce Andino is the name of the company now running the spectacular lake-crossing journey from Bariloche over the border (and the Andes Mountains) to the Chilean Lake District. It's a boat-and-bus combination that terminates in Lago Todos los Santos, near Ensenada and Puerto Varas, although it can also be done in reverse, from Chile to Bariloche. If you're planning to visit Chile, it's a superb option that allows you to take in the beauty of the Andes and the volcanoes, rivers, and waterfalls in the mountain range. I don't recommended making this journey during heavy rain. The trip can take 1 long day or 2 days, with an overnight in the Hotel Peulla or the recommended Hotel Natura in Chile. The 1-day trip costs $230 per person for the boat trip, and an average of $420 per person based on double occupancy for an overnight at the Hotel Natura in Peulla, Chile. Book at any travel agency or from Cruce Andino's offices in Bariloche ((✆02944/426109; www.cruce andino.com).

(usually $15 more) *coche cama* or supercama for chairs that practically become beds. A few daily buses travel from San Martín de los Andes via the scenic Siete Lagos (Seven Lakes) route (summer only); from Villa La Angostura, try **Ko-Ko** (✆ 02944/431135).

Motorists can reach Bariloche from San Martín via several picturesque routes. The 200km (124-mile) scenic **Siete Lagos route,** from San Martín de los Andes, follows rutas 234, 231, and 237 (avoid this route when it's raining, as the dirt roads turn to mud). The 160km (99-mile) **Paso Córdoba** follows rutas 234, 63, and 237. The safest route for night driving or crummy weather, the **Collón Curá** runs 260km (161 miles) along rutas 234, 40, and 237; it's the longest route, but it's entirely paved. To get to El Bolsón, follow RN 258 south; continue down 40 to get to Esquel. To cross into Chile, take the Puyehue Pass via RN 231 (through Villa La Angostura); during periods of heavy snowfall, chains are required. The drive from Buenos Aires will take you upwards of 20 hours, and there are few pit stops en route. Driving here from Buenos Aires, or other far destinations such as El Calafate and Mendoza, is not recommended.

GETTING AROUND   The city center is compact enough to explore on foot. Parking can be atrocious, so best to come in via taxi or public bus. Most visitors spend just a few hours touring the city, however, and then use it as a base for exploring the region. The main streets for shopping and tourist agencies are Mitre and San Martín/Moreno. The center of town is the scenic Centro Cívico (Civic Center) plaza. From here, distances are measured in kilometers to the east or west. While you may be tempted to try to walk into town along Bustillo, the lakeside road, it's a very busy street that isn't very enjoyable for walking; better to hop in a taxi or take the bus.

Many travelers rent a car to visit this area. You'll need wheels if you're staying for more than a night or two outside the city center or planning to explore the sinuous roads that pass through exceptionally scenic landscapes such as the Circuito Chico on your own. All travel agencies offer bus excursions to these areas, which is another way to see them if you don't drive. Private guided tours are also available. Car rental agencies, such as Budget, Dollar, Hertz, and Avis, have kiosks at the airport as well as a number of downtown offices: **Budget,** Mitre 717 (✆ 02944/426700); **Aka Rent**

a Car, Pajaros Azules 210 (© 02944/15-554050 [mobile]); **Dollar,** Palacios 191, 1st Floor (© 02944/439078); **Hertz,** Bariloche Airport (© 02944/450044); and **Thrifty,** Quaglia 352 (© 02944/427904). Rates are reasonable, starting at around $60 per day. Many agencies are booked solid from mid-December through February so plan ahead. Driving west of town, you have two options: the direct **Pioneros** road that locals use, a few blocks uphill from the lake, or **Bustillo,** the lakeside road. Distances, and addresses, are measured in kilometers west from the Civic Center.

Bariloche's **public bus system** is cheap and efficient, whether you're heading to the Cerro Catedral ski resort or exploring the lakeside route of the Circuito Chico. Regular buses depart from Calle San Martín, just in front of the National Park headquarters, or from Moreno and Palacios. Bus no. 20 follows the shores of Lago Nahuel Huapi past the Campanario chairlift to the Llao Llao Hotel & Resort. Bus no. 10 does the same route but continues past the village at Colonia Suiza. Bus no. 50 will take you directly to Cerro Catedral, and snowboards and skis are allowed onboard. Rides cost less than $1.50 (ask the driver for your rate).

When navigating the streets of Bariloche, be aware that two streets have similar names, though they are distinct routes: V.A. (Vice Almirante) O'Connor runs parallel to the Costanera, and J. O'Connor bisects it.

VISITOR INFORMATION The **Secretaría de Turismo,** in the stone-and-wood Civic Center complex between calles Urquiza and Panzoni (© **02944/429850;** www.bariloche.gov.ar/index-turismo.php), has general information about Bariloche and is an indispensable resource if you need last-minute accommodations, especially during the high season. It's open daily 9am to 9pm. They also operate an information stand in the bus terminal (Mon–Fri 8am–9pm; Sat–Sun 9am–9pm). Useful tourism information, as well as the best maps and local books, are available at an information kiosk at the corner of Villegas and Moreno, next to the Artisan Market (no phone).

The **Club Andino Bariloche,** Av. 20 de Febrero 30 (© **02944/422266;** fax 02944/424579; www.clubandino.com.ar), provides excellent information about hiking, backpacking, and mountaineering in the area. They sell maps and provide treks and mountain ascents led by guides from the Club Andino (open daily 9am–1pm and 6–9pm in winter; 8:30am–3pm and 5–9pm in summer). This is an essential stop for those heading into the mountains. For general information about **Nahuel Huapi National Park,** head to the park's headquarters across the street from the Civic Center (© **02944/423111**); it's open Monday through Friday from 8:30am to 12:30pm.

Bringing a Car into Chile

If you're hoping to do a Lake District circuit combining both the Argentine and Chilean lake districts, be warned that you'll need additional insurance and written permission from the car-rental agency to take the vehicle across the border. If you are planning to drive back to Argentina, you'll have no problems but you will need special papers. Few agencies, however, will allow you to leave the car in Chile. I suggest using Budget or Avis for these trips: They're the only companies with offices in numerous towns in both countries; they can offer roadside assistance, and they can quickly provide you with a replacement car if you run into problems. *Note:* The passes into Chile require chains in wintertime.

Good websites for up-to-date travel information about the region include **www. bariloche.org** and **www.interpatagonia.com**.

[FastFACTS] BARILOCHE

Banks & Currency Exchange Most banks exchange currency, including **Banco Galicia,** Moreno and Quaglia (☏ **02944/ 427125**), and **Banco Frances,** San Martín 336 (☏ **02944/430315**). Banks close at 1pm, but have 24-hour ATMs outside. Try also **Cambio Sudamérica,** Mitre 63 (☏ **02944/ 434555**).

Hospital The best hospital in town is **Sanatorio San Carlos,** Bustillo Km 1 (☏ **02944/435-099;** www. ssancarlos.com.ar).

Internet Access Internet cafes are on just about every corner—and almost every hotel has Internet access, which is usually free for guests. Try **CyberFirenza,** Quaglia 262, Loc. 20 (☏ **02944/422038**), or **Net & Cappuccino,** Quaglia 220 (☏ **02944/426128**). The cost is less than $2 per hour.

Laundry Most hotels will send out your laundry for you. There are two reliable laundromats where you can take your own clothes for a reduced rate: **Milco,** at Villegas 146 (☏ **02944/**

422331), and **Lavadero Huemul,** on Juramento 36 (☏ **02944/522067**).

Pharmacy The three main pharmacies in the city center are **Angel Gallardo,** A. Gallardo 701 (☏ **02944/ 427023**); **Zona Vital,** Moreno 301 (☏ **02944/ 420752**); and **Nahuel,** Moreno 238 (☏ **02944/ 422490**).

Police For emergencies, dial **101.** For other matters, call ☏ **02944/423434.**

Post Office The central post office (☏ **02944/ 425100**) is at Moreno 175.

Seeing the Sights

Bariloche's **Centro Cícivo (Civic Center),** Avenida Juan Manuel de Rosas and Calle Panzoni, is a charming stone-and-wood complex that houses most municipal offices and tourism services, such as the information center and national park headquarters. The complex, built in 1940, was inspired by the architecture of Bern, Switzerland. Here you'll find the **Museo de la Patagonia Perito Moreno** (☏ **02944/422309;** www.bariloche.com.ar/museo), open Tuesday through Friday from 10am to 12:30pm and 2 to 7pm, and Saturday from 10am to 6pm (suggested donation: $1.25). The museum has five salons dedicated to the natural science, history, and ethnography of the Bariloche region. The well-tended displays here are intriguing, notably the stuffed and mounted local fauna, such as *pudú* (miniature deer), puma, condor, and more. The second floor has displays of Mapuche artifacts such as weapons, art, jewelry, and other artifacts from the colonial period. A small gift shop sells postcards, books, and crafts.

SHOPPING You'll find everything and anything along Bariloche's main street, Mitre, including shops selling souvenirs and Argentine products such as *mate* (tea), gourds, and leather goods. For the region's famous smoked meats and cheese, and other regional specialties such as trout pâté, try the renowned **Familia Weiss,** V. A. O'Connor 401 (☏ 02944/424829), or **Del Turista,** Mitre 239 (☏ 02944/424725). Del Turista also has an enormous array of chocolates and candy, as do other confectioneries up and down Calle Mitre, such as **Abuela Goye,** Mitre 258 (☏ 02944/433861), and Quaglia 221 (☏ 02944/422276); **Mexicana,** Mitre 288

WHAT'S WITH ALL THE chocolate?

Bariloche is a chocolate-lover's heaven. Within 3 blocks on the main drag, Calle Mitre, dozens of chocolate shops offer tasty morsels of artisan chocolate. The industry sprang from early Swiss pioneers who settled at the nearby village of Colonia Suiza and saw the potential in all those healthy cows. Classic local flavors include *dulce de leche,* chocolate with lemon, and chocolate with local berries. All the shops are quite good and produce high-quality chocolate, but the constant lines in **Mamuschka,** Mitre 298 (**(*** 02944/423294**)**, attest to the fact that this shop sells the absolute best chocolate in town. It's worth waiting your turn for the cute red boxes of delicious treats. Mamuschka also has a nice smoke-free cafe inside, and a branch at the base of Cerro Catedral ski resort. (Take note of the colorful tile work, by a local artist, on the sidewalk when you enter Mamuschka.)

(*** 02944/422505); and **Mamuschka ★**, Mitre 298 (*** 02944/423294). Stop by the Information Center in the Civic Center (see above) for a map of Avenida Bustillo and the Llao Llao Peninsula, which are lined with dozens of shops selling regional goods. One of the best for home furnishings and accents is **El Coihue,** at Bustillo Km 15.5 (*** 02944/448623). Also try the charming tiny shop **Los Juncos,** Bustillo Km 20 (*** 02944/448107).

For local handicrafts predominantly made of wood and wool, stroll the **outdoor artisan market ★** behind the Centro Cívico, held Thursday through Monday afternoons, from noon to 8pm (depending on the time of year). It's also worth checking out the indoor **artisan market** on Moreno between Quaglia and Villegas, which is open daily from 11am to 8pm. There is a small shop of all-natural wool products run by a local Mapuche indigenous group. All the vendors are friendly.

TOUR OPERATORS

A plethora of travel agencies offer everything under the sun along the streets of Bariloche. Most tours do not include lunch, and all charge extra for a bilingual guide. The best of the lot includes **Travelideas,** Villegas 316 (*** 02944/424659; www.travel ideas.com.ar), and **Limay Travel,** V.A. O'Connor 710 (*** 02944/420268; www. limaytravel.com.ar). Both offer a wide variety of land excursions to El Bolsón, Cerro Tronador, and circuit sightseeing routes. **Senza Limiti** (*** 02944/520597) specializes in adventure sports such as kayaking, trekking, and horseback riding, as well as creative and fun multiday outings that combine activities. They can also help with car rentals and hotel accommodations.

Parque Nacional Nahuel Huapi ★★

Nahuel Huapi is Argentina's oldest and most popular national park, with a range of activities for any fitness level. It stretches from the Seven Lakes Road in the north to the Manso River in the south. The park also surrounds the city of Bariloche, and its headquarters are downtown in the Civic Center (see "Seeing the Sights," above). The park's main feature is the 3,500m (11,480-ft.) extinct volcano **Tronador (Thunderer),** named for the rumbling produced by ice falling from the mountain's peak. But the park is also known for its glacial-formed Lake Nahuel Huapi (the largest of more than a dozen lakes), as well as its lovely forested peninsulas and its waterways,

Say What?

You're not the only one who has trouble pronouncing the name of Bariloche's stunning lake and national park, **Nahuel Huapi**—that's *nah*-well *wah*-pee. It means Island of the Tiger in the native Mapuche language. With 524 sq. km (204 sq. miles), this stunning lake is more like an inland sea, connecting the lush forests and high peaks of the Andes with the rugged plains of the Patagonian Steppe.

which are often compared to the channels of southern Chilean Patagonia or the fiords of Norway. During summertime, visitors can take part in day hikes or backpacking trips, with many trails to choose from, or boat out to the lake's largest island, Isla Victoria. The park also has plenty of other outdoor activities such as rafting, horseback riding, and fishing; during the winter, the park's other dominant peak, **Cerro Catedral,** is a popular ski resort, the largest and most-visited in South America. Easy access to all regions of the park makes Nahuel Huapi popular with visitors seeking mellower activities, such as sightseeing drives and chairlifts to magnificent lookout points. The following information applies to all attractions within Nahuel Huapi and around Bariloche.

The Road to the Llao Llao Peninsula ★★★

The **Cerro Campanario ★** provides possibly the best lookout point in the region, with exceptional views of Nahuel Huapi and Perito Moreno lakes, as well as the ravishing beauty of the Llao Llao Peninsula and the peaks surrounding it. The lookout point is accessed by a 7-minute chairlift ride located 18km (11 miles) outside Bariloche on the road to Llao Llao, meaning you'll have to arrange transportation with a tour, drive a rental car, or take the local bus no. 20, which departs from behind the Centro Cívico on Calle San Martín. A cafe and restaurant here offer panoramic views. Call © **02944/448151** for information. The first lift goes up daily at 9am and the last lift of the day comes down at 6pm; the cost for the chairlift is $10, and you don't need reservations. Just show up at the chairlift at Avenida Bustillo, Km 17.5, during operating hours. You can also hike up a 2km (1½-mile) dusty trail for free; it will take you about 40 minutes, but you have to pay for the chairlift ride down ($5).

The Cerro Campanario is along a popular 60km (37-mile) drive around the Llao Llao Peninsula, commonly known as the **Circuito Chico ★★**. This drive affords spectacular views of the Nahuel Huapi and Perito Moreno lakes as well as the snow-capped peaks of Cerro Lopez, Capilla, and Catedral, which tower over the water. The route also goes past countless cottages, cabins, cafes, and boutiques. Head west out of town on the lakeside Avenida Bustillo. Eighteen kilometers (11 miles) from Bariloche, the route changes into Ruta 237, loops around the peninsula as Ruta 77, and meets back at Ruta 237 and eventually Bustillo, all the while meandering through dense forest and picturesque bays with outstanding lookout points. There are short hikes en route as well, including a trail through an enchanting *arrayán* (myrtle) forest at the Parque Municipal Llao Llao, and a trail out to the hidden Lago Escondido. Visitors will find *parrilla* (grill) and fondue-style restaurants along the way, as well as the world-renowned **Llao Llao Hotel & Resort** (p. 318). Overlooking the hotel, the lovely **Capilla San Eduardo chapel ★** displays the unique rustic Andean architecture that so typifies Bariloche. In front of the Llao Llao, **Puerto Pañuelo** is the main dock for boat trips (see below), as well as the boat crossing to Chile. Past the Llao Llao, the Ruta 77 continues to a lookout below Cerro Lopez and then descends to Bahía Lopéz, which has a nice beach and is the trail head for a 45-minute hike out to the tip of **Brazo Tristeza,** another large, lovely arm of Nahuel Huapi Lake. Next along the road is the trail head for the hike up to the Refugio Lopez hut, where there is also a snack bar. Farther along, be sure to stop for a photo op at the incredibly picturesque Punto Panorámico. Before you head out, stop by the tourist information center in town to pick up a detailed Circuito Chico map, which highlights restaurants and shops along the way. Again, most tour operators offer this excursion as a bus tour. Another option is to take the local bus along this route, hopping off and on in accordance with the hourly schedule (the tourist information office can also give you a bus schedule).

Cerro Otto

You can walk, bike, drive, or ride a gondola to the top of **Cerro Otto** for sweeping views of Lake Nahuel Huapi, the Llao Llao Peninsula, and the high peaks of Catedral and Tronador. It's the hill closest to town. Popular local pastimes include paragliding, hiking, rock climbing, and, during the winter, cross-country skiing, tobogganing, and dog sledding. To walk (2–3 hr.) or bike, take Avenida Los Pioneros for about 1km (about ½ mile) and follow the signs to Cerro Otto or Piedras Blancas. Or take the free shuttle bus that leaves from Mitre and Villegas; it runs daily on the hour from 10:30am to 4:30pm and drops you off at the gondola base. The **gondola ride** (© 02944/441035) costs $18 per person and runs January through February and July through August daily from 9:30am to 6pm; the rest of the year, it runs daily from 10am to 6pm. Atop the summit, you'll also find a revolving restaurant (© 02944/441035). The view here is not as nice as that at Cerro Campanario (see above) and it's definitely more civilized—packed with tourists and less wild. Better to avoid Otto altogether in favor of Cerro Campanario.

Colonia Suiza ★

Don't miss the quaint Swiss pioneer village at Colonia Suiza, out on the Circuito Chico, for their twice-weekly *curanto* cook-ups—a centuries-old style of cooking meat and vegetables deep in the ground. Both a lesson and a delight, curantos are held on Wednesdays and Sundays at the main plaza in Colonia Suiza. Founded in 1895 by the Swiss Goye and Mermaud families, who crossed into the area from Chile, this is also where Bariloche's chocolate industry was born. It's a tranquil little hamlet with a few restaurants and good campgrounds.

For more local driving tours, see "South of Bariloche," later in this chapter.

Boat Excursions

Several boat excursions run from Puerto San Carlos or Puerto Pañuelo at Llao Llao. The cost fluctuates between $40 and $55 per person, so to obtain exact prices for any of the following trips and to make a reservation, stop by any travel agency or call © 02944/429850 for more information.

An enjoyable full-day excursion takes you to **Isla Victoria** and the **Bosque Arrayanes** (see also "Villa La Angostura," later in this chapter) by boat from Puerto Pañuelo. The excursion begins with a 30-minute sail to Isla Victoria, a giant midlake island, where passengers can disembark for a walk through a conifer forest or ascend to a lookout point atop Cerro Bella Vista via chairlift. The second stop is Península

Quetrihué and the Bosque Arrayanes, famous for its concentration of the unusual terra-cotta-colored arrayán tree. This handsome "tree" is really a bush, with an odd, slick trunk that is cool to the touch. The peninsula can also be accessed from Villa La Angostura (discussed later). From Puerto Pañuelo to Isla Victoria, trips leave at 10am and return at 5:30pm. Cost is $40 per person. Book via **Cau Cau,** Mitre 139 (© **2944/431372;** www.islavictoriayarrayanes.com).

Another boat trip heads to **Puerto Blest** at the far west of Nahuel Huapi Lake, sailing through classic fiords and exuberant vegetation known as the Valdivian Forest. From this point, there is a lovely hike up to a wide cascade and peaceful mountain lake, with a giant *alerce* tree next door that's more than 1,200 years old. Visitors can dine at the restaurant at Puerto Blest or bring a picnic lunch. These trips are very crowded in the summer. An interesting alternative is to hire a private hiking or naturalist guide (see "Outdoor Activities," below), who will lead you away from the crowds and deep in to the forest while your boat is docked at Puerto Blest. From Puerto Pañuelo, trips to Puerto Blest leave at 10am and return at 5pm. Cost is $40 per person. This is the first leg of the Cruce Andino lake crossing to Chile (see earlier in this chapter).

Outdoor Activities

BIKING   Mountain bike rental and information about bike trails and guided trips in Nahuel Huapi are available from **Bike Way Mountain,** V.A. O'Connor 867 (© **02944/425616);** and **Dirty Bikes,** V. A. O'Connor 681 (© **02944/425616).**

FISHING   This region provides anglers with excellent fly-fishing on the Manso, Limay, Traful, and Machico rivers. Fishermen also troll on Lake Nahuel Huapi for introduced species such as brown trout, rainbow trout, and landlocked salmon. Even hard-core anglers will find enough to keep them busy here for weeks on end. The fishing season opens in November and runs through April. You can pick up information and fishing licenses at the **Baruzzi Fly Shop,** Urquiza 250 (© **02944/424922),** or the office of the Parque Nacional Nahuel Huapi in the Civic Center. Bariloche is home to dozens of fly-fishing guides. Be sure to choose one who is fully licensed and provides lunch, transfers, and the appropriate gear. I recommend Nico Martin at **Bariloche Anglers** (© **02944/462102;** www.barilocheanglers.com.ar) or **Martin Ferrer** (© **02944/15-634752** [mobile]). Costs generally run around $350 per day for up to two people. Trolling and spinning are also available.

GOLF   There are three golf courses in the Bariloche area. The crème de la crème is the par-70 18-hole course at the **Llao Llao Hotel & Resort** (© **02944/445753;** www.llaollao.com). Above the shores of Lago Gutierrez, the **Arelauquen Golf Resort** (© **02944/476110;** www.arelauquen.com), is the newest 18-hole course in the area. There are 9 holes at the **Pinares Golf Club** (© **02944/462416;** www. pinares.us) on the road to the Llao Llao. Most course are open from mid-September through mid-May, and fees run from $35 to $60.

HIKING   The Nahuel Huapi National Park has a well-developed trail system for day hikes, multiple-day hikes, and loops that connect several backcountry *refugios,* some of which offer rustic lodging. The national park office in the Civic Center provides detailed maps and guides to the difficulty level of each trail. Local hiking guides will share their knowledge and make for a safe and rewarding outing. An excellent multilingual local hiking guide and naturalist is **Max Schoffel** (✆ **02944/15-669669** [mobile]; www.patagoniatravelco.com). Another great source for information is **Club Andino,** Av. 20 de Febrero 30 (✆ **02944/422266**; www.clubandino.com.ar), which also has trails, guided trekking, ice walks, and climbing trips on Cerro Tronador.

HORSEBACK RIDING Horseback rides in various areas of the park are offered by **Carol Jones,** M. Victoria 5600 (✆ **02944/426508**; www.caroljones.com.ar); rides run about $40 for 2 hours, $55 for 3 hours. Another nice option is the friendly gauchos at **Cabalgatas Haneck** (✆ **02944/441558**). Across the lake, **Cuyin Manzano** (✆ **02944/15-651946**; www.cuyinmanzano.com) is a step back in time to a truly rural outpost just an hour's drive from Bariloche. They offer trips ranging from 1 day to 5 days. Finally, **Gatomancha** (✆ **02944/523009**; www.gatomancha.com) offers overnight and multiday horseback riding trips.

KAYAK TOURING Recently, the many fiords of Nahuel Huapi Lake have been tempting visitors to explore in sea kayaks, or touring kayaks. It's a lovely outing that's possible in a variety of weather conditions. Operators such as **Senza Limiti** (✆ **02944/520597**; www.slimiti.com) also offer overnight tours, often year-round.

MOUNTAINEERING Experienced climbers, and those looking for a taste of the high peaks, have plenty of options in Bariloche, including the challenging 3-day climb of Mt. Tronador. Contact **Andes Cross** (✆ **02944/15-633581** [mobile]; www.andescross.com) for guiding services.

RAFTING Various companies offer river rafting on the Río Manso in both Class III and Class IV sections, on full-day trips. The Rafting Frontera trip takes you to the Chilean border and is truly a thrill. The average cost for a trip is $85 to $95. Easier floats down the Class I Río Limay are also available, for about $75 for a half-day. Excursions include all equipment, transportation, and a snack or lunch (full-day trips). The two best local rafting companies are **Patagonia Rafting,** San Martín 86 (✆ **02944/525362**), and **Extremo Sur,** Morales 765 (✆ **02944/427301**).

SKIING & SNOWBOARDING Bariloche's main winter draw is the ski resort at **Cerro Catedral ★** (✆ **02944/423776**; www.catedralaltapatagonia.com). When the resort's two former halves joined in 2005, everyone rejoiced. That fusion meant more terrain, better lifts, and close to a dozen on-slope restaurants to choose from, making this perhaps South America's greatest ski hill. The scenery is stunning. Lift tickets range from $28 to $48 for adults, $15 to $32 for kids, depending on high and low seasons. The season usually runs from June through October, with mid-August by far the busiest and most expensive time (when all Argentines have their 2-week winter holidays). Heavy snowfalls in September the past few years have helped keep the top sections open well into spring (which here means mid-Oct). Regardless, experienced skiers will want to stay high and explore the mountain from Punta Princesa to the south to Piedra del Condor on the north. There is lots of terrain for beginners and intermediates, as well as a snowboard park and tons of events throughout the season. For great slopeside atmosphere and a drop-dead view, have lunch at the traditional Refugio Lynch. Nonskiers can also enjoy the scene thanks to pedestrian lifts, open daily, that ferry passengers to the top. Every July, Catedral hosts the **National Snow Party,** with torchlight parades and other events (contact the Catedral ski resort for more information and the current year's dates). The bustling Villa

Catedral is at the base of the resorts, with a jumble of shops, rental stores, and several lodging options. The only ski-in, ski-out hotel is **Pire-Hue Hotel and Resort** (📞 **02944/460040;** www.pire-hue.com.ar). The upscale ★ **Galileo Boutique Hotel** (📞 **02944/460388;** www.galileoboutiquehotel.com) also boasts a world-class astronomy observatory. **Sudbruck Hostería** has a handful of spacious rooms decorated with rustic cypress wood (📞 **02944/460156;** www.sudbruck.com). Rooms start at about $125 per night for a double. **Cabañas Antu Pukem** has cabins for six to eight guests; consult them directly for prices (📞 **02944/460035**).

During the summer, the main gondolas are open to pedestrians for sightseeing Monday to Friday from 9:15am to 4pm.

Where to Stay

If you're looking for luxury, you'll find the most options along Avenida Bustillo, the main road outside town that runs parallel to the lake and leads to the Llao Llao Peninsula. The larger hotels in the city (such as the Panamericano) tend to cater to tour groups or students and aren't especially luxurious or service oriented. If you're planning to rent a car, then by all means stay outside the city and drive in at your convenience. You can also take the local bus or a quick taxi ride.

During the high season (Dec 15–Feb 28 and Easter week), prices double. Many hotels consider the winter months of July and August to be a second high season, with prices to match. The cheapest rates are from March 1 to June 30 and September 1 to December 15. Dates vary; inquire before booking and always ask for promotions or discounts for multiday stays. Rates listed here are generally for high season.

WITHIN THE CITY CENTER
Very Expensive

Hotel Panamericano 〰 You can't miss the massive Hotel Panamericano, somewhat of a white elephant in Bariloche. It's apparently midway through a desperately needed makeover, essential if the hotel wants to keep its five stars (right now I'd say it's a three-plus), but it's slow going. With 300 rooms, a casino, and a conference center, it's the biggest hotel in Patagonia. For the price, it offers none of the warmth, natural setting, or style of the Llao Llao (p. 318), for example. Rooms are spacious if standard. Hallways are particularly dark and dreary. The new spa, however, is the finest in town, with a lovely top-floor pool and deck. Lake views are available only above the fifth floor; in fact, the hotel rarely books rooms on the bottom floors unless they're hosting a convention, although they have plenty of tour groups that keep the hotel busy year-round. The back rooms face an ugly building, but they're cheaper. The junior suites are quite nice and are actually a better deal than the regular suites. inside the lobby, a faux waterfall trickles in the background, and a bar/lounge regularly has live piano music. The hotel has another 100 or so rooms and a casino on the other side of the street, connected by an aerial walkway.

Av. San Martín 536, San Carlos de Bariloche. 📞/fax **02944/425846.** www.panamericanobariloche. com. 306 units. $338 double; $360 double with lake view; from $560 suite. Rates include buffet breakfast. AE, DC, MC, V. Free valet parking. **Amenities:** 2 restaurants; bar; lounge; exercise room; massage; indoor pool; room service; sauna. *In room:* TV, minibar.

Moderate

Alpenglow Boutique Hotel ★ Slip out of the hustle and bustle of downtown Bariloche and relax in this recently refurbished 10-room inn steps from the Centro Cívico. The spacious and fantastically quiet lobby sets a tone of upscale comfort.

Mid-range prices are spot-on. The rooms mainly have lake views. Separated bathrooms have state-of-the-art adjustable shower heads, plus towel heaters. A top floor suite is tucked under the original wooden beams and has a view over the lake to one side and the lights of the Centro Cívico to the other. No other downtown inn has as much heart and such good taste. Ask about regular promotions. This is a much welcomed addition to Bariloche's hotel scene.

Libertad 195, San Carlos de Bariloche. ✆ **02944/422229.** www.alpenglowhotel.com. 10 units. $150 double; $190 studio; $270 suite. Rates include breakfast. AE, MC, V. **Amenities:** Bar; babysitting; concierge; free use of computer; Wi-Fi. *In room:* TV, hair dryer, minibar.

Cacique Inacayal A new hotel right on the waterfront, the Inacayal offers comfortable rooms with great lake views, and it's just steps from town. The hotel clings to the side of the hill reaching down to a stony beach (you enter at the main road level). Traffic noise outside is a problem, as are the discos next door, so request a room on the quieter west side. Still, indoors it's all business, with an efficient atrium-view elevator and bow-tied waiters. All rooms have great views, and the bottom-floor rooms include terraces. Decor is standard, with a dash of modernity. Lacquered wood, wicker, and wool predominate. The "Gran Confort" double rooms are cheaper than a suite but plenty spacious. The hotel has packages that include breakfast and dinner, a strange option as what most appeals is its proximity to so many other restaurants.

Juan M. de Rosas 625, San Carlos de Bariloche. ✆ **02944/433888.** www.hotelinacayal.com.ar. 67 units. $159–$199 double; $230 suite. Rates include breakfast. AE, MC, V. **Amenities:** Restaurant; lobby cafe; wine bar; garden w/beach access; pool; spa; Wi-Fi. *In room:* Minibar.

Inexpensive

Hostería Las Marianas ★★ 🎒 A lovely, cozy inn just a few blocks from the Centro Cívico, this is a great choice if you want both the convenience of downtown and the tranquillity of residential Bariloche. It's a renovated old Austrian-style mansion. The managers are friendly and fun. Beds have luxurious down comforters. The bedrooms aren't large, and bathrooms are particularly tight, but the warmth of the entire place makes up for it. Four new rooms on the top floor have nice views.

24 de Septiembre 218, San Carlos de Bariloche. ✆/fax **02944/439876.** www.hosterialasmarianas.com.ar. 14 units. $94 double; $108 triple. Rates include buffet breakfast. AE, MC, V. **Amenities:** Lounge; high-speed Internet. *In room:* TV, hair dryer.

Patanuk Guesthouse With a hostel vibe and an awesome location right on the lake, the doubles and twins with private bathrooms here are good value. The style is loftlike, with an industrial design and local art on display. The shared rooms have a handful of bunk beds and the best views. Privates have a very simple bathroom with a stall shower. In the evenings, the garden opens up into a funky bar. There's a tiny computer squeezed in by the office that guests can use. If all you want is a fun, safe place to spend the night, then this is a good choice—but opt for the private bathroom.

Juan Manuel de Rosas 585, San Carlos de Bariloche. ✆ **02944/434991.** www.patanuk.com. 30 beds. $60 double with private bathroom; from $17 bunk. No credit cards. **Amenities:** Kitchen; bar; garden.

View Boutique Hotel 🎒 Practical, comfortable, and modern, this boutique-style hotel is just a block up the hill from the heart of town. The main floor is a large, bright lobby, where breakfast is served. As the name suggests, there are great views of the lake. Dark wood and cream walls characterize the rooms, which are a bit small but have cozy chocolate-colored fleece blankets and lots of closet space. Bathrooms have the same look, with dark wood and marble. A triple has a small deck (ask for an upgrade if you've booked a double). The owners, who opened the View in 2008, are here all the time to welcome you and help you organize your days. The convenience of being so close to town is hard to beat, and the modern vibe is refreshing.

Tucumán 221, San Carlos de Bariloche. ©/fax **02944/522221.** www.viewhotel.com.ar. 12 units. $100 double; $126 triple. AE, MC, V. **Amenities:** Bar; concierge; Wi-Fi. *In room:* TV.

OUTSIDE THE CITY CENTER, ON THE ROAD TO THE LLAO LLAO PENINSULA
Very Expensive

El Casco Art Hotel ★★★   Exclusive and elegant, this award-winning upscale inn midway between Bariloche and the Llao Llao is a spectacular place, what all hotel reviewers hunt for. It has remarkable services and amenities for an inn with only 33 rooms, not to mention a lovely lakeside setting. As the name suggests, there is high-brow artwork throughout—320 outstanding paintings and sculptures by some of the most important names in Latin American art to be exact. The hotel is just small enough to feel intimate. The rooms are hard to beat, both for their size (bathrooms are practically palatial) and their tasteful style. Plush marble bathrooms are slick and have separate tub and shower. The spa and pool could be considered small, but don't forget, there are only 33 rooms here. The restaurant offers high art–inspired gourmet food. For all the pluses, there is a high price. But if excellent quality is your priority, and money isn't such a concern, this is a superb choice.

Av. Bustillo, Km 11.5, San Carlos de Bariloche. © **02944/462929.** www.hotelelcasco.com. 33 units. $390–$660 double; $825–$1,210 suite. Rates include breakfast and transfers. AE, MC, V. **Amenities:** Restaurant; bar; free airport transfer; health club; indoor/outdoor pool; spa. *In room:* A/C, TV, DVD player, minibar, stereo.

Hostería Isla Victoria Lodge ★★ 💼   How about a few nights at a remote lodge on an island in the middle of a huge mountain lake? Isla Victoria Lodge, on the island of the same name, is located in the middle of the massive Nahuel Huapi Lake and makes for a divine upscale getaway. The views are truly stunning, with gourmet food, talented guides, and superb all-inclusive packages to match. The lodge itself was originally built in the 1940s and reopened (after a large fire) in 2002. In your spacious, comfortable room perched atop a cliff, you'll have the best view in the entire national park. But you won't be in your room much—most of your time will be spent outside, exploring the island—on foot, horseback, by bike or kayak. When the daily boat tours depart, you'll have the island to yourself. In the evenings, enjoy fine dining with an even finer view in the restaurant. It's romantic and intimate. Although children aren't specifically prohibited, families are gently discouraged, which is a shame as the island is a childhood dream come true. A 2-night stay here is just right.

Nahuel Huapi National Park. © **02944/448088.** www.islavictoria.com. 22 units. 2-night packages from $515 per person double; 4-night packages $1,030 per person double. Packages include transfers, boat crossing, lodging, full board, excursions. AE, DC, MC, V. **Amenities:** Bar; wine cellar; library, outdoor pool; spa.

Llao Llao Hotel & Resort ★★ ☺   This internationally renowned resort is one of the finest hotels in Latin America. Situated on a grassy crest of the Llao Llao Peninsula and framed by rugged peaks, this five-star hotel is reminiscent of Canadian mountain lodges, with cypress and pine-log walls, stone fireplaces, antler chandeliers, and barn-size salons. Maintaining very high standards and offering a slew of amenities, this is *the* place to spend the night if you're willing to splurge for a special evening. A driveway winds upward to the hotel, where a discreet security guard monitors traffic (the hotel tries to keep gawkers at a distance, although visitors may come for a drink, afternoon tea, or a meal, but only with a prior reservation). From the lobby, every turn leads to another remarkable room, including a "winter garden" cafe, whose expansive glass walls look out onto a large patio, the hotel's golf course, and Lake Nahuel Huapi beyond. All rooms are decorated in a rustic country design and have gleaming white bathrooms. Standard rooms are comfortable but quite small; superior suites are split into bedroom and living areas and some come with a wraparound deck and fireplace; a lovely two-bedroom cabin with a splendid view of Lake Moreno is also available. Opened in 2008, the hotel's new Moreno Wing has 43 suites and studios that were designed to please North Americans—they are larger and have wide windows, terraces, air-conditioning, and massive bathrooms. The spa affords views that are nothing less than panoramic. A myriad of daily activities are included in the price of the rooms, from adult watercolor-painting classes to games and events for kids. Transfers to and from the airport and the ski hill are also included. The hotel's fine-dining restaurant, Los Cesares, is currently well overshadowed by nearby restaurants. It's definitely time for the hotel to up the ante with better dining options.

Av. Bustillo, Km 25, San Carlos de Bariloche. ② **02944/448530.** Fax 02944/445789. Reservations (in Buenos Aires). ② **11/4311-3434.** Fax 11/4314-4646. www.llaollao.com. 172 units. $385–$532 double; $532–$954 studio; $587–$1,145 suite; $715 cottage. Rates include buffet breakfast and valet parking. Rates rise substantially during the holidays, Christmas to New Year's, and Easter. AE, DC, MC, V. **Amenities:** 2 restaurants; bar; lounge; babysitting; golf course; exercise room; Jacuzzi; massage; small indoor heated pool; room service; fabulous spa; tennis courts; extensive watersports equipment. *In room:* A/C (some), TV, minibar.

Expensive

Aldebaran ★ 🎁 Serenity, silence, and highly personalized service make this remote retreat one of the Lake District's newest treasures. Far off the typical tourist route, each of the 10 rooms here enjoys lovely views across the Campanario Arm of Nahuel Huapi Lake. The design and construction are very natural, from stone-and-wood walls to cement floors. Thick Mediterranean-style walls have curved ceilings and dark hallways. Rooms are large, with earth-toned blankets, cozy nooks, and a blend of modern and recycled furniture. Rustic bathrooms have large tubs and spotlights. All have either a balcony or a patio. Downstairs, an indoor/outdoor pool and serene spa are deeply relaxing. There's a new lakeside deck and a "dojo" for yoga and relaxing. Ten minutes down a dirt road, on the coast of the San Pedro Peninsula, Aldebaran is a compelling hideaway. (Media junkies be warned: Rooms don't have TV.) Staying here without a rental car, however, can be a headache, as each outing requires waiting for a taxi to come, and many excursions and guides won't pick you up at a place so remote.

Península San Pedro, Av. Bustillo, Km 20.4, San Carlos de Bariloche. ② **02944/465143.** www.aldebaranpatagonia.com. 10 units. From $282 double; $396 suite. Rates include breakfast and free airport transfer. AE, V. **Amenities:** Restaurant; bar; spa; dock; TV/DVD room. *In room:* Hair dryer.

Design Suites It's been open for a few years now, and the trendy chic facade of this hotel is beginning to wane. The exterior look is ultramodern, and the location, 2.5km (1½ miles) from town amid a large garden, is quite good—close enough to town to walk, but outside the hustle and bustle. The interior design is contemporary and minimalist, with local materials such as wood, stone, and glass enhanced by a revolving display of local art. Rooms are among the largest in town, with light hardwood floors, crisp cream walls, plenty of shelving, and small patios. They may remind you of IKEA showrooms. Ample bathrooms have heated floors. All have either a jetted tub or a full hot tub nestled beneath a bay window. They all have advanced technology appliances, from snazzy little stereo systems to flatscreen televisions. Entrance hallways allow rooms to stay clean and dry. The junior suites have the best views. The rooms are spread among four buildings, each with an outdoor elevator. So you must go outside to get to and fro (and up and down a slight hill); be prepared to brave the weather! Breakfast is served in the main building.

Av. Bustillo, Km 2.5, San Carlos de Bariloche. (© **02944/457000.** www.designsuites.com. 78 units. $215–$255 double; $280–$335 junior suite. Rates include continental breakfast. AE, MC, V. **Amenities:** Restaurant; bar; gym; indoor/outdoor pool; sauna; kids' club; spa; art gallery. *In room:* TV, minibar, stereo.

Villa Huinid ★ Villa Huinid is a sprawling complex facing the lake, just 2.5km (1½ miles) from the city center, backed by a thick forest with a walking trail. There are 12 cabins handcrafted of knotty cypress, and graced with some privacy, and a newer hotel complex with 50 high-level rooms that is popular with tour groups. Cabins have stone fireplaces, lovely decks with a full-size barbecue, and a handsome decor of floral wallpaper and craftsy furniture. The units come as four-, six-, and eight-person cabanas with fully stocked kitchens. In the main building, spacious and bright standard rooms have a cozy, country cottage style. The bathrooms are sumptuous, with wooden sinks and hydro-massage tubs. The large spa boasts a spectacular indoor pool.

Av. Bustillo, Km 2.5, San Carlos de Bariloche. (©/fax **02944/523523.** www.villahuinid.com.ar. 62 units. $139–$333 forest-view double; $159–$459 lake-view double; $220–$715 cabins (sleeping 4–6 people). AE, DC, MC, V. **Amenities:** Restaurant; lounge; gym; pool; spa; high-speed Internet. *In room:* TV, fridge.

Moderate

Hotel Sol del Nahuel ★ 🛏 Making full use of a strategic lakeside location, this inn is bright, cheery, and peaceful. It comfortably lets the lake be the star of the scene. Positioned below the main road, the hotel is protected from traffic noise, unlike many of the other inns along Bustillo. The lobby is reminiscent of an Alpine ski chalet, with a massive fireplace and comfy couches. All rooms have spectacular views overlooking the lake. Rooms are large, with wood floors and neutral colors that let the gorgeous blues of the lake shine. Downstairs, a warm indoor/outdoor pool is open year-round. The grounds also encompass a vast garden with a private beach and barbecue.

Av. Bustillo, Km 5.4, San Carlos de Bariloche. (© **02944/520700.** www.soldelnahuel.com.ar. 12 units. $175 double. Rates include airport transfers and breakfast. AE, MC, V. **Amenities:** Restaurant; bar; garden; massage; pool; sauna. *In room:* TV, minibar.

Posada Los Juncos ★★ Some inns just get it right, that elusive mixture of style and substance, warmth and comfort. Los Juncos is run by a sister and brother who've had great success since opening this tiny five-room inn in an old home outside town. Each room is completely unique, but rich in character and mixing old and new. The "air" room has a separate living room, and a nice view of the lake; "water" has a boat theme; and "soul" is the suite on offer, with a romantic feel. There are always fresh flowers, superb coffee and tea, and new friends to be made. They have an excellent little **restaurant** that is open to the public in their candlelit front room (by reservation only). Few places offer this level of personalized service and good taste at such an accessible price. You are far from town, but a bus goes by regularly.

Av. Bustillo Km 20, San Carlos de Bariloche. ℰ **02944/448485.** www.visitlosjuncos.com. 5 units. $155 double; $180 suite. No credit cards. **Amenities:** Restaurant; lounge; computer; concierge; Wi-Fi. *In room:* No phones.

CABANAS

The southern shoreline of Nahuel Huapi Lake is dotted with cabin complexes for visitors. Some have only one or two cabanas for rent, while others have up to a dozen. They're a nice way to be self-sufficient, prepare your own meals, and make yourself at home. Some can be very affordable, especially outside the high-season months of January and August. Bungalows and apart-hotels are similar options. Try the fun **El Bosque de los Elfos,** Avenida Bustillo, Km 5 (ℰ **02944/442356;** www. bungalowsdeloselfos.com.ar), or the upscale lakefront **Puerto Pireo,** Bustillo Km 17.1 (ℰ **02944/448484;** www.puertopireo.com.ar). **Patagonia Vista,** Bustillo Km 21.85 (ℰ **02944/448735;** www.patagoniavista.com.ar), is a new complex also right on the lake, with lake houses available.

Where to Eat

The restaurants in downtown Bariloche, unlike the hotels, are an excellent value. Still, the choicest meals to be had are lakeside. Meals here, often like the service, are leisurely; always allow plenty of time for lunch (2 hr.) and dinner (3 hr.).

WITHIN THE CITY CENTER
Expensive

i latina NUEVO LATINO   Opened by immigrants from Colombia, this trendy restaurant has brought some color and pizzazz to downtown Bariloche. Across from the main cathedral, it is a nice break from the "triple Ps" (pizza, pasta, *parrilla*). The cuisine is a blend of Latino influences, from Mexico to Brazil, with an emphasis on discovering new tastes; *maracuyá* (passion fruit), tamarind, black rice, and mango figure into many dishes. The tamarind pulp is imported from Bogotá. Try the Peruvian *tacu tacu* or the pork with mango chutney and beet risotto. And without a doubt, they have the best ceviche in Argentine Patagonia. The superfriendly staff, many of whom speak English, is eager to please. There's a lively cocktail bar upstairs.

V.A. O'Connor 541. ℰ **02944/428520.** Reservations recommended in summer. Main courses $14–$20. AE, MC, V. Mon–Thurs noon–4pm and 8pm–midnight; Fri–Sat noon–4pm and 8pm–4am.

Kandahar REGIONAL   Named after the famed European ski race, rather than the Afghani capital, Kandahar is one of the best restaurants in town. In this funky and colorful old house with cozy nooks, the food is creative and fresh. The rosehip soup is a great starter, as is the Kandahar salad with greens from the owner's garden and smoked venison. For main dishes, try homemade pastas such as gnocchi with olives, trout with spinach, rabbit with quince sauce, or peppered tenderloin. The desserts are excellent, including grilled spiced apples with ice cream. This place is always busy, so a reservation is essential. Lately, they've been having trouble with their credit card system, so if that's essential to you, call ahead to double-check.

20 de Febrero 628. ℰ **02944/424702.** Reservations highly recommended. Main courses $22–$26. AE. Daily 8pm–midnight.

Naan ★★ 🍴 FUSION   Hard to find but impossible to forget, Naan is a revelation in Patagonia. The couple (he's the chef, she's the service) who operate this small restaurant inside a house in a leafy neighborhood have traveled the world and brought the flavors back to Bariloche. Starters range from Italian and Middle Eastern dishes to Vietnamese and French specialties. Main courses include a lamb curry and a coconut chicken and prawns that will awaken your senses. They also prepare a souvlaki and tofu tempura—practically a revolutionary dish for these parts. And the filet mignon *a la pampa* is divine. Less adventurous diners will delight in the simple, delicate trout. The view is spectacular, and the vibe is slightly chaotic but sensual and delightful. They close for holidays in low season, so call before heading out.

Campichuelo 568. ⓒ **02944/421785.** Reservations required. Main courses $18–$21. No credit cards. Jan–Easter and July 10–Sept daily 8–11:30pm; post-Easter to July 9 and Oct–Dec Tues–Sun 8–11:30pm.

Santos ★ MODERN ITALIAN This location on Calle España has been a revolving door for some of the most interesting restaurants in the area. Right now, Santos is one of the best in the center of Bariloche. It's hip, fun, and stylish, with a menu based on simple, fresh food that is remarkably flavorful. Entrees include superb sirloin-stuffed *panzotti* with spinach and cream sauce. Tourist favorites like fondues (the "Santos" version includes bacon, endives, and cherry tomatoes), a straightforward peppered tenderloin, and local trout are also on the list. There's a living room for chilling out, and a wine list that has lots of excellent midrange options. Try the Corte B from Vistalba.

España 268. ⓒ **02944/425942.** Reservations highly recommended. Main courses $15–$22. No credit cards. Dec–Mar and July–Aug daily 8pm–1am; Apr–June and Sept–Nov Mon–Sat 8pm–1am.

Tarquino 📷 **REGIONAL** Worth visiting for the architecture alone, this friendly family-run grill in front of the leafy Plaza Belgrano feels like a storybook treehouse. After entering through a stunning wooden door that would suit a hobbit, choose a table beside a live towering cypress tree (this is Bariloche's famous rustic building style at its most imaginative). The food is good, especially the beef: There are standard grill selections, such as *bife de chorizo* (a 650g/22-oz. piece of tender flank steak), pork tenderloin, or grilled trout with almond sauce. The servings are large. There is also a salad bar.

24 de Septiembre (corner of Saavedra). ⓒ **02944/431601.** Reservations recommended. Main courses $16–$24. MC, V. Daily noon–3pm and 8pm–midnight.

Moderate

El Boliche de Alberto 🍴 **PARRILLA** Long considered by many to be the best *parrilla* in Bariloche, Alberto is an institution in these parts. Some regulars have been coming back for 20 years, and some make the crossing from Chile just to have a piece of beef here. The menu is brief, with several cuts of beef, chicken, and sausages; salads; and side dishes such as french fries. The dining area is unpretentious and brightly lit, with wooden tables. A typical bife de chorizo steak is so thick you'll need to split it with your dining partner; if you're alone, they can do a half-order for $15. They don't accept reservations, so there is almost always a long line here, which has the waiters hurriedly (rudely, if you ask me) rushing diners through their meals in an effort to keep filling tables fast-food style. The wine list is straight from the supermarket and seriously overpriced. Yes, the meat is good. But for the same price, you can go somewhere less touristy and crowded and actually enjoy your meal at a reasonable pace. There's a second location on Avenida Bustillo, at Km 8, and a third at Eflein 347.

Villegas 347. ⓒ **02944/431433.** Reservations not accepted. Main courses $11–$22. AE, MC, V. Daily noon–3pm and 8pm–midnight.

El Boliche Viejo ★ 📷 REGIONAL   Step back in time to the old Patagonian pioneer days, at this country store dating back more than a century. Little has changed since the days when Butch Cassidy and the Sundance Kid purportedly stopped in for a meal. It's northeast of Bariloche, on the road to Villa La Angostura, past the airport turnoff and the town of Dina Huapi, about a 15-minute drive from the city center. The menu is pure Patagonian, including lamb slow-grilled on a spit and every cut of beef you could imagine, from T-bone to tongue. This makes a great stop for a midday meal if you are on a sightseeing drive.

Ruta 237, at Limay River bridge. ℂ **02944/468452.** Reservations recommended. Main courses $12–$22. MC, V. Daily noon–4pm and 8:30pm–midnight.

Kostelo Lake Bar   With its large menu and giant windows overlooking the lake, this new restaurant has plenty to offer day or night. Most of the tables are low booths, making it a fun place to come with friends. They have great appetizers to share, including a deli platter or a plate of *humita* (steamed fresh corn cake) croquettes. The pork shoulder in black beer sauce is recommended, and, on a wintry night, their waffles are the best in town. For lighter and kid-friendly options, there are pizzas (arugula, cherry tomato, and mozzarella, for example) and sandwiches (I like the beef with bacon, peppers, and black olive tapenade). Very popular with locals, it's also a happening place well into the evenings. Service is a bit sour.

Quaglia 111, corner of Costanera. ℂ **02944/439697.** Reservations recommended for dinner. Main courses $12–$18. AE, DC, MC, V. Tues–Sun 12:30–4pm and 8:30pm–2am.

Inexpensive

La Fonda del Tio REGIONAL   The lines tell the story of just how popular this local joint is. Fortunately, a recent expansion will help shorten the wait. But it's worth it. For more than 22 years, this place has been offering Argentine family favorites, including a wide option of *milanesas* (breaded veal cutlets), with cheese, ham, tomato sauce, or hard-boiled eggs. There are other classics, such as simple cuts of beef, that go well with giant french fries, and daily specials. Portions are enormous. Match them with a soft drink (try the Quatro pomelo grapefruit soda) or a glass of table wine. This a good place to try real Argentine cooking and take a break from the tourist scene.

Mitre 1130. ℂ **02944/435011.** Main courses $7–$14. Reservations not accepted. AE, MC, V. Daily noon–midnight.

Rock Chicken FAST FOOD   Bariloche has no McDonald's or any other multi-national fast-food chain. What they do have is Rock Chicken, a local staple and a great place to grab a quick and cheap bite. The grill is wide open so there is no doubt what is coming your way. Choose from a *choripán* (chorizo sausage on a bun), *milanesa* (breaded beef), grilled chicken, or a slice of sirloin. Menus usually include a drink (beer or wine) and a choice of salad or french fries. There's a second location on Calle San Martín next to the Banco Frances.

Rolando 245. ℂ **02944/435669.** Main courses $6–$11. No credit cards. Daily 10am–4am.

Vegetariano ★ VEGETARIAN   If you need a break from the grills, head to this unpretentious, cozy restaurant for a dose of veggies. Recipes are purely homemade. Meals are served as a large and nutritious daily set menu; you can usually choose either fish or a soy patty. The mixed juice is chock-full of vitamins, and the tea served at the end of the meal is delightful. Try to save room for dessert; the sweets here are excellent. The staff is very friendly.

20 de Febrero 730. ℘ **02944/421820.** Main courses $12–$16. No credit cards. Mon–Sat noon–3pm; Mon–Fri 8–11pm.

OUTSIDE THE CITY CENTER (EN ROUTE TO THE LLAO LLAO PENINSULA)

The intimate restaurant at ★★ **Posada Los Juncos** (see "Where to Stay," above) is another excellent option to the west of town. Note that the majority of these places do not accept credit cards.

Very Expensive

Butterfly ★★★ 🍴 MODERN FUSION   The three young amigos who own and run this amazing, tiny lakeside restaurant could have set up shop just about anywhere in the world—the Michelin-trained chef is Irish, the delightful sommelier's German, and the charming server is a Porteña. That they chose a lovely location just above Bariloche's popular Playa Bonita illustrates their passion for this place. Fresh local ingredients, from rabbit and duck to leeks and berries, are sourced daily and presented in an impeccably intricate seven-course menu. Wine is offered by the bottle or as a highly recommended paired tasting. On summer days, lunch and dinner are served on the outdoor patio.

Hua Huan 7831, at Bustillo, Km 7.9, Playa Bonita. ℘ **02944/461441.** www.butterflypatagonia.com.ar. Reservations required. 7-course set-price menu $58. V. Thurs–Tues 8:30pm–midnight.

Cassis ★ EUROPEAN/REGIONAL   Mariana Muller's inspired restaurant is nestled on a cliff overlooking Lago Gutierrez, just to the south of Bariloche. Inside, with high wooden rafters and gentle candlelight, you may feel like you've come to visit the cottage of your casually stylish friends. The food has its roots in Europe. There are usually three to five fixed four-course menus to choose from. Dishes may include warm shrimp with gin and lemon as an appetizer, followed by sweetbreads in a pecan *panzotti,* and then a slow-cooked salmon or a lamb strudel in sauvignon blanc reduction. The pace is gentle, making for a leisurely experience. The wine cellar has more than 200 labels. Prices are very high for Bariloche standards. Cassis is also a nice spot for a late afternoon cocktail on the deck.

Ruta 82, on Lago Gutierrez, 1km (⅔ mile) past the entrance to the Coihues neighborhood. ℘ **02944/476167.** Reservations highly recommended. 4-course fixed menus $52–$70. No credit cards. Summer daily 6pm–midnight; winter daily 8pm–midnight.

Expensive

Il Gabbiano ★★ 🍴 ITALIAN   If Bariloche's dining scene has a sure thing, this outstanding Italian restaurant is it. Located close to the Llao Llao, Il Gabbiano is a labor of love for its owners. It's set inside a bungalow that has a Mediterranean feel, with brick, iron, and stonework reminiscent of a countryside farmhouse. The menu is authentic *Italiano.* Antipasti include bruschetta and salmon with grapefruit. Delicate homemade pastas are varied and fresh. Main entrees include *osso buco,* rabbit with garlic and rosemary, and a simple trout with lemon. The wine cellar has more than 250 labels, including a good selection of European varieties, rare in Patagonia.

Av. Bustillo, Km 24.3. ℘ **02944/448346.** Reservations highly recommended. Main courses $22–$28. No credit cards. Wed–Mon 7:30pm–midnight.

Bariloche After Dark

Bariloche is home to a handful of discos catering to the 16- to 30-year-old crowd. These discos adhere to Buenos Aires nightlife hours, beginning around midnight or

12:30am, with the evening peaking at about 3 or 4am. The cover charge is usually $3 to $4 per person, and women often enter for free. Try **Roket,** J.M. de Rosas 424 (© 02944/431940), or **Cerebro,** J.M. de Rosas 405 (© 02944/424965). Earlier in the evening, locals gather at the **Roxvury,** San Martín 490 (© 02944/400451), for funky music and big-screen light shows. There are a number of local pubs, including **Wilkenny,** San Martín 435 (© 02944/424444), and **Pilgrim,** Palacios 167 (© 02944/421686). Microbrew pubs are also popular in Bariloche. Downtown, try **Antares,** Elflein 47 (© 02944/431454). **Cervecería Blest,** Avenida Bustillo, Km 11.5 (© 02944/461026), the oldest microbrewery in Argentina. Next door, **Berlina,** Avenida Bustillo, Km 11.75 (© 02944/523336), is hip and fresh.

The **Worest Casino,** Av. San Martín 570 (© 02944/425846), is open from 9am to 5am. There is a multiscreen cinema at Shopping Patagonia, Onelli 447 (© 02944/427189), often showing English-language movies with Spanish subtitles.

SOUTH OF BARILOCHE ★★

The massive Nahuel Huapi National Park extends to the south of Bariloche in a winding maze of majestic mountains and lakes. Whether you're on a day's drive, as part of an overnight getaway from the hustle and bustle of Bariloche, or en route to a world-class fly-fishing lodge, this area is definitely worth exploring. Driving south out of Bariloche on RN 40, you'll pass tall waterfalls and snowy peaks, edge around emerald lakes, and drop through a deep canyon as you head to El Bolsón. This laid-back town has a microclimate that has drawn nature lovers from around the country since the 1960s.

Heading south from Bariloche, you'll find the lovely **Estancia Peuma Hue ★★** (© **02944/15-501030** [mobile]; www.peuma-hue.com) on the south shore of Lake Gutierrez. With two large houses and two cabins, as well as a slew of outdoor activities such as horseback riding and trekking, this high-end complex is intimate. It's one of the only ways to live a more rural Patagonian experience so close to Bariloche. A 3-day all-inclusive plan starts at $255 per person per day.

Continuing south, you'll pass the **Continental Divide**—a wide marsh where the water drains north to Lake Gutierrez and then on to the Nahuel Huapi and the Atlantic; and west through Lake Mascardi, over the border to Chile and the Pacific.

A Driving Tour: Cerro Tronador, Los Alerces Waterfall & Ventisquero Negro

This wonderful, full-day excursion takes visitors through lush forest and past emerald lakes (such as the picturesque Lago Mascardi), waterfalls, and beaches to a trail head that leads to the face of **Ventisquero Negro (Black Glacier).** You'll need a vehicle to drive the 215km (133-mile) round-trip road, including a detour to **Cascada Los Alerces (Los Alerces Waterfall);** it's 170km (105 miles) without the detour. Plan to stop frequently at the various lookout points along the road. Most tour agencies offer this excursion for about $40 to $50 a person. A private bilingual local guide can also take you for around $160 plus transportation.

At 35km (22 miles) south of Bariloche, you'll reach Villa Mascardi. Take RP 81, the road that branches off to the right. You must stop at the National Parks gates and pay an entrance fee of $3.50 for foreigners. Past the turnoff to Pampa Linda and Los Rapidos campsite, continue to the Río Manso bridge, where a road heads left to the

Los Alerces Waterfall. A 300m (984-ft.) walk takes you to a vista point overlooking the waterfall. After doubling back, you reach the bridge again, where you head left, continuing along the shore of Lake Mascardi until you reach the **Hotel Tronador** (© 02944/441062; www.hoteltronador.com), where the views of Mt. Tronador are outstanding. The charming log cabin hotel, built in 1929 by a Belgian immigrant family, is backed by high peaks and makes a good spot for lunch or a quiet getaway for overnight visitors. They have 30 rooms; high-season (Jan–Feb) prices for a double start at $115. The road continues up the valley of the Río Manso Superior, winding through alpine scenery until reaching the lush and expansive Pampa Linda plains, where there is another inn and teahouse. The final leg ends at a stunning cirque (a steep valley with a lake) draped with vegetation and waterfalls. From here a trail leads to the Black Glacier, named for the debris that colors the ice at its terminus. The mountain's power is imposing here. Return to Bariloche the same way you came, and see if you can pick out the heart-shaped Isla Corazón in the middle of Lago Mascardi.

Note that the route to Tronador, RP 81, is a narrow gravel road with restricted hours of transit during the busy summer months. Cars are allowed to travel in toward Tronador in the mornings only (9:30am–2pm), and travel out again in the afternoon only (4:30–7:30pm). Check with the Tourist Information Office before heading out.

El Bolsón

131km (81 miles) S of Bariloche

A lovely town of 11,000 set amid a lush valley, El Bolsón is equally famous for its artisan's fair and its microclimate, which makes it almost 7°F (4°C) warmer than in Bariloche. On Saturdays throughout the year, and on Sundays, Tuesdays, and Thursdays in summer, El Bolsón hosts a wonderful **Artisan and Produce Market** ★★ in its central plaza. Stroll the stands for organic fruit, wool sweaters, homemade jams, wooden cutting boards, and microbrewed beer. There are also vegetarian sandwiches, sweet waffles, and delicious Armenian empanadas to grab as snacks. It usually runs from 10am to 4pm. Because El Bolsón is in a basin surrounded by tall peaks, there is great hiking here. One of the most interesting hikes takes you up to the **Bosque Tallado,** a magical forest with sculpted tree trunks. Inquire at the Tourist Information Center, Avenida San Martín and Roca (© **02944/492604**), for trail maps and other information.

El Bolsón is also known for its production of hops, its microbreweries, and its annual **Beer Festival,** held each year in late February. South of El Bolsón by 15km (9⅓ miles) is **Lago Puelo National Park,** where visitors can swim, boat, hike, camp, and fish.

WHERE TO STAY & EAT

The downtown core has some standard hotels, the best of which is **Hotel Cordillera,** Av. San Martín 3220 (© **02944/492235**). Rooms have balconies. Doubles start at $70. Outside town, you can soak up the authentic El Bolsón lifestyle at **La Casona de Odile,** Barrio Luján, Km 6 (© **02944/492753;** www.interpatagonia. com/odile), a small inn and restaurant serving French cuisine and local produce. Rooms start at $45, and for an extra $17 you can include three fabulous meals a day. On a mountain above town, the **Buena Vida Social Club** (© **02944/491729;** www.buenavidasocialclubpatagonia.com) is a lovely B&B run by an Argentine artist and his Californian partner. Views are excellent. Doubles are $90 with breakfast

The mighty and legendary **Ruta 40** is one of the world's great adventure drives. It takes you along the eastern slope of the Andes from the top of Argentina all the way to the bottom of Patagonia. For travelers with a few extra days, 3-night Ruta 40 trips are organized by **Chalten Travel** (✆ **02944/456005;** www.chaltentravel. com). To drive it on your own, from the Lake District to El Calafate, give yourself a minimum of 2 long days, with a stopover in either the town of Perito Moreno, or at the more interesting **Estancia Cueva de las Manos** (✆ **011/5237-4043** [mobile] or 02963/432730 in Perito Moreno; www. cuevadelasmanos.net), a historic *estancia* that includes the UNESCO World Heritage Site Cave of Hands. A 4WD vehicle will make the drive more comfortable, given that the 1,400km (868 miles) are still at least half unpaved. This land is Patagonia off the beaten track.

included. **Jauja ★**, Av. San Martín 3261 (✆ **02944/493505**), is home to an outstanding ice-cream parlor and a good restaurant next door with delicious trout entrees. Vegetarians will love **La Calabaza,** Av. San Martín 2518 (✆ **02944/492910**), which serves soups, salads, and quiches.

South of El Bolsón

Farther along the road is the village of **Cholila,** where Butch Cassidy and the Sundance Kid hid out and ranched in peace from 1901 to 1906. They became cherished members of this tiny community. You can still spot the old farmhouse the two fugitives built. South of Cholila, the outstanding **Museo Leleque** (✆ **02944/451141;** Tues–Thurs 11am–5pm) is 6km (3¾ miles) from town on RP 15. Situated on an enormous ranch once owned by the South-Land Company and now part of the extensive landholdings of the Italian clothier family Benetton, this excellent museum focuses on the history of rural Patagonia. Nearby is the **Los Alerces National Park ★**, one of the world's finest fly-fishing areas. Its majestic giant alerce trees are more than 2,000 years old, and mesmerizing emerald lakes come into view at every turn. **Esquel Outfitters** (✆ **406/581-1760** in the U.S.; www.esqueloutfitters.com) will hook you up on a dreamy weeklong fishing adventure, with accommodations in their luxurious and remote lodge. The best lodge around is the **Lago Cholila Lodge** (✆ **02944/610310;** www.cholila.com).

Esquel

Continuing south is the small city of Esquel, 310km (193 miles) south of Bariloche and 180km (119 miles) from El Bolsón. It's another mecca for fly-fishing and home to a little-known but gorgeous ski resort called La Hoya. **Las Bayas Hotel ★** (✆ **2945/455800;** www.lasbayashotel.com) is without doubt the nicest hotel in the center of town, with very large rooms and an excellent breakfast. The small in-house bistro has the most upscale dining in town. **Hostería Canela** (✆ **02945/453890;** www.canelaesquel.com) is a lovely B&B in the nicest part of town.

Just west of Esquel is the small town of Trevelín, with an important Welsh heritage similar to that of Gaiman close to the Atlantic Coast, at the other end of the Chubut River. For superb touring of all things **Welsh in Patagonia,** contact Jeremy Wood at www.welshpatagonia.com.

VILLA LA ANGOSTURA ★★

81km (50 miles) N of Bariloche; 44km (27 miles) E of the Chilean border

Villa La Angostura is the loveliest mountain village in Argentina. Meaning "Narrow Village," it takes its name from the slender isthmus that connects the town's center with the Quetrihué Peninsula. The town was founded in 1934 by a handful of simple farmers who were eventually displaced by out-of-towners, who selected this pretty location for their summer homes. Increased boating activity, the paving of the road to Bariloche, increased tourism to Chile (the border of which is just 20 min. from town), and the inauguration of several exclusive hotels and a slew of bungalow complexes have converted Villa La Angostura into an upscale getaway for the rich and famous. Even so, this tiny enclave hosts only a fraction of visitors to the region, unlike Bariloche. This picturesque village, with a smorgasbord of mountains and lakes nearby, is for visitors seeking solitude, although increasing traffic from tractor trailers is making the main street less than serene. Most lodging options are tucked away in the forest or on the shore of the Lake Nahuel Huapi, providing beautiful views and quiet surroundings. Like Bariloche, Villa La Angostura is within the borders of Parque Nacional Nahuel Huapi. If Bariloche is for action, Villa La Angostura is for relaxing by the lake and slowing things down. Note that "villa" is pronounced *"vee-sha"* in Argentine Spanish, and the town is often simply referred to as "La Villa."

Essentials

GETTING THERE   For airport and flight information, see "Getting There," under "San Carlos de Bariloche," earlier in this chapter. To get to Villa La Angostura from the airport, take the 1-hour drive by taxi or transfer service (about $65–$90).

Algarrobal Buses (© 02944/494360) leave for Villa La Angostura from Bariloche's Terminal de Omnibus about every 3 hours from 8am to 9pm. The trip takes about 1½ hours. **Albus** (© 02944/423552) also goes to Villa La Angostura four times a day.

If you drive, Villa La Angostura is a 1-hour trip from Bariloche around the north shore of Lake Nahuel Huapi. Take the coastal road northeast of town past the village at Dina Huapi, and turn left on RP 231.

VISITOR INFORMATION   The **Secretaría de Turismo** is at Av. Siete Lagos 93 (© 02944/494124), open daily from 8am to 8pm. It offers accommodations listings and prices, and information about excursions around the area. For information about Nahuel Huapi National Park or Parque Nacional Los Arrayanes, try the **Oficína de Turismo** at the pier (© 02944/494152), open Monday through Friday from 11am to 4pm (Wed until 2pm), and Saturday and holidays from 2:30 to 5pm.

Seeing the Sights

PARQUE NACIONAL LOS ARRAYANES ★

The Parque Nacional Los Arrayanes is home to the only two arrayán forests in the world (although the arrayán can be found throughout this region, including in Chile), one of which can be visited at the tip of Península Quetrihué. This fascinating bush grows as high as 20m (66 ft.) and looks to the untrained eye like a tree, with slick cinnamon-colored trunks that are cool to the touch. They are especially beautiful in the spring when in bloom.

shopping IN "LA VILLA": WORTH THE DRIVE AROUND THE LAKE

More compact and stylish than its sprawling neighbor Bariloche, Villa La Angostura's main drag, Avenida Arrayanes, is a great shopping destination. Brand-name stores, such as Kill and Cardon, have shops here. The **Paseo de Compras** at Av. Arrayanes 172 (no phone) has lovely upscale silver and leatherwear. Also try **La Candela** (Av. Arrayanes 188; ✆ **02944/495686**) and **Aladino** (Av. Arrayanes 193; ✆ **02944/15-607529** [mobile]). Just down Las Mutisias is

Blumenhaus (Las Mutisias 192; ✆ **02944/495752**) for lovely candles and ceramics. **Patagonia Exquisiteces** (Av. Arrayanes 231; ✆ **02944/495084**) has such gourmet food products as smoked meats and chocolate, as well as Patagonian wines. At the western end of Arrayanes is the handicrafts market. Even nonshoppers will delight in the lovely architecture, and don't forget to stop in at **Jauja** (Av. Arrayanes 40; no phone) for an ice-cream cone!

The peninsula itself offers a pleasant 24km (15-mile) round-trip moderate hiking and biking trail to the arrayán forest. Most visitors either walk (2–3 hr.) or bike (1–2 hr.) half the trail and then boat to or back from the park; you can also take the boat both ways (trip time: 2½ hr.). From the interior side of the port at Bahía Mansa, the **Catamaran Futaleufú** (✆ **02944/494004** or 494405 at the dock; www.bosquelosarrayanes.com.ar) departs daily at 2:30pm, and in high season at 11am, 2:30pm, and 5:30pm. The return trip costs $35 per person; one-way costs $18. Villa La Angostura is a main stop on the popular Ruta de los Siete Lagos from Bariloche. It's also the last stop on the road to the border with Chile. That, unfortunately, means the main street is a thoroughfare for tractor-trailer trucks making their way south from Puerto Montt to southern Chile (there is no road through southern Chile, so all transport has to come through Argentina).

OTHER OUTDOOR ACTIVITIES

BIKING **Free Bikes,** on Las Fucsias behind the bus terminal (✆ **02944/15-642985** cell; www.freebikes.com.ar), has a large selection of rental bikes for $6 per hour, $15 up to 6 hours, and $18 for a full day. They also guide a number of different mountain-bike trips.

FISHING Anglers typically head to the renowned Río Correntoso for rainbow and brown trout, reached just before crossing the bridge just outside town on Ruta Nacional 231, from the Siete Lagos road. **Banana Fly Shop,** at Arrayanes 282 (✆ **02944/494634**), sells flies and gear, and they provide information and can recommend guides. You may pick up a **fishing license** here or at the Bosques y Parques Provinciales office at the port (✆ **02944/494157**); it's open Monday through Friday from 11am to 4pm, Wednesday until 2pm, Saturday and holidays from 2:30 to 5pm.

HORSEBACK RIDING Hop on a horse and ride up to the top of the ridge for views of all the area lakes. Organized by a well-known local character, **Cabalgatas Correntoso** (✆ **02944/15-510559** [mobile]; www.cabalgatacorrentoso.com.ar) has rides lasting from 2 to 9 hours, plus overnight pack trips.

SKIING Villa La Angostura is home to a little gem of a ski resort, **Cerro Bayo,** located about 9km (5½ miles) from downtown. It's a smaller resort than the one at Cerro Catedral, but the crowds are thinner and the view is wonderful. For those reasons, I almost prefer it. There are 250 skiable acres. About 40% of the terrain is intermediate, and 35% is advanced. To reach it, you'll need to take a long lift from the base up to the summit; during the summer, this same chairlift provides access to an excellent short hike and lookout point. Cerro Bayo has ski and snowboard rental and instruction; the season runs from mid-June to mid-September, although it can get fairly patchy toward the end of the season.

To get to Cerro Bayo, ask your hotel to arrange transportation or hire a taxi for the short ride. Tickets are $23 to $52 for adults, $22 to $41 for kids, depending on the season. Kids 5 and under and adults 66 and older ski free. Half-day tickets, 3-day tickets, and weekly passes are also available. For more information, call **ⓒ 02944/494189** or visit www.cerrobayoweb.com.

Where to Stay

VERY EXPENSIVE

Correntoso Lake and River Hotel ☺ Perched above the mouth of the Correntoso River and facing due west across to the Andes, the Correntoso Hotel was founded in 1922 as a fishing destination for Bariloche residents who crossed the lake by boat. Now it feels like a clean, natural, and fresh mountain lodge. The lobby is lovely, with glass ceilings, large leather couches, and an enormous fireplace. The huge library has big sofas, heritage maps, and another fireplace. The gourmet restaurant is open to the public and worth a visit for the views alone—hotel guests have access to the choicest tables. Down at the dock, there is another charming but less formal restaurant that serves excellent trout. The property is full of walking trails and berry bushes. All but six of the rooms have fabulous views over the lake. Corner room nos. 309 and 409 have the very best views. There's a lovely new spa with a gorgeous indoor/outdoor pool, and 16 new suites tucked behind the spa. Multinight packages can help keep costs down. This is a complete hotel experience and the most family-friendly of the upscale options in the area.

Ruta 234 and Río Correntoso, Villa La Angostura. ⓒ/fax **11/4803-0030** in Buenos Aires; 02944/15-619728 (mobile) in Villa La Angostura. www.correntoso.com. 49 units. $355 double; $430–$525 suite. Rates include breakfast. AE, MC, V. **Amenities:** Restaurant; bar; lounge; concierge; deck; heated outdoor pool; spa; Wi-Fi. *In room:* TV, fridge (in suites only).

Las Balsas ★★ The Relais & Châteaux–affiliated Las Balsas has the airs of a country cottage, and an unbeatable lakefront setting (neighbors are among the wealthiest folk in Argentina). From the moment you walk in, you'll feel relaxed and at home. Common areas range from a big-screen TV room upstairs to a living room with a massive fireplace, comfortable couches, and coffee-table books. With only 15 rooms, this place goes for exclusive without being showy or opulent. English-speaking staff members are very charming and attentive without being stuffy or condescending. There is a strong focus on details, from fresh orange slices by the pool to imported teas. Rooms are generally small—this inn was built long before the McMansion-style hotel trends of late—but they make up for their limited size with character. Each room is different, and all have bright windows overlooking the lake; none have televisions. Floors are a bit squeaky and the walls a bit thin, so you may want to bring earplugs. The inn's restaurant is world-class. The spa next door doesn't quite match the inn, and the gym should be moved out of the tranquil relaxation area, but the services are specialized and indulgent. Most things, from the food to the excursions, are very expensive here. Nonguests can enjoy a memorable lakeside lunch at the restaurant.

Bahía Las Balsas. ⓒ/fax **02944/494308.** www.lasbalsas.com.ar. 15 units. $396 double; $636 suite. Rates include breakfast. AE, MC, V. **Amenities:** Exquisite restaurant; bar; lounge; babysitting; massage; indoor/outdoor heated pool; room service; sauna; spa; watersports equipment. *In room:* Hair dryer.

EXPENSIVE

El Faro ★★ The owners of this refined inn aren't the only ones who think Nahuel Huapi Lake resembles the sea. So inspired by the mariner vibe, they've built a hotel around a lighthouse. It's a classy inn throughout—mature, relaxing, and polished. The rooms are quite large, with crisp white curtains, king-size beds, stand-alone showers, and jetted tubs; all have lake views and most have fireplaces. It is definitely romance friendly here. The "boutique" rooms are the most economical. Ask for a superior with a terrace. There are three suites, including one inside the lighthouse. A lovely buffet breakfast is served in a sunny room overlooking the lake, and in summer can be enjoyed on the outside deck. The spa, renovated in 2008, is divine. If you want a big room, you are much better off here than at Las Balsas (see above). For a stunningly romantic dinner, book the single table at the top of the lighthouse.

Av. Siete Lagos 2345, Villa La Angostura. ⓒ **02944/495484.** www.elfaropatagonia.com. 15 rooms. Doubles $238–$336; suites $352–$378. Rates include breakfast. MC, V. Free parking. **Amenities:** Restaurant; bar; concierge; small gym; heated outdoor pool; room service; spa; Wi-Fi. *In room:* A/C, minibar.

MODERATE

Hostería El Establo ★ 🛏 A lovely inn steps from the heart of town, El Establo is a charming oasis, with a lovely garden and warm service. Inspired by pioneers, there is much history on display here—a stable was once situated on the same spot. Inside, the lounge area is spacious and cozy, with a large fireplace and giant sofas. Upstairs, rooms are full of wooden charm, reminiscent of a cottage. Fabrics change room to room, but maintain a country feel. Premium rooms are just a bit bigger, with corner windows and a Jacuzzi. Suites are very spacious with a giant white bed and a sunny bathroom. Breakfasts here are legendary for their abundance.

Los Maquis 56, Villa La Angostura. ⓒ **02944/494142.** www.hosteriaelestablo.com.ar. 14 rooms. $126 double; $160 premium double; $192 suite. Rates include breakfast. AE, MC, V. **Amenities:** Lounge; concierge; Wi-Fi. *In room:* TV.

Hostería Le Lac ★ Just west of town on a hill above the main road, this small inn, run by a family of former world travelers, prides itself on superb attention and simple but tasteful lodging. Eight bright rooms have just enough space to keep you wanting to linger. Opened in 2006, it's got modern amenities like thermopaneled windows and central heating. There's a lovely garden that spreads out to superb views of Lago Nahuel Huapi. A cozy common room has a stone fireplace and decor magazines to peruse. You'll pay a bit more for lake views. Suites have Jacuzzi tubs and multiple windows. Come here for pleasant and personalized service.

Av. de los Siete Lago, Villa La Angostura. ⓒ **02944/488029.** www.hosterialelac.com.ar. 8 units. $105–$120 double; $160–$180 suite. Rates include breakfast. No credit cards. **Amenities:** Lounge; Wi-Fi; TV room.

Villa La Angostura is the last stop before you head over the Andes and on to Chile via Paso Cardenal Samore, also known as **Paso Puyehue.** The border itself is 64km (39 miles) from town, although driving eastward, you'll hit the Argentine Customs building at 34km (21 miles). It's a spectacular drive through virgin forests in two adjoining national parks (Nahuel Huapi in Argentina and Puyehue in Chile). There are lovely picnic spots and short hiking trails en route. In winter, the drive often requires chains. The border crossing itself in- volves first exiting Argentina and then entering Chile. Across the border, you're within an hour of lovely spots such as the Thermas de Puyehue hot springs and the delicious seafood restaurants in the city Puerto Montt on the Pacific Coast. Either makes a great day trip from Bariloche or Villa La Angostura. Remember, though, that the border closes at 11pm in summer and at 8pm in winter. If you are renting a car, be sure to tell the rental agency that you plan to drive to Chile—if you reach the border without the proper paperwork, you will have to turn back.

Where to Eat

Many *parrillas* and cafes line the town's sole main street. The best, however, are either on side streets or are a few minutes' drive outside town. For a cheap meal where the locals eat, try the typical grill-house *parrilla* **El Esquiador,** Las Retamas 146 (© **02944/494331**). It's almost always packed.

La Delfina ★ CONTEMPORARY ARGENTINE   Tucked inside a cozy old cottage next to the La Escondida Inn at the Bahia Manzano community, La Delfina is a gourmet revelation that's full of surprises. The menu changes almost daily to reflect the chef's whimsical tastes, but staples include a spectacular steak with teriyaki sauce and shiitake mushrooms, and a trio of trout. The smoked-trout soup with lime cream is also fabulous. During the summer, you can dine outdoors.

Av. Arrayanes 714, Puerto Manzano. © **02944/475313.** Reservations highly recommended. Main courses $18–$22. AE, MC. Tues–Sun noon–3:30pm and 8:30–11:30pm. Closed for lunch in winter.

La Encantada 🍴 PIZZA   This may be the best pizza joint in the Lake District. The trademark here is the thin crusts cooked in the wood-burning oven. Toppings are fresh and creative, including my favorite: arugula, mozzarella, tomato, and olive oil. Another option combines locally smoked salmon with parsley and mozzarella. The menu also includes some unusual empanadas such as one stuffed with rainbow trout, white wine, and hard-boiled eggs. Soups, salads, and pastas are also available. It's a cozy and fun place with great service.

C. Belvedere 69. © **02944/495515.** Main courses $8–$13. No credit cards. Low season Tues–Sat 12:30–3:30pm and 8–11:30pm; summer daily 12:30–3:30pm and 8–11:30pm.

Tinto Bistro ★★ FUSION   Everything sparkles inside the Tinto Bistro. The lighting is intimate, and the decor is deluxe. Chef Leonardo Andres's food manages to shine as well. An eclectic offering of tapas includes rabbit *escabeche* with endives. The main courses reflect a global palate, with Asian, Middle Eastern, and

Mediterranean influences—from garlic-and–lemon grass chicken to Saigon beef and udon noodles with sautéed seafood in vodka-saffron sauce and coconut milk. It's a very exciting and refreshing change, perhaps a bit too spicy for most Argentine palates but interesting to many travelers. A wide selection of *vino tinto* (red wine), with more than 180 labels, honors the restaurant's name. For dessert, try Princesa Mia, a honey parfait with flambéed fruit—named, perhaps, after the owner's celebrity sister, Princess Maxima of Holland. There's now a second location inside Bariloche's Panamericano Hotel, which unfortunately lacks this bistro's cozy vibe.

Bd. Nahuel Huapi 34, at end of Arrayanes. (C) **02944/494924.** Reservations highly recommended in high season. Main courses $13–$18. MC, V. Mon–Sat 8pm–midnight.

Waldhaus SWISS/REGIONAL   This little restaurant's gingerbread eaves, notched furniture, and woodsy location will make you feel like you're dining in the Black Forest. The location, 6km (3¾ miles) from downtown, is close to hotels in the Bahía Manzano district. In addition to nightly specials, typical menu offerings include wild-mushroom soup, beef fondue, venison marinated in burgundy wine, and typical Tyrolean dishes such as spaetzle with ham.

Ruta Nacional 231, Km 61. (C) **02944/475323.** Main courses $11–$18. MC, V. Summer and winter daily noon–3:30pm and 8:30pm–midnight; spring and fall Wed–Sat 8:30pm–midnight.

DRIVING FROM BARILOCHE TO SAN MARTIN ★★

There are four ways to get from Bariloche to San Martín de los Andes. Each has its pros and cons. All head northeast of Bariloche on RN 237, however, with lovely picnic spots and stunning scenery along the way. If you continue along the Limay River, you'll journey past the river's impressive Amphiteatre and the Valle Encantado, with rare volcanic rock formations, including the Dedo de Dios (Finger of God).

The only fully paved route takes you along the gorgeous Limay River to Rinconada and then loops to San Martín via **Junín de los Andes.** This route is the longest, at 260km (161 miles), but it's the one I recommend for safety if you are traveling in winter or at night.

The second route takes you also along the Limay River but then heads west on a gravel road just past Confluencia and over the incredibly wild and rugged **Córdoba Pass** before joining the traditional Seven Lakes Route, RP 234. This also takes you past the picturesque Meliquina Lake, where you'll find a teahouse and general store. Soon after Meliquina, turn right on RP 234, the Ruta de los Siete Lagos (see below), to continue to San Martín de los Andes. Turn left to return to Villa La Angostura.

The route that heads through **Villa Trafúl** at RP 65 can also be done as the "Circuito Grande," a nice day drive from Bariloche, looping through Villa La Angostura. At Confluencia, you head west along the Trafúl River past the expansive Estancia Primavera, owned by a certain gringo by the name of Ted Turner. It then catches up to RP 234, the Ruta de los Siete Lagos. Again, it's a right turn to San Martín de los Andes and a left turn to Villa La Angostura. The Circuito Grande is 240km (148 miles) total, looping from Bariloche.

Numerous daily buses link along these roads as well. Campers can hop on and off at their own pace.

On what is often referred to as the Circuito Grande (opposed to the Circuito Chico that takes you to the Llao Llao), the delightful little village of Villa Traful makes a great day trip from either Bariloche or Villa La Angostura. This lakeside settlement 63km (39 miles) north of Villa La Angostura is home to some 300 people, many descendants of original settlers. The town includes teahouses, campgrounds, and a few cabins for those who want to spend the night.

The classic **Ruta de Los Siete Lagos (Seven Lakes Route),** is a direct trip from Villa La Angostura to San Martín de los Andes. This road is now mostly paved, 184km (114 miles) from Bariloche, although road work continues at a snail's pace. This route affords many excellent lookouts, short hikes, and picnic spots. You certainly need a full day to complete the drive to San Martín and back to Villa La Angostura. After leaving the shores of Nahuel Huapi Lake and the town of Villa La Angostura on RP 231, turn north on RP 234. The lakes actually amount to more than seven, starting with Correntoso, Espejo, and Espejo Chico. At the juncture of lakes Villarino and Falkner, the rustic **Hostería Lago Villarino (© 02972/427483)** is one of the only places to spend the night en route, besides numerous campgrounds. Shortly thereafter, you cross the border into Lanín National Park. You can check Hermoso, Machónico, and Lácar lakes off your list before dropping into the town of San Martín de los Andes. On the shores of the Río Hermoso is the outstanding Río Hermoso Lodge (see "Where to Stay" under "San Martín de los Andes," later).

SAN MARTIN DE LOS ANDES ★★

1,640km (1,017 miles) SW of Buenos Aires; 200km (124 miles) N of San Carlos de Bariloche

San Martín de los Andes is a charming mountain town of 35,000 nestled on the tip of Lago Lácar between high peaks. The town is considered the tourism capital of the Neuquén province, a claim that's hard to negate, considering the copious arts-and-crafts shops, gear-rental shops, restaurants, and hotels that constitute much of downtown. San Martín has grown considerably in the past 15 years, yet a city law that limits building height and regulates architectural style means the town has kept its lovely character, unlike Bariloche. The town is quieter, more organized and walkable than Bariloche and decidedly more picturesque, thanks to its wide streets, timber-heavy architecture, and Swiss Alpine influence. Because it's in a valley between two peaks, however, it lacks the majestic lake view and can feel dark and closed-in. San Martín overflows with activities including biking, hiking, boating, and skiing. The town is also very popular for hunting and fishing—and, believe it or not, some come just to relax. The tourism infrastructure here is excellent, with every lodging option imaginable and plenty of great restaurants.

Essentials

GETTING THERE   **Aeropuerto Internacional Chapelco (© 02972/428388)** sits halfway between San Martín and Junín de los Andes (see later in this chapter) and, therefore, serves both destinations. **Aerolíneas Argentinas/Austral,** Capitán

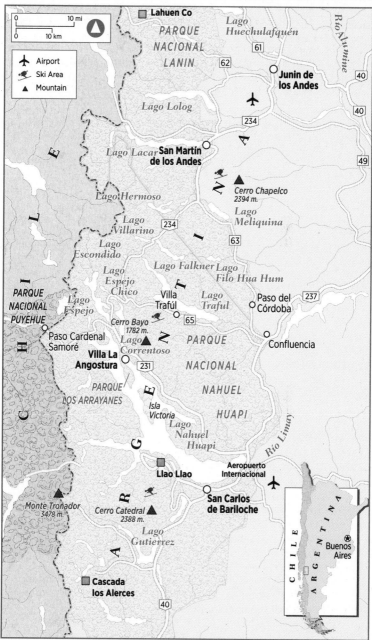

Lahuen Co

PARQUE
NACIONAL
LANIN

Lago
Huechulafquén

Río Aluminé

61

62

40

Junin de
los Andes

40

Lago Lolog

234

49

Lago Lacar **San Martín
de los Andes**

Lago Hermoso

Lago
Villarino

234

Cerro Chapelco
2394 m.

Lago
Meliquina

63

Lago
Escondido

Lago Falkner Lago
Filo Hua Hum

PARQUE
NACIONAL
PUYEHUE

Lago
Espejo
Chico

Lago
Espejo

Villa
Trafúl

Lago
Trafúl

Paso del
Córdoba

237

Cerro Bayo
1782 m.

65

Paso Cardenal
Samoré

Lago
Correntoso

**Villa La
Angostura**

231

PARQUE

NACIONAL

Confluencia

PARQUE
LOS ARRAYANES

NAHUEL

Isla
Victoria

HUAPI

Lago
Nahuel
Huapi

Río Limay

CHILE

ARGENTINA

Llao Llao

Aeropuerto
Internacional

Monte Tronador
3478 m.

Cerro Catedral
2388 m.

**San Carlos
de Bariloche**

Lago
Gutierrez

Cascada
los Alerces

40

Scale:
0 — 10 mi
0 — 10 km

✈ Airport
🎿 Ski Area
▲ Mountain

CHILE

ARGENTINA

⊛ Buenos
Aires

Drury 876 (© **02972/427871;** www.aerolineas.com.ar), flies from Buenos Aires. The hope is that recent improvements in the airport's infrastructure will keep the number of flights canceled due to bad weather to a minimum. A taxi to San Martín costs about $22; transfer services are also available at the airport for $20 per person. A taxi to Junín de los Andes costs $20; transfer services are $14 per person. **By Mich Rent a Car** and **Avis** both have auto rental kiosks at the airport.

The **Terminal de Omnibus** is at Villegas and Juez del Valle (© 02972/427044). **Via Bariloche** (© 02972/422800) runs daily bus service to San Martín de los Andes from Buenos Aires (a 19-hr. trip). **Ko-Ko Chevalier** (© 02972/411295) also offers service to and from Buenos Aires, and serves Villa La Angostura and Bariloche by the paved or by the scenic Siete Lagos route. **Centenario** (© 02972/427294) has service to Chile and also offers daily service to Buenos Aires; Villarrica- and Pucón-bound buses leave Monday through Saturday, and those for Puerto Montt depart Tuesday through Thursday. **Albus** (© 02972/428100) has a handful of daily trips to Bariloche via the Siete Lagos route (about 3 hr.). Bus service can vary due to season, and it's best to evaluate a coach's condition and services before buying a ticket, especially for trips to and from Buenos Aires.

As outlined above in "Driving from Bariloche to San Martín," San Martín de los Andes can be reached from San Carlos de Bariloche following one of four routes. The popular 200km (124-mile) Siete Lagos route takes rutas 234, 231, and 237 and sometimes closes during the winter. The 160km (99-mile) Paso Córdoba route takes rutas 234, 63, and 237; the longest, yet entirely paved 260km (161-mile) Collón Curá route follows rutas 234, 40, and 237. If driving at night, take the paved route. To get to Neuquén (420km/260 miles), take rutas 234, 40, and 22. From Chile, take the Tromen Pass (132km/82 miles from Pucón) to Ruta 62, taking you to Ruta 234 and through Junín de los Andes; note that a large portion of this route is on unpaved roads.

GETTING AROUND San Martín is compact enough to explore by foot. For outlying excursions, tour companies can arrange transportation. **Hertz** is at Av. San Martín 831 (© **02972/430280**), and **Easy Rent A Car** is at Rivadavia 804 (© **02972/427704**). Both also have stands at the airport.

Note that two main streets have similar names and can be confusing: Perito Moreno and Mariano Moreno.

VISITOR INFORMATION San Martín's excellent **Oficina de Turismo** (©/fax **02972/427347** or 425500) offers comprehensive accommodations listings with prices and other tourism-related information, and the staff is friendly and eager to make your stay pleasurable. The office is open daily 8am to 8pm, at Rosas and Avenida San Martín, on the main plaza. The **Asociación Hotelero y Gastronomía,** San Martín 1236 (© **02972/427166**), also offers lodging information, including photographs of each establishment, though service is not as efficient as it is at the Oficina de Turismo. During the off season, it's open daily 9am to 1pm and 3 to 7pm; during high season, it's open daily 9am to 10pm.

For information on Parque Nacional Lanín, drop by the park's information center at Frey 748 (© **02972/427233**), open daily 9am to noon only, or visit **www.parque nacionallanin.gov.ar.**

A website chock-full of valuable information is **www.smandes.gov.ar.**

[FastFACTS] SAN MARTIN DE LOS ANDES

Banks & Currency Exchange Andina International, Capitán Drury 876, exchanges money; banks such as **Banco de la Nación,** Av. San Martín 687; **Banco de la Provincia Neuquén,** Belgrano and Obeid; and **Banco Frances,** Avenida San Martín and Sarmiento, have ATMs and money exchange. All banks are open Monday through Friday from 10am to 3pm.

Emergency Dial ⓒ **107.**

Hospital Hospital Regional Ramón Carrillo is at Avenida San Martín and Coronel Rodhe (ⓒ **02972/427211**).

Laundry The most convenient laundromats are **Laverap Santa Ana,** Belgrano 618 (ⓒ **02972/421898**), and **Laverap Drury,** Capitán Drury 880 (ⓒ **02972/428820**).

Police For emergencies, dial ⓒ **101.** The federal police station is at Av. San Martín 915 (ⓒ **02972/428249**); the provincial police station is at Belgrano 635 (ⓒ **02972/427300**).

Post Office Correo Argentino is at the corner of General Roca and Coronel Pérez (ⓒ **02972/427201**).

Taxi Eco-taxi (ⓒ **02972/428421**) has a stand at Plaza San Martín.

Telephone & Internet The fastest computers are at **Cooperativa Telefónica Cotesma,** Capitán Drury 761 (ⓒ **02972/428900**), open from 9am to 11pm, where you can also make phone calls. One half-hour of Internet use costs less than $2.

Seeing the Sights

San Martín de los Andes's heritage is in agriculture, cattle, and logging, all of which are carefully displayed at the **Museo de los Primero Pobladores,** J. M. Rosas 700 (no phone), open Tuesday and Friday afternoons only. Now San Martín is heavily geared toward tourism; accordingly, its streets are lined with shops selling arts and crafts, wonderful regional specialties such as smoked meats and cheeses, outdoor gear, books, and more. There is a lovely crafts market open most afternoons in the central plaza. Visitors will find most shops on **Avenida San Martín** and **General Villegas.** For regional specialties and/or chocolates, try **Ahumadero El Ciervo,** General Villegas 724 (ⓒ **02972/427361**); **Mamusia,** Av. San Martín 601 (ⓒ **02972/427560**); or **Su Chocolate Casero,** General Villegas 453 (ⓒ **02972/427924**). For arts and crafts, try **Cooperativa De Artesano,** Av. San Martín 1050 (ⓒ **02972/429097**), or **La Oveja Negra,** Av. San Martín 1025 (ⓒ **02972/428039**).

San Martín is a mountain town geared toward outdoor activities. If you're not up to a lot of physical exertion, take a stroll down to the lake and kick back on the beach. Alternatively, rent a bike and take a slow pedal around town. Pack a picnic lunch and head to Hua Hum.

The vast **Parque Nacional Lanín,** founded in 1937, is the third-largest national park in the country. It has 35 lakes, as well as thick forests, abundant wildlife, and an extinct volcano. The park is still home to more than 50 native Mapuche communities. At its heart is the towering, conical, snow-capped and highly picturesque Lanín Volcano (3,776 m/12,293 ft.), which is surrounded by a forest of ancient araucaria (monkey puzzle) trees.

LAHUEN CO: hot springs DEEP IN THE ANDES

Turn west halfway between San Martín de los Andes and Junín de los Andes, head deep into the temperate rainforest of Lanín National Park, over petrified lava flow, past glistening lakes and snowcapped peaks, and you'll end up at this spectacular oasis. The **Lahuen Co ★★** thermal hot springs is a natural thermal spa with boutique services and amenities. There are seven thermally heated pools, four indoors and three out. A typical day here begins with a stunning boat trip across Lago Huechulafquén beneath the Lanín Volcano and then a hike to a waterfall, followed by an hour or so to soak, drift, and relax in an Asian-inspired building with Vichy showers and a sunny deck. A lovely lunch is served to guests in robes. Afternoons involve a shiatsu massage, some fishing, or more soaking. The landscape is divine, and the new building delicately blends modernity, ancient practices, and nature. They are also open in winter, and now have a sweet little hotel so you can *really* get away from it all. Advance booking is essential. Contact their office in San Martín at ℂ **02972/424709** or online at www.lahuenco.com.

Just up the hill above town, the quaint and cozy **Arrayán Tea House ★**, Circuito Arrayán, Km 4 (ℂ **02972/425570**), has the area's best view. Built at a clearing in a cypress forest in 1938 by Renee Dickenson, a spirited young British woman, the house today maintains the same style that first charmed local residents. During the '40s and '50s, this was the hot spot in San Martín, on the old road to Bariloche. Today it's open afternoons for exquisite teas, coffees, and pastries, and for lunch and dinner with a reservation only. Take a taxi up for $8 and walk down.

The **Red Bus** (ℂ **02972/421185**) runs city tours on a double-decker bus that helps orient visitors and gives a glimpse into the town's history. Tours depart daily at 10:30am and 4:30pm from the Plaza San Martín. The tour costs $12.

TOUR OPERATORS & TRAVEL AGENCIES

Both **Huemul Turismo,** Av. San Martín 881 (ℂ **02972/422903**; www.huemul turismo.com.ar), and **Viviendo Patagonia,** Av. San Martín 555 (ℂ **02972/411300**; www.viviendopatagonia.com), offer similar tours and prices, and also operate as travel agencies for booking plane tickets.

Excursions to the village Quila Quina, via a sinuous road that offers dramatic views of Lago Lácar, cost $17; a longer excursion including Chapelco and Arrayán is $25. Scenic drives through the Siete Lagos route are $40 to Villa La Angostura and $65 to Bariloche. A gorgeous circuit trip to Volcán Lanín and Lago Huechulafquén goes for $55. Tours do not include lunch, so pack your own or arrange for one ahead of time.

OUTDOOR ACTIVITIES

BIKING   San Martín is well suited for biking, and shops offer directions and maps. Bike rentals and tours are available at **Andes Bike,** at Avenida Costanera and General Villegas (ℂ **02972/15-552475** [mobile]). You can rent a bike from **Mountain Snow Shop,** Av. San Martín 861 (ℂ **02972/427728**).

BIRD-WATCHING   Horacio Matarasso is a passionate birder who hosts great bird-watching trips out of San Martín. Contact him at **Aves Patagonia** (ℂ **02972/15-568427** [mobile]; www.avespatagonia.com.ar).

BOATING   **Naviera Lácar & Nonthué,** at the Costanera and main pier (✆ **02972/427380**), offers year-round boat excursions on Lago Lácar. A full-day excursion to Hua Hum includes a short navigation through Lago Nonthué. The cost is $45. There's a restaurant in Hua Hum, or you can bring a picnic lunch. Naviera also operates three daily ferry services to the beautiful beaches of Quila Quina (which are packed in the summer) for $16. Naviera also rents kayaks for $15 per hour.

To raft the Hua Hum or the Aluminé rivers, get in contact with Tiempo Tours or Pucará (see "Tour Operators & Travel Agencies," above).

DIVING   For lake dives, including first-timers, stop by the lakefront **Buceo de los Andes,** Costanera and Obeid (✆ **02972/15-696838** [mobile]).

FISHING INFORMATION & LICENSES   **Jorge Trucco,** Ten. Col. Perez 662 (✆ **02972/429561;** www.jorgetrucco.com), organizes day and overnight fishing expeditions to the Meliquina, Chimehuín, and Malleo rivers, among other areas. The other local fishing expert is **Alberto Cordero** (✆ **02972/421453;** www.ffandes. com), who will arrange fishing expeditions around the area. He speaks fluent English; for more information, visit his website. You can pick up a fishing guide at the **Oficina Guardafauna,** General Roca 849 (✆ **02972/427091**). Fanatic anglers with a generous budget should not miss a few days at **Tipiliuke Lodge** (see below).

GOLF   The 18-hole golf course at the **Chapelco Golf & Resort** (✆ **02972/427713;** www.chapelcogolf.com), just north of San Martín, was designed by Jack Nicklaus and his son. It's being called the "best course in Argentina" and is part of the impressive Loi Suites Chapelco (see "Where to Stay," below). A full round of 18 holes starts at $55.

HORSEBACK RIDING   Take a trip with some local gauchos at the **Estancia Chapelco** (✆ **02972/411253;** www.chapelcogolf.com). A 2-hour trip costs $43. For $150, you get a 4-hour ride and a giant *asado* barbecue. The scenery is beautiful.

KAYAKING   The dozens of lakes near San Martín practically call out for kayakers. **Paralelo 40 Expediciones** (✆ **02972/428213;** www.paralelo40.com.ar) organizes full- and half-day outings in touring or sea kayaks.

MOUNTAINEERING   The guides at **Lanín Expediciones** (✆ **02972/429799;** www.laninexpediciones.com) have decades of experience and offer climbing and orientation courses; ascents of Volcán Lanín and Volcán Domuyo; and treks, climbs, and overnight trips in Lanín and Nahuel Huapi national parks. They have creative itineraries for mountaineering.

SKIING   The principal winter draw for San Martín de los Andes is **Cerro Chapelco,** one of the premier ski resorts in South America. Just 20km (12 miles) outside town, Cerro Chapelco is known for its plentiful, varying terrain and great amenities. Although popular, the resort isn't as swamped with skiers as Bariloche is. Instead it draws more families. The resort sports one gondola (which takes skiers and visitors to the main lodge), five chairlifts, and five T-bars. The terrain is 40% beginner, 30% intermediate, and 30% advanced/expert. Chapelco offers excellent bilingual ski instruction, ski and snowboard rental, and special activities such as dog sledding. The resort has open-bowl skiing and tree skiing, and numerous restaurants with an alpine theme. To get here without renting a car, ask your hotel to arrange transportation or hire a *remise* (private taxi).

To drive to the resort from town, follow Route 234 south along Lago Lácar; it's paved except for the last 5km (3 miles). Lift tickets are quite reasonable and vary from low to high season. A 3-day ticket runs $88 to $164 for adults, and $73 to $135 for kids. During the summer, the resort is open for hiking and sightseeing, with lift access. For more information, call (C) **02972/427460** or visit www.cerrochapelco. com. The road is usually passable, but you may need chains during heavy snowfall; check before heading up to the resort.

Where to Stay

If you arrive in town without a reservation, your first stop should be the Oficina de Turismo (see above), next to the main plaza, which has an updated list of availabilities and prices. Rates almost double in most places from December 18 to March 1. For more information, go to **www.sanmartindelosandes.gov.ar**.

VERY EXPENSIVE

Río Hermoso Lodge ★★ 💼   Sometimes a place just gets it right. There is sublime luxury to be had at this delightful mountain lodge that's on the Seven Lakes Road south of San Martín de los Andes. It's natural without being rustic, peaceful without being too isolated (though it is somewhat isolated). A gentle river streams by, birds chirp above, and one feels deeply relaxed. Inside, the background color is white, but with the presence of much wood and the dotting of such bright colors as purple, yellow, and pink, the lodge feels alive and energetic. Rooms have giant windows overlooking the greenery. Bathrooms are a mixture of wood and stone, with large windows. A suite upstairs is ideal for families. Outside, there are paths leading through lush forests. The restaurant is a bit overpriced for dinner. This lodge also makes a good coffee break if you are driving the Seven Lakes Road. Just call first.

Ruta 63, Km 67, Paraje Río Hermoso (2km/1¼ miles south of San Martín, just off the Seven Lakes Rd.). (C) **02972/410485.** www.riohermoso.com. $330–$400 double. MC, V. **Amenities:** Restaurant; library; TV room; Wi-Fi.

EXPENSIVE

El Casco Viejo Patagonia Lodge ★★ 💼   There are only three rooms at this little gem of a fishing lodge run by the smiling Taylor sisters, whose grandfather, an immigrant from Texas, owned the entire Chapelco resort until a few years ago. The lodge is a new building that replicates the old family homestead entirely, with heaps of heart and soul. It's at a truly treasured location, at a bend in the gentle Quiluihue River with a fabulous fishing hole right in front. Rooms are very spacious, with a lush farmhouse style, giant beds, and lots of windows. Food is typical country cooking, delicious and unpretentious. The best moments are at sunset, when the fish are jumping, the fresh-baked cakes are being served, and silence prevails. Besides fly-fishing, there are horseback riding and trekking activities (as well as an 18-hole golf course) right out the door. Rates include all meals and transfers. The lodge also is open to the public as a teahouse (by reservation).

Ruta 234, Km 57.5, Loma Atravesada de Taylor, San Martín de los Andes. (C) **02972/427713.** www. estanciachapelco.com.ar. 3 units. $250. MC, V. **Amenities:** Restaurant; horseback riding; library.

Loi Suites Chapelco ★   Opened in 2008, this is the first five-star hotel in San Martín, hugely important for the town. The location, with sunset views across the outstanding golf course, is lovely. The hotel has a business feel to it, with long corridors, empty spaces and formal (albeit excellent) service. Rooms have Asian-inspired details, particularly in the modern, massive bathrooms. Furniture is chunky and heavy, and wool, leather, and hide predominate in accents. Only two of the junior suites and most of the studios have decks; the lofts are cozy. The spa focuses on

TIPILIUKE LODGE: fly-fishing IN PARADISE

Those who like to fly fish usually like to do it a lot. And there's no place in the area that caters to them better than the historic, beautiful **Tipiliuke Lodge** (© **02972/429466;** www.tipiliuke.com). Located on a sprawling *estancia* just north of the San Martín de los Andes airport, the lodge has private access to 14km (9 miles) along the Chimehuín River, a place of jaw-dropping beauty that happens to packed with rainbow and brown trout. The smaller Quilquihue River contrasts brilliantly. Everything is taken care of here by expert guides, who'll drive you to your own fishing hole, set up a gourmet lunch, and even tie your flies. Nine spacious guest rooms are in the lovely country lodge, and fine meals are served family style. All-inclusive rates start at $680 per day for fishers, $350 for non-fishers. Their "Never Fished Before" program will take you from beginner to the big-time in 3 days; check the website for details.

water-based treatments. Laminate floors, thin doors, and mediocre amenities keep the Loi from being a true five-star. But the lovely views, excellent restaurant, and slew of activities make it the best place to stay in the area.

Ruta 234, Km 57.5, San Martín de los Andes. © **02972/410304** or 11/5777-8950 in Buenos Aires. www.loisuites.com.ar. 85 units. $235–$280 double; $350–$770 suite. AE, MC, V. **Amenities:** 2 restaurants; lounge; wine cellar; golf course; horseback riding; indoor/outdoor pool; spa. *In room:* TV, minibar.

MODERATE

Hostería La Casa de Eugenia ★ 🎁   Built in 1927, this lovely heritage building with bright blue trim used to house the local historical society; now it's a bed-and-breakfast. Eugenia has moved to the States, but she smartly left the place in the hands of her charming brother Agustín. The delightful living room with its large fireplace, piano, and colorful sofas leads to five bedrooms, named by color. The *verde* (green) has a skylight that keeps it bright throughout the day; all the rooms have comfortable beds with down comforters and exquisite linens, gleaming white bathrooms, and little else. Five newer rooms blend modern amenities and bright colors with the inn's historical feel. There's a small outdoor pool and Jacuzzi. An amazingly decadent breakfast is served in the bright dining room overlooking a small park.

Coronel Díaz 1186, San Martín de los Andes. © **02972/427206.** www.lacasadeeugenia.com.ar. 9 units. $150–$170 double. Rates include continental breakfast. AE, MC, V. **Amenities:** Lounge; room service. *In room:* Minibar, no phone.

La Raclette ★ 🎁   The design of this appealing inn is a cross between something you'd find in Morocco and Switzerland—molded white stucco interiors set off by carved wooden shutters and eaves. It might also be described as a Hobbit House—anyone over 1.8m (6 ft.) tall might have to stoop, the ceilings upstairs are so low. Impressive renovations in 2007 make it appealing to those who like modern design. On a quiet street, La Raclette has a cozy seating area and a bar and restaurant downstairs. The public areas and the rooms have nooks and crannies and lovely modern art on display. Rooms have charisma, and they are remarkably private considering the small room sizes inherent in an old house like this. All bathrooms have jetted tubs. Now they need to turn their attention to improving the breakfast.

Coronel Pérez 1170, San Martín de los Andes. ©/fax **02972/427664.** www.laraclette.com.ar. 9 units. $89–$105 double. Rates include breakfast. AE, MC, V. **Amenities:** Restaurant; bar. *In room:* TV.

INEXPENSIVE

Hostería Anay 🖋 A convenient location, economical price, and simple yet comfortable accommodations make this a good value in San Martín. The rooms come with a double bed or two twins, and triples and apartments are available for four and five guests. Second-floor rooms have wooden ceilings and ruby-red bedspreads, a lamp here and there, and nothing else, but they're all clean and neat. The bathrooms are older, yet they have huge showers (no bathtubs). Downstairs, the lobby has a large fireplace, a game table, and plenty of plants. The sunny, pleasant eating area is a nice spot for breakfast. The hotel is owner operated, with direct and professional service.

Capitán Drury 841, San Martín de los Andes. ℂ/fax **02972/427514.** www.interpatagonia.com/anay. 15 units. $50–$65 double; $90 triple; $105 apt for 4. Rates include continental breakfast. No credit cards. **Amenities:** Lounge; limited room service. *In room:* TV.

Hostería Monte Verde A good value, this simple and clean *hostería* is one of the newer inns in town. The lobby is sparsely furnished with a giant stone fireplace. Skiers will like the large and handy ski storage area right at the door. Rooms are large and comfortable, with new beds. Bathrooms are also spacious. All superior rooms have Jacuzzi tubs and fireplaces. Some of the common spaces still need to be filled in, but the staff is friendly, and no one would feel cramped here.

Rivadavia 1165, San Martín de los Andes. ℂ **02972/410129.** www.hosteriamonteverde.com.ar. 16 units. $99–$120 standard double; $105–$135 superior double. No credit cards. **Amenities:** Restaurant; outdoor pool; sauna; grill. *In room:* TV.

CABANAS

San Martín has more than three dozen cabana complexes, ranging from attached units and detached A-frames to newer "apart-hotels." The quality varies somewhat; generally, the real difference between each is size, so always ask if a cabin for four means one bedroom and two fold-out beds in the living room. Cabanas are a great deal for parties of four to six. They're usually less expensive than hotels and come with small kitchens. During the off season, couples will find reasonably priced cabanas; however, many places charge a full six-person price during high season.

On the higher end ($78 double off season; $210 double high season), try the **Claro del Bosque ★**, Belgrano 1083 (ℂ **02972/427451;** fax 02972/428434; www.clarodelbosque.com.ar), a Swiss Alpine–style building tucked away at the end of a street on a wooded lot. The managers are very friendly and accommodating. If they're fully occupied here (which is common), ask about their new complex of charming apartments nearby. In a quiet location close to the water, **Apart del Faldeo,** Coronel Rohde 1250 (ℂ **02972/411317;** www.apartdelfaldeo.com.ar) is also recommended; it's new and open year-round.

If you'd like to get out of town, try **Paihuen**'s beautiful stone-and-mortar attached cabanas in a forested lot at Ruta Nacional 234, Km 48 (ℂ/fax **02972/428154;** www.paihuen.com.ar). It's an upscale resort-style complex with one of the best wine bars in the area. **Aldea Misonet,** Los Cipreses 1801 (ℂ/fax **02972/421821;** www.aldeamisonet.com), has wood-and-stone attached units that sit at the edge of town; some units overlook a gurgling stream, as does the terrace.

Note: Prices fluctuate wildly according to who makes the reservation; speak Spanish and you'll likely get a lower rate. Feel free to bargain when making your reservations. Make your final offer if you find the price too high—the owners may very well take what you offer, especially during low season.

Where to Eat

San Martín has several excellent restaurants. For sandwiches and quick meals, try **Peuma Café,** Av. San Martín 851 (② **02972/428289**); for afternoon tea and delicious cakes and pastries, try **Unser Traum,** General Roca 868 (② **02972/422319**). Food is generally more affordable here than in Bariloche, although it lacks both the innovation and the drama.

EXPENSIVE

La Tasca ★ REGIONAL   La Tasca is a solid choice for its fresh, high-quality cuisine and extensive wine offerings. Regional specialties are the focus, such as venison flambéed in cognac and blueberries, saffron trout, and raviolis stuffed with wild boar. All meats are handpicked from local ranches by the chef-owner, and the organic cheese is made at a local German family's farm. Mushroom lovers will savor the fresh, gourmet varieties served with appetizers and pasta. Appetizer platters are a specialty here. The cozy restaurant is festooned with hanging hams, bordered with racks of wine bottles, and warmed by a few potbellied iron stoves. It's a bit too bright for a romantic dinner, but great for families, as they have several large tables.

Mariano Moreno 866. ② **02972/428663.** Reservations recommended. Main courses $20–$28. AE, MC, V. Daily noon–3:30pm and 7pm–1am.

Piedra Kenaz ★ REGIONAL   The chef who runs this place with his wife has worked in some of the top restaurants in Patagonia, but decided to settle in San Martín de los Andes, like so many do, for the lifestyle. In a heritage building with trendy, colorful decor, they call their menu "sea and mountain cuisine." Sea includes calamari, octopus, shrimp, salmon, and sole; mountain means Patagonian lamb, venison, wild boar, and local produce like mushrooms and berries. There's also a superb vegetarian menu, including homemade spinach tortelloni. The informal but very personalized attention is perhaps the best in town.

General Villegas 657. ② **02972/427585.** www.piedrakenaz.com.ar. Reservations recommended in summer. Main courses $20–$25. AE, MC, V. Daily noon–3pm and 7:30pm–1am.

Torino Bistro ★ REGIONAL   Three of the area's top chefs came together to open this trendy spot that aims to be a bit of everything that is cool. It's funky, intimate, and informal in style, extravagant in cuisine and ambition. Start with a selection from the varied tapas menu: mussels with salami or a plate of local cheeses. For your main course, try salmon in an avocado emulsion or venison tenderloin with foie gras. Like many restaurants in Argentina, this one is "sponsored" by a handful of *bodegas,* meaning their wine list is limited. In the evenings, great music (often including DJs) makes this one of the most happening late-night hangouts in town.

Mariano Moreno 846. ② **02972/412614.** Reservations recommended. Main courses $22–$28. AE, MC, V. Daily 7pm–1am.

MODERATE

El Regional BREWPUB/REGIONAL   The *picadas* here are massive plates of delicious local nibbles, like smoked meats, olives, cheese, and pickles, served with dip and fresh breadsticks. They're great for sharing. The fish and seafood arrives fresh from Chile, making it the best in town. The atmosphere is a bit hectic and harried, but unassuming. There are more than 10 different artisan-brewed beers on tap as well. If you get here before 8:30pm for dinner, ask for a discount!

General Villegas 965. ② **02982/425326.** Main courses $14–$22. AE, MC, V. Daily noon–3pm and 7pm–midnight.

Ku Parrilla ★ 📷 REGIONAL   In a heritage house just north of the downtown core, this is a mountain grill, with trout, lamb, and your usual selection of beef cuts. More unique meats include venison, wild boar, and buffalo. I loved the sweet-and-sour venison with local fruit. The wine list is one of the best in town. The historical ambience adds style and romance.

Ruta 234 and Callejón de Bello. 📞 **02972/425953.** Reservations recommended in summer. Main courses $18–$22. AE, MC, V. Daily noon–3pm and 7pm–midnight.

La Costa del Pueblo ☺ INTERNATIONAL   This restaurant is a good bet, with a lake view and an extensive menu with everything from pastas to *parrilla*. The establishment ran as a cafe for 20 years until new owners expanded it to include a dozen more tables and a cozy fireside nook. La Costa offers good, homemade pasta dishes such as cannelloni stuffed with ricotta and walnuts, grilled meats, pizzas, and sandwiches. A kids' menu and vegetarian sandwiches help please any crowd. The restaurant is a great place to down a cold beer and a platter of smoked cheese and venison while you watch the lake lap the shore. Just don't come here in a rush; service can be really slow.

Av. Costanera and Obeid. 📞 **02972/429289.** Main courses $14–$22. AE, DC, MC, V. Daily 11am–1am.

La Fondue de Betty ★ FONDUE   A San Martín classic for 36 years, Betty's friendly service and bubbling fondue pots make this cozy restaurant an enchanting place for dinner, especially if you are with friends. Cheese fondue is the classic starter. Follow it with either beef bourguignon (beef in oil), which comes with six sauces, or beef chinoise (beef in broth). Both come with french fries. A local favorite is *bagna cauda,* a Northern Italian fondue of anchovies, garlic, and cream, in which you dip vegetables. The menu also includes some nonfondue dishes, such as tenderloin with mushroom sauce and trout with saffron. The wine list is very good. For dessert, don't miss the chocolate fondue, of course!

General Villegas 586. 📞 **02972/422522.** Reservations recommended in winter. Main courses $16–$23. No credit cards. Daily 7pm–midnight.

La Reserva ★ 📷 ARGENTINE   This lovely old stone-and-wood house was transformed into one of the most romantic restaurants in Patagonia, with a stone fireplace, elegant cloth-covered tables, soothing music, and superb service. La Reserva is run by talented Chef Alejandro Marchand, who lets many ethnic cuisines influence him while using mostly Patagonian ingredients. Begin with a cold glass of Argentine champagne to go with an order of tapas—a tasting of cheeses and dried meats. Then move on to grilled trout, tender venison with fresh berry sauce, or chicken breast stuffed with feta cheese and herbs. More than 250 wines are available, including excellent regional wines for under $14 a bottle. Desserts include a divine selection of homemade fruit tarts and ice creams.

Belgrano 940. 📞 **02972/428734.** Reservations recommended. Main courses $16–$24. AE, DC, MC, V. Daily noon–3pm and 7:30pm–midnight.

INEXPENSIVE

La Nonna Pizzería PIZZA   La Nonna's pizza, calzones, and empanadas are so good they're sold packaged and ready-to-bake at the supermarket. Toppings generally run the repetitive gamut of ham and onion, ham and pineapple, ham and hearts of palm. But there are a few deviations, such as anchovy, Roquefort, and Parmesan, or mozzarella with chopped egg. La Nonna also offers specialty regional pizzas with trout, wild boar, and venison. Calzone fillings include chicken, mozzarella, and bell pepper. For a quick snack, try one of eight types of empanadas or a piece of *faina*, a traditional and delicious garbanzo bread. La Nonna also delivers.

Capitán Drury 857. (*C* **02972/422223.** $7–$10 small pizza; $7–$12 large pizza. AE, MC, V. Daily noon–3pm and 8pm–12:30am.

San Martín After Dark

With its nice outdoor patio and cool wood and stone interior, the **Dublin South Pub,** on the corner of Mariano Moreno and San Martín (*C* **02972/424938**), has a huge list of microbrewed beers and cocktails.

JUNIN DE LOS ANDES

40km (25 miles) N of San Martín de los Andes

The main draw in the tiny town of Junín de los Andes is fly-fishing. The sport has caught on so well here that even the street signs are shaped like fish. But it also provides stunning scenery for other outdoor sports such as hiking and boating, and some lovely nearby ranches may appeal to those searching for a rural getaway. Junín is spread out in a grid pattern, a fertile little oasis along the shore of the Río Chimehuín, surrounded by dry pampa. You'll pass through Junín if you're crossing into Argentina from the Pucón area in Chile.

Essentials

GETTING THERE   See "Getting There" under "San Martín de los Andes," earlier in this chapter. It is also common for drivers to arrive in Junín from Pucón, Chile, coming over the gorgeous Paso Tromen.

For travel by bus **Ko-Ko Chevalier** (*C* **02972/427422**) has service from San Martín de los Andes and Buenos Aires; they also serve Lago Huechulafquén. The **bus terminal** (*C* **02972/492038**) is at Olarama and Felix San Martín.

GETTING AROUND   Most visitors find that the only real way to get around is to rent a car, although if they've come to fly-fish transportation is generally provided by their guide. Car-rental agencies can be found at the airport and in San Martín (see "Getting Around," under "San Martín de los Andes," earlier in this chapter).

VISITOR INFORMATION   The **Secretaría Municipal de Turismo** is located at Padre Milanesio 596 (*C* **02972/491160**); it's open daily from 8am to 9pm, 8am to 11pm during summer.

Seeing the Sights

Puerto Canoa is the central entrance to the splendid **Parque Nacional Lanín,** 30km (19 miles) from Junín. Here, you'll find a 30-minute interpretive trail and the departure spot for catamaran excursions across Lago Huechulafquén, which looks out onto the snowcapped, conical Volcán Lanín. See the earlier box, "Lahuen Co: Hot Springs Deep in the Andes," for an excellent day trip into the park's interior. Río Chimehuín begins at the lake's outlet and offers outstanding fishing opportunities. Several excellent hiking and backpacking trails traverse the area, with a few rustic backcountry huts; you can pick up information at the ranger station at Puerto Canoa. Towering behind Junín is the park's namesake volcano, Volcán Lanín, standing

3,776m (12,400 ft.) tall. Experienced mountaineers can mount the summit with a licensed guide (see "Mountaineering," under "San Martín de los Andes," earlier in this chapter). If you're in San Martín de los Andes, stop by the park's headquarters, the **Intendencia Parque Nacional Lanín,** Emilio Frey 749 (✆ **02972/427233**).

Founded in 1883, but populated by native Mapuches for centuries, Junín is one of the older towns in the area. The **Mapuche Museum,** Ginés Ponte 550 (✆ **02972/492322**), is worth a stop. Nearby, the **Museo Don Mosés,** C. Juarez and San Marín (no phone), is a turn-of-the-20th-century general store that has been totally preserved. Outside town on the road to Volcán Lanín, you can visit the wool and woodworking workshop of the local native Mapuche people at **Reserva Indígena Chiuquilihuin,** open daily from 9:30am to 7:30pm. Take RP 60 toward Tromen, turning right at Km 13. Local guides also run short hikes in the area. Ask at the workshop for more information or book a tour of the Mapuche villages with **Alquimia Viajes** in San Martín (✆ **02972/491355;** www.alquimiaturismo.com.ar).

FISHING INFORMATION & LICENSES   Visitors can obtain licenses at the **Tourism Office,** the office of the Guardafauna (✆ **02972/491277**), open Monday to Friday 8am to 3pm; the **Fly Shop,** Pedro Illera 378 (✆ **02972/491548**); **Bambi's Fly Shop,** Juan Manuel de Rosas 320 (✆ **02972/491167**); or **Patagonia Fly Fishing,** Laura Vicuña 135 (✆/fax **02972/491538**).

Where to Stay & Eat

Junín de los Andes has a few lodges that specialize in fly-fishing, such as the **Hostería de Chimehuín,** Suarez and Avenida 21 de Mayo, on the shore of the Chimehuín River (✆ **02972/491132;** $120 double). Accommodations are basic, including rooms with balconies and apartments, but the atmosphere is friendly and homey, and it has a good breakfast. An excellent fly-fishing lodge is the **San Huberto Lodge,** on a picturesque 20km (13-mile) stretch of the Malleo River (✆ **02972/491238;** www.sanhubertolodge.com.ar), which charges $185 to $280 for a double, including all meals. The San Huberto consists of six chalets with twin beds, units that are separate from an enormous, rustic lodge. The restaurant is excellent, and so are the fishing guides. Run by a British expat, the similarly rural **Estancia Huechahue** (no phone; www.huechahue.com) is a working cattle ranch open to visitors for daylong and overnight horseback trips. Their eight-room main house doubles as a charming inn. Rates are $356 per guest per night. They also have interesting multiday horseback-riding expeditions that cross the Andes. Dining options are limited here; try the **Ruca Hueney,** Milanesio 641 (✆ **02972/491113**), which serves pasta dishes, venison, and, of course, trout.

PENINSULA VALDES & SOUTHERN PATAGONIA

by Christie Pashby

Drawn to its emptiness, its wind-swept horizons, and its promise of discovery, many adventurers are driven to Patagonia by the sense that it's the end of the world. A traveler can drive for days without seeing another soul on the vast Patagonian Steppe. The unrelenting wind spins your head in circles and conspires with the emptiness of the landscape to warp your perception of time and distance and convince you that you're the only human left on the planet. It is a seduction, but also an illusion; people do live here, after all—though just a scant few hardy survivors. Sheep still outnumber humans here.

Patagonia's harsh, blustery climate and curious geological circumstances have produced some of the most beautiful natural attractions in the world: the annual congregation of the Southern Right Whale at Península Valdés, the granite towers and expansive glaciers of Los Glaciares National Park, the Southern and Northern Patagonian Ice Fields with their colossal glaciers, and the flat steppe, broken by multicolored sedimentary bluffs. Wildlife lovers and divers explore the rugged coastline of the spectacular Península Valdés; mountaineers stage elaborate excursions through rugged territories, only to be beaten back, like their predecessors, by unrelenting storms.

The area has a fascinating human history as well. Native groups eked out a life in this vast land. European explorers, such as Magellan and FitzRoy, put it on the map. Brave and gutsy settlers turned the emptiness into home. Recently, mountaineers and adventurers have reached amazing heights here. The ample presence of gauchos further heightens the air of romanticism that distinguishes the region.

Exploring the Region

In Argentina, Patagonia technically begins at the Río Colorado, which forms the border between the provinces of La Pampa and Neuquén. Thus, Bariloche is in Patagonia, and that region is known as "Andean

Patagonia," "The Lake District," or Northern Patagonia (and is covered in chapter 11). This chapter covers the Atlantic Coastal area and the far south of Patagonia, and it includes Torres del Paine National Park in Chile.

The big challenges in Patagonia are the extreme distances and the weather. Destinations can be upwards of 1,000km (620 miles) apart—and many of those kilometers are on unpaved roads, although roads like the mythical Ruta 40 and Hwy. 23 to El Chaltén are being paved at a steady rate. Yet thanks to modern amenities and air travel, it's nonetheless easy to travel to Patagonia's most compelling areas today. It's entirely feasible to visit such main highlights as Puerto Madryn and Península Valdés on the coast and then head inland to El Calafate and El Chaltén (or reverse), making for a trip that is just over a week long. If you're planning to hike the trails of Los Glaciares National Park, beneath the lofty peaks of Mt. FitzRoy and Cerro Torre, for example, you'll want to spend between 3 and 5 days in El Chaltén. The minimum amount of time for a worthwhile stop at Península Valdés is 3 days. A quick trip to Argentine Patagonia might include 2 days in El Calafate, 2 in El Chaltén, and 3 in Península Valdés. If you want to work in a trip to Chilean Patagonia, add at least another 5 days.

Prices jump and crowds swell during the summer months (early Nov to late Mar), and some businesses open only during this season. In November, the Península Valdés is busiest with visiting foreigners, who come to see the Southern Right Whales. The southern area around Parque Nacional Los Glaciares is busiest in January and February, but these summer months are not necessarily the best time to visit Patagonia; calmer weather usually prevails from mid-March to late April, when the leaves turn gold and rust in the autumn air, and winds generally die down a bit.

Exploring Península Valdés/Puerto Madryn

In the middle of Atlantic Patagonia, in the vast province of Chubut, lies the remote and barren Península Valdés, declared a World Heritage Site by UNESCO in 1999.

The bays and shores on this peninsula that juts out into the Atlantic serve as a marine-life preserve for sea elephants, sea lions, and the enormous Southern Right Whales, which come into the calm waters of the peninsula from July to December. Penguins and orca whales also swim past. Visitors come here to see the whales, penguins, and elephants up close.

Other animals that run wild here include guanacos (similar to llamas), *maras* (large wild rabbits), *choique* (similar to an ostrich), and a bevy of birds and smaller animals.

The region is very well controlled—in fact, in some areas, beach access is restricted unless you are with a certified "naturalist guide." When whales are in the bays (from July–Dec), beach activities are generally not allowed. This is a nature preserve, after all, not a playground. A handful of outfitters now have permits for kayak tours during whale season. Diving is allowed offshore throughout the year, but only on certified boats with government-sanctioned guides.

On the peninsula itself (the entire area is a national park), the tiny village of **Puerto Pirámides** (100km/62 miles from Puerto Madryn) is the departure point for all the whale-watching and diving trips. Some visitors opt to stay overnight here. But most of the tourist infrastructure is in **Puerto Madryn,** a small, laid-back, beachside city of 80,000 people. The town went from a tiny, sleepy hamlet of 6,000 people to a bustling small city that serves as a center for industrial products in eastern Patagonia. It's the most pleasant base for travelers—a jumping-off point for day trips to the peninsula and to **Punta Tombo** (2 hr. south), where Magellan penguins come to mate every year.

Patagonia

Bahía Blanca

Zapala

Neuquen

Río Colorado

NEUQUEN

RIO NEGRO

Río Negro

San Martín de los Andes

Viedma

Parque Nacional Lanin

4

Mt. Tronador

San Carlos de Bariloche

3

Puerto Montt

Parque Nacional Nahuel Huapi

Parque Nacional Lago Puelo

El Maitén

ARGENTINA

Parque Nacional Los Alerces

Esquel

Río Chubut

Puerto Madryn

Reserva Faunística Península Valdés

Puerto Pirámides

Gaiman

Dolavon

Rawson

Trelew

CHUBUT

25

Reserva Provincial Punta Tombo

20

Río Chico

1

26

Comodoro Rivadavia

ATLANTIC OCEAN

Puerto Aisen

Las Heras

43

40

Río Deseado

281

SANTA CRUZ

3

Puerto Deseado

Gobernador Gregores

CHILE

ARGENTINA

Buenos Aires

Mt. Fitzroy

El Chaltén

Río Chico

27

Puerto Santa Cruz

Parque Nacional Los Glaciares

PERITO MORENO GLACIER

El Calafate

Parque Nacional Monte Léon

3

Parque Nacional Torres del Paine

Puerto Natales

Río Gallegos

Strait of Magellan (Estrecho de Magellanes)

Falkland Islands (Islas Malvinas)

SOUTH PACIFIC OCEAN

Punta Arenas

Porvenir

Río Grande

TIERRA DEL FUEGO

Parque Nacional Tierra del Fuego

Ushuaia

Cape Horn

0   200 mi
0   200 km

The typical visit to this area includes a travel day; then a jampacked day tour of the Península Valdés, which could include whale-watching; and a third day to visit the penguin colony at Punta Tombo.

Visitors with more than 3 nights available should consider renting a car and spending a few nights at a rural hotel on the peninsula itself, such as Faro Punta Delgada or Rincón Chico (reviewed later in this chapter), or in the beach town at Puerto Pirámides. This will allow you to explore the area away from the crowds, and also to relax. You could consider skipping Punta Tombo if you visit the penguin colony at Estancia San Lorenzo instead, on the northern tip of Península Valdés. A car is necessary to explore the peninsula on your own; there is no public bus system, and distances are vast. Most of the roads are not paved, so a 4WD is a good idea.

The capital of Chubut province is the nearby residential town of **Rawson** (only 20,000 inhabitants), where there's not much to see. Nearby, the bigger city of **Trelew** has the area's largest airport and handles most flights. Trelew has a good museum, but the pickings for hotels are very slim; it's not of much interest to visitors. The Welsh town of **Gaiman** is much more interesting and makes for an excellent afternoon excursion. Settled primarily from 1865 to 1870, this is one of the few places outside of Wales where Welsh is still spoken. Houses here are reminiscent of those in the Welsh countryside. A handful of teahouses offer traditional tea service (which came in handy when the late Princess Diana visited in 1995).

Exploring Southern Argentine Patagonia

The popular image of Patagonia—wind-swept plains, towering granite spires, hard-working pioneers, endless stretches of dirt road—still exists today in the southern part of Argentina. It's way down there, though. The main tourist center is El Calafate, which is 2,727km (1,691 miles) or a 3-hour flight southwest of Buenos Aires. It's easier than ever to get here, however, which means an increasing number of visitors from North America and Europe are making a pilgrimage to see the glaciers, peaks, and emptiness of Patagonia; their primary destination being Los Glaciares National Park, which is split into two areas. The southern part of the park near El Calafate is the jumping-off point for seeing the beautiful glaciers like Perito Moreno, and the northern part is centered at Chaltén, a hiking town at the base of Cerro Torre and Mt. FitzRoy. You could feasibly see this area in a short week, which would include 2 travel days for travel to and from Buenos Aires, from where all international flights depart.

I recommend you start in El Calafate and spend a few days exploring the glaciers—Perito Moreno and the more remote ones such as Upsala. Then head to El Chaltén for some hiking; to make it worthwhile, you need at least 1 full day and 2 half-days there.

Many people visit this area on a trip combined with Torres del Paine National Park, next door in Chile. It's worthwhile, given that they are so close. "Paine," however, as the park is known here, is much busier and more expensive.

You'll also find a growing list of inns and some very good restaurants. If you're anything like me, you'll find yourself deeply moved and inspired by the vast stretches of wilderness unique to this remote part of the world.

PUERTO MADRYN

1,374km (852 miles) S of Buenos Aires; 62km (38 miles) N of Trelew; 1,798km (1,115 miles) N of Ushuaia

A laid-back city of 80,000, Puerto Madryn's population boom came in the mid-1970s. Until then, the city had only 6,000 inhabitants, but the Aloar aluminum factory

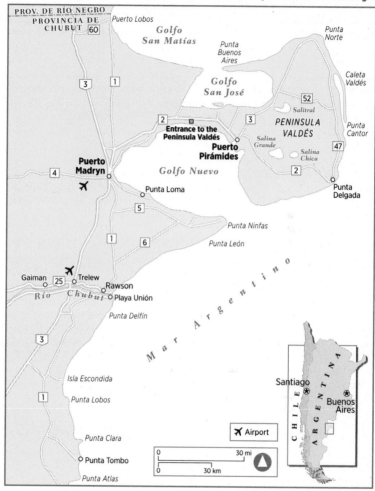

completely changed the town when it opened its doors here in 1973. Now there are tile, fish, and ceramic factories on the outskirts of town. Tourism is booming, and Aloar is still expanding. In fact, Puerto Madryn is now one of the fastest-growing cities in Argentina. Mostly used by foreign visitors, the coastal street, Avenida Roca, is lined with restaurants, bars, and hotels. Locals tend to patronize establishments at least 1 block inland. The wide beach is great, with frequently calm waters that make swimming possible from mid-December to mid-March. I also recommend that you take 30 minutes to stroll to the tip of the Old Dock for a great view of the area. The streets a few blocks inland are buzzing with locals. Here you'll find inexpensive clothing stores, and cafes and bars catering more to residents than to tourists. Very few visitors take the time to walk around here, but it's worth meandering in the residential neighborhood for at least an hour. With the bay shimmering in front, there's an easy-going and relaxed feeling about Puerto Madryn, and you may want to spend an extra day relaxing here, before continuing your journey.

Essentials

GETTING THERE **LADE (Líneas Aereas del Estado),** Roca 119 (© 2965/451256 or 0810/810-5233), has flights on Sunday, Monday, and Thursday from Buenos Aires aboard a small commuter jet (the flight makes one or two stops along the way) for $185. Weekly flights depart from Ushuaia ($265) and El Calafate ($210). The fares are much cheaper than those of Aerolíneas Argentinas, but the service is very basic. **Andes Líneas Aereas** (© 0810/777-26336 or 11/4508-6750; www.andesonline.com) departs Buenos Aires Sunday through Friday (round-trip flights from $400). Both airlines are the only ones that fly into **Aerodromo El Tehuelche** (© 2965/451909), saving you an hour-long transfer from the other airport, Trelew (see below). A taxi from the airport to the center of Puerto Madryn, 10km (6¼ miles) away, should cost no more than $12 for the 10-minute ride.

Most visitors to this region fly into Trelew Airport, **Aeropuerto de Trelew** (© 2965/433443), 62km (38 miles) away. **Aerolíneas Argentinas** (© 0810/222-86527) has three to four daily flights to Trelew from Buenos Aires and several weekly flights from El Calafate and Ushuaia. A shuttle bus meets all flights (just outside the airport to the left) and will take you to your hotel in Puerto Madryn for $10. A taxi or *remise* from Trelew airport to Puerto Madryn costs $40 to $50, and the trip takes 40 minutes.

The **Terminal de Omnibus** is on García and Independencia. The fastest bus from Buenos Aires takes 19 hours aboard **Andesmar** (© 2965/473764; www.andesmar.com). One-way fares range from $145 for the least expensive to $200 for a reclining *cama* chair with onboard meal service. Andesmar also has daily services to Mendoza ($110–$130 one-way; 18–23 hr.) and Bariloche ($75–$94 one-way; 13 hr.). Both connect in the city of Neuquén. Other reputable bus companies to try are **QueBus** (© 2965/455805), **Mar y Valle** (© 2965/472056), and **Don Otto** (© 2965/451675).

VISITOR INFORMATION You can pick up maps and detailed park information from the **Puerto Madryn Secretaria de Turismo (Tourist Office),** located at Roca 223 (© 2965/453504; www.madryn.gov.ar/turismo). Their office is open daily from 7am to 9pm.

GETTING AROUND Puerto Madryn is compact enough that you can pretty much walk everywhere. Taxis are available, however, in case you need them. A trip within the city center should cost no more than $8 or $10. Taxis are lined up near the Plaza San Martín, or you can call one at © 2965/472214. A reputable *remise* company is **Remise Madryn,** España 1560 (© 2965/453444).

Buses run by the company **28 de Julio** (© 2965/472056) depart every hour for the 45-minute journey to Trelew. The cost is $3 one-way. **Mar y Valle** (© 2965/472056) buses depart the central bus station twice a day to Puerto Pirámides on the Península Valdés at 9:45am and return at 6pm, making it handy for independent day-trippers.

You can rent a car at Trelew Airport, at the Puerto Madryn airport, or from the center of Puerto Madryn. **Avis,** Av. Roca 493 (© 2965/475422), and **Hertz,** Av. Roca 115 (© 2965/474287), have similar rates of about $75 per day for a small car.

If you think you'll want a car, it's best to book it before leaving home, for the lowest rate. If not, try bargaining at **Fiorasi Rent a Car,** Av. Roca 165 (© **2965/456300;** www.fiorasirentacar.com), a local company that offers lower rates if they have cars available. For exploring the Península Valdés, where virtually none of the roads are paved, consider renting a 4WD. Rates start at $130 per day.

[FastFACTS] PUERTO MADRYN

ATMs There are quite a few ATMs around town. **Banco Galicia,** Mitre 25 (© **2965/452323**), and **Bansud,** corner of R. Saenz Pena and Marcos A. Zar (© **2965/451489**), are the most conveniently located.

Currency Exchange The Casa de Cambio Thaler, at Av. Roca 493 (© **2965/455858**), is open until at least 10pm every night.

Emergency Dial © **101** or 2965/451449 for police; © **100** for fire.

Hospital The **Hospital Subzonal** is at R. Gomez 383 (© **2965/453030**).

Internet You'll find many Internet cafes around town. Rates are under $2 per hour, and most are open from 8am until midnight. Try **Cyber World,** at Roca 650 (© **2965/475370**), or **El Tucán,** Mosconi 36.

Laundry The laundromat at Roca 2040 (© **2965/456969**) is open Monday to Saturday from 10am to 9pm.

Pharmacy FarMadryn, corner of Roca and Belgrano (© **2965/474555**), is open 24 hours.

Post Office The main post office for **Correo Argentino** (the official name of the Argentine postal service) is located at Belgrano and Maíz (no phone).

Where to Stay

Nearly all Puerto Madryn hotels are situated along the main coastal road, Avenida Roca (which turns into Bd. Brown farther south), or a few blocks inland. Besides the avant-garde Hotel Territorio, most are still family-run, old-fashioned hotels that aren't exactly chic. The giant white 170-room Hotel Rayentray (© **2965/459300;** www.cadenarayentray.com.ar; doubles starting at $245), just south of town on the waterfront, is operated by a local hotel chain and offers unreliable service.

Most visitors to Puerto Madryn spend only 2 or 3 nights here. They visit the peninsula 1 day and Punta Tombo the next, and then fly out. Prices have soared here over the past few years, especially during the busy months of October and November; some hotels will offer you a cheaper price if you pay in cash. Rates listed here are for high season, September through March.

EXPENSIVE

Hotel Bahía Nueva ★★ This is Puerto Madryn's best-kept traditional hotel. The staff is friendly and helpful, and they take great pride in maintaining a spick-and-span hotel. Rooms are simple, with small windows, but about half of them have been renovated, so book early to ensure you get one with a modern bathroom, decent TV, and a fresh feel. Older rooms are getting a bit desperate. Four rooms have sea views; ask at check-in if one is available, and you'll likely be upgraded at no extra cost. The full breakfast buffet, including fresh fruit and eggs (a rarity in these parts), may be the best in town; it's served in a cheerful dining room on the second floor. The ground-level bar area has a pool table and a lovely fireplace in the cozy lounge. The staff is knowledgeable about the area and can help arrange excursions. My main concern is that they have drastically raised their prices without making any renovations to the common spaces. It is no longer a bargain.

Av. Roca 67, 9120 Puerto Madryn. ℂ/fax **2965/451677.** www.bahianueva.com.ar. 40 units. $179 double; $210 triple. Rates include breakfast. AE, MC, V. Free parking. **Amenities:** Bar; lounge. *In room:* TV.

Hotel Península Valdés ✋ For decades, this was the top place in Puerto Madryn, and it retains a certain elusive highbrow feel that would appeal to business travelers. The owners (a well-known local family) have recently tried to be hipper and more modern. Many of the rooms have been renovated, including the bathrooms, which are brighter now, though most tubs are still tiny. Upper-level rooms are certainly in better shape. Rooms on the top floor are the most spacious. The charge for "panoramic" rooms with sea views (plus king-size beds and flatscreen TVs) is 20% extra, though it never hurts to ask at check-in for a free upgrade. I find it annoying that they charge $16 for use of the sauna and $14 for the unattractive indoor Jacuzzi; at least Internet access is free. The staff is efficient, if a bit snotty. I recommend the Territorio over this place, if you can afford it, but if you must stay here, particularly if you're traveling with a tour group, you will likely find it satisfactory, if unimpressive.

Av. Roca 155, 9120 Puerto Madryn. ℂ **2965/471292.** Fax 2965/452584. www.hotelpeninsula.com.ar. 76 units. $185 double standard; $223 superior with ocean view. Rates include buffet breakfast. AE, DC, MC, V. Free parking. **Amenities:** Bar; lounge; Jacuzzi; massage; room service; sauna. *In room:* A/C, TV, hair dryer, minibar.

Hotel Territorio ★ This hotel is small enough to be classified as an inn (36 rooms), but considers itself upscale enough to be a five-star. The hotel itself does not cry for attention, and you may even miss it for how well it blends into the natural setting. It's built in an inconspicuous style with local materials such as stone and tin sheeting. Inside, it's much more flashy. The views are superb: The lobby, restaurant, and bar look out over the water and have towering windows and a sleek, modern look. Rooms are the largest in town, and all face the water to varying degrees. They too feel natural, with washed-cement floors, cream walls, dark-wood furniture, and crisp white linens. Bathrooms are long and narrow, and all have small tubs with ocean views. A new pool is scheduled to open in late 2011. By far, Territorio is the ambitious, comfortable, and stylish lodging option.

Bd. Brown 3251, 9120 Puerto Madryn. ℂ **2965/470050.** www.hotelterritorio.com.ar. 36 units. From $256 double; from $463 suite. Rates include buffet breakfast. AE, MC, V. Free parking. **Amenities:** Restaurant; bar; lounge; room service; spa. *In room:* A/C, TV, hair dryer, minibar.

MODERATE

Hostería Solar de la Costa 🏨 An oceanfront inn in an upscale neighborhood, this hotel has a friendly, breezy vibe. Most of the rooms are doubles with king-size beds, tiny TVs, and clean, compact bathrooms. Ocean-facing rooms cost the same as those with a garden view, so reserve early to get the front ones. Top-floor rooms sleep four and have a fully equipped kitchen and a Jacuzzi. Breakfast includes home-baked breads, pastries, and pies. A big shady garden out back has a barbecue.

Bd. Brown 2057, 9120 Puerto Madryn. ℂ **2965/458822.** www.solardelacosta.com. 14 units. $125 double; $190 quad with kitchen. Rates include breakfast. AE, MC, V. Free parking. **Amenities:** Family room; garden; high-speed Internet. *In room:* A/C, TV.

INEXPENSIVE

Hotel Gran Madryn ★ Small, comfortable and clean, and just a half-block from the beach, this traditional hotel has been slowly getting a face-lift, and it remains a good

Although reservations are not required anywhere in Puerto Madryn, you can usually score a better table and a warmer greeting if you call ahead. Even if you don't arrive exactly on time, the mere fact that your name is on a "list" gives you a bit more leeway with the waitstaff. If you see a table you like (by a window, for example) and you have a reservation, they are more likely to give it to you. If you plan to come around 9:30pm, you'll find most places packed. For earlier diners (7:30–8:30pm), you should have less of a problem.

deal. The 11 top-floor rooms are largest and all have sea views; some have balconies and the corner units have Jacuzzis. Bathrooms are bright and clean. Service is upbeat.

Lugones 40, 9120 Puerto Madryn. ⓒ **2965/472205.** www.hotelgranmadryn.com.ar. 43 units. $70 double; $86 triple; $92 superior. Rates include breakfast. AE, MC, V. Free parking. **Amenities:** Room service; free Wi-Fi (in public areas). *In room:* TV.

Where to Eat

Fish is big in Puerto Madryn. The fishermen go out into the bay every morning and reel in white salmon, cod, and sole. Meat is double the price here, compared to Buenos Aires, because everything has to be flown or trucked in. If you are craving meat, the best place is where the locals go—the simple **Estela Parrilla,** R. S. Pena 27 (ⓒ **2965/451573**). For $14 to $18, you can have tenderloin or filet mignon and a salad. A variety of sausages is also available, as well as chicken on the grill. They're open Monday to Saturday from 8pm to midnight and Sunday from noon to 11pm. For an upscale "behind closed door" gourmet experience, try chef Gustavo Rapretti's acclaimed **En Los Fuegos de Mi Casa** (ⓒ **02965/476375**).

EXPENSIVE

Cantina El Náutico SEAFOOD   A local tradition, this is a great spot for seafood, pasta, and fresh fish. The owners (father and son) are almost always there to make sure the service is smooth, that diners are happy, and that everyone's impressed with the dozens of photos of celebrities who've dined here in the past. Dining a la carte can be pricey; stick with the daily specials when possible, especially if paella is on offer. And they have the best *milanesas* (breaded veal cutlets) in town!

Av. Roca 790. ⓒ **2965/471303.** Main courses $16–$24. AE, MC, V. Daily 11:30am–3pm and 7pm–midnight.

Mar y Meseta ★★ SEAFOOD/INTERNATIONAL   This excellent seafood restaurant manages to be both upscale and relaxed, and it has a kids' menu. Service is top-notch, and the chef uses Patagonian ingredients whenever possible to create his masterpieces. Start with a bottle of cold Argentine sparkling wine and the chef's appetizer platter, consisting of steamed mussels, smoked mackerel, fried cod fingers, and pickled carrots and cauliflower. Move on to what may very well be the most creative dish in Puerto Madryn: fresh local cod baked with Patagonian honey, served on a bed of toasted cinnamon sticks and sweet-potato chips. Other seafood dishes include a mixed grill of seafood and fish for two people for $24, and a daily selection of fresh grilled fish filets (depending on the catch of the day). The seafood stew is a hearty meal on a cold evening.

Av. Roca 485. ⓒ **2965/458740.** Main courses $18–$28. AE, MC, V. Daily 11am–3pm and 7pm–midnight.

Nativo Sur ★★ ☺ REGIONAL/INTERNATIONAL   This is the best beachfront restaurant in town. A small playground for kids faces the pleasant patio area. The large windows overlooking the bay give the entire place an airy and relaxed feel. The owners, a husband-and-wife team, buy fish daily from a local fisherman, and vegetables are trucked in fresh from a nearby farm. The focus here is fish—whatever is fresh (usually white salmon, sole, or cod), made to order. The best appetizer is a seafood sampler with calamari, scallops, oysters, prawns, and the like. I highly recommend fish of the day with stir-fried vegetables for $12.

Corner of Brown and Humphreys. ✆ **2965/457403.** Main courses $11–$18. MC, V. Tues–Fri 8pm–midnight; Sat–Sun noon–3:30pm and 8pm–midnight.

Plácido ★ INTERNATIONAL   Puerto Madryn's fanciest restaurant has a great location in the center of town. An airy, expansive dining room with plenty of windows, large wineglasses, crisp white tablecloths, and heavy silverware sets the stage for an elegant evening. Unfortunately, management has overzealously sought out foreign visitors, which has made the cuisine schizophrenic, at best. Paella, cod in hollandaise sauce, Patagonian lamb with rosemary, and shrimp in curry sauce with white rice are just a few of the many main courses available. The wine list is impressive, and service is very refined. Stick with simply prepared fresh fish or prawns or the good selection of homemade pastas, and you'll have a memorable meal. The vegetarian tagliatelle with wild mushrooms, for example, is delicious. Call ahead and reserve a table by a window overlooking the bay.

Av. Roca 506. ✆ **2965/455991.** Reservations recommended. Main courses $16–$28. AE, DC, MC, V. Daily noon–3:30pm and 7:30pm–1am.

MODERATE

Ambigú ★ 🍴 PIZZA   Elegant but very affordable, Ambigú has a huge menu with a mélange of dishes, ranging from chicken curry to beef chop suey and all kinds of pizzas. The most interesting is the asparagus-and-provolone pizza with black olives. There's also a limited selection of seafood and fish. It's a fun, boisterous, and informal place that is busy every night. Service can be spotty when they're swamped, but nobody's in a rush here. Order a bottle of Mendoza Malbec to go with your meal, then sit back, and watch all the people walk by on the coastal Avenida Roca.

On the corner of Roca and Roque Saenz Pena. ✆ **2965/472541.** Main courses and pizzas $3–$16. MC, V. Daily noon–2pm and 7:30pm–midnight.

Taska Beltza ★ BASQUE/SEAFOOD   A local favorite, this spot is hip without being flashy. It's all about good food served in an atmosphere that's not trying to be something it isn't. Chefs garnish local fish and seafood with the classic Basque quartet of seasonings: garlic, lemon, butter, and parsley. Try blackened *merluza* (hake) with red-pepper sauce or *pejerrey* (mackerel). Shrimp with cognac and scallops on the half shell are also excellent. For dessert, don't miss the Beltzan apples. Service can be a bit slow, but it could just be that the staff is that relaxed.

9 de Julio 345. ✆ **2965/15-66-8085** (mobile). Main courses $10–$16. AE, MC, V. Tues–Sun 7:30pm–midnight.

Puerto Madryn After Dark

Although it's open all day, serving good food from 11am and going strong through 4am, **Margarita Pub** (✆ **02965/475871**), Roque Saenz Pena 15, really comes into its own at cocktail hour. Trendy and friendly, it has the coolest vibe in town.

Getting to the Ecocentro

There are four ways to get to the Eco-centro, which is 3km (1¾ miles) south of the center of town. The fastest is by taxi, which will cost around $5. If you have an hour or so, and it's a nice day, walk down the coast to the south, just over the point on the horizon to the museum. Or rent a bike and pedal for about 30 minutes in the same direction.

For about 50¢, you can take the local bus no. 2 from downtown. It will drop you off just down the hill from the Eco-centro. En route, you'll also pass the Punta Cuevas historical monument to the Welsh settlers as well as the Tehu-elche Monument to the area's original inhabitants. Remember, Ecocentro is open mainly in the afternoon.

Seeing the Sights

There's not much to see in Puerto Madryn itself, apart from a couple of museums. Most visitors are here because of the town's proximity to the Península Valdés. If you have time to kill, however, grab a bike or walk up the lovely beach road or stroll the shops along Roca.

Ecocentro ★★   This is more like an interactive learning center, where you can educate yourself on the marine ecosystems of Atlantic Patagonia. I recommend coming to Ecocentro on your first day in Puerto Madryn, after settling into your hotel and before heading out to the Península Valdés. The view of the ocean is exquisite from this lovely modern building, and the nautical and topographical maps afford deep insight into this region. A tank re-creates a tidal pool, where you can see species that inhabit the coastal areas. A soundtrack plays whale sounds, and a good movie about the Península Valdés explores the habits of Magellan penguins in Punta Tombo, as well as local elephant seals and sea lions. Ask for the English-language handbook to get even more out of your visit. You'll need about 2 hours to visit Ecocentro. A very pleasant on-site cafe serves snacks.

Julio Verne 3784. ✆ **2965/457470.** www.ecocentro.org.ar. Admission $9.50. Mar–Dec Wed–Mon 3–7pm; Jan–Feb Wed–Mon 5–9pm. Hours can fluctuate; call to confirm hours.

Punta Tombo National Reserve

Most visitors spend a day on the Península Valdés and then a day at Punta Tombo National Reserve, the second-most-visited attraction in Atlantic Patagonia. The largest sanctuary for Magellan penguins, Punta Tombo is 248km (154 miles) south of Puerto Madryn, a 2-hour trip. Every year from September to April (the park is closed May–Aug), up to a million of these penguins return to Punta Tombo to mate. Visitors are able to walk just a few feet away from thousands of penguins guarding their nests. Baby penguins are visible in December and January. Bird lovers will enjoy views of king and rock cormorants, giant petrels, kelp gulls, and oystercatchers as well.

The drive from Puerto Madryn is all highway, until you pass Trelew; then you head south on RP 1, a monotonous gravel road that seems to go on forever. The entrance to the national reserve is clearly marked, and the entrance fee is $8, payable in dollars or pesos. Be sure to observe all the posted signs (stopping your car is strictly prohib-ited except in the designated parking lots). Walkways and handrails point you in the right direction as you explore. Veering off the trail is prohibited, as is going down to the beach. There is a cafeteria at Punta Tombo, but consider bringing a picnic instead. Plan on 2 hours to visit the reserve and observe the penguins. Tour operators run trips daily for about $105, and some stop for tea in Gaiman (see later in this chapter).

Tour Operators

Puerto Madryn's coastal street, Avenida Roca, is lined with travel agencies. Shop around for a space if you are booking at the last minute. Unless you are bilingual, it's very important to ensure that your tour has an English-speaking guide. Almost all quote the same price for standard tours, such as the 1-day Península Valdés or Punta Tomba tours, most of which start at 7:30am (depending on whether you are staying in Trelew or Puerto Madryn) and get you back before dinner. One-day tours of the Península Valdés start at $80 per person, not including a whale-watching trip (an additional $35) or lunch.

If you have a group of six or more, it is worthwhile—and surely more relaxing—to take a private tour for the same price, rather than signing up for a standard group tour.

Flamenco Tour, Av. Roca 331 (© 2965/455505; www.flamencotour.com), is perhaps the largest tour operator in the area. The 1-day guided tour to the Península Valdés lasts from 7:30am to 7pm and includes a stop at the museum, a chance to go on a whale-watching cruise, and guided walks on the Punta Delgada beach and Caleta Valdés, to view the elephant seals.

Huinca Travel, Av. Roca 353 (© 2965/454411; www.huincatravel.com), has traditional tours in small groups as well as active options, including a nighttime whale-watching tour and mountain biking on the Península Valdés. **NieveMar Tours ★,** Av. Roca 493 (© 2965/455544; www.nievemartours.com.ar), has very friendly and knowledgeable guides. They offer the standard Península Valdés tour with a long lunch break, to stretch your legs, at Caleta Valdés; a full day at Punta Tombo; and a 6-hour trip to discover the Welsh heritage of Gaiman. They can also set up multiday tours that include accommodations.

Outdoor Activities

BIKING For short-term bike rentals, try **El Retorno,** Mitre 798 (© 2965/456044). A 1-day bike rental costs around $15.

DIVING Most of the diving companies here offer the same tours for the same price. It's a question of which schedule you prefer. All have been licensed and have high safety standards. The main draw is swimming with the sea lions and elephant seals, and some also arrange for diving close to the whales. **Aquatours,** Av. Roca 550 (© 2965/451954), offers a variety of diving trips in the bay off Puerto Madryn and also off the Península Valdés.

FISHING Raúl Díaz (© 2965/450812) is a seasoned fisherman who is happy to take visitors out with him on a fishing trip.

GOLF The **Puerto Madryn Golf Club** (http://golf.madryn.com) is on RN 4, on the road to the airport. Call the club manager, Juan González (© 2965/471947), to arrange your tee times and get detailed information on the rates.

HORSEBACK RIDING For rides between 2 and 4 hours in the steppe above Madryn and along the coast, try **Nativo Adventure** (© 2965/15-695232).

KAYAKING Huellas y Costas, 1995 Morgan (© 2965/470143; www.huellasy costas.com), runs unique sea-kayaking expeditions from late December through March, during the whale season.

You can rent a sailboard and sail from the **Vernardino Club Mar,** Bd. Brown 860 (© **2965/474289**).

PENINSULA VALDES

Most visitors to the peninsula come for the day on guided excursions, aboard small nine-passenger vans. There is enough here, however, to keep you busy for 3 or 4 days. If you choose to drive on your own in a rental car, remember that the peninsula is very isolated and barren, and the only gas station is in Puerto Pirámides. Sometimes you can go for hours without seeing another soul. All roads on the peninsula are gravel, and driving is hazardous. Consider renting a 4WD truck for more comfort.

Península Valdés is not a national park but a Natural Protected Area managed by the Province of Chubut. Within its protected borders, families continue to run the ranches that they have managed for more than a century, although some are now turning to tourism. Human activity is restricted, and although tourism is now the major player, the balance game between conservation and recreation is monitored closely.

At the park gates, foreign visitors have to stop and pay an entrance fee of $18 per person (it's good for the length of your stay in the park, be that an afternoon or 3 days). Just past the entrance to the national park (which is about a half-hour's drive northeast of Puerto Madryn), the **Interpretive Center** makes a good consolation prize if you don't have time for the excellent Ecocentro museum in Puerto Madryn (see above). It's open from 8am to 8pm daily, and admission is free. From the park entrance, after driving east for about an hour on Ruta 2, you'll reach the tiny village of Puerto Pirámides (pop. 202), which is only 2 blocks wide. This is the main launching spot for the whale-watching boats that depart from this area from April to late December. Whale-watching trips cost $45 per person and last about 1½ hours.

The rest of the year, warmer weather transforms Puerto Pirámides (see below) into more of a beach town, popular with vacationing Argentines on their summer holidays. The Southern Right Whales that swim past here once verged on extinction (they earned their name because they move slowly and float easily, making them "right" for hunters). Today, these gentle giants gather to mate in these bays just off the peninsula from April to December. They each weigh 35 to 40 tons and measure about 17m long (56 ft.). About 800 whales show up each year, after feeding in Antarctica for 3 months. Whale-watching trips almost always bring visitors within meters of these very social whales. It's a rare and moving experience.

From Puerto Pirámides, if you continue east on Ruta Provincial 2, you'll reach **Punta Delgada,** a stretch of beach favored by elephant seals from mid-June to late December. You can stop for lunch at the upscale Faro Punta Delgada hotel (see below) and also take a tour of the lighthouse.

Heading north on RP 47 will bring you to **Caleta Valdés,** which has a cafeteria on the bluff overlooking the ocean. This is where most visitors on excursions eat lunch, so it is very busy from 1 to 3pm. The stairs leading down to the beach take you to another stretch of sand covered by elephant seals, which are usually sleeping. Pleasant interpretive walks with placards explain the natural history of the area, with beautiful views of the Atlantic Coast.

At the northeastern tip of the peninsula is Punta Norte, where hundreds of sea lions congregate from January to June. Orcas can sometimes be seen off this point too, attracted by the sea lions—their favorite snack. Count yourself very lucky if you

When to Visit

Timing is critical when you're visiting the Península Valdés. If you want to see penguins, forget about coming here between May and August. If you're hoping to watch whales, don't come between mid-December and April. All things considered, the ideal time to visit Atlantic Patagonia is in October or November. The penguins have laid their eggs and are guarding their nests, the whales are happily swimming in the bays with their offspring, and schools in Argentina are still in session, so crowds are thin.

manage to see the orcas hunting baby sea lions during dramatic high-tide attacks. Just to the west of Punta Norte is **Estancia San Lorenzo** (© **2965/455888;** www.pinguinospuntanorte.com.ar), which welcomes a colony of up to 200,000 Magellan penguins each year from August to April. Tours are expensive ($55 per person) but worthwhile, because you get to see penguins up close, in a very quiet setting. Come early in the morning if possible.

Because the peninsula is barren and dry, you'll be able to spot guanacos; reminiscent of small llamas, they're found only in Patagonia. Because they are so shy, however, they usually run in the opposite direction when they see a car coming. Also keep an eye out for choiques (ostrichlike birds); the strange-looking mara, which is a rabbit that runs on four-legs like a dog; and lots of sheep. In the middle of the peninsula, three giant salt flats appear like mirages on the horizon.

In 1 day, it's possible to quickly sample the area and spot some whales, sea lions, elephant seals, and guanacos. You will spend the bulk of the day in the tour operator's van, however, especially if you are staying in Trelew. Wildlife lovers should plan to spend 2 or 3 days exploring the peninsula. For more information and good interactive online maps, visit **www.peninsulavaldes.org.ar**.

Where to Stay & Eat

The peninsula has a handful of newer upscale lodging options—namely ranches or lighthouses that have opened their doors to the public. Most are expensive and offer packages that include all meals and daily activities. They're a relaxing way to really live the wonders of Península Valdés, to see the wildlife in silence, and to get away from it all. I recommend you spend at least 2 nights in any of the following places. Highly recommended, **Estancia La Elvira ★** (© **2965/474248;** www.laelvira.com.ar) is inland, at the working heart of a ranch, which also runs a restaurant overlooking Caleta Valdés. The ranch house has eight large rooms that start at $340 with breakfast or $395 for full board. You don't get the coastal views or the ocean breezes here, but you will delight in excellent service and a charming rural facility. At the tiny and elegant **Rincón Chico ★★** (© **2965/471733;** www.rinconchico.com.ar; all-inclusive doubles at $545), a local family has opened the doors to their eight-room guesthouse near the beach, with great success. There's heaps of character, and access to a restricted sea lion colony, but the restaurant is substandard. The most visitor-friendly is the **Faro Punta Delgada ★★** (© **2965/458444;** www.puntadelgada.com; all-inclusive doubles at $406 per night), inside a refurbished government lighthouse facility. The setting is beautifully wind-swept, and the rugged outdoor setting is balanced by the charming staff and nice amenities inside the hotel. Rooms are cozy and country style, with blue-gingham bedspreads and simple bathrooms. Guests can explore the lighthouse, which brings a sense of romance to dark evenings, or the many nearby trails that lead to deserted beaches on their own. The bar is a great place to gather and share stories with other travelers in the evening. The restaurant is packed with tourists during the day, but it's much more intimate for breakfast and dinner. All three of the above are heads above the hotels in Puerto Madryn in terms of warmth, service, natural setting, and ambience.

PUERTO PIRAMIDES

100km (62 miles) NE of Puerto Madryn

The only village inside the Península Valdés National Park, Puerto Pirámides is tiny—about 4 blocks. Once a bustling salt-exporting port, today it's a quiet village. It's the sole launching point for the many whale-watching trips that depart from here, from April to late December. During the day, the beach is mobbed with day-trippers, but it's a much more intimate experience in the evening. Some travelers choose to stay here overnight instead of in Puerto Madryn (see earlier in this chapter), especially if they have their own transportation. You can venture to other parts of the park much more quickly from here. There is no fresh water here—salt water is just barely treated before hitting your taps—so you must make an effort to conserve water and drink only bottled water.

Essentials

GETTING THERE See "Essentials," under "Puerto Madryn," earlier in this chapter.

You can rent a car in Puerto Madryn or in Trelew. From Puerto Madryn, the trip is 100km (62 miles) and takes about 1½ hours. There's only one road here: Ruta 2.

Daily buses depart Puerto Madryn's terminal at 9:45am and return at 6pm. Contact **Mar y Valle** (⟨©⟩ **2965/472065**). The cost is $6 each way.

A taxi or *remise* from Puerto Madryn should cost no more than $100; from Trelew, the cost is about $150.

Seeing the Sights

See also "Península Valdés," above.

Since Puerto Pirámides is the only town on the peninsula, it's entirely tourist-oriented and, therefore, very expensive. The only gas station on the peninsula is here. Whale-watching tours depart from here, so it is a stopover point for people who are visiting the park. Diving trips also leave from here, and the few hotels are frequently filled with groups of divers from Europe. From late December to late March, when the whales leave the bay, it's possible to kayak and swim, and the area becomes a destination for beach-seeking Argentine vacationers. But the main draw is the whale-watching trips. The cost is about $55 per person, but if you're staying overnight, I encourage you to bargain with Captain Pinino to arrange your own excursion. Staying here also gives you best access to the sunset whale-watching trips, which are beautiful. Sometimes you can even hear the whales at night from your room. A few nights here will leave you relaxed and in touch with nature.

Perhaps the most respected whale-watching outfitter is **Southern Spirit ★★** (⟨©⟩ **2965/473043**; www.southernspirit.com.ar). They have two speedy boats that are more intimate than their competitors'. The sunset departure is the best of the day.

There's usually a group whale-watching trip at around 10:30am daily, but private trips may be arranged for later in the day.

For kayaking (in the summer), try **Patagonia Explorers** (© 2965/15-350619 [mobile]; www.patagoniaexplorers.com). For longer kayak expeditions in the remote reaches of the Peninsula, contact **Huellas y Costas** (© 02965/470143; www.huellasycostas.com). Even if you've never dived before, **Master Divers Patagonia** (© 2965/15-681004; www.masterdivers.com.ar) will take you out for a first dive and will take more seasoned divers for night and deep dives, as well as dives with sea lions. They have English-speaking PADI-certified instructors.

Where to Stay

Choices are limited in Puerto Pirámides, and prices are very high. There are a handful of private campgrounds in town, but you'll need a tent. Camping is prohibited elsewhere in the peninsula. For other alternatives, see "Where to Stay & Eat" in the Península Valdés section, above. Rates listed here are for high season (Sept–Mar).

Del Nomade Hostería ★★ Calling itself an eco-lodge, this new inn was built with green technologies like solar panels to provide heat and hot water, and it employs other practices like waste reduction and water conservation. Rooms are simple, modern, comfortable, and decorated in natural colors. Breakfast includes home-baked cookies, and bathroom amenities include homemade natural soaps. They also have the friendliest staff in town. A small, self-catering apartment is also available. Check the website for discounts.

Av. De las Ballenas s/n. © **02965/495044.** www.ecohosteria.com.ar. 8 units. $160–$190 double. V. Rates include breakfast. **Amenities:** Wi-Fi.

Las Restingas You'll pay a lot to be able to watch whales from your bed at this small hotel. Of their 12 rooms, 8 are oceanfront. The airy lobby and adjacent dining room, with its exposed stone, are pleasant, with an understated elegance. Rooms have tiled floors, wooden beds, wrought-iron lamps, ceiling fans, and TVs, but no cable (instead you can borrow DVDs). I highly recommend splurging for the sea view; the other rooms are darker and less cheery. Marble bathrooms have bathtubs.

1st right as you enter the village, Puerto Pirámides. © **2965/495101.** www.lasrestingas.com. 12 units. $240 double w/village view; $300 double w/sea view. Rates include breakfast. AE, MC, V. **Amenities:** Restaurant; bar; room service; DVD library. *In room:* TV/DVD player, hair dryer, minibar.

Where to Eat

El Refugio ★ SEAFOOD The owner of this quirky restaurant-bar is a fisherman, so you can be assured that what you're eating is fresh from local waters. Ask what he caught that day, and order it. The small dining room, filled with antiques, has a very cozy feel to it. They now have small cabins that sleep up to five.

Puerto Pirámides. © **2965/495031.** Main courses $12–$22. No credit cards. Daily noon–11pm.

La Estación ★ ARGENTINE This place is a great choice for lunch on a warm day, with a very pleasant patio outside a building with a historical feel. Fresh seafood is the focus, but they also have homemade pastas, salads, and some grilled meats. In the evening, it's a lively pub. Note that the restaurant is closed the last week in December.

Puerto Pirámides. © **2965/495047.** Main courses $9–$22. No credit cards. Daily 10am–11pm.

TRELEW

67km (42 miles) S of Puerto Madryn

Trelew's airport is the gateway to the region; many travelers pass through here on their way to and from the Península Valdés. The largest city in the region (pop. 100,000), Trelew is industrial and certainly not as charming at its neighbor Puerto Madryn. Crime is also a concern here. The town has a pleasant square and an excellent paleontological museum, but little else of interest. The nearby Welsh town, Gaiman, is worth an afternoon visit.

Essentials

GETTING THERE **Aerolíneas Argentinas** (© 0810/222-86527) is the sole operator at **Almirante Zar** airport, 5km (3 miles) from the city center. They fly at least twice daily from Buenos Aires, with extra flights on weekends. Aerolíneas also has several weekly flights from El Calafate and Ushuaia. **28 de Julio** buses (© 2965/472056) arrive every hour from Puerto Madryn at the OmniBus station, at Urquiza 100 (© 2965/420121). The cost is $10 one-way. Buses from Buenos Aires take 20 hours and cost $125 one-way.

VISITOR INFORMATION The tourist office is on the Plaza San Martín, at Mitre 387 (© 2965/420139; www.trelew.gov.ar). The English-speaking agents are very helpful and have lots of maps and information about the Península Valdés and the region. The office is open from 8am to 8pm daily.

GETTING AROUND A taxi *(remise)* from the airport to the city center will cost no more than $5. From Puerto Madryn to Trelew, a *remise* is about $45; from Puerto Pirámides it's about $200.

Fiorasi Rent a Car has offices at the airport and at Urquiza 31 (© 2965/435344; www.fiorasirentacar.com) in the city center. **Hertz** has an office only at the airport (© 2965/436005). The average cost for a compact car is $70 per day.

Seeing the Sights

There's not much to see here except for one museum, but if you have a bit of extra time, you may want to take a walk around the pleasant San Martín square.

Museo Paleontológico Egidio Feruglio (Paleontological Museum Egidio Feruglio) ★★ The MEF, as it is widely known, is one of the best paleontological museums in South America, a must for dinosaur fans. Opened in 2000, it houses an amazing collection of fossils and dinosaur bones. Inside the museum (and visible when you visit) is a working lab where a team of scientists studies and cleans fossils. Try to come here during the week when the scientists are at work (Mon–Fri), and you'll get a sense of how much they do to study just one fossil. An amazing skeleton of a titonausaur, which walked on this land 70 million years ago, fills one room. Other rooms take you through a chronological order of dinosaur discoveries over the years, from past to present. There's also a good movie with English subtitles showing sea fossils found in Patagonia. You'll need about 1½ hours to visit the museum. See if you can spend the night at one of their excavation sites. The lobby houses a gift shop and a snack bar.

Av. Fontana 140. © **2965/420012.** www.mef.org.ar. Admission $9. Mid-Sept to end of Mar daily 9am–8pm, Apr to mid-Sept daily 10am–6pm.

Where to Stay & Eat

The most centrally located hotel is **Hotel Rayentray,** San Martín 101 (© **2965/434702;** www.cadenarayentray.com.ar; $88–$120 double; Amex, Master-Card, Visa accepted), just steps from the main plaza. The building is modern on the outside and dated on the inside. It has 110 rooms that are comfortable but neither luxurious nor elegant, and some complain it is too noisy. There's a restaurant, a bar, and a small indoor pool, and massages are available. The only other decent place to stay is the classic **Hotel Touring Club,** Fontana 240 (© **2965/433997;** www. touringpatagonia.com.ar; doubles starting at $55), which dates back to the days of Butch Cassidy (who allegedly stayed here). Rooms are dated, but the atmosphere is unbeatable. It also has a good cafe.

The best *parrilla* in town is **El Viejo Molino,** Av. Gales 250 (© **2965/428019**). In a heritage building, the wood-fired grill offers up classics of sausages, beef, chicken, and lamb. They also serve grilled vegetables and interesting pastas. Main courses cost $8 to $15; no credit cards accepted. They are open from noon to 3pm and from 8 to 11:30pm Tuesday through Sunday.

GAIMAN

17km (10 miles) W of Trelew

Just a 10-minute drive west of Trelew, you'll find the lush, green town of Gaiman, settled in 1870 by immigrants from Wales. It's a pleasant place to take a walk and to admire the very English-looking houses. Almost every house in this town of 4,500 residents is open to the public in some way, as a teahouse, a small inn, or some other type of hospitality center. People in Gaiman—many of them descendants of the original families such as the Joneses and Roberts—are both exceedingly friendly and proud. They cling to their unique heritage with the same sense of purpose that brought their ancestors all the way here more than 130 years ago. Gaiman is also known for its singing choirs that blend traditional Welsh tunes with Argentine folk music. Each October, the town hosts the Eisteddfod music and poetry festival, which draws people from Wales and other Welsh communities around the world. Some of the choirs perform at the teahouses (see below). For an excellent bilingual tour that focuses on all things Welsh, your best choice is Jeremy Wood at **Welsh Patagonia** (www.welshpatagonia.com), who is a wealth of information and stories.

Getting There

From Trelew, buses such as **28 de Julio** (© **2965/472056**) depart regularly for Gaiman from Plaza Roca. Fewer buses run on the weekends. The trip is about 25 minutes and costs about $5. A *remise* from Trelew to Gaiman should cost around $20. If you are driving, take Ruta 25 west from Trelew.

Seeing the Sights

The Welsh museum, **Museo Histórico Regional Gales,** at the corner of Rivadavia and Sarmiento (no phone), is an interesting place to get the lowdown on the town and its origins. The Welsh immigrants built the Chubut railway, and the museum is housed in the old railway station. It contains some interesting documents and relics from the late 1800s and early 1900s. Admission is $2.

high tea IN GAIMAN

Most visitors come to Gaiman to have real Welsh tea, a tradition that was built on the difficult life of the early settlers, who came home in the afternoons and found solace in a cup of warm brew sent specially to these outposts from the United Kingdom. The tradition lives on, and it's now shared with the public: The late Princess Diana herself enjoyed tea here in 1995, when she made an official visit. The chair she sat on is displayed inside a lovely house that has become one of the best teahouses in Gaiman: **Ty Te Caerdydd,** Finca 202 (℗ **2965/491510**), serves Welsh tea complete with sandwiches, scones, homemade jams, cakes, and lemon pie every day from 2 to 8pm. The cost is $12 per person. **Ty Nain,** Yrigoyen 283 (℗ **2965/491126**), will fill you up with *torta galesa* (Welsh cake) and a bottomless pot of tea, also for $12. The lovely 1890 home is sparkling clean and has a small museum of Welsh-Argentine history out back. Note that the Gaiman tea experience is popular with bus tours; if you are on your own, look for a spot that doesn't have a bus parked out front if you want some personal attention.

If you are keen on continuing to explore the Welsh scene, take a side trip to the nearby village of **Dolavan,** 18km (11 miles) west of Gaiman via RN 25. It's an authentic little farming village, with wooden water wheels and a historic town center with old brick buildings, including the old mill known here as the **Molino Harinero,** Maipú 61 (℗ **2965/492290**). Built in 1880, it still operates, has a small cafe serving hearty sandwiches, and opens sporadically for guided tours. The little brick chapel, built in 1917, is typical of the Welsh architecture that blends so naturally with the environment. It's one of a handful of similar constructions that dot the countryside of the Chubut River valley.

Where to Stay & Eat

Many of the small teahouses (see above) have a room or two available for rent. They are generally spanking clean. Try the friendly three-room B&B at **Plas Y Coed Hostería,** M. de Jones 123, Gaiman (℗ **2965/491133;** www.plasycoed.com.ar; from $80), which also has superb Welsh cooking. It's right in front of the plaza. The most charming place to stay near Gaiman is the rural **Posada los Mimbres,** Chacra 211, Gaiman (℗ **2965/491299;** www.posadalosmimbres.com.ar), which is housed on a sprawling riverside farm 6km (4 miles) from town. There is an old house, built more than 100 years ago, and a new one that is much brighter; both have three doubles that run a pricey $210, with breakfast included.

EL CALAFATE ★★

222km (138 miles) S of El Chaltén; 2,727km (1,691 miles) SW of Buenos Aires

El Calafate was once a rough frontier town that served as the center for a vast community of remote *estancias* (ranches). Today, it is primarily a tourist-oriented town that has seen phenomenal growth in the past 8 years. It's best known for being the base from which to see the spectacular Perito Moreno Glacier. The town hugs the shore of turquoise Lago Argentino, and this location, combined with the town's leafy streets, gives it the feel of an oasis in the desert steppe. The town's population has grown from 5,000 in 1996 to 20,000 in 2010 and has a remarkable 8,000 hotel beds—there are a lot of hotels here! Besides the natural wonders in the Los Glaciares National Park, the town depends heavily on the many daily flights that arrive at the El Calafate International Airport packed with foreign and national tourists. Thousands of visitors come for the chance to stand face to face with tremendous walls of ice, including one of the few glaciers in the ice field that isn't retreating (scientists say the Perito Moreno Glacier is "in balance," meaning it shrinks and grows constantly).

The town was named for the *calafate* bush found throughout Patagonia, which produces a sweet berry commonly used in syrups, ice creams, and jams. Legend says that if you try *calafate* fruit, you'll return to Patagonia one day. As the economy in Buenos Aires deteriorated, following the country's financial collapse in 2001, many Porteños (residents of Buenos Aires) fled to the south, to El Calafate, which had suffered from a tourist-trap mentality for years. While urban planning is nonexistent, the town is quite pleasant, tidy, and clean, and there are more and more efficient and creative businesses meant to serve visitors. But you won't find many attractions here—they are almost all within the confines of Los Glaciares National Park. What you will find, however, are several good restaurants and a charming main street lined with boutiques boasting fine leather goods and shops selling locally manufactured chocolates, jams, and delicious caramel cookies called *alfajores*.

Most of the time you spend in the town will be on your arrival and departure days as you transfer in or out of the airport.

[FastFACTS] EL CALAFATE

ATMs There are only a few ATMs around town. **Banco Patagonia,** Av. del Libertador 1355 (© **02902/429-39**), and **Banco Santa Cruz,** Av. del Libertador 1285 (© **02902/492320**), are the most conveniently located. *Note:* At press time, there was no ATM in El Chaltén. If you're headed there, be sure to withdraw extra cash in El Calafate.

Currency Exchange The **Casa de Cambio Thaler** is at Av. del Libertador 963 (© **02902/493245**).

Emergency Dial © **101** or 02902/451449 for police; © **100** for fire.

Hospital The **Hospital Districtal José Formenti** is at Av. Julio A. Roca 1487 (© **02902/491001**).

Internet You'll find many Internet cafes around town. All have fast connections, for about $1 per hour. Try **El Calafate Cyber,** 25 de Mayo 23 (© **02902/492706**), or the **Cooperativa Telefónica,** Cte. Espora 194 (© **02902/491011**), which has the fastest connections, at about $1.50 per half-hour. They are open Monday to Saturday from 8am to midnight, and Sunday from 9am to midnight.

Laundry El Lavadero is at 25 de Mayo 43 (© **2965/492182**), and **Lava Andino**

is at Cte. Espora 88 (© **2965/493980**).

Pharmacy Farmacia Del Cerro is at Av. del Libertador 1337 (© **02902/491496**).

Post Office The main post office for **Correo Argentino** (the official name of the Argentine postal service) is located at Av. del Libertador 1133 (© **02902/491012**).

Taxi There are a number of taxi or *remise* agencies in El Calafate. A good one is **Lago Argentino,** which has an office at the corner of Avenida del Libertador and 15 de Febrero (© **2902/491479**).

PACIFIC
OCEAN

Cochrane

Bajo
Caracoles

CHILE

ARGENTINA

Buenos
Aires

Peninsula
Valdes

Map
Area

Villa O'Higgins

24

Lago
O'Higgins

Lago
San Martín

Lago
Cardiel

Parque
Nacional

Puerto Edén

ISLA
WELLINGTON

Mt. Fitz Roy

El Chaltén

Gobernador
Gregores

Chico

Bernardo

O'Higgins

Parque Nacional
Los Glaciares

Lago
Viedma

Lago
Argentino

Glaciar
Perito Moreno

El Calafate

Santa Cruz

Puerto
Santa Cruz

CHILE

ARGENTINA

Parque Nacional
Torres del Paine

Bahía
Grande

Cueva del Milodón

Coig

Reserva
Nacional
Alacalufes

Puerto Natales

Gallegos

Río Gallegos

9

Punta Delgada

ATLANTIC
OCEAN

Estrecho de Magallanes

Reserva Nacional
Magallanes

Penguin
colony

Magallanes

Isla Magdalena

Seno
Otway

Punta Arenas

Porvenir

Reserva Nacional
Laguna Parrillar

Fuerte
Bulnes

Estrecho

Camerón

ISLA

GRANDES
VENTISQUEROS

GRANDE

Río Grande

Parque
Nacional

de

DE

Alberto
de Agostini

Parque Nacional
Tierra del Fuego

TIERRA

DEL

Mar

Ushuaia

FUEGO

✈ Airport
▲ Mountain

Chileno

Puerto Williams

0   50 mi
0   50 km

Parque Nacional
Cabo de Hornos

Cabo de Hornes

Essentials

GETTING THERE

BY PLANE El Calafate's **Aeropuerto Lago Argentino** (© 02902/491220) is a modern complex that was built in 2000. It's already proving to be too small, though, for the increasing traffic. Service is from Argentine destinations only: **Aerolíneas Argentinas** (© 11/4340-3777 in Buenos Aires; www.aerolineas.com.ar) has up to six daily flights from Buenos Aires and flights from Bariloche, Trelew, and Ushuaia several times a week. A daily 747 flight also arrives directly from Ezeiza International Airport in Buenos Aires during high season (all flights used to leave from Aeroparque, downtown, and you would have to change airports). Be sure to specify which airport you'd like to fly from. **LAN** (© 0810/999-9526; www.lan.com) has two flights per day from Buenos Aires in summertime, less the rest of the year. **LADE** (Líneas Areas del Estado; © 0810/810-5233; www.lade.com.ar) has a weekly flight from Buenos Aires and weekly connection to Puerto Madryn, Ushuaia, and Bariloche. Their flights have no onboard service and are generally much cheaper than the other airlines.

The airport is 23km (14 miles) from the center of town, which seems like a long way in the wide-openness of Patagonia. From the airport, **Ves Patagonia Airport Shuttle** (© 02902/494-355; www.vespatagonia.com) operates a bus to all the hotels in town for $8; they can also pick you up for your return trip with 24 hours' notice. A taxi into town should cost no more than $18 for up to four people. There's also a handful of rental car desks at the airport. Please note that on the exit from this airport, all travelers are required to pay an airport exit tax of $18.

BY BUS El Calafate has a bus terminal on Julio A. Roca, reached via the stairs up from the main street, Avenida del Libertador. To and from Puerto Natales, Chile: **Turismo Zaahj** (© 02902/491631; www.turismozaahj.co.cl) has six weekly trips leaving El Calafate at 8am, returning from Puerto Natales at 8am. **Cootra** (© 02902/491144) leaves El Calafate at 8:30am, returning at 7:30am. The trip takes 4 to 5 hours, depending on how long it takes to get through border-crossing procedures. To get to El Chaltén, your options are **Chaltén Travel** (© 02902/491833), which departs El Calafate daily at 8am, 1pm (in high season only), and 6:30pm; or **Caltur** (© 02902/491842), which has buses leaving El Calafate at 7:30am and 6:30pm. The trip takes approximately 3 hours, with a snack break at a cafe midway. To Río Gallegos, the provincial capital Santa Cruz, buses depart El Calafate daily at 12:30pm and return at 8pm with **Sportsman** (© 02902/492680) and departing El Calafate at noon and 2:30pm with **Taqsa** (© 02902/491843), returning at noon and 2pm. Buy all bus tickets at least 1 day before your trip to ensure you'll get a seat.

BY CAR Ruta 5, followed by Ruta 11, is paved entirely from Río Gallegos to El Calafate. From Puerto Natales, in summertime you can cross through the border at Cerro Castillo, which will lead you to the famous Ruta 40 and up to the paved portion of Ruta 11. Buses and commercial vehicles go via Río Turbio. The drive from Puerto Natales is roughly 4 hours, not including time spent at the border checkpoint.

GETTING AROUND

For information about transportation to and from Perito Moreno Glacier, see "Parque Nacional Los Glaciares & Perito Moreno Glacier," later in this chapter. If you'd like to rent a car, you can do so at the locally owned **Servi-Car,** Av. del Libertador 1341 (© 02902/492634; www.servicar4x4.com.ar). Rates begin at $80 per day, including insurance and taxes. To connect El Calafate with other Patagonian destinations, such as Puerto Madryn, via rental car, try **Fiorasi Rent a Car,** Av. del Libertador 1341 (**℡ 02902/495330;** www.fiorasirentacar.com). Rental cars may be of interest if you're in a group of four people and want to cover longer distances of 4 hours or more, including the drive to El Chaltén or Torres del Paine National Park in Chile. Most of the town can be explored on foot, although many new hotels are either up a good-size hill or well out of town, so make sure your hotel offers a shuttle. Taxis in El Calafate are reasonably priced. More and more people are also visiting El Chaltén in a rental car, thanks to the road improvements. Buses are frequent, though, so it's not really necessary.

VISITOR INFORMATION

The city's **visitor information kiosk** is inside the bus terminal. They offer an ample amount of printed material and can assist in planning a trip to Perito Moreno Glacier; they're open October through April from 8am to 10pm daily and May through September from 8am to 8pm daily (**℡ 02902/491476**). All other spots that look like information centers are travel agencies trying to sell tours.

Two good websites for impartial information are **www.elcalafate.com.ar** and the municipal government's site at **www.elcalafate.gov.ar.**

Seeing the Sights

El Calafate serves mostly as a service town for visitors on their way to the glaciers (see "Parque Nacional Los Glaciares & Perito Moreno Glacier," later in this chapter), but it does present a pleasant main avenue for a stroll. As expected, there are lots of souvenirs, bookstores, and crafts shops to keep you occupied. Heading out of town on the Laguna de Nimes, you'll find the **Calafate Historical Interpretation Center** (Calle G. Bonarelli s/n; **℡ 02902/492799;** free admission), open Monday through Friday from 10am to 8pm, with a collection of farming and ranching implements, Indian artifacts, and historical and ethnographical displays. It's worth a stop if you have the time. The **Los Glaciares National Park Headquarters,** Av. del Libertador 1302 (**℡ 02902/491755**), has a good visitor information center and a lovely garden. New to town is the **Glaciarium: Museum of Patagonian Ice** (www.glaciarium.com), which opened in January 2011. Located 3km (2 miles) from town, it focuses on interpretation of the ancient ices of Los Glaciares National Park, with a 3-D theater, interactive exhibits, and a thorough catalog of the planet's glaciers.

Attractions & Excursions Around El Calafate

For information about visiting the glaciers and the national park, see "Parque Nacional Los Glaciares & Perito Moreno Glacier," later in this chapter. Other typical excursions from El Calafate include El Chaltén, for trekking beneath the famous peaks of Cerro Torre and Mt. FitzRoy in 1 day, or a jampacked day visiting Chile's Torres del Paine National Park. For either of these, try **Cordillera del Sol,** 25 de Mayo 43 (**℡ 02902/492822;** www.cordilleradelsol.com), or **Patagonia Extrema,** Av. del Libertador 1215 (**℡ 02902/492393**). More and more adventure activities and excursions are popping up in El Calafate, capitalizing on the tourism boom.

FISHING **Calafate Fishing,** Av. del Libertador 1826 (**℡ 02902/496545;** www.calafatefishing.com), has half- and full-day fishing (mainly fly-fishing) trips in remote areas of Los Glaciares National Park, in search of brown, rainbow, and brook trout. Full-day trips start at $265.

HOW TO KILL A half-day IN EL CALAFATE

Because of flight and bus schedules, many people are "stuck" in El Calafate the day they arrive or depart.

Here's our list of the best things to do to make use of this extra time:

o Who knew there were flamingos in Patagonia? Take your binoculars and stroll along the shallow shore of Laguna Nimez, on the edge of town. Other birds include cauquén geese, black-necked swans, and ibis birds. Entrance fee is $3.50. Rent binoculars and borrow a guidebook at the reserve's headquarter on Av. Leandro Alem. That's where the 2km (1¼-mile) walk starts. Give yourself 30 minutes to 2 hours.

o Opened in early 2011, the new **Glaciarium** (www.glaciarium. com) is a state-of-the-art glaciology facility, inspired by the Ecocentro museum at Puerto Madryn, and a worthwhile visit.

o **Calafate Historical Interpretation Center** (see above) is a exhibition center that covers 14,000 years of history, located just 5 blocks from downtown.

o Let your inner gaucho ride free on a half-day **horseback** riding trip. See below for details on outfitters.

o Linger with a *café con leche* at one of the many **cafes** along the main street (Av. del Libertador); consider **Borges y Alvarez** (Av. del Libertador 1015, upstairs; ℂ 02902/491464) or **Casablanca** (Av. del Libertador 1202; ℂ 02902/491402).

o The **Estancia 25 de Mayo** (see below) has a late afternoon program that includes a sheep-shearing show, a nature walk, and evening folklore dinner show.

HORSEBACK RIDING Patagonia is horseback-riding heaven, and a number of agencies offer good trips. Whenever possible, try to get away from tours that depart directly from El Calafate. A company called **Cerro Frias**, Av. del Libertador 1857 (ℂ 02902/492808; www.cerrofrias.com), offers half-day horseback riding trips in the wide-open plains of Patagonia that take you up to a gorgeous view point. Excursions include a barbecue lunch or dinner. **Cabalgata en Patagonia,** Av. del Libertador 4315 (ℂ 02902/493278; www.cabalgataenpatagonia.com), offers a 2-hour ride from Bahía Redonda to Punta Soberana for a panoramic view of El Calafate ($70).

OFF-ROADING Four-wheel-drives have become a popular way to explore the landscape around El Calafate. **Mil Outdoor Adventure,** Av. del Libertador 1029 (ℂ 02902/491446; www.miloutdoor.com), takes you across rivers, over boulders, along ridges, and up to the El Calafate Balcony for a panoramic view. There are also fossils and rock mazes en route. **Calafate Extremo,** Av. del Libertador 1185 (ℂ 02902/491095; www.calafateextremo.com) takes Land Rover Defender 4×4s up the Huyliche lookout, where you can see FitzRoy on a clear day. **Cerro Frias** (see above) also has 4×4 trips in Land Cruisers.

VISITING AN ESTANCIA As the world's wool market declines, many of the *estancias* (ranches) in Patagonia have opened their doors to tourists, including some very close to El Calafate. This is the heart of the real Patagonia. Trips typically run day activities and restaurant services, and many even offer lodging, should you opt to spend the night. They're a lovely way to experience the local history, immerse yourself in the wild landscapes, and live Patagonia as authentically as possible. Most day excursions include a choice of horseback riding, hiking, or bird-watching, as well as a hearty traditional meal, usually of barbecued local *cordero* (lamb). All of the following *estancias* offer meals, excursions such as horseback riding and trekking, and transportation from El Calafate. Most also have museums in the old family ranch homes. Close to town, **El Galpón del Glaciar** (© 02902/491793; www.elgalpon delglaciar.com.ar) adds traditional *estancia* activities, such as sheep-shearing, and has a lovely afternoon tea. It's also a good spot for an evening visit; dinner shows with folklore dancing start at 6pm (reservations required). **Estancia 25 de Mayo** (© 02902/491450; www.estancia25demayo.com.ar) has a nice late-afternoon excursion with a simple gaucho show, nature walk, and barbecue. It's very close to town and is rich in history and culture. My favorite of the bunch is **Estancia Cristina ★★**, situated at the end of the remote north arm of Lago Argentino. See "Where to Stay," below, for more information. You take a spectacular 4-hour boat trip to get there, sailing past floating icebergs and the enormous Upsala Glacier. Day trips include a short hike with excellent views of Cerro Norte and the Patagonian Ice Cap, or a 4WD trip. Contact their office in El Calafate at Av. del Libertador 1033 (© 02902/491133; www.estanciacristina.com).

The meticulously maintained **Estancia Alta Vista** (© 02902/491247; www. hosteriaaltavista.com.ar), 33km (20 miles) from El Calafate, on the dirt road RP 15 near the beautiful area of Lago Roca, is open October through March and offers ranch activities and fishing. It has an English-country style that has made it popular with British genteel types. **Estancia Nibepo Aike** (© 02902/492797; http:// nibepoaike.com.ar) is picturesquely nestled on the southeast edge of the national park, about 60km (37 miles) from El Calafate. It's also near Lago Roca, offering fishing and ranch activities October through April. An overnight here costs slightly less than at other local *estancias*.

Where to Stay

Really good value is hard to find here, as most places are capitalizing on the short tourist season. Prices soar from springtime (Oct–Dec) and remain high through February, making March to April the most economical time to visit. The main issue to resolve when selecting lodging in El Calafate is if you want to stay in town or not. You can find a slew of mediocre inns within walking distance of the main drag, Avenida del Libertador. Then there are more about 10 to 15 minutes away, and most of these hotels offer complimentary shuttles to town, as well as better views. Finally, there are options much farther out of town, which will appeal to those looking to relax and stay put.

VERY EXPENSIVE

Casa los Sauces   Not only is the current president of Argentina, Cristina Fernández de Kirchner, the owner and next-door neighbor of this exclusive boutique hotel, she was also the interior designer. And she's obviously got highbrow taste, exemplified in the opulent, formal Argentine country style that oozes throughout the buildings. It's all very refined, luxurious and, frankly, quite snobby. There's a large staff ready to wait on you, from offering glasses of champagne at check-in or a ride in a golf cart to massages and private transfers. The 38 über-plush suites, each drastically different in style, are located in five houses dotted about a meticulously maintained green garden by a lake. There is a minimum 2-night stay, and most guests come here as part of an all-inclusive program. For just a taste of the exclusivity, have dinner at the excellent **La Comarca.**

Los Gauchos 1352–1370, El Calafate. ✆ **02902/495584** or 11/4348-5288 in Buenos Aires. www.casa lossauces.com. 38 units. $325 double; $450 corner suite; $650 master suite. Rates include breakfast, airport transfers, spa access, and breakfast. AE, DC, MC, V. **Amenities:** Restaurant; bar; airport transfer available; bikes; Jacuzzi; indoor pool; free downtown shuttle; spa; archery; reading room; Wi-Fi. *In room:* Minibar.

EXPENSIVE

Posada Los Alamos ♨   The sprawling Posada Los Alamos is as conservative as a Brooks Brothers suit, perhaps better suited to a golf resort than wild Patagonia. Because of the low-key design of the complex and the slightly aloof service, you can't help the feeling that you're in a private country club or thousands of miles north in a Buenos Aires province. But they have just about everything here, including a spa with a huge pool, wine bar, convention center, and hair salon. There are a number of comfortable lounges in the hotel's various buildings, all with large windows looking out onto an expansive, perfectly manicured lawn. Rooms have ample space, and each has a slightly different color and style. Ask for one that looks out onto the quiet, grassy backyard instead of the dusty dirt road.

Gobernador Moyano and Bustillo, El Calafate. ✆ **02902/491144.** Fax 02902/491186. www.posada losalamos.com. 144 units. $254 double; from $373 suite. AE, MC, V. **Amenities:** Restaurant; bar; lounge; golf course; massage; room service; tennis court. *In room:* TV, minibar.

MODERATE

Cauquenes de Nimez   Nature lovers will appreciate this smart and friendly new inn located close to the Laguna Nimez Ecological Reserve. It's run by a veteran local mountain guide whose passion for Patagonia outshines so many of the other very standard hotels in town. Twelve simple rooms have standard but chic bathrooms and superb views (watch for flamingos, swans, herons, falcons, and ibises!), although the rooms are small. There is a basic living room with a great library. It's just a 10-minute walk to town, but you should take a taxi in the evenings. Breakfasts are magical, with beautiful sunrises, homebaked pastries, and bird life right out your window.

Calle 303 79, El Calafate. ✆ **02902/492306.** www.cauquenesdenimez.com.ar. 12 rooms. From $85 double. AE, MC, V. **Amenities:** Restaurant; library; Wi-Fi. *In room:* No TV.

Hotel Edenia ★   This is a very comfortable and functional hotel on the outskirts of town. The view out your window just may include an iceberg or two here. Rooms are similar to what you'd find in a business hotel, with crisp linens, satellite TV, a workable desk, and individually controlled heaters. Bathrooms are large and have heated floors. Edenia's best asset, though, is its friendly, multilingual staff who'll welcome you with a glass of champagne and take good care of you as you rush in and out from the many excursions typical of a visit to El Calafate. Visit their website for online promotions.

Punta Soberana, Manzana 642, El Calafate. ✆ **02902/497021.** Fax 2902/496210. www.edeniahoteles. com.ar. 68 units. $120–$170 double. AE, MC, V. **Amenities:** Restaurant; bar; airport transfer available; gym; room service; free downtown shuttle; library; Wi-Fi. *In room:* Satellite TV, hair dryer.

Kau Yatún Hotel de Campo ★   Long before El Calafate was a major tourist destination, it was the heart of a rugged area populated by remote *estancias*. Kau Yatún is a country inn located on the Estancia 25 de Mayo, only 5 blocks from El Calafate's main drag. It's got lovely rural charm, with generous green spaces, quiet corners, and a relaxed air; use one of their bikes to ride into town. Rooms are very large, with thick walls and ceilings. Watch out for those that are set aside for smokers. Bathrooms, likewise, are very large but are dated. The hallway can be noisy. The restaurant and bar are both pricey, but breakfasts are generous. Out back, there are 7 hectares (17 acres) of natural paradise. When you are stuck trying to kill time in El Calafate, you'll be glad you choose Kau Yatún.

Estancia 25 de Mayo, El Calafate. ☏ **02902/491059** or 11/4523-5894 in Buenos Aires. Fax 11/4523-5894; www.kauyatun.com. 44 units. $143–$173 double; $236 triple. AE, MC, V. **Amenities:** 2 restaurants; bar; airport transfer available; excursions; library; free downtown shuttle. *In room:* Hair dryer, Wi-Fi.

Kosten Aike   If being close to the action is important to you, this large family-run downtown hotel is a good choice since it's only 2 blocks from the main drag, Avenida del Libertador. Neither deluxe nor luxurious, Kosten Aike is standard issue, and popular with European tour groups. The linens and overall decor could use an update. Bathrooms have deep tubs and most have small windows. Upstairs, there is a small gym, with a sauna and Jacuzzi and a deck for those rare Patagonian days when you can suntan. Downstairs in the lobby there is a stone fireplace, comfortable sofas (a place to wait for your early morning tour pickups), and free Wi-Fi.

Gob. Moyano 1243, El Calafate. ☏ **02902/492424.** www.kostenaike.com.ar. 82 units. From $183 double. AE, MC, V. **Amenities:** Restaurant; lounge; airport transfer available; gym; Jacuzzi; room service; sauna; free downtown shuttle. *In room:* Hair dryer, Internet.

Patagonia Rebelde 📷   History buffs will love the heritage items on display in this train-themed tin-walled *hostería* on the hill above town. Every item has a story behind it: The main room floors are recycled from a Buenos Aires *conventillo*, furniture is from auctions, even key chains are from old train cars. Others may find it noisy. Rooms are small but bright, with yellow walls and refurbished bureaus. All have showers only. The suite, in the corner, is slightly bigger and brighter.

José R. Haro 442, esq. Jean Mermoz, El Calafate. ☏ **02902/494495.** www.patagoniarebelde.com. 12 units. $110 double; $125 suite. Rates include breakfast. AE, MC, V. **Amenities:** Bar; library; Wi-Fi.

INEXPENSIVE

America del Sur Hostel ★   With a friendly vibe and nightly all-you-can-eat *asado* barbecues for only $16, this is a great budget option. Located a 7-minute walk up the hill from downtown, it affords a lovely panoramic view. Guests have the choice of a simple bunk bed in a shared room that sleeps up to four people at a time, or one of the newer doubles with private bathrooms. All dorm rooms have private lockers and bathrooms with separate tubs, showers, and toilets that allow for some privacy in an otherwise shared room. The big kitchen is an upbeat place in which to mix and mingle with other travelers while saving some cash by dining in.

Puerto Deseado 153, El Calafate. ☏ **02902/493523.** www.americahostel.com.ar. 60 beds. $70 double with private bathroom; $15 bed in shared room. Rates include breakfast. No credit cards. **Amenities:** Restaurant; airport transfer available; free downtown shuttle; high-speed Internet; kitchen; luggage storage. *In room:* Lockers.

Casa de Grillos B&B 🍴   This small inn, 8 blocks from Avenida del Libertador in the old part of town, is in one of El Calafate's only lush, green areas. Steps from Laguna Nimez and the shores of Lago Argentino, it's somewhat of an oasis and a nice choice for nature lovers who still want the convenience of being walking distance from town. It's a true bed-and-breakfast, in that a lovely couple rents a handful of rooms in their home. Rooms are cozy, and each of the five rooms has a private bathroom. There is a charming common area for TV watching, Internet surfing, and visiting.

Los Condores 1215, esq. Las Bandurrias, El Calafate. ☏ **02902/491160.** www.casadegrillos.com.ar. 5 units. $70 double. Rates include breakfast. No credit cards. **Amenities:** TV room; Internet; library.

ESTANCIAS

Eolo Patagonia's Spirit ★★ 🏕   Inspired by the ever-present Patagonian winds, Eolo is a new take on the old-style ranch. Built around a protected courtyard, it is upscale through and through, yet casual and comfortable. Expansive cream-colored rooms have huge windows and a mixture of new and antique furnishings. Bathrooms have refurbished mirrors, vanities, and deep tubs with windows looking out to the vastness. The corner suite has a view of the Torres del Paine on a clear day. No matter which way you look, there are sublime expanses outside with no trace of civilization in sight. Only 25km (15 miles) from El Calafate, and en route to the Perito Moreno Glacier, the location is convenient to town, the airport, and the main tourist attractions, making it much more convenient than its competitors, and a good place to base a trip lasting from 3 to 5 days. Most people opt for the all-inclusive package, which includes transfers and all meals, as well as trekking, bird-watching, and horseback riding. Or you can just relax by the indoor heated pool. The unpretentious and flexible staff will call you by name and make you feel at home. For a place with only 17 rooms, Eolo offers a remarkably complete experience.

RP 11, Km 23, El Calafate. 🕿 **02902/492042** or 11/4700-0075 in Buenos Aires for reservations. www. eolo.com.ar. 17 units. 2-night packages start at $720 per person double; 4-night packages start at $1,120 per person double. Rates include all meals, airport transfers, and excursions on the *estancia*. AE, MC, V. **Amenities:** Restaurant; lounge; indoor pool; sauna; guided excursions; Wi-Fi; library; TV room. *In room:* No TV.

Estancia Cristina ★★★ 📷   If seclusion is the new luxury, this *estancia* is the ultimate indulgence. Situated at the end of the north arm of Lago Argentino, it's the well-preserved former ranching outpost of the Masters family, early-20th-century British pioneers. To get here (see "Visiting an Estancia," above), you take a spectacular 2-hour boat trip, sailing past floating icebergs and the enormous Upsala Glacier. One- and 2-night packages allow you to choose from a selection of day excursions such as treks, a 4WD trip, or a wonderful horseback ride. Upon return, you'll have the place to yourself, once the day-trippers have headed back to town. At night, the silence and darkness will astound you. Relax in a soaker tub, explore the Masters family museum, roam the English gardens, enjoy bird-watching, or sidle up to the bar for a glass of *vino tinto*. Sixteen rooms have been designed to resemble the older ranch buildings, with light green roofs and white walls. Inside, they're clean, spacious, and fresh, with large beds and huge bay windows that open onto the Cerro Norte. The food is quite good considering the location, and the service is friendly and charming. The modern facilities don't detract from the history or majestic setting of the place. Both gentle and rugged, new and old, Estancia Cristina is a gem, making it a favorite of so many Patagonian travelers. If you can splurge for just 1 night in Patagonia, do it here.

9 de Julio 57, local 10, El Calafate. 🕿 **02902/491133** or 11/4814-3934 in Buenos Aires for reservations. www.estanciacristina.com. 1 night from $500 per person double; 2 nights from $824 per person double. Rates include all meals, excursions, and transfers. AE, MC, V. **Amenities:** Restaurant; bar; hiking trails; Internet; library; museum. *In room:* No TV.

Where to Eat

A number of cafes and espresso bars run along the main drag, Avenida del Libertador, and its side streets. Try **Elba'r,** in the De los Pajaros plaza at 9 de Julio 57 (🕿 **02902/493594**), or the interesting **Borges & Alvarez Libro-Bar,** Av. del

Libertador 1015 (✆ **02902/491464**), which has a fantastic selection of books to peruse while you sip a *café con leche*.

EXPENSIVE

Casimiro Biguá ★★ ▣ REGIONAL The chic and modern black-and-white decor, thick tablecloths, flickering candles on every table, and young and energetic waitstaff make this place a winner. You can sample one of the many wines while enjoying an appetizer platter of regional Patagonian specialties such as smoked trout, smoked wild boar, and a variety of cheeses. Main courses change frequently but usually range from a simple steak to an elaborate pasta with salmon, cream, and capers in white-wine sauce; there's always a chicken, risotto, and seafood offering as well. A few doors down is the sister restaurant, the town's most upscale steakhouse, called, unsurprisingly, Casimiro Biguá Parrilla, and farther down the street is its Italian country-inspired trattoria (see below).

Av. del Libertador 963. ✆ **02902/492590.** www.casimirobigua.com. Reservations recommended. Main courses $13–$24. AE, MC, V. Daily 10am–1am.

Casimiro Biguá Trattoria ☺ ITALIAN A breath of Mediterranean sunshine in the Patagonian wilderness, locals are raving about this informal Italian restaurant, run by the same folks as the popular bistro of the same name (see above). The open kitchen and red-and-white checkered tablecloths are bright and friendly. Mix and match homemade pastas with one of a huge variety of sauces—ricotta and nut ravioli goes great with pesto. Or try such classics as *osso buco* or lamb risotto. It's also a good option if you want a light dinner. Late afternoon, stop by for a glass of wine and a cheese plate. The wine list is long and includes plenty of options by the glass. There's a kids' room out back and Wi-Fi indoors.

Av. del Libertador 1369. ✆ **02902/492993.** Main courses $13–$28. AE, MC, V. Daily noon–midnight.

La Cocina ★ 🍴 BISTRO This recently expanded restaurant serves bistro-style food, including fresh pastas, such as raviolis and fettuccine, fresh trout, and meats prepared simply but well. Try the cannelloni stuffed with vegetables or combinations such as ham and cheese, or meat items such as steak with a pepper-and-mustard sauce. There's a huge list of pasta options as well. Of all the restaurants on the main street with a similar appearance, La Cocina is the best. There is something here for everyone, and when it's busy, the friendly staff maintains an upbeat vibe.

Av. del Libertador 1245. ✆ **02902/491758.** Main courses $10–$19. MC, V. Tues–Sun noon–3:30pm and 7pm–midnight.

MODERATE

Casablanca CAFE/BAR The Casablanca is the local hangout for a beer and a quick meal, and one of the few places around where you can grab a meal at odd hours. There's a wooden bar and a dining area with tile floors and metal chairs and tables, and an elevated TV that's usually on. The menu is mostly pizzas, sandwiches, and empanadas, but sandwiches are your best bet here. This is a good spot for writing out postcards and sipping a cold beer on a warm afternoon.

Av. 21 de Mayo and Av. del Libertador 1202. ✆ **02902/491402.** Main courses $6–$16; sandwiches $4.50–$8. No credit cards. Daily 10am–3am.

Don Pichón ★★ PARRILLA   With a menu that's classic Argentine grillhouse and a gorgeous view of glaciers and mountains, Don Pichón has risen to the top in El Calafate. The specialties are rustic local lamb (freshest in springtime) and the very abundant *parrillada* (mixed grill) to share. If you pick a simple cut of beef, don't forget to add vegetables and salad as well. Otherwise your meal will be teeny tiny. And remember, beef in Argentina is generally well-done, so be sure to order to your liking if that's not it. Reserve early for a windowside table. It's on a hill just north of town, a good walk but they'll also pick you up at your hotel and bring you there directly.

Puerto Deseado 272. ✆ **02902/492577.** Reservations recommended. Main courses $10–$18. AE, MC, V. Daily 8pm–midnight.

La Tablita ★ 🍖 PARRILLA   This is 100% typical Argentine food—the stuff that families from Iguazú to Ushuaia enjoy on any given Sunday afternoon. Carnivores, look no further. La Tablita is one of the local favorites in town, known for its heaping platters and giant *parrilladas* that come sizzling to your table on their own minibarbecues. The *parrilladas* for two cost $24, but it really serve three diners, given the size and assortment of chicken, sausage, beef, lamb, and a few innards you may or may not recognize. The sunny, airy restaurant can be found on the other side of the bridge that spans the Arroyo Calafate, about a 2-minute walk from downtown.

Coronel Rosales 24. ✆ **02902/491065.** Reservations highly recommended. Main courses $13–$17. AE, MC, V. Thurs-Tues 11am-3pm and daily 7pm–midnight.

Pura Vida ★ 🍴 VEGETARIAN/REGIONAL   The friendliest place in town is a short walk from downtown, but it's worth finding. Set in a woodsy location overlooking the lake, it's the best place in El Calafate for home-style cuisine that offers good options for vegetarians. Try the delicious pumpkin soup (great after a blistery day in the wilds of Patagonia) or the gnocchi in saffron sauce. If you want to try a regional specialty, go for the *cazuela de cordero* (hearty lamb stew with mushrooms). For dessert, both the rice pudding and the pumpkin ice cream are delicious. Fresh fruit shakes and sandwiches are also offered. Despite the outdated A-frame exterior, the service is laid-back, the crowd is young and relaxed, and the view of the lake is divine.

Av. del Libertador 1876. ✆ **02902/493356.** Main courses $10–$17. AE, MC, V. Thurs-Tues 7:30–11:30pm.

INEXPENSIVE

Viva la Pepa ★ ☺ SNACKS   Viva la Pepa has fun vibes and healthy lighter options, specializing in crepes (both savory and sweet), salads, and sandwiches. Lots of juices, and a hearty breakfast, are also available. Hang out in the afternoon on the outdoor patio, or indoors with a sweet treat. This is also a good spot to sample yerba *mate*; the friendly staff are happy to show you how!

Emilio Amado 833. ✆ **02902/491880.** Main courses $7–$13. No credit cards. Daily 9am–11pm.

El Calafate After Dark

La Tolderia, Av. del Libertador 1177 (no phone), serves fast food during the day and funky music at night. **Humus,** Gobernador Moyano and Bustillo (✆ **02902/491144**) is a very popular wine bar at the Posada los Alamos (p. 372). **Don Diego de la Noche,** Avenida del Libertador and 17 de Octuber (✆ **02902/493270**), remains the town's most happening late-night pub.

PARQUE NACIONAL LOS GLACIARES & PERITO MORENO GLACIER ★★★

The Los Glaciares National Park covers 600,000 hectares (1.5 million acres) of rugged land that stretches vertically along the crest of the Andes and spills east into rolling steppe. Most of Los Glaciares is inaccessible to visitors except for the park's two dramatic highlights: the granite needles, such as FitzRoy near El Chaltén (see below), and this region's magnificent Perito Moreno Glacier. The park is also home to thundering rivers, blue lakes, and thick beech forest. Los Glaciares National Park was formed in 1937 and declared a World Heritage region by UNESCO in 1981. It is a wild, rugged, and yet sublimely beautiful landscape—one that offers up surprise, wonder, adventure, and serenity all at once.

Named after famed Argentine scientist Francisco "Perito" Moreno ("perito" is the title given to someone considered an expert in their field), the famous glacier Perito Moreno is a must-see, as important to Argentine culture and tourism as Iguazú Falls or the Casa Rosada. Few natural wonders in South America are as spectacular or as easily accessed as this glacier. It's just one fingertip in the imposing Southern Patagonian Ice Cap, the fourth-largest frozen mass in the world after the two poles and Greenland. Perito Moreno is one of the few glaciers in the world that is not receding. Scientists like to stay that it is "stable," or constantly growing and receding. Around 1900, Perito Moreno was measured at 750m (2,460 ft.) from the Península Magallanes; by 1920, it had advanced so far that it finally made contact with the peninsula where tourists now walk the lovely and newly refurbished boardwalk and take in views. Each time the glacier reached the peninsula, which would occur every 3 to 4 years, it created a dam in the channel that drastically altered water levels on either side. Over the period of a few years, the built-up pressure would set off a calving explosion for 48 to 72 hours, breaking the face of the glacier in a crashing fury. The last time this happened was in July 2008, making news across the country. Perito Moreno is usually reliable for sending a few huge chunks the size of buses hurling into the channel throughout the day. Sit in silence with your camera ready and you're almost certain to get a fabulous photo opportunity of a calving glacier.

What impresses visitors most is the sheer size of Perito Moreno Glacier—a wall of jagged blue ice measuring 4,500m (14,760 ft.) across and soaring 60m (197 ft.) above

Glaciology 101

A glacier is a large body of snow and ice that slowly moves down a valley or spreads across a surface due to accumulation and gravity. Glacial ice forms when heavy snowfall crushes first into snow crystals and then into pellets, finally becoming a dense mass that takes on transparency and hardness over time. Heavy precipitation and low temperatures are the most significant factors in glacial growth. Dark lines in the glaciers, called moraines, are produced by rock debris, sand, and clay that accumulate on the ice. They are useful for indicating past positions of the glacier.

the channel. You literally could fit the entire city of Buenos Aires on it. From the parking lot on the Península Magallanes, a series of vista-point walkways descend, which take visitors directly to the glacier's face. It's an unforgettable, spellbinding experience, worth taking in slowly so you can savor the view and capture the ice cracking off in photos or videos. You can join an organized group for a walk on the glacier, and there are boat journeys leaving from Puerto Banderas for visits to the neighboring glaciers. In 2008, a major infrastructure expansion project began at the Península Magallanes and includes more than 4km (2.5 miles) of refurbished boardwalk paths, an elevator for tourists with disabilities, and a new cafeteria. Down the hill, at the dock, there's another large restaurant and a giant visitor center in the works.

There are other magnificent glaciers in the national park; all are much harder to access than Perito Moreno but equally stunning. The Upsala Glacier is the largest in South America, and the Spegazzini Glacier has the largest snout of all the glaciers in the park. Onelli, Seco, and Agassiz are also gorgeous. All can be seen as part of the **All Glaciers** tour, organized by René Fernández Campbell, whose main office is at Av. del Libertador 867 (© **02902/492340**).

Getting There & Getting Around

At Km 49 (30 miles) from El Calafate, you'll pass through the park's entrance en route to the Perito Moreno Glacier, where there's an information booth with erratic hours (no phone). Here, they charge the entrance fee of $25 per person. They'll also give you a map if you ask for one. If you're looking for information about the park and the glacier, pick up an interpretive guide or a book from one of the bookstores or tourist shops along Avenida del Libertador in El Calafate.

ARRIVING AT THE PARK

BY CAR   Following Avenida del Libertador west out of town, the route turns into a well-maintained road that is almost completely paved. From here, it's 80km (50 miles) to the glacier. Give yourself an hour and a half as the final stretch is on a winding road with a few unpaved sections. If you have a rental car, you'll be able to linger late into the afternoon after all the other tourists have left.

BY TAXI OR REMISE   If you want to see the glacier at your own pace, hire a taxi or *remise*. The cost averages $115, although many taxi companies will negotiate a price. Be sure to agree on an estimated amount of time spent at the glacier, and remember that the park entrance fee of $25 per person is not included.

BY BUS   **Caltur** buses, Av. del Libertador 1080 (© **02902/491368;** www.caltur. com.ar), leave downtown El Calafate twice a day (7am and 3pm, returning from the glacier at 11:30am and 7:30pm), allowing you to explore the glacier lookout area on your own. The bus ride costs a very reasonable $20, plus the $25 park entrance fee. **Los Glaciares Turismo,** Av. Almirante Brown 1188 (© **02902/491158;** www. losglaciaresturismo.com.ar), has buses departing town at 7:30am, 8am, and 3pm, returning at 7pm. They take 90 minutes to get to the lookout. All depart from the bus terminal.

BY ORGANIZED TOUR   Several companies offer transportation to and from the glacier, such as **Gigantes Patagones,** Av. Del Libertador 1315, Loc. 3 (© **02902/495525;** www.gigantespatagones.com.ar); **Caltur** (see contact info, "By Bus," above); and **Los Glaciares Turismo** (© **02902/491159;** additional info above). These minivan and bus services provide bilingual guides and leave around

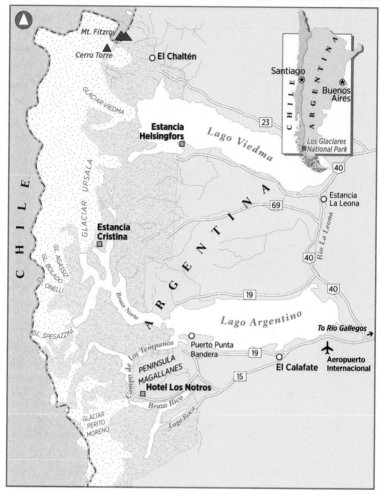

9am and again at around 2:30pm, spending an average of 4 hours at the peninsula; the cost is $40 to $50 per person, not including lunch or park entrance fee. **Patagonia Backpackers,** Av. del Libertador 587 (© **02902/491792;** www.patagonia-backpackers.com) has what they call an "alternative" tour to the glacier, which starts with a short hike and ends with a short boat trip; the cost is $56 per person, not including lunch or park entrance fee.

Outdoor Activities

You can see the Perito Moreno glacier close up on your own in a half-day's outing by taxi, rental car, or bus (give yourself a minimum of 1 hr. at the glacier). But several exciting activities in the Perito Moreno region afford a more in-depth and thrilling

Upsala: A Bottleneck of Icebergs

In 2008, a massive chunk of ice, measuring 2.5km (1.5 miles) wide, cracked off the front of the Upsala Glacier. It spilled kilometers of chunks of ice forward, essentially closing off the bay that leads to the Upsala and Spegazzini glaciers. Experts say the bay will need at least 5 years to unclog; until then, the only way to see Upsala is from the lookout above Estancia Cristina (see "Where to Stay," earlier in this chapter). René Fernández Campbell's All Glaciers trip (see below) still cruises in the area, stopping for photos of the icebergs floating at the bay, but can't access these glaciers themselves.

experience. **"Minitrekking"** (although there is nothing "mini" about it) takes guests of all ages and abilities for a walk upon the glacier. The trip begins with a 20-minute boat ride across the Brazo Rico, followed by a 30-minute walk to the glacier. From here guests are outfitted with crampons and other safety gear, and then they spend approximately 1½ hours atop the ice, complete with a stop for a whiskey on the thousand-year-old "rocks." This great trip gives visitors the chance to peer into the electric-blue crevasses of the glacier and fully appreciate its size. More experienced, fit, and adventurous visitors under the age of 45 can opt for the **Big Ice ★★** option, which has a more technical approach and gives you much more time (upwards of 4 hr.) to walk on the glacier. Both Big Ice and Minitrekking are organized exclusively by **Hielo y Aventura,** which has its main office at Av. del Libertador 935 (© **02902/492205;** www.hieloyaventura.com). Big Ice costs $180 including the transfer from El Calafate. Minitrekking will run you $125 with transfer. Remember, you have to bring your own lunch from town. And don't forget the sunscreen!

René Fernández Campbell, Av. del Libertador 867 (© **02902/491105;** www. solopatagonia.com), offers visitors navigation trips through the Brazo Rico to the face of Perito Moreno for $13, departing hourly from 10:30am to 3:30pm from the Muelle Moreno port next to the glacier's visitor center. Their **Todo Glaciares (All Glaciers) ★★** trip departs from Puerto Punta Bandera and navigates more remote areas of Lago Argentino, including cruising past the entrance to the Spegazzini (the tallest glacier in the park), and Uspala (the largest) glaciers as well as the Onelli glacier for $295.

Lodging near the Glacier

Los Notros ★★★ 📷 Few hotels in Argentina (in the world, really) can boast as spectacular a view as Los Notros—but it doesn't come cheap. This luxury lodge sits high on a slope looking out at Perito Moreno Glacier, and all common areas and rooms have been fitted with picture windows to let guests soak up the marvelous sight. Although the wood-hewn exteriors give the hotel the feel of a mountain lodge, the interior decor is contemporary. Each room is slightly different, with personal touches such as antique lamps and regional photos; crocheted or gingham bedspreads; and padded floral headboards or iron bed frames. Bathrooms are gleaming white if a bit small, and premium rooms in the newer wing have whirlpool tubs. The older "Cascada bungalow" rooms have very thin walls; if you're a light sleeper, be sure to request a top-floor room or a room in the newer (and pricier) "Premium" wing. Inside the main building is a large and expansive restaurant that serves regional cuisine. Guests at Los Notros must opt for one of the multiday packages that include airport transfers, meals, box lunches for expeditions, guided trekking, boat excursions, and ice walks. The guides are great, but hotel service is a bit spotty, and the restaurant is definitely understaffed. Although Los Notros offers 4-night packages, you might find that length of time too long, limiting your chance to see other parts of Patagonia. Note that prices jump substantially during Christmas, New Year's, and Easter weeks. One-night stays are on request only and subject to availability. The $25 park fee is extra.

Main office in Buenos Aires: Arenales 1457, 7th floor. ⓒ **02902/499510;** 11/4813-7285 in Buenos Aires. Fax 11/5277-8222. www.losnotros.com. 32 units. $1,029 per person for 2-night package Cascada bungalow; $1,401 per person for 2-night package in double superior; $1,643 per person for 2-night package in double premium. Rates include all meals, park entrance, excursions, and transfers. Room-only rates available by request only, depending on availability. AE, DC, MC, V. **Amenities:** Restaurant; bar; lounge; room service; video library. *In room:* Minibar.

EL CHALTEN & THE FITZROY AREA ★★

222km (138 miles) N of El Calafate

El Chaltén is a rugged village of about 800 residents whose lifeblood, like El Calafate's, is the throng of visitors who come each summer. Visitors here, however, are generally more active and adventurous than those who stay only in El Calafate; they include some of the world's greatest mountaineers as well as avid trekkers. This is the

HOW TO SEE THE glacier

Every Patagonian pilgrimage requires a stop at the majestic Perito Moreno Glacier, one of the world's most stunning sites and a great lesson in nature. You've got a number of options for making your visit worthwhile, depending on your time frame and budget.

○ **Rent a car and drive to the glacier from town.** This option is not cheap unless you are in a party of four, but it gives you freedom to come late in the afternoon, when the crowds have thinned out. It's helpful if you have a midday flight.

○ **Take the local bus that has three departures daily.** This is the best budget option, and a good choice if you want to stick to your own schedule.

○ **Hop on a local tour.** You get more information and a better understanding of what you're looking at, but you're beholden to the tour's timetable. Some tours offer a short hike along Icebergs Channel (Canal de los Témpanos) or boat trips along the north wall. Most are bilingual, and some include snacks.

○ **Sign up for Hielo y Aventura's Minitrekking tour** (p. 380), to take a walk on the ice and get a good look at its southern wall along the Rico Arm of Lago Argentino. It's a half-day outing; you can include a stroll on the boardwalks.

○ **For an in-depth and unforgettable exploration** of the big white sheet, Hielo y Aventura's Big Ice tour (p. 380) is the most complete glacier experience. A good level of fitness is required.

DEEP IN THE heart of patagonia:
HOSTERIA HELSINGFORS

Remote, warm, and widely admired, **Hostería Helsingfors,** open from October to March, is located on the shore of Lago Viedma about 150km (93 miles) from El Calafate. On a clear day, it has amazing views of FitzRoy. With a lovely main lodge and endless miles of untouched wilderness at its doorstep, Helsingfors offers lodging, horseback riding, over-flights, bird-watching, boat trips, and fine dining. For more information, contact their offices in Buenos Aires at Av. Córdoba 827, 11th floor (©/fax **011/4315-1222;** www.helsingfors.com.ar).

second-most-visited region of Argentina's Los Glaciares National Park. It's quite possibly the most exquisite as well due to the singular nature of the granite spires that shoot up, torpedo-like, above massive tongues of ice that descend from the Southern Patagonian Ice Field. In the world of mountaineering, the sheer and ice-encrusted peaks of Mt. FitzRoy, Cerro Torre, and their neighbors are considered some of the most formidable challenges on the planet, and they draw hundreds of elite climbers here every year. The valleys beneath them provide world-class trekking trails that any hiker can enjoy. Besides trekking, there are also interesting new options for kayaking, bird-watching, and mountain biking.

El Chaltén is known as the "trekking capital of Argentina," and it ranks up there with the best trekking destinations in the world. What it offers—excellent trails in spectacularly wild scenery, mixed with cozy inns and bistros that you can return to at night—is quite rare. Another bonus is that the hiking here doesn't require many serious uphill (or downhill for that matter) climbs, as most trails generally follow valley floors. Altitude is not a concern either, meaning that your lungs should have no problem taking in some of the cleanest air on the planet.

Little more than 10 years ago, El Chaltén counted just a dozen houses and a *hostal* or two, but FitzRoy's rugged beauty and great hiking opportunities have created somewhat of a boomtown. The town sits nestled in a circular rock outcrop next to the FitzRoy River, and it's fronted by the vast, dry Patagonian Steppe. It's a wild and windy setting, and the town has a ramshackle feel, although recent street paving has helped clean things up a lot. Visitors use El Chaltén either as a base from which to take day hikes or as an overnight stop before setting off for a multiday backpacking trip. This area is also remarkably rich in human history, from its hardy early settlers and courageous alpinists, to more recent political border disputes with Chile.

Populated by folk with a pioneering spirit, El Chaltén has a cool, young vibe. But in some respects the town has also taken a turn upscale over the past few years, first with the opening of Hotel Los Cerros hotel (p. 387), and now with the planned arrival of two more luxury lodges—one on the road north from town toward Lago del Desierto (run by the owners of explora Hotel Salto Chico in Torres del Paine), and another right in town, from the people behind Chaltén Travel.

Most visitors come here for 3 nights, with 2 travel days on each end and two full days for hiking. If you take the early morning bus from El Calafate, you'll be here with time for a good half-day hike. Most hotels offer a catering service that prepares box lunches you can take with you on the trail. Do *not* hit the trail without food.

The town's layout is somewhat haphazard, but a new bus terminal at the entrance to town helps orient tourists when they hop off the bus from El Calafate. Güemes and San Martín are the main drags; most hotels and restaurants don't have street numbers.

Essentials

GETTING THERE All transportation to El Chaltén originates from El Calafate, which has **daily plane service** from Ushuaia and Buenos Aires. From El Calafate, you need to take a bus or rent a car; the trip takes 3 to 3½ hours.

By car from El Calafate, take RN 11 west for 30km (19 miles) and turn left on RN 40 north. Turn again, heading northwest, on RP 23 to El Chaltén. The only place for a midtrip pit stop is the historic Estancia La Leona, where you can grab a snack and a coffee. The route is now almost entirely paved.

From the El Calafate airport, there are three daily shuttles to El Chaltén run by **Las Lengas Transporte** (✆ 02962/493023; www.transportelaslengas.com.ar) for $23. From your hotel in El Calafate, you can take one of two daily transfers run by **Hostel del Glaciar** (✆ 02902/496242; www.glaciar.com) directly to your hotel in El Chaltén for $23. **Chaltén Travel,** with offices in El Chaltén at Avenida Güemes and Lago del Desierto (✆ 02962/493092; www.chaltentravel.com), leaves El Calafate daily at 8am, 1pm (Jan and Feb only), and 6:30pm, and El Chaltén at 7:30am, 1pm (Jan–Feb only), and 6pm, departing from the Rancho Grande hostel, for $23. **Caltur,** which departs El Chaltén's Hostería Fitz Roy, at Av. San Martín 520 (✆ 02962/493062; www.caltur.com.ar), leaves El Calafate daily at 7:30am and 6:30pm, and leaves El Chaltén at 3pm.

VISITOR INFORMATION When you first get to town, stop at the **APN Intendencia office** (park service; ✆ 02962/493004) for a good introduction to the park in English. Here you'll find an interpretive exhibit, a helpful staff, and a variety of maps and pamphlets. El Chaltén also has a well-organized visitor center at the town's entrance—the **Comisión de Fomento,** Perito Moreno and Avenida Güemes (✆ 02962/493011), which is open daily 8am to 8pm. Here you'll find maps, pamphlets, and brief interpretive displays about the region's flora and fauna. In El Calafate, the **APN Intendencia** has its offices at Av. del Libertador 1302 (✆ 02962/493004). Its visitor center is open daily from 9am to 3pm.

There is currently an ATM (with a spotty cash supply) in El Chaltén, but no bank. Many inns, restaurants, and stores don't take credit cards, because phone lines are sketchy, so be sure to stop in for cash at a bank in El Calafate.

Finally, I can't emphasize enough how prepared you must be for the weather in El Chaltén. Often, severe winds, rain, and storms will keep you indoors for your entire stay and offer not a single glimpse of the glorious peaks. Dress appropriately, and try to embrace the wild weather that brings so much character to Patagonia.

Outdoor Activities

TOUR OPERATORS

Fitz Roy Expediciones ★★, Av. San Martín 5 (✆/fax **02962/493017;** www.fitz royexpediciones.com.ar), offers a variety of trekking excursions, including a complete 9-day circuit around the backside of the FitzRoy and Cerro Torre peaks on the spectacular Patagonian Ice Cap, for $1,850 per person, all equipment and meals included, as well as 2 nights' lodging in an *albergue.* This is a trip for hard-core adventurers only. They also have an excellent day trip to Lago del Desierto, which includes a short hike or boat cruise and lunch at their adventure camp, which offers rafting trips. The full-day trip costs $90 and is a good option on a stormy day, as the weather is often better toward Lago del Desierto than in El Chaltén. Finally, they have multisport trips, with river kayak trips, mountain biking, and horseback riding from their lovely FitzRoy Adventure Camp, just north of El Chaltén.

BOAT TRIPS

The rugged and wild Viedma Glacier is accessed from El Chaltén. It's a powerful place where you can strap on some crampons and explore the magical ice. **Patagonia Aventura ★** (✆ **02962/493110;** www.patagonia-aventura.com) currently has the concession to run this excursion. Choose from four options: Viedma Light is a half-day boat trip, where you don't step on the ice ($35); Viedma Trek includes a light hike at the base of the glacier ($53); Viedma Ice Trek is a crampons-on trek atop the glacier ($110); and finally, Viedma Pro is an ice trek that includes a short course in ice climbing ($135). All include transfers from El Chaltén, but not lunch, so bring your own. Another interesting boat trip offered by Patagonia Aventura is across the remote Lago del Desierto, which, despite its name, is in one of the most lush valleys in southern Patagonia.

HIKING & CAMPING

El Chaltén is Argentina's national trekking capital and home to some very good hiking guides who'll take you out for an afternoon stroll, a full-day trek, or even a multiday hiking expedition. The best can be found at **Mountaineering Patagonia,** whose office is at San Martín 16 (✆ **02962/493194;** www.mountaineeringpatagonia.com). Also try Manuel Quiroga's **El Chaltén Mountain Guides,** San Martín 187 (✆ **02962/493329;** www.ecmg.com.ar). These groups also can arrange more-challenging mountaineering objectives, such as climbs of local peaks, multiday treks to Paso Marconi, and weeklong traverses of the majestic Southern Ice Field.

Although the trails here are generally very well marked, enlisting a local guide will give you a much more enjoyable experience. Guides will explain the natural history, tell you about amazing mountaineering feats that took place in the area, and ensure your safety. If you're planning to hike in the park, you'll want to pick up a copy of Zagier & Urruty's trekking map, *Monte FitzRoy & Cerro Torre,* available at most bookstores and tourist shops in El Calafate and El Chaltén. You'll also need to register at the park service office at the entrance to El Chaltén. The best thing about hiking in El Chaltén is that almost all trails start and end in the town itself, meaning you can return each evening for a hot shower, a nice meal, and a good bed. Two standard half-day hikes leave from town: Laguna Capri, which offers a marvelous view of FitzRoy, and the Laguna Torre Lookout. For full-day hikes, the best are Laguna Torre and Laguna de los Tres. Trails here run from easy to difficult, and they take anywhere from 4 to 10 hours to complete. See below for trail descriptions.

Trails in the El Chaltén Area

The El Chaltén area of Los Glaciares National Park has incredible trails for hikers, not to mention imposing challenges for alpinists and mountaineers. The beauty of this area, besides the stunning scenery, is that the valleys are long and don't require too much uphill or downhill hiking, and you can make it back to town each night. While overnight camping trips are available, El Chaltén excels in its proximity to day-hike trail heads. Unlike the Torres del Paine hikes, which generally require a few nights of camping, all of the main highlights here can be seen in a few day hikes.

What makes hiking in El Chaltén so good is the varied terrain and the relatively little climbing required to get amazing views. These hikes all leave from town and range from easy to difficult; each of them allows you to see the famous spires from many angles. The times given below are estimates for the average walker from El Chaltén. **Note:** These trips are listed according to difficulty, from easy to strenuous.

Cascada Chorrillo del Salto The easiest and flattest hike in the area, this trail is level and stays along the El Chaltén valley floor. Follow the Río de las Vueltas riverbank northeast of town to the Chorrillo del Salto waterfall, which emerges from a dense forest. Give yourself an hour each way to walk at an easy pace.
Return 90 min. 4km (2.5 miles) one-way. Easy.

Cerro Torre Lookout Known as "El Mirador del Cerro Torre" in Spanish, this is a nice half-day hike. The trail head is behind the Los Cerros hotel. After climbing 200m (656 ft.) to get above the El Chaltén valley, you'll stroll along a raging glacial FitzRoy River, through thick beech forests, meeting a spectacular view of the needle-like Cerro Torre, with its namesake lake and glacier in front. This is an excellent way to sample some of the world's finest trekking and a great choice if you arrive midday. Climb off to the left (river side) of the trail for the lookout at Cerro Dos Condores.
Return 3 hr. 3km (2 miles) one-way. Easy to moderate.

Laguna Capri ★ A bit longer than the other great local half-day hike to the Cerro Torre Lookout, Laguna Capri is the must-see destination for lovers of the FitzRoy massif. The trail leads north from town past Cerro Rosado before heading west toward Mt. FitzRoy. Many trekkers come here as a pilgrimage to one of the world's finest granite mountains, saving some time to scour the walls of FitzRoy with binoculars, to look for climbers. It's a 2-hour hike into the lagoon, following the same trail that leads to the Poincenot camp.
Return 4-hr. 7km (4 miles) one-way. Easy to moderate.

Laguna Torre ★★ Continuing past the Cerro Torre lookout (see above), the trail winds its way up the FitzRoy River to the sheltered nook at the D'Agostini campground, which is a good spot for a protected picnic. From here, you climb up over the moraine and face first into the howling wind for a jaw-dropping close-up of Cerro Torre, its glacier, and its milky blue lake. Next to the Torre Glacier, you have a glimpse of the Grande Glacier. This is a 22km (12-mile) round-trip; plan for 3 hours each way. There are also good views of Mt. Solo and the Adela chain en route. If you have time left at the lake, scramble to the north shore of Laguna Torre to Mirador Maestri. For an even fuller day, you can include a hike with crampons on the Torre Glacier as well, though this must be done with a guide from Fitz Roy Expediciones (see "Tour Operators," above).
Return 6–7 hr. 11km (7 miles) one-way. Moderate.

Laguna de los Tres ★★ The best full-day hike in El Chaltén takes you along the Chorrillo del Salto river past the campground at Poincenot—which is probably the best and most centrally located campground in the area—and over the Río Blanco before the final steep climb (400m/1,312 ft., which will take you an hour) up to the gorgeous Laguna de los Tres, nestled beneath the giant granite walls of Mt. FitzRoy.
10-hr. return. 13km (8 miles) one-way. Moderate to difficult.

PATAGONIA'S FAMOUS peaks

The Cerro Torre and FitzRoy groups may be two of the alpine world's most recognized skylines, made famous by decades of unbelievable mountaineering feats, and by the U.S.-based Patagonia Inc. clothing company, which chose this horizon as its company's logo. Climbers consider these among the toughest challenges on the planet. They are also a remarkable display of natural beauty, with a rich human history of struggle, controversy, and extraordinary achievement. Whether you're a serious climber or a nonclimbing mountain lover, these peaks are sure to inspire. From left to right, on those exceptional clear days, here is what's making your jaw drop:

○ **Cerro Torre:** At 3,102m (10,174 ft.), this granite needle sticks straight into the sky. Its first ascent has been the subject of debate for 50 years, since photographer and climber Tony Egger disappeared on what climbing partner Cesare Maestri claimed was the first summit. Maestri's account has been long doubted and debated. A recent team of climbers followed the route Maestri described and found it impossible to climb, with no apparent evidence of previous attempts.

○ **Cerro Standhart:** The granite needle Standhart, at 2,650m (8,692 ft.), is seen as a good warm-up for those attempting the summit of Cerro Torre.

○ **Torre Egger:** Named after Tony Egger, who allegedly climbed what was considered the hardest mountain climb in the world with Maestri in 1956. When Egger disappeared on the descent, along with his camera, he shattered the credibility of the summit Maestri claimed.

○ **Pico Poincenot:** The big one to the left of FitzRoy group, this spire reaches 3,002m (9,846 ft.).

○ **Mt. FitzRoy:** Named for Sir Robert FitzRoy, the captain of HMCS *Beagle*, which brought Charles Darwin on his first voyage to South America, this magnetic giant stands 3,405m tall (11,168 ft.). For generations, the local Tehuelche people have called FitzRoy "El Chaltén," or volcano, because it is almost always covered by clouds, which they confused for smoke. To the left of FitzRoy are the spires Agujas, St. Exupery, and Rafael Juarez. To the right are Mermoz and Guillaumet.

Pilar-Río Blanco–Poincenot This alternative to the Laguna de los Tres trek starts at Hostería El Pilar and heads back to El Chaltén via Río Blanco. The advantage is that it's a one-way trail (one of the only), so you are not retracing your steps. To make it to Laguna de los Tres, though, you need to get a very early start. You'll need a shuttle one-way to get to the trail head on the banks of the Río Eléctrico, at Hostería El Pilar, 17km (11 miles) from El Chaltén. Many local companies, including Mountaineering Patagonia (see above), can help you organize this. From here it's a gradual climb to Laguna Capri (see above) before dropping back into El Chaltén.

Circuit 9 hr. 20km (12 miles) total. Moderate to difficult.

HORSEBACK RIDING

There's nothing like horseback riding in Patagonia, and the gauchos at **El Relincho,** Avenida del Libertador (📞 **02962/493007**), have been leading rides from their stables in "downtown" El Chaltén for years.

Where to Stay

As the distances from El Calafate shrink, thanks to highway pavement, El Chaltén is taking a swing upscale. Formerly a destination for backpackers and hostelgoers, it now affords interesting new lodging options. A new explora hotel from the legendary Chilean innovators is in development stages, and a handful of other upscale lodges are also in the works.

VERY EXPENSIVE

Hotel Los Cerros ★   The Los Cerros inn sits above everybody else physically and is by far the most highbrow, luxurious place in town. The common spaces have a new-cottage feel, with comfy sofas and tall ceilings. The rooms, on either side of green hallways, are large and open to fabulous views stretching above the village and across the valley. Bathrooms come in a variety of setups, all with modern fixtures and a jetted soaker tub. Top-floor premium rooms have sloped ceilings and an alpine chalet feel. There are no TVs or phones in the rooms; but there is a common living room with picture books and a large TV where you can watch movies. I found the service a bit too formal for a laid-back mountain village such as El Chaltén. Breakfasts are excellent, particularly the scrumptious baked goods. The downstairs spa is minimal but relaxing enough. Los Cerros will appeal to those looking for a Patagonian version of white-glove formality.

San Martín s/n, El Chaltén. 📞 **02962/493812.** www.loscerrosdelchalten.com. 44 units. $328–$494 double with breakfast; $770–$954 3-night packages including transfer and half-pension. AE, MC, V. **Amenities:** Restaurant; lounge; excursions; gift shop; high-speed Internet; library; mini-cinema; room service; small spa. *In room:* Hair dryer, jetted tubs, no phone.

EXPENSIVE

Kaulem Hostería ★ 🎁   If you are looking for peace and quiet, very personalized service, and comfortable rooms with a great view, this charming (albeit tiny) B&B may be just right. Dark woods and natural colors fill up the two-story main room, where FitzRoy is on display. Rooms are simple, perhaps too simple for the price, but the upstairs ones have superb views. With only four rooms, the staff really goes above and beyond to make you feel at home in this unique setting; they'll happily meet just about any request, from a sewing kit to a latte.

Av. Antonio Rojo and Comandante Arrua, El Chaltén. 📞/fax **02962/493251.** www.kaulem.com.ar. 4 units. $175 double. Rates include breakfast and transfers from bus stop. MC, V. **Amenities:** Lounge.

MODERATE

Hostería El Pilar ★   Seventeen kilometers (10 miles) from El Chaltén, this hotel is isolated and a bit austere, but with lovely, peaceful surroundings. The red-roofed El Pilar was once an *estancia;* now it's tastefully and artistically decorated with just enough detail to look great without distracting you from the outdoors. Rooms are rustic and simple but attractive. Superior rooms are all doubles and have bigger bathrooms. Transfers from El Chaltén are included. Guests normally take their meals at the hotel's restaurant, which serves decent cuisine. The hotel offers guided excursions, and it's located next to several trail heads. If you're driving here, keep an eye open for the sign to this hotel, because it's easy to miss. It is open to the public as a teahouse.

Ruta Provincial 23, 17km (10 miles) from El Chaltén. ✆/fax **02962/493002.** www.hosteriaelpilar.com. ar. 10 units. $128 double. Rates include breakfast and transfers from El Chaltén. No credit cards. Must reserve ahead Oct–Apr. **Amenities:** Restaurant; bar; lounge.

Senderos Hostería ★★ 🎒 This lovely little mountain lodge with an excellent restaurant offers superb service, cozy rooms (the nicest ones have wooden ceilings), and great service; it's gentle luxury is just upscale enough for this informal town. Built with traditional Patagonian architecture (tin and wood), rooms are bright and sunny. Top-floor rooms are the quietest. The location, on the edge of town facing the new bus terminal, isn't great, but inside, there is a lot of heart, warmth, and good vibes.

Perito Moreno s/n, El Chaltén. ✆ **02962/493258.** www.senderoshosteria.com.ar. 21 units. $145–$170 double; $185–$230 suite. Rates include breakfast. No credit cards. **Amenities:** Restaurant; wine bar; transfers; reading room; TV room w/DVD library.

INEXPENSIVE

In-Land-Sis ★ 🗡 This fresh, new spot in town is run by two funky young mountain lovers. It's a small step up from a *hostal* and particularly appealing to young couples on a budget. There are eight doubles, each with a private bathroom. Four have double beds, and four have bunk beds squished in. All have views of the peaks; room no. 6 has a great view of FitzRoy. Discounts are given to those who pay in cash.

Lago del Desierto 480, El Chaltén. ✆ **02962/493276.** www.inlandsis.com.ar. 8 units. $63 double with queen-size bed; $48 double with bunk. AE, MC, V. **Amenities:** Small restaurant.

Where to Eat

For a casual town where everyone wears hiking boots, El Chaltén has surprisingly good dining options. Climbers gather during a stormy day at **Patagonicus,** Güemes at Andreas Madsen (✆ **02962/493025**). Patagonicus serves mostly pizza and enormous salads in a woodsy dining area with fair prices; no credit cards accepted. It's a good spot for an afternoon coffee. **Fuegia ★**, San Martín 342 (✆ **02962/493243**), has an eclectic, global menu including coconut chicken with cashews and excellent salads. There are also good vegetarian options. In a ramshackle old house loaded with character, **Ruca Mahuida ★★**, at Lionel Terray 55 (✆ **02962/493018**), has the feel of an old alpine hut. The food is pure Patagonia, with stews, trout, and hearty pastas to fill you up after a day on the trail. Diners gather around a handful of tables, making this a great spot to make new friends. Reservations are recommended. For a funky scene with cool music and creative food, head to **Estepa,** at the corner of Cerro Solo and Antonio Rojo (✆ **02962/493069**). The lamb in soft mint sauce, pizzas, and pumpkin sorrentinos are superb. The restaurant at the **Senderos Hostería ★★** (see "Where to Stay," above) is also excellent.

TORRES DEL PAINE NATIONAL PARK, CHILE ★★

113km (70 miles) N of Puerto Natales; 360km (223 miles) NW of Punta Arenas

Across the border from Argentina's Los Glaciares National Park is Chile's prized jewel—a national park so magnificent that few in the world can claim a rank in its class. Torres del Paine is a major tourist destination whose popularity has grown tenfold over the past 8 years. Granite peaks and towers soar from sea level to upward of 2,800m (9,184 ft.). Golden plains and the rolling steppes are home to llamalike guanacos and more than 100 species of colorful birds, such as parakeets, flamingos, and ostrichlike rheas. During the spring, Chilean firebush blooms a riotous red, and during the autumn, the park's beech trees change to crimson, sunflower, and orange. A fierce wind screams through this region during the spring and summer, yet flowers, such as the delicate porcelain orchids and lady-slippers, somehow weather the inhospitable terrain. Electric-blue icebergs cleave from Glacier Grey. Resident gauchos ride atop sheepskin saddles. Condors float effortlessly even on the windiest day. This park is not something you just visit; it is something you experience.

Although it sits next to the Andes, **Parque Nacional Torres del Paine** is a separate geologic formation created roughly 3 million years ago when bubbling magma began growing and pushing its way up, taking a thick sedimentary layer with it. Glaciation and severe climate weathered away the softer rock, leaving the spectacular Paine Massif, whose prominent features are the *Cuernos* (which means "horns") and the one-of-a-kind *Torres*—three salmon-colored, spherical granite towers. The black sedimentary rock is visible on the upper reaches of the elegant Cuernos, named for the two spires that rise from the outer sides of its amphitheater. *Paine* is the Tehuelche Indian word for "blue," and it brings to mind the varying shades found in the lakes that surround this massif—among them the milky, turquoise waters of Lagos Nordenskjold and Pehoé. Backing the Paine Massif are several glaciers that descend from the Southern Ice Field.

Torres del Paine was once a collection of *estancias* and small-time ranches; many were forced out with the creation of the park in 1959. The park has since grown to its present size of 242,242 hectares (598,338 acres), and in 1978 was declared a World Biosphere Reserve by UNESCO for its singular beauty and ecology. This park used to be a backpacker's dream, for adventurous trekkers only. These days, more and more visitors are choosing shorter hikes and fancier lodges, and Torres del Paine is closer to becoming a destination on the beaten path. Hiking along the main trails in January or February, you may find yourself in a queue and stumble upon places to spend money at every corner. Still, it's a big place, with big skies and room for many. There are options for everyone, which is why the number of visitors to this park grows by nearly 20,000 per year.

Essentials
WHEN TO GO & WHAT TO BRING

This is not the easiest of national parks to visit. The climate in the park can be abominable. Wind speeds can peak at 161kmph (100 mph), and it can rain and snow even in the middle of summer. It is not unusual for visitors to spend 5 days in the park and never see the Towers. On average, the windiest days happen between late October and mid-March, but the only predictable thing about the weather here is its unpredictability. But besides the weather, spring is a beautiful time for budding flowers and birds; during the fall, the beech forests turn colors, which can be especially striking on walks up to the Towers and to the glacier. The winter is surprisingly temperate, with relatively few snowstorms and no wind—but short days. You'll need to stay in a hotel during the winter, but you'll practically have the park to yourself. Summer is, ironically, the worst time to come, especially from late December to mid-February, when the wind blows at full fury and crowds descend upon the park. When the wind

12

Torres del Paine National Park, Chile

PENINSULA VALDES & SOUTHERN PATAGONIA

blows, it can make even a short walk a rather scary experience. But just try to go with it, rather than fight it, and revel in the excitement of the extreme environment that defines Patagonia.

I can't stress enough the importance of bringing the right gear, especially waterproof hiking boots (if you plan to do any trekking), weatherproof outerwear, and warm layers, even in the summer. The ozone problem is acute here, so you'll need sunscreen, sunglasses, and a hat as well.

VISITOR & PARK ENTRANCE INFORMATION

Your visit to Torres del Paine will require logistical planning, unless you've left it up to an all-inclusive tour or hotel (this option is increasingly popular and there are more choices available for all-inclusive trips). Begin your research at **www.torresdel paine.cl**, which offers an English-language overview of the park and its surroundings, including maps, activities information, events, photos, hotel listings and links, and more. The park service **CONAF** has a relatively unhelpful Spanish-only website at www.conaf.cl. The park's administration and visitor center are at the southern end of the park (© **56/61-691931**). The park is open daily year-round from 8:30am to 10pm. The cost to enter is $32; during the winter, the cost is $16 for adults. It's a lot—"Paine" as the park is called, is the most visited park in the country and thus is the money-grabber for the entire Chilean National Park system.

GETTING THERE & AWAY

Many travelers are unaware of the enormous amount of time it takes to get to Torres del Paine. From the Argentine side, semiregular buses run to the park, but most go first to the town of Puerto Natales, where you will need to spend the night before heading to the park. Remember that if you are planning to camp in Torres del Paine, you'll need to buy most of your food in Puerto Natales, as there are very limited grocery options in the park, and you cannot take fresh food across the border from Argentina. From the nearest Chilean airport in Punta Arenas, it's a 5-hour drive to the park. From Puerto Natales, the park is about an hour north by car.

BY BUS To get to Torres del Paine from Argentina by bus, your best bet is to take the regular bus to Puerto Natales, spend the night there, and then head into the park the next morning. **Bus Sur Zaahj,** at the Bus Terminal (© **02902/491631**), runs this route on Tuesdays, Thursdays, and Saturdays, leaving El Calafate at 8am. **Cootra** (© **02902/491144**), departs El Calafate at 8:30am. Buy tickets at least 1 day before to ensure yourself a seat. **Cordillera del Sol,** whose office is at 25 de Mayo 43, in El Calafate (© **02902/492822;** www.cordilleradelsol.com), offers transfers from El Calafate to Torres del Paine directly.

From Puerto Natales, buses to Torres del Paine enter through the Laguna Amarga ranger station, stop at the Pehoé catamaran dock, and terminate at the park administration center. If you're going directly to the Torres trail head at Hotel Las Torres, there are minivan transfers waiting at the Laguna Amarga station that charge about $5 one-way. The return times given below are when the bus leaves from the park administration center; the bus will pass through the Laguna Amarga station about 45 minutes later. Some buses will pick you up from your hotel, but it depends on the relationship your hotel has with the various bus companies, so ask at the hotel reception.

Trans Via Paine, Bulnes 516 (© **56/61-413672**), leaves daily at 7:30am via Laguna Amarga; **Gomez,** Arturo Prat 234 (© **56/61-411971**), also leaves at 7:30am, returning from the administration building at 1pm; and **Buses JB,** Arturo Prat 258 (© **61/410242**), departs also at 7:30am, returning at 1pm. The cost is around $30 one-way.

BY TOUR VAN From El Calafate, a handful of similar "Paine in a Day" tours include one organized by **Chaltén Travel** (© **02902/492212** in El Calafate; www.chaltentravel.com) for $135. It's a long but unforgettable day. They will also pick you up or drop you off in the park. **Comapa** (© **56/61-414300**; www.comapa.com) has an 11-hour tour of Paine from Puerto Natales that includes a few short hikes and lunch at the Hostería Lago Grey.

BY CAR From El Calafate, the direct drive to Torres del Paine is 342km (212 miles). Head south on Ruta 11 to Ruta 40, past the small town at El Cerrito, to the border at Cerro Castillo, also known as Cancha Carrera. The border is open daily in summertime from 8am to 10pm. On the Chilean side of the border, head north on Ruta 9 at Cerro Castillo, 84km (52 miles) to the park's administration building, or right/south on Ruta 9, for 63km (39 miles) to Puerto Natales. Be sure to tell the rental car agency that you will be taking your car to Chile, which requires special permits. The drive takes approximately 3½ to 4 hours. *Note:* Fill your tank in El Calafate and again at El Cerrito before crossing into Chile.

CROSSING LAGO PEHOE BY CATAMARAN Day hikers to the Glacier Grey trail and backpackers taking the W or Circuit trails will need to cross Lake Pehoé at some point aboard a catamaran, about a 45-minute ride. The cost is $22 one-way or $36 round-trip. Buses from Puerto Natales are timed to drop off and pick up passengers in conjunction with the catamaran (Nov 15–Mar 15 leaving Pudeto at 9:30am, noon, and 6pm; and from Pehoé at 10am, 12:30, and 6:30pm; Oct 1–30 and April from Pudeto at noon, and from Pehoé at 12:30pm; Nov 1–14 and Mar 16–31 from Pudeto at noon and 6pm, and Pehoé at 12:30 and 6pm; closed May–Sept). Hikers walking the entire round-trip Glacier Grey trail can do so only by taking the 9:30am boat, returning at 6:30pm from mid-November to March 15. The boat fills up quickly, so try to be there early; it's first-come, first-served. For more information call © **56/061-411380** or visit www.hielospatagonicos.cl.

Where to Stay & Eat
HOTELS & HOSTERIAS

explora Hotel Salto Chico ★★★ 📷 The explora in Patagonia has garnered more fame than any other hotel in Chile, and deservedly so. It's a one-stop shop for an unforgettable Patagonian experience, with a stunning view, perched above the milky, turquoise waters of Lago Pehoé and facing the dramatic granite amphitheater of the Paine massif. Of course, it's terribly expensive, too. The hotel's style is comfortable elegance, and its contemporary interiors belie the rather bland modernist exterior: softly curving blond-wood walls built entirely from native deciduous beech, but with large windows all around. An expansion from 30 to 50 guest rooms has made the explora more of a hotel than a cozy mountain inn, so much of the intimacy has been lost. Explora is all-inclusive, meaning prices cover everything from airport transfers to fabulous excursions such as photo safaris and horseback riding and a dozen other choices. It must be said that the food quality has at times been uneven—never bad, but not as outstanding as one would expect from a hotel of this caliber. Four-day packages start every 4 days. Note, however, that the first-day arrival to the hotel is around 6pm, leaving time for a short hike to a lookout point only. And the last day isn't really a day at all, as guests leave after breakfast for the drive back to the airport.

In Santiago, Américo Vespucio Sur 80, 5th floor. © **2/395-2533.** Fax 2/228-4655. www.explora.com. 50 units. Packages per person, double occupancy: 4 nights starting at $2,780; 6 nights starting at $4,410. Rates include all meals, transportation, excursions, gear, and guides. AE, DC, MC, V. **Amenities:** Restaurant; bar; lounge; large indoor heated pool; outdoor Jacuzzi; sauna; shop; massage; laundry service; high-speed Internet. *In room:* Minibar.

Hostería Lago Grey   This classic little white *hostería* is tucked within a beech forest, looking out onto the beach at Lago Grey and the astounding blue icebergs that drift to its shore. It's well on the other side of the park, but the view is better here than at the Hotel Las Torres (see below). A new wing with 30 "superior" rooms has essentially doubled the size of the hotel, leaving the common areas crowded during high season. The price suggests more luxurious rooms, but the walls are a tad thin and have little decoration. On the plus side, there are plenty of trails that branch out from here. You can also arrange rafting trips down the Río Grey and kayaking among the icebergs. The downside is that a stay here includes nothing but a room and breakfast—you will end up coughing up much cash for overpriced meals, bar service, and transfers.

Office in Punta Arenas, Lautaro Navarro 1077. © **56/61-712143.** www.turismolagogrey.com. 60 units. Oct–Apr $308 double standard; $368 double superior. Rates include buffet breakfast. AE, DC, MC, V. **Amenities:** Restaurant; lounge; tours.

Hotel Las Torres ★ ☺   This used to be an original working cattle *estancia*, sitting at the trail head to the Torres. But due to recent expansion, it's now a full-blown hotel, with traffic to match. The complex now includes a low-slung, ranch-style hotel, a two-story hotel wing next door, a large campground, and a hostel. Their on-site stables and access to the Towers are convenient; however, it is a long drive to the other side of the park. Las Torres also offers a small spa, with mud therapy, massage, and sauna. The buffet-style restaurant is above par, but pricey. The hotel offers pricey packages that include guided tours, meals, and transportation, much like explora, and excellent off-season trips to little-explored areas. Packages run from 3 to 7 nights, or you can pay separately for day trips. Try spending 2 nights here and 2 at Hostería Lago Grey (see above), thereby avoiding the steep price of an excursion there. Rooms have no views.

Office in Punta Arenas, Sarmiento 846. ©/fax **56/61-617450.** www.lastorres.com. 84 units. $270 double standard; $305 double superior; 4-night packages from $1,674 per person double. Rates include buffet breakfast. AE, DC, MC, V. **Amenities:** Restaurant; lounge; room service; horseback riding.

Patagonia Camp ★★ ☺ 📷   The most appealing new lodging option in the area is a camp for grown-ups. With a mountaineer's heart and a luxury bent, this is not a hotel, it's an experience in nature. Set on a slope above Lago del Toro, with stunning views of the Paine massif, its layout is similar to safari camps found in the African

Due to the soaring popularity of Torres del Paine, it is recommended that travelers book well in advance, if they're planning to visit the park between late November and late March. Nearly every business now has a website or, at the very least, an e-mail address, so trip planning is easier than ever. Hotels can be booked directly and often they offer their own transportation from the airport. At the very least, they can recommend a service to call or e-mail. One-stop local agencies such as **FantásticoSur,** Esmerald 661, in Puerto Natales (© **56/61-614185;** www. fantasticosur.com), and **Chile Nativo,** Eberhard 230, in Puerto Natales (© **56/ 61-411835,** or toll-free from North America 800/649-8776; www.chile nativo.com), are good places for *refugio* reservations, horseback-riding trips, or camping equipment rentals; and they can sometimes offer lower hotel rates at *hosterías* in the park. They can also solve tricky transfer problems.

savanna. There are 18 wood-framed yurts (Mongolian-inspired wood-framed tents) situated along wooden walkways tucked inside beech forest. Incredibly bright, cozy, and plush, the yurts have high-end touches, such as woven blankets, central heating, and copper shower heads. Each has a luxurious bathroom with a soaker tub. But it's not a walk in the park: If you have trouble sleeping, you may curse the tents that flap loudly in a strong storm. If the night's clear though, you'll have delightful stargazing from your bed. If it's raining, you'll get wet here just going from place to place. But the atmosphere is incredibly natural, secluded, and romantic. In the main lodge, meals (and pisco sours) are served. Their all-inclusive packages, again, mirror those of explora, but Patagonia Camp is much more quiet and intimate.

Hernando de Aguirre 414, Santiago. © **56/2-335-6898.** www.patagoniacamp.com. 18 units. $260 double with breakfast; 3-night programs $2,320 single, $1,554 double. Rates include all meals, excursions, transfers, and guides. AE, DC, MC, V. **Amenities:** Restaurant; library.

REFUGIOS & HOSTALES

Four cabinlike lodging units, all with shared accommodations and distributed along the park's Circuit and W trails, are moderately priced sleeping options for backpackers who are not interested in pitching a tent. Although most have bedding or sleeping bags for an expensive rental price, your best bet is to bring your own. The price, $60 on average per night for a simple dorm bed (about $76 for room and full board), is not cheap, but the units all come with hot showers, a cafe, and a common area for hiding out from bad weather. Meals served here are simply prepared but hearty. Alternatively, guests can bring their own food and cook. Each *refugio* has rooms with two to six bunks, which you'll have to share with strangers when they're full. During the high season, consider booking weeks in advance; although many visitors have reported luck after calling just a few days beforehand (due to cancellations). All agencies in Puerto Natales and Punta Arenas book reservations and issue vouchers, but the best bet is to call or e-mail (see below).

The first three *refugios* are owned and operated by **FantásticoSur.** Rates are $37 for a bed, plus $10 for breakfast and $19 for dinner. They can be booked by contacting ©/fax **61/614185** or by visiting www.fslodges.com:

- **Refugio Torres:** This lodge is the largest and most full-service *refugio* in the park; it sits near the Hotel Las Torres and the trail head for the W-circuit and Full Circuit. You may dine in the hotel or eat simple fare in the *refugio* itself. Horseback rides can be taken from here.
- **Refugio El Chileno:** This is the least-frequented *refugio* because it is located halfway up to the Towers (most do the trail as a day hike). Hikers will find it more convenient to stow their stuff in the campground at the *hostería,* but, then again, this *refugio* puts you away from the hubbub below.
- **Refugio Los Cuernos:** This may be the park's loveliest *refugio,* located at the base of the Cuernos. The wood structure (which miraculously holds up to some of the strongest winds in the park) has two walls of windows that look out onto Lago Nordenskjold.
- **Paine Grande Mountain Lodge:** This *hostal*-like "lodge" replaces the old *refugio* Pehoé, at the busiest intersection in the park. It is the hub for several of the trail heads to the park administration center, Glacier Grey, and French Valley, as well as the docking site for the catamaran. Utilitarian in style, the *hostal* has 60 beds, two lounges, and a cafeteria. Day walks to Glacier Grey and French Valley can be taken from here. Call © **56/61-412742** or write to contact@verticepatagonia.cl.

CAMPING IN TORRES DEL PAINE

Torres del Paine has a well-designed campground system with free and concession-run sites. **Camping Pehoé** (www.campingpehoe.com) is a roadside campground with great facilities, including electricity, phones, gear rental, a small supermarket, firewood, fresh water, hot showers, and a restaurant. All *refugios* have a campground, too, and these and other concession sites charge about $8 to $10 per person, which includes hot showers, clean bathrooms, and an indoor dining area in which to escape bad weather and eat under a roof. The site at Las Torres provides barbecues and firewood. Free campgrounds are run by CONAF, and they can get a little dingy, with deplorable outhouses. Beginning in March, mice become a problem for campers, so always leave food well stored or hanging from a tree branch. The JLM hiking map (available at every bookstore, airport, kiosk, and travel agency, and at the park entrance) denotes which campgrounds are free and which charge a fee.

Trails in Torres del Paine

Torres del Paine has something for everyone, from easy, well-trammeled trails to remote walks through relative wilderness. Which path you choose depends on how much time you have and what kind of walk you're up for. Pick up one of **JLM's Torres del Paine maps** (sold everywhere), or visit **www.torresdelpaine.com** and download a map, to plan your itinerary. Walking times shown below are average.

LONG-HAUL OVERNIGHT HIKES

The Circuit The Circuit is a spectacular, long-haul backpacking trip that takes hikers around the entire Paine Massif. It can be done two ways—with the W included or without. Including the W, you'll need 8 to 11 days; without it, from 4 to 7 days. The Circuit is less traveled than the W because it's longer and requires that you camp out at least twice. I don't recommend doing this trail if you have only 4 or 5 days. This trail is for serious backpackers only, because it involves several difficult hikes up and down steep, rough terrain and over fallen tree trunks. You'll be rewarded for your effort, however, with dazzling views of terrain that varies from grassy meadows and winding rivers to thick virgin beech forest, snowcapped peaks, and, best of all, the awe-inspiring view of Glacier Grey, seen from atop the John Garner Pass. If you're a recreational hiker with a 4- to 6-hour hike tolerance level, you'll want to sleep in all the major campgrounds or *refugios*. Always do this trail counterclockwise for easier ascents and with the scenery before you. If you're here during the high season and want to get away from crowds, you might contemplate walking the first portion of this trail, beginning at Laguna Azul. This is the old trail, and it more or less parallels the Circuit, but on the other side of the river, passing the gaucho post La Victorina, the only remaining building of an old *estancia*. At Refugio Dickson, you'll have to cross the river, in the *refugio*'s dinghy, for $5. To get to Laguna Azul, you'll need to hitchhike or arrange private transportation. Do not underestimate the isolation of most of this hike—snowstorms, injuries, having minimal food, a lot can go wrong on this trek so please be fully prepared.

Approx. 60km (37 miles) total. 7–10 days. Beginning at Laguna Amarga or Hotel Las Torres. Terrain ranges from easy to difficult.

The W This segment of the Paine Massif is so called because hikers are taken along a trail that forms a W. This trail leads to the park's major geological features—the Torres, the Cuernos, and Glacier Grey—and it's the preferred multiday hike for its relatively short hauls and a time frame that requires 4 to 5 days. In addition, those who prefer not to camp or carry more gear than a sleeping bag, food, and their personal goods can stay in the various *refugios* along the way. Most hikers begin at Hotel Las Torres and start with a day-walk up to the Torres. From here, hikers head to the Los Cuernos *refugio* and spend the night, or continue on to the Italiano campsite near the base of the valley; then they walk up to French Valley. The next stop is Pehoé *refugio*, where most spend the night before hiking up to Glacier Grey. It's best to spend a night at Refugio Grey and return to the Pehoé *refugio* the next day. From here, take the catamaran across Lago Pehoé to an awaiting bus back to Puerto Natales.

4–5 days. Approx. 56km (35 miles) total. Beginning at Hotel Las Torres or Refugio Pehoé. Terrain ranges from easy to difficult.

DAY HIKES

These hikes run from easy to difficult, either within the W or from various trail heads throughout the park. Again, the times given are estimates for the average walker. **Note:** These trips are listed according to difficulty, from easy to strenuous.

Lago Grey 📷 Not only is this the easiest walk in the park, but it is one of the most dramatic for the gigantic blue icebergs that rest along the shore of Lago Grey. A flat walk across the sandy shore of the lake takes visitors to a peninsula for a short hike to a lookout point with Glacier Grey in the far distance. This walk begins near the Hostería Lago Grey; they also offer a recommended boat ride that weaves past icebergs and then takes passengers to the face of the glacier.

Departing from the parking lot past the entrance to Hostería Lago Grey. 1–2 hr. one-way. 2km. Easy.

Mirador Nordenskjold The trail head for this walk begins near the Pudeto catamaran dock. This trail begins with an up-close visit to the crashing Salto Grande waterfall. Then it winds through Antarctic beech and thorny bush to a lookout point with dramatic views into the French Valley and the Cuernos, looking over Lago Nordenskjold. This trail is a good place to see wildflowers in the spring.

1 hr. one-way. 5km. Easy.

Lago Pingo 🏛 Lago Pingo consistently sees fewer hikers, and it's an excellent spot for bird-watching for the variety of species that flock to this part of the park. The trail begins as an easy walk through a pleasant valley, past an old gaucho post. From here the trail heads through forest and undulating terrain, and past the Pingo Cascade until it eventually reaches another old gaucho post, the run-down but picturesque Zapata *refugio*. You can make this trail as long or as short as you'd like; the return is back along the same trail. The trail departs the same parking lot as the Lago Grey trail.

Departing from the Lago Grey parking lot past the entrance to Hostería Lago Grey. 1–4 hr. one-way. 11km, 8km to Pingo River. Easy to moderate.

Valle Francés (French Valley) There are several ways to hike this trail. From Refugio Pehoé, you'll pass by the blue waters of Lake Skottsberg and through groves of Chilean firebush and open views of the granite spires behind Los Cuernos. From Refugio Los Cuernos, you won't see French Valley until you're in it. A short walk through the campground leads hikers to direct views of the hanging glacier that descends from Paine Grande, and enthusiastic hikers can continue the steep climb up into the valley itself for a view of French Valley's enormous granite amphitheater.

Departing from Refugio Pehoé or Refugio Los Cuernos. 2½–4½ hr. one-way. 8km. Moderate to difficult.

Glacier Grey Hike here for an up-close look at the face of Glacier Grey, though warm summers of late have sent the glacier retreating. There aren't as many steep climbs as the trail to Las Torres, but it takes longer to get there (about 3½ hr.). I recommend that hikers in the summer walk this lovely trail to the glacier lookout point, and then take the boat back to Hostería Lago Grey. The walk takes hikers through thick forest and stunning views of the Southern Ice Field and the icebergs slowly making their way down Lago Grey. A turnoff just before the lookout point takes you to Refugio Grey.

3½ hr. one-way. 11km. Difficult.

Las Torres (The Towers) The trail to view the soaring granite Towers is a classic hike in the park but certainly not the easiest. Those who are in decent shape will not want to miss this exhilarating trek. The trail leaves from the Hotel Las Torres and begins with a steep 45-minute ascent, followed by up-and-down terrain for 1½ hours to another 45-minute steep ascent up a slippery granite moraine. Midway is the Refugio Chileno, where you can stop for a coffee or spend the night. Don't give up—the Torres do not come into full view until the very end.

3 hr. one-way. Difficult.

Horseback Riding in the Park

A horseback ride in Torres del Paine can be one of the most enjoyable ways to see the park. Hotel Las Torres has its own stables, which are open to the public; rides range from 1 hour ($26 per person) to a full day ($120 per person). For daylong outings on horseback both inside and just outside Torres del Paine National Park, contact **Baqueano Zamora** (© **56/61-613531;** www.baqueanozamora.cl). Full-day rides cost $95. For longer, multiday horseback-riding trips, contact **Chile Nativo,** Eberhart 230 (© **56/61-411835;** www.chilenativo.com). Chile Nativo can plan custom-made journeys within the park and to little-known areas, some of which include an introduction to the gaucho and *estancia* way of life. Most trips require prior experience.

TIERRA DEL FUEGO & ANTARCTICA

by Christie Pashby

13

This is the end of the world. It's a place cut off from everywhere else, facing south toward the stormy waters of the Drake Passage, Cape Horn, and, ultimately, Antarctica. It's a magical and alluring location that continues to draw tourists. Nearly 500 years have passed since Ferdinand Magellan cast his eyes on the dark headlands, silver shores, and craggy peaks of Tierra del Fuego. As he sailed past, flames blazed in the darkness along the coastline—bonfires lit by the Yamanas tribe—inspiring him to name the place "Land of Fire." Since then, this wind-swept island, washed by the Strait of Magellan to the north and the Beagle Channel to the south, has witnessed a rich parade of shipwrecks, penal colonies, gold prospectors, and missionaries. The Yamanas have disappeared, but Chile and Argentina have repopulated the area, while conducting a bad-tempered tug of war over its icy inlets and penguin-populated rocks. This wild, romantic island is now divided in two: Argentina controls the more populated lower eastern coast, and the rest belongs to Chile.

Vast sheep *estancias* (ranches) to the north cover a rolling tundra of brown furze and isolated farmhouses. Here the wide, meandering Río Grande holds the world's biggest sea brown trout, making it a mecca for fly fishers. Farther south, the land rises into forests of beech trees and wind-chopped lakes. The snow-flecked summits of the Andes give way to the bustling pioneer town of Ushuaia and its eclectic mix of resettled Argentines, eccentric sailors, and silver-haired European and American baby boomers stopping off on cruises bound for Antarctica. But they also come for rich coastal wildlife, stunning views, the best seafood in Argentina, and off-season skiing beneath hanging glaciers.

And when you think you can go no farther, you remember that another continent lies farther south. If you're lucky enough to have Antarctica as your final destination, it's from Ushuaia that you get there.

USHUAIA

461km (286 miles) SW of Punta Arenas; 594km (368 miles) S of Río Gallegos

Pinned snugly in a U-shaped cove facing the Beagle Channel, Ushuaia is a substantial and growing metropolis of 75,000 people. Colorful clapboard

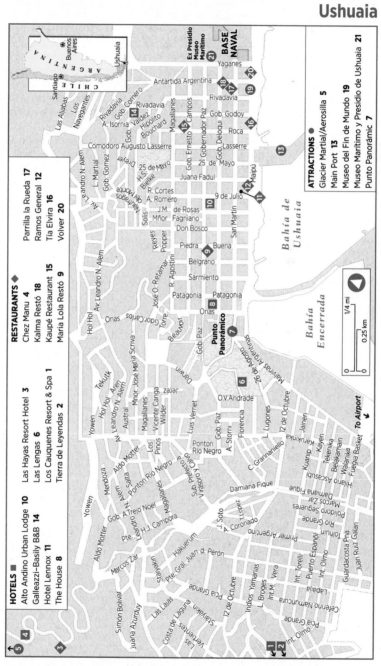

Ushuaia

HOTELS ■
Alto Andino Urban Lodge **10**
Galleazzi-Basily B&B **14**
Hotel Lennox **11**
The House **8**
Las Hayas Resort Hotel **3**
Las Lengas **6**
Los Cauquenes Resort & Spa **1**
Tierra de Leyendas **2**

RESTAURANTS ◆
Chez Manu **4**
Kalma Restó **18**
Kaupé Restaurant **15**
María Lola Restó **9**
Parrilla la Rueda **17**
Ramos General **12**
Tía Elvira **16**
Volver **20**

ATTRACTIONS ●
Glacier Martial/Aerosilla **5**
Main Port **13**
Museo del Fin de Mundo **19**
Museo Marítimo y Presidio de Ushuaia **21**
Punto Panorámic **7**

13

TIERRA DEL FUEGO & ANTARCTICA | Ushuaia

houses with rickety staircases and corrugated roofs at impossible angles are punctuated by the occasional bland block of brick or concrete. All rise steeply into a backdrop of beech trees and spirelike mountain summits. Not only is it the most southerly city in the world (Chile's Puerto Williams is actually farther south, but hardly qualifies as a city), but it also has the distinction of being the only Argentine city on the "other" side of the Andes. At its tail end, the mountain range is dragged eastward by restless tectonic plates that rattle frequently. To reach Ushuaia by car, you must cross briefly through Chile and then cross the Andes. Most people these days arrive by plane or cruise ship. What you find is a frontier town with lots of character, a rich outdoor life, and a surprisingly cosmopolitan feel. One hundred years ago, the only people crazy enough to live here were convicts in chains. Indeed, the city owes its existence to the prison: Inmates built the town railway, hospital, and port. Now it attracts Argentines from all over the country who come for tax breaks and plentiful jobs. Visitors find lots to do—whether it's visiting that same prison, which is now a fascinating museum, or exploring the many attractions of the Beagle Channel. Local residents are welcoming and friendly, with a refreshing hardiness and eccentricity that likely come from living at the end of the world.

Essentials

GETTING THERE

BY PLANE The **International Airport Malvinas Argentinas** is 5km (3 miles) from the city (© **2901/431232**). There is no bus service to town, but cab fares are about $7; always ask for a quote before accepting a ride. **Aerolíneas Argentinas** (© **0800/222-86527** or 2901/437265; www.aerolineas.com.ar) operates four or five daily flights to Buenos Aires, one of which leaves from Ezeiza and stops in El Calafate. Average round-trip fare is around $600. Flight frequency increases from November to March, when there's also a daily flight from Río Gallegos and twice-weekly flights from Trelew. **LAN** (© **0810/999-9526** or 2901/424244; www.lan.com) flies from Buenos Aires daily via El Calafate. **Aerovías DAP,** Deloqui 575 (© **2901/431110;** www.aeroviasdap.cl), runs charter flights from Punta Arenas and over Cape Horn. It costs around $3,000 for a group of seven people (round-trip), leaving whenever you want.

BY BUS There is no bus station in the city. Buses usually stop at the port (Maipú and Fadul). The service from Punta Arenas, Chile, costs $35 to $45 and takes about 12 hours. **Tecni Austral** (© **2901/431408** in Ushuaia, or 61/613423 in Punta Arenas) leaves Punta Arenas, via Río Grande and Río Gallegos on Tuesday, Thursday, and Saturday at 8:30am; tickets are sold in Ushuaia from the Tolkar office, at Roca 157, and in Punta Arenas, at Lautaro Navarro 975. They can also connect you to El Calafate. **Pacheco,** San Martín 1267 (© **2901/437727;** www.busespacheco.com), has trips to Punta Arenas via Río Grande, leaving on Tuesday, Thursday, and Sunday at 9am; it costs $56. To go to Río Grande, try **Lider LTD, Transporte Montiel,** or **Tecni Austral;** both offer eight daily departures, and the $21 trip takes around 4 hours.

BY BOAT **Crucero Australis** operates luxurious cruises between Ushuaia and Punta Arenas aboard its ships the M/V *Mare Australis,* the M/V *Via Australis,* and the M/V *Stella Australis.* Departures are Saturday from Punta Arenas and Wednesday from Ushuaia, from late September to April. See "Cruising from Punta Arenas to Ushuaia," below.

cruising FROM PUNTA ARENAS TO USHUAIA

Crucero Australis operates an unforgettable journey between Punta Arenas and Ushuaia aboard its ships, the M/V *Mare Australis* and the M/V *Via Australis* or the new M/V *Stella Australis*. This cruise takes passengers to remote coves and narrow channels and fiords in Tierra del Fuego, and then heads into the Beagle Channel, stopping on Isla Navarino and later Ushuaia, Argentina. There's also a stop at the absolute end of the world, Cape Horn, although the chances that you will be able to get off the boat and touch *tierra firma* there aren't likely, due to notorious winds. The trip can be done as a 4-night one-way from Punta Arenas or a 3-night one-way journey from Ushuaia. I recommend that you take just the one-way journey, ideally departing Punta Arenas, leaving you to explore a new city and then travel by air or land from there. Compared to the many massive cruise ships plowing these waters, this is an intimate, more adventurous journey, allowing you to access more solitary routes. Daily excursions include visits to penguin colonies and glaciers, always by zodiac boats. The accommodations are comfortable, ranging from suites to simple cabins. All-inclusive, per-person prices (excluding alcoholic beverages) range from $1,050 to $2,350 one-way from Punta Arenas and $1,400 to $3,136 one-way from Ushuaia. It's not really worth it to pay extra for an upper deck; second-floor berths are the most stable, quiet, and comfortable. This cruise operates from late September to April. For reservations or information, contact their U.S. offices in Miami at 4014 Chase Ave., Ste. 215 (© **877/678-3772**).

GETTING AROUND

BY CAR   Everything in and around Ushuaia is easily accessible via bus, taxi, or an inexpensive shuttle or tour service. Ushuaia's taxi drivers must be the nation's friendliest, and they're fonts of information concerning the region. The multitude of excursion options obviates the need for a car, though if you are staying at a hotel outside downtown (and many of the best are too far to walk), a car will certainly free you up for dining and exploring options. **Hertz,** San Martín 245, has an office in town right next to the Crucero Australis office and another at the airport (© **2901/437529;** www.hertz.com). **Avis,** Godoy 46, drops its prices for multiday rentals (© **2901/436665;** www.avis.com); **Cardos Rent A Car** is at Av. San Martín 845 (© **2901/436388**). Rates start at $55 a day in high season. Most of them rent 4×4 Jeeps with unlimited mileage. If you wish to cross into Chile at San Sebastian, you will need a special-permission document costing $50. Rental car companies can provide the document; request it when booking.

VISITOR INFORMATION

The **Subsecretaría de Turismo** has two very helpful and well-stocked offices on Av. San Martín 674 (© **2901/432000;** fax 2901/434550) and another on the tourism Pier, Maipú 505 (© **2901/437666;** fax 2901/430694; www.turismoushuaia.com). They also have a counter at the airport which is open Monday to Friday according to flight arrival times. The offices are open Monday through Friday from 8am to 10pm, Saturdays and Sundays from 9am to 8pm. For information on visiting Tierra del Fuego National Park, visit the helpful national park administration office at Av. San Martín 1395 (© **2901/421315;** Mon–Fri 9am–3pm).

[FastFACTS] USHUAIA

Currency Exchange
Thaler, Av. San Martín 209 (☏ **2901/421911**), is an old-fashioned currency-exchange house. **Banco Patagonia,** Avenida San Martín and Godoy (☏ **2901/432080**), and **Banco de la Nación,** Av. San Martín 190 (☏ **2901/422896**); both exchange currency and have 24-hour ATMs.

Laundry Soles del Milenio, Gobernador Paz 219 (☏ **2901/424108**) offers same-day service and is open Monday through Saturday from 10am to 6pm.

Pharmacy Andina, Av. San Martín 638 (☏ **2901/}423431**), is the most centrally located.

Post Office Correo Argentino is at Avenida San Martín and Godoy (☏ **2901/421347**), open Monday through Friday from 9am to 7pm, Saturday from 9am to 1pm; the private postal company **OCA** is at Maipú and Avenida 9 de Julio (☏ **2901/424729**), open Monday through Saturday from 9am to 6pm.

Travel Agency & Credit Cards American Express travel and credit card services are provided by **All Patagonia,** Juana Fadul 60 (☏ **2901/433622**).

Where to Stay

It seems that anyone with a large house in Ushuaia is offering rooms, and the plethora of hotels, B&Bs, and cabins can be bewildering. Nevertheless, accommodations here are not cheap, and price is often not indicative of quality. It's best to shop around before committing to lodgings. There is also a **Sheraton Hotel** being built on the hillside, as well as a handful of other important new hotel investments planned (but as of press time still under wraps).

VERY EXPENSIVE

Las Hayas Resort Hotel For years, this was the top hotel in Ushuaia, on the road to Glacier Martial. It has traditionally welcomed all VIPs and major events and has appealed to those looking for old-world elegance. But times have changed, and the market is much more competitive. Las Hayas needs to up the ante if it wants to stay on top. The best part of staying here may be the view out your window. It's at least 3km (1¾ miles) from downtown, however, so you'll need to take a cab, hike, or use one of the hotel's summer-only transfer shuttles. Service is mediocre, formal, and fails to provide any kind of special welcome. The lounge stretches the length of the building; here you'll find a clubby bar, formal restaurant, and fireside sitting area. The rooms are decorated with rich tapestries, upholstered walls, and big and bright bathrooms. A nice indoor pool and spa is tucked out back in the forest. The owner of Las Hayas promotes an air of old-fashioned genteel exclusivity, making the hotel less than entirely suitable for children. Le Martial, the gourmet restaurant on-site, changes its menu weekly but specializes in black hake and king crab dishes. Breakfasts are standard, and the public space could use a freshening up. Still, rooms are large and bright, if not modern and deluxe.

Av. Luis Fernando Martial 1650, Ushuaia. ☏ **2901/430710.** Fax 2901/430719. www.lashayashotel.com. 102 units. $253 double; $338–$510 suites. Rates include buffet breakfast. AE, DC, MC, V. **Amenities:** 2 restaurants; bar; lounge; concierge; exercise room; access to nearby golf club; Jacuzzi; massage; indoor pool; room service; sauna; squash court. *In room:* TV, hair dryer.

EXPENSIVE

Hotel Lennox This recently renovated hotel exudes style and modernity. In the lobby, floor lighting illuminates tall, mirrored walls, punctuated by dark-rock tiles and light-wood paneling. Modish sofas, in moody tones of black and gray, look out onto busy Avenida San Martín. On the third floor, a comfortable and spacious communal room houses more sofas and a widescreen TV. The dining room has elegant, urbane furnishings in red and brown. Here you can enjoy a continental breakfast while taking in fantastic views of the bay. Rooms are small but adequate, and some of the sparkling bathrooms have a Jacuzzi. Be sure to ask for a room at the back facing the bay. The street side can be noisy, and the inward facing rooms (facing a tiny, somewhat over-stated "Zen garden") can lack privacy. In general, staff members are very friendly, and the hotel's contemporary feel is very refreshing and reassuring. Still, they've tripled the price over the past few years, and service hasn't improved accordingly.

Av. San Martín 776, Ushuaia. ©/fax **2901/436430.** www.lennoxhotel.com.ar. 30 units. $205 double. Rates include continental breakfast. AE, DC, MC, V. **Amenities:** Restaurant; room service; Wi-Fi. *In room:* Jacuzzi (in some rooms).

Las Lengas Hotel Back on the scene after a smart renovation, this hotel has the most modern feel of all the multistory properties in town. The look is sparse and natural, almost Scandinavian. The views of the Beagle Channel are maximized every-where from the lobby to the restaurant to the guest rooms, so be sure to ask for a water view. Rooms are not large, but they are comfortable and colorful; the hotel makes extra ecological efforts like water conservation. The location is midway between downtown and the more remote places (like Los Cauquenes and Tierra de Leyendas), a decent 15-minute walk into the heart of the city. Staff is friendly with a good level of English.

Goleta Florencia 1722, Ushuaia. © **2901/423366.** www.laslengashotel.com.ar. 46 units. $180 double. Rates include continental breakfast. AE, MC, V. **Amenities:** Restaurant; bar; free Wi-Fi.

Los Cauquenes Resort & Spa ★★ ☺ Ushuaia's most casual upscale hotel has an outstanding location, perched right on the Beagle Channel and meters from the beach. The red-roofed, beechwood, and stone-walled main building looks like a mountain lodge. The lobby has massive windows, comfortable, oversize wool and leather furniture, and a giant fireplace. For a hotel with only 54 rooms, there are a lot of amenities here, including the area's top spa and an acclaimed restaurant. Opt for one of the superior rooms, which are large and have bright windows overlooking the channel—standards often have little or no view. Suites have wooden terraces. All have modern bathrooms with marble and stainless steel fixtures, lush robes and towels, and flatscreen TVs. The staff tries hard to exceed your expectations. It is far from town though. There are 10 daily transfers into town, although after a busy day explor-ing the area, you may not want to budge. Six cabins work well for families on extended stays.

Calle Reinamora 3462, Ushuaia. © **2901/441300** or 11/4735-2648 in Buenos Aires. www.loscauquenes. com. 60 units. $315–$445 double; $541 junior suite with ocean view. AE, MC, V. **Amenities:** Restaurant; wine bar; babysitting; gym; indoor/outdoor pool; spa; Wi-Fi. *In room:* Satellite TV, minibar.

Tierra de Leyendas ★★ Maia Muriel and Sebastian Garcia Cosoleto met while working at the Marriott in Buenos Aires. They married and traveled the world before opening Tierra de Leyendas in Ushuaia, a hotel that caters to hedonists, foodies, and coastal walkers. It's been a huge success. Sebastian's experience as a trained chef and Maia's background in the hotel business go to good use here. The entire bottom floor is open plan, comprising a lounge room, restaurant, and reception with huge windows overlooking the bay. The attention to detail is incredible; they comb the sheepskin seat covers every day, and deliver with breakfast every morning a little note explaining a local anecdote (this is what the legends in the hotel's name refers to). The dining room tables are mini-museum exhibits, with indigenous arrowheads and flints beneath the glass dining surface. The five rooms are all named after a local fable. Ask for the Los Yamanas room, with its stunning view and incredibly relaxing, giant hot tub. Some rooms have only showers. The small restaurant is open to the public Monday to Saturday, so if you do decide to lodge elsewhere, at least book a table here to experience Sebastian's excellent cooking. Located on the outskirts of town, it's a $5 taxi ride into town.

Calle Sin Nombre 2387, Ushuaia. © **2901/443565.** www.tierradeleyendas.com.ar. 5 units. $169 double. AE, MC, V. **Amenities:** Restaurant; bar; DVD library; room service; Wi-Fi. *In room:* TV/DVD player, Jacuzzi.

MODERATE

Alto Andino Urban Lodge 🛍   Probably the best value in all of Ushuaia can be found at this new apart-hotel. Funky modern art welcomes you in the lobby. Then head up the escalator to one of the 10 standard double rooms. For just a bit more, you can get a suite, which comes with a sofa bed and kitchenette. All decor is done in shades of rusted red and chocolate brown. Ask for a third-floor room for the best views. Breakfast is served in a sunny, bright space on the top floor. Out back is their backpackers' hostel called Freestyle.

Gobernador Pax 868, Ushuaia. © **2901/430920.** www.altoandinohotel.com. 18 units. $155 double; $170 suite; $180 apt for 4. AE, MC, V. **Amenities:** Bar; Wi-Fi. *In room:* Minibar.

The House ★   This stylish, green-roofed boutique hotel (formerly known as Macondo) has a young, bohemian feel. Wall-to-wall Georgian windows surround the common room, with a black stone floor and colorful, cubed armchairs. The spacious, loftlike bedrooms have red roof beams and rafters, clean cream-colored linens and walls dotted with red and orange accents. Bathrooms are fair-size, with shower enclosures and wooden platforms. Stairs are in the style of a fire escape, leading you down to a common room with a giant fireplace and comfortable couches. Simple, modern, and attractive, this hotel also boasts a good central location with a great view.

Gobernador Paz 1410, Ushuaia. ©/fax **2901/437576.** www.thehouseushuaia.com. 7 units. $95 double. Rates include continental breakfast. AE, DC, MC, V. **Amenities:** Room service; free Internet and Wi-Fi; TV room.

INEXPENSIVE

Galeazzi–Basily B&B 🍴   Long before there were giant cruise ships docking at the port, Frances Basily and Alejandro Galeazzi have been receiving a steady stream of guests, some lodging in the family home and others in some well-appointed cabins out back known as the "Aves del Sur" cabins. The house itself is tall, with a picket fence out front guarding a small forest of beech trees. A wooden walkway leads you into a comfortable, if somewhat worn, suburban home of white walls, plants, family photos, and a long dining room table. The house rooms are small and basic and a little gloomy. They offer two single beds and a shared bathroom. The cabins are much more spacious with lots more light. Yet you do not come here for luxury—what you get instead is a much more elusive sense of welcome and belonging. Everyone in the family speaks perfect English, and they're all very engaging and helpful. The kitchen is accessible any time of day or night, as is the living room sofa and TV, and Internet is free.

Gob. Valdez 323, Ushuaia. ✆ **2901/423213.** www.avesdelsur.com.ar. 5 shared units. $50 double; $95 cabin for up to 4. No credit cards. **Amenities:** Lounge/TV room; bike rental; free Internet; use of kitchen.

Where to Eat

In Ushuaia, king crab rules, and you'll find it on all menus, along with other excellent seafood dishes, such as sea bass, hake, and mussels. In general, dining out is much pricier here compared to the rest of the country. A dozen cafes are on San Martín, between Godoy and Rosas; all of them offer sandwiches and quick meals. The most popular among them is **Tante Sara,** Av. San Martín 137 (✆ **2901/435005**), where a two-course meal of salad and ravioli or gnocchi costs $8. A block away, the Tante Sara Café, Av. San Martín 701 (✆ **2901/433710**), is the place to sip coffee with locals in the afternoon. A few of the hotels in the area also have fine restaurants, including **Los Cauquenes Resort & Spa** (✆ **2901/441300;** reviewed above) and **Tierra de Leyendas** (✆ 2901/443565; reviewed above). It is wise to book ahead.

Chez Manu 🖿 SEAFOOD/FRENCH   The Chez Manu offers great food and even better views, seen through a generous supply of windows. A French expat, Emmanuel Herbin, runs the place. True to his roots, he has crafted a French-style menu that optimizes the abundance of fresh local ingredients, most of them coming from the sea. Start with a sample of the house-smoked fish. Main entrees include black hake cooked with anise and herbs, or Fuegian lamb. Before taking your order, ask your server to describe the catch of the day, usually a cold-water fish from the bay, such as *abadejo* or *merluza* from Chile. Side dishes include a delicious eggplant ratatouille, made with extra-virgin olive oil and herbes de Provence. Service is so-so and the decor could use an update. The wine list includes several excellent regional dry whites.

Av. Luis Fernando Martial 2135. ✆ **2970/432253.** www.chezmanu.com. Reservations recommended. Main courses $16–$29. AE, MC, V. Daily noon–2pm and 8–11:30pm.

Kalma Resto ★★ CONTEMPORARY ARGENTINE   Since it opened in early 2010, everybody in Ushuaia has been talking about this chef-owned and -operated bistro. Certainly, there's a unique passion for cuisine and dining, and unlike Chez Manu, Kalma is walkable from downtown. It's small and service is very personable; chef Jorge Monopoli will even give you a tour of the kitchen if you ask. The dishes are small and intricate, with details like edible flowers and foamed reductions. The menu will please locavores and vegetarians as it's heavy on local specialties like octopus, black hake, lamb, and sea bass (here with tomato sauce and spinach gnocchi). Non–meat eaters will appreciate intricately prepared pastas, soups, and salads. Desserts include ice cream with figs, chocolate, and olive oil.

Antartida Argentina 57. ✆ **2901/425786.** Reservations recommended. Main courses $15–$22. AE, MC, V. Tues–Sun 7:30–11:30pm.

Kaupé Restaurant ★★ ARGENTINE FINE DINING   This has long been considered one of the best restaurants in Ushuaia, having built an award-winning reputation on its superb cuisine and lovely view. Lately, portions have become smaller and prices bigger. The menu is limited, but the offerings are delicious. Don't start your meal without ordering a sumptuous appetizer of king crab wrapped in a crepe and bathed in saffron sauce. Main courses include scallops, fish, and beef; sample items include tenderloin beef in a plum sauce or a subtly flavored sea bass steamed in parchment paper. The extensive gourmet wine list ranges in price from $14 to $58; there's also wine by the glass. Finish it all off with a sorbet in a frothy champagne sauce. Kaupé's dining area is cozy, and candlelit tables exude romance.

Roca 470. © **2901/422704.** www.kaupe.com.ar. Reservations recommended on weekends. Main courses $15–$27. AE, MC, V. Mon–Sat 8:30–11pm.

Maria Lola Restó ★ ☺ ARGENTINE This laid-back, relaxing restaurant is situated on a hill, 4 blocks from main street San Martín. In a modern house with large windows, it overlooks the bay, with the town's clapboard church in the foreground. The dining area is large and spacious, and the decor is modern if a little bare. The clientele is a healthy mix of locals of various backgrounds and visitors. There's a kids' menu, so families come for the early sitting (before 9pm). All come for the seafood menu, which includes the ubiquitous king crab, homemade pasta, and enormous desserts of cream and fresh fruit. A more recent addition includes a wine list and sommelier. Maria Lola may not leave you speechless gastronomically, but it makes for very pleasant evening dining. Its charm lies in its understatement.

Deloqui 1048. © **2901/421185.** www.marialolaresto.com.ar. Reservations recommended. Main courses $12–$18. AE, MC, V. Mon–Sat noon–3pm and 7pm–midnight.

Parrilla la Rueda ★ PARRILLA There is a long line of *parrillas* along the far east end of San Martín. All offer "all you can eat" buffet-style service. This is the best of the bunch. Lamb, beef, and chicken are all slow-roasted on the grill and then offered table by table. The meat is complemented by a large salad bar and friendly, unpretentious service from people who honestly care that you enjoy your meal. Eat as much as you like for $15, with a dessert like homemade *flan* included.

San Martín 193. © **2901/436540.** Main courses $13–$19. MC, V. Daily noon–11pm.

Ramos General ★★ COFFEEHOUSE/DELI This quirky, renovated general store is over 100 years old and loaded with personality. It's been lovingly and passionately restored; there are pieces of Ushuaia's amazing heritage all around. A piano sits in the corner, along with old-fashioned typewriters. Situated in front of the port, the restaurant's menu offers generous king crab salads, and outstanding breads and sweet treats by their fantastic French baker. Recommended are the panini, fisherman's salad, and the superb cheese boards. It makes for the perfect midmorning coffee stop, afternoon teatime, or last stop on land before boarding a cruise. Bring a book and relax. In keeping with its old-world vibe, the coffeehouse also serves as a bakery, a chic ladies fashion store, and bar with draft beer.

Maipú 749. © **2901/424317.** www.ramosgeneralesushuaia.com. Main courses $7–$15. AE, MC, V. Daily 9:30am–12:30am.

Tía Elvira ARGENTINE BISTRO Tía Elvira is part restaurant, part mini-museum, with walls adorned by antique photos of the region and various artifacts collected by the owners during their 30-plus years in business. The menu is aimed squarely at tourists, featuring fairly straightforward Argentine dishes such as grilled meats, but the restaurant serves mostly simple seafood preparations, including king crab, trout, sea bass, and cod in a variety of sauces, such as Provençal or Parmesan. Homemade pastas include lasagna and stuffed cannelloni. The restaurant is directly on the waterfront, with up-close views of the canal and the pier. It's packed when cruise ships are in port.

Maipú 349. © **2901/424725.** www.tiaelvira.com. Main courses $13–$28. MC, V. Daily noon–3pm and 7–11:30pm.

Volver ARGENTINE   It is worth stopping by just to see this crazy, kitschy restaurant on the waterfront. Volver is inside a century-old yellow tin-pan house. Old newspapers and signs wallpaper the interiors, which are also packed with oddball memorabilia, photos, football shirts, gadgets, spider crabs swimming in a tank, trinkets, and antiques. The food is decent and includes regional dishes such as trout, crab, and lamb, plus homemade pastas. King crab comes a dozen different ways, in soups, casseroles, or with a side sauce. Desserts are primarily crepes with local fruit such as *calafate*. Service is a bit hit-or-miss, and the toilets ought to be better cleaned.

Maipú 37. ℂ **2901/423977.** Main courses $12–$21. MC, V. Tues–Sun noon–3pm and daily 7:30pm–midnight.

Seeing the Sights

Because Ushuaia rests on a steep hill, most businesses, traffic, and people seem to converge on the main street that lies near the bottom, Avenida San Martín. You will soon tire of walking up and down this busy thoroughfare, however, so it's worth making the effort to climb up and explore the city's other big streets, Deloqui or Gobernador Paz. The best way to get a feel for the landscape is to walk to the city park and up to the **Punto Panorámico,** a great lookout point, from where you get sweeping views of the city and the channel. The trail, which begins at the southwestern end of Avenida San Martín, is free. The port area has been fixed up significantly, making it more pedestrian and tourist friendly.

Acuario de Ushuaia ★ 🛍   If the idea of jumping into the frigid waters of the channel is out of the question, visit this basic but interesting aquarium on the east side of town for a look at what it's like under the surface of the Beagle Channel. Be warned: You might be charmed by the king crabs and refuse to eat one again. Admission is on the steep side, but the aquarium gets top marks for environmental awareness and was born from local, grass-roots efforts, receiving no government funds. Except for injured animals, all specimens are returned to the water after a few months on display. You'll want to take a taxi, as it's on the channel, 3km (2 miles) east of downtown.

Av. Perito Moreno 2564, 3km (2 miles) from town. ℂ **2901/422980.** Admission $11 adults, $5 children 4–16, free for children 3 and under; group discounts available. Daily noon–8pm.

Glacier Martial/Aerosilla 🛍   Glacier Martial is a pleasant excursion that sits in Ushuaia's backyard. Avenida Luis Fernando Martial winds 7km (4¼ miles) up from town to the base of a beautiful mountain amphitheater. From here, a chairlift takes you on a thrilling ride to the small Glacier Martial ($12). It's a long walk up the road, and no buses can take you there. Visitors usually hire a taxi for $12 up to the lift's base and walk all the way back down, or arrange for the driver to pick them up later. At the base of the chairlift, don't miss a stop at **La Cabaña** ★ (ℂ **2901/424257**), an excellent teahouse with a wraparound outdoor deck and mouthwatering cakes and pastries.

Av. Luis Fernando Martial, 7km (4¼ miles) from town. ℂ **2901/15-512204** (mobile). Admission $12 adults, free for children 9 and under. Daily 10am–4:15pm.

Museo del Fin de Mundo ★   The main room of this museum displays an assortment of Indian hunting tools and colonial maritime instruments. There's also a natural history display of stuffed birds and a "grandfather's room" set up to resemble an old general store, packed with antique products. But the strength of this museum is its 60 history and nature videos available for viewing, and its reference library with more than 3,650 volumes, including a fascinating birth record. Its store has an excellent range of books about Patagonia for sale.

Maipú 173. © **2901/421863.** www.museodelfindelmundo.org.ar. Admission $8 adults, $2 students, free for children 13 and under. Oct–April daily 9am–8pm; May–Sept Mon–Sat noon–7pm. Guided tours at 10am and 2 and 5pm.

Museo Marítimo y Presidio de Ushuaia ★★ 🔲 Ushuaia was populated primarily by the penal colony set up here in the late 1800s for hundreds of Argentina's most dangerous criminals. The rehabilitation system consisted of forced labor to build piers and buildings, and creative workshops for teaching carpentry, music, tailoring, and other trades—all of which, coincidentally, fueled the local economy. The museum offers a fascinating look into prisoners' and prison workers' lives through interpretive displays and artifacts. Here you can dwell in the cells of mass murderers and teenage anarchists and read about their unenviable existence in what must have been a grim place. The on-site restaurant serves "prison" meals and other theme items. The maritime museum displays famous ships and shipwrecks from the area. It's an outstanding museum.

Yaganes and Gobernador Paz. © **2901/437481.** www.museomaritimo.com. Admission $13 adults, free for children 11 and under. Daily 9am–8pm. Guided tours at 11:30am and 6pm.

OUTDOOR ACTIVITIES

BOATING The best way to explore the Beagle Channel is by boat. Numerous companies offer a variety of trips, usually in modern catamarans with excellent guides. Many of them run kiosks near the pier; you'll see a cluster of them by the water. The most popular excursion is a half-day cruise of the Beagle Channel to view sea lions, penguins, and more. **Catamaranes Canoero** (© 2901/433893; www.catamaranescanoero.com.ar) has a variety of options ranging from 3 hours to 9 hours, on four different boats. Their full-day trip stops at Estancia Harberton, returning to Ushuaia via bus. **Motonave Barracuda** (© 2901/437066) leaves every afternoon for its 3-hour trip around the channel for $35 per person, stopping at Isla de Lobos, Isla de Pájaros, and a lighthouse. **Motovelero Tres Marías** (© 2901/421897; www.tresmariasweb.com) also leaves twice daily and sails to the same location; they accommodate a maximum of nine guests at a time, and they add an hour-long walk, crab fishing, cognac, and an underwater camera to the package, for $36 per person. From November through February, most companies visit the teeming penguin colony and pull the boats up to the shore where travelers can close in tight to watch these marvelous animals. It's roughly $75 per person. **Pira Tur,** B. Yaganes Casa 127 (© **2901/435557** [mobile]; www.piratour.com.ar), offers walking tours onto the penguin colony with controlled groups. **Motovelero Patagonia Explorer** (© **2901/15-465842** [mobile]; www.patagoniaadvent.com.ar) has an 18-passenger maximum and leaves daily; it visits the sea lion colony and includes a walk on the Isla Bridges for $46. This company also works with the Aventuras Isla Verde in the park for a full-day sail; inquire at their kiosk. **Ushuaia Boating,** Gob. Godoy 190 (© **2901/15-609030;** www.ushuaiaboating.com.ar), operates a small, speedy zodiac ferry to Chilean Puerto Williams. It costs $240 round-trip.

FISHING For a fishing license and information, go to the **Club de Pesca y Caza,** Av. San Martín 818 (no phone). It costs about $15 for foreigners per day. Keen fishers need only book a week at one of Tierra del Fuego's incomparable fly-fishing lodges to find heaven (see "Monster Trout on the Río Grande," below).

HIKING One of the best mountain guides in the area is Juan Pablo Terrado, who runs **Gotama Expediciones** (© **2901/15-550807;** www.gotama-expediciones.com). The company offers guided half- and full-day hiking outings, multiday treks deep into the mountains of Tierra del Fuego, even mountain biking and sea kayak trips. Trips can also include transportation, meals, and accommodations.

SKIING   Ushuaia's ski resort, **Cerro Castor** (📞 2901/499301; www.cerrocastor. com), is surprisingly good, with more than 400 skiable hectares (988 acres), 15 runs, three quad chairs and one double, a lodge/restaurant, and a slopeside bar. Day tickets cost $30 to $47, depending on low or high season. The resort is open from June 15 to October 15. To get there, take the shuttle buses **Pasarela** (📞 2901/433712) or **Bella Vista** (📞 2901/443161); the fare is $15.

TOUR OPERATORS

One of the better agencies in town, **All Patagonia Viajes y Turismo,** Juana Fadul 60 (📞 2901/433622; www.allpatagonia.com), is the local American Express travel representative. It acts as a clearinghouse; if they don't offer a trip themselves, they'll arrange an excursion with other outfitters. They can also reserve excursions in other destinations in Argentina and Chile. All Patagonia offers three glacier walks for those in good physical condition, impressive scenic flights over Tierra del Fuego ($95 per person for 30 min.), and treks and drives in its Land Rover with nature guides. **Catamaranes Canoero** (📞 2901/433893; www.catamaranescanoero.com.ar) arranges a bus and boat trip to Estancia Harberton and the penguin colony ($60 per person), and they are one of the few agencies to operate afternoon tours of the national park. It is a very good company to approach if you're not sure what you want. **Canal Fun & Nature,** Rivadavía 82 (📞 2901/437395; www.canalfun.com), specializes in "unconventional tourism." It's a fun company of passionate Ushuaia folks who should be your choice if you're hankering for some hair-raising adventure. They staff excellent guides who provide 4WD trips and walks culminating with a barbecue. The company also leads kayaking and nighttime beaver-watching trips, and they'll custombuild a trip for you. They run private tours only on request. **Rumbo Sur,** Av. San Martín 350 (📞 2901/422275; www.rumbosur.com.ar), and **Tolkeyen Patagonia Turismo,** San Martín 1267 (📞 2901/437073; www.tolkeyenpatagonia.com), are two more conventional operators that deal with larger groups and arrange more classic excursions, such as a city tour and guided visits to the national park and Lagos Escondido and Fagnano.

Ushuaia After Dark

Nocturnal activities are somewhat sedate in this city. That is not to say it is completely dead, however, and there are some good bars to help you wash down that king crab dinner with some locally brewed beer. Two to try are **Dreamland,** 9 de Julio and Deloqui (📞 2901/421246), and **Dublin Irish Pub,** 9 de Julio 168 (📞 2901/430744). A local tango club has regular shows throughout the year at the **Milonga del Fin del Mundo,** Maipú 1210 (no phone).

Café Latino   With a long list of cocktails and a packed agenda of live music and DJs on weekends, the current incarnation of Café Latino is going strong. There's Argentine rock (known as "Rock Nacional") on Sunday, karaoke on Thursday, and a local R&B band most Saturdays. Whenever there's a touring band passing through town (which unfortunately doesn't happen too often down here at the end of the world), they'll usually be given the mic here. Walanika 140. 📞 **2901/424446.**

Kuar   With its cushioned mini-amphitheater facing a giant, shoreline view of the bay, Kuar is certainly the most avant-garde of Ushuaia's nightspots. The rustic wooden counter goes well with the ironclad menus, and the decor is a hip arrangement of

A Ride in the Park

If you don't feel like walking but still want to take in the sights at Parque Nacional Tierra Del Fuego, you can ride **El Tren del Fin del Mundo,** a vapor locomotive replica of the train used to shuttle prisoners to the forest to chop wood (☎ 2901/431600; www.trendelfindelmundo.com.ar). It is very touristy and may put you to sleep. The train departs from its station (with souvenir shop and cafe) near the park entrance three times daily. Just go one-way; a return trip is tediously slow. And don't bother with first class—it's not worth the light snack and souvenir. The 1-hour, 50-minute round-trip journey costs $28 for adults, $50 for first class, $7.50 for passengers 4 to 14, and free for children 3 and under.

chunky wooden tables, faux leather furniture, and colored-glass beading. The bar brews its own beer, and patrons can view the fermenting tanks through a glass panel beneath the dining room. There is decent restaurant adjacent. But you'll want to make the effort later in the evening for regular live music and theater performances. The bar is located 2km (1¼ miles) east of the city center. It's open Tuesday to Sunday from 5pm until 2am. Av. Perito Moreno 2232. ☎ **2901/437396.**

EXCURSIONS AROUND USHUAIA

One of the most intriguing destinations around Ushuaia is the **Estancia Harberton** (www.estanciaharberton.com), the first ranch founded in Tierra del Fuego. Now run as a museum, it affords a fascinating glimpse into the area's pioneering past. The tour begins with a walk through a small nature reserve, where the guides discuss, in good English, the different plants from the area. The *estancia's* missionary founders are buried in the graveyard, and nearby are some reconstructed houses used by the original natives. Just as interesting is the mothballed shearing shed, a marvelous step back in time to when this was a thriving sheep farm. There is also a curious natural history museum of marine life bones and fossils. (*Note:* To visit the museum, you must make reservations in advance; it's not included in the ordinary tour.) The ranch is located on the shore of the Beagle Channel, accessible by road (it's 85km/53 miles east of Ushuaia) or boat; entrance $5. Most travel agencies in town provide transportation to the *estancia,* 90km (56 miles) from Ushuaia, for an average cost of $65 per person, plus the entrance fee, provided you are among a group of four or more. Roughly from October to April, several tour companies offer a catamaran ride to the *estancia,* a 6-hour excursion for $85 per person; try **Catamaranes Canoero** (☎ **2901/433893;** www.catamaranescanoero.com.ar), the only agency that lets you stop for more than an hour at the *estancia.* Tour groups will also arrange a boat excursion to a **penguin colony** from the *estancia,* an add-on excursion that costs about $67 per person.

After the turnoff for Estancia Harberton, RN 3 begins to descend down to **Lago Escondido,** a beautiful lake about 60km (37 miles) north of Ushuaia. It provides a quiet spot for relaxation or for fishing the mammoth trout that live in the lake.

North of Ushuaia and in the middle of the island of Tierra del Fuego, the landscape changes. Icy mountains give way to dry rolling hills. A massive lake, **Lago Fagnano,** dominates. It almost slices the island in half. This is a nice place for a day trip—the weather is almost always sunnier at Tolhuin, the sleepy village on the east side of Lago Fagnano. The easiest option is to rent a car and drive yourself here. The nicest hotel, by far, is red-roofed **Hosteria Kaiken,** RN 3 Km 2942

(© **02901/492372**). It's 100km (62 miles) from Ushuaia. A visit to Tolhuin is not complete without a visit to the local bakery **Panadería La Union,** Cerro Jerujupen 450 (© **2901/492202**), for empanadas and pastries.

PARQUE NACIONAL TIERRA DEL FUEGO

Parque Nacional Tierra del Fuego was created in 1960 to protect a 63,000-hectare (155,610-acre) chunk of Patagonian wilderness that includes mighty peaks, crystalline rivers, black-water swamps, and forests of *lenga*, or deciduous beech. Only 2,000 hectares (4,940 acres) are designated recreation areas, some of which offer a chance to view dams built by the beavers that were introduced to Tierra del Fuego in the 1950s. Another eyebrow-raiser is the multitude of rabbits that roam the park.

It's the only Argentine national park with both mountains and a maritime coast, but chances are you won't be blown away by it if you've been traveling around southern Argentina or Chile. Much of the landscape is identical to Patagonia's thousands of kilometers of mountainous terrain, but it does afford a handful of easy and medium day hikes to let you stretch your legs, breathe some fresh air, take a boat ride, or bird-watch. In some areas, the road runs through thick beech forest and then abruptly opens into wide views of mountains, whose dramatic height can be viewed from sea level to more than 2,000m (6,560 ft.). Anglers can fish for trout here in the park but must first pick up a license at the **National Park Administration office,** Av. San Martín 1395 (© **2901/421315;** Mon–Fri 9am–3pm), in Ushuaia. The park service issues maps at the park entrance showing the walking trails here, ranging from 300m (984 ft.) to 8km (5 miles); admission into the park is $9. Parque Nacional Tierra del Fuego is 11km (6¾ miles) west of Ushuaia on RN 3. Camping in the park is free; there are no services, but potable water is available. At the end of the road to Lago Roca, there is a snack bar/restaurant. At Bahía Ensenada, you'll find boats that take visitors to Isla Redonda, where there are several walking trails. The cost is about $10, or $16 with a guide. All tour companies offer guided trips to the park. Trips last 4 hours and cost $40. If all you need is transportation there, call these shuttle bus companies: **Pasarela** (© 2901/433712) or **Patagonia Transfers** (© 2901/445486). The round-trip cost $15. Buses leave from Avenida Maípu in front of the main pier.

PUERTO WILLIAMS, CHILE

Puerto Williams is the southernmost town in the world, though it functions primarily as a naval base with a population of fewer than 2,100 residents. The town occupies the northern shore of Isla Navarino in the Beagle Channel, an altogether enchanting location framed by towering granite needles called the Navarino's Teeth. It's much more wild, remote, and undiscovered than Ushuaia, its Argentine neighbor across the channel. Getting here has become much easier now thanks to a new twice-daily service from Ushuaia (see "Getting There," below), but that doesn't ensure stress-free travel—there's still a good chance you'll get stuck here due to bad weather that rules out boat or plane travel. There are some outstanding hiking trails; some say it's set to be Chile's next Torres del Paine (p. 388).

The Yamana culture, which so perplexed the first Europeans in their ability to withstand their harsh environment with little clothing, is long gone; but visitors may still view the last vestiges of their settlements and a well-designed anthropological museum

monster trout ON THE RIO GRANDE

The north of Tierra del Fuego is a brown plain of gentle, undulating hills and meandering rivers, punctuated by the occasional lonely *estancia*. It is a serene and desolate place without so much as a tree or a hedge for miles. Indeed, for many years, the only things you could find here were hardy ranchers, thousands of sheep, and wild herds of graceful guanacos.

One of those hardy ranchers decided to introduce trout to the local rivers, with the aim of creating a diversion for himself and his fly-fishing friends. Little did John Goodall know, when he first slipped some fingerlings into the gentle waters of the Río Grande back in the 1930s, that the area would become world famous for its trout. It's now a place of annual pilgrimage for thousands of fly-fishing fanatics. The trout thrived on the river, but they did even better when they discovered the rich Antarctic fishing grounds out to sea. The **sea run brown trout** had found its ideal habitat and grown accordingly; anglers are astounded to find fish as heavy as 30 pounds. Many say the Río Grande is the world's top location for fishing this type of trout.

Overfishing depleted stocks in the mid-1980s. In response, several *estancias* that controlled the upper Río Grande introduced strict conservation methods and catch-and-release restrictions. Their methods worked, and now those same

estancias enjoy a steady stream of visitors seeking luxury accommodations on their fishing trips. The most famous is **La Villa de Estancia María Behety,** owned by the affable Alejandro Menéndez, who must be one of the few people in the world who can boast a river named after his family. The elegant family home, with a sparkling blue roof and commanding glass porch, has six opulent rooms. When guests are not fishing, they can partake of Alejandro's 10,000-bottle wine cellar and magnificent full-size snooker table—a relic of the Anglo-Argentines who used to work here. The property has another more modern but just as welcoming **Estancia María Behety Lodge** closer to the river that accommodates 12.

Estancia La Despedida is another popular fishing lodge. This ample log cabin offers very comfortable rooms and an inviting lounge with bar. The charismatic owner Danny Lajous speaks perfect English and regales guests with stories about the area.

For bookings from overseas, all three lodges work exclusively through a Californian outfitter called the **Fly Shop,** 4140 Churn Creek Rd., Redding, CA 96002 (✆ **800/669-3474** or 530/222-3555; fax 530/222-3572; www.thefly shop.com). All-inclusive 1-week packages start at $4,895 per person. All the *estancias* are close to the town of Río Grande, 180km (112 miles) north of Ushuaia.

in town. A new ferry service connects Puerto Williams with Ushuaia (see "Getting There," below) three times a week. There are also plans to improve the airport.

Getting There

BY AIR   Aerovías DAP, O'Higgins 891 (✆ **61/223340** in Punta Arenas, or 621051 in Puerto Williams; www.aeroviasdap.cl), runs a handful of flights per week from Punta Arenas.

BY BOAT   Fernández Campbell (✆ **2901/433232;** www.fernandezcampbell. com) offers two sailings per day Friday through Sunday throughout the summer for

$125 each way. You could combine a morning crossing with a day exploring the area and then depart on the 3pm boat back to Ushuaia. The passenger and cargo ferry **Transbordadora Austral Broom** offers cheaper passage to Puerto Williams, with a 34-hour journey from Punta Arenas (Av. Bulnes 05075; © **61/218100;** www.tabsa. cl). During the summer, the ferry leaves Punta Arenas four times a month on Wednesday and returns on Saturday; sleeping arrangements consist of reclining seats ($175 adult one-way) and bunks ($210 adult one-way). Kids receive a 50% discount. **SIM Expeditions,** in Puerto Williams (office located in the Coiron Guesthouse; © **61/621150;** www.simltd.com), is an interesting agency with a 6-passenger and a 12-passenger yacht that take visitors on 5- to 12-day journeys around Cape Horn and past the Darwin mountain range; contact the agency for prices. For general travel agency needs, including city tours, airline tickets, and hotel reservations, contact **Turismo Akainij,** Uspashum 156 (© **61/21327;** www.turismoakainij.cl).

Seeing the Sights

The **Museo Martín Gusinde,** Aragay 01 (© **61/621043**), is open Monday to Thursday and Saturday from 10am to 1pm and 3 to 6pm, and features a good collection of Yaghan and Yamana Indian artifacts, ethnographic exhibits, and stuffed birds and animals. The museum's docent is an anthropologist, naturalist, and all-around expert in the region; he is usually on hand to provide tours in the area. About 3km (1¾ miles) southeast of Puerto Williams on the main road, at the La Virgen cascade, is a medium-level **hiking trail** with an exhilarating, sweeping panorama of the Beagle Channel, the Dientes de Navarino mountain range, and Puerto Williams. The hike takes 3 hours round-trip. One of Chile's best backpacking trails, the **Dientes de Navarino Circuit ★★**, is here, thanks to an Australian who blazed the trail in 1991. The circuit is 53km (33 miles) in length, goes through very remote mountains, and takes at least 4 days to walk; the difficulty level is medium to high. The trail is open only from late November to April; otherwise, snow makes this walk dangerous and disorienting. The best map is JLM's *Tierra del Fuego* map, sold in most shops and bookstores.

Where to Stay & Eat

There's a new option in town that's filled the void for those looking for more than a bed with a pillow: **Hotel Lakutaia,** Seno Lauta s/n (© **61/621721;** www.lakutaia. cl), offers simple luxury in 24 rooms, all with private bathrooms. They offer all-inclusive 4-day package that include flights from Punta Arenas, trekking, sailing, horseback riding, and all meals starting at $1,970 per person. Otherwise, pickings are slim but reasonably priced. Basic, clean accommodations can be found at the **Hostería Camblor,** Calle Patricio Capdeville 41 (© **61/621033;** hosteriacamblor@hotmail.com), which has four simple, modern rooms for $42 or $58 per person (including meals and transfer). Some rooms come with a kitchenette. The Camblor also has a restaurant that occasionally serves as the local disco on Friday and Saturday nights, so noise could be a problem. Another simple but comfortable place is the **Hostal Coirón,** Ricardo Maragano 168 (© **61/621150;** hostalcoiron@tie.cl), with doubles for $50. For dining, try the convivial **Club de Yates Micalvi** (© **61/621042**), housed in an old supply ship that is docked at the pier. It serves as the meeting spot for an international crowd of adventurers sailing around Cape Horn. Or try **Los Dientes de Navarino** (© **61/621074**), on the plaza.

ANTARCTICA

The coldest spot on the planet is one of the hottest destinations for travelers seeking the next great adventure. Antarctica is its own continent, but the hook of the Antarctic Peninsula is closest to the tip of South America, and so the majority of visitors depart for Antarctica from Ushuaia.

Antarctica is home to exotic wildlife and landscapes that are equally savage and beautiful. Be prepared for ice like you've never seen it: monumental peacock-blue icebergs shaped in surreal formations, craggy glaciers that crash into the sea, sheer ice-encrusted walls that form magnificent canals, and jagged peaks that jut out of icy fields. A major highlight here is the penguins—colonies of several hundred thousand can be found nesting and chattering away throughout the area. Humpback, orca, and minke whales are often visible, nosing out of the frigid water, as are elephant, Weddell, leopard, and crabeater seals. Bird-watchers can spend hours studying the variety of unique seabirds that reside here, including petrels and albatrosses.

Most importantly, Antarctica sits at the end of the world, which is reason alone to compel many people to venture here. If you're itching to really get away from it all, you couldn't pick a better destination—the vastness here heightens the sensation of humanity's insignificance. Like the early explorers who first visited this faraway continent in the 1800s, travelers today revel in the chance to explore a pristine region where relatively few humans have stepped foot before. But Antarctica's remoteness comes with a toll: No matter how you get here, it's not cheap. The tediously long travel time, amid sometimes uncomfortable conditions, heightens the price that this region exacts from travelers. Nevertheless, many of Antarctica's 15,000 yearly visitors would agree that it's worth the effort.

A Brief History

The history of exploration and the discovery of the Antarctic continent are littered with claims, counterclaims, tall tales, intrigue, and suffering. Captain James Cook discovered the South Sandwich and South Georgia Islands in 1773 (a part of Antarctica, these islands are a British possession), but he never spotted the Antarctic continent. He did, however, set off a seal-hunting frenzy, after reporting the large colonies he found there; it's estimated that sealers eventually discovered around a third of the islands in the region. Two sealers were the first to actually step foot on the continent: the American John Davis, at Hughes Bay in 1821, and the British James Weddell, at Saddle Island in 1823. During a scientific expedition in 1840, the American navy lieutenant Charles Wilkes finally concluded that Antarctica was not a series of islands and ice packs, but rather a contiguous landmass.

The South Pole eluded explorers for another 90 years, until Norwegian Roald Admudsen and his well-prepared five-man team reached it on December 4, 1911. Amundsen's arrival at the pole accounted for one of history's most remarkable expeditions ever. His feat, however, was eclipsed by tragedy: His rival, the British captain Robert Scott, reached the pole 33 days later, only to find Amundsen's tent and a note. Scott and his party, already suffering from scurvy and exposure, froze to death on their return trip, just 18km (11 miles) from their ship.

No other destination has held such cachet for adventurous explorers. In 1915, the Irish explorer Ernest Shackleton deemed Antarctica "the last great journey left to man." Shackleton attempted to cross the Antarctic continent but never achieved his

Map of Antarctica

0 — 1000 mi
0 — 1000 km

ARGENTINA
CHILE
Ushuaia
Falkland Islands (U.K.)
Drake Passage
To South Georgia Island

SOUTH PACIFIC OCEAN

ANTARCTIC CIRCLE

Bellinghausen Sea

Palmer
Archipelago
GRAHAM LAND
S. Shetland Islands
ANTARCTIC PENINSULA
S. Orkney Islands

Amundsen Sea
ELLSWORTH LAND
Walgreen Coast
ELLSWORTH MTNS.
Vinson Massif
PALMER LAND

Weddell Sea

SOUTH ATLANTIC OCEAN

Ronne Ice Shelf
Mt. Sidley
MARIE BYRD LAND
Mt. Seelig
Filchner Ice Shelf
PENSACOLA MTNS.
COATS LAND

Ross Sea
LESSER ANTARCTICA

Ross Ice Shelf

SUNDAY / MONDAY
DATE LINE
Mt. Kirkpatrick
TRANSANTARCTIC MOUNTAINS
POLAR PLATEAU
South Pole
Meridian of Greenwich

C. Adare
VICTORIA LAND
Mt. Markham
ADÉLIE LAND

GREATER ANTARCTICA

QUEEN MAUD LAND

AVERAGE PERIMETER OF SEA ICE

GEORGE V LAND
Thickest Ice 15,670 feet (4785 m)
WILKES LAND
PR. CHARLES MTNS.
MAC ROBERTSON LAND
ENDERBY LAND

South Magnetic Pole

AMERICAN HIGHLAND

INDIAN OCEAN

QUEEN MARY LAND
Amery Ice Shelf
Shackleton Ice Shelf

goal: Pack ice trapped and sank his boat. The entire party miraculously survived for 1 year on a diet of penguin and seal, before Shackleton sailed to South Georgia Island in a lifeboat to get help.

Today, 27 nations send personnel to Antarctica to perform seasonal and year-round research. The population varies from 4,000 people in the summer to roughly 1,000 in the winter. A total of 42 stations operate year-round, and an additional 32 run in summer only. The stations study world climactic changes and can be instrumental in improving the environment. In 1985, for instance, researchers at the British Halley station discovered a growing hole in the ozone layer. This prompted the Montreal Protocol, in 1987, to cut back on CFC emissions.

Planning Your Trip to Antarctica

VISITOR INFORMATION

Numerous websites offer helpful information about Antarctica. A few of the best are:

o **www.iaato.org:** This is the official website of the International Association of Antarctica Tour Operators. It is important that your tour group be a member of the IAATO. Most cruise operators are members. Membership in the organization ensures a safe and environmentally responsible visit to Antarctica. Statistics, general information, and news can be found on this website.

o **www.discoveringantarctica.com:** This educational site has the nuts and bolts behind natural and human life on the frozen continent.

o **www.antarcticconnection.com:** This site offers travel information, tour operator links, and Antarctica-related items for sale, including maps and videos.

ENTRY REQUIREMENTS

No single country claims Antarctica as its territory, so visas are unnecessary. You will need a passport, however, for unscheduled stops and for your first stop in either Argentina or Chile (see chapter 3 for information about entry requirements).

WHEN TO GO

Tours to Antarctica are conducted between October and March—after March, temperatures dip to lows of –100°F (–38°C), and the sun disappears until September. The opposite is true of the summer months (Dec–Mar), and visitors can expect sunlight up to 18 to 24 hours a day, depending on where you are in Antarctica. Summer temperatures near the Antarctic Peninsula vary between lows of 5°F to 10°F (–15°C to –12°C), and highs of 35°F to 60°F (2°C–16°C).

What you see during your journey to Antarctica may depend on when you go. November is mating season for penguins and other birds, and visitors can view their offspring in December and January. The best months for whale-watching are February and March.

SAFETY

EXTREME WEATHER   Cold temperatures, the wind-chill factor, and perspiration conspire to prohibit the human body from keeping itself warm in Antarctica. Travelers need to outfit themselves in the highest-quality outdoor clothing available. Tour operators are constantly amazed at how under-prepared people can be when they visit Antarctica, and so they will provide clients with a packing checklist. Ask your tour company if it provides its guests with waterproof outerwear or if you are expected to bring your own. The thin ozone layer and the glare from snow, water, and ice make a high-factor sunscreen, a hat, and sunglasses imperative as well. Days during the Austral summer are long, with up to 20 hours of sunlight. You may be surprised at how sunny it is.

SPECIAL HEALTH CONCERNS   *Everyone* should bring anti–motion sickness medication on their trip to Antarctica. If you are suffering from a special health problem or taking prescription medication, bring a signed and dated letter from your physician for medical authorities, in case of an emergency. Delays of up to 4 weeks aren't uncommon on guided trips to the interior, so visitors should seriously consider the extremity of such a journey, submit themselves to a full medical exam before their departure, and bring the quantity of medication necessary for a long delay.

MEDICAL SAFETY & EVACUATION INSURANCE   All passenger ships have a physician on board in the event of a medical problem or emergency; however, passengers should discuss an evacuation policy with each operator. Emergency evacuation can be hindered by bad weather, and anyone with an unstable medical condition needs to keep this in mind. Also, check your health insurance to verify that it includes evacuation, because it can be unbelievably expensive. From the Shetland Islands alone, it costs $40,000 to evacuate one person.

Getting There

BY SHIP

Few would have guessed that the collapse of the Soviet Union in the early 1990s would spawn tourism in Antarctica. But when Russian scientific ship crews found themselves without a budget, they spruced up the ships' interiors and began renting the vessels out to tour operators on a rotating basis. These ships (as well as others that have since come on the market) are specially built for polar seas, complete with antiroll stabilizers and ice-strengthened hulls. A few of these ships have icebreakers that can chip through just about anything.

Before you go, it helps to know that a tour's itinerary is only a rough guide of what to expect on your journey. Turbulent weather and ice conditions can cause delays or detours. Schedules are always changing and adapting. Wildlife sightings may prompt your group to linger longer in one area than the next. The ship's crew and the expedition leader of your tour will keep you informed of any changes to the program.

Typical Itineraries

Tour companies offer roughly similar trajectories for cruises to Antarctica, with the exception of a few over-the-top cruises. (Got a month and $25,000? Then Quark Expeditions conducts a semi-circumnavigation of Antarctica.) Apart from the destinations listed below, cruises attempt to land at research stations when it's convenient. Most Antarctic cruises leave from Ushuaia, in Argentina, but a tiny fraction leave from New Zealand. Chile used to be a departure site for Antarctica, but few if any travelers now leave from Chile; those who do make the journey aboard a military ship. Plan to leave from Ushuaia; it's the fastest departure point.

Remember to factor in 2 days to cross the Drake Passage (4 days total for the return trip, if you're traveling to the Antarctic Peninsula). During this time, you won't do much more than hang out, relax, take part in educational lectures, and suffer through occasional bouts of seasickness. Conditions range from utterly terrible to gentle—the rare "Drake Lake" phenomenon. Cruises typically last 8 to 13 days for the Antarctic Peninsula, and 18 to 21 days for journeys that include the Subantarctic Islands. Seasoned travelers have frequently said that 8-day trips are not much of a value; consider tacking on 2 extra days for a 10-day trip.

THE ANTARCTIC PENINSULA This is the easiest site to visit in Antarctica. Due to its rich variety of wildlife and dramatic scenery, it makes for a magnificent introduction to the "White Continent." If you have a short amount of time and/or a limited budget, these trips are for you.

Most tours stop at the **South Shetland Islands.** Historically, sealers and whalers used these islands as a base; today they're home to research stations, colonies of elephant seals, and a variety of nesting penguins and seabirds. Popular sites here are **King Island, Livingston Island,** and **Deception Cove**—a collapsed, active volcanic crater with bubbling pools of thermal water.

Tours continue on to the western side of the Antarctic Peninsula, making stops to view wildlife such as Weddell and leopard seals and vast colonies of Adélie, chinstrap, and Gentoo penguins. At the peninsula, sites such as the **Lemaire** and **Neumayar** channels afford camera-worthy views of narrow, sheer-walled canals made of ice and rock. At **Paradise Harbor,** calving icebergs theatrically crash from the harbor's main glacier, and throughout the area, outlandishly shaped gigantic icebergs float by. Other popular stops include **Port Lockroy,** a former British base that is now run as a museum; **Cuverville** and **Rongé** islands, with their penguin colonies; and **Elephant Island,** named for the huge, sluglike elephant seals that inhabit it.

THE POLAR CIRCLE   Ships with ice-breaking capabilities can transport guests past the Antarctic Circle, below 66 degrees 33'S, and into the zone of 24-hour sunlight. The highlight here is **Marguerite Bay** (or Margaret Bay), with its abundant orca, minke, and humpback whales, and multitudinous Adélie penguins. These expeditions typically stop for a fascinating tour of research stations, both ultramodern and abandoned ones.

THE WEDDELL SEA   Longer tours to the peninsula (18–21 days) usually include visits to its east side of the peninsula, known as "iceberg alley" for the mammoth, tabular chunks of ice floating by slowly. Stops include the rarely visited **Paulet Island,** an intriguing crater island, and **James Ross** and **Vega** islands, known for their nesting colonies of Adélie penguins.

An even longer trip (or simply a different itinerary) takes travelers to the distant **Weddell Sea,** which is blanketed with a vast expanse of pack ice, looking much like a frozen sea. But that's just one of the highlights here; the real reason visitors pay extra time and money to reach this white wonderland is because of the colonies of emperor penguins that reside here. Rugged mountains and glaciers are also part of the view.

SUBANTARCTIC ISLANDS   Tours to the Subantarctic Islands begin or end with a trip to the Antarctic Peninsula and the Shetland Islands, which is the reason why these tours run 18 to 21 days. A few of these faraway islands are little visited by tourists, and they instill a sense of adventure in the traveler for their remoteness and fascinating geography, not to mention their important historical aspects.

The first stop is usually the **Falkland (Malvinas) Islands,** to view bird life, especially king penguins, and to tour the Victorian port town of Stanley. Some tours fly directly from Santiago, Chile, to the Falklands, and then begin the sailing journey there.

One of the most magnificent places on earth, **South Georgia Island** is surely a highlight of this trip. Its dramatic landscapes, made of rugged peaks, fiords, and beaches, are home to a staggering array of wildlife. South Georgia Island is also subject to unpredictable weather. Trip landings here risk cancellation far more frequently than other sites. Some tours tack on visits to the **South Orkney Islands** (with their dense area of Antarctic hairgrass—an indigenous flowering plant) and the actively volcanic **South Sandwich Islands.**

Tour Operators

Prices vary depending on the length of the trip, the company you choose, and the sleeping arrangements you require. A 9-day journey in a room with three bunks and a shared bathroom runs about $4,500 per person. A 21-day journey with lodging in a corner-window suite runs between $8,500 and $15,000 per person. Shop around to find something to suit your needs and budget.

Prices include passage, meals, guides, and all excursions. Some tours offer scuba diving, kayaking, over-flights, or alpine trekking, usually at an additional cost. Beginning in August 2011, a ban on high-sulfur fuels in Antarctic waters will effectively limit ships to those carrying no more than 500 passengers. When researching trips, also consider the size of the ship: Tour companies offer space for anywhere from 50 to 500 passengers. Most travelers like to share their space with fewer people; even for those who enjoy the camaraderie of a crowd, more than 100 to 150 guests is overkill. The International Association Antarctic Treaty Organization limits landings to 100 people, meaning large ships must conduct landings in turns.

A few well-known tour operators include:

o **Abercrombie & Kent,** 1520 Kensington Rd., Ste. 212, Oak Brook, IL 60523-2141 (© **800/544-7016** or 630/954-2944; fax 630/954-3324; www.abercrombiekent. com). A&K offers deluxe and comprehensive journeys, with trips that last 11 to 20 days.

o **Antarctica Expeditions,** Guido 1852, Office B, 4th Floor, Buenos Aires C1119AAB (© **54-11/4806-6326;** fax 54-11/4804-9474; www.antarcticacruises.com.ar). Based in Buenos Aires, Zelfa Silva and her husband Gunnar are seasoned Antarctica travelers and expert trip-planning consultants.

o **Antarctic Shipping,** Ebro 2740, Las Condes, Santiago, Chile (© **877/972-3531;** www.antarctic.cl). With a renovated decommissioned Chilean naval ship, this Chilean company began trips in 2004. Their trips are slightly more affordable.

o **Antarpply Expeditions,** Gobernador Paz 663, Ushuaia 9410 (© **54-2901/433636;** fax 54-2901/437728; www.antarpply.com). From their office in Ushuaia, Antarpply runs 9-night, 10-day cruises that start at $3,350.

o **Aurora Expeditions,** 182A Cumberland St., The Rocks, NSW 2000, Australia (© **02/9252-1033;** fax 02/9252-1373; www.auroraexpeditions.com.au). This Australian company organizes a variety of educational, photographic, and climbing tours for small groups, including uncommon trips to the Eastern Antarctic.

o **Fathom Expeditions,** 416 Moore Ave., Ste. 204, Toronto, Ontario M4G 1C9 (© **800/621-0176** or 416/646-2688; www.fathomexpeditions.com). A Canadian company that is run by former expedition leaders, Fathom's trips tend to be a bit longer, more personalized, and a bit less hurried.

o **Ice Tracks,** main office in Radway, Warwickshire, UK (© **44/078-3187-7129;** www.ice-tracks.com). A new operation run by two women who've crammed a huge amount of polar experience into their years, Ice Tracks will appeal to independent-minded travelers. They have seasoned staff and interesting "special guests" on board most trips, from conservationists to artists.

o **Lindblad Expeditions,** 720 Fifth Ave., New York, NY 10019 (© **800/397-3348** or 212/765-7740; www.expeditions.com). This venerable Swedish-run company was the first to bring tourists to Antarctica. They've now teamed up with *National Geographic* for perhaps the most educational trips offered, ranging from 11- to 28-day tours, with trekking.

o **Peregrine Adventures,** 258 Lonsdale St., Melbourne, VIC 3000, Australia (© **1300/854444** in Australia, or 03/9662-2700 outside Australia; fax 03/9662-2442; www.peregrine.net.au). This Australian company has trips leaving from Auckland, Tasmania, and Ushuaia.

o **Quark Expeditions,** 93 Pilgrim Park, Ste 1, Waterbury, VT (© **800/892-0334** or 203/803-2888; www.quarkexpeditions.com). This highly esteemed company offers the industry's most outrageous trips, including complete circumnavigations and a trip that includes a flight across the Drake Passage for a head start.

Last-Minute Reduced Fares to Antarctica

Some travel agencies in Ushuaia offer reduced fares for last-minute bookings, but this is by no means guaranteed. Be prepared to hang around Ushuaia for up to 2 weeks without any certainty that you will score a berth. If you do, however, prices can be 10% to 50% lower than the advertised rate. Try **All** Patagonia, Juana Fadul 60, Ushuaia, Argentina (© **2901/433622;** fax 2901/430707; www.allpatagonia.com). Note that the best time to snag discounted rates is late November to early December, before the onset of the high-travel season in southern Argentina.

BY PLANE

Apart from working for a research station, one of the few ways to get out and really explore the Antarctic continent is by plane. A handful of companies offer a small selection of astonishing, out-of-this-world journeys to the Antarctic interior and beyond.

Flights to the Antarctic can be divided into two distinct categories: flights that access man-made airstrips on certain islands close to the peninsula, and flights that penetrate the frigid interior, relying on natural ice and snow runways for landing areas. The logistics involved in flying to the Antarctic are complicated, to say the least, and fuel becomes an issue. Make no mistake: Air travel to the Antarctic is a serious undertaking. The rewards, however, can be unforgettable.

From Punta Arenas, Chile, King George Island on the peninsula is the preferred destination. The island houses a number of research stations, some of which can be visited. It boasts extraordinary wildlife and sightseeing opportunities. The average stay is 1 or 2 days, but weather delays can alter itineraries.

The severity of the landscape and the remoteness of the Antarctic interior call for special considerations when you're planning and preparing for an unexpectedly prolonged stay. All travelers attempting a trip to the interior should be aware of the extreme climatic conditions. Travel delays caused by severe weather are the norm. These trips, however, represent adventure travel in its purest form.

Tour Operators

Prices vary depending on the company and the destination. In general, flights to the peninsula are much cheaper than those to the interior. As expected, these all-inclusive trips can cost anywhere from $15,000 to $38,000 per person, depending on the destination. Logistical support for extended expeditions can easily run to over $40,000. Prices typically include transportation, meals, and guides.

o **Adventure Network International,** 79 W. 4510 South, Ste. 2, Salt Lake City, UT 84107 (© **801/266-4876;** fax 801/266-1592; www.adventure-network.com). This company began as a private plane service for climbers headed for Vinson Massif, the highest peak in Antarctica. They now include several 7- to 22-day tours, such as flights to the South Pole and the Transantarctic and Ellsworth mountain ranges, an emperor penguin safari, and a 60-day ski trip to the South Pole. Activities planned during these trips can include hiking, skiing, and Ski-Doo trips; overnight camping; and ice hockey, igloo building, and just about anything else related to ice.

- **Aerovías DAP,** O'Higgins, Punta Arenas (© **56/61-223340;** fax 61/221693; www.aeroviasdap.cl). This small Chilean airline specializes in charter flights to the peninsula, in particular King George Island. They have a unique 2 day–1 night flight that costs $3,950 per person.
- **Antarctica Flights** (© **56/61-28814-5701;** www.antarcticaflights.com.au). This is an Australian operation that runs one-day trips aboard Qantas 747 planes. There are lectures onboard. Seats start at A$999 for middle rows, and go up to A$6,799 for first class.
- **Antarctica XXI S.A.** (© **877/994-2994** or 61/614100; fax 61/614105; www. antarcticaxxi.com). A new Chilean company, this group offers trips combining flights and cruising. Departing from Punta Arenas and based out of King George Island, they'll save you the adventure (or perhaps the agony?) of the Drake Passage. A week-long trip starts at $9,000.

FAST FACTS: ARGENTINA

FAST FACTS: ARGENTINA

American Express   Offices are located in Buenos Aires, Bariloche, Salta, San Martín, and Ushuaia. In Buenos Aires, the Amex office is at Arenales 707 (© **11/4310-3000**).

Business Hours   Banks are open weekdays from 10am to 3pm. Shopping hours are weekdays from 9am to 8pm and Saturday from 9am to 1pm. Shopping centers are open daily from 10am to 8pm. Some stores close for lunch.

Climate   See "When to Go," in chapter 3.

Currency   See "Money & Costs," in chapter 3.

Documents   See "Entry Requirements & Customs," in chapter 3.

Driving Rules   In cities, Argentines drive exceedingly fast and do not always obey traffic lights or lanes. Seat belts are mandatory, although few Argentines actually wear them. When driving outside the city, remember that *autopista* means motorway or highway, and *paso* means mountain pass. Do not drive in rural areas at night, as cattle sometimes overtake the road to keep warm and are nearly impossible to see.

Drugstores   Ask your hotel where the nearest pharmacy *(farmacia)* is; they are generally ubiquitous in city centers, and there is always at least one open 24 hours. In Buenos Aires, the chain **Farmacity** is open 24 hours, with locations at Lavalle 919 (© **11/4821-3000**), and Av. Santa Fe 2830 (© **11/4821-0235**). Farmacity will also deliver to your hotel.

Electricity   If you plan to bring any small appliance with you, pack a transformer and a European-style adapter because electricity in Argentina runs on 220 volts. Note that most laptops operate on both 110 and 220 volts. Luxury hotels usually have transformers and adapters available.

Embassies   All in Buenos Aires: **U.S. Embassy,** Av. Colombia 4300 (© 11/5777-4533); **Australian Embassy,** Villanueva 1400 (© 11/4779-3500); **Canadian Embassy,** Tagle 2828 (© 11/4808-1000); **New Zealand Embassy,** Carlos Pellegrini 1427, 5th Floor (© 11/4328-0747); **United Kingdom Embassy,** Luis Agote 2412 (© 11/4808-2200).

Emergencies   The following emergency numbers are valid throughout Argentina. For an **ambulance,** call © **107;** in case of **fire,** call © **100;** for **police** assistance, call © **101.**

Information   See "Visitor Information," in chapter 3.

Internet Access   Cybercafes called *locuturios* are found on every corner in Buenos Aires and in other cities and towns as well, so it won't be hard to stay connected while in Argentina. Access is reasonably priced (usually averaging just under $1 per hour) and connections are reliably good.

Mail   Airmail postage for a standard letter from Argentina to North America and Europe is about $5. Mail takes, on average, between 7 and 10 days to get to the U.S. and Europe.

Maps Reliable maps can be purchased at the offices of the **Automóvil Club Argentino,** Av. del Libertador 1850, Buenos Aires (© **11/4808-4040;** www.aca.org.ar).

Safety See "Health & Safety," in chapter 3.

Smoking People who hate smoke can rejoice. Antismoking laws are in effect in Buenos Aires, as well as a few other Argentine cities; however, no restrictions exist in many small towns and the interior.

Taxes Argentina's value added tax (VAT) is 21%. You can recover this 21% at the airport if you have purchased certain local products totaling more than 70 pesos ($17 per invoice) from stores participating in tax-free shopping. Forms are available at the airport and participating stores, but know that you may be asked to display your purchases on your departure.

Telephone The country code for Argentina is **54.** When making domestic long-distance calls in Argentina, place a 0 before the area code. For international calls, add 00 before the country code. Direct dialing to North America and Europe is available from most phones. International, as well as domestic, calls are expensive in Argentina, especially from hotels (rates fall from 10pm–8am). Holders of AT&T credit cards can reach the money-saving **USA Direct** from Argentina by calling toll-free © **0800/555-4288** from the north of Argentina or 0800/222-1288 from the south. Similar services are offered by **MCI** (© **0800/555-1002**) and **Sprint** (© **0800/555-1003** from the north of Argentina, or 0800/222-1003 from the south).

Public phones take either phone cards (sold at kiosks on the street) or coins (less common). Local calls cost 20 centavos to start and charge more the longer you talk. Telecentro offices—found everywhere in city centers—offer private phone booths where calls are paid for when completed. Most hotels offer fax services, as do all Telecentro offices. Dial © **110** for directory assistance (most operators speak English) and © **000** to reach an international operator.

Time Argentina is 1 hour ahead of Eastern Standard Time in the United States in northern summer. In 2007, the country introduced daylight saving time in the east of the country with Buenos Aires and the coast moving forward 1 hour from December 30 to March 16. This means the capital will be 3 hours ahead of Eastern Standard Time in northern winter, while the Andean provinces will be 2 hours ahead.

Tipping A 10% tip is expected at cafes and restaurants. Give at least $1 to bellboys and porters, 5% to hairdressers, and leftover change to taxi drivers.

Water In Buenos Aires, the water is perfectly safe to drink. But if you are traveling to more remote regions of Argentina, it's best to stick with bottled water for drinking.

TOLL-FREE NUMBERS & WEBSITES

MAJOR U.S. AIRLINES

American Airlines
© 800/433-7300 (in U.S. and Canada)
© 084/4499-7300 (in U.K.)
www.aa.com

Delta Air Lines
© 800/221-1212 (in U.S. and Canada)
© 084/5600-0950 (in U.K.)
www.delta.com

Northwest Airlines
© 800/225-2525 (in U.S.)
© 870/0507-4074 (in U.K.)
www.nwa.com

United Airlines
© 800/864-8331 (in U.S. and Canada)
© 084/5844-4777 (in U.K.)
www.united.com

MAJOR INTERNATIONAL AIRLINES

Aerolíneas Argentinas
℡ 0810/222-VOLAR (86527; in Argentina)
℡ 800/333-0276 (in U.S.)
℡ 800/688-0008 (in Canada)
℡ 0800/0969-747 (in U.K.)
℡ 61-2-9234-9000 (in Australia)
www.aerolineas.com.ar

Air Canada
℡ 888/247-2262 (in Canada)
www.aircanada.com

Air France
℡ 800/237-2747 (in U.S.)
℡ 800/375-8723 (in U.S. and Canada)
℡ 087/0142-4343 (in U.K.)
www.airfrance.com

Air India
℡ 212/407-1371 (in U.S.)
℡ 020/8745-1000 (in U.K.)
www.airindia.com

British Airways
℡ 800/247-9297 (in U.S. and Canada)
℡ 087/0850-9850 (in U.K.)
www.british-airways.com

Cathay Pacific
℡ 800/233-2742 (in U.S. and Canada)
℡ 20/8834-8888 (in U.K.)
www.cathaypacific.com

Emirates Airlines
℡ 800/777-3999 (in U.S.)
℡ 087/0243-2222 (in U.K.)
www.emirates.com

Gol
℡ 0810/266-3131 (international)
www.voegol.com.br

Iberia
℡ 0845/601-2854 (in the U.K.)
www.iberia.com

Japan Airlines
℡ 012/025-5931 (international)
www.jal.co.jp

KLM
℡ 866/434-0320 (in U.S. and Canada)
℡ 0871/222-7740 (in U.K.)
www.klm.com

Korean Air
℡ 800/438-5000 (in U.S. and Canada)
℡ 0800/413-000 (in U.K.)
www.koreanair.com

LAN Airlines
℡ 866/435-9526 (in U.S.)
℡ 305/670-9999 (international)
www.lan.com

Lufthansa
℡ 800/399-5838 (in U.S.)
℡ 800/563-5954 (in Canada)
℡ 087/0837-7747 (in U.K.)
www.lufthansa.com

Qantas Airways
℡ 800/227-4500 (in U.S. and Canada)
℡ 084/5774-7767 (in U.K.)
℡ 13-13-13 (in Australia)
www.qantas.com

Qatar Airways
℡ 877/777-2827 (in U.S. and Canada)
℡ 0870/389-8090 (in U.K.)
www.qatarairways.com

Singapore Airlines
℡ 800/742-3333 (in U.S. and Canada)
℡ 0844/800-2380 (in U.K.)
www.singaporeair.com

South African Airways
℡ 271/1978-5313 (international)
www.flysaa.com

Swiss Air
℡ 877/359-7947 (in U.S. and Canada)
℡ 084/5601-0956 (in U.K.)
www.swiss.com

Taca
℡ 0810/333-8222 (international)
www.taca.com

TAM
℡ 888/2FLY-TAM (235-9826; in U.S.)
www.tam.com.br

Thai Airways International
℡ 800/426-5204 (in U.S.)
℡ 020/7491-7953 (in U.K.)
www.thaiair.com

FAST FACTS: ARGENTINA | Toll-Free Numbers & Websites

MAJOR HOTEL & MOTEL CHAINS

Crowne Plaza Hotels
☎ 800/227-6963 (in U.S.)
☎ 0800/8222-8222 (in U.K.)
www.crowneplaza.com

Four Seasons
☎ 800/819-5053 (in U.S. and Canada)
☎ 0800/6488-6488 (in U.K.)
www.fourseasons.com

Hilton Hotels
☎ 800/HILTONS (800/445-8667; in U.S. and Canada)
☎ 087/0590-9090 (in U.K.)
www.hilton.com

Holiday Inn
☎ 800/315-2621 (in U.S. and Canada)
☎ 0800/405-060 (in U.K.)
www.holidayinn.com

Hyatt
☎ 888/591-1234 (in U.S. and Canada)
☎ 084/5888-1234 (in U.K.)
www.hyatt.com

InterContinental Hotels & Resorts
☎ 800/424-6835 (in U.S. and Canada)
☎ 0800/1800-1800 (in U.K.)
www.ichotelsgroup.com

Marriott
☎ 877/236-2427 (in U.S. and Canada)
☎ 0800/221-222 (in U.K.)
www.marriott.com

Sheraton Hotels & Resorts
☎ 800/325-3535 (in U.S.)
☎ 800/543-4300 (in Canada)
☎ 0800/3253-5353 (in U.K.)
www.sheraton.com

Westin Hotels & Resorts
☎ 800/937-8461 (in U.S. and Canada)
☎ 0800/3259-5959 (in U.K.)
www.westin.com

SURVIVAL SPANISH

Argentine Spanish has a rich, almost Italian sound, with the double "ll" and "y" pronounced with a "j"-like sound. So *llave* (key) sounds like "*zha*-ve" and *desayuno* (breakfast) sounds like "de-sa-*zhu*-no." *Usted* (the formal "you") is used extensively, and *vos* is a form of "you" that's even more familiar than *tú* (informal "you"). Peculiar terms you may come across only in Argentina include *bárbaro* (very cool); Porteño (a resident of Buenos Aires); *pasos* (steps in a tango); *bandoneón* (a cousin of the accordion, used in tango music); and *subte* (the Buenos Aires subway). Uruguayan Spanish closely resembles the Spanish spoken in Buenos Aires.

BASIC WORDS & PHRASES

English	Spanish	Pronunciation
Good day	**Buenos días**	bweh-nohss dee-ahss
How are you?	**¿Cómo está?**	koh-moh ehss-tah
Very well	**Muy bien**	mwee byehn
Thank you	**Gracias**	grah-syahss
You're welcome	**De nada**	deh nah-dah
Goodbye	**Adiós**	ah-dyohss
Please	**Por favor**	pohr fah-bohr
Yes	**Sí**	see
No	**No**	noh
Excuse me (to get by someone)	**Perdóneme**	pehr-doh-neh-meh
Excuse me (to begin a question)	**Disculpe**	dees-kool-peh
Give me	**Déme**	deh-meh
Where is . . . ?	**¿Dónde está . . . ?**	dohn-deh ehss-tah
the station	**la estación**	lah ehss-tah-syohn
a hotel	**un hotel**	oon oh-tel
a gas station	**una estación de servicio**	oo-nah ehss-tah-syohn deh sehr-bee-syoh

English	Spanish	Pronunciation
a restaurant	**un restaurante**	oon res-tow-*rahn*-teh
the toilet	**el baño**	el *bah*-nyoh
a good doctor	**un buen médico**	oon bwehn *meh*-dee-coh
the road to . . .	**el camino a/hacia . . .**	el cah-*mee*-noh ah/*ah*-syah
To the right	**A la derecha**	ah lah deh-*reh*-chah
To the left	**A la izquierda**	ah lah ees-*kyehr*-dah
Straight ahead	**Derecho**	deh-*reh*-choh
I would like . . .	**Quisiera . . .**	kee-*syeh*-rah
I want . . .	**Quiero . . .**	*kyeh*-roh
to eat	**comer**	koh-*mehr*
a room	**una habitación**	*oon*-nah ah-bee-tah-*syohn*
Do you have . . . ?	**¿Tiene usted . . .?**	*tyeh*-neh oo-*sted*
How much is it?	**¿Cuánto cuesta?**	*kwahn*-toh *kweh*-stah?
When?	**¿Cuándo?**	*kwahn*-doh?
What?	**¿Qué?**	kay?
There is (Is there . . . ?)	**(¿)Hay (. . . ?)**	eye
What is there?	**¿Qué hay?**	keh eye
Yesterday	**Ayer**	ah-*yer*
Today	**Hoy**	oy
Tomorrow	**Mañana**	mah-*nyah*-nah
Good	**Bueno**	*bweh*-noh
Bad	**Malo**	*mah*-loh
Better (best)	**(Lo) Mejor**	(loh) meh-*hor*
More	**Más**	mahs
Less	**Menos**	*meh*-nohss
No smoking	**Se prohibe fumar**	seh pro-*hee*-beh foo-*mahr*
Postcard	**Tarjeta postal**	tar-*heh*-tah poh-*stahl*
Insect repellent	**Repelente contra insectos**	reh-peh-*lehn*-teh *cohn*-trah een-*sehk*-tohss

MORE USEFUL PHRASES

English	Spanish	Pronunciation
Do you speak English?	**¿Habla usted inglés?**	*ah*-blah oo-*sted* een-*glehss*
Is there anyone here who speaks English?	**¿Hay alguien aquí que hable inglés?**	eye *ahl*-gyehn ah-*kee* keh *ah*-bleh een-*glehss*
I don't understand Spanish very well.	**No (lo) entiendo muy bien el español.**	noh (loh) ehn-*tyehn*-doh mwee byehn el eh-spah-*nyol*
The meal is good.	**Me gusta la comida.**	meh *goo*-stah lah koh-*mee*-dah
What time is it?	**¿Qué hora es?**	keh *oh*-rah ehss

English	Spanish	Pronunciation
May I see your menu?	**¿Puedo ver el menú (la carta)?**	*pweh*-doh vehr el meh-*noo* (lah *car*-tah)
The check, please.	**La cuenta, por favor.**	lah *kwehn*-tah, pohr fah-*bohr*
What do I owe you?	**¿Cuánto le debo?**	*kwahn*-toh leh *deh*-boh
What did you say?	**¿Cómo?** (colloquial expression for American "Eh?")	*koh*-moh?
I want (to see) . . .	**Quiero (ver) . . .**	*kyehr*-oh (vehr)
a room	**un cuarto** or **una habitación**	oon *kwar*-toh, *oon*-nah ah-bee-tah-*syohn*
for two persons	**para dos personas**	*pah*-rah dohss pehr-*soh*-nahs
with (without) bathroom	**con (sin) baño**	kohn (seen) *bah*-nyoh
We are staying here only . . .	**Nos quedamos aquí solamente . . .**	nohs keh-*dah*-mohss ah-*kee* soh-lah-*mehn*-teh
1 night	**una noche**	oo-nah *noh*-cheh
1 week	**una semana**	oo-nah seh-*mah*-nah
We are leaving . . .	**Partimos (Salimos) . . .**	pahr-*tee*-mohss (sah-*lee*-mohss)
tomorrow	**mañana**	mah-*nya*-nah
Do you accept . . . ?	**¿Acepta usted . . . ?**	ah-*sehp*-tah oo-*sted*
traveler's checks?	**cheques de viajero?**	*cheh*-kehss deh byah-*heh*-roh
Is there a laundromat?	**¿Hay una lavandería?**	eye *oo*-nah lah-*bahn*-deh-*ree*-ah
near here?	**cerca de aquí?**	*sehr*-ka deh ah-*kee*
Please send these clothes to the laundry.	**Hágame el favor de mandar esta ropa a la lavandería.**	*ah*-gah-meh el fah-*bohr* deh mahn-*dahr* ehss-tah *roh*-pah a lah lah-*bahn*-deh-*ree*-ah

TRANSPORTATION TERMS

English	Spanish	Pronunciation
Airport	**Aeropuerto**	ah-eh-ro-*pwer*-toh
Flight	**Vuelo**	*bweh*-loh
Rental car	**Arrendadora de Autos**	ah-rehn-dah-*doh*-rah deh *ow*-tohss
Bus	**Autobús**	ow-toh-*boos*
Bus or truck	**Camión**	kah-*myohn*
Local bus	**Micro**	*mee*-kroh
Lane	**Carril**	kah-*reel*
Luggage storage area	**Custodia**	koo-*stoh*-dyah
Arrivals gates	**Llegadas**	yeh-*gah*-dahss
Originates at this station	**Local**	loh-*kahl*
Originates elsewhere	**De Paso**	deh *pah*-soh

English	Spanish	Pronunciation
Stops if seats available	**Para si hay lugares**	*pah*-rah see eye loo-*gah*-rehss
First class	**Primera**	pree-*meh*-rah
Second class	**Segunda**	seh-*goon*-dah
Nonstop	**Sin Escala**	seen eh-*skah*-lah
Baggage claim area	**Recibo de Equipajes**	reh-*see*-boh deh eh-kee-*pah*-hehss
Waiting room	**Sala de Espera**	*sah*-lah deh eh-*speh*-rah
Toilets	**Baños**	*bah*-nyoss
Ticket window	**Boletería**	boh-leh-teh-*ree*-ah

NUMBERS

1   **uno** (*ooh*-noh)

2   **dos** (dohs)
3   **tres** (trehss)
4   **cuatro** (*kwah*-troh)
5   **cinco** (*seen*-koh)
6   **seis** (says)
7   **siete** (*syeh*-teh)
8   **ocho** (*oh*-choh)
9   **nueve** (*nweh*-beh)
10   **diez** (dyess)
11   **once** (*ohn*-seh)
12   **doce** (*doh*-seh)
13   **trece** (*treh*-seh)
14   **catorce** (kah-*tor*-seh)
15   **quince** (*keen*-seh)
16   **dieciseis** (dyeh-see-*sayss*)
17   **diecisiete** (dyeh-see-*syeh*-teh)
18   **dieciocho** (dyeh-*syoh*-choh)

19   **diecinueve** (dyeh-see-*nweh*-beh)
20   **veinte** (*bayn*-teh)
30   **treinta** (*trayn*-tah)
40   **cuarenta** (kwah-*ren*-tah)
50   **cincuenta** (seen-*kwen*-tah)
60   **sesenta** (seh-*sehn*-tah)
70   **setenta** (seh-*ten*-tah)
80   **ochenta** (oh-*chen*-tah)
90   **noventa** (noh-*behn*-tah)
100   **cien** (*syehn*)
200   **doscientos** (doh-*syehn*-tohss)
500   **quinientos** (kee-*nyehn*-tohss)
1,000   **mil** (meel)

15

SURVIVAL SPANISH | Numbers

Index